Dictionary of Puget Salish

Dictionary of Puget Salish

Thom Hess

UNIVERSITY OF WASHINGTON PRESS

Seattle and London

Library of Congress Cataloging in Publication Data

Hess, Thom.
    Dictionary of Puget Salish.

    Bibliography: p.
    Includes index.
    1. Salishan languages—Dictionaries—English.
2. English language—Dictionaries—Salishan.
I. Title.
PM2263.H4   497'.3   75-42197
ISBN 0-295-95436-1

Dedicated

to

Mrs. Louise George, Cisxʷisał

and to the

memory of

Mr. Levi A. Lamont, Dxʷsdiłiliyus

Foreword

This collection of Puget Salish vocabulary represents most of the
lexical information I have gathered since 1962. It goes without saying
that this is only a small part of the total vocabulary; and further study
continues. No one person, especially one who is not native to the culture
of the language being recorded, can amass a large portion of the lexicon
and study each item for its full semantic and grammatical range. Therefore,
it is fervently hoped that the general distribution of the information con-
tained here will stimulate the Indian elders to expand upon it and make
whatever emendations they see as needed thereby passing on to their grandchildren, none of whom now knows the language, a fuller record of their
rich ancestral tongue. It is also hoped that other scholars may become in-
terested in the language and carry the study into such areas as componen-
tial analysis and semantic domains. Extensive cross-referencing for synonyms and antonyms is included to facilitate such further investigations.
Also, within the limits of this researcher's knowledge, complete derivational and grammatical information is given for each item.

Occasionally, it has seemed useful to refer to one or another anthropological or linguistic work where further explication of objects denoted
by certain words is to be found. Therefore, a short bibliography has been
included to which the reader is referred at these particular entries.

Mrs. Vi Hilbert of the Skagit has taken the time and effort to proof-
read this work checking the transcription and glosses for all those words
used in Skagit. Her assistance is deeply appreciated.

The extremely long and tedious task of typing this very difficult
manuscript was done by Mrs. Anneliese Hlavac; and the English to Puget
Salish section is entirely her contribution. This dictionary would never
have proceeded beyond card files had it not been for her industry and
belief in this undertaking.

The following agencies and institutions contributed financial support
for the research and typing of this work: The National Science Foundation,
the Graduate School Research Committee of the University of Washington,
the Department of Anthropology of the University of Kansas, the Department
of Linguistics of the University of Victoria, Canada Council, and American
Indian Studies of the University of Washington.

Thom Hess

Victoria 1974

Contents

Introduction

Language Setting

Puget Salish is the American Indian language spoken in the vicinity of Seattle, Washington. Its domain encompasses all the Puget Sound watershed and the adjacent Skagit River drainage (at least as far upstream as Diablo Dam), the Samish River region, Whidbey Island and the eastern portion of Fidalgo Island. (It does not include the area around Hood Canal. This is the Twana language territory.)

Puget Salish is one of just over twenty related languages belonging to the Salish language family. These languages, spoken in an area extending from the Pacific to western Montana and from central British Columbia into Oregon, all descend from a single ancestor language spoken thousands of years ago. It is not yet known whether other languages in the Northwest or elsewhere are related to the Salishan group at a still greater time depth.[1]

Dialect Differences

Along each of the rivers that flows to the Sound and on the many islands and bays small differences of accent and vocabulary have developed during the many centuries that the Indian people have dwelled here. Today these varieties of Lushootseed are named after those who use them. The most well known are Skagit (also spoken by many Nooksack though again with slight variations), Snohomish, Snoqualmie, Suquamish, Duwamish, Muckleshoot (of the Green and White Rivers), Puyallup, Nisqually, and Sahewamish. See map, p. iv.

In strict usage the name Skagit applied only to those living on Whidbey Island from Snakelum Point to Crescent Harbor; but today the name includes all those living at Swinomish and along the Skagit River and its tributaries. Although linguistic diversity within this region is not as great as that encountered throughout the entire Lushootseed region, there are sufficient differences to merit at least a three way division within

[1]
In a famous article by Edward Sapir, Central and North American Languages *in* Encyclopaedia Britannica, (14th Edition 1929) 5: 138-141, it is suggested that Salish languages are distantly related to those in the Wakashan, Chimakuan, and Algonkian groups. (Wakashan and Chimakuan languages are also located in British Columbia and Washington.) However, intensive studies of all Northwest languages since Sapir's time and especially in the last decade have not revealed supporting evidence for such a connection.

For a detailed discussion of locations of and current research on Northwest languages see the article by Laurence C. Thompson, The Northwest *in* Current Trends in Linguistics, edited by T. A. Sebeok, Vol.X, 1973.

Skagit as follows: Sauk-Suiattle on the Sauk and Suiattle Rivers; Upper
Skagit from the most upriver group, the Miskaiwheewh (bəsq̓íx̌ʷix̌ʷ), downstream to about Mount Vernon; and Lower Skagit from below Mount Vernon
to the estuary and islands.

Even this threefold division is not exact. It should always be remembered that slight differences existed from village to village, not only
in the Skagit territory, but also within the boundaries of every Lushootseed group. Most of these less pronounced differences were lost after the
people were relocated on reservations.

Detailed information on the location of Lushootseed tribes and villages
is to be found in the following sources:

Collins, June McCormick. Valley of the Spirits. University of
    Washington Press, 1974. (Skagit)

Roberts, Natalie. A History of the Swinomish Tribal Community.
    PH. D. Dissertation, University of Washington, 1975. (Skagit)

Sampson, Martin J. Indians of Skagit County. Skagit County Histo-
    rical Society, Mount Vernon, Washington, 1972. (Skagit)

Smith, Marian W. The Coast Salish of Puget Sound. American Anthro-
    pologist 43. 197-211, 1941. (Sahewamish, Nisqually, Puyallup)

_____. The Puyallup-Nisqually. Columbia University Press. New York,
    1940. (Duwamish, Snoqualmie, Suquamish)

Snyder, Warren A. Southern Puget Sound Salish: Texts, Place Names
    and Dictionary. Sacramento Anthropological Society 9. Sacramento,
    California, 1968. (Suquamish)

(The reader should bear in mind that, except for Chief Sampson who is
    fluent in Skagit, the above authors do not speak the language. There-
    fore, mistakes in writing the Indian names sometimes occur.)

Among the various Puget Salish groups, a major set of differences separa-
rates Skagit and Snohomish in the north from the others to the south.[1]
The most striking divergence between these two groups is that of stress.
In the north the accent is often on the second stem vowel while in the south
it is usually on the first. A very few words reverse this pattern, e.g.,
s.tə́qxʷ NPS and stəqáxʷ SPS beaver. In vocabulary, it is the names for
flora and fauna that vary the most although a substantial number of more
"basic" vocabulary differences are also found, e.g., šuɫ NPS and lab SPS
see, -čəc NPS and -kʷiƛ SPS red.

---

[1]
 This division corresponds very roughly to the Snohomish–King County line.

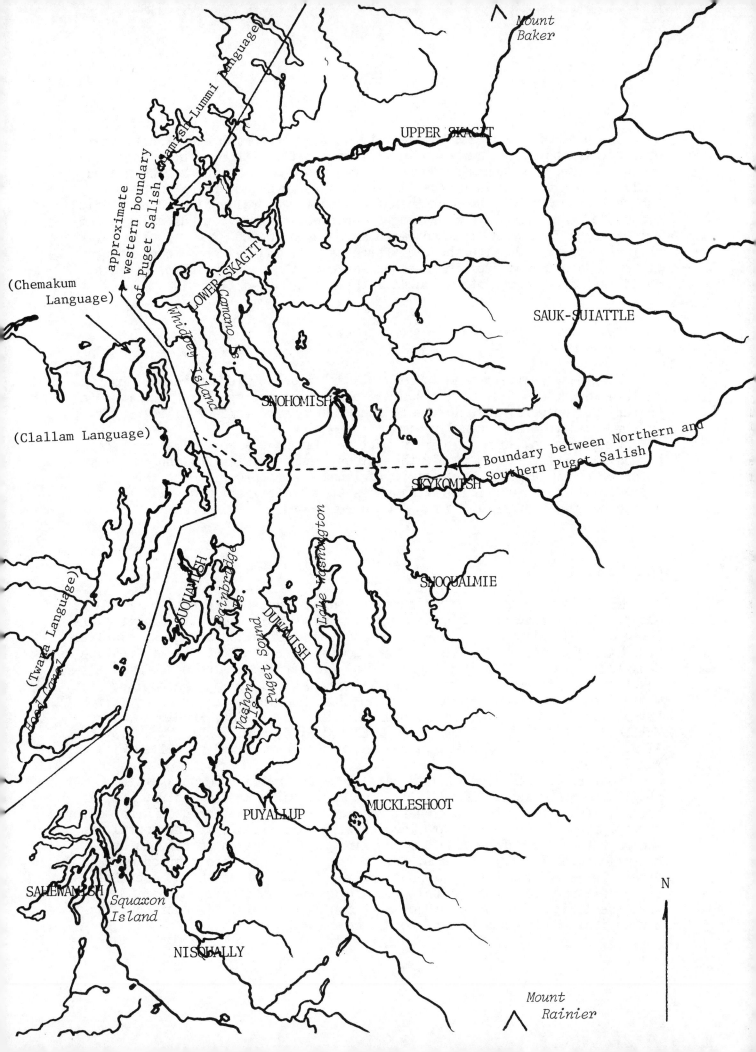

Mount
Baker

UPPER SKAGIT

SAUK-SUIATTLE

(Chemakum
Language)

Samish-Lummi Language

approximate
western boundary
of Puget Salish

LOWER SKAGIT

Camano Is.

Whidbey Island

(Clallam Language)

SNOHOMISH

Boundary between Northern and
Southern Puget Salish

SKYKOMISH

SNOQUALMIE

(Twana Language)

Hood Canal

SUQUAMISH

Bainbridge Is.

Vashon Is.

Puget Sound

DUWAMISH

Lake Washington

MUCKLESHOOT

PUYALLUP

SAHEWAMISH

Squaxon
Island

NISQUALLY

N

Mount
Rainier

In spite of the greater similarity between Snohomish and Skagit, there
do occur a substantial number of differences between them. Where these two
groups differ, the Snohomish term is often found also in the southern area
while the Skagit name is frequently related to words occurring in Lummi-
Samish to the north. The Sauk-Suiattle area is generally classed as Skagit
because of the common river drainage. However, this region has a large number of forms in common with Snohomish as opposed to the Skagit spoken further downstream. Despite these differences, all Indians from Mount Baker
to Mount Rainier and from the Cascade Range to the western shores of Puget
Sound understand one another and call their language dxʷləšucid.

Language Name

The Indian name for the language is dxʷləšucid, pronounced variously as
dxʷləšucid, txʷəlšucid, or xʷəlšucid depending on the speaker. The root (or
center) of the word, ləš, designates the Puget Sound region while the affixes
dxʷ-...-ucid together mean *language*.
Linguists and anthropologists call the language Puget Salish or Skagit-
Nisqually. However, the people themselves, when speaking English, usually
refer to their language by specific regional name appropriate to the imme-
diate local. This particularizing shows tribal affiliation as well and is
apt to be more meaningful to non-Indian neighbors.

Consultants

The following people contributed to this study: Mr. Ernest Barr, Muckle-
shoot; Mr. Charlie Boome, Upper Skagit; Mrs. Minnie Campbell, Skagit; Mrs.
Joyce Cheeka, childhood on Squaxon Island; Mrs. Emma Conrad, Sauk-Suiattle;
Mrs. Harriette Dover, Snohomish; Mrs. Louise George of the Skagit-speaking
Nooksack; Mrs. Vi Hilbert, Skagit; Mrs. Eva Jerry, Muckleshoot; Mrs. Eli-
zabeth Krise, Snohomish (from sbâda?ɫ); Mr. Levi A. Lamont, Snohomish; Mrs.
Martha Lamont, Snohomish; Mrs. Bertha McJoe, Muckleshoot; Mr. Dewey Mitchell,
Lower Skagit; Mr. Alfred Sam, Snohomish; Mr. Edward Sam, Snohomish; Mr.
Martin J. Sampson, Lower Skagit; Mr. Edward Sigo, Suquamish; Mrs. Florence
Sigo, Puyallup; Mrs. Bernice Tanewasha, Muckleshoot; and Ms. Ellen Williams,
Muckleshoot.
Most forms and grammatical details were collected from speakers of
Skagit and Snohomish and especially from Mrs. Louise George and Mr. Levi A.
Lamont. Therefore, this dictionary is biased toward the northern area. Over
three-fifths of the entries are labeled with the initials of the consultant
who gave the form. (Mr. Edward Sigo's initials are given as ESi. to avoid
confusion with Mr. Edward Sam's, ES.) Often forms are also labeled more
generally as NPS for Northern Puget Salish and SPS for Southern Puget Salish
or by more specific geographical provenience such as Skagit, Snohomish, etc.
when the limits of a word's usage are known. (See point #7 under Spelling
Conventions and Explanations of Format below.)

Technical Terms Used in Definitions

lexical:
A suffix having relative concrete meaning, *e.g.*, -ačiʔ *hand, lower arm*, -iʔɬ *baby*, -čup *fire, firewood*. Typically, the lexical and an independent word of the same or similar meaning are mutually exclusive. One may say either ʔuɬíčačiʔ čəd or ʔuɬíčid čəd tə dčáləs both meaning *I cut my hand*. (čáləs is Northern Puget for *hand, lower arm*. The Southern Puget equivalent is čáləš.) It is not grammatical to say *ʔuɬíčačiʔ čəd tə dčáləs. Of the two (correct) sentences, the former with the lexical is by far the more common.

lexical connective:
1. An affix which connects two forms having relatively concrete significance, *e.g.*, -al- in qʷágʷəbalqʷuʔ *soda pop* linking qʷágʷəb *sweet* and qʷúʔ *(fresh) water*.
2. An affix which alters (usually by rendering more specific) the meaning of a lexical, *e.g.*, -y- and -l-. Contrast -l-ax̌ad *arm* and -y-ax̌ad *edge, attached by the side* with -ax̌ad *side*.

reduplication:
The repetition of a part of a word, *e.g.*, the first three sounds in bədbədáʔ *(one's own) children* based on bədáʔ *(one's own) child*.

thematic suffix:
A vowel certain roots require before inflectional endings may be added. Compare ʔubə́č *fell down* and ʔubə́čad *set it down*. The -a- is a thematic suffix; the -d is an inflectional ending.

thematic stem:
A stem having a thematic suffix or a root to which a thematic suffix can be added.

athematic stem:
A stem which does not require a thematic suffix for the addition of inflectional endings.

Spelling Conventions and Explanations of Format

1. The raised ᵊ indicates an epenthetic vowel, that is a sound inserted between certain consonants to facilitate pronunciation.

2. The vowel /a/ is very often reduced to /ə/. The convention followed here writes ə (on the line) to represent the 'reduced' /a/. In many examples the same word is spelled sometimes with ə and sometimes with a. However, the main entry is always written with a.

3. The dot found in many words separates prefixes from the root. This convention should aid the reader in looking up any word that occurs in examples or definitions. For example, dxʷdaʔəb *shaman, Indian doctor* is written as dxʷ.daʔəb, the dot separating the prefix from the root. This indicates that the word dxʷdaʔəb is entered under the root daʔ(əb), page 127, and not under the prefix dxʷ-. The only place where the dot has not been constantly used is with reduplications.

4. The raised dot indicates rhetorical lengthening.

5. Parantheses are placed around letters which represent sounds that are not pronounced in a particular environment, *e.g.*, ʔəs(h)áydxʷ *know it* versus ʔuháydxʷ *find it out*.

6. A slight distinction is maintained between using *Cf.* and writing out *See (under)*. With the latter cross reference, considerable more information is found or there is a list of synonyms. With the former only a single synonym is given or the cross reference is deemed somewhat less important.

7. Many of the entries are followed by the initials of the speaker who contributed the form. This information will aid studies concerned with the distribution of particular usages.

8. If the reader cannot find a word whose root consists of two consonants without a vowel, he should look for that word with the root having a ə between the two consonants.

9. At the beginning of each letter there is a brief non-technical description of the sound that letter represents followed by the linguistic label for the sound (in articulatory terms). It is hoped that this description may give those who have never heard the language some vague conception of its sounds.

10. The reader will note little arrows, →, along the left hand margin of some pages. These indicate that there is more information for a particular entry in the addendum or that a totally new form has been added there.

11. The alphabetic order is: a b c c̓ č č̓ d ə g gʷ h i j ǰ k k̓ kʷ k̓ʷ l (l̓) ɬ ƛ̓ p p̓ q q̓ qʷ q̓ʷ s š t t̓ u w (w̓) xʷ x̌ x̌ʷ y (y̓) ʔ . An explanation of the sounds these letters represent is to be found at the beginning of each letter section in the Puget-English portion of the dictionary. (The letters in parantheses stand for sounds which never occur initially. These are usually heard as sequences of /ʔl/, /ʔw/, or /lʔ/, /wʔ/, and /yʔ/ depending upon syllabification. Occasionally, they are heard as /lʔl/, /wʔw/, and /yʔy/ - this last especially in reduplications.)

Dictionary of Puget Salish

a

The letter a represents a sound very similar to the *a* of English *father*, although, sometimes it is more like the *a* of *at* or the *a* of *hall*. When the vowel represented does not receive major stress, it is usually replaced by ə which stands for a sound similar to the *u* of English *cut*. (However, in some instances the spelling system retains a even though the pronunciation would indicate ə. Such cases are like English spelling which maintains the letter *o* for the second vowel of the three words *photo*, *photographer*, *photograph* even though this second o in each word is pronounced quite differently.)

Strictly heard, no word in Puget Salish begins with a vowel. Therefore, if the reader is seeking a word that he believes to begin with a, he should look under ?, the last letter of the alphabet. (This letter is called a glottal stop.)

1.   a   'sequence connector'
            Links one independent predication to another. It is found
            only with the personal pronominal particles, that is, in
            first and second persons only. This unit is the first ele-
            ment in the second predication.

            ʔu.húdčup čəɬ čəɬa ʔu.hə́gʷəb

            We made fire and we warmed ourselves.

            kəpúubəxʷ ɬi čələpa šíqʷəb čəɬa ɬu.ʔúx̌ʷ

            You folks coat and hat yourselves and we will go.
            (I.e., Put your coats and hats on and we will go.)

2.   -a$_1$-   A thematic suffix for those distributive stems that derive
            from roots which are normally (i.e., always except when found
            with distributive reduplication) athematic.

3.   -a$_2$-   derivational suffix of unknown significance

            Compare:

qʷcáb	slip	qʷə́cəd	slide it
kʷxʷád	helper, luck	kʷáxʷad	help him
túʔad	salivate	túʔud	spit on him
səʔsxʷáb	broad jump	sáxʷəb	jump, run
putáb	travel by boat	pút	boat

1. -a₃-   lexical connective

   See under -al-.

2. -abac   lexical suffix   'body; bulk'

c̓ág̓ʷəbàcᵊb	wash self
ʔu.k̓ʷásəbəc čəxʷ ʔu	Is your body roasting? (Said to person sitting close to stove.)
ʔəsƛ̓í.ƛpabəcᵊb	hold blanket around self with hand (the blanket is not fastened)
s.ƛ̓áləbac	garment
ʔu.ƛ̓úyəbəc	ran into something
ʔu.k̓x̌ábactəb	gave him a dressing down for several minutes
s.ƛ̓íqabac	smallpox
ʔàɫx̌ədábac	on the downstream side (of it)
čəg̓ʷábac	on the lower side, below the driftwood, i.e., on the water side of the logs and stuff washed up on the beach. (/čəg̓ʷ-/ is from čaʔkʷ.)
č̓itábac	Saturday (i.e., on the near side)
p̓əɫq̓ʷábac	Monday (on the 'after' side) Snohomish and Suquamish. Not Skagit.
dxʷ.diʔábac	to the other side of the division
g̓ʷədábac ʔal ti *table*	It is under the table.
šqábac ʔə tiʔiɫ č̓ƛaʔ	It is on the rock.

3. -ac   lexical suffix   'tree, (upright cylindrical object)'

   Contrast with -alc.

čəbídac	Douglas fir tree
s(ə)k̓ʷəbác	alder tree
x̌páyʔəc	cedar tree
čálasəc	brake fern
s.x̌ədíʔac	devil's club

-alikʷ-ac

pədálikʷəc	seed

    Cf. pəd   bury

        dxʷs.pədálikʷ   farmer

→

2.   -ačiʔ   lexical suffix   'hand, lower arm'

     Requires thematic suffix -i- before -t.

qəláčiʔ	left hand
jəháčiʔ	right hand
yəláčiʔ	both hands
q̓ʷəbxʷačiʔ	knuckle
xʷ.ʔəcúsačiʔ	palm of hand
xʷ.təbúsačiʔ	palm of hand LG.

      Cf. s.ʔácus   face

lúpačiʔ	glove(s)/mitten(s)
ší.šqáčiʔd	'Indian hammer'
łəq̓łəq̓táčiʔəc	white fir tree (lit. 'wide hands')
ʔu.tsáči(ʔ)b čəd	I pounded my hand. EK.
šqáči(ʔ)b	Raise your hand. EK.
x̌ədx̌ədáči(ʔ)b	pushing with the hands

     Contrast with x̌ədx̌ədyálc under -alc.

jəláči(ʔ)b ʔə tə səxʷ.x̌al	Put the pencil in your other hand.	
kʷədáči(ʔi)c	Shake hands with me.	

-ay-ači?

kʷədáyači?	knife in hand	LL.
təɫáyači(ʔ)b	see into the future (with arm across forehead)	AS.

-gʷas-ači?

p̓əsq̓ʷəgʷásači?	wrist

-qs-ači?

q̓ʷəx̌ʷqsači?	fingernail
šicqsači?	ring (for finger)
s.yáylupqsači?	ring (for finger)	LG.

In numbers

jəláči?	SPS	six (lit. 'change to other hand')
tqáči?		eight (lit. 'closed hands')
(s.)saliʔači?		twenty
s.ɫíxʷači?		thirty
s.tqáči?ači?		eighty
dəc̓uʔ s.bək̓ʷàči?		one hundred (lit. 'one all hands')

2. -ad   I, me
This suffix belongs to a class of five suffixes.
Three persons and two numbers are marked except that third
person has no number distinction.

1.	-ad	I, me		-aɫi	we, us
2.	-axʷ	thou, thee		-alap	ye, you
3.		-as	he, him, she, her, it they, them		

These suffixes are bound to the independent clause marker
č-. In the absence of č-, i.e., in dependent clauses, they
are the last order of elements in the predicate head. If
an adverb occurs within the predicate of a dependent clause,
they are suffixed to it instead of to the head. In this respect, they resemble predicate particles.

Allomorphs:

Under weak stress /a/ is replaced by /ə/. After č- the vowel
is always /ə/ and -aɫi is shortened to /-əɫ/.

The exception is -as. In predicates of independent clauses,
there is no overt mark for third person. (č- is also lacking.)
Thus, in predicates of independent clauses the forms are:

1.	čəd	čəɫ
2.	čəxʷ	čələp
3.		

1. -adəc   lexical suffix   'tackle, equipment, gear'

xʷíʔxʷiʔàdəc   hunting tackle

2. -adis   lexical suffix   (Appropriate gloss uncertain.)

ʔəs.x̌ɫádis čəd   I am sickly.

x̌i.čcádis   red meat, red cloth

x̌ʷi.qʷ ̓q̓ʷádis   white meat, white shirt

   Cf. -aɫči ̓

3. -adi ̓   lexical suffix   'ear, side, sound'
(derived from di ̓)

x̌ʷíqʷadi ̓   thunder

ƛ̓əládi ̓   noise

ʔu.túčadi ̓ čəd cut ɫ(u)as.x̌əjàs
I shot (at random) just to scare him.

ʔəs.tkʷadi ̓   deaf; not understand

q̓ʷəládiʔ	ear
čílqadiʔ	the fish fin close to the gills
s.ƛ̓əgʷádiʔ	earring
kʷədˀbádiʔ	bail, hoop handle
ʔəs.kʷədádi(ʔ)b	He has it by the bail.
(Cf. kʷədˀbáləp	straight handle LL.)
tč̓ádiʔ	point with finger
díʔadiʔ	other part of house/room on the other end of the house (inside) other room
t̓əq̓tádiʔ	upper (landward) side of house (inside)
čəgʷálatxʷ t̓əq̓tadiʔ	outside the house on the landward side
ʔal ti šq̓ádiʔ	It is (stored) up above.
šq̓ádiʔbid	on top of something
čəgʷádiʔ	side toward the water
q̓ádadiʔ	behind the house
x̌č̓ádiʔ ʔə ti ʔàlʔal	It's up on end in the corner of the house.

-al-adiʔ

ʔudxʷ.tsáladi(ʔ)dˀb	I want to sock him in the side of the head.
títəɬaledi(ʔ)b	cock head to one side; lay head so as to expose temple
čəxʷa xʷəbəbxʷəbáladib	...and you will toss your head from side to side.
ʔəs.jəƛ̓əládi(ʔ)bid čəd	I misunderstood it.
ƛ̓udxʷ.jəƛ̓áladiʔ čəd	Generally my ears get twisted (lit. 'wander'). (I.e., I generally don't understand.)

lúhəlàdi?	hear
dxʷ.ʔílaledi?	cheek

-əl-di?

háchacəldi?	long ears
c̓àgʷəldí?ᵊb	wash your ears
c̓àgʷəldí?c	wash my ears

-ay-di?

ʔəs.t̓əbt̓əbšáydi?	braided hair
t̓əbšáydi(?)d	braid her hair
k̓ʷčáydi?	rabbit (wild ears) LG.
	(See under k̓ʷəč.)

1. -agʷ-(il)   (-aw-il with attenuative stems)

> derivational suffix

> An agent puts himself into the act (rather than performing it on someone or something else). And, in the case of stems already intransitive, a patient becomes agent.

bəc̓agʷil	lie down for a rest
Cf. bəc̓	fall down from a standing position
bəc̓ad	put it down
ǰíqagʷil	enter the water
Cf. ǰíq	drown
ǰíqid	immerse it
ǰíqcut	soak self in water

2. -agʷəl   'reciprocal'   (-agʷəl̓ with attenuative stems)

q̓ʷúlutəgʷəl	hug each other

8

tʼúčutəgʷəl   shoot at each other

háydəgʷəl   know each other

titx̌ʷútəgʷəl   tug-of-war (pull each other a bit)

x̌íx̌ʌustəgʷəl   converse with each other (lit.
                                         'bite each other's faces a little')

1. -akʷ-   See under -aʔkʷ-.

2. -al-   lexical connective
            Lexical connectives particularize the meaning of the lexical.
            There are nine:

            -a-   -al-   -l-
            -i-   -il-   -y-   -ay-
            -u-   -ul-

→
→

5. -alc   lexical suffix   '(usually cylindrical) object'
            etymologically perhaps -al-c (?)

            kʷədálc   get hold of someone to keep self
                                         from falling or to prevent him from
                                         doing something.

            ləs.kʷədálc čəd   I take (your) arm (as I go down the
                                         steps so I won't fall).

                Contrast with kʷədláx̌ədid under -ax̌ad.

            ləs.x̌ʌ́alc ʔal tə sčupč ʔə ti k̓ʷàʔtəd

            (While going along) the mice were biting the tails (of the ones
            ahead). (I.e., they were holding on to each other going single
            file.)

            tíx̌alc   spread out arms quickly for protection
                                         or to keep canoe from hitting something.

            ʔu.píx̌ʷilalc čəxʷ ʔə tad.pàʔkʷ   You dropped your pipe.

            xʷəltəbálc   gun

s.ċqʷálc	home-made ammunition
səxʷ.ʔíkʷigʷədalc	ramrod for cleaning gun
túx̌ʷ čəd ƛus.čulʔalc	I just borrow it.
ƚu.čulʔálcᵊd čəd kʷi yəq̓ùs	I'll lend her a basket.
ʔu.x̌ʷílalcbid čəd	I lost it.
ʔu.k̓ʷƚálc čəd ʔə ti s.xʷiʔxʷiʔ	I spilled what I'd gathered.

-y-alc

x̌ədx̌ədyálc	pushing with the hands

Contrast with x̌ədx̌ədáči(ʔ)b (under -ači?).

1. -alap 'ye, you'

   See under -ad.

2. -ali lexical suffix 'place where'

húdali	stove
cəƚdálbəli	pressure point, pulse; breath
sáx̌ʷilali Skagit	hayfield
xʷ.dəgʷígʷsali	pocket
jədísali	gums
xʷ.lábali	bottle

3. -alikʷ lexical suffix 'creative activity'

júbalikʷ	dance	júb	kick
pədálikʷ	to plant	pə́d	bury
tsálikʷ	hammering	təs	hit with fist
xʷšálikʷ	sow	xʷəš	broadcast
x̌čálikʷ	counting	x̌əč	seat of emotions and understanding

→
→

4. -ałči? lexical suffix 'meat'

    šəbáłči?   dried meat

    s.qíg^wəcàłči?   venison

5. -ałi 'we, us'

    See under -ad.

    The non-ego part of -ałi is often specifically mentioned with a phrase naming the other person(s):

    tu.šúdx^w čəł ?i ci mali   Mary and I saw it, we saw it.

    This sentence does not mean ego and someone else, we, saw it and Mary too.

    Attraction is also possible with (h)əlg^wə?.

6. -ap ~ -ah-

    lexical suffix 'bottom'

    dx^w.šqáp   high off the ground (referring to a house that stands on posts)

    ?ácəp   in the middle of the bottom, at the very end of bay

    dx^w.líləp   Tulalip Reservation named after the very deep bay there. (Lit. 'the distant bottom'.)

    x^w.tábəp   rump   Skagit

    s.?áləp   thigh, hind leg

    x^w.čłíčəp   sacrum

    x^w.?iləlúg^wəp   hip, buttocks

    dx^w.(h)ájəp   long hipped person

    dx^w.(h)íg^wəp čəd I have a big rear.

    łíw?əp   a slang word for someone who can't control his rectum   LL.

    x^w.ƛáləp   pot

-al-ap

    kʷədᵊbáləp   (straight kind of) handle

    xʷ.kʷədᵊbáləp   same gloss

    húdaləp   burning on the bottom

    tu.gʷədáləp čəd   I was under the tree.

    tu.gʷədáləpəd čəd I put it under that tree.

-ah-

    ʔudxʷ.jx̌áhᵊbitubuɬ   (He always) gets his butt up here (i.e., over to us) (in order to eat).

    ʔudxʷ.təx̌ʷtx̌ʷáhəb   He's dragging his hind end around.

    ʔudx̌ʷ.ǰíq̓ahəb   put rear in the water

1. -apsəb lexical suffix 'neck'

    ʔudxʷ.ɬíc̓əpsəbdùbut čəd   I happened to cut the nape of my neck.

    ʔudxʷ.pqʷápsəbəd   He decapitated someone.

    ʔu.čík̓ʷapsəb   He gagged/choked.

    ʔu.ƛ̓ípəpsəbəd čəd   I choked him.

    čəlíǰəpsəb   upper end of spine

    s.cqápsəb   front part of neck

→

3. as- An aspectual prefix having static reference. Contrast ʔəsq̓axʷ 'frozen' with sq̓axʷ 'ice' and ʔuq̓axʷ 'froze'. as- plus a root are very often glossed with English predicate adjectives.

    Allomorphs:

    /ʔəs-/ when initial, /əs-/ after a consonant, /as-/ after a vowel. as- plus dxʷ- result in /ʔəxʷ-/.

4. -as 'he, him, she, her, it, they, them'

    See under -ad.

1.   -aw̓   lexical suffix   (Appropriate gloss uncertain.)

          ʔu.ɫqáw̓əd   licked it, lapped it up

            Cf. čib(i)   lick, dip

          x̌.dədáw̓šəd   marrow

2.   -axʷ   'thou, thee'

        See under -ad.

3.   -axʷ ~ -əxʷ

        aspectual suffix   'change affected'

4.   -ax̌ad lexical suffix   'edge, side appendage'

        Requires -i- if -t follows.

          qətqáx̌əd   axilla

          gəd(ə)gáx̌əd   axilla

          q̓čáx̌əd   SPS   seagull (lit. 'bent wing')

          s.ʔíləx̌əd   hired hand, employee, people who work under someone's direction

          xʷ.ʔíləx̌əd   side of body

          q̓əláx̌əd   fence

          ʔu.kʷədáx̌ədid   a net in water, a drag seine

          daʔxʷ ʔu.q̓ígʷəx̌əd   the edge is just showing

          p̓u.p̓sabəx̌əd   wood floats on a gill net

          ʔu.jəláx̌ədəxʷ čəd dxʷ.díʔàx̌əd   I'm going visiting on that side/end.

          q̓ʷúʔəx̌əd   neighbor

-1-ax̌ad

kʷədláx̌ədid   grab by the arm to help him or simply to be friendly

     Contrast with kʷədálc.

s.təbláx̌əd   shoulder   LG.

   (LL. gives s.ʔílʔalubid.)

qʷəbxʷláx̌əd   elbow

čəbtəláx̌əd   wing (of bird or plane)

-y-ax̌ad   (See -ucid.)

títsyàx̌əd   knock on the door

ʔəxʷ.ʔəƛ̓ʷyáx̌əd   The door is open.

ʔudxʷ.(ʔ)əƛ̓ʷyáx̌ədid   Open the door.

ʔudxʷ.(ʔ)əƛ̓ʷyáx̌ədyic   Open the door for me.

gʷədyáx̌əd   down on the edge (of a piece of paper)

1.   -ay-   lexical connective

          See under -al-.

          Probably etymologically related to -i-.

2.   -aʔkʷ ~ akʷ

          lexical suffix   'group viewed distributively'

          dəčáʔkʷbixʷ   foreigner, one from a different village

          ləlíʔəkʷbixʷ   a different class, breed, type, group

          bəkʷáʔkʷbixʷ   all nations, everyone

          stábakʷbixʷ čəxʷ   What sort of a person are you? (This is a rather rude way of asking what group you belong to.)

s.ɬíčəkʷčup	wood saw
ləs.čəbáʔakʷčup	carrying firewood on back
bəqʷíčaʔakʷčup	shouldered the firewood

1. -aʔɬdəɬ ~ -ʔaʔɬdəl-

       lexical suffix   'parts of the mouth'   (See -ucid.)

       Requires -i- if -t follows.

təsˀbáʔɬdəɬ	lips are chapped
šqáʔɬdəɬ	upper lip, the name for Snoqualmie Falls
gʷədáʔɬdəɬ	lower lip, below a waterfall
tḱáʔɬdəlitˀb	slapped in the mouth
cɬílaʔɬdəɬ	mouth bleed
dxʷ.čágʷəʔɬdəlb	wash your (own) mouth out
ƛəláʔɬdəlb	stop eating
q̓xʷáʔɬdəɬ	above a waterfall DM.

2. (h)aʔs   (well) then   LG.

      ɬílc aʔs   Give me some food then.   LG.

      ɬíld aʔs   Give him some food then.   LG.

b

This letter represents a sound similar to that of the English *b*. However, the sound is a recent development from an original nasal consonant. Within the past one hundred years or so /m/ was spoken where /b/ is used today. (Note that words in English borrowed from Puget Salish retain the nasal whereas today the Indians use oral sounds, e.g., Snoqualmie versus sdúkʷalbixʷ from earlier *snukʷálmixʷ.)

Even today /m/ is sometimes heard instead of /b/ in special vocabularies such as some proper names and religious terms, and in certain styles of speaking and singing. This is especially the case for prayer, talking endearingly to children, and quoting the speech of certain animals and other supernatural beings. Whether the nasal or oral consonant is used depends upon style; the difference does not alter the significance of individual words. Therefore, b and m are listed together under b. (See Thompson and Thompson.)

1. -b   middle voice

    /-b/ after vowels and also usually after /l/

    /-əb/ elsewhere

2. s.bábibəł   evil thoughts

→

4. báčus   a kind of buʔqʷ

    This bird is unidentified. It is both a good diver and a good flier. Typically, it is lined up with others on a drifting log with wings spread to dry. With the wings thus extended, it looks as though they are playing sləhál. Hence, in mythology, they are represented as good gamblers.
    LL.

    Other names for the same bird are bəčúł, qʷátqs.

5. bád   father

    See under bədáʔ.

    bábaʔ   vocative

    šəłbádəb   step-father (Snohomish)

    čəłbádəb   step-father (Skagit) (lit. 'make a father')

    ciłbəsbád   half-sibling with father in common

    xʷíʔ šbà (or) xʷíʔ šmà   No, Sir.   ESi.

1. s.báda?ɬ   name for site of Snohomish, Washington

2. s.bádəš   tobacco

     dxʷsbádəš   someone who smokes

     ?əs.təbáš čəd kʷi sbàdəš   I'm craving a cigarette.

3. bádil   blind, no sense of sight

     ?əsbadil čəd   I'm blind.

4. s.bádil   mountain   EK., ES.

     reduplication

         sbábədil   small mountain   EK.

         sbábdil   small mountain   ES.

     s.bádit   mountain   LL.

→

6. s.bágʷə?əc   unidentified tree

7. bak̓ʷ(a)   move rapidly

     Cf. béjqᵊb

     See under jakʷ(a).

     -at

         ?ubák̓ʷəd ti?iɬ   He made them run all about.
                                (i.e., disturbing animals in a small area.)

         x̌ʷuɬ ?ubák̓ʷacut ti?ə? qədxʷs
         Only his mouth was moving and that was moving fast.

     -txʷ

         ?ugʷəbák̓ʷtxʷ čəd   I kind of got a glimpse of it.

1.   bakʷɬ   See baʔkʷɬ.

2.   balac-   See under bəɬ(bíd), ƛəl.

   -t

       xʷiʔ kʷ(i) adsubalac⁼d tiʔiɬ s.čətxʷəd.   JC.
       Don't disturb/distract the bear!

3.   bálbal   confused, mistaken

       See under jaƛ.

       ʔubálbəl čəd   I made a mistake.

       ʔəsbálbəl čəd   I am confused.

   -dxʷ

       ʔubálbəldub čəd ʔə ci s.ɬàdəy?
       The woman mistook me for someone else.

4.   bálbaliʔ   bait for fishing

5.   báli   forget

   root

       ʔubáli čəd   I forgot.

       ʔəsbálihəxʷ čəd čəda ʔəsbàli   I forgot now.

       ƛəbasbálihəxʷ čəd   I'm forgetting (these days).

   -c

       ʔəs.ƛúbil. x̌ʷúƛ čəxʷ ʔəsbáliic.
       That's OK. Just forget it. (This is a way of expressing 'you are
                                   welcome' for some favor.)

       ʔubáliic čəd tə hùd.   I forgot the wood.

xʷíʔ lə.líl čəda gʷəbali(ic) xʷíʔ kʷi ds.q̓p̓úcid
I almost forgot to pay you.

jíxʷbid ʔə kʷi gʷədsbəlìic kʷi gʷəds.q̓p̓ùcid
Before I forget it, I will pay you.

ʔubaliicᵊbš čəxʷ   You forgot me.

lexical

ʔudxʷbálihigʷəd čəd čəda sìx̌ʷicut
I forgot myself and made noise with the water.

reduplication

híkʷ čəd bəlbàli   I'm forgetful.

tílᵊb bàlaɬbali   Suddenly (I) am forgetting.

1.   bál(y)i   marry   (ultimately from French *marier*)

   Compare ʔiɬ.húygʷas under huy(u).

2.   s.báliʔxʷ   name of a Skagit River extended village
                        (lit. 'mixture of people')

   (See Sampson p. 2.)

   Compare báli and bálbal, báluqʷ.

3.   s.bálucid   in-law when link is deceased   LG.

   s.bəlúcid   Same gloss: in-law when link is deceased
                                                               EK., AS.
       See under yəláb, s.kʷəlwás.

   -b

       bəlúcidᵊb   court a girl, be going with someone   AS.

       Compare kʷì.kʷədátəgʷəɬ 'going steady' under kʷəd(a).

19

1. báluqʷ   mixed up, messed up, entangled

   -t

     xʷiʔ ləbáləqʷəd tə c̓ic̓əb   Don't mess up the blankets.

   -dxʷ

     ʔubáluqʷədxʷ čəd   I inadvertently messed it all up.

2. bał(a)   cure by a shaman, Indian doctor

   -at

     gʷəl łudəxʷbáłads ciʔəʔ s.ładəyʔ ʔəs.x̌əł...
     And he is going to "doctor" this woman who is sick...

     huy, tubáłatəbəxʷ ʔə tiʔił dəs.càpa
     Then, my grandfather treated her.

3. bap(a)   busy

   Cf. x̌ʷaq̓ʷ(a)

   root

     ʔəsbáp čəd   I'm busy.

     cíck̓ʷ čəd ʔəsbàp   I'm very busy.

   -at

     See under bəł(bíd).

     bápətəb   pester, annoy

     ləc̓ubápəd (h)əlgʷəʔ tiʔił čxʷlùʔ   They are pestering the whale.

4. s.báqbaq   A kind of short reed that can be peeled and eaten
                     without further preparation.

5. xʷ.báqʷabus   meadow

     báqʷəb   cranberry marsh

1. báqʷuʔ   snow (noun)

     -b

        baqʷu(ʔ)b   snow (verb)

          Cf. təqʷúbəʔ   any snow-capped mountain

2. básil   damp, a little wet

    Synonymous with łíʔ.łqʷ.   See under łə́qʷ.

       tux̌ʷ čəd básiligʷadəbəxʷ   I just wet my insides a bit.

3. bástəd   Synonymous with šəlá ʔ, *q.v.*

4. báwəč   complain, growl

       ʔubáwəc tə s.čə̀txʷəd   The bear is growling.

       ck̓ʷáqid ʔubàwəč   He is always complaining.

     For 'growl' LL. gives x̌ídib.

5. báyəc   SPS   meat

     See under biác.

6. báʔ   wide, width measured from inside

     Cf. łəqt   wide, flat

       p̓il(i)   flat

   lexical

     dxʷbá(ʔ)wił   wide canoe ("wide inside") LG.

     ʔəs.ʔəx̌íd kʷi sxʷbàwił ʔə tiʔił ad.q̓ìlbid   LG.

     How wide is your canoe?

     ʔəs.ʔəx̌íd kʷi sba(ʔ)wił ʔə tiʔił ad.q̓ìlbid   DM.

     How wide is your canoe?

dəčáxʷ táɫ xʷbàwiɫ ʔə tiʔiɫ dᵊ.q̓ìlbid   LG.
My canoe is six feet wide.

   rejected: *ɫəq̓tgʷíɫ   LG.

1. baʔkʷɫ   get hurt

   Cf. q̓iƛ(dxʷ)   wound

     x̌əɫ   sick

     ʔila   hurt

  root

    ʔubákʷɫ čəd   I got hurt.

    xʷiʔ čələp ləbàʔkʷɫ   Don't you folks get hurt.

    xʷiʔtubš ɫi ləbákʷɫ   Don't you folks let me get hurt. EK.
                      Don't you folks try to get me hurt. LL.

    gʷə.kʷáxʷatubuɫəd čəd cut ɫəxʷíʔələp ləbákʷɫ
    I help you folks so that you won't get hurt.

  -dxʷ

    xʷiʔ ɫi ləbákʷɫdubš   Don't you folks let me get hurt.

  lexical

    -ačiʔ

    ʔubákʷɫačiʔ čəd   I hurt my hand/arm.

    ʔəs.čál kʷ(i) adəxʷubákʷɫačiʔ How did you hurt your hand/arm?

    díɫ cəxʷubákʷɫačiʔ   That's how I hurt my hand/arm.

2. maʔman   See under biʔbad.

3. baʔs   stationary

  root

    ʔəsbáʔs   a child who won't move (when told to)

-t

    bá?sᵊd łi   Anchor it, you folks!

lexical

    ?ubá?sgᵂił   anchored canoe

-təd

    ba?stəd   anchor (noun)

      Cf. púbᵊb   resist being drawn through the water, "drag anchor"

1.   bə-   auxiliary prefix   'anew'

    See under gᵂə-.

2.   s.bəbí?   hoop

    See under búluxᵂ   'round'.

3.   bəč̓ac   NPS   snake

    bə́č̓əc   SPS   snake

      bəč̓acqs   kettle (lit. 'snake nose')

4.   bəč̓ulᵊb   pus

5.   bəč(a)   fall from standing position
                       set down

    Equivalent to łaq̓(a) in Skagit.

    See under xᵂí?til.

    root

    ?ubə́č čəd   I fell down.

    ?ubə́č čəd dxᵂ?al *cement*   I fell down on the cement.

-at   (Note: <u>as-</u> is never found with bəč-at.)

  bəč̓ád   NPS   set it down

  bə́č̓əd   SPS   set it down

  ʔubəč̓ád čəd ʔal tudiʔ   I laid it over there.

  huy, bəč̓átᵊbəxʷ tiʔił k̓ʷàtaq   So they laid out the mat.

  ʔubəč̓átᵊb čəd   I was put down.

    See under qʷat(at).

-dxʷ

  ʔubəč̓dúb čəd ʔə tiʔił ʔu.yàbuk̓ʷ

  In the fight I was knocked down.

  ʔubəč̓dúb čəd   (My work) is getting me down.

-txʷ   (Note: <u>ʔu-</u> is never found with bəč-txʷ.)

  ʔəsbə́č̓txʷ čəd   I laid it down.

  ʔəsbəč̓túb t(i) ad.bədàʔ ʔal tiʔił haʔł s.łàgʷid

  Your son was laid on a nice bed.

-agʷ-il

  híwil, bəč̓ágʷil   Go, lie down. (This is a pleasant way of talking more or less equivalent to "Why don't you lie down a while?")

dxʷ-...-b

  dxʷbə́č̓ᵊb   sink   (Occurs in Skagit as well.)

    Cf. łəbáʔ   fall into water; drown

      gʷál   capsize

  ʔudxʷbəč̓ᵊb čəd   I sank.
                         I drowned.

dxʷ-...-b-t

  ʔudxʷbəč̓ᵊbᵊd čəd   I sank it.

ʔudxʷbəč̓ᵊbt̓ᵊb ʔə tiʔił   That man sank it.

lexical

bəč̓álikʷ   bet, wager
                            something to lay something on, e.g.,
                            a clip board

bəč̓álq   kill game; carcass

ʔu· siʔáb; tux̌ʷ čəł ʔubəč̓álq ʔə tiʔə?
Oh, Sir! We only killed this (game).

ʔubəč̓álq (h)əlgʷə? ʔə kʷi s.qìgʷəc ʔə kʷi s.čətxʷəd ʔə kʷi stab
They killed deer, bear, and whatever (they could get).

→

2.   bəč̓úł   See under báč̓us.

3.   bəč̓úʔᵊb   lump

4. x̌i.bə́č̓ NPS   black

   Cf. x̌i.túč̓ SPS   black

5.   bədáʔ NPS   offspring, (one's own) child

   bə́dəʔ SPS   same gloss

   Contrast čačas.

   -b

   tubədáʔᵊb (h)əlgʷə? ʔi tiʔə? təkʷtəkʷəlùs
   They had a baby (Frog) and Owl.

   ...xʷəbt̓ᵊbáxʷ ʔəs.q̓ʷúʔ ʔə tiʔə?cəc biʔbəda?s mìʔman

   səsbədáʔᵊbs ciʔə? cədił wáq̓waq̓

   Thrown (down) together with this little baby, the small
   one which Frog bore.

25

reduplication

bíbədà?   small or young offspring; referring to
                 one's own offspring modestly

bí?bədà?   ML.

  sbíbədà?   A bluff near to but south of the present site
                 of Spee-Bi-Dah, Washington. At one time this
                 cliff looked like a woman carrying a baby.

bíbibədà?   young progeny

bədbədá?   progeny

bíbədbədà?   young of an animal; dolls

bədá? is a kin term for first descending generation. The following
is the complete set of lineal terms in Puget Salish:

3, 4 and 5 are reciprocal

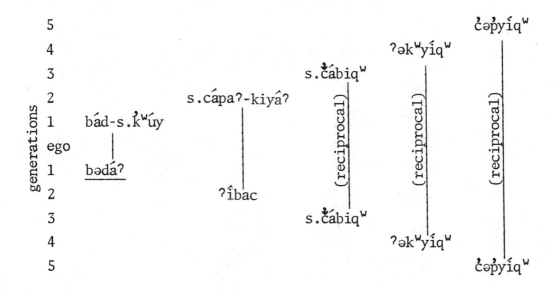

1. bədč   lie, fib, exaggerate

    -b

      ?əlc̓ubə́dc̓ᵊb   telling a lie   LG.

-bi-t

    tùx̌ʷ čəd ʔubə́dčəbìd tiʔəʔ   I'm just feeding the bull.

    tux̌ʷ ʔubə́dč̌ᵊbitəb

    They are implicating him although he is innocent.

dxʷ-s-

    dxʷsbə́dč̣   a liar

    tiʔił dəxʷsbə́dč̣   He's a liar.

reduplication

    dxʷsbáhəbàdč   a person who pretends to be more than
                           he is (e.g., Raven)   LL.

    dxʷsbáhəbədč   person who thinks he's smart, a big shot,
                           thinks he's really it, feels as though
                           he's above everybody.   LG.

Compare biawcut and yəwaʔq.

1.   bə́jqᵊb   move rapidly in a small area

    Cf. bak̓ʷ(a)

    See under jak̓ʷ(a).

2. s.bə́kʷ   ball

    See under búlux̌ʷ   'round'.

3. bək̓ʷ   all

    root   The uninflected form occurs in a variety of syntactic
                      positions. The following sentences examplify the
                      possibilities:

    adverb

      bək̓ʷ čəł dxʷx̌ʷi.q̓ʷús   We all have white faces.

    head of complement

      xʷiʔ gʷədsəs.ƛ̓əlábut ʔə kʷi bək̓ʷ

      I don't understand it at all.

modifies noun phrase

cə̌x̌ʷ.cəx̌ʷálu? ti?ił səs.čàjils bə̌kʷ ti?ə? q̓ilbids (h)əlgʷə?

They hid in the willows including their canoe.

?ululú?b ?i ti?ił dìⁱču? bə̌kʷ ti?ił kikəwič

There were eleven of them including Little Hunchback.

xʷi? gʷədsəs.ləqálbutbid bə̌kʷ t(i) adsgʷəd.gʷátəd

I don't understand all your language.

modifies noun

?u.?í?ub čəł bə̌kʷ s.łax̌il   We cried all night.

bə̌kʷ cqʷú́ł   every day

bə̌kʷ s.pà?c ƛ(u)as.?ìtut ?al pə(d).tə̀s   Skagit

All bears sleep in the winter.

ƛ̓ub čəł xʷu?ᵊlə? ?u.q̓ʷu?ᵊd kʷi bə̌kʷ titčulbixʷ

Hadn't we better gather all kinds of little animals?

modifies pronoun

gʷəl (h)uy bə.qʷú́?qʷa? ?al ti?ił bə̌kʷ čàd

And then he drank everywhere.

ƛ(u)as.lú́(h)utᵊb ?ə ti?ə? su.?ululuł ?ə ti?ə? bə̌kʷ gʷàt

?al kʷi sə.łax̌il

Everyone hears her as she paddles about (lit. 'water travels
about') in the evening.

qʷátqʷatatᵊbəxʷ ti?ə? bə̌kʷ s.tàb

They lay all the things (i.e., cuts of meat) all about.

bə̌kʷ s.tàb ?əs.?ə̀bstálətxʷ (h)əlgʷə?

They had to have money for everything.

?əs.jə̌ctxʷ ti?ił tàlə dxʷ?al bə̌kʷ s.tàb

Money is used for everything.

-t

    bə́k̓ʷəd   Take it all.

-il

    ʔubək̓ʷíləxʷ   all used up, all gone

    ʔəsbək̓ʷíləxʷ   That's all of it.

         Cf. xʷíʔil

-il-dxʷ

    bək̓ʷíldxʷ   took everything
                                finished it off

lexical

    dəču̓ʔ sbək̓ʷáči?   one hundred

    bək̓ʷáʔkʷbixʷ   all people

    ʔu.q̓ʷúʔtəbəxʷ tiʔił bək̓ʷáʔkʷbixʷ

    All the people were gathered.

    tuⱡil sbək̓ʷaʔkʷbixʷ   foreigners

    s.duhúbš čəd, bək̓ʷáʔkʷbixʷ, xʷiʔ gʷəds.yàyaʔ

    I'm Snohomish, all you people. I (recognize) no (one as a) friend.

         Cf. ʔádəkʷ   each and every one of you

  -idup

    bək̓ʷídup s.ʔulàdxʷ   all types of fish

1.   bək̓ʷ(u)   take what one finds (often referring to what can
                                   be eaten)

         Cf. dxʷ.bəx̌ʷíqad   scavenge

          xʷíʔxʷiʔ   forage for food (berries, small game etc.)
                                 (from xʷiʔ 'negative')

          gʷəč̓-   seek

Cf. čqʷíb	be able to share in receiving something (usually food)
kʷədálikʷ	help oneself to (from kʷəd 'grab, get')
bis(i)	select (one out of many)
ʔəy̓	find

-ut

bək̓ʷúd	pick up various eatable items (such as apples) from the ground gather up from the ground or floor

-b

sbə́k̓ʷəb	plunder gotten in a raid

lexical

ʔubə́k̓ʷálps čəd	I brought home an animal that I happened to find.
bək̓ʷúcid	help yourself (to eatables)
ʔubək̓ʷúcid čəd	I picked up something worth eating. I picked up stuff that no one else wanted.

reduplication

smíʔmk̓ʷàlps ML.	A favorite or loveable little stray animal that attaches itself to someone. (Lit. 'little pick-up') (The change from b to m adds an endearing quality.)

1. s.bə́k̓ʷbək̓ʷ — blue grouse

2. s.bələwíʔ — An unidentified bottom fish. It is similar to the saltwater bullhead. It eats salmon eggs.
Its other name is s.čə́bək̓ʷ. LL.

Cf. s.x̌ʷədíʔ — saltwater bullhead

1. bəláⁱgʷəʔ EK., LL. navel, according to EK., this is also the name for Mount Pilchuck

    bəláⁱwəʔ LG., LL. navel

      -b

        bəláⁱwə(ʔ)b tag along, as would a younger sibling after an older brother

2. bəlídəgʷəs blue-head, blue-bill, a buʔqʷ

3. bə́lkʷ return

    root

        ʔubə̀lkʷ čəd I returned.

      -txʷ

        bə́lkʷtxʷ return it

        bə́lkʷtxʷ dxʷʔal kʷədiʔ dəxʷ.ʔà̀ʔs Put it back where it was.

        ƛ́ub čəd ʔu bə̀lkʷtxʷ Should I put it back?

4. bəlqʷəyíʔqʷᵊb somersault
→
        lədxʷbəlbəlqʷəyíʔqʷᵊb He's doing somersaults. LG.
        (Heard as ...qʷiʔiqʷᵊb once.)

5. s.bəlúcid See under s.bálucid.

6. bə̀ləwᵊb bubbling up, spring of water, boiling

        ʔubə̀ləwᵊbáxʷ tiʔəʔ qʷùʔ The water is boiling.

          Cf. bú́ʔlac 'spring of water' LL.

            s.bú́ʔcᵊb 'spring of water' EK.

7. bəlúps SPS raccoon

          Cf. x̌áʔx̌əlus NPS raccoon (x̌al)

1. bə́lx̌ʷ   Skagit   'after' in time and space, pass, surpass

           pə́lq̓ʷ   'after' in other dialects

       bə́lᵊx̌ʷəɬdàt   Monday (lit. 'the day after')

       bəlᵊx̌ʷáx̌ʷ ʔəs.bùus   It's after 4 o'clock.

       bəlᵊx̌ʷáx̌ʷ dxʷʔal s.buus   Same gloss: It's after 4 o'clock.

       ʔəsbə́lᵊx̌ʷ ʔə kʷi cəlàcs tiʔəʔ ʔəs.(hə)d?ìwʔ
       There are more than five here.

    -t

       bə́lᵊx̌ʷəd   pass him

    reduplication

       bíʔbəlx̌ʷəd   pass him by a little

2. bəɬ   full (from food and drink)

    Cf. ləč̓   full (container)

    root

       bəɬáxʷ   NPS   full now

       bə́ɬəxʷ   SPS   full now

    -b-i-t

       dxʷ.ʔáləxʷ sbəɬbídəxʷ ʔə tiʔəʔ təkʷtəkʷəlùs   LG.
       Owl had had more than enough/ had gotten more than plenty
       of it.

    Compare:

       bəɬbíd   LG.   get more than enough of something
                                or someone

       biɬáʔil   ML., LL.   Same gloss: get more than enough of
                                something or someone

Compare:

čájax̌bid	get sick and tired of it
bápad	annoy/pester someone
x̌ʷáq̓ʷbid	bothered/worried/troubled by it
bálacᵊd	disturb/distract it

1. bə́qłti(y)uʔ   LL. Mukilteo

    Also recorded bək̓ʷəłtíwʔ from ES.

→

3. bəq̓   put in mouth, swallow

    See under ʔəł-.

    root

    tux̌ʷ ʔəbsbə́q̓   He has something in his mouth.

    -t

    bə́q̓ᵊd   swallow it

    bəq̓tᵊb   be swallowed

    ʔu.húydx̌ʷ čəd dx̌ʷʔal tiʔił gʷədəx̌ʷbə̀q̓ᵊds
    I entreated him until he swallowed it (a pill).

    lexical

    dx̌ʷbəq̓ʷúcid   Skagit   kiss him

    bəq̓ʷúci(di)c   Skagit   kiss me

       Cf. Snohomish lək̓ʷúcid   kiss

                    lək̓ʷúcidic čəxʷ   You kissed me.

    bəq̓ʷúcidači(ʔi)c   kiss my hand

4. bəqʷ   heavy set, fat, big

    Cf. hikʷ   big

        x̌ʷəs   fat of meat

root

    b̓ə́qʷ s.tùbš   heavy set man, fat/big man

    (hə)lá?bəxʷ čəd b̓ə̀qʷ   I'm really fat.

-il

    (hə)lá?bəxʷ čəd ?ubəqʷìl   I'm getting really fat.

    hí?i?əbəxʷ čəd ?ubəqʷìl   Same gloss: I'm getting really fat.

lexical

    bəqʷíča?   carry on shoulder

      Cf. čəbá?   backpack

    ləsbəqʷíča? čəd ?ə tə hud   I'm carrying wood on the shoulder.

    bəqʷíča?akʷčup   carry wood on shoulder

    ləsbəqʷíča?alc   carrying a rifle on the shoulder

    stábəxʷ ti ləsbəqʷíča?ᵊd   What's he carrying on his shoulder?

1. s.bəq̓ʷá? NPS   heron (not a bu?qʷ)

    s.bə́q̓ʷə? SPS heron

               xʷi? lə.bú?qʷ ti?ə? s.bəq̓ʷá? yəx̌i xʷi? gʷəʌsu.tíčibs
               x̌ʷúləb ?ə ti?ił bu?qʷ. xʷi? gʷəʌsu.?úsils. díł
               də(xʷ).xʷí?s lə.bu?qʷ ti?ił.   IM.

               A Heron is not (classed as) a bu?qʷ because it does
               not swim like a bu?qʷ. It does not dive. That is
               why it is not a bu?qʷ.

               The wife of s.bəq̓ʷa? was x̌ʷú?x̌ʷəy? 'Little Diver'.

    lexical

      bəq̓ʷá(?)qs bayonet

1.   bəs   thin

          See under tíʔttiš   'narrow'.

          Cf. λ̣u   thin person

               qʷəqʷqʷíʔs   thin, slender

     -il

          bəsíl   It came to be thin (as a worn cloth).

     reduplication

          bésbəs   thin board

2.   bəs-   derivational prefix indicating possession, especially territory over which a person or group has authority

       Cf. -bš, -bixʷ

          bəsíkʷigʷìlc   name of a Skagit River extended village (lit. 'people of the big rocks') See under hikʷ. (See Sampson, p.2, 21.)

          bəsq̓íxʷixʷ   name of a Skagit River extended village (lit. 'people way up river') See under q̓ixʷ. (See Sampson, p.2, 22.)

     -bəs-

          ciɬbəsbád   half-sibling with father in common

          ciɬbəsk̓ʷuy   half-sibling with mother in common

3.   bəsád   grow dark (evening)

          See under ɬax̌.

          Cf. səláx̌il   evening

          ʔubəsádijəxʷ čəxʷ   It's getting dark on you.

          λ̓álal uʔxʷ gʷəl ləbəsàd It's early yet, but it's getting dark.

1. bə́sqʷ   crab

2. bə́ščəb NPS   mink

       bíbščəb   small mink

       Cf. čəbálqid SPS   mink

3. bəxʷ   scavenge

       See under bə́kʷ(u).

       xʷuləxʷ čələp p̓aλaλ ɬudxʷbəxʷíqad liɬ.ʔilgʷiɬ

       You low counts will just scavenge along the water's edge.

4. -bi-   secondary suffix

       Cf. -i-

5. biác NPS   meat

     báyəc SPS   meat

       Note lexical suffixes -aɬči? 'meat' and -adis   'meat, hide, cloth'.

6. biáw

     s.biáw   coyote

        -t

         biáwcut   act smart. A person who pretends first to know then that he doesn't.

          Cf. yəwá?q

7. -bicid   object suffix   'thee'

       See under -bš.

1.   bík^w(i)   give slack

        -it

           bík^wid   Give it slack. (Says nothing about the rope.)

           bik^w(ə)yíbᵊd   Give the rope slack.

           híqəbəx^w čəx^w ʔubik^wid   You give it too much slack.
                                            (As when trying to land a fish.)

2. dx^w.bílcəp   fall on rump

        See under x^wíƛil.

        Cf. k̓^wə́q   fall on back

           tác̓x̌   fall forward (on the face)

3. g^wə.bíləd   well-done, overcooked

        Cf. bíʔw

        putəx^w ʔəsg^wəbíləd   It was very well-done.

4.   biƛáʔil   get more than plenty of it, have more than enough.
                              (Used figuratively in the sense of annoyed with
                              someone/something as well as literally.)

        See under bəɬ.

        dx^w.ʔáləx^w sbiƛáʔiləx^w ʔə tiʔəʔ tək^wtək^wəlùs   ML.
        Owl had gotten more than plenty of it/had had more than enough.

5.   biƛ(i)   smash, crush

        See under k̓aw-.   Contrast with juq̓^w(u).

        -it

           bíƛid   smash, crush it

-il

    təɬ bíƛil

In truth he (Slug) became smashed (when the bark fell on him).

-il-dxʷ

    ʔubíƛildxʷ   inadvertantly smashed it up
                                      (as "when I cook smelt, it all crumbles up.")
                                                               LL.

-il-txʷ

    ʔəsbíƛiltxʷ   already has it smashed up

    xʷî? ləbíƛiltxʷ t(i) ads.ʔùkʷukʷ   Don't smash your toy.

    xʷi?txʷ ləbíƛil   Don't let it smash up (e.g., a pie when
                                     cutting it).

lexical

    dxʷbíƛustəb   smashed up face

lexical (following root-il)

    bíƛildup   muddy, dirt

        Cf. ləqʷdúp   mud

            dxʷ.tíq̓ʷəb   murky water

            pədíxʷ   earth, ground, soil

            číq̓ʷil   filth

rejected:

    *bíƛdxʷ, *bíƛdub

→

2.   bísid   select it (out of many)

    See under bək̓ʷ(u).

3.   bit   ten cents

    sali?ilc ?i kʷi buusbit   2 dollars 40 cents

    c̓ú(?)kʷsbìt ?i kʷi ɬixʷìlc x̌ič̣ì.čc   73 cents

x̌ʷəlílc ʔi kʷi x̌ʷəlbìt ʔi kʷi ʔił.čəxʷbìt

ti ʔił x̌əčalc ʔə ti ʔił pùʔtəd

That shirt is dollars 9.95

reduplication

bitbit   ten per cent

1. s.bít   SPS   soup

     Cf. s.łúʔb   NPS   soup

2. bíwʔ   AS.   borrow

     Cf. čuł-   borrow

     ʔəxʷsʔalbíwʔəb čəd ʔə t(ə) ads.gʷàʔ

     I want to borrow yours.

3. -bixʷ   lexical suffix   'homogeneous group or cluster'

     Cf. -bš, bəs-

     gʷədbíxʷ   blackberry

     s.ʔəlʔəlbíxʷ   a mountain blueberry that grows on a low bush and is sweet

     sáʔqʷəbìxʷ   Sauk

     -aʔkʷ-

     bəkʷá(ʔ)kʷbixʷ   everyone

     (də)čákʷbixʷ   from a different tribe, others

     ləliʔákʷbixʷ   foreigners

     -al-

     p̓íc̓albixʷ ciʔəʔ qʷìst   milk the cow

     ƛ̓íp̓albixʷ   squeeze/hold the teat

39

ʔu.čəšál	suckle
ʔáciɫtalbixʷ	Indian; human as opposed to animal
tátačulbixʷ	animal
títčulbixʷ	small animal
s.dúkʷalbixʷ	Snoqualmie

1. bíʔ — river banks are washed away

-t

ləbíʔtəb — river banks are being washed away

2. miʔman — small, little

bíʔbad MS. (sometimes EK.) small, little

míʔmad LG. same gloss

míʔməʔn JC. same gloss

míʔman (or) mímaň (all other consultants) same gloss

míʔmad gʷəs.ʔíšɫs (h)əlgʷəʔ
They paddled only a little (and the magic boat skimmed over the water.)

míʔman čačas — baby

t(u)a(s).šuucəbš čəxʷ ʔal tudsmìʔman
You looked after me when I was little.

distributive

máʔman — group of small items

3. bíʔw — overcooked

See under xícil.

Cf. bil

ckʷaqid ʔəxʷbíʔwusəb
His face is always angry looking (lit. 'overcooked')

1. blás   molasses   (from English *molasses*)

2. -bš   object suffix   'me'

The pronominal object suffixes of Puget Salish are:

	singular		plural	
	(a)	(b)	(a)	(b)
person 1	-s ~	-bš	-ubuɫ ~	-buɫ
2	-sid ~	-bicid	-ubuɫəd ~	-buɫəd
3		(not marked)		

	(a)	(b)
reflexive	-sut ~	-but

All allomorphs labeled (a) follow -<u>t</u>. /-t/ plus /-s/ becomes /-c/:

čálac   chase me

čálacid   chase thee

čálacut   chase self

čálatubuɫ   chase us

čalatubuɫəd   chase you

(čálad   chase him, her, it, them)

Allomorphs labeled (b) occur with the other four transitive suffixes. The variants with /ə/ before <u>b</u> follow consonants:

ʔúx̌ʷcᵊbš   go after me

ʔúx̌ʷcᵊbicid   go after thee

ʔúx̌ʷcᵊbut   go after self

ʔúx̌ʷcᵊbuɫ   go after us

ʔúx̌ʷcᵊbuɫəd   go after you

(ʔúx̌ʷc   go after him, her, it, them)

1. -bš   lexical suffix   'people of'

        Cf. bəs-, -bix^w

čubə?ábš	Skagit people who live in the area of Lyman, Washington
s.duhúbš	Snohomish
dx^w.dəw?ábš	Duwamish
dúk^wəčàbš	Skagit people who live on the duk^wač River
s.q^wədábš	name of a Skagit people
s.q̓íx^wəbš	Skykomish
s.túləg^wábš	Stillaguamish
s.(y)u?q̓^wábš	Suquamish
s.wə́dəbš	Swinomish
s.wádəbš	the people east of the mountains
?íhiwəbš	(same gloss)

         (Note also the final element in s.tubš 'man'.)

2. bšč̓ád   louse

3. cis.bújał   a woman's name, LG.'s husband's father's father's sister

4. búbx̌əd   horsetail (scouring-rush)

      (Gunther, p.15, says it means 'makes it smooth'.)

5. búlux̌^w   round; sphere

        Cf. s.bə́k^w   ball

           s.bəbí?   hoop

      Contrast p̓íl   flat, broad.

ʔəsbúlux̌ʷ tiʔəʔ čáwəyʔ ʔə tiʔəʔ s.x̌əṗáb. ləlí tiʔəʔ čáwəyʔ
ʔə tiʔəʔ haʔac. gʷəl tux̌ʷ huy ʔəs.ṗil tiʔəʔ čáwəyʔs.

The shell of the cockle is round. The shell of the horse
clam is different. In contrast, its shell is flat.

1.   búlcəb   swamp blueberry

2.   -buɫ   object suffix   'us'

      See under -bš.

3.   -buɫəd   object suffix   'you (pl.)'

      See under -bš.

4.   -but   reflexive

      See under -bš.

5.   búus   four

      lexical

          sbúusəɫdàt(il)   Thursday

          sbúusàči?   forty

          buusálgʷiɫ   four canoes

          búusali   four growing plants

          buusálps   four animals, esp. horses

          buusál?txʷ   four houses

          buusáɫčup   four fires

          buusáɫič   four bundles

          búusəlus   four squares in a net, four stitches
                                    in knitting

          búusilc   four dollars

          búusqs   four points

búusulč	four baskets, four containers
dxʷsbúusus	four rows, four layers

reduplication

bəbúʔs	four people
bíʔbuus	four little ones

1. buyus   slang for primping

   -t

   búyu(s)cut   primping (slang)

   lexical

   ʔubúyusqi(d)c   fixed my head (i.e., had my hair done
                        (at the beauty parlor))

2. s.búʔcᵊb EK.   spring of water

   Cf. búʔlac, bə́ləwᵊb

3. búʔqʷ NPS   waterfowl
                       This word is a generic term for all waterfowl that
                       are good swimmers such as ducks, geese, mergansers,
                       and the like. It does not include shorebirds.

   Cf. s.q̓ʷálaš   SPS   waterfowl   See under s.bəq̓ʷáʔ.

4. búʔlac LL.   spring of water

   Cf. búʔcᵊb, bə́ləwᵊb

c

This letter represents a sound similar to the *ts* of English *cats* and *tsetse* fly. [voiceless alveolar affricate]

1. -c   a transitive suffix
         (Vowels are lengthened before -c.)
         Compare with -s. -c and -s may turn out to be
         allomorphs of the same morpheme. Their meanings
         appear similar and they are in complementary
         distribution. However, until their significance
         is more fully understood, they are treated as
         representing different morphemes.

2. cáadiɫ   See under cədíɫ.

3. s.cácəlqid   man's name for LG.'s father's older brother (John)

4. cág^{w}əl   (meaning unknown)

   cág^{w}əl s.duhùbš   I am Snohomish.

    Cf. s.duhúbš čəd   I am Snohomish.

5. cág^{w}ič(əd)   tiger lily bulb

6. cáləɫ Puyallup lake

  Cf. x̌áču? NPS lake

    q^{w}əlút (Suquamish; possibly a misrecording of q^{w}əlúlt, *q.v.*)

7. s.cápa   grandfather

  cápa (no /s-/) vocative for grandfather

  See under bədá?.

8. cáq̓(a) NPS jab, poke

  See under k̓aw.

  Compare: cíq(i) poke, jab   cə́q̓   spear

      cíki   poke with a stick cq^{w}úɫ post, sticking up

root

ʔucáq̓ čəd ʔə tiʔəʔ s.x̌ədìʔac I got stuck by the devil's club.

-at

ʔucáq̓ətᵊb čəd ʔə tə čəsày I've been jabbed with a spear.

-dxʷ

ʔucáq̓dxʷ I hit him.

ʔucáq̓ᵊdub ʔə tə q̓ìlbid There was an automobile accident.

lexical

ʔucáq̓àči̓ čəd dxʷʔal ti s.x̌ədìʔac

I got stuck in the hand by the devil's club.

reduplication

cácq̓ NPS act of spearing big game on the salt water

 Compare cácq̓ with tpíl and x̌ág̓ʷič. The SPS equivalent of cácq̓ is cícq̓.

cáq̓caq̓ad poking it

1. cay SPS   adverb 'very'

Cf. cickʷ NPS   very

cáy ʔəs.pìxʷil tə d.x̌ə̀č JC.

I'm completely disorganized. ("This is a slang use of pixʷil.")

cáy čəxʷ ʔəs.jə̀wil ʔal ti s.lə̀x̌il JC.

You are elegantly dressed.
You are acting in a dignified way.

2. cáʔagiʔ   sound made by unidentified kind of duck
          (also nickname for that duck)   ESi.

3. cə   article 'known to addressee'

  See under ti.

1. cəb   second, two

      Cf. sáliʔ   two

      cəbáb kʷi s.tàšətˤbs ʔə kʷi səs.ʔìtuts
      Twice they rubbed him down while he slept.

      cəbágʷił   two canoes

      cəbdát kʷi s.ʔàs   Two days he was there.

      scəbdát(il)   Tuesday

      cəbálʔtxʷ   two houses

      cəbaƛ́ádiʔ   heard it twice

      cəbádxʷ   two years

      cəb x̌ʷiƛ   two spans

2. cədíł   as pronoun: the particular one (who)

                   as modifier: the very (one)

      Cf. dił

   as pronoun

      ʔəs.qʷíbicut tiʔəʔ cədíł
      He is all fixed up.

      kʷi s.čətxʷəd dił ʔəxʷ.cutˤb cədíł kʷi dəxʷə.ʔibəš ʔə ciʔił k̉aʔk̉aʔ
      Bear thought he was the one Crow was travelling for.

      ʔalil tiʔił cədíł bədəxʷ.łalils (h)əlgʷəʔ
      It came to be the place where they went ashore again.

      k̉ʷəłk̉ʷłád ciʔəʔ cədíł tusəs.x̌acbids ʔal tiʔił q̉iƛ̉q̉ilbid
      She kept pouring that which she had along for her lunch into the canoes.

as modifier

gʷədiltub ʔəs.q̓ʷuʔ ʔə tiʔəʔ <u>cədił</u> dəbəł tiʔəʔ xʷ.či̓łqs

They sat her down next to <u>this</u> worthy son of Oyster.

təqdúbəxʷ ʔə tiʔəʔ <u>cədił</u> dukʷibəł

<u>This</u> (<u>very</u>) Transformer blocked her (way).

reduplication

tu.ǰúʔiləxʷ tiʔəʔ <u>caadił</u>

<u>Those</u> (<u>people</u>) had a good time.

diłəxʷ dəxʷ.ǰuʔil ʔə tiʔił <u>caadił</u> ʔaciłtalbixʷ

That is what made <u>those</u> people glad.

→

2.　cə̓kʷ　　　　　　straight　　See 50.3.

root

cə́kʷ　　　　　　　　　straight

cə́kʷ čəxʷ　　　　　　　You are right.

húyud cə̓kʷ　　　　　　make it straight

cíckʷ cə̓kʷ　　　　　　It's very straight.

-t

cə́kʷəd　　　　　　　　tell the truth　　EK.
　　　　　　　　　　　make it straight　LG.

cə̓kʷcut　　　　　　　　straighten up (posture)

ʔəxʷcə̓kʷcutəb čəd　　　I want to straighten it out.

-dxʷ

dáʔxʷ čəd ʔucə̓kʷədxʷ　I just now understand it.

cə̓kʷdxʷáxʷ čəxʷ　　　　You got it right.　　LG.

See under <u>ləq̓ał-</u>.

-il

c̓k̓ʷíldxʷ   understand, have straight

-txʷ

c̓ə́k̓ʷtxʷ   Make sure it is straight.

c̓ə́k̓ʷtxʷ kʷ(i) ads?u.g̓ʷàag̓ʷəd   Make your story straight.

lexical

c̓k̓ʷíč   short cut

c̓ək̓ʷədúp   level

1.   cəlác   five

cəlácači?   fifty

cəlác s.bək̓ʷàči?   five hundred

cəllác   five people

cícəlàc   five small ones

scəlácəɫdàt(il)   Friday

2.   cəlq   halve, divide into two equal parts

-t

cə́lqᵊd tə d.?àyəd   Share equally with my friend.

cə́lqc čəxʷ   Give me half; divide it into two.

lexical

?ucə̀lqg̓ʷásᵊd   Divide it up; share it.

3.   cəɫ

cəɫdálbali   pulse, pressure point

cəɫcəɫdálb   the sharp, fairly loud sigh that the
                                               old people make

xʷcəɫdálbali   trachea

-il

    cə́ƛil   SPS   bleed

    cƛíl   NPS   bleed

-il-t

    cƛíld   bleed him (as in treating a snake bite)

lexical

    cƛíla?ɬdəɬ   bloody lip

    cƛílqs   nosebleed

1. s.cəqí   sockeye salmon, a s.?uladx^w LL.

    Cf. s.čí?ɬ, x^w.bádi?, čəwádx^w

2.   cəqɬcút   sizzle

    rejected: *cə́qɬ^{ə}d

3.   cəq̓   jab, spear

    Compare: caq̓(a), cik̓(i) and ciq(i).

   -t

    ?ucə́q̓^{ə}d čəd tə p̓uày?   I speared the flounder.

   lexical

    cəq̓^{ə}dís^{ə}bəd   fork (lit. 'something to stick with')

      Cf. čəč̓^{ə}dísbəd   toothpick

   reduplication

    cícq̓   SPS   act of spearing big game on the salt water

4. cə́q^w rectum

→

1. cəx̌ʷálu?   willow   ML.

        Compare:

            x̌ʷəx̌ʷálu?(ac)   willow (tree)   LG.

            s.x̌ʷálu?(əc)   willow (tree)   MC.

            s.čáp(ac)   willow (tree)   ESi.

2. ci   article

                        1. new information
                        2. emphasis

        See under ti.

3. cíckʷ   NPS   adverb 'very'
                        (Perhaps an original reduplication etymologically
                          related to cək̓ʷ 'straight' and ck̓ʷaqid 'always')

        Cf. cay   SPS   'very'

        cíckʷəxʷ čəd ?əs.tàgʷəxʷ   I'm really hungry.

        cìckʷ q̓íč ci?ə? s.łàdəy? ?ə kʷədi? tu.hà?kʷ
        Women were very expensive a long time ago.

4. cícu?/cícuh

        dxʷcícu?ap ~ dxʷcícuhap   sit down   LL.
        "Kind of a joking word - used only with friends and children.
         Literally, 'put (your) seat down a bit'."   LL.

        /cu? ~ cuh/ does not occur.

        Cf. gʷədíl

5. cigʷ

        xʷcigʷədid   take parts out of something

1. cík̓(i)

    Cf. caq̓(a), ciq(i), cəq̓

    -it

    cík̓id   poke it with a stick

    lexical

    ck̓áy̓staq   poke a fire

2. cikʷ(i)   move, jerk, tug

    See under ɬəlp̓ and təx̌ʷ(u).

    -it

    cík̓ʷitˀb   (A fish) jerked (on the line).

    ləcucík̓ʷicut   twitching

    gʷə-...-ad

    x̌ʷi? k̓ʷ(i) adsgʷəcík̓ʷəd   Don't move!

3. cil(i)   upbear, place on/in a receptacle; dish up

    root

    ʔúx̌ʷtubəxʷ tiʔiɬ s.t̓əlù?b ?al tiʔiɬ ʔəscílcil
    Dried salmon is to be taken and served up.

    ləscíl tiʔiɬ jəsəds ?al tiʔiɬ sə.ʔibəšs
    Her feet are protected when she walks.

    ?ə(s)cíləxʷ tə s.?əɬˀd
    The food is on the table/in the dish.

    -it

    cílid   serve food, dish it up

    ƛúb x̌ʷùl ɬucílitˀb tiʔiɬ s.?əɬˀd
    Just let someone dish up the food.

-dxʷ

ʔucíldub tiʔił ads.ʔə̀łᵊd

Your food was mistakenly put on the wrong plate.

-txʷ

ʔəscíltxʷ   It's put on something.

ləscíltub   It's already put on (the platter).

-yi-

bələcílyitᵊbəxʷ   They dished it up for him again.

lexical

húyutᵊbəxʷ tiʔił s.łàgʷid cícəĺšaad

A mat was made to support (her) feet.

húyutᵊbəxʷ tiʔəʔ dəxʷcícəĺšaadᵊbəxʷ ʔə ciʔəʔ k̓àʔka?

They made a carpet for Crow's feet.

cíliwʔ   basin, pan   (See under ła?x̌.)

reduplication

cicəĺšaad   diminutive

húyutᵊbəxʷ tiʔił s.łàgʷid cícəĺšaad

A mat was made to support (her) feet.

cílcilitᵊbəxʷ   dish up (for a group)

1.   cił   emphatic particle (emphasizes what is being talked
                                            about)

díł tiʔəʔ cił dəxʷu.yáyusčəł

It is for this that we are working.

2.   cił-   Snoh.   derivational prefix   'half-sibling'

cíłbəs.bad   half-sibling with common father

cíłbəs.k̓ʷuy   half-sibling with common mother

1.　ciq(i)　　　　　　　poke, jab

　　　　Compare:

　　　　　　cáq̓(a)　　poke, jab　　　　　LL.

　　　　　　cík̓(i)　　poke with a stick　LL., ID.

　　　　　　cə́q̓　　　spear it　　　　　　SPS

　　　　　　cqʷúɫ　　post sticking up

　　　-it

　　　　cíqid　　　poke, jab it

　　　lexical

　　　　dxʷcíqəp　　poke in the rear with something sharp

2.　cixʷ-　　　　　　　derivational prefix　'-in-law'

　　　　See Hoard/Hess, p.51.

　　　　cixʷʔíbac　　　　　grandchild's spouse

　　　　dəcixʷʔíbac　　　　my grandchild's spouse

3.　cix̌(i)

　　　　See under səx̌əb.

　　　-it

　　　　cíx̌id　　　　　　　an abrupt rhythm

　　　lexical

　　　　ləcíx̌aci(ʔ)b　　　trotting

　　　　　Cf. t̓ít̓ədàči(ʔ)b　loping (of a horse)

4.　ciʔə́ʔ　　　　　demonstrative　'this'

　　distributive: tiiʔə́ʔ

　　　rejected: *ciiʔə́ʔ

　　　　See under ti.

1. ciʔíɬ   demonstrative 'that'

       distributive: tiiʔíɬ

         rejected: *ciiʔíɬ

       See under ti.

2. c̓k̓ʷálidxʷ   thank you (not the same as dàhᵊdubš)   MC.

      LG. and VH. give ʔəs.cuk̓ʷálid.

3. c̓k̓ʷáqid NPS   adverb 'always'

      Cf. c̓ᵊqáqid SPS   always

      (Perhaps etymologically related to cíck̓ʷ 'very'.)

      c̓k̓ʷàqid čəxʷ ɬ(u)as.x̌əɬ
      You will always be sick.

4. c̓kúsəd   cane, walking stick   LG.

      "In another dialect there is the word cə́k̓ᵊd 'poke it',
         but it is not a Skagit term."   LG.

      Cf. čk̓ʷúsəd   cane, walking stick   LL.

5. cɬíl   See under cə́ɬil.

6. s.cqápsəb   front part of neck

7. cqíws Skagit   trousers

      Cf. yəlábcəd Snoh. and SPS   trousers

8. cqʷáb

      ʔəscqʷáb   tight, taught

9. cqʷúɬ

      ʔəscqʷúɬ   post, sticking up

...dxʷʔal tus.ʔəy̓dxʷs kʷi sc_ə_q̓ʷuɬs šaqʷiləxʷ...

...until he found a log across...

    Cf. s.t̓ə̓k̓ʷəb   SPS   log, tree

xʷ_cq̓ʷú̓ɬ   day

bək̓ʷ _cq̓ʷù̓ɬ_   everyday

    Cf. t̓agʷt   noon

      s.ləx̌il   day

1.   cúbəd   eyebrow

2.cis.cúcəblu   one of VH.'s names

    Her other names are: táqʷšəblù

                        q̓ʷəstányə

                        cis.q̓ʷálaɬq̓ʷàl

3.   cukʷ   Skagit   adverb; also serves as predicate head   'only'

    Cf. day?   Snoh. and Sauk   only

    (It is possible that a /ʔ/ was missed before the last consonant, i.e., the form might be cuʔkʷ.)

    adverb

        ləs.čálad čəɬ yəxi cùkʷ ʔəs.(h)áydxʷ ti ši̓ʔ.šəgʷɬ

        We followed him because he is the only one who knows the trail.

    -txʷ

        cùkʷtxʷ ʔu.ʔúx̌ʷ   Let just him go.

    lexical

        díɬəxʷ ɬucùgʷáɬəxʷ   That will be the last.

    reduplication

        cúgʷukʷ čəd ʔal tiʔə?   I'm alone here.

cíʔccugʷad čəd   I'm all alone. (Usually /ʔ/ replaces /d/.)

x̌ʷuɫ čəxʷ ʔu cəcugʷa Are you all alone?

1. ʔəs.cuk̓ʷálid   thank you   LG., VH.

    ck̓ʷálidxʷ   thank you   MC.

    See also dáhᵊdubš.

2.   cúluq̓ʷyus   man's name for LG.'s father's father

3.   cut   adverb   'in order that/to'

    ʔu.tučadiʔ čəd cut ɫ(u)as.x̌əjàs
    I shot at random just to scare him.

    gʷə.kʷáxʷacid čəd cut ɫə.xʷiʔəxʷ lə.bàkʷɫ
    I'll help you so you won't get hurt.

4.   cut   say, tell

    Compare:

ʔíl(i)		speak
gʷád		speak, speak a language, speech
yə́c		inform
túɫ(u)		interpret
-ucid		language, speech
ʔuʔíd(i)gʷət čəxʷ		What did you say?
təjúcid		answer
qʷíʔad	Snoh.	shout, announce in a loud voice
wíʔəd	Skagit	shout, announce in a loud voice
(yə)yəhúbtxʷ	NPS	recite a myth
(s)x̌ʷiʔáb	SPS	recite a myth

ləlǝʔúlᵊb	recite the history of a people
gʷíh(i)	invite
híl(i)	tell someone to do something
júhəb	talk
dxʷʔəhádəd	talk about
kǽskᵊb / qəsqᵊb	chatting away all the time; never quiet
x̌íx̌λ̣ùstəgʷəl̓ (fig.)	converse (lit. 'nibble each other's faces')
státabəb	gossip
x̌áλil	argue
-udəq	conference, parley, agenda
gə́lgəb	mumble
c̓ú(h)àyucid (fig.)	mumble (lit. 'weak chin') Said of those who do not speak loudly enough for everyone at a gathering to hear.
ʔə́č̓ʔəč	stammer, stutter
k̓ʷíčicut	stammer, stutter
ʔíwb	cry
ƛ̓íqicut	scream, loud crying
ƛ̓ílib	sing
x̌ʷíw̓ʔad	whistle
ƛ̓íʔəb	war cry
kší	shoo
šá	shoo

58

root

ʔucút ciʔił kàʔkaʔ   Crow said.

x̌əł ti ƛ̓ucut tiʔəʔ qyuuqs
Just like seagulls always talking.

ʔəscút tə ƛ̓su.ʔílitᵊbs
That's the way they were saying it.

ʔəcà gʷəl łu.kʷədád tiʔił s.ƛ̓àlabəc ʔə tiʔił dᵊs.qa
cut tiʔił diič̓uʔ
"I will take the garment of my older brother,"
said one.

pronominal suffix

(A very few roots can take a pronominal suffix directly --
no transitive suffix occurs. In this respect compare
łəgʷł ~ łəgʷ(ᵊ)l- 'leave'.)

ʔucútᵊbš čəxʷ   You said to me.

reduplication

ʔucútcut ti tab   Thom said so.

ʔu.č̓ígʷisəxʷ čəd ʔə tiʔił ʔucútcut
I'm getting irritated with her jabbering.

ʔalč̓ucútcut   He said so.

-b

(These forms with -b pattern syntactically as though they were
derived from *cut-t-b with the subsequent loss of one t. However, the pronominal suffix allomorphs -s, -sid, etc. do not
occur, suggesting that the transitive -t does not, in fact,
follow cut. A very few other roots, e.g., łəgʷł, suxʷt- take
-b without -t and the pronominal object suffixes of set (b)
instead of set (a). The construction, however, is equivalent
to the far more numerous type root-t-b; and it is not like the
middle voice construction root-b. (Whether or not there are two
homophonous suffixes of the shape -b is not yet known.))

-b

cút^əb ʔə tiʔił tu.luλluλ

The old people (used to) say so.

dəc̓áx^wəs k^wədà g^wəl g^wə.λəlábut g^wəcut^əbəs ʔə k^wi stab

For once he would mind if ever you tell him anything.

-bi-t

cút^əbid ʔə tiʔił tu.luλluλ

The old people (used to) say that.

reduplication

cútcut^əbəx^w ʔə tiʔəʔ wiw̓su

The children talked (it over among themselves).

-c

díłəx^w dəx^wəscùucs ciʔəʔ cədił qiʔqəl̓adiʔ

That is why she tells Little Uprooted Tree.

tədəx^wcúucs ciʔəʔ bədàʔs

Therefore, he told his daughter. (This form,
<u>tu</u>-<u>dəx^w</u>-<u>cu(t)</u>-<u>uc</u>-<u>s</u>, is equivalent to
<u>tu</u>-<u>dəx^w</u>-<u>yəc</u>-<u>^əb</u>-<u>tx^w</u>-<u>s</u>.)

cúucəx^w tiʔəʔ stə.tudəqs qyuuqs

She told her seagull slaves.

tucùuc čəd g^wə.x^wiʔəs g^wəsu.k̓^wíts dx^wʔal tə s.tùlək^w

I told him not to go down to the river.

łucúucbułəd čəd ʔəs.ʔəx̌id g^wəs.huyləp

I will tell you folks what you are to do.

-c-b

cúuc^əbəx^w ciʔəʔ bədàʔs

They told her daughter.

ʔəs.cúucᵊb cədił ti t̓uc̓ud tə s.paʔc

They say he (is the one who) shot the bear.

gʷə-...-ad

huy, x̌əł ti ʔugʷəcútad

Then they made a fuss (noise) like that.

dxʷ-...-b

dxʷcutᵊb   think (wish to say?)
   Cf. ptidəgʷasᵊb, t̓ukʷ/gʷu-

ʔəxʷcútᵊb čəd, ƛub xʷiʔ kʷi gʷ(ə)ads.ʔəx̌ dxʷʔal tə d.ʔalʔal
ʔal tiʔəʔ x̌aʔx̌aʔ

I think it is better that you do not come to my house this week.

ʔəxʷcútᵊb čəd ʔə kʷi dsəs.x̌ə̀ł

I think I'm ill.

ʔəxʷcútᵊb čəd xʷi̓ʔ   I doubt it.   LL.
   Cf. ʔəs.qʷácdxʷ čəd   I doubt it.   LG.

      xʷiʔ gʷədsəs.tłíldxʷ   I don't believe it.
      xʷiʔ gʷədsəs.q̓álbid   I don't believe it.

-b-i-t

ʔəxʷcútᵊbid čəd

I thought so.

ʔəxʷcútᵊbid čəd dəgʷí kʷi ʔu.k̓ʷə̀łᵊd

I think you are the one who spilled it.

xʷùʔᵊləʔəxʷ ʔəxʷcútᵊbitᵊb ʔə tiʔəʔ cədił dùkʷibəł,
dayʔəxʷ (h)áʔł tiʔacəc q̓ʷəlb ʔə tiʔacəc bəščəb

Dukʷibəł must have thought, "That roasted (salmon)
of Mink's sure is good."

reduplication

ʔəxʷcúcutᵊbid čəd   I sort of think so.   LL.

1. s.cuʔíɬ   pudenda

c̓

The letter c̓ stands for a sound somewhat like that of c̲ except that the former has a simultaneous abrupt closure of the vocal cords, a sort of catch in the throat. [glottalized alveolar affricate]

1.   c̓ábid   blue camas, crow potato

     xʷ.c̓ábiǰigʷəd   March, i.e., the time of the camas tubers

2.   s.c̓ábt   red elderberry, a s.q̓ʷəlaɬəd

3.   c̓ájax̌   See under bəɬ(bíd).

     huy, ʔuc̓ájax̌bitəbəxʷ ciʔəʔ čəgʷàs ʔə tiʔiɬ təkʷtəkʷəlùs
     Then, they got sick and tired of the wife of Owl.

     huy, ʔəsc̓ájəx̌bitəbəxʷ ciʔəʔ čəgʷàs ʔə tiʔəʔ ʔaciɬtalbixʷ
     ʔəs.ɬaɬlil
     Then, the people who lived there were sick and tired of (his) wife.

4.   c̓al-   obstruct the view

     Contrast wəlí   'appear, be visible'.

     root

        ləc̓áləxʷ tə ɬùkʷəɬ
        The sun is going out of sight (setting or going behind a cloud).

     -t

        c̓ald   obstruct the view of it

        ʔuc̓aləd čəd   I blocked the view of him.

        ʔuc̓álcut čəd   I hid myself.

           Cf. čaj, tigʷil

     -bi-t

        c̓álbid   shadow

lexical

    čaličtəd   umbrella

1.   čáladi?   side of the head

2. s.čáli? Snoh., SPS heart

    Cf. yədwás Skagit heart

3. s.čáp(ac) SPS   willow (tree)   ESi.

    Cf. cəx̌ʷálu? willow   ML.

        x̌ʷəx̌ʷálu?(ac) willow (trec) LC.

        s.x̌ʷálu?(əc) willow (tree) MC.

→

5.   čáqᵊb   a strong and unpleasant odor

    See under sub(u).

6.   čáq̓ab SPS   gooseberry, a s.q̓ʷəlaɬᵊd

    Cf. (s)čəq̓áb Snoh. gooseberry

        ƛ̓ábxʷ Skagit gooseberry

7.   čáqalus   eye matter

    reduplication

        čáqčaqalus   'cheese-eyed', i.e., a lot of matter in one's eyes -- an insult

→

9.   s.čáx̌əč   sole (fish)

    Cf. čə́x̌   worn out

10. čáxʷəy(əc)   white pine (tree)   EK., ESi.

    Cf. jújəbàlikʷ(ac) white pine (tree) (under jub)

1. čáwč̓   bracelet

2. č̓áyə   fur seal

    Cf. sup̓qs   hair seal

      ʔašx^w/ʔasx^w   hair seal

      ʔəš̓ás   sea lion

3. čayk̓-   [Considered by some to be a vulgar word; others
               do not think it objectionable.]

    Cf. bə́jq^əb   move rapidly in a small area

    -t

      ʔəl̓čučáykcut   always chattering

    lexical

      <u>čáyk̓alùs^əb</u>   squint

        Cf. q^wícalus   squint

      ʔəx̌íd əẃə <u>čàyk̓əp</u>   unladylike behavior

4. č̓áyq   a power for procuring any and all kinds of food.
               It chases the food to you or shows you where it is.
                                          MC.

    s.č̓áyq   a slowly danced power for hunting   LG.

    See under <u>s.qəlalítut</u>.

5. s.č̓áy(ʔ)t SPS   gills

    Cf. s.x̌əyáy̓   Snoh.   gills

        s.x̌áy̓ay̓   Skagit   gills

6. č̓aʔk^w ~ č̓ag^wa-   wash

    Cf. t̓it̓^əb   bathe

root

čə̓scá?kʷ   washed

-at

čágʷəd   wash it

čágʷəcut   wash self up

lexical

čágʷəbàcᵊb   wash own body

čagʷəldí?ᵊb   Wash your ears!

dxʷčagʷəldí?ᵊd   She washed his ears.

   rejected: *dxʷčagʷəldi?ᵊb

ča?kʷdáliɬᵊd   wash food

ck̓ʷàqid ƛučà?kʷdáliɬᵊd tə x̌a?x̌əlus
A raccoon always washes its food.

čágʷidup   scrub floor

čə?kʷqídᵊb   Wash your head/hair!

čə?kʷqí?ᵊd   Wash his head/hair!

   rejected: *dxʷčə?kʷqidᵊb

           *dxʷčə?kʷqi?ᵊd

čəgʷúlč   wash dishes

dxʷčəgʷúlč   dishwashing machine   LG.

səxʷučəgʷúlč   what is used to wash dishes
                                                 LG.

sixʷ(u)čəgʷúlč   person who washes dishes   LG.

sixʷučəgʷúlč həlgʷə?   She is their dishwasher.   LG.

ʔudxʷc̓agʷusᵊb   He washed his (own) face.

ʔəxʷc̓agʷusᵊbəxʷ   He has his (own) face washed now.

rejected:

*ʔixʷ(u)c̓əgʷúlč   "because you can't belong to the machine"   LG.

*c̓ágʷil, *c̓ágʷagʷil, *c̓ágʷᵊb

1.   c̓áʔsuč   bow (archery)   ESi.

Cf. q̓číc NPS   bow   Also recorded as c̓ácus EW.

See under q̓əč.

2.   c̓əb-

c̓əbál̓qid SPS   mink

Cf. bə́šc̓əb NPS   mink

sc̓əbqíd   brain

3.   c̓əb- NPS   pick berries/fruit

kʷil SPS   pick berries/fruit

-yi-

tu.bákʷɫačiʔ čəd gʷəl díɫ cə ds.qà tuc̓əbyic ʔə tə s.qʷəlàɫᵊd
I hurt my hand so my older sister picked berries for me.

-b

ʔuc̓əbᵊb čəd tə s.təgʷàd   I picked salmonberries.

-b-iluɫ

c̓əbᵊbíluɫ   go to pick berries

t(u)asc̓əbᵊbíluɫ čəd   I went berrying (long ago).

4.   s.c̓əbáyʔus   blue/black huckleberry, a s.q̓ʷəláɫᵊd
→

1. čəčáʔus   thimbleberry sprouts

    Cf. ɫáqəʔ   thimbleberry

2. s.čədčəd   kidney   EK.

    Cf. čƛ̓alúb   kidney   LG.

        s.p̓ús   kidney   ML.

3. čəjáqʷ   red-shafted flicker

4. s.čə́jx̌   stinging nettles

5. čək-   See under x̌aƛ̓.

    ʔəsčək̓ᵊbíd čəd kʷi gʷəds.ʔùx̌ʷ dxʷʔal kʷi lı̀l s.wàtixʷtəd
    I'm eager to go to a distant land.

6. s.čə́k̓ʷ   worm (generic), bug   LG.

    Cf. s.ʔúləč̓   worm

    reduplication

        sč̓íč̓k̓ʷ   a small worm or bug

7. čəl-   win, get the better of

    Contrast ʔu.x̌ʷál̓.

    -dxʷ

        čə́ldxʷ   win

    lexical

        čəlálikʷ čəd   I won.

        ʔiɫ.čád kʷi ʔučəlálikʷ   Which side won?   LG.

        dxʷsčəlálikʷ   He's a winner.

ƛub čəxʷ ʔučəlálikʷtubuɬ dxʷʔal gʷəl bək̓ʷ jək̓ʷadədčəɬ

It is well that you win us over from all our error.

(From the translation of the Lord's Prayer and corresponds
to the English translation, "And lead us not into temp-
tation.")

čəlálq   sticks used in the bone game   DM.

1. s.čəlíč   NPS   backbone (of mammals including humans)

    s.čə́lič   SPS   backbone

    Cf. s.x̌ə́x̌əč   backbone of a fish

    lexical

    čəlíǰəpsəb   upper end of spine

2. čəlčəlkáyus   chickadee   VH.

    či̓čəlkáyus   "Another way of saying chickadee."   VH.

3. čəlk̓ádiʔ   See under či̓lk̓àdiʔ.

4. čəlqáy̓ac   spruce tree   LL.

    (Also recorded   čəl̓qáyəc   spruce tree   MC., VH.

                     čəl̓káyəc   spruce tree   LG.)

5. čəlqíws   cut all up

    See under ɬič̓(i).

    tux̌ʷ čəɬ ʔu.bəčálq ʔə tiʔəʔ čəɬ ʔučəɬqíwsᵊd

    We just killed this (game animal); we cut it all up.

    (Or perhaps, because of the unusual position of the second
    čəɬ, a better gloss would be: We just killed this (big
    game animal) which we cut all up.)

1. čəlqʷcút   glitter, sparkle

2. s.čəpálič   swamp, stagnant water

   Cf. qʷəlúlt   marsh

   čəp̓čəp̓dúp   a lot of puddles of water

3. čəp̓yíqʷ   great-great-great-grandparent
                       great-great-great-grandchild

   See under bəda?.

4. s.čəq   SPS   fermented salmon eggs,
                      "Indians' Limburger cheese"   ESi.

   Cf. du?áyus   fermented salmon eggs   LL.

      dəw?áyus   fermented salmon eggs   LG.

5. čəq̓

   lexical

       ?učə̓q̓qs čəxʷ   (Something) you (ate) went down the wrong
                        'pipe'.

       č̓q̓áp   a pole for poling a canoe

       č̓q̓á(hə)b   act of poling a canoe

6. (s)čə̓q̓áb   Shoh.   gooseberry, a s.q̓ʷəlaɫᵊd   LL.

   Cf. s.čəq̓áb   gooseberry   EK.

      čáq̓ab SPS   gooseberry   ESi.

   sč̓q̓ábac   name for the site of Langley, Washington;
                       literally 'gooseberry bush(es)'   LL.

   Cf. t̓ə́bxʷ Skagit   gooseberry   MC.

1. s.čəqʷálc   home-made ammunition (cylindrical in shape)

     Cf. q̓íwədìlc   buckshot

2. čəs   See under čis(i).

3. čə́tq   pinch

    -t

      čə́tqəd   pinch it

      čə́tqtəb   got pinched

    -yi-

      ʔiɬčətqyíc   Give me a pinch of it.

    lexical

      číčtqapəd   pinch on the bottom

    reduplication

      ʔiɬčíčətq   little pinch of some (food)

      Compare the construction ʔiɬ.čə́tq with pəqʷ(u).

→

5. čəwíl   good-looking

    dayʔəxʷ ʔəsčəwíl ciʔə lə.ʔìbəš   LL.
    That one walking (this way) is sure good-looking.

      Cf. háʔɬ šùɬ   Snoh. good-looking

         háʔɬubš   Skagit good-looking

6. čə́x̌   wear out

    root

      ʔučəx̌   worn out

      Cf. s.čáx̌əč   sole (fish), "Sounds as if its back were
                               worn out."   LL.

1. čəx̌bíd(ac)   yew (tree)

    (Sometimes LL. says čx̌əbídac.)

2. čib(i)   lick, dip

    Cf. łqáw?   lap up, lick

        dəx̌ʷčibs ?ə ti?ił k̓ayəyə? ?ə ti?ił bəs.x̌ʷəs   ES.
        So he could dip the dried salmon in the grease.

        k̓ayəyə? ti dəx̌ʷčibs ?ə ti?ił bəs.x̌ʷəs   LG.
        Same gloss: So he could dip the dried salmon
                    in the grease.

        dəx̌ʷ?učibs   what he uses to dip with

        dx̌ʷsčib   someone who is always dipping, a dipper

    -it

        čibid   lick it

    lexical

        dx̌ʷčiba?łdàlᵊb   lick lips

        dx̌ʷsčiba?łdàlᵊb   always licking the lips

        ?udx̌ʷčibusc tə s.qʷəbày?
        The dog licked me in the face.

        ?udx̌ʷčibusᵊb tə s.qʷəbay?
        The dog licked its (own) face.

        dx̌ʷčibwild tə ła?x̌   Lick the pan!

        ?əx̌ʷčibwild tə ła?x̌   The pan has been licked.

    rejected:

        *dəx̌ʷdx̌ʷčibs

        *dəx̌ʷdx̌ʷsčibs

1. čičal   long feathers with thick 'stems'

    Cf. s.tú?q̓ʷ

    s.k̓ʷík̓ʷəlč

2. číčq̓ᵊb   a small unidentified shore bird that bobs up and
                             down and gives a high pitched cry; a títčulbixʷ

    (Also recorded číčkəd.)

3. čikadax̌əd   man's name, great-grandfather of ES.

    (Stress?) (Probably /k/ should be /q/.)

→

5. čík̓ʷik̓ʷ   blue elderberry, a s.q̓ʷəĺáɬᵊd

6. čílk̓àdi?   pectoral fin area (has triangular shape)   LG.

    Cf. čìl(?)k̓ádi?   pectoral fin area LL.

        čəlk̓ádi?   pectoral fin area VH.

    reduplication

        čílčilk̓àdi?   distributive

7. čip̓l-

        číp̓əlil   close eyes

    Contrast qx̌íl   open eyes

    -s

        číp̓əlis   close eyes to avoid seeing something;
                             close eyes to avoid getting something into them

    -bi-t

        číp̓lilbid   shut eyes to avoid seeing something

→

1. čis(i)   nailing

    See under <u>təs</u>.

    -it

        čísid   nail it   LG.

        čə́s^əd   nail it   ESi.

    lexical

        ʔučsálik^w   hammering; pecking (as a bird)

    -təd

        čə́stəd   a nail

2. číx^wčix^w   fish hawk   EK., HD.

    Cf. číx̌cix̌   fish hawk   ES.

3. čix̌(i)   fry

    See under q̓ʷəl-t.

    root

        scíx̌s   boil

            Cf. qálc

    -it

        číx̌id   fry it

    -b

        číx̌^əb! číx̌^əb! ...

    What Fish Hawk says as he holds his hands over the fire so that
    fat (to use as a dip for eating dried salmon) would come out of
    his hands and drip into a little pan/bowl set at the edge of the
    fire. It boils out from between his fingers which he holds spread
    apart.   ES.

lexical

c̓íx̌alikʷ	frying
səxʷc̓íx̌alikʷ	frying pan

    See under ɫaʔx̌.

cəxʷc̓íx̌alikʷ	my frying pan
acəxʷc̓íx̌alikʷ	your frying pan
səxʷc̓íx̌alikʷs	her frying pan
dəxʷʔuc̓íx̌alikʷ	what someone uses to fry with
cəxʷʔuc̓íx̌alikʷ	what I use to fry with
adəxʷʔuc̓íx̌alikʷ	what you use to fry with
dəxʷʔuc̓íx̌alikʷs	what she uses to fry with

rejected:

    *c̓íx̌alikʷtəd

    *c̓íx̌təd

1. dxʷ.c̓íx̌   stingy   LL.

    (However, LL. commented that 'stingy' was not too good a gloss, but he could not think of a better one.)

    Cf. dxʷs.qaqáx̌aʔ   stingy   LG.

2.   c̓íx̌c̓ix̌   fish hawk   ES.

    Cf. c̓íxʷc̓ixʷ   fish hawk   EK., HD.

3.   c̓iyúuqʷ   wart

4.   c̓iʔátkʷuʔ   See under c̓yátkʷu(ʔ).

1. čk-

    See under ɫič̓(i).

    (d)xʷčkápsəbᵊd   decapitate him   LL.

       Cf. dxʷp̓q̓ʷápsəbᵊd   same gloss   LG.

          dxʷp̓q̓ʷúsᵊd   same gloss   LL.

2. čk̓ʷúsəd   cane, walking stick   LL.

       Cf. ck̓ʷúsəd   cane, walking stick   LG.

    reduplication

        č̓íčk̓ʷúsəd   little walking stick

3. č̓ᵊqáqid   SPS   adverb   'always'

      Cf. čk̓ʷáqid   NPS   always

       diɫ č̓ᵊqáqid gʷəɫ dᵊgʷi

       That will always be yours.   JC.

       ʔəs.tíx̌ᵊdxʷ čələp, č̓qáqid

       You folks take care of it, always.

4. č̓qáysəb   flower   EK.

       Cf. s.kʷíʔkʷəlùs   flower   LG.

    reduplication

        sč̓ič̓qáysəb   flower   JC.

5. s.č̓q̓álqsəd   scapula

6. č̓q̓áb   See under čəq̓, 69.5.

7. č̓qʷ-

       ʔəs.čál kʷi gʷ(ə)adsč̓qʷàd   How are we related?

1.　　ċqʷíb　　　　　　　　be able to share in receiving something
　　　　　　　　　　　　　　　(usually food)

　　See under bək̓ʷ(u).

　　　λaləxʷ bəċqʷíb tiʔəʔ kawʔqs
　　　Raven also happened to get in on it, be there at the right time.

　　　gʷəl bəċqʷíbəxʷ ʔə tiʔił bə.ʔà
　　　And he got in on some more.

　　　ʔu· ċqʷíb čəd ʔə tiʔił s.q̓əjax̌ ʔə tiʔił s.qigʷəc
　　　Oh, I picked up (what nobody wanted) the entrails of the deer.

　　　díʔłəxʷ s.tab adsċqʷìb
　　　Anything (you see) help yourself to.

　　　díł cəxʷəs.čəbáʔ, dsəsċqʷíb ciʔəʔ
　　　That is what I'm packing, this that I got in on.

　　　x̌ʷuí díł bəsʔuċqʷíbčəł ciʔił
　　　We only got in on just that/ We only picked up just that.

2.　　čƛ̓ʷə́ƛ̓　　　　　　　　butter clam　　　　　　ESi.

　　See under s.ʔáx̌ʷuʔ.

　　Cf. səxʷúb　　　butter clam　　　　　　EK., LL.

3.　　čúbid　　　　　　　　See under ču̓ʔbid.

4.　　čúbčub　　　　　　　barnacles

5.　　čud　　　　　　　　　weak (muscles), sickly

　　See under x̌əł.

　　root

　　　ʔəsču̓dəxʷ　　　He's weak now.

ʔi· gʷətu.ʔux̌ʷ čəɫ gʷə.xʷíʔəs ti ʔəs.həláʔb čəɫ

x̌əɬx̌əɫ čəlà (a)sc̓ùd

Yes. We would have gone but we are much too sick,
too much under the weather.

lexical

   c̓ú(h)àyucid   weak chin, i.e., a voice that does not
carry well, a speech that is not clearly
articulated.

     Cf. gəlgᵊb   mumble

      See under cut.

1.   c̓ukʷ(u)   suck

  Cf. c̓əš-

  -ut

    c̓úkʷud   suck it

    c̓úkʷud čəd tə qʷùʔ

    I sucked the water (through a straw).

  lexical

    c̓úkʷàči(ʔ)b   I sucked my hand (or finger).

    c̓ùkʷálqsačiʔ   suck finger

     ʔəlc̓uc̓úkʷqsàčiʔ   He's sucking his finger.

  rejected:

    *c̓úkʷᵊb

2.   c̓úkʷəb   flesh   EK.
                 skin of human or salmon   LG.

    Cf. k̓ʷə́luʔ   (animal) hide

k̓ʷə́ləwʔ seems to refer to hair or fur covered skin, while čúk̓ʷəb designates glabrous skins such as those of humans and fish.

Cf. s.čə̂bîd

1. c̓ú?bid   fish bone   LL., EK., ESi.

    Cf. čúbid   fish bone   LG.

2. c̓ú(?)kʷs   seven

    c̓ú(?)kʷs bit ?i kʷi łixʷîlc x̌ičìčc   seventy three cents

    lexical

        c̓u?kʷsál̓čup   seven fires

        c̓u?kʷsál̓ič   seven bundles

        c̓ú?kʷsəlus   seven squares in a net,
                                   seven stitches in knitting

        dxʷc̓ú?kʷsus   seven layers/rows

    reduplication

        c̓úkʷukʷs   seven people

3. c̓xʷáy̓s

    ?əsc̓xʷáy̓sus čəd
    I cannot see because it is too bright.

    ?əsc̓əxʷc̓xʷáy̓s čəd   Same gloss: I cannot see because it is
                               too bright.

    See under t̓qʷus.

4. ?əs.c̓x̌ʷádub s.x̌ə̀ł   unidentified sickness

    See under x̌ə̀ł.

1.   čyátkʷu(?)   very vicious wild Indians who live in
                          the Cascades near Tulalip   LL.

     čyákʷu   some kind of monster   ESi.

     čiʔátkʷuʔ   wild people   VH.

     See under s.ƛálqəb.

     Cf. s.títaʔɬ   wild people

          qʷ(ə)qʷ(ə)stáybixʷ   forest dwarf, Eskimo   LL.

          s.wáw̓tixʷtəd   nocturnal beings
                                 who take care of
                                 plants and trees   JC.

č

The sound value of this letter is similar to *ch* of English *church*. [voiceless palatal affricate]

1. č-   independent predication marker

2. -č   See under -ač; -ič, -alič; -ilč; -ulč.

→

4. čad   where

    Cf. čayɫ, čal, k̓ʷid, tab, ʔəx̌id

      č̓ád kʷi x̌ʷubt   Where is the paddle?

      č̓ád t(i) ad.ʔàlš   Where is your brother?

      č̓ád kʷ(i) adəxʷəxʷ.cutᵊb gʷədəxʷəs.ɫaɫlils
      Where do you think he lives?

      tučádəxʷ čəxʷ   Where have you been?

      bə́k̓ʷ čàd   everywhere

→

with directional prefixes:

dxʷ-

      lədxʷč̓ádəxʷ čəxʷ   Where are you going?

      ʔəs.(h)áydxʷ čəxʷ ʔu dxʷč̓àd kʷi s.ʔúx̌ʷs
      Do you know where he went?

      xʷì̓ʔ gʷədsəs.(h)áydxʷ gʷ(ə)udxʷč̓àdəs
      I don't know where he went.

liɫ-

      ʔuliɫč̓ád čəxʷ   Which way did you go/come?

      ɫuliɫč̓ád čəxʷ   Which way will you go?

      liɫč̓ád kʷi ɫ(u)adsu.ʔúx̌ʷ   Which way are you going to go?

tuɫ-

    tuɫčád čəxʷ   Where are you from?

    (Contrast tuɫčad with sčads below.)

s-...-s

    sčáds čəxʷ   Where are you from?

The difference between tuɫčád and sčáds is a matter of
origin (or, perhaps, permanency). The second form asks about
one's lineage, home village, tribal affiliation, and the like.
It could be answered, for example, by saying s.duhúbš čəd
'I am Snohomish.' While the first form could be used to question someone's origins, it has much broader application. For
example, it could be answered, tuɫ.ʔál čəd (s)ji.jəlàɫič
'I am from Seattle' meaning simply that I live there now.
tuɫčád could also (with appropriate aspectual affixes) simply
ask where someone is coming from.

→

lexical

    ʔiɫčádgʷas   which

    ʔiɫčádgʷəs kʷ(i) ad.wə̀q̓əb   Which is your chest?

    ʔiɫčádgʷəs kʷi gʷ(ə)ads.x̌aƛ   Which do you want?

    ʔiɫčádgʷəs ʔə ti tsùlč kʷi gʷ(ə)ads.x̌aƛ(txʷ)
Which drum do you want?

People differ in their usage. LG. most often uses
ʔiɫčád while JC. seems to prefer čádgʷas, though both accept
ʔiɫčádgʷas. This last form is recorded most frequently from
DM.

1.   čáj   hide

    Cf. čalcut (under čal), tíg̓ʷil, qaǰət

čáj	hide it
ʔəsčac	It's hidden.

-il

ʔəsčajil	Someone is hiding.
ɬučajil čəd	I'm going to hide.

reduplication

čáčjibᵊb	kill without anyone knowing or suspecting, hide the body of one whom you have murdered LL.

See under gʷəlál-.

1. čájax̌ʷəb   man's name, LG.'s father and older brother, David

2. čal NPS   how, why

Cf. ʔəx̌id, k̓ʷid, tab, čad, čayɬ

ʔəsčál(əxʷ) čəxʷ	How are you?
ƛ(u)asčáləxʷ čəxʷ	How have you been?

Contrast with the following:

ʔəs.ʔəx̌id əẁə čəxʷ	What is the matter with you?
x̌ʷuɬ čəxʷ ʔu ʔəs.ƛúbil	Have you been all right?
ʔəsčál ɬuhùy	Whatever it will be; However it will turn out.
ʔəsčál ʔə kʷi ɬus.hùys	same glosses
ʔəsčál gʷə(ɬu).hùyəs	same glosses
ʔəsčál kʷ(i) adəxʷu.bàk̓ʷɬšəd	How did you hurt your foot? DM.
ʔəsčál kʷ(i) adəxʷudxʷ.ɬičus	How did you cut your face? DM.

83

ʔəsčál kʷ(i) adəxʷəs.x̌əc kʷi gʷ(ə)ads.ʔux̌ʷ

Why are you afraid to go?   LG.

p̓áλaƛ gʷə.ʔáhas kʷi səsčáls gʷəłu.hùyəs

It makes no difference which way it's going to be done.

...gʷəʔəsčáləs tiʔił dəxʷ.ʔàs ʔal tiʔił

       ...why are you there?
       ...what are you doing there?

ʔəsčál kʷ(i) adsgʷə.gʷàdəd   How did you say it?
                            What did you say?

ʔəsčál kʷi sgʷə.gʷàdəds   What did he say?

ʔəsčál kʷi gʷ(ə)ads.cùuc tiʔə?   How did you say this?

ʔəsčál əw̓ə kʷi səs.ʔùx̌ʷs   How would that go?

  Contrast with the following:

  s.táb əw̓ə kʷi s.dàtubs tiʔił...

  What is ... named?

  s.táb əw̓ə kʷi s.dàtubs ʔal tiʔił ḍxʷ.1(ə)šucid

  What is the name of it in Puget Salish?

ʔəsčál əw̓ə ʔəsčál   What?
                        (This is a nice way of asking
                         someone to repeat something.)

ʔəsčál čəd kʷa?   How am I? Well, I don't know.
                        (This is the answer often given
                        to the question, ʔəsčál(əxʷ)
                        čəxʷ. The gloss is not literal.)

1. čal(a)   chase, follow

    Compare čəj-   sneak up on, stalk; k̓ʷə́čtxʷ   track.

    -at

      ʔučáləc   He chased me.

      ʔučálətubuł   He chased us.

ʔučáləd čəɫ   We chased it.

ləsčáləd   We followed it.

-dxʷ

ʔučáldubš   He caught up with me.

-txʷ

dày?(ʔə)cáʔ tiʔiɫ ƛučəčəláɫtubəxʷ

It's only me who is almost caught.

-əɫ

ʔučáləɫ čəd pìšpiš   I chased the cat.   LG.

ʔučáləɫ pìšpiš cə d.ʔàlš   My sister chased the cat.   LG.

lexical

ƛudxʷčáligʷəd čəd

I go along (with you) in my thoughts.

reduplication

ckʷàqid ʔəlčučáɫčalac   He is always chasing me.

čəláɫ

čəláɫəxʷ čəd gʷəs.q̓ʷəlàdubəd!

My dinner is almost ready!

čaʔčəláɫ

ʔučà(ʔ)čəláɫ čəd čəda gʷə.kʷə̀dəxʷ

I almost got caught.

dày? (ʔə)cá tiʔiɫ ƛučəčəláɫtubəxʷ

It is only me who is almost caught.

    Compare xʷíʔ lə.lìl to (čaʔ)čəláɫ.

rejected:

*ʔučalil, *čal čəd, *čálagʷil   LG.

1. čáləs   NPS   hand, forearm

      čáləš   SPS   hand, forearm

      Cf. -ači?

      -ab

         čələsáb   by means of the hands

         čələsáb tə sə.ʔìbəšs   He is walking on his hands.

      reduplication

         čáčələs   little hand

         čálčaləs   hands (distributive)

2. s.čálub   liver   EK., LL.

      Cf. s.táqʷuʔ   liver   LG.; LL.

3. čáɫaʔ   fail to recognize   LG.

      Contrast with suxʷt- 'recognize'.

      See under hay- 'know'.

      -dxʷ

         ʔučáɫaʔdxʷ čəd   I didn't know who/what it was.

         ʔučəlᵊdúb čəxʷ ʔə tə dsqʷəb.qʷəbày?
         My dogs didn't recognize/remember you.

      -bi-t

         ʔučáɫaʔbid čəd   I don't know it; I don't recognize it.

4. s.čátqɫəb Skykomish, Muckleshoot   grizzly bear   LL., EB.

      Cf. s.təbtábəɫ Skagit, Snoh.   grizzly bear   LL., MC.

1. čáydi   Chinese

    λu.lə́k^wtəb ƛ^wəɬ ʔə tiʔiɬ čáydi tiʔiɬ k̀àdayuʔ. λ̓su.šə́ɬs
    (h)əlg^wəʔ s.ɬùʔb

    It's said that the Chinese eat rats. They make soup of them.

2. čáyɬ   'go for what reason?'

    Cf. čad, čal, k̓^wid, tab, ʔəxid

    čáyɬ čəx^w   Why do you want to go? (You are foolish
                        to go.)   VH.

    ləčáyɬ čəx^w   Where are you going?   LG.

        Cf. lədx^w.čád čəx^w   Same gloss: Where are you going?
    (Note that čad without the prefixes lə-dx^w- means
        'where is something located'; while čayɬ is necessarily
        dynamic, never static.)

    g^wəl bələčáyɬəx^w čəd čəx^wa ʔəs.dúk^wtubš

    Why should I want to come? You don't like me.   LL.

    g^wəl bələčáyɬəx^w čəd k^w(i) ads.dùk^wtubš čəx^w

    Same glosses: Why should I want to come? You don't like me.

    g^wələčáyɬəx^w čəd

    Why should I want to go over there?

3. čáʔaj(ac)   oak (tree)

4. čáʔk^w   seaward, toward the water (river, lake, or sound)

    Note čáʔk^w in the following sets:

	Locative		Dynamic	
I.	a. q̓íx^w	'located upstream'	təyíl	'go upstream'
	b. ʔáɬx̌ad	'located downstream'	q^wíc	'go downstream'
II.	a. táq̓t	'located away from shore, up landward'	čúbə	'go up from shore, go up river bank'
	b. čáʔk^w	'located toward the river/ sound or out in the river, lake or sound'	k̓^wíɬ	'go down to shore, go down river bank'

In group II, both lə.k̓ʷiƛ čəd and lədxʷ.čáʔkʷ čəd mean
'I'm going down to the water', but the latter can also mean
'I'm going on out from shore', whereas k̓ʷiƛ stops at the water's
edge. Similarly, both lə.čúbə čəd and lədxʷ.t̓áɋt čəd signify
'I'm going up from shore', but the first always begins at the
water's edge while the second can be used if someone is out
from the shore and heading back to the beach (or to the river
bank) and also if he is already on land (and not necessarily
right on the shore) and heading toward the mountains away from
the water.

root

čáʔkʷ tə s.gʷádil
A way out the salmon are jumping.

dxʷčáʔkʷ   toward the water

tul̓čáʔkʷ   from the water, south wind   ES.

gʷəl ɬu.bə́č dxʷʔal tudiʔ tul̓čà ʔkʷ
and setting in the west (i.e., in the direction of Puget Sound). ES.

-t

dxʷʔučagʷcut   go out from shore

híkʷ čəd ʔučakʷt^əb   I'm being forced out. (Someone is
                                  trying to get me to do something I don't
                                  want to do and he is a skillful talker.)

-dxʷ

ʔučaʔkʷdub tiʔiɬ s.qìgʷəc ʔə tiʔiɬ s.qʷəbày?
The dog drove the deer to the water.

ʔučáʔkʷdxʷ čəd   I managed to get it down to the shore.

But this gloss isn't very good. Actually the English means more:

ʔu.ʔúx̌ʷtxʷ čəd dxʷčàʔkʷ   LL.

-bi-t

čáʔkʷbic   came down to shore where I was   LL.

ʔučáʔkʷbitᵊb čəd   Something came down to the water
                          where I was.   LL.

čəʔkʷᵊbíd ʔə tə ʔálʔal   in front of the house   LG.

lexical

With the lexical suffixes beginning with a vowel, čaʔkʷ is
heard in its reduced form /čəgʷ-/.

The word čəgʷálətxʷ NPS   '(anywhere) outside a house'
shows a shift of reference. Etymologically, it is čaʔkʷ
'seaward' plus -alatxʷ 'building', the expected opposite
of təq̓tálətxʷ 'landward side of house'. In precontact times
the door of a house was on the water side, so 'outside'
necessarily meant going first to the sea or river side.
Today, two terms are required (for some speakers) to designate the front or water side of a house, čəgʷálətxʷ čəgʷádiʔ
'outside house (on) water side'; but note čəʔkʷᵊbíd ʔə tə
ʔálʔal above. Like unmodified locative terms, čəgʷálətxʷ
has a corresponding dynamic term, šəjál 'go outside' q.v.
Cf. šálbixʷ SPS   'outside (but close to) house.'

čəgʷálataxʷ tə s.qʷəbàyʔ
The dog is outside (the house).

čəgʷábac   on the lower side;
                       below the drifts, on the beach

čəgʷádiʔ   side toward water

čəgʷáyucid   lower side of the road

ti ʔálʔal čəgʷáyucid ʔə tə šəgʷɫ
The house is on the lower side of the road.

      sčəgʷúcid   island   EK.

rejected:

    *ča?kʷtub

-il

    ?učagʷil čəd   I got too far out.

-il-dxʷ

    ?əs.dúkʷtxʷ čəd ti?ił jəxʷčagʷildxʷ

    I'm angry with him, that's why I picked on him.

    ?učagʷildub   be shoved out into the water without
                             a paddle; to be ganged up on   EK.

    ?učagʷildub čəd   They ganged up on me. They got the
                             best of me because I was alone.   LL.

    ?učagʷildubš   He has me cornered and is threatening
                             me.   LL.

    reduplication

    ?uča?čagʷildub čəd   I was forced to do something undesirable
                             because they overpowered me.

1.   čəbá?   carry on back, backpack

    Cf. bəqʷiča?   carry on shoulder

    root

    ləsčəbá?   packing something on back

    ?učəbá? ci?ił xʷi? lə.ha?ł s.ƛalqəb ?ə ti?ił

    That no-good she monster packed them off.

    xʷi? lə.ha?ł s.ƛalqəb ?učəbá? ?ə ti?ił   same gloss

    -t

    híwiləxʷ čəbà?ᵊd   Go on, pack it!

ləsčəbáad tiʔəʔ wiw̓su

She is carrying the youngsters.

ʔučəbáʔtᵊb ʔə ti d.bàd tə s.qìg̓ʷəcáłči? dxʷʔal ʔalʔal   DM.

My father carried the venison home.

-txʷ

ləs<u>čəb</u>áʔtxʷ tiʔił

Make him pack it. (I already have enough to carry.)

ʔu<u>čəb</u>áʔtxʷ

He made someone else backpack it.

lexical

<u>čəb</u>aʔák̓ʷčup   carry firewood on back   LL., DM.

<u>čəb</u>áʔiʔł   carry a baby on back

-təd

<u>čəb</u>á(ʔ)təd   tumpline   LG.

Cf. s.t̓k̓ʷálšəd   tumpline   LG., LL.

s.łidálšəd   tumpline   EK.

1. s.<u>čə</u>bčəb   carbuncle boil

    See under x̌əł.

2. <u>čə</u>bəqəb   Chemakum (near Port Ludlow around a deep lagoon)   EK.

3. <u>čə</u>béš   mist   ML.

    This word occurs in a song sung by ML., but it
    is a SPS word.

    Cf. łə́cᵊb   heavy mist   LL., ESi.

    qə́lb   rain

1.　čəbíd(ac)　　　　Douglas fir (tree)　　　MC., LG., EK.

　　s.čəbídəc　　　Douglas fir (tree)　　　ESi.

　　s.čəbíd　　　　bark (esp. fir bark, the bark par excellence)

　　Cf. čᵊx̌álc (under čəx̌)

2.　č(ə)c　NPS　　　red

　　Cf. kʷiƛ　SPS　red

　　　　liq̓(i)　　　paint self red

　　　　tábł　　　　ochre

　　x̌i.čə́c　　　　　red

　　-il

　　　ʔəsččíl　　　reddish, light red, becoming red

　　lexical

　　　ʔəxʷččíligʷəd　　　red inside

　　　*dxʷččíligʷəd　　　rejected

　　　pùt yú tiʔəʔ sʔəsčiččìls　　It was a really nice red color.

　　-b

　　　dxʷčə́cəb　　　red river

　　　Cf. dxʷ.kʷiƛᵊb　　Pilchuck River

　　　(Although the river is in NPS territory, its name has a SPS
　　　root. Snohomish speakers use the SPS form in this one case
　　　instead of the expected dxʷčə́cᵊb.)

　　lexical

　　　x̌iččálus　　　red color

číčcyusac   unidentified berry plant (lit. 'little red face plant')

The bark turns red. The berries are white and in a bunch. The plant grows alongside the road. Take the "outer" skin off and steep it to prepare medicine for colds.
                                                                              MC.

reduplication

  x̌ičíčc   penny   ES.

    Cf. s.q̓ʷíq̓ʷx̌ʷ   penny   LL.

      s.qəqəlíbəɬ   penny   EK.

1. čəcxʷílč   shinny

      ʔučəcxʷílč   shinny

    See under ʔúkʷukʷ.

2. čəc̓ᵊdísbəd   toothpick

      Cf. cəq̓ᵊdísᵊbəd   fork (something to stick with)

3. čəd   from č plus ad

    See under -ad.

5. čədúqq   Chinook jargon   LG.

      Cf. qqájətᵊb   speak Skagit

6. čəgʷás   NPS   wife

    Cf. čəgʷəš   SPS   wife

    reduplication

      čəgʷčəgʷás   look for a wife

      čáagʷəs   wives

1. čə́jq̓ʷ(ᵊd)   rub about (as two pieces of cloth rubbed together);
                        rub bark together (to extract juices for medicine,
                        or to make it stringy for making clothing)

    See under šíc(i)   'rub, file'.

    Cf. xʷíkʷ(i)   rub hard   (as two canoes tied too close
                        to each other)

        sáx̌(a)   scrape

    lexical

        cickʷ čəd gʷəčəjᵊq̓ʷúsᵊd
        I'd very much like to twist his head off.

2. čəl   See under čała̓ʔ.

3. čəláxʷali   quiver (for arrows)   LL.

    Cf. čsíč   arrow quiver   AS.

4. čələp   from č plus aləp

    See under -ad.

5. čə́lpᵊb   itch

    čə̀lpᵊbábac   itch on the body

    Compare x̌íq̓   'scratch to relieve an itch'.

6. čəlqʷúbəʔ   blackcaps (raspberries q.v.), a s.qʷəlałᵊd   LG., MC.

    čəlqʷúba   EK.

7. čəł   surprise, shock

    root

        (hə)lá·b čəd ʔučə̀ł   I was really shocked.

    -t

        ʔučə̀łᵊd čəd   I surprised him.

dx^w

    ʔučəɫdúbš tiʔiɫ   He surprised me.

-bi-t

    ʔučəɫbíd čəd tiʔiɫ   I got shocked by him.

    (hə)lá·b čəd ʔučə̀ɫbid tiʔiɫ He really shocked me.

1.   čəɫ   Skagit   make, build

Three root stems čəɫ/šəɫ, təx^w, and λ̉a are special in that their goal or object does not have a determiner. Compare this class with the suffix -aɫ.

Cf. šəɫ   Snoh. make, build

    q^wíb(i)   prepare, fix, make

    p̉áyəq   hew out, make a canoe

root

    ləcučə́ɫ čəd x̣^wùbt   I'm making a paddle.

      Cf. ləcu.húyud čəd tiʔə̉ʔ x̣^wubt   I'm making a paddle.

    ləčə̀ɫ čəd   I'm on my way to make something.

    čə́ɫ ʔàlʔal   build a house

    ʔučə́ɫ hùd   make a fire

      Cf. ʔu.húdičup čəd   Same gloss: make a fire

    ʔəlc̉učə́ɫ čəd yìq̉us   I'm making a cedar-root basket.

      Cf. ʔəlc̉u.yíq̉ib čəd   Same gloss: I'm making a cedar-root basket.

    ʔučə́ɫ čəd yìq̉us   I made a cedar-root basket.

    čí̉ʔ.čəwàt čəd dx^wʔal čə̀ɫ x^w.ʔàx̣^waʔəd
    I'm good at making clam baskets.

    ʔučə́ɫ čəx^w s.ɫàg^wid   You made mats; You made the bed.

      Cf. ʔu.λ̉ág^{wə}b čəx^w   You made mats.

ʔučə́ɬ čəd s.tùdəq   I made him a slave.

ʔučə́ɬ čəd x̌ʷùbt tuʔ̓al tə luƛ s.x̌əlà?s   LG.
I made a paddle out of the old board.

    Cf. ʔu.húyud čəd x̌ʷùbt   I made a paddle out of it.   LG.

ču?ɬac tə dəxʷučə́ɬ x̌ʷubt; ƛ̓ál bədəxʷučə́ɬ ɬaṗqs
Maple is what they use to make paddles and also to make ladles.
                                               LG.

ʔučə́ɬ šə́bəd tuʔ̓al tə s.tìdgʷəd   LG.
They make a fishtrap out of cedar boughs.

s.tígʷəd tə dəxʷučə́ɬ šə́bəd   LG.
Cedar boughs are used to make a fish trap.

ɬ(u)adčə́ɬ s.tàb tə tsùlč   LG.
What are you going to do with a drum?

-dxʷ

  ʔučə́ɬdxʷ čəd puʔtəd   I made him a shirt.

in compounds

Terms for 'step-relatives' are derived from čə́ɬ plus the consanguinal terms:

(Note that the Snohomish say šə́ɬ-.)

čə́ɬbádəb	step-father
čə́ɬtádəb	step-mother
čə́ɬʔíbacəb	step-grandchild
čə́ɬbədá?əb	step-child
čə́ɬkiyáb ~ čə́ɬkiə́?əb	step-grandmother
dəsčə́ɬstálə́ɬəb	my step-nephew, step-niece
adčə́ɬscápa?əb	your step-grandfather
sčə́ɬstálə́ɬəbs	his step-nephew, step-niece

rejected:

*čə́ɫˀd   LG.

*ləcučə́ɫ čəd tiʔəʔ x̌ʷubt   DM.

1.   čə́ɫ   from č plus -aɫ(i)

   See under -ad.

2.   -čəɫ   our

   See under d-   'my'.

3.   čə́ɫqs   name of one of the four principal Snohomish villages.
                         (Haeberlin and Gunther give what would be čə́čɫqs,
                         p. 7.) The site today is known as Brown's Point or
                         Sandy Point.

4.   čə́pˀb

      ʔučə́pˀb   bruised   EK

      ʔəsčə́pˀb x̌i.čə̀c   dark red   EK.

        Cf. čə́qʷˀb   bruised   EK.

5.   čəq   dirty, soiled
        Cf. číq̓ʷ(il)   dirt, dirty, soiled;
                         dirt, earth

   root

      ʔəsčə́q ti s.ƛ̓əlàličaʔ
      My clothes are dirty (but not the ones I'm wearing).

      tuʔəbs.qəlíkʷ čəd ʔə ti ʔəsčə́q
      I had a dirty blanket.

   lexical

      ʔəsčq̓áličaʔ čəd   My clothes are dirty.

1.   č(ə)s(a)   send someone on an errand

    Cf. hil   tell someone to do something

    -at

      č̲s̲ád   send him; send him away

      č̲s̲át^əb   be sent

      dííɫtxʷ tiʔiɫ kʷi ʔuč̲s̲àd čəxʷ
      He's the one you should send.

      ʔuč̲s̲ác   He sent me.

      ʔuč̲s̲át^əb čəd dxʷʔal xʷuyubàlʔtxʷ
      They sent me to the store.

      č̲š̲àd gʷə.teláwiləs   Tell him to run.

      xʷiʔ gʷəɫudsč̲š̲àd, dəgʷítxʷ kʷi ʔəsč̲š̲àd
      I'm not going to tell him to, you tell him to.

    -dxʷ

      č̲ə́sdxʷ   finally persuaded him to go

    -bi-t

      č̲s̲ádbid   animal track   ES.

      číč̲s̲àdbid   little animal track   ES.

      Cf. dxʷ.š̲ádbid   imprint on the ground

    rejected:

      *ʔəsčəstxʷ

2. s.čə́š   rival

3. s.čə́txʷəd   Snoh., SPS   black bear

    s.číčtxʷəd   bear cub

      s.číčičtxʷəd   bear cubs

    s.čə́tčətxʷəd   bears

Cf. s.pá?c   black bear   LG., DM., CB.

s.čátqɬəb   grizzly bear   Skykomish LL.

s.təbtábəɬ   grizzly bear   Skagit, Snohomish LL.

1. čə́tx̌ʷ-   gobble food

   -t

     čə́tx̌ʷəd   gobble it up

     čə́tx̌ʷtəb   gobbled it up

2. čəwá(?)t   know how to; be good at doing

See under (h)ay-.

     ?əsčəwát čəd dxʷ?al kʷi gʷədsu.t̓ilib   EK.
     I know how to sing.

     (hə)lá?b čəd ?iɬ.jìxʷ sčəwà?t dxʷ?al dəgʷì   LG.
     I'm a lot better at it than you.

   -il

     čəwá?tiləxʷ čəxʷ   VH.
     You are catching on; You are learning.

     xʷì? gʷəsəčəwá?til (h)əlgʷə? dxʷ?al kʷi gʷəsuq.qáǰətəbs
     (h)əlgʷə?   LG.
     They will never learn to speak Skagit.

     ləčəwá?til čəd ?ə dsugʷəd.gʷadad ?ə tə gʷəɬ q.qaǰatəbs
     gʷəd.gʷatəd   LG.
     I'm learning how to speak our Skagit language.

     (hə)lá?bəxʷ čəd sčəwà?til dxʷ?al kʷi gʷədsu.p̓ayəq
     I'm very knowledgeable about making canoes.

   reduplication

     sčəčəwá?t   be good at doing something, really know how   LG.

      opposite of ?əsǰáƛ̓b

číčəwàt   know how to do something well

    číčəwàt čəd dxʷʔal čəɬ xʷ.ʔàx̌ʷaʔəd   EK.

    I'm good at making clam baskets.

    čičəwát čəd dxʷʔal ƛ̓ičib   EK.

    I'm good at swimming.

1.   s.čəwáʔcən   Skagit name for site of Tsawwassen, British Columbia

2.   čəxʷ   from č plus -axʷ

   See under -ad.

3.   čə́x̌   crack, split; half

  See under xʷəƛ̓ 'break' and ɬič(i) 'cut'.

root

   ʔəsčə́x̌ ti d.q̓ílbid   My canoe has a crack.

   ʔiɬčə́x̌   half

     saliʔílc ʔi kʷi ʔiɬčə̀x̌   two dollars and a half

     x̌ʷəlbít ʔi kʷi ʔiɬčəx̌bít   ninety-five cents

-t

   ɬučə́x̌ᵊd čəd   I'm going to split it.

   čə́x̌ᵊdàx̌ʷ čəxʷ tiʔiɬ s.tìdᵊgʷəd   Split the cedar boughs. JC.

lexical

   čᵊx̌álc   "another word for čəbíd 'fir' because fir is easy to split."   DM.

   čx̌(ᵊ)gʷás   person of mixed blood

   čx̌gʷásəxʷ tə s.p̓əɬq̓ʷ ʔə tə bùus

   half past four o'clock

ʔáliləxʷ čə̌x̌gʷàs   after midnight   EK.

čə̌x̌gʷâsᵊd   Split it in two.

1.   čəyáɫqʷuʔ   name for site now called Potlatch Beach
                      (just to the west of Priest Point) Tulalip, Wash.

2.   číc

      ʔučícəxʷ   It's blowing hard and getting bad at sea.

  See under šə́xʷᵊb.

3.   číkʷ(i)   stuff into, caulk; narrow; swallow

  See under ƛuq̓ʷ(u); and compare bəq̓.

  root

    ʔəsčíkʷ ʔal ti s.wàtixʷtəd   JC.
    It is tucked in the ground.

  -it

    číkʷid   swallow it (equivalent to bə́q̓ᵊd),
                 caulk, stuff into

    ʔudxʷčíkʷid   (The road) narrowed.   LL.

      Cf. k̓ílc   narrow place   EK.

  lexical

    číkʷàpsəb   choke

      diɫ cəxʷčíkʷapsəb tiʔiɫ
      That's what I choked on.

        Cf. ʔaq̓

  -il

    číkʷilgʷiɫ   narrow part of a river

1. s.čílčil   lazy (will not work)   DM., LG.

        sčílčil tiʔił   He is lazy.

    Cf. q̓əyíl, q̓ʷíč̓

2. číit(ᵊ)bixʷ   great horned owl   LG.

        Cf. (təkʷ)təkʷəlús   great horned owl

3. číx̌ᵊb   rancid   LG.

                        a bit too strong to eat,
                        kind of spoiled   VH.

        See under -q̓əp.

4. s.číʔyu   wild strawberry

        s.čiʔú?   Skagit   wild strawberry   MC.

        s.číy̓u? Snoh.   wild strawberry   EK.

        s.číʔyuhəc   wild strawberry plant LL.

            Cf. t̓íləqʷ SPS   wild strawberry   ESi.

5. xʷ.čłíčəp   sacrum

→

7. čúbə   go up landward, proceed away from shore

    See under ča?kʷ.

    root

        čúbəhəxʷ   She went up from the shore.

        ʔučúbə čəd dxʷ.šqùs   I went up hill.

    -txʷ

        s.tábəxʷ tiʔił ləčúbətxʷ What is he taking up landward?

-c

    čúbaac   go up landward after it

lexical

    čubəhák^wčup   carry wood up from beach   DM.

    čubə(ʔ)ábš   name of the people who live along the Skagit River around Lyman, Washington. The people had to go to higher ground when the river flooded.   DM. See Sampson, pp. 20-21.

1.   čúbəx̌ad   man's name for Tommy George (He is from La Conner, Washington.)

2.   čuɫ-   borrow, lend items other than money

Compare g^wi(h)ači ʔ.

Contrast ʔábaq   'return something borrowed'.

lexical

-alc

     tux̌^w čəd ƛusčuɫalc
     I just borrow it (every week).

     ɫučuɫalcəd čəd k^wi yiq̓ùs
     I'll lend her a basket.

     čuɫalc čəd ʔə tiʔiɫ q̓iɫbid
     Lend me your canoe.

-tx^w

     ʔəsčúɫtx^w   rented house

-idup

     ʔəsčúɫidup   rented land

1. čúƛ(u)   sharp rattling noise

        -ut

        čúƛucut   sharp rattling noise (like dishes)

        lexical

        čúƛqid   unidentified species of swan (lit. 'rattle head')
                                                     LL.

        xʷčúƛqid   Same gloss: unidentified species of swan (lit. 'rattle head')   EK.

2. -čup   lexical suffix   'firewood, a laid fire'

        Cf. -ay̓staq   flame, fire

        hud   fire, firewood; burn

        húdčup   light the fire

        ƛáčup   fetch firewood

        ʔuƛáƛčup   brought the firewood

        -aɫ-čup

        ʔəspúkʷəbàɫčup   a stack of firewood

        -aʔkʷ-čup

        ləs.čəbákʷčup   carrying firewood on back

        bəqʷíčaʔakʷčup   carrying firewood on shoulder

        s.ɫíčəkʷčup   wood saw

        (hə)dʔiwákʷčup   bring the firewood in the house

        -i-čup

        qʷíbičup   fix the fire

        húdičup   Skagit light the fire

3. čúqʷilb   foot race

        Cf. x̌íx̌q̓

1. čúqʷ(u)   whittle

    See under ɬič(i).

    root

       ləcučúqʷ čəd ʔə tiʔəʔ qʷí.qʷɫayʔ   DM.
       I was whittling a stick.

    -ut

       ləcučúqʷud čəd tiʔəʔ qʷí.qʷɫayʔ gʷəl qʷcáb tiʔiɬ dᵊs.duukʷ   DM.
       I was whittling a stick and my knife slipped.

2. čúsəd   star   LL., MC., ESi.

    s.čúsəd   star   EK.

    reduplication

       čúščusəd   stars

3. s.čútx̌   halibut   LG., ML.

4. čx̌ʷ(ə)lúʔ   whale   ES., LL.

    Cf. qʷə́dis   whale   ESi.

       qʷədís   whale   LL.

          Cf. qáɬqaləx̌ìč   killer whale, blackfish   LG., LL., EK.

5. čx̌ʷucid   cover, lid, top   EK.

    (Perhaps a mistake for č(ə)x̌- 'crack, split' plus -ucid 'mouth, opening')

    Cf. x̌k̓ʷucid   cover, lid, top   EK., LG.

č̓

The sound represented by this letter is similar to that of č
except for the added simultaneous abrupt closure of the vocal cords,
a sort of catch in the throat. [glottalized palatal affricate]

1.   č̓aabəs ~ č̓ahəbəs   See under č̓əbás.

2. s.č̓ábyəqʷ   great grandparent, great grandchild

    See under bədá?.

3.   č̓ačas   NPS   child (up to 10 or 12 years); any child

     č̓ačaš   SPS   child

        Contrast with bədá?   'one's own child'.

          Cf. wíwsu   Snoh. and SPS   children

               s.táwixʷə?ł / s.táwigʷəł   Skagit   children

               lə́gʷəb   youth   q̓ábəy?   maiden

               púsəč̓   puberty (male only?)

     č̓ačas čəd x̌ʷuɬ̓ab ?ə dəgʷí   LG.
     I am as young as you.

     ƛ̓àl čəxʷ bəč̓ačas x̌ʷuɬ̓ab ?ə ?əcà
     You are just as young as I am.

          Contrast luƛ̓ 'old'.

       reduplication

          č̓aačas   mature acting child

4. č̓ádəsq̓idəb   man's name, VH.'s MoMoMoBr and VH.'s son, Ron

1. s.čájəp   cedar bark skirt   EK.

     Cf. s.čáyəp (in addendum)

→

2. čájajᵊb   inherit   EK.

      ʔučájajᵊb čəd ʔə tə s.wàtixʷtəd

      I inherited the land.

3. čájuʔ   a wooden float carved to represent a duck which is attached to a harpoon or spear line and which resists being pulled through the water

     Cf. púbᵊb

4. čálas(ac)   NPS   brake fern (plant)

     čáləš   SPS   brake fern

      ʔəbìɫəxʷ čəxʷ ɫu.lábᵊdxʷ kʷi slə.ƛ̓àx̌ʷ ʔə ti čàləš

      čəxʷə əs.(h)áydxʷəxʷ. ʔi, téɫəxʷ ʔu.ɫə̀čil ti s.q̓ʷəlᵊb s.lə̀x̌il.

      When you see the growing of the brake fern, you know [lit. Yes,] truly warm days have arrived.   JC.

5. čápᵊb   sour (like a sour apple)

     See under -qəp.

     lexical

      čápᵊbàlikʷ   make it sour

6. čásᵊb   It has a good taste.

     See under -qəp.

      ʔučásᵊb   delicious

7. s.část   branch, limb

     Cf. s.tídgʷəd   cedar bough

reduplication

    ščásčast   branches

1.   čáwəyʔ   seashell (of any type)

    Cf. łáʔx̌ , qʷłəy(ʔ)úlč, cíliwʔ

    lexical

       čáwəyʔ(ùlč) dish (the modern, store-bought kind)

2.   čáw̓   SPS   smelt   ESi., JC.

    (Also recorded čáʔuʔ.)

    Cf. šíjus   NPS   (under šic)   smelt

3.   čáxʷ(a)   club

    root

       ʔučáxʷ čəd   I got hit (by a branch in the thicket).

       ʔučáxʷ tiʔił stubš   That man got hit.

    -at

       ʔučáxʷəc čəxʷ   You clubbed me.

       ʔučáxʷəd čəd   I clubbed him.

       ʔučáxʷətᵊb   Someone clubbed him.

       ʔučáxʷətubuł   He clubbed us.

       čáxʷəcut   self-flagellate

    -dxʷ

       ʔučáxʷdxʷ   He finally got a "lick" in (with his switch).

       ʔučáxʷdub (h)əlgʷəʔ   They happened to club him.

       ʔučáxʷdubuł   He accidentally clubbed us.

108

lexical

| čáxʷadiʔ | sticks for keeping time | LG. |

See under tílib 'sing, sə́x̌ə̆b 'dance'.

Cf. gʷədáčiʔ, čix̌(i)

ʔudxʷčáxʷahə̆bid	(The cougar) beat him with its tail.
ʔudxʷčáxʷahə̆bitə̆b	(The cougar) beat him to death (or at least injured him severely) with its tail.
ʔučáxʷqid	broken skull

reduplication

| čáčxʷəd | hit it lightly with a stick |
| čáxʷčaxʷəd | beat him with a stick or club |

rejected:

*ʔučáxʷətub, *čáxʷil, *čáxʷagʷil

→

2. čáʔ   dig, dig out,
               loosen ground for planting

Cf. gʷil(i)   dig up something buried

yaƛ(a)   dig into, dip out, gore

x̌ʷič(i)   plow; mark up

s.qáləx̌   digging stick for clams

-t

| čáʔə̆d | dig it, dig it up, dig it out |
| ʔučáʔtə̆bəxʷ | They are digging it. |

lexical

| čáʔalikʷ | digging it |

rejected:

*čáʔatəb, *čáʔacut, *čáʔcut

1. ča²a SPS play

    Cf. ²úkʷukʷ NPS play

    ²učá²ahəxʷ ti²ił qá wiẁsu ²al tə s.tù²tələkʷ
    Many children were playing in the creek.

    ²učá²ahəxʷ tə ²àciłtalbixʷ
    The people are playing.

> "These are the words to a little song and dance engaged in by young and old. Everyone sang and danced it over from person to person. When everyone had had his turn, the people would take turns performing their own 'little dance'. These were improvised for the occasion and were a way of encouraging youngsters to perform -- thus leading them into participation in tribal affairs. This song and dance is also used as of means of taking a break during a long meeting. It is danced with two steps forward and to the right, then two steps forward and to the left." JC.

2. čá²ad animal hair (e.g., dog hair)

    Cf. łábid fur

3. ččádi² name for site of Lowell, Washington

4. čəbás NPS siblings-in-law including cousins exclusive of those that are both male, i.e., a man's wife's sister and female cousins, a man's brother's wife and her female cousins, a woman's husband's siblings and cousins, and a woman's sibling's spouse and his/her cousins.

    čə́bəš SPS ESi.

    Contrast x̌ə́łtəd and see under s.k̓ʷəlwás.

    reduplication

      čaabəs ~ čáhəbəs several siblings-in-law LL.

5. s.čə́bək̓ʷ an unidentified kind of bottom fish similar to a bullhead. It eats salmon eggs. It's other name is s.bələwí. (Cf. s.x̌ʷədi²) LL.

1.   čə́bs   dried herring eggs (ready for eating)
      See under qə́lx̌.

2.   čəbtəláx̌ᵊd   wing (of bird, airplane)

3.   čə́c̓qs   mosquito

4.   čə̀c̓ᵊsəlí   name of Hat (Gedney) Island in Port Gardner Bay
                             of Puget Sound

5.   čə́dᵊb   shiver (from cold or fear), the shaking of the
                                                                    Shakers
      See under ƛ̓ə́lp̓.

          ʔalc̓uč̓ə́dᵊb čəd   I'm shivering.   LG.

          ʔuč̓ə́dᵊb ʔə ti ds.kìis ʔu.gʷəgʷàdad   LG.
          I shivered when I got up to talk.

6.   čəj-   See under čal(a).
      Cf. k̓ʷəč̓
      -t
          čə́jᵊd   sneak up on someone
      lexical
          čəjálikʷ   stalk prey

7.   čə́lp   twist, turn, sprain
      See under q̓(ə)č̓.
      root
          ʔəsčə́lp   It's turned.
      -t
          čə́lpᵊd   turn it, twist it
          čə́lpcut čəd   I twisted myself.

lexical

čəlpúsᵊd	turn the head (of a horse when riding)
ʔučəlpúsəbᵊd čəd	I wrung its neck.
ʔučəlᵊpúsc	He wrung my neck.

ʔəs.x̌ác čəd gʷəčəlpšádəd gʷə.təlàwiləd

I fear that I will turn my ankle if I run.

   (čə́lp is here equivalent to jə́lq.)

čəlpáciʔ	Twist his arm!

1. čə́ɬ   ripped through (flesh usually but could be
                                     a car fender)
               Typical use of word would be when a fish hook
               pulled through a fish's mouth and it got away
               by ripping its mouth.   LL.

   Cf. sík̓ʷ   tear, rip apart, take apart

   -b

       xʷčə́ɬᵊb   gully   EK.

   lexical

       čəčə́ɬᵊdís   teeth mostly extracted

2. čə́λ̓əʔ   SPS   rock

   See under čλá̓ʔ.

3. čə́qʷᵊb   bruised, getting blue

   Cf. čə́pᵊb   dark color; bruised, getting blue

4. čə́q̓ʷ-

       ʔəsčə́q̓ʷíl   open sore; filth
                       This is the Skagit equivalent to číq̓ʷil.

   See under x̌ə́ɬ.

1.   čəsáyʔ   NPS   straight spear for crabs and bottom fish   EK.

     čə́say?   SPS   straight spear for crabs and bottom fish   ESi.

     Cf. ƛəgʷíʔčad   straight spear   LL.; ESi.

The act of using a straight spear (whether it is called čəsáyʔ
or ƛəgʷíʔčad) is ƛágʷič.
However, IM. defines čə́sáyʔ as a two pronged pole for spearing.
(This is, perhaps, what the other speakers mean by s.táʔɫ, a
two pronged salmon harpoon.) IM. comments that it "is usually
made out of fir because fir is easy to split". He says that the
act of using a čə́sáyʔ is təpíl q.v.; while the other speakers con-
sulted gloss təpíl as 'spearing salmon in a river', the act of
'using a s.táʔɫ'. See under ƛágʷič.
A third gloss for čə́sáyʔ is given by LG. who defines it as 'a
stick of firewood' (cf. -čup, hud). The easy splitting quality
referred to by IM. may account for the term's use as firewood
by some speakers. (See also x̌əƛyáčəd.)

reduplication

        číc̓sày?   toy spear   EK.
                          small piece of firewood   LG.

2.   čə́sáy?   stick of firewood

     See preceding entry.

→

4.   čə́t-

     lexical

     -qs

        čə́tqs   point

           Cf. -qs, tč̓-

        sčə́tqs   end of nose, point of land

di?ábac ?ə ti?iɫ sc̣ə́tqs   on the other side of the point
ES., DM.

čə̣́tqsáči?   finger tip

-uɫbix^w

čə̣́tuɫbix^w   a sharp, white grass used as trim on baskets
LL.

-yalus

čə̣́t^əyálus   end of something

Cf. ?i̓lyálus, di̓?yálus

čə̣́t^əyálus ?ə tə čəg^wùcid   end of the island   EK.

other

čə̣́tx̌ NPS   Kingfisher, a títču̓lbix^w

čṭə́x̌ SPS   Kingfisher   ESi.

1.   čə̣́t-   separated (?)

Cf. tix̌

čə̣́tq^ə(s)šád   big toe

See under s.dəx̌q(s)šád 'toe'.

Cf. s.luƛ̓alqsači? (stress?)   thumb

sc̣ə́tšád NPS   fishtail   LG., LA., LL., EK.

sc̣ə́tšəd SPS   fishtail   ESi.

Cf. s.k^wə́ɫt   fishtail   LL.

x^w.čúpč̓   tail, coccyx

2.   čə̣wálc   hibernate   LL.

Cf. ƛ̓x^wíl

114

1. čəxʷ(u)
→
    -yi-

        čəxʷyíc   Add more (to what I have).

    reduplication

        gʷəčičxʷyicid čəd ʔu ʔə kʷi dxʷs.(h)ədálqʷuʔ
        Should I give you more coffee?

2. čə̀xʷtədábut   fall down flat, all spread out, fall down hard,
                      (a child throwing a temper tantrum) threw himself
                      down flat   LL.

    See under xʷítił.

3. čəx̌(i)   See under čx̌(i).
→

5. čígʷil   impatient, disgusted, irritated

    Cf. x̌ícil   angry

        dukʷtxʷ   angry   (under dukʷ(u))

    -il

        ʔučígʷiləxʷ čəd   I'm getting disgusted.

        ʔučígʷiləxʷ čəd ʔə ciʔił ʔu.cùtcut
        I'm getting disgusted with her jabbering.

    -i(l)-s

        ʔučígʷisəxʷ čəd ciʔił ʔu.cùtcut
        I'm getting disgusted with her jabbering.

        xʷìʔ kʷ(i) adsʔučígʷis
        Don't get impatient with her.

        ʔučígʷisəbəxʷ čəd ʔə tiʔił
        He is getting disgusted with me.

-il-bi-t

x̌ʷì? kʷ(i) adsučíg̓ʷilbid

Don't get impatient with her.

?əsčíg̓ʷilbid čəd ti?iɬ s.qʷəbày? ləcu.gʷuhᵊb

I'm getting irritated with that dog's barking;
that dog's barking is getting on my nerves.

?əsčíg̓ʷilbicut   irritated with self

→

2. xʷ.č̓íɬqs   a very large oyster. The shell was used as 'money'.
In at least one of the Old Stories xʷ.č̓íɬqs becomes
Crow's father-in-law.

3. č̓íq̓icut   scream, loud crying

See under cut.

Cf. ?íwb x̌áhəb   cry

4. č̓(i)q̓ʷ-

reduced grade with -il

č̓q̓ʷíl   become rotten, decay

Cf. p̓x̌ác   rotten wood

-t

č̓q̓ʷíld   make it rot/decay

normal grade with -il

č̓íq̓ʷil   filth, infection, dirt, dirty

(The Skagit equivalent is č̓əq̓ʷíl where the /ə/ replaces
/i/ and is not an epenthetic vowel. That is, the Skagit
form č̓əq̓ʷíl belongs to the normal grade (along with
č̓íq̓ʷil of the other dialects) and contrasts with the reduced grade č̓q̓ʷíl.)

Cf. čə́q	dirty	
pədíxʷ	soil, earth, dirt	LG
qá scíq̓ʷil	There was a lot of dirt.	EK.
łəqʷdúp cíq̓ʷil	wet dirt (i.e., mud)	LL.
ʔəscíq̓ʷil	infection, dirty	ESi., EK.
ʔəscíq̓ʷiʔ	same gloss	FSi.

-il-t

ʔəscíq̓ʷilcut	infection is spreading	EK.
Cf. gʷə.łə́x̌ čəxʷ	You might catch a disease/ become contaminated.	LG.

lexical

ʔəscíq̓ʷàčiʔ	dirty hands
cíq̓ʷilus	dirty face

1. s.čístxʷ   husband

See under s.k̓ʷəlwás.

Cf. čəgʷás   wife

-il

gʷəsʔábsscístxʷils	to have a husband (lit. 'to have her becoming husbanded')
łudəxʷbəscístxʷil	she will become husbanded (i.e., get a husband)

reduplication

ləbscíscistxʷ	go about seeking a man to marry

2. čit   near

Opposite of lil   'far'.

root

łu.húyud č́ìt tiʔəʔ łudəxᵛ.ʔuxᵛˇčəł

He will make our journey near (i.e., short).

-t

č́itcut   draw self closer

-il

č́itil   draw near

hiʔáb čəd ʔuč́itil ʔə tə hù̀d   I got too close to the fire.

-i(1)-s

č́itis   approach someone/something

-bi-t

dəč́itbid čəxᵛ   You are near me.

ʔəs.gᵛəd́il čəxᵛ ʔal ti dč̀itbid   You are sitting near me.

ʔəs.ḱiis tiʔił s.tù̀bš ʔal ti č́itbids

That man is standing near her.

in compounds

č́itsqà   older sibling next to ego

č́itsù̀q̔ᵛaʔ   younger sibling next to ego

lexical

č́itábac   'near side', metaphorically extended
                       to mean Saturday, i.e., on the near
                       side of the Sacred Day   LL.

čətábac   same gloss   ESi.

č́itáləp kᵛ(i) adsəs.k̀iis

Stand by the foot of the tree.

č́itəlus   surprised (lit. 'near eyed')

ʔuč́itəlusbid ci ds.ḱù̀y dxᵛʔal tiʔił s.ʔà̀xᵛuʔ

My mother was surprised about the clams.

118

1. čít(i)

    -it

    čítid   chewed it up (destroyed it as would an insect)

    See under k̓aw.

2. s.číyùya?   twins

3. čí?əb   war cry

    See under cut.

4. s.čí?ɬ Skagit   sockeye salmon (red, blueback), a s.?uládxʷ LG.

    Cf. s.cəqí (Snoh.), čəwádxʷ (Muck.), xʷ.bádi? (Snoqu.)

5. čƛá? NPS   rock

    čəƛə? SPS   rock

    Cf. s.bádil   mountain

        ƛáq̓t   landward

    lexical

        čƛá(?)qs   rock point; the name for the site of Priest Point,
                        Tulalip Reservation, Washington

    reduplication

        c̓əƛcƛá?   rocks scattered about

        číčƛa?   small rock, stone

        číčičƛa?   gravel

6. čƛàlúb   kidney   LG.

    Cf. s.čədčəd   kidney   EK.

        s.p̓ús   kidney   ML.

1. čq̓ʷíl   See under c̓(i)q̓ʷ-.

2. čsáy?   See under čəsáy?.

3. čsíč   arrow quiver   AS.

     Cf. čəláxʷali   arrow quiver   LL.

4. čtíɬq̓ʷəbš   name for people who live(d) at site of Steilacoom, Washington

5. čučgʷas   twisting in the process of weaving blankets

     See under ?əq̓ʷál, q̓ác.

6. ču(?)k̓ʷ   NPS   skunk cabbage   LG.

     Cf. q̓ílt   SPS   skunk cabbage; name for site of Port Gamble Bay, Kitsap Co., Washington   ESi.

     lexical

        čuk̓ʷali   the whole skunk cabbage plant   LG., EK., MC.

     rejected:

        *ču(?)k̓ʷac   "The -ac would make it a whole tree."   LG.

7. s.čuɬəy?   leaf (in general)   HD.

     Cf. ču?ɬac   broadleaf maple

     lexical

        čuɬəy?àlus   leaf color, green   EK.

          Cf. x̌ʷi.q̓ʷác

8. -čup̓č   tail, coccyx

     Cf. s.čətšád   fishtail

     xʷ.čup̓č   tail, coccyx   LG.

     s.čup̓č   tail, coccyx   LL., DM., EK.

120

1.   čútəp   flea

2.   čúʔɫac   broadleaf maple   HD., EK., ESi.

   Cf. s.čúɫəyʔ   leaf (in general)

      čúʔɫac tə dəxʷu.čəɫ x̌ʷùbt. ƛ̓àl čúʔɫac bədəxʷu.čəɫ ɫápqs
      Maple wood is used to make paddles and also ladles.   LG.

   reduplication

      sčúcuʔɫəc SPS   vine maple   ESi.

         Cf. təqt̓qác Skagit   vine maple

            kiúʔkiwəc Snoh. vine maple

3.   čx̌(i)

   See under ƛ̓uq̓ʷ(u).

   -it

      ʔəsčx̌id   It is jammed, stuffed, crowded.

         qá ʔàciɫtalbixʷ pút ʔəsčx̌id tiʔəʔ d.ʔàlʔal
         A lot of people were crowded into my house.

      ʔəsčəx̌id   It is too tight. squeezed into it (e.g., clothing)
                                                          DM.

d

This letter represents a sound very much like that of the English *d* except that in Puget d̲ also encompasses n̲-sounds. (See discussion under b̲.) [voiced alveolar stop]

1.   d-   'my'

The possessive system comprises five morphemes distinguishing three persons and two numbers, singular and plural. Number in third person is not indicated. The first two persons singular are prefixes. The other three morphemes are suffixes:

d-	'my'	-čəɬ	'our'
ad-	'thy'	-lap	'your'
	-s	'his, her, its, their'	

Third person /-s/ combines with preceding alveolar stops (including those of roots): /d-s>j/ and /t-s>c/. (However, most of the examples in this dictionary are written without this assimilation, e.g., bad̲s instead of baj̲.)

The prefix representation is complex. A few of the allomorphs are:

d̲ᵊbad	my father	badčəɬ	our father
ʔədbad	thy father	badləp	your father
	baj̲	his, her, its, their father	

/də-/ 'my'   when initial in a syllable if not followed by an /s-/ prefix.

/ʔəd-/ 'thy'   *ibid.*

ti d̲bad	my father	ti badčəɬ	our father
tadbad	thy father	ti badləp	your father
	ti baj̲	his, her, its, their father	

/d-/ 'my'   when final in a syllable and not followed by an /s-/ prefix.

/tad-/ 'thy'   *ibid.*
When two vowels are juxtaposed, the first drops.

ci c̲k̓ʷúy   my mother   ci sk̓ʷúyčə̵ł   our mother

cack̓ʷúy   thy mother   ci sk̓ʷúyləp   your mother

ci sk̓ʷuys̲   his, her, its, their mother

/d/ plus an /s-/ prefix become /c/ (occasionally /j/).

The first person plural suffix, -čə̵ł, is etymologically related to the sequence č̲-a̲ł(i).

While -la̲p is the underlying form of the second person plural suffix, it is always realized as -lə̲p.

1.   -d   allomorph of -t̲   'transitive'

2.   dab   contrastive emphatic

      dábəxʷ dəgʷí   Let it be you.

      dábəxʷ cədił   Let it be he.

      də̲b ʔəcá tiʔił ƛ̓ə.x̌ə̵łqìd   It's me who gets the headache.

      də̲b dəgʷí   It is you.

      də̲b díbə̵ł   It is we.

Note: This form is not used in answer to the question, Who's there (at the door)? For that, the response is simply

       ʔəcá   (It's) I/me.

or   ʔəcá ti *Thom*.   (It's) me, Thom.

də̲b dəgʷí t(i) as.(h)àydxʷ

You (instead of me) know it.

   Cf. dił dəgʷí t(i) as.(h)àydxʷ

     You are the one who knows it.

3.   dah-   thank for gift of food/drink

    Cf. daʔ

-dx^w

dáh^ədubš čəx^w   (I) thank you. (Lit. 'You make me live'.)

ʔudáh^ədx^w čəx^w   Thank you for helping him.

   Cf. həlíʔdx^w   thank for gift of food/drink

      ʔi   (as in ʔí· siʔàb ʔə tə ʔabyic ʔə tə talə
                     Thank you, Sir, for the money.)

   čk^wálidx^w, tíg^wid

In expressing thanks, one often lifts both hands, palms up, and with elbows bent at right angles and arms kept parallel, moves the forearms up and down slightly (much as English speakers might gesture to someone to get up) and while thus lifting and lowering the arms, moves them from first one side of the body to the other.

   To say 'you are welcome', the usual expression is

      x̌^wuƚ čəx^w ʔəs.balíic   'Just forget it.' or
      ʔəs.ƛúbil   'That is O.K.'

→

2.   dat   day, 24 hour period

ƚix^w dát tiʔiƚ ʔàcig^wəds (h)əlg^wəʔ ʔə tiʔiƚ čəx^{wə}lùʔ
Three days they were inside the whale.

   s.cəbdátil   'second day'   Tuesday

ʔəƚ-

   ƚubə.ƚčíl čəd ʔal k^wi ʔəƚdàt
   I'll arrive again the day after tomorrow

   dúk^wəƚdàt   'changed day'   yesterday or tomorrow

      ʔal k^wi tu.dúk^wəƚdàt   yesterday

      ʔal k^wi dúk^wəƚdàt   tomorrow

      ʔal (k^wi) k̓^wídəƚdàt   in a few days

      díʔəƚdàt   the day before yesterday

   (lit. 'on the (other) side of dúk^wəƚdàt')

x̌áx̌aʔəɬdàt	'great day', i.e., Sunday	
bə́lᵊx̌ʷəɬdàt	Skagit	'after the day', i.e., Monday

Cf. p̓əɬq̓ʷábac   Snoh., SPS   'after side', i.e., Monday

ʔəɬ-...-il

s.ɬíx̌ʷəɬdàtil	'third day'	Wednesday
s.búusəɬdàtil	'fourth day'	Thursday
s.cəlácəɬdàtil	'fifth day'	Friday

sáliʔàči ʔəɬdàtils ʔi tə sàliʔ   the 22nd of the month

k̓ʷídəɬdàtiləxʷ   What day is it?

dádatu   morning, early   LL.; ES.

ʔəs.t̓ígʷid ʔal k̓ʷi dàdatu   LG.
Praise Him in the morning (lit. 'Thank Him in the morning')
Christian hymn (in Snoqualmie?)

Cf. ɬukʷáčiləs   tomorrow morning   LG.

ɬup   morning, early part of day

1. daw   an interjection
   dá·w ti dəgʷí!   Hey, you!   LG.

2. dáwʔ   adverb 'just now'   LL.
   See under daʔxʷ.

→

4. dáx̌aɬ   a shiny black cloth
   Cf. -adis

5. dáyəsqidəb   man's name, LG.'s younger brother, Elison

6. dáysuʔìčaʔ   woman's name, LG.'s MoMoBrDa and younger BrDa,
   Ruby

125

1. dayʔ   Snoh.,   adverb; can also serve as head of predication
           Sauk   (Sometimes recorded as /daẏ/.)
                         Equivalent to cukʷ of most Skagit groups.

    as predicate head

    diłəxʷ łusdáyʔsəxʷ   That will be the last.   LL.

       Cf. diłəxʷ łucugʷáłəxʷ That will be the last.   LG.

    as adverb

    dáyʔəxʷ čəd ʔəs.x̌ʷìduł   I'm very melancholy.

    dáyʔəxʷ čəd ʔəs.x̌ə̀ł(əł)x̌əč   I feel real bad.

    dáyʔəxʷ čəd ʔəs.x̌ik̓ʷəb   I'm really lonely.

    dáyʔəxʷ (h)à?ł šə.šìqʷ   a nice looking hat

    dáyʔəxʷ (h)à?ł ti s.q̓ʷəlàłᵊd   real good berries

    tiʔił gʷədáyʔəxʷ (h)à?ł   That is real good.

    dàyʔ ʔu.tə̀ł   That's certainly true.

    dàyʔ ʔəcá kʷ(i) as.(h)áydxʷ   I'm the only one who knows.

    dáyʔ tiʔəʔ čál̓.čaləs dəxʷə.ʔìbəšs
    He just walked with his hands.

    dáyʔ čál̓.čaləs lə.j̓ə̀ctxʷ   He just used his hands.

    díł čəd dàyʔ ʔəs.(h)àydxʷ   That is all I know.

    díł čəxʷ dàyʔ ʔəs.(h)àydxʷ gʷ(ə)adsu.xʷì?xʷiʔ
    All you know is hunting.

    dáyʔ čəd łu.hàydxʷ   I'll know after a while.

    dáyʔ čəd łu.šùdubicid ʔal kʷi dəc̓úʔ x̌àx̌aʔ
    I'll see you again in one week.

    reduplication

    dáyayʔ   alone (more or less permanently)

      dáyayʔ   She lived alone.

dáyay? čəd   I live alone.

həláʔb čəd dàyay?   I'm really alone.

dáy?diəy?   (from day?-di-ay??)   alone (temporarily)

dáy?diəy? bəščəb. xʷi? gʷəsəs.gʷátxʷs ti?ił tətyiqa?,
su?suq̓ʷə?s. dáy?diəy?

Mink was alone. His little younger brother, Tətyiqa?
(who usually accompanies him) was not with him. He
was alone.   ML.

Equivalent to Skagit cúgʷukʷ.   DM.

It, dáy?diəy? or cúgʷukʷ, would be used if someone
were out in the woods by himself.   DM.

rejected:

*?əsdáy?diəy?

1.   daʔ(a)   name, call

   root

      gʷát kʷ(i) adsdà?   What is your name?

      Hedli tə dsda?   Henry is my name.

      gʷat kʷi sda? ?ə c(i) ads.k̓ʷuy   What is your mother's name?

      Mali ti sda?s   Her name is Mary.   LG.

      gʷát kʷi bək̓ʷ adsdà?   What is your full name? LG.

      stab kʷi sda?s   What would that be called?

      q̓číc tə sda? ?ə ti?ə?   This is called a bow.

      s.təčás sdà? ?ə ti?ə? s.wàtixʷtəd
      Oyster Bay is the name of the place.

      dxʷ?al kʷ sná?s kʷə máns ?i tə məná?s ?i tə sanḵtus pli
      In Nomine Patris, et Filii, et Spiritus Sancti.

   -at

      dáʔəd   Name it!

stàb kʷi ɬ(u)adsdáʔəd t(i) ad.bədàʔ

What are you going to name your baby?

ʔudáʔatᵊb ʔə kʷi dxʷs.qàda

The statement was made that he is a thief.

dəxʷəsdaʔətᵊbs tiʔəʔ diʔəʔ s.qʷalíʔabš dxʷʔal tiʔəʔ
sqʷì.qʷəli(ʔ) s.wàtixʷtəd

So the Nisqually are named after this grassy land.

-at-sut-bi-t

dáʔəcutbid   Tell them your name!

reduplication

dídaʔa-

ʔudídaʔətᵊb tə d.bədàʔ ʔə kʷi dxʷs.qàda

They are calling my son a thief.

ʔudídaʔətᵊb ʔə kʷi dxʷs.qàda

It was said over and over that he is a thief.

ʔudídaʔətᵊb (h)əlgʷəʔ ʔə tiʔəʔ dxʷs.qàda

This thief is calling them names.

1. dxʷ.dáʔᵊb   shaman, Indian doctor

   Cf. baɬ(a)   (The etymology of dxʷ.dáʔᵊb is not certain.
                  It is perhaps to be linked to daʔ(a) 'call,
                  name' or to daʔ- 'support'.)

2.   daʔ-   support (?)

   Cf. dah-, higʷᵊd (under hikʷ)

dáʔdaʔ   that which gives emotional support, satisfac-
                tion; that which is important to someone.

háʔɬ kʷ(i) adsə(s).šùuc t(i) ad.bədàʔ; dàyʔ ɬ(u)addáʔdaʔ
ʔal kʷi ɬus.luʎils

Take good care of your son; when he grows up, he will be
your mainstay in old age.

128

1. dáʔxʷ   adverb   'just now'   LG., JC.

        Cf. dáwʔ   LL.

            dáʔxʷ ʔu.ɫčìl   He's just now arrived.

            dáʔxʷ čəd ʔu.cə̀kʷədxʷ   I just now understand it.

            ʔəs.ʔəx̌íd kʷ(i) adəxʷəs.tágʷəxʷ. dáʔxʷ čəxʷ ʔu.huyədxʷ   LG.
            Why are you hungry? You just ate.

            dáʔxʷ ʔal tiʔəʔ   Right now.

            ʔal tiʔəʔ dáʔxʷ   same gloss

2. də́b   See under dáb.

3. dəbə́ɫ   offspring of a siʔáb

        Cf. bədáʔ

4. -dəč   lexical suffix (Appropriate gloss uncertain.)

        -áldəč   abdomen

        See under ƛač.

            ʔu.tsáldəčdub čəd   I got punched in the belly.

            ʔu.čəxʷčxʷáldəčtəb   Someone clubbed him (repeatedly)
                                    in the abdomen.

            təǰəǰáldəč   rolling belly along (metaphor for
                                    extreme fatigue, sort of just manag-
                                    ing to roll it along the ground.
                                    See under wáwɫqayuʔ.)

            ləčáldəč   belly filled (jocular way of saying
                                    bəɫ, q.v.)

            tə s.qʷəbáyʔaldəč   the belly of a dog

            pə́čáldəč   feces on anus   VH.

-adəč

ʔəs.x̌əɬádəč   stomach ache   VH.

1.   dəčú?   NPS   one

       də́ču?   SPS   one

       Cf. sáli?   two

          ɬíxʷ   three

          búus   four

          cəlác   five

          yəlá?c   NPS   six   (jəláči?   SPS)

          čú?kʷs   seven

          tᵊqáči?   eight

          x̌ʷə́l   nine

          ?úlub   NPS   ten   (pádəc   SPS)

          ?úlub ?i kʷi d(ə)čù?   NPS   eleven

          (pádəc yəxʷ tə dəčú?   SPS   eleven)

          sáli?ači?   twenty

          dəčú? s.bəkʷàči?   one hundred

          ?úlubìlc ?i kʷi d(ə)čù?   eleven dollars

       lexical

          dəča?ágʷəp   one thing to plant

          dəča?álps   one animal

          dəča?ál?txʷ   one house

          dəča?aɬčup   one fire

          dəča?áɬič   one bundle

dəčá(ʔ)kʷbixʷ   from a different tribe, group, class

    dəčákʷbixʷ dxʷʔal tiʔəʔ (hə)làʔb s.ʔulàdxʷ   MS.
    It is different from the real salmon.

dəčáʔəlus   a square in a net, one stitch in knitting

dəčaʔič

    dxʷ(də)čaʔijᵊd dxʷʔal tiʔəʔ dxʷ.líʔil   MS.
    one way from the other

dəčáʔidup   one of a class of

    diɬ dəčáʔidup s.ʔulàdxʷ
    That is one of a class of salmon.

dəčaʔílc   one dollar

dəčəʔílc   one month

    haʔkʷ dəčəʔìlc s.ɬukʷàlb tiʔiɬ s.ʔàs
    For one month he was there.

dəčáʔqs   one point

    didčáʔqs   single barrel gun

dəčáxʷ   once

    dəčáxʷaɫadiʔ   heard it once

-agʷ-txʷ

    dəčágʷtxʷ tə səs.ɫaɬlil ʔə cə ds.k̓ʷùyʔ
    My mother lives next door.

    tiʔəʔ diʔəʔ ʔəs.ɫaɬlil dəčàgʷtxʷ
    Here neighbors are living.

-agʷ-txʷ-b

    ʔəsdəčágʷtxʷᵊb   She is visiting.

      Cf. jəláx̌ədbid (under jal), jəx̌əx̌

    dxʷsdčágʷtxʷᵊb   One who is always visiting.

131

-agʷ-txʷ-bi-t

ʔux̌ʷ čəd łud(ə)č̓agʷtxʷbid tə d.ʔiìšəd łu.kʷàčiləs
I'm going to visit my relatives tomorrow.

dxʷdəč̓ágʷus   one row, one layer

reduplication

dídč̓uʔ   solitary   LG.

dídč̓uʔ   one small person, article etc.   LL.

gʷəl tiʔəʔ x̌ʷúʔx̌ʷayʔ gʷəl (hə)láʔb bìʔbad. x̌əł tì
dìdč̓akʷbixʷ   MS.
But the Little Diver is really small -- as if
from a different class.

díič̓uʔ   one human being   LL.; LG.

dìdədíič̓uʔ   one child   LG.

dídidʔč̓uʔ   one by one   LG.

dədíč̓uʔ   be alone   EK. (rejected by LL.; LG.)

1. x̌.dədáw̓šəd   marrow of a bone

    See under šáw̓ 'bone'.

2. dədícx̌ayʔ   lizard

3. dəgʷí NPS   you (sg.)

    də́gʷi SPS

    See under ʔəcá.

4. dəgʷásx̌   Possession Point, the southernmost tip of
                     Whidbey Island, Washington

                     "This is where the summer longhouse was." HD.

                     Haeberlin/Gunther write what would be trans-
                     cribed here as nəgʷáasx̌, p. 7.

1.   dəkʷ ~ dəw- ~ dəgʷ(a)   inside a small, confining place

    Contrast with həd?iw̓ 'inside building'.

    See under ʔac-.

    root

        ʔəcá ti?ə? ?əsdə̀kʷ   I'm inside (the cave).

        ?əsdə̀kʷ ?al ti wə̀q̓əb   It's inside the box.

    -at

        dəgʷád NPS   Put it inside.

          dəgʷád dxʷ?al tə xʷdəgʷigʷsali
          Put it into the pocket (bag).

        də́gʷəd SPS   Put it inside.

          də́gʷəd ?al tə wəq̓ə̀b   Put it in the box.   JC.

        dəgʷátᵊb   It was put inside.

        dəgʷácut   I put myself inside.

    -aš

        dəgʷáš NPS   Put it inside. (Said to be
                             equivalent to dəgʷád.)

        də́gʷəš SPS

          See under -š.

          ?udə́gʷəš čəd ?al ti syà lt   JC.
          I put it in the cedar-root basket.

    -agʷil

        ?u.ƛ̓íqagʷil ti?iɫ s.čə̀txʷəd tul̓?al ti?iɫ ?àl?als
        ƛudəxʷdəgʷágʷils ?al ti?iɫ pə(d).tə̀s
        The bear came out from his house where he goes
        into in the winter.

lexical

    xʷdəgʷígʷsali   pocket, bag

    dxʷdəwʔábš, dxʷduʔábš   Duwamish ('the people inside
                                             (the bay)')

rejected:

    *əgʷášᵊb, *dəgʷíb

1.   dəqʷáləd   house post   LL.

    reduplication

    dəqʷdəqʷáləd   house posts

2.   dəš   lean, be on side

    Cf. ʔil

    root

        ʔəsdə́š   It's on its side.   LG.

        ʔəsdə́š   lean over   AS.

        lədə́š tə s.ɬáq̓s   fall on side from standing
                                         position   LG.

        lədə́š tə s.xʷìtils   fall on side from high place   LG.

        lədə́š tə s.pìxʷils   Same gloss: fall on side
                                            from high place   LG.

    -t

        də́šᵊd   put it on its side

        də́štᵊb   It was set on its side.

    -agʷ-il

        ʔəsdəšágʷil čəd   I'm leaning against something.

reduplication

dəšdəšád　　　　　　set many things on their side

1.　dəwʔáyus　　　　See under du?ayus.

2.　dəxʷ-　　　　derivational prefix　'reason for (an act)'
　　　　　　　　　or 'place where (an act occurs)'. Usually
　　　　　　　　　glossed as 'because, why, that is where, what'.
　　　　　　　　　When preceding the prefix u-, it is glossed
　　　　　　　　　as 'what use made of'.

See Hoard/Hess, p. 48 and following.

3.　s.dəxʷíɫ　NPS　　small, fast canoe　　　　　　LL.; EK.
　　　　　　　　　especially for duck hunting

　　s.də́xʷiɫ　SPS　　　　　　　　　　　　ESi.

See under q̓íˑlbid.

　　gʷəl tiʔəʔ kʷa sdəxʷíɫ gʷəl x̌əɫ ti ʔəs.tújil. bíʔbad tiʔiɫ
　　sə(s).š(ə)qìl ʔə tiʔiɫ šəjts. x̣ál bəs.ʔìstəʔ tiʔiɫ ʔìlaqs.
　　bíʔbad q̓ìlbid tiʔiɫ sdəxʷíɫ.　　　　　　　　　MS.

　　As for the hunting canoe, it seems bent over. It's bow
　　is raised a little and so is its stern. The hunting canoe
　　is a small canoe.

　　reduplication

　　sdíʔdəxʷiɫ　　　　a model of a s.dəxʷiɫ　　　　DM.

4.　dəx̌-

　　Cf. q̓ʷəx̌ʷ-

　　　jə́səd　　　　　foot, lower leg

　　sdəx̌q(s)šád　　　　toe　　　　　　LG.

　　　Cf. čə́tq̓ə(s)šád　　big toe　　　　DM.

　　sdəx̌álqsači?　　　fingers　　　　LL.

　　　Cf. s.lúx̣qsačiʔ　　thumb (lit. 'old finger')　LL.

Cf. t̓isuhálqsači?   little finger (lit.'young finger') EK.

mi?man(?)álqsači?   little finger (lit.'small finger') LL.

jixʷálqsači?   index finger (lit.'lead(ing) finger') LL.

<u>sdəx̌álači?</u>   whole open hand, palm
                      fingers and all   EK.

<u>dəx̌álači?</u>   space between fingers   LL.

1.   díbəɫ   we, us

    See under <u>?əcá</u>.

2.   dídi?ɫ   adverb   'still'

    Cf. di?ɫ, u?xʷ

      <u>dídi?ɫ</u> čəd ?əs.x̌ə̀ɫ   I'm still sick.

      <u>dídi?ɫ</u> čəd lə.təlàwil   I'm still running.

      <u>dídi?ɫ</u> u?xʷ ?u čəxʷ ?ə(s).šuɫàlbut

      Are you still able to see? (i.e., not yet blind in
                           your old age)

      bə.lə́x̌iləxʷ ?al ti?iɫ bə.də̀ču? s.lə̀xil. <u>dìdi?ɫ</u>
      ?əs.x̌ə́ɫəɫx̌ə̀č ti?iɫ

      Came the light of another day (and) he was still unhappy.

3.   dídšəlqid   small sized 'sawbill' (hooded merganser(?)),
                    a <u>bú?qʷ</u>   LL.

→

5.   díɫ   the one who/ the thing that/ the event mentioned

    Cf. cədíɫ, ?əcá (and the other emphatic pronouns
              listed under ?əcá)

    Different from <u>cədíɫ</u> and like the emphatic pronouns, <u>díɫ</u>
can (and usually <u>does)</u> occur as head of a predication. Occasionally, however, its syntactic position in the clause is
like the adverb's.

syntactically like an adverb:

díɫ qádadic   He's the one who stole from me.

gʷəl díɫ ʔu.ʔátəbəd   And he died.

huy, díɫəxʷ ʔu.cùtˀbəxʷ   Then, that is what they said.

as predicate head:

gʷədíɫəxʷ   That might be he now!

níɫ tə!   He's the one!

He's the one! (The n replaces d in 'seagull language'
(quoted here) and in a number of other specialized
speech styles.)

xʷíʔ lədìɫ   He/it is not the one.

bədíɫ əẁə sixʷ xʷùʔˀləʔ!   It must be that one again!

díɫ tiʔəʔ ƛu.cútˀb stìq.tiqàyuʔ tiʔəʔ ʔu.bəčalq

They who made the kill used to be called Wolves.

díɫ kʷi dúkʷibəɫ kʷi ʔu.ɫčísˀbš

It was Transformer who came to me.

x̌ʷùì díɫ b(ə)u.ċqʷìbčəɫ

We just got in on it too.

díɫ dəxʷəs.ʔístə ʔə ciʔiɫ p̓uày?

That's why Flounder is like that.

reduplication

díɫiɫ   just as soon as   ML.
                 upon (doing something) LG.

díɫiɫ ƛubəs.xʷìʔxʷiʔiluɫ ʔə tiʔəʔ s.bəq̓ʷàʔ

That is why Heron kept going out hunting.

díɫiɫ sə.ɫčìls...

Just as soon as he arrived,...

díɫiɫəxʷ tiʔiɫ q̓əjà x̌ ʔə ciʔiɫ s.qìgʷəc kʷi ɫad.q̓əjà x̌

The entrails of Deer will be your entrails.

137

gʷəl díɬiɬ s.ʔùx̌ʷ ʔə tiʔəʔ diʔəʔ lə̀gʷəb s.ʔílids tiʔəʔ
s.qəlàlitut tələs.ʔə̀y̓dxʷ, ləs.ʔə̀y̓gʷásbid

Thereupon the youth went on (and) sang the power song
he had found, he had met.

diɬdiɬ   same, alike

Cf. pus

diɬdiɬgʷəs tiʔəʔ q̓ilbid   The canoes are alike.   LG.

díʔɬdiɬ   It's just the same way yet.

1. s.níƛəm   a point near Coupeville, Washington

2. -dis   lexical suffix   'tooth, straight pin'

Cf. -adis

A few lexical suffixes are transparently related
derivationally to the nouns they replace. Examples are:

1.	-dis	tooth	jədís	tooth
2.	-šad	foot, lower leg	ǰə́səd	foot, lower leg
3.	-qs	nose, point	bə́qsəd	nose
4.	-idᵊgʷas	upper part of torso, mind, mental attitude	yədwás	heart (Skagit, not Snohomish)

In (2) dissimilation and stress shift account for the
replacement of šad by səd in ǰə́səd. In (4) the entire noun
occurs as the lexical suffix. This appears to be a clear
case of noun incorporation, although yədwás might be derived from the suffix (if, for example, the operation of
word taboo required the replacement of s.čáliʔ among the
Skagit). This second possibility is less likely since gʷ
is thought to derive from w and not the reverse.

-dis   tooth

x̌ə́ɬdís   toothache

č̓ə.č̓əɬᵊdís   teeth mostly extracted

-dis   straight pin

x̌ʷúq̓ʷədisəd   pin with a straight pin in order to put
a wrap on someone

lexical composition

cəq̓ᵊdísᵊbəd   fork

čəč̓ᵊdísbəd   toothpick

x̌tádis   very hard wood

1.   díšə?   See under di?a?.

2.   di?   to/at the side of

See under ?ac-.

Cf. ?il

root

    tuɫ?ál čəd di? s.ləx̌îl   I am from the daylight.   LL.

    ... ?al dì? šə́q   ... in Heaven

-bi-t

    dí(?)bid   on the other end

lexical

-ábac

    di?ábac ?ə ti q̓əláx̌ad   other side of the fence

    di?ábac ?ə ti?iɫ s.čə́tqs   on the other side of the point

    ?al kʷi di?ábac   dead (lit. 'on the otherside')

      Cf. ?atəbəd

-adi?

    di?ádi?   other part of the house   LG.
                               other room   LG., JC.
                               on the other side of the house (inside) LG., JC.
                               end of room/next room   DM.

-al̓-ič

    <u>dí?əl̓ič</u>   (on the) other side of the ridge
                           (on the) other side of hill/rise

-ál?txʷ

    <u>di?ál?txʷ</u>   house on the other side,
                          on the other side of the house (outside)

-á-qid

    <u>di?á</u>qid   headed opposite way

-ax̌ad

    <u>dí?ax̌əd</u>   other side of something   LG.

        Cf. líilax̌əd   on the far side of something

        təláwiləxʷ ci?ə? lúƛ dxʷ?al <u>dí?ax̌əd</u> ?ə tə
        qá ?àcił talbixʷ   EC.
        The old lady ran <u>next</u> <u>door</u> (where) there
        were a lot of people.

    <u>dídi?ax̌əd</u>   next door neighbor

        Cf. dəc̓agʷtxʷ (under dəc̓ú?)

-ay-ucid

    <u>di?á</u>yucid   other side of the road, trail

-úcid

    <u>di?ú</u>cid   located on the other side of the river

        Cf. jəlúcid (under jál), šáqʷil, túlil

        ?u<u>di?ú</u>cid(d)xʷ čəxʷ gʷəl jíx̌ tə x̌àlšəd   EK.
        You crossed over and the bridge collapsed.

-ulic-bi-t

    <u>di?ú</u>licbid   on the other side of the bay, room, trail,
                    road   JC.

-y-alus

di?yálus   on the end

Cf. čət°yálus   end of something

?ilyálus   edge/end of something

-(?)əɬ-dat

dí?əɬdàt   the day before yesterday
(lit. 'on the other side of
dúkʷəɬdàt' 'yesterday')

lexical composition

di?ílaq   stern of canoe, back seat of car

Cf. laq

?al di?ílaq kʷ(i) ads.q̓il   You ride in the stern.

as an element in certain deictic words

di?a? NPS   here

díša? SPS   here

túdi?   there

tádi?   (same gloss. All consultants claim that tudi?
and tadi? are exactly the same.)

túdi(?) dì?i   way over there

kʷədí?   far off into the misty past

as an element in lexical suffixes

-adi?

-aldi? ~ -əldi?

reduplication

dí?i?

?al túdi(?) dì?i   way, way over there

tuɬ?ál čəd di?i s.b°čáx̌ad

I'm from there where the edge lies down.

lədxʷdíʔi tə sə.ʔìbəš ʔə dìiču̓ʔ s.tùbš

That man is walking <u>that</u> <u>way</u>.

dìł ʔiłs.(h)ájᵊb tiʔił ʔiłdì̓ʔi

That person on the other side is taller.

dxʷdíʔi ti s.ʔùx̌ʷs

He went the opposite way.

dədídiʔ   Move over!

    See under <u>jəx̌</u>.

dídiʔax̌əd   next door neighbor

1.   díʔaʔ   NPS   here

    díšaʔ   SPS   here

    Cf. ʔá

        łu.šúuc čəxʷ tà ʔə <u>diʔə</u>ʔ: tiʔəʔ bək̓ʷídup s.ʔulàdxʷ,
        tiʔəʔ <u>diʔə</u>ʔ yúbəč, tiʔəʔ <u>diʔə</u>ʔ qíwʔx̌, tiʔəʔ <u>diʔə</u>ʔ
        (s).kʷxʷíc, tiʔəʔ s̓ʔu.ʔuládxʷ ʔal tiʔəʔ x̌ʷə̀lč   EC.

        You will see this (right) here: all kinds of salmon,
        (this here) king, (this here) steelhead, (this here)
        dog salmon, (this here) silver salmon, many salmon
        from the sea.

    as head of predication

        ... čədà łubəd<u>íʔə</u>ʔ ... and I'll be here again.

        <u>díš</u>əʔəxʷ čəd   I'm here.   ESi.

        cəq̓áqid čəxʷ ʔu <u>dìšə</u>ʔ   Are you always here?   JC.

        <u>díš</u>əʔ ʔu kʷ(i) ad.bàd   Is your father here?   JC.

        xʷiʔ kʷi łudsdíšə ʔal kʷi s.buusil   ESi.
        I won't be here on Thursday.

        gʷát kʷə <u>dìšə</u>ʔ   Who is here?   JC.

-bi-t-

díʔəbic   my company

díʔəbicid   your (sg.) company

... čədà lə.híiɫ dxʷʔal ti diʔəbic
... and I'm glad for (having) guests.

1.   díʔɫ   adverb 'suddenly'

   Cf. dídiʔɫ

   díʔɫ kʷi s.čaʔkʷ ʔə tiʔiɫ xaʔ.x̌əlus ʔəxʷ.x̌àlus(ᵊb)   ML.
   All at once Raccoon came down to the shore with
   (his) face marked up.

   díʔɫ kʷi gʷ(ə)ads.ɫəbɫəbčqs   Your nose might run.

   díʔɫ kʷi gʷə(s).šùdubuɫ   They might see us.

   díʔɫ stab, ads.ʔábyic, ʔəbʔil qʷùʔ, ʔəbʔil s.qəbùʔ
   Give me either some water or some milk.

2.   -du-   allomorph of -dxʷ

3.   s.duhúbš   Snohomish

4.   dukʷ(u)   change, transform

   -ut

   lədúkʷudəxʷ tiʔəʔ tu.huy ʔə tiʔəʔ s.qigʷəc   ML.
   He (i.e., Transformer) was changing the way Deer was.

   díɫ səs.hùytubs dxʷʔal kʷədìʔ tudúkʷud ta ʔàciɫta(1)bixʷ
   That is the way he has been made since the person
   (i.e. he) was changed.   DM.

   ʔudukʷutᵊb   He was changed into something else.

lexical

dúkʷəɫdàt	yesterday	LG.
ʔal ti tudúkʷəɫdàt	yesterday	EK.
dùkʷəládxʷ	next year	ES.
dúkʷibəɫ	Transformer, the being who changed the world from its earlier state into its present form.	

1. dukʷ(u)   worthless, bad

Cf. p̓aƛ-, jíx̌(i)

root

sdúkʷ	nothing; worthless; broken down	ES.
ʔəsdúkʷ	does not fit	LG.
	it is not fixed right	LG.
	worn out (and now no good)	LG.
	not right	LG.

ʔəsdúkʷ tə d.ʔàlʔal. yáw̓əxʷ čəd ɫu.qʷìbid   JC.

My house is not right. Now I'll have to repair it.

-ut

dúkʷucut   worry

pútəxʷ tudúkʷucut ciʔiɫ tus.k̓ʷùys (h)əlgʷə?

Their mother was very worried.

See under x̌ʷaq̓ʷ(a).

-il-dxʷ

ʔəsdúkʷildxʷ čəd   I'm dissatisfied with it.

-txʷ

ʔəsdúkʷtxʷ   Someone is angry with him.

ʔudúkʷdxʷ   Someone got mad at him.

Cf. x̌ícil   angry

č̓ígʷil   disgusted, irritated, impatient

ʔəsdúkʷtub čəd   They are angry with me.   DM.

ʔudúkʷtub čəd ʔə ci ds.k̓ʷùy dxʷʔal ti dsu.bədč̓ʷə́bíd ti?iɬ

My mother got mad at me because I told him a lie.

-ab

ʔəsdukʷáb   get sicker, get worse   DM.

   ʔəsdúkʷab čəd   I'm not quite well.   LL.

   ʔəsdúkʷab sixʷ ti?iɬ dᵊ.q̓íɬbid   LL.

My car isn't right (and it's the same trouble I have been having with it.)

   ʔəsdúkʷab čəd ʔu.wəlíʔil sixʷ ti dsx̌ìʔ.x̌ɬ   LL.

I'm not so well; my little sickness has (re)appeared.

lexical

   sdúkʷàlbixʷ   Snoqualmie   ES.; LG.

   The name may derive from the Coastal peoples' low opinion of these upriver dwellers; or, more likely, the root dukʷ may also connote ferocity. In the latter case, the name would signify the 'ferocious people' rather than the 'worthless people'. (In this connection, it is interesting to note that the Snohomish have a song they sing about themselves which includes the line xʷi? gʷəds.yaya?   'I have no friend/relative', the idea being 'I'm so warlike no one is safe near me'.)

reduplication

   sdúdkʷəb   bad weather

    ʔəxʷsdúdkʷəbəb   it's threatening to storm

   sdú?dukʷ   riffraff, no-counts, rabble

    equivalent to p̓áp̓ap̓λàλ (q.v. under p̓aλ-)

    xʷú?ᵊlə? ?al kʷi jìxʷ ti?iɬ sdù?dukʷ

    I guess first (came) the riffraff.

   sdədúkʷəb   unidentified sort of game and power

    See under ?ukʷukʷ.

1. dúqʷač   name of the river that flows into Clear Lake
    where whitefish used to spawn   DM.
    Nookachamps River

    dúqʷəčàbš   name of the Skagit group who lives along or
    near the Nookachamps River
         See Sampson, p. 4, 20.

2. -dup   lexical suffix   'distributive'

    Cf. -i-dup   ground, floor

    lə.čáxʷdup   hitting things with a stick as one goes along

    q̓ílduptubuɫ   load us and all our belongings

    šíldup   dig around (looking for something)

    ʔu.púsdupᵊb   (They all) got hit (by things thrown).

    x̌í.x̌ƛᵊdup   snack, lunch (from x̌əƛ 'bring (jaws/teeth)
                                     together, bite')

    See under ʔəɫ- 'eat'.

    c̓əp̓c̓əp̓dúp   a lot of puddles of water

    s.gʷistáldup   sandy place

    dxʷ.sácᵊbdup   a place where water goes fast

3. s.dúukʷ   knife; iron

    Cf. ƛ̓áltəd, yíyəq̓ʷ

    reduplication

    sdíduukʷ   small knife

    sdídiduukʷ   small knives

    sdúduukʷ   knives

    sdáduukʷ   Same gloss as sdúduukʷ.

    dúukʷəli   (I'm) a big blade.
        díduukʷəli   (I'm) a little blade.   MC.
    These are some of the words of a s.qí(yə)p.

146

1. du?áyus   fermented salmon eggs   LL.
                        (Indians' Limburger cheese)

     dəw?áyus   fermented salmon eggs   LG.

       Cf. s.čə́q   fermented salmon eggs   ESi.

2. dx^w_1-   derivational prefix

See Hoard/Hess, p. 55ff.

3. dx^w_2-   toward   (In rapid speech this prefix is usually realized as /tx^w-/.)

See Hoard/Hess, p. 63ff.

Cf. tuɫ-   from

     liɫ-   by what route, by what means, located where

Stems designating specific locations become <u>directions</u> <u>toward</u> that location with the addition of dx^w_2-:

dx^w-čad

     lə<u>dx^w</u>čádəx^w čəx^w   Where are you going?

     lə<u>dx^w</u>čád k^w(i) adsə.?úx̌^w   Where are you going?

     lə<u>dx^w</u>čád k^wi t(i) ads.?úx̌^w   Where did you go?

     ?u<u>dx^w</u>čád əẃə   Where is he going?

x^wi? g^wədsəs.(h)áydx^w g^wə(u)<u>dx^w</u>čadəs k^wi s.?ùx̌^ws
I don't know where he went.

     lə.?íbəš bək̓^w <u>dx^wčàd</u>   He was walking everywhere.

dx^w-di?-

     <u>dx^wdi?ábac</u>   (taken) over the divide

     <u>dx^wdi?áx̌ad</u>   to that side

     <u>dx^wdi?ílc</u>   over the hill

dxʷ-gʷəd

ləcuʔu.təȷ̆ᵊd (h)əlgʷəʔ tiʔəʔ s.bəbíʔ dxʷgʷə̀d
They were rolling this hoop down.

dxʷgʷədíʔqad   down the hill, toward the foot of the hill

ʔəs.k̓ʷə́ɫ ʔal tiʔiɫ cədiɫ x̌pày dxʷgʷə̀d
It was pouring down from that cedar.

gʷəl gʷə.x̌ʷit̓il dxʷgʷəd (dxʷʔal tiʔiɫ) čəɬa gʷə.k̓ʷə̀d(d)xʷ
And let her fall down (from there) and we will get her.

sáx̌ʷᵊb dxʷgʷə̀d   Jump down.

dxʷ-lil

ʔu.ʔúx̌ʷtxʷ čəd dxʷlì̓l   I took it a way off.

dìɫəxʷ ləs.kʷədád ɫu.ʔux̌ʷəs ʔə kʷi dəxʷ.ʔúx̌ʷs dxʷlil
He will be taking that when he goes, when he goes far away.

dxʷ-q̓ixʷ

lədxʷq̓íxʷ   going upriver

dxʷ-šəq

dxʷšə́q   high from ground up

  Cf. liɫšə́q   up high (free in the air)

  λu.púkʷəb hìk̓ʷ dxʷšə̀q   It (snow) would pile up very high.

  ʔu.čúbə čəd dxʷšqùs   I'm going uphill.

dxʷ-taq̓t

x̌ʷúluɫ q̓ʷásduličaʔ tiʔiɫ ʔu.ɫə́x̌tᵊb dxʷtáq̓t dxʷʔal tudiʔ ʔalʔal
Nothing but this best kind of blanket was spread out,
up from shore, way up to the house.

huy gʷəl ʔúx̌ʷ dxʷtáq̓t, liɫ.táq̓t
And then he went up, up along the edge (of the bluff).

With ʔal plus nominal complements: dxʷʔal means 'toward (the complement)' when the predicate indicates a change of location, e.g., 'go, run, climb'. When the predicate has other meanings, the gloss of dxʷʔal varies; but the significance always seems derivable from the general concept 'toward'. (dxʷʔal is usually pronounced /txʷəl/.)

toward

ʔúx̌ʷ čəd dxʷʔal skuwəl	I'm going to school.	LG.
ʔu.ɬčíl čəd dxʷʔal skuwəl	I'm coming to school.	
dəgʷád dxʷʔal tə xʷ.dəgʷigʷsali	Put it in the bag.	

kʷátačaac tiʔiɬ s.x̌ʷiƛəyʔ dxʷʔal tə s.bàdil   LG.
Climb the mountain in pursuit of that mountain goat.

dxʷʔal tə s.túləkʷ kʷi ɬus.təláwilčəɬ   LG.
Let's run to the river.

xʷíʔ lədxʷʔal tə s.tùləkʷ kʷi (gʷə)ads.təlàwil   LG.
Don't run to the river!

təláwil dxʷʔal tə s.tuləkʷ   LG.
Run to the river!

ʔu.tíwiɬtxʷ čəd lə.q̓ílidəs gʷàtxʷ dxʷʔal sjì.jəlàƛič   EK.
I asked him to please take her along to Seattle.

ʔəs.ɬə́x̌ dxʷʔal tudiʔ q̓ilbid   ML.
It is spread out all the way to the canoe.

x̌ʷúluɬ q̓ʷásduliča? tiʔiɬ ʔu.ɬə́x̌t̓əb dxʷ.táq̓t dxʷʔal
tudiʔ ʔalʔal   ML.
Nothing but this best kind of blanket was spread out,
up from shore, way up to the house.

x̌alalikʷ dxʷʔal c(i) ads.k̓ʷuy   LG.
Write to your mother.

tukʷásačiʔ čəd gʷəl ʔu.x̌alalikʷyic ci ds.k̓ʷuy dxʷʔal
ti d.qəsìʔ   LG.
I burned my hand so my mother wrote to my uncle for me.

149

čitəxʷ ʔu dxʷʔal kʷi ɫadəxʷ.tùkʷ   LL.

Is it getting close to your going home (time)?

dxʷʔal kʷ snáʔ ʔə kʷə máns ʔi tə mənáʔs ʔi tə
sánctus plì. ƛúm ʔəs.ʔìstə

In nomine Patris, et Filii, et Spiritus Sancti. Amen.

until (toward then)

dᵊs.x̌áƛ kʷi gʷədsəs.ʔàʔsil dxʷʔal kʷi ta.tᵊgʷət

I want to wait until noon.

ɫ(u)as.ʔáʔsil čəd dxʷʔal kʷi ɫ(u)ads.ɫčil

I'll wait until you **arrive**.

   (same gloss: ɫuʔəs.ʔáʔsil čəd ɫu.ɫčiləxʷ)

ʔu.húydxʷ čəd dxʷʔal tiʔiɫ gʷədəxʷ.bəq̓ᵊds

I entreated him until he swallowed it (a pill).

concerning, concerned with

ʔu.x̌ʷáq̓ʷigʷəd čəd dxʷʔal ti s.pàpstədčəɫ   LL.

I'm worried about our young white boy.

ʔudxʷ.idáwligʷəd čəd dxʷʔal tiʔiɫ tə q̓ìlbid   LL.

I'm worried about the car.

x̌ʷáx̌ʷaq̓ʷəxʷ tiʔəʔ kawqs dxʷʔal ciʔəʔ ʔàlšs ʔəs.x̌əɫ

Raven pondered his sister's sickness.

in order to

ʔabcutəxʷ dxʷʔal kʷi gʷəs.càq̓atᵊbs

He (seal) extended himself so they could spear him.

ʔu.ʔúx̌ʷcᵊb ʔə tiʔiɫ s.tùbš ci s.ɫàdəyʔ dxʷʔal kʷi
gʷəs.ʔəɫdíluɫs (h)əlgʷəʔ

That man went after the woman so he could take her
to lunch.

ʔu.sáx̌adəx ti ʔəʔ ǰə̀səds <u>dx^wʔal</u> s.x^wì ʔs k^wi g^wəsə.sìx̌^wicuts

ʔal k^wi sə.tíčibs ʔal k^wi ʔilg^wił ʔə k^wi x̌^wəlč

He scraped his legs so he wouldn't make splashing noises
as he walked along the edge of the sea.

tu.p̓áacut čəd <u>dx^wʔal</u> g^wəds.ʔə̀ƛ   I tried to come.

tu.p̓áacut čəd <u>dx^wʔal</u> g^wəds.tìčib   I tried to swim.

tu.p̓áacut čəd <u>dx^wʔal</u> g^wəds.g^wàdədg^wəd   I tried to talk.

tu.p̓áacut čəd <u>dx^wʔal</u> g^wədsəs.làx̌dx^w

I'm trying to think of it.

ləbə.qíx^wqix^w kayəyə <u>dx^wʔal</u> k^wi bədaʔ ʔə x̌əyáliwəʔ?   ML.

Crow is going to marry the son of X̌əyáliwəʔ.
(Going there in order to marry him).

ləbs.čisčistx^ws <u>dx^wʔal</u> k^wi bədà ʔ ʔə ti ʔił x̌əyáliwəʔ?   ML.

She is going in order to marry the son of X̌əyáliwəʔ.

ʔudx^w.ʔəq̓^w(ə)yax̌adid tə šəg^wł <u>dx^wʔal</u> ʔəcà

He opened the door for me.

qá spàʔc ʔəlču.šáyil <u>dx^wʔal</u> k^wi s.ʔulàdx^w   LG.

Many bears are hunting for fish.

ʔəs.húdčup <u>dx^wʔal</u> ti s.ʔulàdx^w

Keeping up the fire for the salmon.

for the purpose of

ʔəs.čəwát čəd <u>dx^wʔal</u> k^wi g^wədsu.tilib   EK.

I know how to sing.

x^wiʔ g^wəsə.čəwáʔtil (h)əlg^wəʔ <u>dx^wʔal</u> k^wi g^wəsʔuq.qáǰətˀb

(h)əlg^wəʔ

They will never learn to speak Skagit.

či.čəwát čəd <u>dx^wʔal</u> čəł x^w.ʔàx̌^waʔəd   EK.

I'm good at making clam baskets.

as a result of

ʔu.ʔábš čəd tiʔiɫ s.tuligʷəd dxʷʔal tiʔiɫ ʔu.gʷiid
tiʔiɫ s.tuligʷəd

I gave the blood they asked for.

ləxʷs.x̌ʷáɫdxʷəb dxʷʔal tiʔəʔ tus.qadaditəbs ʔə tiʔəʔ
tus.ʔulàdxʷs

He wants to get the best of him because he stole his salmon.

ʔu.čítəlusbid ci ds.k̓ʷùy dxʷʔal tiʔiɫ s.ʔàx̌ʷuʔ

My mother was surprised about the clams.

síʔƛub dxʷʔal dəgʷì   DM.

It is just right on you (i.e., it fits you).

comparison

ʔiɫ.qʷíq̓ʷ čəd dxʷʔal dəgʷì

I am stronger than you.

   Cf. ʔiɫ.qʷíq̓ʷ čəxʷ tuɫʔal ʔəcà
       You are stronger than I.

ʔəs.ʔəx̌íd kʷi s.ləlìʔ ʔə tə qìwx̌ dxʷʔal yùbəč

What is the difference between a steelhead and a king salmon?

ləlíʔ tiʔəʔ səs.hùy ʔə tiʔəʔ qìwx̌ dxʷʔal tiʔəʔ yùbəč   DM.

A steelhead is (made) different(ly) from a king salmon.

1.   dxʷs₁-   derivational prefix   'profession, occupation;
                                                proclivity'

See Hoard/Hess, p. 51ff.

   dxʷskʷátač   a mountain climber

   dxʷsčəbáʔ   a porter

   dxʷsjúbalikʷ   a dancer

   dxʷsbə́dč   a liar

   dxʷsqáda   a thief

1. dx^{w}s$_2$-   derivational prefix

   See Hoard/Hess, p. 52ff

2. -(ə)dx^w ~ -du-   A transitive suffix indicating that the agent,
                            while responsible for an act, is not in full
                            control of it. Contrast the following:

   ʔu.k̓ʷə́ɫdx^w spilled it

   ʔu.k̓ʷə́ɫ^{ə}d   poured it

   ʔu.húd(d)x^w (finally) managed to get it lit

   ʔu.húdud   lit it

ə

This letter stands for a sound similar to that of the English *u* in <u>bu</u>t and *a* in <u>a</u>bout.

1. -ə-   variant of <u>lə</u>- occurring after <u>s</u>-

2. -əd   suffix marking second person following -(u)bu<u>ł</u>, thus -(u)bułəd 'you (pl.)'

3. -əd   variant of -<u>ad</u>, *q.v.*

4. -ələp   variant of -<u>alap</u>. See under -<u>ad</u>.

5. əlgʷə?   variant of <u>hə</u>lgʷə? found most frequently after <u>s</u>, <u>ł</u>, <u>xʷ</u>, and <u>x̌ʷ</u>

6. -əlus   variant of -<u>alus</u>

7. -əł   variant of -<u>ał</u> 'class membership'

8. -əł   variant of -<u>ał</u> 'agent acts in own interest'

9. -əł(i)   variant of -<u>ałi</u>. See under -<u>ad</u>.

10. -əs-   variant of <u>as</u>-

11. -əs   variant of -<u>as</u>. See under -<u>ad</u>.

12. əẃə   rapid speech variant of <u>haẃə</u>?

13. -əxʷ   variant of -<u>axʷ</u>. See under -<u>ad</u>.

14. -əxʷ   variant of -<u>haxʷ</u>

(Many other suffixes beginning in <u>a</u> have variants where <u>a</u> is replaced by <u>ə</u>.)

g

This letter represents a sound similar to that of the English
g of *get*.

1. gədg   tickle, axilla

    -t

    ʔugə́dᵊgᵊd čəd   I tickled him.   LG.; EK.

    ʔugə́dᵊgᵊc   He tickled me.   LG.

    lexical

    gədgáx̌əd   axilla   LG.; EK.

        Cf. qətqáx̌əd   axilla   LL.

    reduplication

    gə́dgə̀dᵊd   tickling someone   LL.

2. gədú   a no-good so and so; a x̌ʷiʔ-lə.haʔɫ   ML.

3. gə́lgᵊb   mumbling

    See under cut.

    Cf. c̆ú(h)áyucid

4. gəl.gəlásəlus   eye glasses (based on English *glasses*)

5. gəlk̓   wind around something; entwine, entangle

    See under ɫid.

    root

    ɫugə́lk̓ čəd   I might get tangled up.   LG.

    ʔugə́lk̓ ʔə tə qʷɫ̓ày̓   wound around the stick   EK.

    ɫugə́lk̓ čəd ʔə kʷi s.ʔàx̌ʷuʔalc   JC.
    I'm going to make a clam basket.

-t

ɬugəlk̓ʼəd čəd kʷi s.ʔàx̌ʷuʔalc   JC.

I'm going to make a clam basket.

gəlk̓ʼədəxʷ čəxʷ dxʷʔal ti   JC.

Now you wind it around this.

lexical

ɬugəlkádiʔ čəd ʔə kʷi s.ʔàx̌ʷuʔalc   JC.

I'm going to make a clam basket (of this I've already started to work on).

ɬugəlkálikʷ čəd ʔə kʷi s.ʔàx̌ʷuʔalc   JC.

I'm going to make a clam basket. (Said in talking to a small child.)

ɬugəlkálikʷ čəd   I'm going to knit.   LG.

reduplication

ʔəsgə́lgəlk̓   It's all tangled up.   LG.

1.   gəq   brightness, sunshine

   Cf. gʷəq   sunshine   LG.

      čəlqʷcút, gʷílič̓ʼb

-b

ʔəsgə́qʼb   The sun is shining.   LL.

sgəqʼb   sunshine   LL.

-il

ʔəsgəqíl   brightness   EK.

ʔugəqíləxʷ   The weather cleared up and the sun came out.   EK.

→
→

1. gə́t   a certain party

> This term is used when the speaker does not want to indicate the identity of whom he is speaking.
> It is also used with mildly disrespectful or indifferent connotations to mean 'who is that?' and 'so and so (whose name I can't at the moment remember'). Cf. gʷat

ɫčíl tiʔəʔ gə̀t   A certain party arrived.

cutəxʷ tiʔacəc ʔihišəd ʔə tiʔəʔ čətx̌ ʔi tiʔiɫ cədiɫ gə̀t, x̌ʷuʔx̌ʷayʔ   ML.

The relatives of Kingfisher and of this one, Little Diver, said, ...

x̌ʷù̀ɫəxʷ čəxʷ ʔu.kʷədád gə̀t, táʔa

You just take that.

2. gəx̌(á)   untie, bail out (of jail), get loose

Cf. gʷəx̌   Skagit   get loose

λ̓iq   emerge

Contrast ɫid.

root

ʔugə́x̌   (a horse) got loose   EK.

-at

gəx̌ád   Untie him! Bail him out (of jail).   LL., EK.

gəx̌átᵊb   He was untied/bailed out.   EK.

-dxʷ

gəx̌dúbutəxʷ   He managed to get himself untied.   EK.

g^w

The sound represented by this letter is much like the English _Gw_ in _Gwendolyn_. [voiced, labialized velar stop]

1. g^wáaldup   ?

> putəx^w g^wáaldup tə s.tulig^wəd ʔal tiʔił tree ʔal tudiʔ g^wəd
> Very ____ blood on the tree all the way down.   ML.

2. g^wad   speak

> See under cut.

> g^wədg^wát

> -t

>> g^wədg^wát^əd   the language   LG.

>> x^wg^wədg^wát^əd   voice   LL.

> g^wəg^wadg^wat

> -tx^w

>> ʔug^wəg^wádg^wat(t)x^w čəd   I got after him.   LG.
>>   I scolded him.   VH.

>>   Cf. k̓x̌at

> g^wádg^wəd

>> g^wádg^wəd   speak, give a speech   EK.

>> ʔá tiʔił ług^wádg^wəd   ES.
>> There's a man going to talk.

>> dx^w.yəqqídəx^w tə sug^wádg^wəds   LG.
>> She's talking loudly.

> g^wáag^wəd

>> dx^w.yəqqíd ług^wàag^wədəs   LG.
>> When she's talking, she talks loudly.

gʷaadgʷəd

    dəxʷu.x̌al ʔə kʷi <u>sgʷahəgʷəd</u>   tape recorder   LG.

      Cf. under gʷəgʷádəd

gʷəgʷát (or) gʷágʷət

  -txʷ

    <u>gʷágʷət</u>(t)ubš   Talk to me.   VH.

    ʔu<u>gʷəgʷát</u>(t)ubš   He spoke to me.   LG.

    ʔu<u>gʷəgʷát</u>(t)xʷ čəd   I spoke to him.   LG.

  -txʷ-əgʷəl

    gʷagʷət(t)əgʷəl   talk to one another   VH.

gʷádədgʷəd

    s<u>gʷádədgʷəd</u>   a story   LG.

    <u>gʷádədgʷəd</u>   converse   EK.

    <u>gʷádədgʷəd</u>əxʷ tiʔił bì.bščəb ʔi tiʔił suq̓ʷaʔ tətyìqaʔ   ES.
    Little Mink and his younger brother, Tətyiqaʔ,
    talked it over.

    ʔəs.hî́ił čəd ʔə ti ds.ʔàcił̓talbixʷil čəd
    gʷə<u>gʷádədgʷ</u>ədtubicid ʔə kʷi dxʷ.ləšucid   ES.
    I'm glad I'm becoming Indian so I can talk to you
    in Puget Salish.

    ʔu.ʔəx̌íd t(i) adəxʷu<u>gʷàdədgʷəd</u>   EK.
    What happened that you are talking about?

    stáb t(i) adsu<u>gʷàdədgʷəd</u>   EK.
    What are you talking about?

gʷəgʷádəd (or) gʷəgʷátad

    <u>gʷəgʷádəd</u>   a formal talk   EK.
                         Speak!   LG.

    sáʔ s<u>gʷəgʷádəd</u>   bad word   EK.

šəq siʔáb sgʷəgʷádəd   Divine word   EK.

gʷəgʷəgʷádəd čəxʷ ʔu ʔə kʷi dxʷ.ləšùcid   EK.
Can you speak Puget Salish?

dəxʷu.x̌al ʔə kʷi sgʷəgʷadəd   tape recorder   LG.

     Cf. under gʷáagʷəd

ʔal kʷi tu.jíxʷ
gʷəl tuʔá tiʔəʔ sgʷədgʷátad
gʷəl tiʔəʔ sgʷədgʷátad
gʷəl t(u)as.q̓ʷúʔ ʔə ti šəq siʔab
gʷəl tiʔəʔ sgʷədgʷátad
gʷəl díɫiɫ šəq siʔab.   MS.
    from the Gospel according to St. John 1 : 1

1.   gʷáda ʔkʷ   horn, antler   LG.; HD.

    gʷádgʷada ʔkʷ   horns, antlers

2.   gʷádil   leader of a school of fish   ES.
            especially large fish such as salmon
            that leap

            the jumping of salmon   LG.

3.   gʷah   accompany

   root

     ɫugʷa čəxʷ ʔu   Are you going along?   LG.

-txʷ

     xʷiʔ gʷəsəsgʷahtxʷs tiʔiɫ tətyiqaʔ su.suq̓ʷaʔs   ML.
Tətyiqaʔ, his little younger brother, was not with him.

ʔu.t̓íwiltxʷ čəd lə.q̓ìlidəs gʷà(h)txʷ dxʷʔal (s)jì.jəlàɫič
I asked him to please take her along to Seattle.

-bi-t-

g^wábid　　　　　　go along with someone　　　HD.

g^wábic　　　　　　Come with me.　　　　　　LG.

g^wábicid čəd　　　　I'll go with you.　　　　LG.

x̌aƛ ʔu k^w(i) adsg^wabic　　　　　　　　　　LG.
Do you want to accompany me?

lexical

ʔug^wášəd čəd　　　　I accompanied him.　　　EK.
　　　　　　　　　　　join in　　　　　　　　EK.

1.　　g^wál　　　　　　capsize

See under x̌ək̓^w(ú), x^wítil.

Cf. x̌t̓áb　　　fall over board

　t̓əbá?　　　fall into water, capsize

ʔug^wál　　　　　　　　It capsized.　　　LG.

ʔug^wál k̓^wəɬ (h)əlg^wə?　　　　　　　LG.
It's said that they tipped over.

ʔug^wál čəd ʔal tudi? ča?k^w　　　　　LL.
It tipped over quite a ways out.

lə.ɬálilƏx^w čəd čədà g^wàl　　　　　LL.
I was getting close to shore and I tipped over.

-t (Note -a- occurs only with -t-sut.)

ʔug^wálacut　　　　I tipped myself over.　LG.

ʔug^wált^əb čəd　　　Someone tipped me over.　LG.

ʔug^wált^əb (h)əlg^wə?　　Someone tipped them over.　LG.

-dx^w

ʔug^wáldub čəd　　　Someone happened to tip me over. LG.

ʔugʷáldub (h)əlgʷəʔ   Someone happened to tip them over.   LG.

1.   -gʷas   lexical suffix   'pair'

ʔu.cəlqgʷásəd   Divide it up, Share it.

čəx̌gʷásəxʷ tə ʔəs.p̓əłq̓ʷ ʔə tə buus   4:30 o'clock

čəx̌gʷás   mixed blood

dxʷ.xʷəλgʷás   half of quantity   EK.

ʔił.čad(gʷəs)   which (of two)

s.ʔácgʷəs   waistline   EK.

λuč̓əgʷás̓b   Tighten your belt.   LG.

xʷiʔ lə.líl gʷə.díłgʷəsəs They are almost alike.   EK.

ʔu.k̓ʷəλ(ə)gʷásil   LL.
We missed each other (although we intended to meet).

q̓ʷú(ʔ)gʷəs̓d   put it together   LG.

ṭəq̓ʷgʷás   It came apart.

(ʔə́λtxʷ) ʔu.ʔábgʷəs   (Bring things) piece by piece. LG.

x̌ə̓λgʷásulàdxʷ
'ends' of the year come together, winter and spring meet

2.   gʷat   who

Cf. čad, čal, čaył, gət, k̓ʷid, tab, ʔəx̌id, ʔidigʷət

as predicate head:

gʷat čəxʷ   Who are you?

gʷat tiʔił s.tubš   Who is that man?

gʷat ciʔił s.ładəy?   Who is that woman?

gʷát kʷə díš̓ə̀?   Who is here?   JC.

gʷat kʷi gʷə.kʷaxʷac   Who would/will help me?   LG.

gʷat kʷ(i) ads.da?   What is your name?

gʷát kʷi bə́k̓ʷ ads.dà?   What is your full name?   LG.

head of dependent clause

xʷi? gʷədsəs.(h)aydxʷ gʷəgʷatəs
I don't know who he is.

xʷi? gʷədsəs.(h)aydxʷ gʷəgʷatəs kʷi s.da?s
I don't know what his name is.

as head of phrase

bək̓ʷ gʷát   everyone

gʷəɬ gʷát   whose

as complement

díɬ gʷàt   anyone   ES.

diɬ gʷat kʷi gʷə.kʷaxʷac   Would/will anyone help me?   LG.

lexical

gʷátgʷəs ?ə gʷəlàpu   which of you (two)?

with partitive prefix

?iɬgʷat kʷi gʷ(ə)əxʷ.kʷaxʷacᵊb   Which (person) would/will help me?
                                          LG.

1.   gʷáx̌ʷ   stroll, go for a walk (always more than one)

See under ?ux̌ʷ.

?ugʷáx̌ʷ čəɬ liɬ?al ti ?íl.gʷiɬ ?ə ti?ə? di?ə? qʷù?   EC.
We (will) walk along the shore of the water.

ƛ́ubəxʷ čəɬ ?ugʷáx̌ʷ   We had better go for a walk.   EC.

gʷáx̌ʷ (h)əlgʷə? bə.bu?s   EC.
The four of them went for a walk.

reduplication

gʷáx̌ʷgʷax̌ʷ	walk to and fro	ES.
gʷáx̌ʷax̌ʷgʷax̌ʷ	two lovers walking about	ES.
ługʷáx̌ʷax̌ʷgʷax̌ʷ čəł	We're going to walk around.	EK.
gʷáx̌ʷax̌ʷgʷax̌ʷ	They went strolling about.	EC.

rejected:

*gʷáx̌ʷšəd	LG.

Note that ?ibəš(š̲)əd 'go on foot' is possible.　　LG.

1.　s.gʷa?　　　　　　　　　one's own

　　Cf. gʷəł

ti ds<u>g</u>ʷá?	It's mine.	EK.
xʷi? ləds<u>g</u>ʷa?	It's not mine.	LG.
cₖ̌ʷáqid ł(u)ads<u>g</u>ʷa?	It will always be yours.	MS.

(díł) ?ił.čád(gʷəs) q̓ìlbid kʷ(i) ads<u>g</u>ʷà?
Which canoe is yours?

　　Cf. ?ił.čád(gʷəs) kʷ(i) ad.q̓ilbid
　　　　Which is your canoe?

díł tə hikʷ ?al?al tə ds<u>g</u>ʷa?	The big house is mine.	LG.

díł ?ił.qá tə ds<u>g</u>ʷa? dxʷ?al gʷəlàpu　　LG.
I have more than you folks.

s<u>g</u>ʷá?čəł gʷədgʷàtəd	our own language	VH.

díł dᵊs<u>g</u>ʷá? ds.qà　　LL.
That is my own older brother.

3.　gʷá?xʷ　　　　　adverb　'eventually, soon'

<u>g</u>ʷá?xʷ čəxʷ gʷələ.bàkʷł　　　You might get hurt.　　LG.

gʷàʔxʷ ɬəčil   He arrives soon.   JC.

gʷáʔxʷ čəxʷ ɬu.háydxʷ   Eventually you will know.   LG.

1.   gʷə-   auxiliary prefix   'subjunctive'

   Auxiliaries are non-obligatory prefixes that expand full words of all classes. They occur most frequently when the word is predicate head; but they are also found when the word is complement head and when it is an adverb. They also (especially gʷə- and ɬu-) introduce dependent clauses. In such cases they are partners to the entire clause thus resembling particles by virtue of their ability to modify a sequence of words.

gʷə- 'conjectural'   ɬu- 'expective'   bə- 'anew'

λ̓u- 'habitual'   tu- 'remote in time/space'

   ɬu- and tu- are mutually exclusive. With this exception, any two of the prefixes can cooccur in the following order:

$$\text{gʷə-} \quad \text{λ̓u-} \quad \begin{matrix}\text{ɬu-}\\\text{tu-}\end{matrix} \quad \text{bə-} \quad \text{STEM}$$

   No examples of three or four auxiliary morpheme sequences are known. There are no restrictions between auxiliaries and any other affix class.

   With gʷə- the action, state, or object is either contingent upon something else (e. g., if) or it is conjectured, doubted, or negated.

2.   gʷəcíl   wade or stand in shallow water

   See under t̓ičib.

   -il

      ʔugʷəcíl   waded in shallow water

      ləgʷəcíl   wading in shallow water

      ... ʔal ti səsgʷəcíls   ... while standing in shallow water

   -i(l)-s

      ... ʔal ti səgʷəcíss   ... while wading after it in shallow
                                        water

1.   gʷəč   search for, look for, seek

      -t   (Note <u>a</u> occurs only with -<u>t</u>-<u>sut</u>.)

         <u>gʷəč</u>əd   Look for it!   HD.

         ʔu<u>gʷə́č</u>təb   They were looking for it.   LL., LG.

         ʔu<u>gʷəč</u>əd tiʔił s.tùbš   LL.
         Someone looked for that man.

         <u>gʷəč</u>ácut   (try to) find one's self   LG.

      -b

         ʔu<u>gʷə́č</u>əb tiʔił s.tùbš   LL.
         That man looked for it.

         ləcu<u>gʷə́č</u>əb ʔə kʷi s.tàb gʷəs.ʔə̀łəds   ES.
         searching for something to eat

      -bi-t

         ʔu<u>gʷəč</u>bíd čəd tə s.q̓ʷəlàłəd   JC.
         I'm searching for berries.

      lexical

         ʔu<u>gʷəč</u>əlúsəb čəd   I looked around for it.   LL.

      reduplication

         ʔu<u>gʷəč</u>gʷəčád   several search for it

         ʔu<u>gʷəč</u>gʷəčáb čəd ʔə tiʔił s.dùukʷ   ·   LL.
         I looked all over for that knife.

2.   gʷəd   down

     Opposite of <u>šəq</u>.

     Cf. ƛ̓əp

     root

        ... ʔal tudiʔ <u>gʷəd</u>   ... all the way down

166

dxʷ₂-

dxʷgʷə́d   downward

ʔəs.k̓ʷə́ɬ ʔal tiʔiɬ cədiɬ x̌pày dxʷgʷə̀d   ML.
It was pouring down that cedar.

gʷə.xʷí̓til dxʷgʷə̀d   may fall downward   ML.

ʔəs.bíq̓itᵊb tiʔəʔ ƛaʔtəd dxʷgʷəd   MS.
The net is pressed downward.

-il

g̲ʷədí̲l   NPS   sit down, get up from prone position

g̲ʷə́di̲l   SPS   same gloss

Cf. t̓ədús   sit right beside

ʔəsg̲ʷədiɬ ʔal tiʔiɬ ad.hiwilbid   LG.
He is sitting in front of you.

gʷát kʷi ləsg̲ʷədí̲l ad.jəbìd   DM.
Who is sitting on your right?

čád kʷi gʷ(ə)ads.x̌aƛtxʷ kʷi gʷ(ə)adsg̲ʷədì̲l   DM.
Where do you want to sit?

qə́ɬcutəxʷ, qə́ɬcutəxʷ!   Wake up now. Wake up now!
g̲ʷə́di̲l, gʷə́dil   Get up. Get up.
hágʷəxʷ tu.jàx̌ tə s.wàtixʷtəd   The world has been shaking
                     for a long time.   JC.

qə́ɬcut, qəɬcut!   Wake up. Wake up!
tíləb čəxʷ ʔugʷədil   Get up right now.
ɬu.xʷí̓ʔəxʷ bələ.ʔìtut   (So) you won't go back to sleep. JC.

liɬš̓əjt tə dsəsg̲ʷədì̲l   I'm sitting in the bow.

səxʷg̲ʷədí̲l   chair   AS.

səxʷgʷíg̲ʷədì̲l   little chair   EK.

Cf. xʷ.t̓ágʷtəp   chair   LG.

-i(l)-s

g^wədís   sit down for some specific purpose;
sit down next to someone

-il-tx^w

g^wədíltx^w   marry (lit. 'cause to sit with')

See under ʔił.huyg^was.

-bi-t

g^wədbídčəł   He is below us.   LG.

lexical

-abac

g^wədábəc   beneath bulk

g^wədábac ʔal ti tibu ti yìx̣us   LG.
The basket is under the table.

ʔu.čálət^əb ʔə tə s.q^wəbàyʔ cə pišpiš g^wədàbac ʔə
tə səx^wg^wədìl
The dog chased the cat under the chair.

g^wədábac haẃəʔ ʔə tə pìit   LL.
Maybe it's under the bed.

ʔəs.báč ʔə tə g^wədàbac ʔə tə tibu
It's lying under the table.

-ači?

g^wədáči?   the board which was pounded to keep time   LG.

Cf. čáx^wadi?   sticks for keeping time

-alap

g^wədálap   foot of a tree   DM.

tug^wədáləp čəd   I was underneath a tree.   LG.

-alg^wił

  d^ə<u>g</u>^w<u>əd</u>álg^wił   under my canoe

-ap

  <u>g</u>^w<u>əd</u>áp   down on the bottom   LL.

    łu.kaw̓ad dəx^w<u>g</u>^w<u>əd</u>àp ʔə tiʔəʔ ʔəs.cq^wuł
    They chew the bottom of trees (lit. 'post')

-aqid

  lə<u>g</u>^w<u>əd</u>áqid tə s.łàq̓s   He fell on his head.   LG.

-ayucid

  (s)<u>g</u>^w<u>əd</u>áyucid   chin   LL. (sans /s-/)
                                      EK. (with /s-/)

    Cf. č̓ú(h)àyucid   weak chin

-ič̓aʔ

  <u>g</u>^w<u>əd</u>íč̓aʔ   underwear   ES.
                                 (Not used by LL., ML.)

-iqad

  <u>g</u>^w<u>əd</u>íqad   down below; foot of hill   LL., EK., LG.

    <u>g</u>^w<u>əd</u>íqəd   foot of a hill   DM.

    <u>g</u>^w<u>əd</u>íqad^əb   go down hill

-ulg^wa-

  <u>g</u>^w<u>əd</u>úlg^waədx^w   lower world   EK.

-yax̌ad

  <u>g</u>^w<u>əd</u>yáx̌əd   lower edge (e.g., of a piece of paper) LL.

reduplication

  sg^wig^wədilál?tx^w   outhouse

rejected:

    *ʔugʷədáləp čəd   LG.

    *ʔəsgʷədáləp čəd   LG.

    *gʷədᵊb čəd

1.   gʷədbíxʷ   Snoh.   blackberry

      gʷə́dbixʷ   SPS   blackberry

        Cf. s.x̌ə́gʷəd   Skagit   blackberry

        pədgʷədbíxʷ   blackberry time (Given as July, "but the berries
                               don't ripen until August".) HD.

2. s.gʷədígʷs   paraphernalia

    See under s.tábigʷs.

3. s.gʷədílič   a kind of power   EK.

    See under s.qəlálitut.

      s.gʷədíličuɫ   the s.gʷədílič that comes from one's ancestors MC.

4. gʷəháw̓ə?   He found it out.   LL.

      -a-d

        gʷəháw̓ə?ad   (You thought about something and) blurted it out.
                                                   LL.
    Cf. haw̓ə?

5. gʷəl   connector particle   'and, but, next'

    Cf. ʔi, yəxʷ

      xʷí?əxʷ lə.líl gʷəl ʔál s.bùuss

      Soon it (will) be four o'clock. (Lit. 'Not far and it (will)
                              be four o'clock.')

1. gʷəlápu   you (pl.)

    See under ʔəcá.   Cf. ɬi

        gʷəlápu tə ʔu.ti̓lib   You folks sing.   EK.

        ti gʷəlápu dᵊ.ʔi̓išəd   You my people.   ES.

        ʔiɬs.(h)ájᵊb čəd dxʷʔal gʷəlàpu   LG.
        I am taller than you folks.

2. gʷəlál-d/tᵊb   kill, injure

    This term is used only for the fate of important people.   LL.

    Cf. təš

3. s.gʷəlúb Snoh.   ring-necked pheasant

    s.gʷə́lub SPS

    Cf. s.tə́xʷəb Skagit   ring-necked pheasant

4. s.gʷəlúlč   loosely woven basket   LL.

    See under yiq̓ib.

5. gʷəɬ   belonging to

    Cf. s.gʷaʔ   one's own

        gʷəɬ díbəɬ bàd   our father

        gʷəɬ gʷát ti?iɬ t(ə)sùlč ʔəs.bəč (ʔal ti?iɬ) gʷədàbəc
        ʔə tə tibu   LG.
        Whose drum is that lying under the table?

        gʷəɬ gʷatəs kʷəd?a?   It must be someone's.   LG.

        gʷəɬ ti ds.qa ti?iɬ q̓ilbid   LG.
        It is my older brother's canoe.

        gʷəɬ x̌ʷə́lč s.wàtixʷtəd ti?iɬ ƛ̓ux̌ʷƛ̓ux̌ʷ yəxʷ tə s.ʔàx̌ʷu?
        The oyster and the clam belong to the realm of the sea.

1.   -gʷap   lexical suffix (?)

    dxʷ.jálgʷəp   walk along the beach   LL.

2.   gʷəq   Skagit   brightness

   Cf. gəq   Snoh.

   root

    ʔəsgʷə́q   The sun is shining.   LG.

   -il

    ləgʷəqíləxʷ   It's getting light now.
                   dawn   LG.

3.   gʷəq̓   open, opening, clearing

   See under x̌əc.

   Cf. x̌ájaƛ(a)   pry open/up

    káad   open mouth

    qx̌íl   open eyes

   (ʔə)x̌íd əẃə gʷə.yəcᵊbtùbšəxʷ ʔəsgʷə́q̓ tiʔiɬ dxʷši?.šɬəb   ES.
   Why didn't you tell me the window was open?

4.   gʷəsəbád   be quiet, shut up   LG.

   Cf. x̌ʷúbil

5.   gʷətq̓ʷád   faint, pass out   EK.

6.   gʷə́x̌   Skagit   get loose

   Cf. gəx̌-   untie, get loose, bail out of jail

   Contrast ɬid(i).

-t

g^wəx̌^əd   Set him loose.   LG.

g^wə̀x̌t^əb   He was let out (of jail).   LG.

-dx^w

ʔug^wəx̌dúbut   He got loose.   LG.

1.   g^wídəq   geoduck   ESi.

2.   g^wih(i)   call to, ask, invite

     See under cut.

     root

       ʔug^wíh čəd   I asked them to come.   EK.

     -it

       ɬ(u)asg^wíid čəɬ   We will invite someone.

       x^wì? k^w(i) adsug^wíid cə s.ƛ̓àlqəb   LA.
       Don't call the monster (or she'll come).

       ʔug^wíid čəd ti?iɬ sq^wəb.q^wəbày? ɬu.túk̓^wəs   LL.
       I called the dogs (home).

       ʔug^wíic čəx^w   You called me.   EK.

       ləg^wíicid čəd   I'm inviting you.   EK.

     lexical

       g^wíhači? čəd ?ə k^wi yəla?cìlc ?i k^wi ?iɬ.čəx̌   DM.
       Lend me six dollars and fifty cents.

          (According to DM. good usage does not permit čuɬalc
          when borrowing money.)

       g^wíhalik^w   payment of wealth in retribution, wergild
                      "asking for whatever can be gotten equal to
                        the murdered man's station in life."   LL.

                      pray   EK.

     See under q̓p̓(u).

reduplication

    sgʷígʷih   potlatch   EK.

1.   gʷil(i)   dig up something buried

      See under čaʔ.

      -it

        ʔugʷilid   He dug it up.   EK.

2.   gʷíličᵊb   shine (as fur), luster

      Cf. čəlqʷcút, gəx̌

3.   -gʷił   lexical suffix   'canoe, waterway; curved side; narrow passage way' See -ucid.

        híqᵊgʷił   shove the canoe out   LL.

        ʔu.təx̌ʷgʷíł čəd   I dragged the canoe. (Canoes were dragged not carried except for s.dəxʷił.) LL.

        ʔu.ƛəkgʷíł   patch the canoe   LL.

        x̌əƛʷgʷíł   turn the canoe over   LG.

        ʔu.ʔáƛgʷíł   He choked (by getting something caught in his throat). LG.

        ʔúdəgʷił   middle of a canoe

        (s)ʔílgʷił   shore, edge of water

        ʔácgʷił   middle of a lake/river

          ʔúdəgʷił ʔə ti ʔácgʷił
        The middle of the canoe in the middle of the river.

         ʔu.tíčib dxʷ.ʔàcᵊgʷił   Swim to the middle.   EK.

        ƛʷádgʷild   bailer   EK.

-al-gʷił

ʔu.tḱálgʷił	patch gunnel	LL.
s.ʔílalgʷił	side of canoe	EK.
húdalgʷił	steamboat	EK.
ʔəs.k̓ʷítalgʷił	be down on the shore	ML.
x̌ix̌q̓álgʷił	canoe race	LL.

-ul-gʷił

x̌łúlgʷił	side ache	LL.
ʔu.x̌ƛúlgʷił	He broke his ribs (up under the axilla).	LL.
ʔu.c̓əxʷc̓xʷúlgʷiłtəb	Someone clubbed him in the side.	LL.

-wił

→

x̌ix̌q̓əwił	racing canoe	LL., EK.
ʔə(xʷ)x̌ílix̌əwił	battle ship, war plane	LL.
s.tək̓íwił	double-ended canoe from the s.tək̓í	LL.
dxʷ.c̓ibwiłd (tə ła?x̌)	lick the pan	LG.

-al-wił

x̌əłəlwíłd	thwart	LL.

See also names for types of canoes some of which end in a labial sound plus ł.

1. (s)gʷistálb   NPS   sand

   gʷístələb   SPS   sand

   s.gʷistálbdup   sandy place

   gʷís.gʷistalb   the Indian name for site of Sandy Beach, Whidbey Island, Washington   HD.

1.   gʷíx̌ʷəb   drip

     gʷíx̌ʷəbìčdxʷ   drip on him

2.   s.gʷúgiyəʔ   See under s.k̓ʷúy.

3.   gʷúhəb   dog bark

     Cf. q̓ʷáʔq̓ʷab   seal bark

h

This letter stands for a sound very similar to that of the English letter *h* in *hat* and *hard*. [voiceless glottal fricative]

1.　　haac　　　　　　　　　long, tall　　　　　　　　　EK., DM.

　　　head of predication

　　　　　ƛ̓ùb háac tiʔiɬ t̓iyùʔsəd　　　A long smelt trap is best. JC.

　　　head in complement

　　　　　ʔəs.ʔəx̌id kʷi sháac ʔə tiʔiɬ s.dəx̌ʷìɬ　　　　　　DM.
　　　　　How long is that 'duck hunting' canoe?

　　　　　cəbtáɬ tiʔiɬ hàac ʔə tiʔiɬ s.dəx̌ʷìɬ
　　　　　That 'duck hunting' canoe is twelve feet long.

　　　　　tiʔiɬ shaac ʔə tiʔiɬ s.dəx̌ʷìɬ　　　　　　LG.
　　　　　That is how long that 'duck hunting' canoe is.

　　　　　diɬ səshaac ʔə tiʔiɬ s.dəx̌ʷìɬ　　　　　　LG.
　　　　　same gloss: That is how long that 'duck hunting' canoe is.

　　　　　tiʔiɬ háac ƛ̓làyʔ gʷəl ds.gʷá̓ʔ　　　　　　LG.
　　　　　That long shovel-nose canoe [which can be seen] is mine.

　　　　　díɬ ti hàac ƛ̓làyʔ ti ds.gʷà̓ʔ　　　　　　LG.
　　　　　The long shovel-nose canoe [which cannot be seen] is mine.

　　comparison

　　　　　(dìɬ) ʔiɬháac tiʔiɬ ad.q̓ílbid tuɬʔal tiʔə(ʔ) d.q̓ílbid　　LG.
　　　　　Your canoe is longer than my canoe.

　　modifying head of complement

　　　　　ʔu.ʔíg̓ʷəɬ čəd (dx̌ʷ)ʔal tiʔiɬ hàac x̌páyac　　　　DM.
　　　　　I climbed that tall cedar tree.

　　　s(h)áj^əb (or) s(h)ajəp　　　　　tall (person)

　　　　　Opposite of q̓íq̓x̌ʷuʔ 'short'.

　　　　　cáy čəd s(h)àjəp　　　　　I am very tall. JC.

cíckʷ čəd s(h)àjᵊb   I am very tall.   LG.

s(h)ájᵊb čəd x̌ʷuɫab ʔə dəgʷì   LG.
I'm as tall as you are.

s(h)ájᵊb tiʔiɫ ləgʷəb x̌ʷuɫàb ʔə ti bàds   LG.
That youth is as tall as his father.

x̌ʷuɫab ʔə ti bàds ti s(h)âjᵊbs tiʔiɫ ləgʷəb   LG.
Same gloss: That youth is as tall as his father.

x̌ʷuɫab ʔu ʔə ti bàds kʷi s(h)ájᵊbs ʔə tiʔiɫ ləgʷəb   LG.
Is that youth as tall as his father?

ʔiɫs(h)ájᵊb čəd dxʷʔal dəgʷì   LG.
I'm taller than you.

ʔiɫs(h)ájᵊb tiʔiɫ ləgʷəb dxʷʔal ti bads   LG.
That youth is taller than his father.

ʔiɫs(h)ájᵊb ʔu tiʔiɫ ləgʷəb dxʷʔal ti bads   LG.
Is that youth taller than his father?

ʔiɫs(h)ajᵊb tiʔiɫ s.tubš ʔal tudiʔ dxʷʔal tiʔiʔaʔ diʔəʔ
bəkʷ s.tububš   LG.
That man there is taller than all these men here.

lexical

-abac

   x̌ʷuɫ háacəbəc tiʔəʔ qìw̌x̌   DM.
   A steelhead is just long (and skinny).

-ap

   [Note that some speakers use this suffix instead of -b
   to designate people's height. See above.]

   dxʷ(h)ájəp   long hipped person   ES.

-apsəb

   gʷəl tiʔəʔ šəjts gʷəl ʔa tiʔəʔ hájəpsəb   LG.
   And its bow has a long neck [speaking of an ʔəʔútəx̌s].

reduplication

    hác(h)ac   a group of tall or long things   LL.

       dìɬ tiʔəʔ dəxʷ(h)ác(h)əc ʔə tiʔəʔ jədìs   DM.

       That is why (its) teeth are long.

1.   há·mu·ʔ   NPS   exhortative to story teller said periodically
                              by audience. Children were told that if they
                              did not say this they would become humpbacked.
                                                      LG.

     həmúʔ   SPS

       ʔəbíɬ xʷiʔ kʷə ɬ(u)adsu.cút ʔə tiʔiɬ 'həmúʔ kayʔ, həmúʔ
       kàyʔkawič', čəxʷ[ə] gʷə.káwič.   JC.

       If you do not say 'həmuʔ kayʔ, həmuʔ kayʔkawič', you
       will become a hunchback.

2.   hagʷ   See under <u>haʔkʷ</u>.

3.   hahəláyʔtəd   rainflower berry   MC.

     Cf. p̓əp̓áyəqəd(əc)   rainflower berry(bush)   LL.

4.   hakʷ   See under <u>haʔkʷ</u>.

5.   haqʷ(a)   smell

    See under <u>sub(u)</u>.

    -at

      <u>háqʷad</u>   smell it

    -dxʷ

      <u>háqʷdub</u>   was smelled   VH.

    -b

      <u>háqʷəb</u>   smell of something spoiled

6.   hásəb   sneeze

1.   haw?   exhortative

   Cf. yəháw?tx^w

2.   hawə?   emphatic particle

   Cf. g^wəhawə?

        ti?ił x^w.čiłqs hawə? ti?ił x^wəyàliwa ti?ił lədì.da?ad   ML.
        The big-oyster-like shell, X^wəyaliwa!, she was repeating
        his name.

        x^wəyáliwa ti?ił s.dà? ?ə ti?ił lədəx^w.?ùx̌^ws hawə?   ML.
        X^w. is the name of him to whom she's going!

        čádəx^w hàwə? ti?ə? dəs.?à   Where am I?   ES.

        ?u.?əx̌íx̌əd čələp əwə   LL.
        What are you folks doing, anyhow?

        dił (h)awə? hig^wəx^w ?udx^w.qədíd ti?ə? s.?ušəbàbdx^w
        s.bəq̓^wa? ?ə ci?ə? čəg^wàss x̌^wu?x̌^wəy?   ML.
        Indeed, he (Kingfisher) really made a cuckold (?)
        of poor Heron by his (Heron's) wife, Little Diver.

        tə́ł cədił əwə ti?ił ?u.lək̓^wyíc ?ə ti?ił dᵊs.?əłᵊd   ML.
        Truly, he <u>must</u> be the one who ate my food from me.

3.   -hax^w   'change affected'

   This suffix contrasts the action or state with a former
condition. It occurs with verbs, adverbs and nouns (especially when the noun is head of predication). Frequently,
this suffix is found twice in the same clause, once with
an adverb and again with the verb.

   allomorphs:

	after vowels (except -a$_2$- 1.3)	after consonants (and very occasionally after vowels)
stressed	-háx^w	-áx^w
unstressed	-həx^w	-əx^w

x^w (after -a$_2$- 1.3)

1. hay   next, then

     Cf. gʷəl, huy

2. hay(a)   know

     Cf. laX̌-   remember

       suxʷt   recognize

       čáɫaʔ   not recognize   LG.

       čəl-   not recognize   LL.

       čəwaʔt   know how to

       qəyíqəl   not know how to

       ləqálbut   understand   Skagit

       ƛ̓əlábut   understand   Snohomish

   -at

       háy̓ad   try to learn something mental   LL.

         See under p̓aʔ.

         ʔuháy̓ad čəd kʷi gʷəds.háydxʷ tiʔiɫ dxʷ.ləšùcid   LL.
         I'm trying to learn the Indian language.

   -dxʷ

       ʔuháydxʷəxʷ čəxʷ ʔu   Do you know that now?   ES.

       dayʔ ʔəcá kʷi ʔəs(h)áydxʷ   I'm the only one who knows.   EK.

       ɫàw̓t čəd ʔuhàydxʷ   I'm learning something new.   EK.

       ʔuháydxʷ čəd ti s.tùbš   I found out who the man was.

       ʔuháydubš ti s.tubš   The man found out who I was.

       xʷiʔ kʷi dsəs(h)áydxʷ   I don't know.

xʷiʔ kʷi stab ʔəs(h)áydxʷ čəd   EK.

I don't know anything.

xʷíʔ gʷədsəs(h)àydxʷ gʷə.čàdəs kʷi səs.ɫaɫlil

I don't know where he lives.

xʷíʔ gʷədsəs(h)àydxʷ gʷəpə(d).tàbəs kʷi s.ʔùx̌ʷs

I don't know when he went.

gʷə-...-dxʷ

ʔəsgʷəháydxʷ čəd   I kind of know it.   EK.

tuʔəsgʷəháydxʷ čəd

I used to kind of know that (but it's half buried in
                    my memory).   EK.

-dxʷ-əgʷəl

ʔacəc t(u)as(h)áydəgʷəl tuɫʔal tus.wiw̌sus (h)əlgʷəʔ   ES.

They knew each other from childhood.

gʷə-...-txʷ

ʔugʷəháytub čəd   LL.

'They caught on to me (the shenanigans I was up to)'

(This expression is more or less equivalent to

ʔu.yíčəbitəb čəd (based on yíčb 'notice, observe, figure out').

1.   háʔəc   black nose clam, also called horse clam ESi.; EK.

                    One of the class s.ʔax̌ʷuʔ q.v. It is good
                    eating all year round.

     Cf. híʔhaʔc   'eastern clam'   which looks like a small horse clam.

2.   háʔkʷ ~ hágʷ-   ago

     háʔkʷ

        (ʔal) kʷədíʔ tuhàʔkʷ   long ago

        (ʔal) ti tuháʔkʷ   ago

hág^w(əx^w)

as head of predication

> hág^wəx^w ti tus.təlàwil ʔə tə hùpt
> Some time ago the deer ran.

> hág^wəx^w ti tus.ʔùx̌^ws g^wəl x^wiʔ uʔx^w g^wə.ɫčìls
> He's been gone a long time and he hasn't come back yet.

as adverb

> hág^wəx^w tu.jax̌ tə s.watix^wtəd   JC.
> For a long time the world has been moving.

1. haʔl(a)   stop someone from crying

    -at

    > háʔləd   stop him from crying.   LL.

    > háʔlacut   stop self from crying   LL.

    lexical

    > ... ɫuháʔliʔɫəx^wəs   LL.
    > ... be better to stop the baby from crying.

2. haʔɫ   good

    Compare ƛ́úb 'well'. Cf. yúʔ

    root

    > ʔuháʔɫ   It was nice.

    > pùt (h)áʔɫ   It was very good.   ML.

    > háʔɫ tə tusə.ʔúx̌^ws ʔal ti s.yəhúb...   ML.
    > He goes right along well with the old tales...

    > dày?əx^w (h)áʔɫ   That is good.   EK.

    > day?əx^w (h)áʔɫ tiʔəʔ q̓ìlbids (h)əlg^wəʔ   EK.
    > They had a very good boat.

dày?əxʷ (h)à?ɬ (s).šúɬ ci?iɬ s.ɬàdəy?   HD.
That is a nice looking lady.

há?ɬ t(ə) ads.?àcus   You have a nice face.   LG.

ha?ɬ ti?iɬ adǰəs.ǰəsəd   You have nice legs.   LG.

ha?ɬ ?u t(i) ad.kùpi   Is your coffee good?   FSi.

ha?ɬ šúɬ s.ɬadəy?   nice looking woman   EK.

gʷəl há?ɬ (h)əlgʷə? ?əs.ɬàɬlil ti?iɬ s.bəq̓ʷà?
?i ci?ə? x̌ʷù?x̌ʷəy?   ML.
And Heron and Little Diver lived happily (after that).

díɬ ha?ɬ ləs.kʷəd(d)ùb ?ə ti?ə? čačasčəɬ ɬ1?iɬ
gʷədgʷàtəd ?ə ti tusluƛ.luƛčəɬ gʷəɬ tus.(h)á?kʷ   ML.
It is good that our youngster has gotten the
language of our old people of long ago.

s.duhúbš, ha?ɬ s.dà?   ML.
Snohomish. It is a good name.

ti?iɬ gʷəl x̌ʷi? ləhà?ɬ   That is not good.   EK.

k̓àwad čəxʷ ?ə tə ha?ɬ   I chewed it well.   EK.

šuucbicut ?ə kʷi ha?ɬ
Look after yourself carefully.

há?ɬ kʷ(i) ads.šùucbicut
Same gloss: Look after yourself carefully.

ha?ɬ ti su.(?ə)ƛ̓àləqəps   It smells good.   LL.

há?ɬ ti?iɬ ƛsə(s).šùucᵊb ?ə ti?iɬ s.čistxʷs s.bəq̓ʷa?   ML.
Her husband, Heron, watches over her carefully.

tu.ɬílc čəxʷ ?ə ti là?b ha?ɬ səplìl   LG.
You brought me real good bread.

lá?b hà?ɬ səplil ti t(u)ads.ɬilc   LG.
Same gloss: You brought me real good bread.

?a·! tə xʷi?-ləhá?ɬ   Oh! You no-goodnik!   ML.

comparison

ʔiɫ(h)áʔɫ dxʷʔal kʷi gʷəs.xʷíʔs   LG.
It's better than nothing.

ʔiɫ(h)áʔɫ dxʷʔal kʷi p̓àƛaƛ
It's better than junk.

adverb

háʔɫ gʷə.ʔəƛáhəxʷ   (You) should come.   LG.

    Cf. ƛúb gʷə.ʔəƛáhəxʷ
        Same gloss: (You) should come.   LG.

xʷúʔəˀləʔ hàʔɫ gʷə.ʔəƛáhəxʷ   LG.
Maybe (you) should come.

-txʷ

haʔɫtxʷ čəd   I like it, I enjoy it.   VH.

    Cf. x̌aƛtxʷ 'want it'

háʔɫtxʷ čəxʷ ʔu tə d.kùpi   FSi.
Would you like some of my coffee?

xʷiʔ gʷədsháʔɫtxʷ t(i) ad.kùpi   ESi.
I wouldn't care for any of your coffee.

xʷiʔ kʷə dsháʔɫtxʷ t(i) ad.kùpi   FSi.
Same gloss: I wouldn't care for any of your coffee.

-il

ʔəsháʔɫil   a person is well/good   LL.

    (More or less equivalent to ʔəs.ƛúbil.)

-it

ʔuháʔlid tiʔiɫ gʷàdaʔkʷs   ML.
He cleaned up his antlers.

háʔlicutəxʷ tiʔiɫ s.čətxʷəd   ES.
Then Bear made himself happy/ had a good time.

185

-b

?əshá?1ᵊb   good weather   LL.

calm, no storm   EK.

lexical

dxʷ(h)á?ɬus   nice face

day?əxʷ dxʷ(h)á?ɬus ci?iɬ s.ɬadəy?   HD.
That woman has a nice face.

dày?əxʷ čəxʷ dxʷ(h)á?ɬus   HD.
You have a nice face.

há?ɬubš   Skagit   Someone is good-looking.

há?ɬùbš čəxʷ   You are good-looking.   LG.

cíckʷəxʷ čəxʷ há?ɬubš   LG.
You are very good-looking.

ha?ɬubš ci s.ɬàdəy?   LG.
The woman is pretty.

há?ɬàləqəp   It tastes good.   LG., EK.

1.   həbú?   pigeon   LG.; HD., EK.

Cf. há·mu·?

2.   həmú?   See under há·mu·?.

3.   həd   warm, hot

See under hud(u).

root

[The h is lost if preceded in the same syllable by s.]

?uhə́d čəd   I got warmed up (after being outside).   LG.

?uhədáxʷ čəd   I've gotten warmed up now.   LG.

lá?b dxʷs(h)əd   It's real hot.   LG.

-b

pədhə́d^əb   summer time   EK., LG.

ʔu.ƛáx̌ʷ tə shə̀d^əb   spring (lit. 'growing of summer') EK.

-il

 lədxʷs(h)ədíləxʷ   It's getting warm.   LG.

là́ʔb udxʷs(h)ədíl   It's gotten quite warm.   LG.

lá́ʔb ʔəsdxʷs(h)ədi̇̀l   It's quite warm.   LG.

là́ʔb d^əxʷs(h)ədíl   It's quite warm.   LG.

     Cf. là́ʔb d^əxʷs.q̇ʷəl   (Same gloss: It's quite warm.) LG.

lexical

ləcuhədhədáči(ʔ)b   warming the hands   DM.

dxʷs(h)ədálqʷuʔ   coffee, tea   LG.

     Cf. kúpi 'coffee'

extended root

hədg^{wə}b   SPS   warm self   JC.

hədq^{wə}b čəd   NPS   I am warm.   DM.

1.   hədú   NPS   humpback salmon, one of the class of s.ʔuladxʷ. LL.

    hə́du   SPS   humpback salmon   ESi.

2.   (hə)dʔíwʔ   enter a building

   root

     ʔəs.bə́l^əx̌ʷ ʔə kʷi cəlàcs tiʔə́ʔ ʔəs(hə)dʔi̇̀wʔ   LG.
     There are more than five in here.

   -t

     hədʔíwʔd   Bring it in.

187

həd?íw?t^əb čəd   Take me in.

həd?íw?c   Same gloss: Take me in.

-tx^w

həd?iw?tubš   Take (carry) me in.

-b

həd?íw?b   Come in! Go in!

lexical

həd?ìw?ák^wčup   Bring the wood in.

1.   həká?ł   hiccup

     ?əĺcuhə̀khəká?ł čəd   I'm hiccuping.

2.   həláytəd   D-adze   (Cf. p̓ayəqəd)   LG.

     há?li?təd   carving tool, adze   VH.

3.   (hə)lá?b   adverb   'really, very'

     həlá?b čəd qə̀d   I'm real slow.   EK.

     həlá?b čəd dày?ay?   I'm really alone.   EK.

     həlá?b s.q̓àšəd   real moccasins   EK.

     lá?b əw?ə ?u.?ùx̌^w   Did he really go?   LG.

     cick̓^w lá?b qəd s.təqíw   Quite a slow horse.   LG.

         (Note contrast: cick̓^w qə̀d s.təqíw

                       A very slow horse. LG.)

     là?b há?ł s.ləx̌ìl   It's a real good day.   LG.

     x^wi? ?u k^wi ƛ(u)adshəlà?b ?u.x̌əłqìd   LL.
     You don't get too much of a headache, do you?

     x^wi? g^wədshəlá?b ?u.tìbicut   LL.
     I didn't really try very hard (to do something physical).

1.   həlgʷəʔ   they, them, their; a particle for third person marking plural

                        [The h̲ is usually lost if preceded in the same syllable by a fricative.]

šúuc həlgʷəʔ	Look at them.	LG.
Cf. šuuc tiʔiʔiɫ	Same gloss: Look at them.	LG.

ʔəlču.púsutəgʷəl həlgʷəʔ ʔə tə č.č̓λà?   LG.
They are throwing rocks at each other.

tu.šúdxʷ čəɫ həlgʷəʔ ʔi mali   LG.
Mary and I saw them.

tu.bədáʔᵊb həlgʷəʔ ʔi tiʔəʔ təkʷtəkʷəlùs   ML.
They had a baby (lit. 'child') and Owl.
Frog is already clearly designated from context as the mother. Owl is added to specify who the other person in həlgʷəʔ is.
Attraction is also found in -aɫi.

ʔəs.tágʷəxʷ ʔu həlgʷəʔ	Are they hungry?	LG.
cíckʷ həlgʷəʔ ʔəs.tàgʷəxʷ	They are very hungry.	LG.

cíckʷ ʔəs.tàgʷəxʷ (h)əlgʷəʔ?   LG.
Same gloss: They are very hungry.

cíckʷ həlgʷəʔ k̓ʷəɫ jəɫ ʔəs.x̌əɫ   LG.
It is said they must be very sick.

láʔb k̓ʷəɫ (h)əlgʷəʔ ʔəs.x̌ə̀ɫ   LG.
It is said they are very sick.

láʔb ʔu həlgʷəʔ ʔəsx̌əɫ.x̌əɫ̀il   LG.
Are they very sick?

láʔb ʔu ʔəsx̌əɫ.x̌əɫ̀il həlgʷəʔ
Same gloss: Are they very sick?

láʔb ʔu ʔəs.x̌əɫ (h)əlgʷəʔ?   LG.
Same gloss: Are they very sick?

    *laʔb ʔu həlgʷəʔ ʔəs.x̌əɫ   rejected   LG.

báds (h)əlgʷə?   their father

1.   həlíʔ   live, alive

     [The h is lost if preceded in the same syllable by a fricative.]

     root

         həlíʔ čəd   I'm alive.   EK.

         həliʔ čəd qʷìq̓ʷ   I'm alive and strong.   EK.

         (hə)láʔb ʔəshəlì? tiʔił qʷùʔ   JC.
         That is very healthful water.

         s(h)əliʔ   life

     -dxʷ

         həliʔdubəxʷ čəd   I saved him.   LL.

         húy čəxʷ həlìʔdubšəxʷ   LL.
         Thank you (Said only when receiving food or drink).
              (Lit. 'You save my life.')

             Compare dáhᵊdubš and cuk̓ʷálid.

         tuhəlíʔdubut   ES.
         She recovered/ came back to life.

             Cf. qəł   wake up, come to

     -txʷ

         həlíʔtub uʔxʷ jəł čəxʷ ʔə kʷi s.qʷùtab   LL.
         You are still permitted by (all) the sickness
         (going around now) to live.

         -il   heal, recover health

         ʔəsəlíʔil   getting well   EK.

2.   həwúʔ   have nothing

         Cf. ʔušəbábdxʷ   (under ʔušəb)

root

    həwúʔ čəd   I have nothing (either spiritual or material). LG.

-il

    həwúʔiləxʷ čəd   I'm getting poor.   LG.

1.   hibúləb   name of the principal Snohomish village. See Haeberlin and Gunther, p. 7.

2. dxʷ.híidəʔ   the spirit power that provides an abundance of fish and game, a type of s.qəlálitut.   LL., HD.

3.   híił   happy, glad

    cìck̓ʷ čəd ʔəshíił ʔə tiʔił adsu.kʷáxʷdubš   ES.
    I'm very glad that you helped me.

    ... čədà ləshíił dxʷʔal ti diʔəʔbic   EK.
    ... and I'm glad for my company (glad to have had visitors).

    ʔəshíił čəd ʔə tə ds.húyəxʷ ʔacíłtalbixʷ   ES.
    I'm glad I'm becoming Indian.

    ʔəshíił čəd ʔə tiʔə(ʔ) ds.šudubicid   DM.
    I'm glad to see you.

    -bi-t

    cáy čəd ʔəshíiłbid tə ds.làbdubicid   JC.
    I am very glad to see you.

    cáy čəd ʔuhíiłbid   I'm very happy about it.   JC.

4.   hikʷ ~ higʷ-   big

    [The h̲ is usually lost if preceded in the same syllable by another consonant.]

root

as modifier

hí·kʷ əs.ɫáɫlil qa ʔal tiʔacəc s.wàtixʷtəd ʔə tiʔiɫ gʷəɫ
dibəɫ ʔal kʷədíʔ tu.hàʔkʷ   ML.
Many dwelt in this place that belonged to us long ago.

dáyʔəxʷ jəɫ hĭgʷəxʷ ʔu.k̓ʷəɫk̓ʷɫátəb ti tud.qʷùʔ   LL.
Gee, they must have spilled all my water.

cíck̓ʷ jəɫ hìkʷ s.tùbš   LG.
He must be a big man.

tiʔəʔ ʔəʔútx̌s gʷəl híkʷ q̓ìlbid   MS.
The 'family' canoe is a big canoe.

as head of predication

ɫuhíkʷ čəd s.tùbš ɫu.lùx̌iləd   LG.
I'm going to be a big man when I grow up.

xʷiʔ lə.làʔb hìkʷ   He's not very big.   LG.

x̌ʷúləxʷ čəd jəɫ hìkʷ   I wish I were big.   LG.

-t

x̌ʷùɫ čəxʷ ʔəshĭgʷəd t(ə) ad.ʔìišəd   ES.
Uphold your people.

ʔəshíkʷcut   big feeling, proud   LL.

láʔb ʔəshìkʷcut   big shot   LG.

tùx̌ʷ bashíkʷcut   JC.
But he conducts himself with high, personal respect.

-il

huy, hígʷiləxʷ siʔàb tiʔiɫ bì.bščəb   ES.
Little Mink became an important (big) man.

ʔuhígʷiləxʷ tiʔiɫ xə̀čs   LL.
He has his courage now.

-il-d

  híg^wild   make it bigger   LG.

    rejected: *híg^wis

-tx^w

  háʔɬ tiʔiɬ g^w(ə)adsəshìk^wtub ʔə t(i) ad.ʔìišəd   ES.
  Your people will have great respect for you.

comparison

-bi-t

  g^wəl tiʔəʔ s.wúq^wa[d] g^wəl díɬ hìk^wbid dx^wʔal tiʔəʔ x̌^wətìs   MS.
  The loon is bigger than the regular diver.

  tiʔəʔ ʔəʔútx̌s g^wəl hík^w q̓ilbid. hík^wbid ʔə tiʔəʔ s.dəx^wìɬ
  The 'family' canoe is a big canoe. It is bigger than the
  'duck hunting' canoe.

ʔiɬ-

  ʔiɬhík^w čəd dx^wʔal dəg^wì
  I am bigger than you.

lexical

  dx^w(h)íg^wəp čəd   I have a big rear.   LG.

  hík^w(h)ik^{wə}dis   (two) big teeth   LG.

  híg^wəlìdəg^wəs   brave   EK.

  hík^w(h)ig^wìlc   name of a large rock located
                      on a bluff south of Tulalip
                      shores, Washington.   ES.

  bəsík^w(h)ig^wìlc   name of a Skagit River group
                      (lit. 'people of the big rocks')
                      (See Sampson, p. 2, 21.)

  dx^w(h)ík^wqid k^w(i) adsu.g^wàdg^wəd   LL.
  Speak in a loud voice.

reduplication

  ʔəshík^w(h)ik^wcut   much pride   LL.

1. hil(i)   tell (to do something)

    (Etymologically related to ʔil(i) 'repeat'?)

    See under <u>cut</u>.

    Cf. čə́s ~ čsá- send someone on an errand

       hílid   Tell him to do something.   LG.

       ʔuhílic   He sent me to do a task.   LG.

       hílid gʷə.yáλabəs   Tell him to get water.   LG.

       ʔuhílitəb čəd   I was told.   LL.

2. hiq(i)

    Cf. x̌əd 'push'

    -it

       híqid   push it, shove it

       híqicut   shove self off   LL.

    lexical

       híqəgʷił   shove the canoe out

    -a-b   too, excessively

    (Some speakers say hiʔáb instead of híqab.)

    Contrast ʔíλub 'just right' (under ʔi).

       híqəb miʔmad   too small   LG.

       híqəb hikʷ   too big   LG.

       hiʔáb hikʷ tiʔəʔ pùʔtəd   This shirt is too big.   DM.

       híqəb łəq̓   too wide   LG.

       híqəbəxʷ   too much, over large   LL.

       híqəb q̓ìč tiʔił pùʔtəd   That shirt is too expensive.   DM.

hi?áb q̓ič ti?ił pù?təd   DM.

Same gloss: That shirt is too expensive.

hiqəbəxʷ čəxʷ ƛu.kəskᵊb   LL.

You talk too much.

xʷ̓i kʷ(i) adshíqəb ?u.kəskᵊb ?ə kʷi dxʷ.(h)ìkʷqid   LL.

Don't converse overly loud.

?əs.hə́gʷᵊb čəd čəda hi?áb ?u.či̓til ?ə ti?ił hùd   DM.

I was warming myself and I got too close to the fire.

reduplication

  híhi?əb tì?ᵊttiš   It's too narrow.   LG.

-a-b-il

  ?uhíqəbiləxʷ   get too much of someone   LL.
                           be too much   LL.; LG.

reduplication

  hìqhiqábiləxʷ čəxʷ   You're getting too smart
                           for your britches.   LG.

-a-b-il-dxʷ

  hìqhiqábildubicidəxʷ čəd   LG.

I think that you are getting to be just too much.

1.   hiq̓ʷab

  -i-d

   híq̓ʷabidəxʷ ci?ił ləlì? sɫə.ɫàdəy?   ES.

  He got stuck on different women.

2.   híwil   go ahead, be ahead; go away

    Compare jíxʷ, súla, lílcut.

    Contrast láq, qád(a), ?alq̓ʷ.

-il

híwiləxʷ lił.jìxʷ	Go ahead first.	EK.
híwil čəd lił.jìxʷ	I'll lead/go first.	EK.
híwil!	Go away!	ES.

-i(l)-s

híwis	go after something

-bi-t

adhiwilbid čəd	I'm in front of you.	
?əs.gʷədíl čəd ?al t.(i) adhiwilbid I'm sitting in front of you.		LG.

reduplication

híhiwil	Go on ahead a bit.	EK.

1. hí?ab   See under híq-a-b.

2. hí?ha?c   Eastern clam, one of the class of s?aX̌ʷu?
This clam looks like the horse clam, há?əc,
only it's smaller.   ESi.

3. s.hí?wəbš   name for site of Olympia, Washington
(as opposed to s.t̉əč̓as which refers more
specifically to Budd Inlet.)   JC.

4. hu-

húma? Snoh.   endearing address to a boy
    The Skagit equivalent is ?i?áb   LG.
(With -ma? compare bə- of bədá? 'offspring'.)

húk̉ʷuy Snoh.   endearing term to address a girl
    The Skagit equivalent is s.k̉ʷuyə? and s.k̉ʷuk̉ʷiyə?   LG.

EK. gives s.k̓ʷúk̓ʷi   (Snohomish)

Cf. s.k̓ʷuy 'mother'

1.   hud(u)   burn, fire, (fire)wood, light (something)

Compare həd, həgʷəb, k̓ʷas, q̓ʷəl, šəƛ̓, xʷəq̓ʷəx̌ʷ, x̌ʷik̓ʷicut; ləx̌.

Contrast qaʔt, t̓əs.

root

ʔuhúd   It's burning.

xʷiʔ ʔu gʷəshúd ʔə tiʔił ʔu.bəc̓ad čəxʷ   LL.
That which you set down won't burn?

xʷiʔ gʷəshùds. t̓əs tiʔił hùdali   LL.
It won't burn. The stove is cold.

-ut

húdud tə ləx̌šàd   Turn the light on.   EK.

húdud   Burn it.   EK.

-dxʷ

ʔuhúd(d)xʷ   Inadvertently burned something. LG.

ʔuhúd(d)xʷəxʷ tə hùd   LG.
Finally managed to get the fire started.

húd(d)xʷəxʷ ʔu t(i) ad.hùd   LG.
Did you get your fire built?

-txʷ

ʔəshúdtxʷ čəxʷ tiʔił hùd   LG.
Keep the fire going.

-ad

xʷ(h)údad   ashes   EK.; LG.

Cf. p̓íc̓t   coals

lexical

húdčup	firewood (all speakers)	
húdičup	firewood	LA., LG., JC. (rejected by LL.)
səx^w(h)údali	stove	LL.
húdalg^wił	steamboat	EK., LL.
húdaləp	burning on the bottom	EK.
ʔəshúdqs	candles	LL.

→   reduplication

ʔuhúdhud čəd	I'm burned out.	EK.

1.   húpt   deer (This word is used by Skagit-speaking Nooksack.)

   Cf. s.qíg^wəc

2.   huy(u)   make, do, finish; be thus

   Compare čəł, q^wib(i).

   root

húy(ʔ)	good-bye	
húyəx^w	all finished now; Hush now!	EK.
łuhuyəs tiʔəʔ dsu.yayus, ...		LG.
When my work is finished, ...		
łuhúyəd tiʔəʔ dsu.yàyus, ...		
When I finish my work, ...		
ʔəshúyəx^w ʔu tə kùpi		EK.
Is the coffee ready now?		
x^wíʔ k^wi səshúys		EK.
It's never been finished.		

198

... siʔab ciʔəʔ k̓aʔk̓aʔ ʔal tiʔił tusəshuys
ʔal tiʔəʔ ʔaciłtalbixʷ ...

... Crow was high class when she was made
as a person ...   ML.

dił tusəshuys (h)əlgʷəʔ ʔal kʷi
tusəshuys (h)əlgʷəʔ ʔaciłtalbixʷ
That is the way they were (acted)
when they were people.

tusəshuys (h)əlgʷəʔ tu.ʔaciłtalbixʷ tiʔəʔ bək̓ʷ stab
That was when everything was made like people.

ləlíʔ tiʔəʔ səshùy ʔə tiʔəʔ qiẁx̌ dxʷʔal tiʔəʔ yùbəč MS.
A steelhead is made differently from a king salmon.

ʔu.ləlliʔcut tiʔəʔ s.x̌əy̓us ti səshuys s.q̓əjuʔs ...   ML.
(His) head changes (colors) [because of] the way
his hair was ...

put ʔu.ləlliʔcut tiʔəʔ səshuys   ML.
The way he is made he changes color beautifully.

ʔu.čəlqʷcuts tiʔəʔ s.ƛ̓alabac səshuys   ML.
The [nicely] made outfit sparkles.

-ut

ʔəs.(ʔə)x̌íd kʷi ł(u)adsuhùyud kʷə səpləl ł(u)ads.q̓ʷəlʔb
ʔal kʷi gʷístəlʔb   JC.
How would you prepare bread to be baked in the sand?

łuhúyudəxʷ čəd   EK.
I'm going to work on it now.

ʔuhúyud čəd tiʔəʔ x̌ʷùbt   LG.
I made this paddle.

ʔuhúyud čəd x̌ʷùbt   LG.
I made a paddle out of it.

ʔuhúyud čəd x̌ʷùbt tulʔal tə luƛ s.x̌əlàʔs   LG.

I made a paddle out of an old board.

ʔuhúyutᵊbəxʷ čəgʷàs   ML.

She has been made (his) wife now.

húyucut   Get ready.   LG.

-dxʷ

  ʔuhúydxʷ čəd   LL.

  I got it done, fixed, solved; I pieced it together.

  ʔuhúydxʷ čəd dxʷʔal tiʔił gʷədəxʷ.bə̀q̓ᵊds   LL.

  I entreated him until he swallowed it (e.g., a pill).

  ʔu.láx̌ᵊdxʷəxʷ čəd. čəda húydxʷəxʷ   LL.

  I remember it now, and now I've got it figured out.

  tux̌ʷ čəxʷ s.talx̌ tiʔił ƛəlàdəxʷ ʔə hùydxʷ   LL.

  You are rather unusual in that you are able to
  get the work put together.

-txʷ   cause to be thus; dismiss from employment,
              fire someone

  ʔəshúytxʷ ƛə̀q̓ʷ   He made it solid.   LH.

  ʔuhúytxʷ čəd   I fired him.   LL.

  ʔuhúytub čəd   I got fired/let go.   EK.

    (*ʔuhúytxʷ rejected LG.)

-il

  ʔuhúyil čəd kiyáʔ ʔal ti dùkʷəłdat   LG.

  I became a grandmother yesterday.

  húyiləxʷ t(i) ads.gəlk̓ᵊd   JC.

  (When) it is finished, you wind it around.

-a-txʷ   plead a cause

  gʷəl huyátubš łi siʔàb cəxʷs.tùdəq   ES.

  My noble masters, I should like to plead a cause.

-aɬ

ʔuhúyaɬ čəd yìq̓us   I made myself a cedar-root basket.   LG.

ʔuhúyəɬ čəd x̌ʷùbt   I made a paddle.   LG.

lexical

-alc

ʔəs.x̌aʔx̌aʔtib dxʷʔal kʷi gʷədshùyalc ʔə ti d.ʔàlʔal   LG.
I'm in a hurry to finish my house.

-alikʷ

ɬuhúyalikʷ čəd ʔə kʷi s.yàlt   JC.
I'm going to make a cedar-root basket.

-daliɬᵊd

s(h)uydáliɬᵊd   cooking   EK.

-ičup

t(u)as.ƛáx̌ čəd gʷəl ʔuhúyičupyic tə d.bàd   LG.
I was cold so my father made a fire for me.

-gʷas

ʔiɬhúygʷəs   make a pair (i.e., marry)   ML.

    Cf. balyi   marry (ultimately from French)

    kʷədátᵊgʷəl   grab one another (This usually refers to a fight, but it can mean to get married.)

      kʷik̓ʷədátəgʷəl   going steady   ES.

      bəlúcidᵊb   Same gloss: going steady

      húyutᵊb čəgʷàs   make her his wife

      čəgʷčəgʷás   seek a woman to marry

      č̓isč̓istxʷ   seek a man to marry

      k̓íxʷk̓ixʷ   Crow talk for č̓isč̓istxʷ

      gʷədíltxʷ   cause to sit with, i.e., marry

1. huy   then, next

     Cf. gʷəl, hay

2. húy-   Skagit   eat it, put it in mouth   LG.

     Equivalent to lək̓ʷəd in Snohomish and SPS.

     See under ʔəɬ-.

     -dxʷ

        ʔuhúydub ʔə tə s.pàʔc tə yùbəč   LG.
        The bear ate the king salmon.

        ʔolčuhúydub ʔo ǰàl ʔi co màli to soplìl   LG.
        John and Mary are eating bread.

     lexical

        dáʔxʷ čəxʷ ʔuhuyucid ʔə tə hikʷ x̌ax̌yəƛ   LG.
        You just ate a big dry salmon.

3. húyəq   gill net

     See s.ƛəlájad 'trap' (under ƛəl).   Cf. ɬičáʔa   SPS

4. huʔxʷ   still, yet

        ƛalal uʔxʷ gʷəl lə.bsàd   LL.
        Early yet, but it's getting dark.

        ʔəs.ʔítut uʔxʷ   He's still sleeping.   HD.

        ʔu.ʔə́ydxʷ ùʔxʷ čəxʷ ʔu kʷi ʔalʔal   LG.
        Have you found a house yet?

        həlí(ʔ)tub uʔxʷ jəɬ čəxʷ ʔə kʷi s.qʷùtəb   LL.
        You are still alive yet from all the sickness?

        čáčas uʔxʷ   very young   EK.

        wiw̓su huʔxʷ   children   LL.

202

líɫgʷəb u̱ʔx̱ʷ tiʔiɫ   He's a little fellow.   LL.

míʔman (u̱ʔx̱ʷ) s.ɫáɫdəyʔ   little girl   LL.

ƛ́al u̱ʔx̱ʷ čəd sixʷ bələs.làqil   LG.
I'm late still again.

ƛ̀al u̱ʔx̱ʷ ʔu sixʷ bələs.láqil (h)əlgʷə?   LG.
Are they late still again?

xʷiʔ u̱ʔx̱ʷ gʷ(ə)ads.yəcəbtùbuɫ pə(d)tàb kʷi ɫəb(ə)ads.ɫčil   LL.
You haven't told us yet when you will arrive again.

hágʷəxʷ ti tus.ʔừx̌ʷs gʷəl xʷíʔ u̱ʔx̱ʷ gʷə.ɫči̇ls   LG.
He's been gone a long time and hasn't come back yet.

i

This letter stands for a sound which English speakers tend to hear as being sometimes similar to that of *i* in *machine* and sometimes to *ei* in *eight* -- this last when the vowel is preceded or followed by a velar consonant or when it is long.

1. -i-   suffix providing for a change in resolution (usually from medio-passive to transitive).

    Cf. -bi-, -yi-

2. -ič̓aʔ   lexical suffix   'clothing'

    ʔu.ɫágʷiča(ʔ)b   took clothes off   LL.

    ʔu.ƛ́áliča(ʔ)b čəd   I put my clothes on.

        Cf. ʔu.ƛ́álabacᵊb čəd   Same gloss: I put my clothes on.

    -al-ič̓aʔ

    ʔəs.t̓q̓álič̓aʔ čəxʷ   There is something stuck on your clothing.
                                                                          LG.
    ʔudxʷ.t̓q̓áliča(ʔ)did tiʔiɫ   LG.
    Someone stuck something on his clothing.

    ʔəs.čq̓álič̓aʔ čəd   My clothes are dirty.   LG.

    ɫu.ʔay̓wáʔsaliča(ʔ)b   I'm going to change my clothes.   LG.

    ʔəs.ƛalálič̓aʔ   clothes   LG.

    ʔəs.ƛiq̓álič̓aʔ čəd   My clothes are caught.   LG.

    t̓k̓álič̓aʔ   patch/mend clothes   LG.

    dəxʷs.t̓k̓álič̓aʔ   a clothes mender   LG.

    ɫik̓ʷálič̓aʔ   clothes hooked on something   LG.

    k̓ìlč̓álič̓aʔ   clothes caught in a door   LG.

    ʔu.sik̓ʷálič̓aʔ čəd   I ripped my clothing.   LG.

    s?íč̓əb   Snoh.   blanket   EK., LL.

    ǰəsgʷíč̓aʔ Skagit   the old type of blanket made of dog
                           or goat hair   LG.

-ul-iča?

ق̓ʷasdùliča?   Snohomish equivalent to the Skagit ǰəsgʷíča?

EK., LL.

See under s.qəlíkʷ.

gʷədíča?   underwear, undershirt   ES.

(Rejected by LL. and ML. See under ƛ̓əp.)

The original meaning of -iča? may be shoulder. Note the form bəqʷíča? 'carry on the shoulder'. The semantic extention to clothing would be what hangs from the shoulder or what covers the shoulder.

Names for women frequently end in ul-iča?:

sá?sxʷəbuliča?   LG.'s nickname   LG.

dáy?suliča?   LG.'s mother's mother's niece   LG.

jəlúliča?   IM.'s wife's mother's mother   DM.

x̌ənimúliča?   Crow's Myth Age name (Crow was a woman.)

1.   -ič ~ -iǰ-   lexical suffix

Cf. -wič   back

?u.ləx̌ʷíǰ°d   It covered him.   LL.

*?u.ləx̌ʷ°d   rejected   LL.

x̌áčiǰ°b ?ə tə s.qʷəlikʷ   LG.
Cover yourself with the blanket.

Cf. x̌áčəd   Cover it!

*x̌ačat°b rejected (Only x̌áčičt°b is possible.)   LG.

?u.x̌k̓ʷíč čəd   (The canoe) turned over on me.   LL.

Cf. ?u.x̌ə́k̓ʷ čəd   Same gloss as above. "This is a possible thing to say but not much used." The form with -ič is preferred. LL.

ʔu.jáq̓ič	A tree fell on it/him.	LG.
ʔu.jáq̓ič čəd	A tree fell on me.	LG.
ʔu.k̓ʷ(ə)łíč čəd	It spilled on me.	LG.
ʔu.k̓ʷ(ə)łiǰᵊd čəd	I poured it on him.	LG.

xʷiʔ lə.k̓ʷ(ə)łíč dxʷs.(h)ə́d tiʔił q̓ʷúʔ   LG.
Don't spill that hot water!

pədíǰᵊd	Bury it!	EK.

ʔu.xʷítilič čəd ʔə tə xʷ.làbali   LG.
The bottle fell on me.

ʔəsx̌ʷílič	kneel	EK.
ʔu.pədíč	dust covered	EK.
	It caved in and got covered.	EK.
ʔu.qəlᵊbíč čəd	I got caught in the rain.	EK.
ʔu.qʷatič čəł	Snowed on us.	LL.
ʔu.bəsádič	got caught in the dark	EK.
s.č̓əlíč	backbone (of mammals)	EK., LG.
č̓əlíǰəpsəb	upper end of spine	EK., LL.
xʷ.łídič	bow string	MS.
q̓əčíc	bow (archery) (with dissimilation of -ič to -ic)	
ck̓ʷíč	short cut	EK.
ʔúdəgʷìč	middle of house, road, rope, pile of things	EK.
dxʷ.qʷíq̓ʷìč	strong backed bow Possibly this should be dxʷ.qʷíq̓ʷwič.	ES.
s.qʷədílič	a type of s.qəlálitut, spirit power	

-ič-ap

xʷ.č̓łíčəp	small of back, sacrum	EK.

čəlíǰəpsəb   nape, upper end of spine

-al-ič

     s.čəṗálič   stagnant water, swamp   LL.

     jəlálič   go over a rise/hillock   LL.

     q̓ílalič   canoe load of gifts   DM.

     šqálič   the very top, high on top   EK.

     šəqəlíč   on top of the water   DM.

1.   -i-čup   See under -čup.

2.   -idg^{w}as   lexical suffix 'torso area'

     Possibly the same etymon as yədwás 'heart'.

     Cf. -g^{w}as 'pair'

       ʔíd-

     s.ʔílìd^{ə}g^{w}əs   chest   EK., LG.

     šáw̓id^{ə}g^{w}əs   collar bone   EK.

     s.ptíd^{ə}g^{w}əs^{ə}b   mind, memory   EK.

       ʔəlču.ptídg^{w}əs^{ə}bid čəd   LG.

       I'm thinking about someone.

     -al-idg^{w}as

     híg^{w}alid^{ə}g^{w}əs   brave   EK.

     qəqəlál̓id^{ə}g^{w}əs   coward   EK.

3.   -i-dup   lexical suffix 'ground, floor'

     See also -dup.

     ʔəs.k^{w}ədídup   land settlers, sqwatters   LL.

     ʔəs.ču̓l̓idup   rented land   LL.

čágʷidup	mop (floor)	LG.
ʔík̓ʷidup	sweep (floor)	EK.
x̌əlídup	floor	EK.

1. -igʷəd   lexical suffix 'inside'

ʔácigʷəd	inside (a whale)	ES.
yúbiligʷəd	miscarriage	LL.
s.túligʷəd	blood	
łəgʷəlígʷədᵊb	orphan	LL.
qələbigʷəd	body waste	JC.
dxʷs.łíligʷəd	one who gives food, is not stingy	LG.
xʷiʔ gʷat ʔu.łiligʷəd	No one food-gave him.	ML.
səxʷ.ʔík̓ʷigʷədalc	ramrod for cleaning a rifle	ES.
dxʷ.x̌ʷáligʷəd	give up on mental problem	EK.
dxʷ.x̌ʷáq̓ʷigʷəd	worry	ML., EK.
dxʷ.(ʔ)idáwligʷəd	worry	LL.
dxʷ.bálihigʷəd	forget one's self	LL.
dxʷ.qáhigʷəd	cunning, clever	ES.
	manipulator, tricky	LG.
ʔəxʷ.čcíligʷəd	red inside	LL.
-al-igʷəd	on/at side of	
jəháligʷəd	right side	
qəláligʷəd	left side	
s.ʔiláligʷəd	whole side; division of two sides, one side as opposed to the other	LG.
... čəxʷa xʷəbəbxʷəbáligʷəd		LG.
... and you will toss your body about.		

1. -ig^ws   lexical suffix   'things, possessions'

      (perhaps -ik^ws)

s.tábig^ws	possessions	LL.
s.g^wədíg^ws	paraphernalia	LL.
x^w.dəg^wíg^wsali	pocket, bag	
x̌^wuɫ čəd ʔu.x̌íbig^ws^əb		LG.

     I just grabbed my things (because I didn't have time to pack
                 carefully).

2. -ik^w   lexical suffix   'shirt'

ʔúʔƛ^əbik^w	stretch shirt, T-shirt	LL.
sáʔsx^{wə}bik^w	jumper (short denim jacket)	ES.
ƛíƛpik^w	undershirt	LL.

3. -il   a voice suffix having the following meanings:

    1.   'reach or achieve a state or position'

    2.   'becoming'

    3.   'begin'   (This last sense is most certainly the meaning
            of the etymologically related root [ʔil], *q.v.*)

    /-i-/ before the transitive suffix -s.

    /-il/ elsewhere

4. -ilc   lexical suffix   'rounded/curved object:
                                      money, forehead, buttocks

ɫíx^wilc	three dollars	
ʔudx^w.bílcəp	He fell on his seat.	LG., EK.
s.ʔilílc	forehead	LG.
ʔəs.ɫəq̓tílc	He has a wide forehead.	LG.
p̓ílilc	He has a flat forehead.	LG.

?əs.bulux̌ʷílc His forehead is round. LG.

q̓əcílc bump forehead LG.

1. -ilč lexical suffix 'shank (of leg)'

Cf. -šad 'leg, foot', -ƚx̌a 'thigh'

?əs.x̌ʷáⱡx̌ʷalilč čəd LL.
I can't manage my legs (from knees down). (An expression
used to mean that one is very tired from walking, standing, etc.)

2. -iⱡ°d lexical suffix 'food'

Cf. ?əⱡ-, -aⱡ°d

-dal-iⱡ°d

cìldáliⱡ°d table LG.

ča?kʷdáliⱡ°d wash food LG.

s.(h)uydáliⱡ°d cook EK.

3. -iqad lexical suffix 'incline, slope, bank, hill'

?ilǰíqad bank, slope, water's edge LL.

šqíqad up hill LG.

gʷədíqad down below LL.

4. -i?ⱡ lexical suffix 'baby'

ləs.čəbá?i?ⱡ čəd EK.
I'm going along with a baby on my back.

ƛu.x̌ah°bi?ⱡəxʷ ML.
She would let the baby cry continuously.

... gʷəƛu.há?li?ⱡəxʷəs ML.
... that she would stop the baby from crying.

ləs.kʷədy̓əɬ   She is carrying the child.   LG.

s.wáxʷi?ɬ   litter of whelp wolves still
with mother   LL.

j

This letter represents a sound which English speakers might spell
dz. It is like the *ds* in *rods*. [voiced alveolar affricate]

1. s.jábtač   doe   VH.

   See under s.qigʷəc 'deer'.

2. jáhak̓ʷuʔ   intensive particle   'really do something'   LL.

3. jakʷ(a)   shake, rock, wag

   Compare: bák̓ʷ(a), bəjqᵊb, č̓ə́dᵊb, jax̌(a), t̓íxʷicut, xʷəbəbxʷáligʷəd

   -at

       jákʷəd   shake it up, move it   EK.
                               shake it   DM.
                               rock it   LL.

       jákʷədəxʷ ʔucu.cuucəxʷ ...   ML.
       She rocks (her baby) while saying ...

       ləjákʷad ʔal kʷədiʔ ǰə̀səds   EC.
       He shakes her at her feet.

       ʔujákʷatᵊb   got shaken   LL.

   gʷə-...-əd

       xʷiʔ kʷ(i) adsgʷəjákʷəd   Don't move!   LL.

       xʷiʔ kʷi sgʷəjákʷədləp   Don't you folks move!   LL.

   -a-b

       jəkʷáb   wag (tail), switch (back and forth) like a tail DM.

   lexical

       dxʷjákʷakʷusᵊb   toss head from side to side

4. ják̓ʷadiʔ   invite   VH.

   See under cut.

ʔuják̉ʷadi(ʔ)cid čəd dxʷʔal gʷ(ə)ads.ʔux̌ʷ   EK.
I asked you to go.

ʔuják̉ʷadi(ʔ)tubuɬ dxʷʔal gʷəs.ʔùx̌ʷčəɬ   EK.
He asked us to go.

1.   ják̉ʷiyus   man's name. LL.'s step-father

2.   jal-   reverse the side of, turn over/around,
                    go around/over some obstruction

     Cf. x̌ək̉ʷ(u)   turn face down

         qit(i)   circle around something

         səlp   spin

         jəpíl   turn

     lexical

         jəlábac   climb over a fence/ pile of logs   LL., EK.
                          (no dxʷ- prefix)

         jəlálič   go over a rise/hillock   LL., EK.
                          (no dxʷ- prefix)

             sjíjəlàl̉ič   name for site of Seattle. This was
                               the place where canoes were hauled
                               over the little rise of land separating
                               Lake Washington from Puget Sound.   LL.

         jəláx̌əd Snoh.   visit   EK.

             Cf. jə́x̌əx̌   Skagit   visit

                 dəčág̉ʷtxʷəb   visit

             jəláx̌ədbic   visit me   EK.

         sjəlgʷás   name for site of Stanwood, Washington

         dxʷjálgʷəp   walk along the beach   LL.

         jəlálgʷiɬ   the command to change side of canoe
                           on which one is paddling   DM.

jálqs   go around a point   LL.

jəlúlč   go around   LL.

jəlúcid   cross river, lake

    Cf. šáqʷil, túlil; diʔúcid

    diłəxʷ dəxʷjəlúcids

    That is where he crossed to the other side of the river.   EC.

root extention q̲:

-t

jálqᵊd   turn it over

                 turn (the fish) around (in order to
                 cook the other side)   LL.

jálqcut   turn self around, turn self over   LG.

lexical

jálqus   turn face to opposite direction

jəljəlqálus   a kind of knitting stitch that involves
                 turning the yarn over in such a way that
                 the socks when finished will not curl down
                 at the top   LG.

reduplication

jáljəlq   turn around several times

jálǝlq   turn part way around

jáləljəlq   turn part way around several times

    x̌ʷułəxʷ čəxʷ łuləjələlqúsbic

    You just turn part way around toward me now
    and again as you go (away).   ES.

sjíjəlàlič   Snoh. and SPS   site of Seattle

sjíjəlàbac   Skagit   site of Seattle

root extention č̲:

sjə́lč̓   Skagit   year, turning of seasons

s.ǰə́lč   Snoh.   year

Cf. -ladxʷ   lexical suffix for year

ʔúlub ʔi kʷi təqàči? s.bək̓ʷàči? sǰə́lč ʔi tiʔə? cəlàcači?
ʔi tiʔə? cəlàc
the year 1855 (lit. 'ten and eight hundred year and fifty-five')
                                                            MS.

1.   ǰáƛ   confused

   Cf. bálbal   confused, mistaken

      báli   forget

      s.báliʔxʷ   mixed people

      báluqʷ   mixed up, entangled

   root

      ǰáƛ   confused   EK.

      ʔəsǰáƛ   be confused   HD.

   -b

      ʔəsǰáƛ°b   be wrong   HD.
                      not know how, mixed up, confused LG.

      ʔəsǰáƛ°b čəd   I'm wrong.   EK.

      ʔəsǰáƛ°b čəd ʔə kʷi gʷəds.sàq̓ʷ   LG.
      I don't know how to fly.

         Cf. qəʔíqəl

      ƛu.wáhi tə s.čàčasčəɫ ƛujàƛ°b   LL.
      Our child made a mistake unintentionally.

   -bi-t

      ʔəsǰáƛbid čəd   I don't know how to do it.   HD.

      ʔəsǰáƛ°bid čəd   I don't understand.   LL.

ʔəsjáƛəlàdi(ʔ)bid čəd   I don't quite understand.   LL.

lexical

ʔəsjáƛəlàdi(ʔ)bid čəd   I don't quite understand.   LL.

ƛudxʷjəƛáladiʔ čəd   LL.
Generally my ears get twisted/ (they) wander.
(i.e., I don't usually understand.)

1.   jaq(a)   mourn

   See under x̌ahᵊb.

   -at

      jáqad   mourn   DM., LL.

      ləjáqəd   She was going along mourning.   ML.

      tiʔił dəxʷujaqadsəxʷ   That is why she was mourning. DM.

   -bi-t

      jáqəbitᵊb   mourn for someone   LG.

2.   jáq̓   more than one (person or animal) runs   EC., LL.

   Cf. təláwil   run

      sáxʷəb   jump, run

         ləjáq̓ ti lə.ʔùx̌ʷ   They are running by.   LG.

         lə.ʔúx̌ʷ ti ləjáq̓   Same gloss: They are running by.   LG.

3.   jáq̓(a)   fall/topple over
                      fell something

   See under bəč̓.

   Cf. x̌iƛ(i)

   -at

      jáq̓ad   fell (a tree), make it fall   LL., LG.

-dxʷ

jáq̓dxʷ He fell. LG.

-txʷ

ʔəsjáq̓txʷ have sex LG.

lexical

jáq̓alikʷ fell (a tree) LG.

  Cf. x̌íƛap chop a tree down LL., LG.

dxʷsjáq̓alikʷ a tree feller LL., LG.

  Cf. dxʷs.x̌íƛap a tree feller, lumber jack LL.

ʔujáq̓ič (A tree) fell on him/it. LG.

reduplication

jáq̓aq̓ totter, titter back and forth, stagger LG., LL.

  Cf. xʷíc̓ic̓ab balance, teeter LG.

x̌ʷúləxʷ ʔudxʷjàkʷakʷusᵊb LL.
He's just tossing his head from side to side.

  Cf. xʷəbəbxʷəbáligʷəd toss body about

rejected: *dxʷsjáq̓ LL.

1. jax̌(a) SPS move, shake

jəx̌ NPS move

See under jakʷ(a).

root

hágʷəxʷ tujàx̌ tə s.wàtixʷtəd
For a long time this world has been moving.

-at

ʔujáx̌ad tiʔił hikʷ s.t̓ək̓ʷəb He shakes that big tree. JC.

ʔujáx̌acut moving self (about) JC.

1. jáx̌ʷ(a)

    root

        ʔujáx̌ʷ   thaw, melt   EK., LL.

        ʔujáx̌ʷ tə s.q̓àx̌ʷ   The ice melted.   EK.

        -at

        jáx̌ʷatˀb   It was thawed.   LL.

→

3. x̌ʷ.jədálbali   trachea   EK.

4. jədís   tooth

    lexical

        jədísali   gum(s) (lit. 'where the teeth sit in')   EK.

    reduplication

        jəjədís   teeth

          (jəǰədís 'teeth' AS.)

5. jəgʷá?   professional, one who is famous for doing
                       something   ES., LL.

        jəgʷá? dx̌ʷs.ʔítut   a great one for sleeping   LL.

        ci?ił λ̓áλačəpəd jəgʷà? dx̌ʷ.ʔùlus   ES.
        Ant was famous for being a dedicated worker.

    reduplication

        jəgʷə?gʷá?   gloss uncertain   ES.

6. jə́gʷə   a kind of monster

    See under s.λ̓álqəb.

7. jəh-   right (direction, location, position)

    Contrast qəl- 'left'.

-bi-t

  jəbíd   right side   DM.

    gʷát kʷi ləs.gʷədíl adjəbíd   DM.
    Who is sitting at your right?

-alal-bi-t

  jəhálalbid   right side   DM.

-ači?

  jəháci?   right hand

-ay-ucid

  jəháyucid   right side of the road   EK.

-igʷəd

  jəháligʷəd   (whole) right side   EK.
                 right side   DM.

  jəháligʷəds   He's on the right.   LG.

  ?al tudi? jəhàligʷəds   LG.
  She's over there on his right.

  ?al túdi? adjəhàligʷəd   LG.
  He's over there on your right.

  gʷát kʷi s.dà? ?ə ti?ił ?əs.gʷədíl ?al t(i) adjəháligʷəd   LG.
  What is the name of him sitting on your right?

-igʷəd-bi-t

  adjəháligʷədbid čəd   I'm on your right.

  ?əs.gʷədíl čəd ?al t(i) adjəháligʷədbid
  I'm sitting on your right.

  dᵊjəháligʷədbid čəxʷ   You are on my right.   LG.

1.   jək̓ʷ   travel, wander, be unstable

  Cf. ?íbəš, ?úluł

root

?əsjə́k̓ʷ   a person who is not stable, who is
emotionally disturbed   HD., LL.

ɬujə́k̓ʷ čəd bək̓ʷ ti?ə? s.ləx̌ìl   LG.

I'm going to travel all (this) day.

?ujə́k̓ʷəs   wind changes   LL.

jə́k̓ʷádəd   sin, wrongdoing

ƛub čəxʷ ?u.baliicyitubuɬ ?ə tə jə́k̓ʷàdədčəɬ

Dimitte nobis debita nostra ...
         Translation of Matthew 6:12

x̌ʷuɬab ?ə tə s.baliicyidčəɬ tə ləli? ?aciɬtalbixʷ

?ə tə jə́k̓ʷàdəds dxʷ?al dìbəɬ

... sicut et nos dimittimus debitoribus nostris.
         Translation of Matthew 6:12

ƛub čəxʷ ?u.čəlálikʷtubuɬ dxʷ?al gʷəɬ bək̓ʷ jə́k̓ʷàdədčəɬ

Ne nos inducas in tentationem.
         Translation of Matthew 6:13

reduplication

jə́k̓ʷək̓ʷ   The wind is changing all the time. It is
coming from every direction.   LL.

jə́k̓ʷjə́k̓ʷálu?   driftwood and other debris   LL.

1.   jəláči?   SPS   six

     Cf. yəlá?c   NPS   six

→

3.   jəlúliča?   a woman's name, DM.'s wife's mother's mother

4.   jəɬ   modal particle   'so it would seem'

Compare:	Not certain of	Perhaps	Certain of
	k̓ʷa?	k̓ʷəd?á?	k̓ʷə́dšəd
	k̓ʷəɬ	x̌ʷú?ᵊlə?	jə́ɬ

ʔəxʷs.ʔítutəb jəɬ   He must be sleepy.   LG.

ʔəs.x̌íc̓il jəɬ sixʷ   He must be cranky.   LG.

həlítub uʔxʷ jəɬ čəxʷ ʔə kʷi s.qʷùtab   LL.
So you are still alive in spite of (all) the sickness.

ʔəxʷs.lək̓ʷdxʷyitᵊbᵊb jəɬ cə x̌ənimulic̓aʔ ʔə tə
s.ɫúʔᵊms, t̓əlúʔᵊms   ML.
It must be that the people want to eat Crow's
dried dog salmon and king salmon.

x̌ʷúləxʷ čəd jəɬ hìkʷ   I wish I were big.   LG.

x̌ʷùləxʷ jəɬ ʔáɬ kʷi gʷəds.ƛ̓ax̌ʷ   LG.
I wish I would grow fast.

x̌ʷuləxʷ jəɬ xʷiʔ gʷədsəxʷs.ʔìtutᵊb   LG.
I wish I weren't so sleepy.

x̌ʷùləxʷ jəɬ kʷi gʷəds.luƛ̓il   LG.
I wish I'd be grown up.

1.   jəɬ-

     jə́ɬtᵊb   They bought her (for a wife).

     jəɬálikʷ   marriage payment
                   (what is paid to the bride's family)

     See under q̓p̓(u).

2.   jəɬígʷəd   name for present site of Everett, Washington

3.   jəɬíxʷ   creek

       jíjɬixʷ   tiny creek

       Cf. s.túləkʷ river

4.   jəpíl   turn

221

ləjəpílǝxʷ   It's turning spring.

See under jal-.

1.   jəqíl   crawl, have head down   LL.

        ʔujəqíl čəd   I crawled.   LG.

        ʔəxʷsjəqílˀb čəd   I feel like crawling.   LG.

        -s

        ʔujəqís čəd tə čačas   LG.
        I crawled after the boy.

        reduplication

        jíjqił   crawl just a bit   LG.
                          have head down being bashful   LL.

2.   jəq̓   grind, sharpen

        See under šic.

        Cf. x̌ʷəc 'sharp'

        -t

        jə́q̓ˀd   grind it, sharpen it   LG.
                          (cannot mean sharpen a stick)   LG.

        lexical

        jə́q̓usˀd   sharpen it (knife, axe)   LL., LG.

        ʔu.húyəxʷ ʔu kʷ(i) adsujəq̓ùs   LL.
        Is your sharpening finished?

3.   jətásəbqiʔ   man's name from the Snoqualmie, VH.'s grandson, Jay
                                                               VH.

4.   jətgʷád Skagit   salmonberry   LG., MC.

        Cf. s.təgʷád, s.tə́gʷəd

1. jə́ẃil   dignity, graciousness   JC.

     cáy čəxʷ ʔəsjə̀ẃil ʔal ti s.lə̀x̌il

     You are looking/acting very nicely today;
     You are acting in a very dignified way today;
     You are elegantly dressed today.   JC.

     sjə̀ẃil   JC.'s childhood name

2. jəx̌   NPS   move

     jax̌(a)   SPS   move

     Cf. jakʷ(a); síd̓q̓cut (under sid̓q̓), dədídiʔ (under diʔ)

     -t

     ʔujə́x̌əd   move it   AS.

     jəx̌tə́báxʷ čəd   I've been moved.   AS.

     lexical

     dxʷjəx̌áhəb   move your buttocks   ES.

     ck̓ʷáqid ʔudxʷjəx̌áhəbitubuɫ   LL.

     He always gets his rear up here to eat with us.

     jəx̌šádəb   move your feet   AS.

     jəx̌ílcəb   kneel, bow head, and tell future   AS.

     reduplication

     jə̀x̌jəx̌   move household   DM.

       Cf. ʔúʔuluɫ (under ʔúluɫ)

     jíjx̌   move a little bit   DM.

       jíjx̌əd   move it a bit   LL.

       jíjx̌əcut   move self a hair   LG., LL.

     jə́x̌əx̌   Skagit   visit   DM., LG.

       Cf. jəláx̌əd   Snoh. 'visit' (under jal)

       dəčágʷtxʷəb   'visit'

-bi-t

ɬujəx̌əx̌bícid čəd   I'll visit you.   DM.

dᵊs.x̌áƛ kʷi dsjəx̌əx̌bìd ti ds.càpa   DM.
I want to visit my grandfather.

pə(d)táb kʷi gʷ(ə)ads.x̌àƛtxʷ kʷi gʷədsjəx̌əx̌bícid   LG.
Do you want to visit me?

→

2.   jíjihiʔ   pregnant

huy, jíjihiʔəxʷ ciʔəʔ wàq̓waq̓   Then Frog became pregnant.

3.   jil(i)

-it

jílid   dislike someone or something
            "That's a stronger word than líliildxʷ which is
            more like 'not get along with someone too well'."

                                                      VH.

ʔəsjílid čəd ti s.ʔə̀ɬᵊd   JC.
I don't like this kind of food.

Opposite of x̌áƛtxʷ.

4.   jíxʷ   first, before (in time or space)

	Synonyms:	Synonyms:
Antonyms:	jíxʷ	láq
Antonyms:	híwil	q̓ád
Antonyms:	súla	ʔálq̓ʷ

root

jíxʷ čəd bəɬic   First I forget it. (?)   LG.

ʔal kʷi tujíxʷ   in the beginning   ML.; MS.

x̌ʷùɫ ʔal jíxʷ s.jəlč̓   in the first of the year   MS.

comparison

ʔiɫjíxʷ čəxʷ ʔəs.làx̌ᵊdxʷ   EK.
You remember better (than I).

ʔiɫjìxʷ čəd háʔɫ dxʷs.ʔìgʷəɫ dxʷʔal dəgʷì   LG.
I'm a better tree climber than you.

(hə)láʔb čəd ʔiɫjìxʷ s.čəwàʔt dxʷʔal dəgʷì   LG.
I'm a lot better at it than you.

liɫjíxʷ   They were first.   LL.

   liɫjíxʷ gʷ(ə)ads.ʔùx̌ʷ   You go ahead.   DM.

   híwil liɫjìxʷ   Go ahead first.   EK.

   híwil čəd liɫjìxʷ   I'm going ahead first.   EK.

   háʔɫ kʷi gʷəs.huyutᵊbs liɫjixʷ
   háʔɫ t(i) ads.gʷa ʔə tə s.daʔ
   Sanctificatur nomen tuum.

-bid

   jíxʷbid ʔə kʷi gʷəds.bəliic kʷi gʷəds.q̓p̓ùcid   LG.
   Before I forget it, I'll pay you.

   cíck̓ʷ x̌əɫ ti siʔàb ciʔəʔ k̓àʔkaʔ ʔal tiʔiɫ tusəs.húys
   ʔal tiʔəʔ ʔàciɫtalbixʷ dxʷʔal tiʔəʔ tujixʷbíd ʔə
   tudiʔ dìbəɫəxʷ ʔal tiʔəʔ s.wàtixʷtəd ʔal kʷədìʔ
   tusəs.béčs ʔal kʷədìʔ tu.ləlìʔ s.wátixʷtəd ʔal kʷi
   tu.jíxʷ, jixʷbídəxʷ ʔal kʷədìʔ tus.qʷìbitᵊbsəxʷ
   tiʔəʔ s.wàtixʷtəd.   ML.

Just as though Crow had been high class [She was not.]
when she was (made) like a person in the world before us
when a different world was set down in the beginning before
the world was fixed over.

   jíxʷbids   It's in front of him.   LG.

   adjíxʷbid   It's in front of you (sg.)   LG.

jíxʷbidləp   It's in front of you folks.   LG.

lə.ʔíbəš čəxʷ ʔal tiʔə(ʔ) djixʷbíd   DM.
You're walking in front of me.

ʔu.qəp̓ cə bí.buʔqʷ ʔal tə djíxʷᵊbid   LG.
The bird landed in front of me.

rejected:

*ʔəs.kiis čəxʷ dᵊjíxʷbid   LG.

*ʔəs.gʷədíl ʔal tiʔił adjíxʷbid   DM.

In these sentences, híwilbid must be used and not
jíxʷbid.

lexical

sjíxʷqs   leader   EK.
                       origin   EC.

  cútᵊbəxʷ ʔə tiʔəʔ sjíxʷqs ʔə tiʔəʔ s.qəlálitut   EC.
  He was told about the origin of this power.

sjixʷúdəq   agenda   LL.

  stàb kʷ(i) adsjixʷúdəq
  What's first on your agenda?

reduplication

jíxʷixʷ   even more

1.   jix̌(i)   break down, collapse;
                    breakdown of a mechanical device

Compare x̌ʷə́ƛ̓, x̌ʷítil, dúkʷ(u), júq̓ʷ(u).

root

  ʔəsjíx̌   (The bridge) has collapsed.   EK.
                (The machine) is broken.   EK.

  łu.x̌ʷìʔəs tiləb ləjíx̌   JC.
  So it does not break right away.

-it

    ʔujíx̌id tiʔəʔ s.čəbìdac   He broke down the bark.   LL.

    jíx̌id   Break it down.   DM.

lexical

    ʔujíx̌ič   It collapsed on him.   LL.

1.   jub(u)   kick

    See under k̓aw-.

    -t

    júbutəb   get kicked

    -dxʷ

    júbdxʷ   manage to kick it

    lexical

    júbalikʷ   dance   LG.
                                    a slang word for dance   JC.

        Cf. séx̌əb, tac, tə́l(s)šəd

    jújəbàlikʷac   white pine tree   LG., MC.

        Cf. čáxʷəy(əc)   white pine (tree)

2.   júhəb   talk

    See under cút.

3.   júlaq̓   hand spinning wheel   MC.

    (Perhaps error for júlak̓.)

    See under łáq, táš.

    Cf. łáqtəd   leg spindle   LG.
        səxʷ.łáq   spinning wheel   LG.
        dəxʷu.tášəd   (modern) spinning wheel   MC.

1. júlču?   wave (of water)   EK.

    -b

       júlču?ᵊbəxʷ   The waves are getting bigger and running
                         faster.   LL.

2. júq̓ʷ(u)   ruin, smash up, shatter

    See under k̓aw-. Compare biƛ̓(i), duk̓ʷ(u), jix̌̓(i).

    -ut

       ?u̓.ƛ̓əlájad čəd dxʷ?al ti?iɬ s.čətxʷəd. cíck̓ʷəxʷ

       ?ujùq̓ʷud ti?iɬ ?à?pəlsəc

       I set a trap for that bear. He's been smashing up
       my little apple trees.

    -il

       ?əs.x̌əɬəɬx̌ə̀č čəd dxʷ?al ti dsujúq̓ʷil ?ə ti?iɬ čawəy?ùlč

       I'm sorry I shattered that dish.

3. jux̌ʷət   vomit   LL.

       júx̌ʷəd   vomit   LG.

    reduplication

       jú?jujx̌ʷət   feel like but can't quite vomit   LL.

ǰ

The sound value of this letter is similar to the *j* of English *jump*. [voiced palatal affricate]

1. s.ǰác   necklace   EK.

                  large kerchief that can be tied
                  about the neck   LL.

2. ǰác̓   river rises, it floods

    Opposite of šuƛ, *q.v.*

    Cf. p̓íl²b   high tide, flood

3. ǰə́c-

    -tx^w

        ǰə́ctx^w   use something   EK., DM.

        ʔəs.ʔəx̌íd k^wi g^w(ə)adsuǰə́ctx^w ti?ə? q̓íl̓bid.
        dəx^wu.ʔúluɫ dx^w?al ti?ə? x̌^wùlč

        What do you use a canoe for?
        It's used for traveling on the sea.

    reduplication

        ʔəsǰə́cǰəc   useful person   DM.

            Opposite of ʔəs.čílčil.

4. s.ǰə́lč̓ Snoh.   year, turning of seasons

    Cf. s.ǰəlč̓ Skagit   year, turning of seasons

        lexical suffix -ládx^w

    Cf. ǰəp̓íl   turn (lə.jp̓íləx^w 'turning spring')

        jal-   'reverse the side of'

5. ǰəsg^wíč̓a? Skagit   dog/goat hair blanket   LG.

    Cf. q̓^wasdùlič̓a? Snoh.   dog/goat hair blanket

    See under -ič̓a?, s.qəlík^w.

1. ǰə́səd   foot, leg

    ǰíǰsəd   little foot

    Cf. -šad (~ -šəd) lexical suffix for foot, leg

        -ilč   lexical suffix for shank of leg

        -ɫx̌a   lexical suffix for thigh

2. ǰiq̓(i)   immerse, soak

    Compare tuk̓ʷ 'immerse, soak more thoroughly'

    Cf.   tág̓ʷusəb   put face in water to drink
                           drink without a cup (human)

           q̓ʷúʔàči?   put hand in pan of water

           ɫəlqáy(?)   soak something; ɫəbáʔ   drown

    root

        ʔuǰíq̓ čəd   The tide came over me (because I had been
                      careless in selecting a campsite, and lay
                      within reach of high tide).   LL.

        g̓ʷəl ǰíq̓əx̌ʷ tiʔəʔ diʔəʔ s.x̌àx̌ax̌aʔs   LG.
        And his in-laws were drowned.

    -it

        ǰíq̓id   put it in the water   LG.; LL.

        ʔuǰíq̓id čəd   I put it in the water.   LL.

        ʔuǰíq̓id čəd ʔal tə q̓ʷùʔ ɫu.x̌ʷíʔəs lə.x̌ʷə̀ɫ ʔə k̓ʷi qiʔ.qiyə́ʔ JC.
        I put it in the water so it would not break easily.

        ǰíq̓itə̓b   It was put in the water.   LL.

        ǰíq̓cut   soak in water   LL.

    -tx̌ʷ

        ʔəsǰíq̓tubəx̌ʷ   It is in the water.   LL.
                            It has already been in the water. LL.

-agʷ-il

    ʔujíq̓agʷil čəd   I got in the water.   LL.

-agʷ-i(1)-s

    ʔujíq̓agʷis čəd   I soaked in the (mineral) water
                               (in order to cure my disease).   LL.

other derivation

    jíq̓alájəd   set a net   LG.

      See under λ̓aʔtəd.

rejected: *jíq̓il

1.   ju̓ʔ-   enjoy

    -t

    júʔtᵊb ci k̓aʔk̓aʔ   LL.
    They had a good time due to what Crow (had done, brought).

    ʔəlču̓júʔcut   He is joking.   LG.

    ʔəlču.x̌ayᵊbid čəɬ tə sju̓ʔcuts   LG.
    We were laughing at the joke.

    -il

    jú̓ʔil   enjoy, have a good time

k

The value of this letter is similar to the *k* in English *keep* and *c* in *cup*. [voiceless velar stop]

1. káad   open the mouth   EK., LG.

     also sometimes ká?d and kah^əd

     See under g^wəq̓.

2. káwič   SPS   humpback

     s.kəwíč   NPS   humpback

→

3. káwɫ^əb   try, improvise, make do   LL.
                          do fumblingly, inadroitly   VH.

     See under p̓a?.

         ƛ̓ukáwɫ^əb čəɫ ƛ̓u.kəskəbítəg^wəl   LL.
     We are doing our best to talk to each other.

     lexical

         tùx̌^w skáwɫ^əbàlc   LL.
     That's the best I can do for a gun.

4. káw̓qs   raven; Brother of k̓a?k̓a? in Myth Age.
                          He was noted for being a glutton and
                          always he tried to get food by trickery.

5. káw̓x̌^w   can, metal container

     káw̓kaw̓x̌^wulč   metal containers

6. káyə(?)   vocative for grandmother   EK.

     Cf. kiyá?

7. káykay   steller's jay; one who talks too much   EK., LG.

     ?əskáykay^əb   azure, sky-blue

1. s.káyu   corpse, ghost   EK., LL.

     s.kəyú   corpse, ghost   ES., LG.

    root

      skáyuhəx^w ci?ə? d^ə.bəda?   ES.
      My daughter has become (like) a corpse.

      g^{w}əskáyu wə̀q̓əb   casket   EK.

    -il

      skáyuiləx^w He's dead.   LL.

       See under ?átəbəd 'dead'.

    lexical

      skəyúqs   Indian name for Mission Head on Tulalip Reservation. It is the southern peninsula between Tulalip Bay and Port Gardner Bay. In former times there was an Indian cemetery there.   ES.

2.   kəkí?   Snoh.   unnamed baby   EK.

    skəkí?   Skagit   cradle board   LG.

    skəkkí?   Skagit   baby   LG.

     səs.x̌qí?ɬs ?əskəkì?tx^w ML.
     She has the baby tied in a cradle board.

3.   kəláp^{ə}x̌^{w}ə̀lč   jellyfish

4.   kəlísi   crazy (from English *crazy*)

    Cf. q(ə)p   crazy, senile, childish

      ?əs.x^{w}ə̀lk̓^{w}qíd   turned head, foolish

5.   kəpú   coat (from C. Jargon from French *capote*)

1. kə́skᵊb   chattering all the time (never quiet); converse VH.

     See under <u>cut</u>, qəsqᵊb.

     -i-t

        ʔukəskᵊbitᵊb čəd

        He talked to me (even though I didn't want to listen).

2. kəšú   pig (from C. Jargon from French *cochon*)

     LG. gives kʷəšú along with kəšú.

     kəškəšú   pigs

     (No diminutive reduplication possible.)

3. s.kəwíč   NPS   humpback

     káwič   SPS   humpback

        kíkəwìč   'Little Humpback', name of a little boy in a Basket Ogress myth

4. s.kəyú   See under <u>s.káyu</u>.

5. kíis   NPS   stand up   Skagit, Snoh.; not SPS

     Cf. ɬx̌ílč   SPS   stand up;   cqʷúɬ (54.9)

     root

        ʔəskíis   (man or animal) stands (up)   EK.

        ʔəskíis ti stùbš   The man is standing.   LG.

        s.x̌əýusab tə səskìiss   He is standing on his head.   LG.

        čitáləp kʷ(i) adsəskìis   DM.
        You stand by the foot of the tree.

        ʔəskíis čəxʷ ʔal ti?ə(?) d.suləbìd   DM.
        You are standing in front of me.

-bi-t

    ʔukíisbid čəd   I stood up beside him.

    ʔukíisbitᵊb čəd   He stood up to me.

lexical

    ʔəskísəč   hair standing on end;   LG.
                               bird's crest; hackles of a dog   LG., LL.

reduplication

    ʔəskíksəč   small crest   LL.

1.   kíkiyalus   name of a group of Skagit living along
                        the south fork of the Skagit River   DM.

                    See Sampson, pp. 2 and 19.

2.   kiyáʔ   NPS   grandmother

     See under bədáʔ.

     káyə(ʔ)   SPS   grandmother

     Cf. káyə   vocative of kiyáʔ

       šəɬkiyáʔᵊb   step-grandmother   EK.

3.   kší   shoo! (The vowel is voiceless.)

     See under cut.

4.   kúkcut   cook (from English cook plus -t-sut)

5.   kúpi   coffee (from English *coffee*)

     Cf. dxʷs.(h)ədálqʷuʔ   coffee, tea

     kúkpi   a little coffee

1. kyúʔkiwəc   Snoh.   vine maple   EK.

    Cf. t̓əqt̓əqác   Skagit   vine maple

       s.čúču̓ʔɬəc Suquamish   vine maple

k̓

The sound of this letter is similar to that of k except for the addition of a simultaneous abrupt closure of the vocal cords. [glottalized, voiceless velar stop]

1.   k̓ádəyù   Snoh., SPS   rat   LL., ES., EK., ESi., FSi.

     k̓ədáyuʔ   Skagit   rat   LG., DM.

2.   s.k̓ák̓axʷ   a dried berry of unidentified variety   MC.
                          The Chilliwack term is təs(ə)lác.

3.   k̓aw(a)   chew (food)

     See under ʔəɬ.

     Cf. x̌ʷuƛ, x̌əp̓kʷ, č̓it

     -at

         ʔuk̓áwad čəd ʔə tə haʔɬ   I chewed it well.   EK.

         k̓áwəd   Chew it.   LG.

         k̓áwad ʔə tə hàʔɬ gʷəl x̌ʷiʔ kʷ(i) ads.č̓ík̓ʷapsəb   EK.
         Chew it well so you won't choke.

     -aɬ

         k̓áwəɬ čəd šàw̓   LG.
         I chewed a bone for myself.

         k̓awəɬ šàw̓ čəd
         Same gloss: I chew a bone for myself.

     lexical

         k̓áw̓k̓awšədit˘b   nipping at the heels   LG.

     reduplication

         k̓áw̓k̓aw   chewing   EK.

1.   k̓aw-   touch, bump

       Compare:

       q̓c-   təs   tuk̓ʷ   c̓aq̓   pus

               təq̓/ɬaq̓   (kʷixʷ)   c̓axʷ   ƛ̓uč   biƛ

               jub   čis ~ čəs   juq̓ʷ

               ləč̓

     -dxʷ

       k̓áwdubš   Touch me.   EK.

     lexical

       k̓áwqid   bump head   EK.

2.   k̓áyayə? (also pronounced k̓ayáyə?)

               a very thoroughly smoke-dried fish. Alder is used.
                                       LL., LG., VH.

   Cf. x̌áx̌yəƛ   another name for k̓ayayə?

       q̓ʷás   Suquamish word for k̓ayayə?

   Cf. xʷ.šəbús   (under šab(a))

       s.t̓əlú?əb

       s.ɬú?əb

3.   k̓áyəx̌əd   man's name

4.   k̓áyiɬ   pretend   ML.

    k̓ayíɬ   pretend   LG.

    ?ayíɬ   pretend   VH.

     k̓ayíɬ čəd diɬ ti?iɬ s.tùbš   LG.
     I pretended I was that man.

-bi-t

    ḱayíɫbid   pretend it   LG.

rejected: *ḱayíɫəd

1.   ḱáʔḱaʔ   crow

    ḱáʔkaʔḱaʔ   many crows

    ḱíḱikḱaʔ   a lot of young crows

    Cf. x̌ənimúliča?   myth name of Crow

      In the Myth Age Crow was the sister of Raven. Crow was not high class but often pretended to be.

2.   ḱədáyuʔ   Skagit   rat

    ḱádayuʔ   Snoh. SPS   rat

3.   ḱə́ləwʔ   a greedy person

    (perhaps ḱə́luʔ)

4.   ḱəᵖḱʷəláʔ   some sort of small screech owl

5.   ḱíč(i)

    See under ɫič(i).

    -it

      dxʷḱíčid   eviscerate someone

6.   ḱilc   pinch   VH.

    Cf. čə́ʔtq   pinch

      tíʔttiš   narrow

      ʔəsḱílc   a narrow place   EK.

lexical

    k̓iɫčáliča?   clothing caught in a door   LG.

1.   k̓iɫ(i)   hang on a peg, nail, etc.

    See under šəq.

    Cf. ɫəp̓(u), q̓it̓(i)

    -it

        k̓íɫid t(ə) ad.kəpu   Hang your coat on a peg.   LG.

        k̓íɫitᵊb tə s.kəyù   hang up the dead
                               (as in the old custom)   EK.

2.   k̓í? (~ k̓íy)   (The vowel is [e].)

    Cf. x̌ək̓ʷəd, čəx̌

        x̌k̓í?təd   a split stick for roasting   LG.

        ?əxʷk̓í?adub   a way of cooking with a stick
                               over the fire   LL.

        k̓íyat   cracking   EK.

3.   k̓t̓íl   grow tired, become impatient   LG.

    See under wáwɫqayu?.   Also recorded as q̓ət̓íl by VH.

    -s

        díɫəxʷ kʷi gʷəsk̓t̓ísᵊb ?ə ci?iɫ s.x̌ax̌a?s   LG.
        His mother-in-law was getting impatient with him.

4.   k̓tú?   belly   The term is slangy and mildly insulting.

    See under ƛ̓ač.

    Cf. k̓ʷyə́xʷ (Suquamish)   ESi.

        ?əsk̓tú?   have a fat belly   LG.

        lək̓tú?ᵊbəxʷ   beginning to get a paunch   LG.

1.   k̓yúcᵊb   starved

See under tagʷəxʷ.

Cf. q̓(i)yúq̓ʷ   appetite

kʷ

This letter stands for a sound that is similar to the *qu* in the English word *queen*. [labialized, voiceless velar stop]

1.   kʷ-   bound morpheme occurring in the determiner system representing vague, or imagined matters.

             kʷi

             kʷsi

             kʷədí?

    See under <u>ti</u>.

2.   kʷáčil   Skagit   dawn, getting light   LG.

     <u>łukʷáčil</u>   tomorrow

      Cf. dádatu   morning

         łúp   morning

3.   kʷágʷičəd   elk, Big Dipper (constellation)   LG., ES., LL., HD.

     kʷágʷičədałči? elk meat   DM.

4.   kʷátač   In Skagit this means to climb up hill as opposed to ?igʷəł which means to climb a ladder or a tree.

                        In Snohomish <u>kʷatač</u> seems to cover all these meanings. Snohomish consultants do not recognize ?igʷəł.

                        VH. comments that <u>kʷatač</u> is used for climbing hills and mountains because a person does not generally go straight up but rather switches back and forth, whereas on a stairway or in a tree ?igʷəł is used because the climbing is more or less straight up.

     kʷátač   climb a hill, climb over something high (both Skagit and Snohomish)

                        climb a ladder, tree (Snohomish only)

     <u>kʷátač</u> čəł dxʷ.di?àbac   Let's climb over it.   ES.

ɫukʷátač čəd dxʷʔal tə s.bàdiɫ   MS.
I'm going to climb the mountain.

səxʷkʷátač   Snoh.   ladder, stairway   EK.

    Cf. səxʷ.ʔígʷəɫ   Skagit   ladder   LG.

dxʷskʷátač   a mountain climber   LG.

1.   s.kʷáwəɫ   SPS   steelhead, a s.čədádxʷ   JC.

    See under s.ʔuládxʷ.

    Cf. qiwx̌   NPS   steelhead

2.   kʷáxʷ(a)   help

    -at

      kʷáxʷac   help me

        yəxì čəxʷ hùy ləskʷáxʷac   EK.
        because you are helping me.

        gʷat kʷi gʷəkʷáxʷac   LG.
        Who will help me?

          rejected: *gʷat kʷi gʷəskʷáxʷacs   LG.

        diɫ gʷat kʷi gʷəkʷáxʷac   LG.
        Will anyone help me?

        gʷat kʷi gʷ(ə)axʷkʷáxʷacᵊb   LG.
        Who wants to help me?

        s.táb kʷi gʷəskʷáxʷacs   LG.
        What could he do for me?

    s.táb kʷi gʷədskʷáxʷacid
    What can I do to help you? (E.g., in a store a clerk would
                     say this.)

gʷək̫ʷáxʷac čəxʷ čəɬa šáqᵊd tiʔəʔ wə̀q̓əb   DM.
Would you help me lift this box?

ʔəxʷskʷáxʷadᵊb čəd ti d.bàd ʔə ti su.čə̀ɬs x̌àẃsalʔtxʷ   LG.
I have to help my father build a new house.

-dxʷ

cíck̓ʷ čəd ʔəs.híiɬ ʔə tiʔiɬ adsukʷàxʷdubš   ES.
I'm very glad that you helped me.

-ad

háʔɬ kʷxʷàd   good luck (lit. 'good help')   LL.

   Cf. k̓ʷidá 'lucky'

reduplication

   kʷíʔkʷxʷᵊd

   háʔɬ kʷíʔkʷxʷᵊd   a good little helper   LL.

   dày?əxʷ čəxʷ háʔɬ kʷìʔkʷxʷᵊd   LL.
   You are a very good little helper.

1. kʷaʔ   a modal particle that denies absolute certainty
                      about validity of statement.

   See under jəɬ.

   Cf. k̓ʷəɬ

      lə.ʔúx̌ʷəxʷ kʷaʔ   He is going now.

      ʔəƛ̓áxʷ kʷaʔ tiʔəʔ   This must come next.   MS.

2. kʷáʔ   leave it alone, let it go

   -t

      kʷáʔᵊd   Leave it alone.   HD., EK.

      kʷáʔc   Leave me alone.   HD.

→

244

1.   kʷəd(á)   NPS   take, get, hold

kʷə́d(ə)   SPS   Cf. x̌îb(i)

root

ləskʷə́d   carrying   EK.

ʔukʷə́d ti ʔił.kʷə̀lq   She took some (not all).   EK.

kʷədáxʷ čəxʷ sixʷ   You are getting that way again. HD.

... ʔaləxʷ tiʔił tuskʷədáxʷ ʔə ciʔəʔ čáčas   ES., HD.
... when this child had a spell.

As the last two examples illustrate, kʷəd can be used
to indicate a spirit (or other power) seizing someone.

-at

ləskʷədád čəxʷ ʔu t(i) ads.tàləhali   LG.
Do you have your purse with you?

ʔił.čád x̌əlày? kʷi ʔukʷədàd.   LG.
Which shovel-nose canoe did he take?

ʔukʷədátᵊb čəd   grabbed me

kʷədátgʷəl   'grab one another' as in fighting (can
                          refer to marriage too but usually other
                          words are used for matrimony)

kʷìkʷədátgʷəl   going steady   ES.

ʔukʷədátəgʷəl čəł ʔi ci Sue   ES.
Sue and I are 'hitching up'.

-dxʷ

ʔukʷədxʷ čəxʷ ʔu   Did you get it?   LG.

mí ʔman cəxʷkʷə̀dxʷ   EK.

Very little that I caught hold of him.
(I only just barely caught him.)

-tx^w

ʔuk^wə́dtx^w   He made someone take it.   LG.

ʔəsk^wə́dtx^w tiʔił   Let him take it.
                         Let him hold it.   LG.

-yi

ʔuk^wədyítəb čəd   took (a stick) to me
                         (i.e., whipped me)

ʔuk^wədyíc ʔə tiʔił q^wíʔq^włəyʔ   ML.

She took a switch to me (to hit me with).
She took a switch from me.

s.tab k^wi suk^wədyítᵊb ʔə t(ə) əd.bə̀d tiʔił čáčas   NPS

What is your father taking from that boy.

ʔuk^wə́dšitᵊb čəx^w ʔu ʔə tə s.tubš ʔə tə kəpù   SPS

Did the man take the coat from you?

-bi-t

ʔuk^wədábitᵊb čəd   captured me

ʔuk^wədábicid čəd   I caught you for a slave.

ʔuk^wədábitᵊb   captive

-ibəł

(ʔu)dx^wk^wədíbəł   a person who takes away another's
                         wife, fiancée   LG.

lexical

k^wədáčiʔc   Shake hands with me.   LG.

k^wədáyačiʔ   knife in hand   LL.

ʔəsk^wədídup   squatters, land settlers   LL.

k^wədíg^wəd   indispensable possession   LL.

k^wədᵊq(s)šádᵊb   touch your toes   LG.

skʷədúlč   container   LG.

xʷkʷədábaləp   straight handle (as on a dipper,
                                          pan, axe)   EK.

xʷkʷədádid   bail, loop handle (as on pail)   EK.

kʷədəbádiʔ   bail, loop handle (as on pail)   LL.

reduplication

kʷìkʷədátgʷəl   going steady   ES.

1.   kʷədáʔ   a modal particle emphasizing probability,
                          maybe, might

See under jəɬ.

Cf. xʷúʔᵊlə

dəčáxʷəd kʷədàʔ gʷəl ʔəsgʷə.ƛ̓lád   EK.
For once he would be still!

ɬu.ʔáɬəɬ čəxʷ kʷədàʔ   HD.
I guess next time you'll hurry.

x̌álalx̌al kʷədàʔ   HD.
Now you learned something! (a reprimand in scolding)

xʷiʔ kʷədə̀ʔ kʷi gʷəs.qə̀lᵊbs   LG.
Maybe it won't rain.

gʷə.díɬəxʷ kʷədəʔ   LL.
That one might be the one!

díɬəxʷ kʷədàʔ   Maybe that's he now.   ML.

2.   kʷədíʔ   See under ti.

Compare also túdiʔ, tádiʔ, díʔəʔ and with the article kʷi.

háʔɬ kʷədiʔ sx̌íʔ.x̌iy̓us ʔə tiʔəʔ cədiɬ   ML.
Such a pretty little head he had.

hák^w k^wədí? s.?as g^wəl ?ə(s).šúdx^w ti səs.g^wədìls

He was there a long time before they saw him sitting (there).

?al k^wədí? tu.hák^w   a long time ago   EK.

bə́lk^wtx^w dx^w?al k^wədì? tudəx^w.?ás   AS.

Put it back where it was.

?u.?úx̌^wtubəx^w ƛ̌^wəɬ dx^w?al k^wədi? ?u.x̌áƛil   LL.

They say he's been sent to the Great War.

ɬu.t̓úk̓^wtx^wyicid čəd ?al k^wədi? ad.?àl?al   ES.

I'll take it home for you wherever your house may be.

?á ti?iɬ s.čətx^wəd ?al k^wədi? dəx^wəs.ɬaɬlils   ES.

There was Bear where he lived.

1.   k^wədšəd   modal particle   'surely, certainly, indeed'

      See under jəɬ.

            ?əƛáx^w k^wədšəd ci s.ƛ̓álqəb   LA.

            The monster is surely coming now.

2.   k^wək^wyús   negligent

3.   k^wəlk̓áw?tx^w   stretch of beach on Tulalip Reservation
                                         now called Sunny Shores   EK.

4.   k^wə́lq   other things   LG.

            ƛu.k^watač k^wi ?iɬk^wəl^əq   ML.

            The others would climb up.

      k^wáal^əq   other people   LG.

            ti?iɬ bə?iɬk^wáal^əq ?àciɬtalbix^w   LG.

            these other people

5. s.k^wə́ɬt   fishtail   LL.

      Cf. s.čə́t̓šad

1. kʷəsyú   porpoise   EK., HD., LL.,
                                                                  ESi.

    kʷíʔkʷəsyù   diminutive

2. s.kʷə́xʷic   See under s.kʷxʷíc.

3. kʷi   article   remote, hypothetical

    See under ti.

4. kʷil SPS   pick berries

    Cf. čəbᵊb   NPS   pick berries

        ʔukʷíləxʷ čəł ʔə tiʔił s.q̓ʷəlàłᵊd   JC.
        We are picking berries.

5. kʷíƛ SPS

    Cf. ǰi.čə́c   NPS   red

        ǰikʷíƛ   Suqu.   red   ESi.

        ǰəkʷíƛ   Puy.   red   FSi.

        dxʷkʷíƛᵊb   Upper Snoh. Pilchuck River   EK.

6. kʷíxʷid   sound of pounding, banging

    See under k̓aw-.

    Cf. tuk̓ʷ(u)

        stàb čəxʷ stàb ʔukʷí:xʷi:d
        What are you that's making that pounding noise?
        (from song in myth about Mink and Whale)

7. s.kʷíʔkʷəlùs   flower   LG.

    Cf. čqáysəb   flower   EK.

1. kʷíʔkʷiɬ   skate fish   DM.

2. kʷsi   article   remote, hypothetical

    See under ti.

3. s.kʷúpəc   SPS   hemlock tree   ESi.

    Cf. t̓q̓ədíʔac   hemlock tree   LL., MC.

        t̓úʔxʷəc   hemlock tree   LG.

4. kʷút   'modern' skirt   LL.
                     dress   EK.

    Cf. s.c̓ájəp   cedar bark skirt

    reduplication

        kʷíʔkʷut   skirt for a little girl

5. kʷúʔt   small cattail mat used for sleeping   EK., LL., JC.

                     "This is the word for skate fish too." JC.

    See under ƛ̓akʷ.

    Cf. s.ɬágʷid

6. s.kʷxʷíc   Snoh.   silver salmon (coho), a member of the class of
                        s.ʔuládxʷ   EK.

    s.kʷəxʷic   SPS   silver salmon   ESi., JC.

    Cf. s.q̓əčqs   Skagit   silver salmon, coho (lit. 'crooked nose')

k̓ʷ

The sound represented by k̓ʷ is like that of k̓ with the addition of simultaneous lip rounding or like that of kʷ with simultaneous abrupt closure of the vocal cords. [labialized, glottalized, voiceless velar stop]

1. k̓ʷác̓

        sk̓ʷác̓   dogfish

        k̓ʷác̓təličuʔ   shark (generic?)

2. k̓ʷád(a)   dip out

    Cf. yaƛ(a)   fetch water, dip it out, gore

        tixʷ(i)   bail out a boat

    -at

        k̓ʷádad   dip it out   LL.

        k̓ʷádatəb   dipped out   LL.

    lexical

        k̓ʷádalikʷ   dip it out   LL.

        k̓ʷádgʷild   bailer (made of cedar bark)   EK., MS.

        k̓ʷádgʷiɬ   bailer   MS.

3. k̓ʷalc̓   wrench/twist back (of body)

    See under q̓əč.

    root

        k̓ʷalc̓   wrench back   MS.
                        bend backwards too far and thus injure self   LG.
                        bend backwards   LG.

    -t

        k̓ʷálc̓cut   is equivalent to táłx̌cut   LG.

k̓ʷálč̓ᵊd čəd   I bent him over backward.   LG.

reduplication

k̓ʷálk̓ʷalč̓cut   lean/bend self backward a number
                      of times (as would a seal)   ML., JC.

1.   k̓ʷáltəd   fish skin

See under k̓ʷəlúʔ.

2.   k̓ʷáɬ(a)   examine, scrutinize, look over, size up

See under šuɬ.

-at

   k̓ʷáɬəd   examine it   LG.

   k̓ʷáɬətᵊb   be sized up   LG.

reduplication

   k̓ʷáɬaɬəd   look it over, size it up   LG.

      k̓ʷáɬaɬad jìxʷbid ʔə kʷi gʷ(ə)ads.k̓ʷədàd   LG.
      Examine it before you take it.
      (I.e., Don't take any wooden nickels.)

   ʔuk̓ʷáɬaɬacut čəd
   I looked myself over (in the mirror to see that
   my tie was straight, etc., before going out).   LL.

   k̓ʷək̓ʷáɬᵊb   nearsighted   EK.

1. ǩʷáƛ

    ləcuǩʷáƛ   copulating (?)
                           The more refined term seems to be qə́dəb.

2. ǩʷás(a)   burn body, roast, barbecue

    See under hud.

    root

        ʔuǩʷás čəd   I got burned.   LG.

        łuǩʷás   He'll get burned.   LG.

        xʷíʔtxʷ ləǩʷàs tiʔił   LG.
        Don't let him get burned!

        ʔəs.čal kʷ(i) adəxʷuǩʷas
        How did you get burned?

        díł cəxʷuǩʷàs   That is how I got burned.

    -at

        ǩʷásəd   Heat it up! Barbecue (especially heat up
                           dried fish to bring out the oil and make
                           crisp)!   LG.

        ʔalčuǩʷasətˀb   It's getting barbecued.   LG.

    -b

        ǩʷásˀb   toast, roast (item being cooked is always
                                 held)   LL.

        ǩʷásˀbəxʷ tiʔił s.tàwixʷəł
        The children heated up [the dried fish].   LA.

        s.čətšád tiʔəʔ sǩʷàsˀb dəs.łiltˀb ʔə tiʔəʔ wiẃsu   LA.
        Roasted fishtail is what the youngsters gave me.

        bəǩʷásˀbəxʷ ʔə tiʔił dəču?   LA.
        They roasted another one.

lexical

ʔuk̓ʷásačiʔ čəd	I burned my hand.	LG.
ʔuk̓ʷásači(ʔ)b čəd		LG.
I (intentionally) burned my hand.		
ʔuk̓ʷásláx̌əd čəd	I got burned on the arm.	EK.
ʔuk̓ʷásšəd čəd	I got burned on the foot.	DM.
ʔəs.čál kʷ(i) adəx̌ʷk̓ʷasus		DM.
How did you burn your face?		
Rejected: *ʔəs.čál kʷ(i) adəx̌ʷəx̌ʷk̓ʷàsus		DM.

1. k̓ʷásəd   stomach, tripe

   See under ƛač.

2. k̓ʷátʔad   mouse

   k̓ʷák̓ʷtʔad   tiny mouse

3. k̓ʷátʔaq   large cattail mat for house walls   EK., LL.

   mats used for making portable
   summer houses   JC.

   "This is also the name for a big
    skate fish."   JC.

   Cf. súlič 'mat for making walls'   LG.

   See under ƛakʷ.

4. k̓ʷə́č   wild

   Cf. q̓ʷal   tame

   k̓ʷčíldiʔ   rabbit (lit. 'wild ears')   EK.

   k̓ʷəčdíʔ   rabbit   LL.

   k̓ʷə́čidiʔ ~ k̓ʷčáydiʔ   rabbit   LG.

   k̓ʷə́čdiʔ SPS   rabbit   ESi.

1. k̓ʷəč̓-

    See under č̓al(a).

    -txʷ

    ʔuk̓ʷəč̓túb ʔə ti s.wawàʔ ci kʷàgʷičəd   VH.
    The cougar tracked the elk.

2. k̓ʷədád   forecast the weather   LL., LG.

3. k̓ʷə́dč̓   suspicious

    ʔəsk̓ʷə́dč̓əd čəd   I'm suspicious of him.
    ʔəsk̓ʷə́dč̓əc   He's suspicious of me.

4. k̓ʷədiid   praise someone, thank someone   JC.

    Cf. č̓iɬ(i)

→
5. k̓ʷəlúʔ ~ k̓ʷál-   skin, hide
    k̓ʷəlúqid   scalp
    k̓ʷáltəd   fish skin

6. k̓ʷəl-   affinal relationship

    Cf. s.x̌ax̌aʔ, k̓ʷiɬiwʔ

    Contrast s.yayaʔ.

    s.k̓ʷəlwás   in-law relationship   LG., LL.

        Compare:

        s.č̓ístxʷ   x̌ə́ɬtəd   s.x̌áx̌aʔ

        čəgʷás   čəbás   cixʷ-

    k̓ʷəlwástad   in-laws to one another   LG.

        k̓ʷəlwástad ʔə tə plìləʔàc   MC., LG.
    birch tree (lit. 'in-laws with the wild cherry')

1. k̓ʷəɬ   spill, pour

    -t

        ʔuk̓ʷə́ɬəd   pour it, emptied it   LL.

        k̓ʷə́ɬtəb   got poured out   LL.

    -dxʷ

        ʔuk̓ʷəɬdúb   It was spilled.   LL.

    -txʷ

        ʔəsk̓ʷəɬtúb ʔal tə x̌əlìdup   EK.
        It was emptied on to the floor.

    -yi-

        ʔuk̓ʷɬyíc   Someone poured it for me.   LG.

        ʔuk̓ʷɬyítəb   poured for someone   LL.

    lexical

        ʔuk̓ʷɬíč čəd   poured on me   EK.

        ʔuk̓ʷɬíčtəb čəd   poured on me   EK.

        ʔuk̓ʷɬíčəd čəd   I poured it on him.   EK.

    reduplication

        dáyʔəxʷ jəɬ hìgʷəxʷ ʔuk̓ʷəɬk̓ʷɬátəb ti tud.qʷù?   LL.
        Gee! They must have poured out all my water.

    rejected:

        *k̓ʷəɬbítəb, *ʔuk̓ʷəɬtúb   LL.

2. k̓ʷ(ə)ɬ   modal particle   'quotative, so they say,
                                        it is said'

    See under jəɬ.

    Cf. kʷaʔ

ʔu.húdhud k̓ʷəɬ

It's said that something caught fire.

ʔu.ʔúx̌ʷtubəxʷ k̓ʷəɬ dxʷʔal kʷədiʔ ʔu.x̌àƛil   LL.

It's reported that he's been sent to the war.

dìɬ k̓ʷəɬ dəxʷ.šə́xʷšəxʷs (h)əlgʷə?   LG.

They say that that's made them swell up.

ɬíxʷixʷ k̓ʷəɬ ʔu.xʷíʔil ʔal ti dəčagʷtxʷ   LG.

They say three people died in that house.

1.   k̓ʷəƛ-   miss

        -c

        k̓ʷə́ƛc   missed it (a target)

        lexical

            ʔuk̓ʷəƛgʷásil   (We were going to meet but) we missed each
                                        other.

            ʔuk̓ʷəƛgʷasʔbid čəd   I missed him (although I intended
                                        to meet him.)

2.   k̓ʷəq   fall/lie on back

        See under xʷítil.

        Cf. t̓álx̌, k̓ʷálč

            ʔuk̓ʷə́q   He fell on his back.

            ʔəsk̓ʷə́q kʷ(i) ads.ɬàq̓agʷil   Lie on your back.   LG.

3.   s.k̓ʷəqíq   robin (So named because it tilts its head back
                                        while singing. See 256.2)

4.   s.k̓ʷ(ə)qʷə́b   NPS   axe   DM., LG., HD,

        Cf. qəbə́təd   SPS   axe   EK., ES.

            sk̓ʷík̓ʷqʷəb   hatchet

1. (s)k̓ʷə́spɬ   trout (generic)   LL., ESi.

                          This term excludes steelhead, q̓íw̓x̌,
                          which are classed as s.ʔuládxʷ.

      Cf. čk̓ʷác/ p̓sáč   Dolly Varden trout

        s.tə́čəb   chub

2.   k̓ʷíčadiʔ   sunset

3.   k̓ʷíčicut   stutter   EK. (not recognized by LL.)

      See also ʔə́čʔəč 'stutter, stammer'

      See under cut.

4.   k̓ʷíč(i)   Snoh.   butcher an animal, clean a chicken or fish,
                        operate on someone

      See under ɬič(i).

      Cf. q̓ʷə́x̌ʷəd

      -it

        k̓ʷíčid   butcher it   EK.

        ʔuk̓ʷíčitᵊb   abdominal operation   LL.

      lexical

        ʔuk̓ʷíčšaditᵊb   They opened up his leg.   LL.

           Compare: ʔu.ɬíčšaditᵊb   His leg got cut.

                   ʔu.pəq̓ʷšaditᵊb   His leg got cut off.

5.   k̓ʷíd   how many?, a number of

      Compare ʔəx̌id, čad, čal, tab, gʷat, gət, ʔidigʷət.

      root

        k̓ʷíd čələp   How many of you?   LG.

ƛ̌ʷíd kʷ(i) ads.ʔulàdxʷ   LG.

How many salmon do you have?

(sáliàči? ti?ił s.ʔulàdxʷ ?i kʷi cəlac   LG.

There are twenty-five salmon.)

ƛ̌ʷíd kʷ(i) ad.pù?təd   DM.

How many shirts do you have?

(sali? ti d.pu?təd   DM.

I have two shirts.)

ƛ̌ʷídəxʷ kʷ(i) adstiq.tiqìw   DM.

How many horses do you have?

1. ?əs.báliic čəd ?ə kʷi ƛ̌ʷíd kʷi dstiq.tiqìw   DM.
2. ?əs.báliic čəd ?ə kʷi ƛ̌ʷíd dᵊstiq.tiqìw   DM.

1. and 2. I forgot how many horses (I have).

xʷì? gʷədsəs.láx̌ᵊdxʷ gʷəƛ̌ʷidəs kʷi dᵊstiq.tiqìw

I don't remember how many horses I have.

ƛ̌ʷidəxʷ kʷ(i) ad.yíq̌us   DM.

How many baskets do you have?

?aləxʷ ƛ̌ʷíd   What time is it?   EK.

    ?aləxʷ ƛ̌ʷíd kʷi gʷəds.?ə̀ƛ   EK.
    What time should I come?

?aləxʷ sƛ̌ʷíd   What time is it?   LG.

?əs.(h)áydxʷ čəxʷ ?u ?al(əxʷ) sƛ̌ʷids kʷi s.?ùx̌ʷs   LG.

Do you know what time he went?

?al sƛ̌ʷids kʷi ł(u)ads.ƛ̌ax̌ʷuyubal?txʷ   LG.

When will you go to the store?

    pə(d).táb is given as equivalent to ?al sƛ̌ʷids
    in this instance.

?áləxʷ sƛ̌ʷìd(s) t(ə) ad.wàč   LG.

What time is it (by your watch)?

lexical

k̓ʷidalps   (stress?)   How many animals?   DM.

k̓ʷidál?txʷ   How many houses?   LG.

tùx̌ʷəxʷ k̓ʷídəlàdxʷəxʷ...   Just a few years...   HD., ES.

k̓ʷidəládxʷ(əxʷ) ti?ił s.tubš   LG.
How old is that man?

(sáliàči? ti?ił ?i kʷi dəču̓?   He is twenty-one.
  sáliàči?əxʷ čəd ?i kʷi dəču̓?   I'm twenty-one.)

k̓ʷídəłdàtiləxʷ   What is the date?   LG.

k̓ʷídəłdàtiləxʷ čəł   In what date are we?   EK.

x̌ʷùl k̓ʷídəłdàt   in just a few days   EK.

k̓ʷídəłtàł   How many fathoms?   LG.

k̓ʷídgʷił ?al ti s.tuləkʷ   LG.
How many canoes are on the river?

k̓ʷídgʷił kʷ(i) ads.gʷa? ad.q̓ilbid   LG.
How many canoes do you have/own?

k̓ʷidílc kʷ(i) ad.talə   DM.
How many dollars do you have?

(təqači?ílc ?i ti?ił ?ił.čə́x̌ ti d.tàlə   DM.
  I have eight dollars and fifty cents.)

     Cf. ?əs.?əx̌íd kʷi s.qa ?ə kʷ(i) ad.talə   DM.
       Do you have a lot of money?

k̓ʷidúlč kʷ(i) ads.gʷa? ad.yiq̓us   LG.
How many (cedar root) baskets do you have?

?al k̓ʷídwàč   At what hour?   ES.

reduplication

k̓ʷídid kʷi ?ùx̌ʷ   How many of them went?   LG.

k̓ʷídid kʷ(i) adcixʷs.yàya?   EK.

How many in-laws do you have?

k̓ʷídid kʷi diʔà?   DM.

How many people are here?

xʷíʔ gʷədsəs.(h)áydxʷ gʷək̓ʷìdidəs kʷi diʔà?   DM.

I don't know how many people are here.

x̌əč̓əd k̓ʷídid kʷi diʔà?   DM.

Count them (here).

rejected:

   *k̓ʷídalbixʷ   ("Instead of this, say k̓ʷidid.")

   *k̓ʷidalps kʷ(i) adstiq.tiqíw   (DM.)

1.   k̓ʷidá   lucky

   Compare kʷxʷád under (kʷaxʷ(a)).

   k̓ʷidá ʔə kʷi dəxʷ.xʷiʔ lə.bàkʷɫ ʔə *Thom*

   It's lucky that Thom didn't get hurt.

2. s.k̓ʷík̓ʷaač̓   tule (a swamp grass with tough, round blades)

3. s.k̓ʷík̓ʷəlč̓   eiderdown

   Cf. s.t̓úʔq̓ʷ, č̓íč̓al

4.   k̓ʷíl(i)   peek, peer, look from behind something, peek
                          around something, peek over the shoulder (that is,
                          have to turn head around)

   See under šuɫ.

   Cf. q̓is(i)

   root

      ʔuk̓ʷíl čəd   I peeked.   LL., ES.

dádatu tiʔił sk̓ʷî1 ʔə tiʔił bìbščəb dxʷ.t̓àq̓txʷ   ES.

Early in the morning Little Mink peered up
into the woods.

-it

ʔuk̓ʷîlid čəd   I peeked at it.   LL., EK.

tux̌ʷ čəł ʔuk̓ʷilid tiʔił CB.   DM.

We just looked in on CB. (to see that he was all right,
but we didn't stay to visit).

lexical

ʔəxʷk̓ʷîlusc   ES.

It's staring me in the face. (This is said when
the left arm (upper, inside) twitches. It means
that bad news concerning the family is soon to come.)

łu.diʔəʔ čəł ł(u)axʷk̓ʷilustagʷəl   LL.

We'll be here looking into each other's faces.

reduplication

ʔuk̓ʷîlil čəd   I peered about.   LL.

1.   k̓ʷiłíw̓   go to live with in-laws

     Cf. k̓ʷəl-

2.   k̓ʷît   go down to a body of water, to the water's edge
                    and no further.

     Contrast čaʔkʷ.

root

     łuk̓ʷît čəd   EK.
     I'm going to go down to the water.

     ʔuk̓ʷîtəxʷ dxʷʔal s.tùləkʷ   LG.
     I went down to the river.

dxʷ.čád kʷi gʷ(ə)adsk̓ʷít dxʷʔal kʷi s.tùləkʷ   EK.

Which way will you go down to the river?

ʔu: xʷuʔᵊlə ƛúbəxʷ xʷuʔᵊlə gʷək̓ʷít čəd, čədà

gʷədxʷ.čágʷusᵊb   LG.

Well, I'd better go down and wash my face.

-txʷ-yi-

ʔuk̓ʷít(t)xʷyid čəd (h)əlgʷə? ʔə tə ƛəlày?   EK.

I took the shovel-nose canoe down to the river
for them.

lexical

ʔəsk̓ʷítəlgʷiɬ   be down on the shore   ML.

1.   k̓ʷiʔát   cleansed, pure, taboo

     Cf. x̌aʔx̌aʔ

     ... čəda ləs.tígʷid k̓ʷiʔat s.ptídəgʷəsᵊb ...   EC.
     ... and I thank (Thee for Thy) pure thoughts ...

     -t

     ʔəsk̓ʷiʔátcut   prohibited, taboo   LG.

2.   k̓ʷtílšəd   a rattle made of deer hooves   LA.

3.   s.k̓ʷúbič   dorsal fin

4. ʔəs.k̓ʷúluʔ   hollow   EK.

     lexical

     ʔəxʷk̓ʷulúʔ(igʷəd)   It's hollow inside.   LG.

     ʔudxʷk̓ʷulúʔ(igʷəd)   hollow inside   LG.

     reduplication

     k̓ʷúʔk̓ʷuluʔ   name for site now called Skagit Point
                   (on Whidbey Island)   LL.

1. ƛ̓ʷúxʷdiʔ SPS littleneck/steamer clam ESi.

    See under s.ʔáx̌ʷuʔ.

    Cf. s.x̌áʔaʔ NPS littleneck/steamer clam

2. s.k̓ʷúy mother

    See under bədáʔ.

    See under tad.

    k̓ʷúyə(ʔ)   endearing way of addressing mother   HD., LG.

    s.k̓ʷúyəʔ   term of endearment fo a girl   LG.

      s.k̓ʷúk̓ʷiyəʔ   term of endearment for a little girl   LG.

    s.gʷúgiyəʔ   pet name of a little girl   LG.

    s.k̓ʷúk̓ʷi   term of endearment for a little girl   EK.

    húk̓ʷuy   term of endearment for a little girl   LL.

    xʷíʔ sk̓ʷù   No, Madame   ESi.

    sk̓ʷúyaɬ   name of ES.'s grandmother (lit. 'Little Mother')

    ciɬ bəsk̓ʷuy   half sibling with mother in common

3. k̓ʷyácut cackle

    ʔu.ʔəx̌íd tiʔiɬ sàʔsaʔ pàstəd ʔuk̓ʷyàcut x̌əɬ ti k̓àʔkaʔ ES.
    What are you bad white people cackling like crows for?

4. k̓ʷyə́xʷ SPS belly ESi.

    See under ƛač.

    Cf. k̓túʔ (Skagit) LG.

l

The sound represented by this letter is much like the English *l* in such words as *loud* and *real*. [lateral alveolar resonant]

1. láb   whisky (from English *rum*)   EK.

    xʷlábəli   bottle   LG.

    ləbálqʷuʔ   Alcohol Creek (The third creek going west
                             from Marysville onto Tulalip Reservation --
                             hardly more than a drainage.)   ES.

    làbálʔtxʷ   tavern

2. lab   SPS   see

    Cf. šuɫ   NPS

    -t

    ʔəslabᵊd s.tab ti dsu.x̌ix̌ədbid   Watch what I am doing.   JC.

    lábc   Look at me.

    lábtubuɫ   Look at us.

    ʔulábtᵊb čəd ʔə ti s.tubš   The man saw me.

    ʔəslábcəbut čəlab   You all look after yourselves. ESi.

    -dxʷ

    ʔəslábdxʷ čəxʷ ʔu tə qà ʔaciɫtalbixʷ   ESi.
    Can you see all the Indians?

    ʔulábᵊdxʷ čəd tə s.tùbš   I saw the man.   JC.

    ʔulábdubš tə s.čətxʷəd   The bear saw me.   JC.

    cay čəd ʔəs.hiiɫbid tə dslabdubicid   JC.
    I'm very happy to see you.

    derivation

    xʷlálbuɫəd   window   JC.

    hiiláʔ tə s.qʷəbàyʔ   Look at the dog.   ESi.

1.   labatú   sheep   (from French *le mouton*)

2.   -ladxʷ   lexical suffix   'year'

       kʷidᵊládxʷəxʷ tiʔił s.tubš   How old is that man?

       tùx̌ʷəxʷ kʷìdᵊládxʷ   Just a few years.   ES.

       dùkʷᵊládxʷ   next year   ES.

       dəčùʔládxʷ   one year   EK.

       The word for salmon. s.ʔuládxʷ, probably also contains
       this component.

3. s.lágʷac SPS   inner bark (next to sap - used a lot in making
                            baskets)   ESi.

     Cf. s.łwáyʔ   NPS

→

5.   laq   last, behind

     See under jixʷ.

     Cf. qad(a) 'back up'

     root

        ʔal ti láq   last

        ʔu.yáyus čəd ʔal ti làq s.łukʷàlb   EK.
        I worked last month.

     -bi-t

        ʔal tiʔił adləqbíd   He is behind you.   LL.

          Cf. ad.qádbid   He is behind you.   LG.

     lił-

        lìłláq   behind, last in a row of people   EK.

        lə.jáɋ lìłləqbìd ʔə tiʔəʔ diʔəʔ dxʷʔal gʷə.bəčᵊds   EC.
        They were running down (falling) behind it to the bottom.

díɫəxʷ yəwáɫ liɫlaq   ML.

She was the very last (to get there).

liɫláq gʷ(ə)ads.ʔə̀ƛ   DM.

You can come afterwards.

lexical

ləqábac ʔə tiʔiɫ s.x̌əy̓ùs   back of the head

-il

ʔəsláqil   late

ləsláqil čəxʷ   You are late.   EK.

xʷíʔ kʷ(i) adsláqil   Don't be late.   EK.

reduplication

ʔuláʔlqil čəxʷ   You're a little late.   LL.

in compositions

ʔílaq   stern, back end   EK.

1.   lax̌   remember

See under hay(a).

root

ʔuláǧ   She remembered.

ʔəslax̌   remember   LG.

-c

láx̌c   thinking of it   LG.

ʔəsláǧc čəd s.k̓ʷùy   I'm thinking of mother.   LG.

ʔəsláǧc čəd   I think of things.   EC., EK.

xʷíʔəxʷ kʷi gʷədsəsláǧc   EK.

I don't remember things.

xʷíʔəxʷ kʷi ʔá· gʷəbəs.tàb gʷ(ə)asláǧc čəd   EC.

Not anything else do I think of.

-dx^w

g^wəl <u>láx̌^ə</u>dx^wəx^w tiʔił sùq̓^w.suq̓^waʔ   ES.
And he remembered his younger brothers.

tu.p̓aacut čəd dx^wʔal g^wəds<u>láx̌^ə</u>dx^w   EK.
I was trying to remember it.

ʔəs<u>láx̌</u>dubš čəx^w   You remember me.   LG., EK.

ʔəs.x̌əc čəd g^wə<u>làx̌</u>dubšəs   LL.
I'm afraid he might remember me.

   Cf. ʔəs.x̌əc čəd g^wə<u>làx̌^ə</u>bicəs   LL.
      I'm afraid he might remember the trouble
      he had with me.

ʔəs<u>làx̌</u>dub ʔə k^wi ds.càpa   LG.
My grandfather remembers it.

t(u)as<u>láx̌</u>dub ʔə k^wi ds.càpaʔ tiʔił d^əs.yàyəʔ   LG.
My grandfather remembered my friend.

ʔəs<u>láx̌</u>dub ʔə k^wi ds.càpaʔ k^wi s.dàʔ ʔə tə ds.yàya?   LG.
My grandfather remembers the name of my friend.

-tx^w

ʔəs<u>láx̌</u>tubš čəx^w   Remind me.   LG.

-bi-t

ʔəs.x̌əc čəd g^wə<u>làx̌^ə</u>bicəs   LL.
I'm afraid he might remember the trouble he had with me.

   Cf. ʔəs.x̌əc čəd g^wə<u>làx̌</u>dubšəs   LL.
      I'm afraid he might remember me.

reduplication

ləláḷx̌   reminiscing   ML.

łuləláḷx̌ čəd   I'm going to memorize.   LG.

haʔł sləláḷx̌   a good recounting of the past   LG.

ʔalčuləɫálx̌ čəd   I've been reminiscing.   LG.

tùx̌ʷ čəd ɫuləɫálx̌ ʔə tiʔiɫ tusəs.hùy   ML.

I'm only going to reminisce about how it was.

lələɫálx̌   a group reminisces

ʔalčuləләɫálx̌ čəɫ   LG.
We (a group of us) have been remembering things
away back.

   rejected: *láx̌ad   LG.

1.   láʔ   point out, locate

   -t

    láʔəd gʷə.čàdəs   Show (me) where it is.   LG.

    láʔcut   introduce self   LG.

    láʔcutbid   Same gloss: introduce self to someone   LG.

   -yi-

    tuláʔyitəbəxʷ ʔə tiʔiɫ sq̓ʷi.q̓ʷəlaɫəd   ES.
    Small berries had been set out for him.

    láʔyid   Show him where it is.   LG.

   -txʷ

    ʔəsláʔtxʷ čəxʷ ʔu   LG.
    Do you know where it is?

    ʔəsláʔtxʷ čəd   I know where it is.   LG.

2.   laʔb   See həlaʔb.

3.   lə- ~ -ə-   aspectual prefix 'progressive'
      An action or state begun is continuing through
      space.

   Cf. ləcu-

1. dxʷ.ləbəyʔ(úcid)   Lummi (language)

2.   ləcu-   aspectual prefix 'continuative'
   An action or state begun is continuing
   through time.

   Contrast with lə-.

   Instead of ləcu-, LG. gives ʔalču-.
   Snohomish and the Southern Puget dialects
   lack this morpheme. lə- covers the semantic
   range of both the Skagit lə- and ləcu-.

3.   ləč̓   come down hard on

   See under k̓aw.

   Cf. biƛ(i)

   -t

   lə́č̓əd   Step on it!

   lə́č̓təb   get crushed, come down hard on

   ʔulə́č̓təb čəɬ   LL.
   They came over us (with the new road).

   -dxʷ

   lə̀č̓dúb čəd   inadvertently stepped on me.

   ʔəs.x̌ə́c čəd gʷəxʷìt̓.xʷit̓iləxʷ čəxʷa gʷələč̓dùbš
   I'm afraid you might fall and crush me.

   xʷì̓ʔ kʷ(i) adsxʷəlč̓áp̓ədub
   Don't step on its tail!

   xʷì̓ʔ kʷ(i) adsxʷəlč̓áp̓ədubš
   Don't step on my tail!

   reduplication

   ləč̓ləč̓át̓əb   trampled

1. ləč̓   fill/full (container)

   Cf. bəł   full (of food/drink)

   root

      ləč̓   full (container)   LG., DM.

   -il

      ləč̓íl   it's filling up   DM.

   lexical

      ləč̓áldəč   belly full, gluttony   EK.

2. lə́gʷəb   youth, young man

   reduplication

      líi̇l̓gʷəb   little fellow

      líli̇l̓gʷəb little fellows

      lə́gʷləgʷəb youths, young men

3. s.lə́gʷx̌   rib

   Cf. -ul-gʷił

4. s.ləhál   bone game /hand game

   (This s- might not be a prefix.)
   See under ʔukʷukʷ.

5. ləkəlí   key   (from French *le clef*)

   -t

      ləkəlíd tə šə̀gʷł   Lock the door.   LG.

   lexical

      ləkəlíhalì   a case for a key   LG., EK.

1. lək̓ʷ- Snoh., SPS

    See under ʔəɫ.

    Equivalent to Skagit huydxʷ.

    -t

      lák̓ʷəd   put it in mouth   LL.
                              eat it

      ʔulák̓ʷəd čəd gʷəl bə̀k̓ʷìl   EK.
      I ate it and it's all gone.

      ʔəxʷslə̀k̓ʷədxʷyítəbəb
      want to be able to eat his food (without his consent)   ML.

    lexical

      lək̓ʷúcid   kiss   EK.

      lək̓ʷúcidic čəxʷ   You kissed me.   EK.

          Cf.   Skagit   dxʷbəq̓ʷúcid   kiss him   LG.

                       bəq̓ʷúcic   kiss me   LG.

2. ləláb   oar   (from French *le ramer*)

    -txʷ

      ləlábtxʷ   row it

          Cf. x̌ʷúbt   paddle, -al-waʔs lexical for paddle

             ʔíš̌ɫ   act of paddling

3. lələʔúləb   recite the history of a people

    See under cut.

4. ləliʔ   different, change

    Perhaps derived from lil 'far'.

ləlíʔ s.wàtixʷtəd foreign country EK.

hiq̓ʷábidəxʷ ciʔił ləlì̃ʔ słə.łàdəy? ES.
He got stuck on different women.

ləliʔ tiʔə? səs.huy ?ə tiʔə? qiw̓x̌ dxʷʔal tiʔə? yubəč DM.
A steelhead is different from a king salmon.

ləliʔ tiʔə? čawəy? ?ə tiʔə? s.x̌ə́p̓ab MS.
The shell of the cockle is different.

ʔəs.ʔəx̌id kʷi sləliʔ ?ə tə x̌ʷətis dxʷʔal s.wuqʷad
How does a silver diver differ from a loon?

-t

ləlíʔcut change

lexical

ləliʔák̓ʷbixʷ foreigners

Cf. (də)čak̓ʷbixʷ

ləlíʔucid foreign language EK.

reduplication

ləllíʔcut keep changing LL.

ləʔlíʔcut keep changing ML.

1. ləlús a woman's name; the older sister of JC.

2. ləlwáʔs(əd) sleeping platform

Cf. piit

ləlwáʔsəd tə cəxʷu.təjì̃l
A sleeping platform is where I go to bed.

reduplication

slələlwáʔs tusəs.huy ʔə tiʔəʔ s.badil   EC.

This mountain was shaped like sleeping platforms.

líliłᵊwàʔsəd   name of a small mountain in Skagit county,
                   Washington   EC.

1.   ləpəskʷí   hardtack   (from French *le biscuit*)

2.   ləpyús   hoe   (from French *le pioche*)

3.   ləq   Skagit   hear

     Cf. luh   Snoh., SPS.   hear

        ƛəlábut   understand

        t(ə)qʷadiʔ   deaf

     root

        ʔəsləq čəd   I hear.   LG.

        xʷíʔ gʷəłudsləq   I won't hear.   LG.

        xʷíʔ gʷədsəsləq   I didn't hear.   LG.

        xʷíʔ gʷədsuləqs   He doesn't hear.   LG.

     -t

        léqᵊc   Hear me!   LG.
                              Listen to me.   LG.

        ʔuléqc   He heard me.   LG.

        ʔəsléqcid čəd   I heard you.   LG.

        xʷíʔ gʷədsəsləqᵊd   EK.
        I didn't hear it (because I wasn't paying attention).

        léqtᵊb čəd   He overheard me.   LG.

-c

lə́qcʼəbš	Listen to me.	LG.
lə́qacʼəbšəxʷ	Listen to me.	ML.
	(From ML.'s father's song, so	
	the vowels are probably altered.)	
NB. *ləqcʼəb čəd	rejected	LG.

-al-but

ʔəsləqálbut čəd	I understand.	
xʷiʔ gʷədsəsləqálbut	I don't understand.	LG.
Cf. ʔəsƛəlábut	understand	

-al-but-bi-t

xʷiʔ gʷədsəsləqálbutbid tə ʔaciɫtalbixʷucid   LG.
I don't understand the Indian language.

lexical

| ləqəládi(ʔ)bəxʷ | Hear now! | LG. |
| ləqəládi(ʔ)bic | Listen to me! Hear me! | LG. |

1.   ləq   See under laq.

2.   ləq̓aɫ-

Cf. cək̓ʷ(dxʷ)   have straight, understand,

    hay(dxʷ)   know, comprehend,   talx̌(cut)   do well,

    tɬíldxʷ   believe (under təɫ)

| ʔuləq̓áɫil čəd | I'm correct. | LG. |
| dáʔxʷ čəxʷ ləq̓àɫil | Now you've got it right. | LG. |

-bi-t

| ʔəsləq̓áɫilbic | You are in my way. | LG. |

1. ləqʷá   a soft, pliable basket made of s.łuáyʔ   MS.

    See under yiq̓ib.

→
3. ləš-

        ləšúcid   what is understandable   DM.

        dxʷl(ə)šúcid   Lushootseed, the Salish language
                          spoken in the vicinity of Puget Sound
                          (See Introduction, pages ii, v.)

4. ləxʷ(u)   stab, cut up

    Cf. caq̓(a)   jab, poke

        łič̓(i)   cut

    -ut

        ʔuləxʷútᵊb čəd   I got stabbed.   LG.

        ʔuləxʷútᵊb tə d.čàləs   My hand got cut.   LG.

    -dxʷ

        ʔuləxʷdúbəxʷ čəd   I got stabbed.   LG.

        ʔuləxʷdúb tə d.čàləs   My hand got cut (in a fight). LG.

    lexical

        ʔudxʷləxʷwíčc   He stabbed me in the back. LG.

    reduplication

        ʔuləxʷləxʷútᵊb čəd   I got all cut up.   LG.

        ʔuləxʷləxʷúd čəd   I cut him all up.   LG.

5. ləx̌   light

    Compare and contrast:

        ləx̌ᵊd   light it   łáčad   extinguish it

        húdud   light/burn it

ləx̌íl   day   łáx̌il   night

kʷáčil   Skag.   dawn, tomorrow

łup   morning

dat   twenty-four hour period

  dádatu   morning

  dúkʷəłdat   tomorrow/yesterday

qəq-/gʷəq-   bright, clear   q̓áƛ̓b   cloud(y)
                 weather, sunshine
                                    qʷšáb   fog

root

  ʔəsləx̌   light   LG.

-t

  léx̌ᵊd   light it   LG.

    léx̌ᵊd tə ləx̌šàd   Turn the light on.   LG.
                                Light the lamp.   LG.

      Cf. húdud tə ləx̌šàd   same glosses: Turn the light on.
                                           Light the lamp.   EK.

-yi-

  ləx̌yíd   Light it for him, give him light.   LG.

     Cf. ləx̌šádid   Give him light.   EK.

-il

  ləx̌íl   getting light   LG.

  sləx̌íl   NPS   day (as opposed to night)

  sléx̌il   SPS   day

277

háʔɬ sləx̌íl	nice day (a greeting)	LG.
làʔb háʔɬ sləx̌íl	a real nice day	LG.
pù·t háʔɬ sləx̌íl	a very nice day	ML.
ʔuləx̌íləxʷ	dawn (It is now light.)	LL.
Cf. ləgʷəqíləxʷ	dawn (It's getting light.)	LG.

-ad-b

| ləx̌ílad°b | early breakfast | EK. |

See under -a-(d)-.

lexical

ləx̌šád   lamp

púʔud tə ləx̌šàd	Blow out the lamp.	LG.
ɬáčəd tə ləx̌šàd	Turn out the light. (I.e., Extinguish the light.)	EK.
ʔu.ɬač tə ləx̌šàd	The light went out.	EK.
ʔəlčulíləx̌ləx̌šàd ʔə tə pàstəd	flashlight (lit. 'the little flashing light of the whiteman')	LG.
ləx̌šáhəd°b	Turn the light on.	EK.
ləx̌šádid	Give him light.	EK.
Cf. ləx̌yíd	Give him light, light it for him.	LG.
ʔalčuləx̌ləx̌šád°b tə x̌ʷìqʷadiʔ	lightning (lit. 'flashing thunder')	LG.

reduplication

ʔəlčulíləx̌	it flashes (slowly, dimly)	LG.
ʔəlčuláx̌ləx̌	it flashes	LG.
ləx̌ləx̌ád	light (all the candles)	LG.

1. ləx̌ʷ-   See under x̌áč.

    -ič

        ʔuləx̌ʷíjˀəd   It covered him.

    rejected: *láx̌ʷˀəd

2. s.lihíb   sandhill crane, a kind of buʔqʷ   LL.
→
3. lijúb   devil (of the Christian concept)

4. lík̓ʷil

        (Perhaps a misrecording for líq̓ʷil.)

        ʔəslík̓ʷil   the water is mirror-like, not a ripple on it,
                     i.e., good weather

                     (When the weather is described as being like
                     this near the beginning of a s.yəyəhúb, it
                     means the story will have a good ending.)

            Cf. ʔəsháʔlˀb   good weather

5. lil   far, remove to a distance

        (Perhaps ləlíʔ 'foreign, different' is derived from líl.)

        Opposite of či̓t.

        root

            ʔal kʷi túdiʔ li̓l   a way far off   ES.

            li̓l čəxʷ ʔił.qʷíq̓ʷ tuli̓ʔal ʔəca   LG.
            You are a lot stronger than I.

            li̓l čəd ʔiłs.(h)àjəp dxʷʔal dəgʷi̓   LG.
            I'm a lot taller than you.

        dxʷ-

            ʔu.ʔúx̌ʷtxʷ čəd dxʷli̓l   I took it a way off.   LL.

lədxʷlíl t(ə) ads.ʔíbəš   You are traveling far.   JC.

-t

líld   Put it out of the way.   LL.

   x̌ʷuɫ čəxʷ ʔulíld   Just put it out of the way.   LL.

lílc tuɫʔàl kʷi bə̀kʷ tucəxʷəs.hìwil   EC.
Took me away from all [the bad ways] I used to go [into].

   lílcut   remove self from a location, get away

      lílcut čəxʷa x̌ʷíl   Go away and get lost!   EK.

-il-dxʷ

   lílildxʷ   not get along too well with someone   DM.

      Cf. jíl(i)

x̌ʷiʔ ləlíl   almost (lit. 'not far')

x̌ʷì?əxʷ ləlíl gʷəl ʔàl s.yəllʔàcs   LG.
Pretty soon it will be six o'clock.

x̌ʷìʔ ləlíl gʷə.diɫgʷasəs   EK.
They are almost alike.

x̌ʷiʔ ləlíl čəda bàliic ʔə gʷəds.ʔàbyicid ʔə tə tàlə   EK.
I almost forgot to give you the money.

x̌ʷiʔ ləlíl čəda bàliic sixʷ t(ə) ad.tàlə   HD.
I almost forgot your money again.

lexical

   dxʷlílap   Tulalip Bay   'distant bottom'   EK.

   lilÁyucid   stubborn, mean   Ek.

      Cf. x̌ák̓ʷ

x̌ʷùɫ čəxʷ ʔəxʷlílígʷədbid   Don't pay any attention to it. LG.

      Cf. ƛ̓al(d)

reduplication

ʔulíllilt^əb	They were separated (from the rest of the group). EK.

other derivatives

ʔulílaɬ   The daughter's parents take her away from her husband because he treats her badly.   LL.

1.   lilud   train (from English *railroad*)

2.   liɬ-   by what route, by what means, located where

Cf. dxʷ₂- 'toward', tuĺ- 'from'

ʔuliɬčad čəxʷ	Which way did you go?	LG.
tuliɬčad čəxʷ	Which way did you come?	LG.
ɬuliɬčad čəxʷ	Which way will you go?	LG.
liɬšə́q	up high (free in the air)	LG.
Cf. dxʷšə́q	high (from ground up)	LG.

ƛu.sáq̓ʷ (ʔal ti) liɬšə́q   LG.
It habitually flies high.

x̌ʷùɬ (h)əlgʷəʔ liɬčáʔkʷ ʔal tə x̌ʷəlč ʔal ti tu.hàkʷ
They were way out at sea long ago.

lə.ʔíbəš liɬʔílgʷiɬ ʔə tiʔəʔ x̌ʷəlč, bəliɬtáq̓t,
gʷəl bəliɬčáʔkʷ   ML.
He was walking right down along the shore of the Sound, and again up along the bluff (or up in the trees), and again down by the water. (I.e., depending on the tide)

huy gʷəl, ʔúx̌ʷ dxʷ.taq̓t, liɬtaq̓t   ML.
And then he went up, along the edge (of the bluff).

liɬʔílgʷiɬ   shoreline, very edge of the water

liɬjixʷ   (They) were first.   LL.

hiwil čəd liɬjìxʷ   I'm going ahead first.   EK.

haʔɬ kʷi gʷəs.huyutᵊbs liɬjixʷ haʔɬ t(i) ads.gʷaʔ
ʔə tə s.daʔ   HD.
Sanctificetur nomen tuum.

lìɬláq   behind, last in a row of people   EK.

díɬəxʷ yəwáɬ liɬlaq   She was the very last.   ML.

ləjáq̓ liɬləqbìd ʔə tiʔəʔ diʔəʔ dxʷʔal gʷəs.bəčəds   EM.
They were running down (falling) behind it to the
bottom.

liɬšə́jt adsəs.gʷədil   You're sitting in the bow.   LG.

liɬʔúdəgʷič   in the middle   EK.

liɬʔúdəgʷiɬ   Someone is in the middle of the canoe. LG.

   liɬʔudəgʷiɬ čəxʷ   You sit in the middle of the canoe. LG.

liɬʔílaq   Someone is in the stern.   LG.

liɬʔal

   ləs.q̓il čəd liɬʔal ti lìlud   LG.
   I came by means of the train.

   Cf. ləs.q̓íl čəd ʔal ti lìlud   EK.
       I'm riding on the train.

ɬu.túlil liɬʔal x̌ʷə̀lč dxʷʔal Alàska   EK.
She is going to Alaska by sea.

ləs.t̓ágʷt čəd liɬʔàl tə s.tiqìw   LG.
I'm riding the horse.

ʔu.cɬíl liɬʔal tə qədxʷs   EK.
bleed through his mouth

... yəx̌i čəxʷ huy ləs.kʷaxʷac <u>liɬʔal</u> ti?iɬ ha?ɬ

ads.gʷa? ads.ptídəgʷəsᵊb   EC.

... because you are helping me through Thine
own good thoughts.

?u.q̓ʷə́lq̓ʷəl čəd <u>liɬʔal</u> ti ds.ɬičid tə s.qʷîqʷali   EK.

I've been sweating ever since I cut that hay.

... čəda ləs.tígʷid k̓ʷi?at s.ptídəgʷəsəb <u>liɬʔal</u>

kʷi dsəs.hiiɬ <u>liɬʔal</u> kʷi ?əs.hiwil ?əs.?ušəbítubuɬ   EC.

... and I (give) thanks (for Thy) pure thoughts
because I am glad for (Thy) great kindness.   EK.

1.   liq̓(i)   red

Cf. čəc, kʷiƛ̓, təbɬ

-it

<u>líq̓icut</u>   paint self red   LL.

-təd

<u>líq̓təd</u>   red paint   LL.

lexical

dxʷ<u>liq̓u</u>səxʷ   He painted his face (red).   ML.

2.   líqʷil

(Probably a misrecording for lík̓ʷil, *q.v.*)

3.   lí?ɬ*   lullaby

<u>?ulí?ɬ</u>   sang a lullaby. (Actually, it is not a song
but rather a soothing sound made by trilling
the tongue against the upper lip while keeping
the lips rounded.)

4.   luh   Snoh., SPS   hear

Cf. ləq Skagit   hear

---

* This form is misanalyzed. The root is ?ul (Cf. ?il(i) (671.1) and -i?ɬ
'baby' is a lexical suffix (209.4.)

Cf. ƛ̓əlábut   understand

   t(ə)q^wadi?   deaf

-t

ʔəslúud čəd	I hear it.	LL.
ʔəsluucid čəd	I hear you.	JC.
ʔuluudəx^w ti?iɫ lùƛ ləcu.ṕáyəq		ES.
He heard an old man hewing out a canoe.		
lúudəx^w ti?iɫ hə̀dli	Listen to Henry.	LL.
ʔulúuc	He heard me.	LL.
ʔulúut^əb čəd	He overheard me.	LL., ES.
	He heard me (and I didn't want him to).	LL.
tulúut^əbəx^w ?ə ci?iɫ s.ɫaɫdəy?s		ES.
His girl heard (about his escapades).		

-dx^w

ʔulúdx^w čəd	LL.
I heard about it (in a roundabout way).	
ʔulúdubicid čəd k^w(i) adsu.huyəx^w	LL.
I heard about what you are doing.	
ʔulúdub ?ə hə̀dli	LL.
Henry heard about it (and it's vital news).	

-c

lúucəx^w	Listen!	LL.
lúuc^əbš	Listen to me!	LL.

    This is equivalent to Skagit ləq^əc^əbšəx^w according to   LL.

lexical

ʔəsluhəládi?əx^w (h)əlg^wə?	They heard it.	LG.

X̌əllá čələpa ɫuluhəlàdiʔ   LG.

(There will be) awhile and (then) you all will hear it.

1.   lúk̓ʷ   Snoh.   dip net   LL.

    See under ƛ̓áʔtəd.

    Cf. qʷúləč   dip net   LG.

→

3.   luƛ̓   old

    Cf. s.qəlíbut   old and infirm

    root

       lúƛ̓ čəd   I'm old.

       ʔu.čə́ɫ čəd x̌ʷùbt tuɫʔal tə luƛ̓ s.x̌əlà̓ʔs   LG.
       I made a paddle out of an old board.

       ƛ̓àl čəd bəlúƛ̓ x̌ʷuƛ̓àb ʔə dəgʷì   LG.
       I am just as old as you.

       lúƛ̓ čəxʷ x̌ʷuƛ̓àb ʔə ti ds.qà   LG.
       You are as old as my older brother.

       xʷíʔ čəd lə.x̌ʷuƛ̓àb ʔə dəgʷì kʷi gʷədsluƛ̀̓   LG.
       I'm not as old as you are.

       ʔiɫlúƛ̓   He's the oldest.   LG.
                      older   EK.

    -il

       ɫuləlúƛ̓il čəxʷ   as you get older   ES.

       ... s.cápaʔ tucəxʷlùƛ̓il   ES.
       ... grandfather reared me.

    -i(l)-s

       ʔulúƛ̓is   LL.
       He grew up to do something (e.g., avenge his family
       for what befell them when he was young).

-il-t

    ʔulúƛild čəd tiʔəʔ səxʷ.gʷədìl   LG.

    I antiqued the chair.

-ᵊb

    lùƛᵊbəxʷ čəd   I'm getting old.   ES.

    xʷìʔ gʷədsəslùƛᵊb   I'm not very old.   EK.

    xʷìʔ kʷi gʷədsəlùƛᵊb   I'm not getting older.   EK.

    ƛàl čəxʷ ɬubəlúƛᵊb x̌ʷuɬàb ʔə ʔəcà   LG.

    You too are going to get old like me.

lexical

    sluƛálqsačiʔ   thumb   LG.

reduplication

    lùƛluƛ   ancestors

      tudəxʷəs.ɬáɬlil ʔə tiʔiɬ tusluƛ.luƛčəɬ   ES.

      There lived our ancestors.

      cútᵊb(id) ʔə ti lùƛluƛ   EK.

      The old people (used to) say it.

    rejected: *ʔəsluƛ čəd

1.   lúpačiʔ   gloves   LL., LG.

    lúplupàčiʔ   several pairs of gloves, mittens

      Cf. s.yay̓lúpqsačiʔ   ring for finger   LG.

2.   lúxʷus   pry bark off

3.   luʔ(u)   hole in the ground; a hole in something but not through it

    Cf. ƚuʔ   hole in cloth, a hole through something

      k̓ʷúluʔ   hollow

root

ʔəslúʔ	hole in the ground, a cave
ʔəslúʔ ʔal tə s.bàdil	a cave in the mountain EK.

-ut

ʔulúʔud čəd	I bored a hole.
wàyəxʷ gʷəl lúʔucut	And finally they spawn (lit. 'make holes for themselves'). LG.

reduplication

ʔəslíʔluʔ	a little hole in the ground

ł

The sound represented by this letter is quite different from any heard in English. It is an *l* sound made without moving the vocal cords and resembles a lateral lisp. [voiceless lateral alveolar fricative]

1. łábac   seaweed (common green)

2. łač̣(a)   extinguish

    See under ləx̌.

    root

        ʔułáč tə ləx̌šàd   The light went out.   EK.

    -al

        łáčad tə ləx̌šàd   Put the light out.   EK.

        łáčəd tə hùd   Put out the fire.   LG.

        łáčət°b   They put it out.   LL.
                            They turned the electricity off.   LL.
                            Mechanical failure.   LL.

    -dx^w

        łáčdub   They got it out before it
                            did much damage.   LL.

    lexical

        ʔułáčalik^w čəd   I fought a forest fire.   EK.

        dx^wsłáčalik^w   fire department; fire extinguisher   EK.

3. łáda-   some member of one's family is sick   LL.

    See under x̌əł.

        ʔułádad čəd   Someone (not me) in my family got sick. LL.

4. s.łádəy?   woman

    słəłádəy?   women

    słáł(ə)dəy?   girl, little woman

sɫáaɫədəy?	girls, little women
sɫádadəy?	woman (living) alone

1. ɫagʷ-

kinds of mats:

ƛ̓úbuɫ, kʷú?t, k̓ʷátaq, s.qəq̓ʷús, súlič

ləlwá?s   sleeping platform

sɫágʷid	pallet	LL.
	mat, mattress	LG.
sɫágʷidac	sheet (for a bed)	EK.

lexical

ɫágʷič̓a(?)bəxʷ	Take your clothes off.	LG.
?uɫágʷič̓a(?)b	took clothes off	LL.

Compare xʷəc 'take off'.

Contrast ƛ̓al- 'encase, put on'.

2. ɫák̓   give food (?)

Cf. ɫíl

3. ɫál   take off/out of the fire

Cf. ?alq̓ʷ   away from center, away from fire

-š ~ -t-

ɫálš   Take it off the fire.

ɫálšəxʷ ti ds.qʷàlc   Take my boiling off the stove.   LL.

ɫálatᵊb   taken out of the fire

(earlier given as ɫáltᵊb)

1.   łal(a)   (Perhaps etymologically related to łəl, 297.1)

    -at

        łálad   park (a car)   VH.

    -il

        łálil   go ashore, land a boat/canoe, dock/moor a boat;
                        reach the end of a row in commercial harvesting

    -i(1)-s

        łális   go ashore after something, e.g., for game   LL.

    lexical

        łáladali   parking lot   VH.

2. łálə   Snoh.   raspberry   EK.

    Cf. q̓ʷələstáb(ac)   Skagit   LG.

3. łáləp̓   tongue

4. łáłlil   dwell

    -i(1)-s

        łáłlis is glossed the same as łáłlil by LL.

        čád kʷ(i) adsəsłáłlil   Where do you live?   EK., DM.

        ƛ̓t(u)asłáłlil čəd ʔal (s)ǰiǰəláˀlič gʷəl ʔáləxʷ čəd jəłíg̓ʷəd EK.
        I used to live in Seattle, but now I'm in Everett.

5. łápqs   ladle, spoon

6. łaq   Skagit   spin   LG.

    Cf. taš Snoh.   spin

    Cf. júlaq̓   old-fashioned hand spinning wheel   MC.
        səxʷłáq   spinning wheel   LG.
        łáqtəd   leg spindle   LG.
        səxʷułáq   what one spins with   LG.

1. ɬáqəʔ Skagit   thimbleberry, a s.q̓ʷəlaɬᵊd   LG., MC.

   s.ɬəɬáq EK., ɬaq DM.

2. ɬáq̓(a) Skagit   lie, set, or fall from standing position

   Cf. bəč(a)

   root

     ʔuɬáq̓ čəɬ   We fell down.   LG.

     ʔuɬáq̓ tiʔiɬ   He fell down.   LG.

   -at ~ -aš

     ʔuɬáq̓ad tiʔiɬ   He put it down.   LG.

     ʔuɬáq̓aš tiʔiɬ   same gloss: He put it down.

         * ɬáq̓acut "This would mean 'lay yourself down'
                     but we don't use it."   LG.

          See ɬáq̓agʷil.

   -txʷ

     ʔəsɬáq̓txʷ tiʔiɬ   He has it laid down.
                     He laid it down already.   LG.
                     He took her to bed.   VH.
     *ʔuɬáq̓txʷ rejected LG.

   -yi-

     tləsɬáq̓yitᵊb čəɬ ʔə kʷi s.ʔulàdxʷ   EC.
     He put down (gave) salmon for us.

     qa· bək̓ʷ stab ʔal ti s.wàtixʷtəd ti səsɬáq̓yitᵊbs
     (h)əlgʷəʔ ʔə kʷi x̌àʔx̌aʔ šᵊq siʔab bads (h)əlgʷəʔ   EC.
     A lot of all things were set down in the world
     for them by the great high Lord, their Father.

   -agʷ-il

     ɬáq̓agʷil   lie down   LG.

ʔəs.də́š kʷ(i) adsɫáq̓agʷil Lie on your side. LG.

ʔəs.k̓ʷə́q kʷ(i) adsɫáq̓agʷil Lie on your back. LG.

lexical

 dxʷsɫáq̓alikʷ He's a planter (of potatoes). LG.

 ɫəq̓úlč set the table LG.

 ʔal tə ɫəq̓ᵊyálus on the edge (of the table)

rejected:

 *ʔuɫáq̓txʷ, *ɫáq̓il LG.

1. ɫáq̓ʷ Skagit See under k̓aw-.

 Cf. təq̓ Snoh. slap

 dxʷɫáq̓ʷusᵊd Slap him in the face. LG.

2. ɫáw̓t Snoh. new, fresh, what is actually new, what is
        new to someone LL.

 Cf. x̌áw̓s Skagit new

 ɫáw̓t čəd ʔu.háydxʷ I'm learning something new. EK.

 ɫáw̓t lə.ʔə̀ƛ čqaysəb flower just coming out EK.

 ɫáw̓t ʔu.ɫči̓l a new-comer EK.

3. ɫax̌   night, darkness

 Cf. bəsád grow dark/night

 Contrast ləx̌ 'light', ləx̌íl 'day'.

 root

  hìkʷ čəd ʔusə.saʔalítut, tuɫàx̌ LG.

  I had a real bad dream last night.
        'when it came, night'.

292

-il

   sɬax̌il   night

   səɬax̌il   evening (lit. 'coming night')   EK.

      xʷíʔ gʷəds.ʔítut ʔə kʷi haʔɬ ʔal ti səɬax̌il   LG.
      I didn't sleep well (last) night.

      ɬax̌il gʷəl bə.ləx̌il
      Night then again day. (These are the words Ant sang when
      arguing with Bear about the length of night and day. Ant
      wanted a roughly equal division between night and day so
      she could get a lot of work done. Bear wanted a year of
      night (and then one day) so he could sleep more.)   ES.

  lexical

    ɬáx̌iləlus   'evening star'   name for site of Clinton, Wash.,
                               on Whidbey Island   HD.

1.   ɬaʔ   arrive there

   Cf. ɬčíl   arrive   ʔá   be located (there)
     ʔə́ƛ̓   come

  root

    tuɬáʔ čəd   I got there.

    pə(d).táb kʷi t(u)adsɬàʔ   When did you get there?

    xʷùʔələ ʔuɬáʔəxʷ kʷədàʔ   Maybe he's arrived now.

    ɬuɬáʔ čəd ʔal kʷi dadatu   I'll get there in the morning.

    ləɬáʔ čəd dxʷʔal ti ʔàlʔal   I got there to my house.   LG.

  -c

    ɬuɬáʔc čəd   I'll go pick it up.

  -c-bi-t

    ɬuɬáʔcbicid čəd ʔal kʷi dadatu
    I'll get there (to pick) you (up) tomorrow.

293

-txʷ

ɬuɬáʔtxʷ čəd   I'll get it there.

lexical

ɬáʔači(ʔ)bid   touch it

rejected:

*ləɬaʔ čəd ʔalʔal   LG.

1. ɬáʔx̌   plate, platter

    Cf. qʷɬəyʔúlč wooden platter

        čáwəyʔùlč modern, store-bought dish, china dish

        cíliwʔ   basin, pan

    ɬíʔɬaʔx̌   (diminutive)

2. ɬčíl   See under ɬəč.

3. ɬə́bč-   mucus

    ɬíʔɬəbčqs   little snotty-nose   LL.

    ʔəxʷɬə́bčqs   (You have) a snotty nose.   LL.

    reduplication

    díʔɬ kʷi gʷ(ə)adsɬəbɬəbčqs   Your nose might run.   LL.

4. ɬə́cᵊb SPS   heavy mist prior to a general rain

    Cf. ɬə́ltᵊb   sprinkle, mist

5. ɬəč   arrive

    Cf. ɬaʔ   arrive there

        ʔəƛ̕   come

root

ʔuɫə́č čəd	I got started (under the influence of a spirit).	LG.
ʔuɫčáxʷ	He got started (under the influence of the spirit); (He received the spirit and) got started.	LG.

-il

ɫə́čil	SPS	arrive
ɫčíl	NPS	arrive

ʔuɫčíləxʷ čəd	I've arrived.	EK.
tuɫčíl ʔu (h)əlgʷə?	Have they returned yet?	LG.
ʔuɫčil ʔal ti dàdatu	They came this morning.	EK.
ləɫčíl čəd dxʷʔal tə d.ʔàlʔal		LG.
I got here to my home.		
ɫáẃt ʔuɫčil	newcomer	EK.

-il-txʷ

ɫčíltxʷ	Bring it!	EK.
ʔuɫčíltxʷ	He brought it.	EK.
ʔuɫčíltxʷ ti?iɫ	That was brought.	LL.
ʔu.tígʷəd čəd ʔə tə sɫčíltxʷs (h)əlgʷə? ti ləs.x̌ə́ɫ		EK.
Thank you for bringing the sick person.		

-i(l)-s

ʔuɫčís čəd	LG.
I got there just in time for some particular event.	
ʔuɫčís čəd ʔə ti səs.x̌ə̀ɫs	LG.
I got there in time when she was sick.	

-i(1)-s-b

ʔuⱡčisᵊb čəd   He came to (see) me.   LL.

-i(1)-s-bi-t

ʔuⱡčisbitᵊb čəd   He came to my place to see me.
                            (That's why I was detained.)   LL.

-i(1)-s-lexical...

ʔuⱡčisičdub čəd

They happened to come in on me when I was not ready
for visitors. ("The whiteman's equivalent is, 'they
caught me with my pants down'.")   LL.

1.   ⱡə́čəb   weasel

2.   ⱡə́gʷⱡ   leave, leave behind

     Cf. šə́gʷⱡ   door, way, path

     root

       ʔuⱡə́gʷᵊⱡ čəd diʔucid   I left him across the river.   LG.

       ⱡuⱡə́gʷᵊⱡ čəd tiʔəʔ   I leave this (behind).   LG.

       huy, ʔúx̌ʷəxʷ ⱡə̀gʷⱡəxʷ tiʔiⱡ s.biàw   ES.
       Then, he went. He left Coyote.

       ʔuⱡə́gʷᵊⱡ čəd ti d.ʔàlʔal   LG.
       I left my house.

       ʔuⱡə́gʷᵊⱡ čəd ʔal ti d.ʔàlʔal   LG.
       I left someone at my house.

       ʔu.jəqílab ti dsⱡə̀gʷᵊⱡ   By crawling I left.   LG.

         rejected:

            *ʔuⱡə́gʷⱡ čəd tulʔal tə d.ʔalʔal   LG.

-dxʷ

g^wəháẃə x̌ʷuɫ ʔuɫə̀g^{wə}ldxʷ ciʔəʔ čəg^wə̀ss   ML.

He found out what transpired when he would
leave his wife (to go fishing).

ʔuɫəg^{wə}ldúb čəxʷ ʔə tiʔiɫ   LG.

He left you.

ʔuɫəg^{wə}ldúb čəd ʔə ti lìlud   LG.

I got left by the train.

ʔuɫəg^{wə}ldúbš   They left me.   LL.

-b   (See remarks under cut-b, p. 58.)

ɫə́g^{wə}1ʔb čəxʷ   leave you (sg.)   LG.

ʔuɫə́g^{wə}1ʔb čəxʷ ʔə tiʔiɫ   LG.

He left you (sg.)

ʔuɫə́g^{wə}1ʔb həlg^wəʔ ʔə ti kìkəwič   LG.

Little Hunchback left them.

ʔuɫə́g^{wə}1ʔb ʔə tiʔiʔiɫ ti kìkəwič   LG.

They left Little Hunchback.

ɫə́g^{wə}1ʔb čəɫ   leave us   LG.

     rejected:

         *ɫəg^{wə}1tʔb   LL.

-bi-t-

ɫəg^{wə}1bítubuɫ   left us   LL.
     (This form is rejected by LG.)

pronominal suffix (See remarks under cut.)

ʔuɫə̀g^{wə}1bícid čəd   I'm leaving you (sg.)   EK.

ɫuɫəg^{wə}1búɫəxʷ   He will leave us.   LL.

ɬəgʷəlbúɬədəxʷ čəd čədà gʷə.t̓úk̓ʷəxʷ   LL.

I'm leaving you folks now to go home.

lexical

ɬəgʷəlígʷədᵊb   orphan

1. ɬəl   turn off (to the right or left)

(Perhaps etymologically related to ɬal(a),
289.1.)

Cf. jál, sídǫ, x̌əƛ́álap

-t

ɬəld   turn it off (the road)   LG.

ɬəlcút   steer to right or left

ɬəlcút dxʷʔal t(i) ad.qəlálig̓ʷəd   LG.
Turn off to your left.

2. ɬəlp̓   vibrate, quiver, wriggle

Compare: čə̌dᵊb   shiver

cikʷ   jerk, move, tug

jakʷ(a)   shake, rock, wag

3. ɬə́ltᵊb   See under qəlb.

Cf. ɬə́cᵊb   SPS   heavy mist prior to a general rain

ʔəlčuɬə́ltᵊbəxʷ   It's starting to rain, sprinkle.   LG.

reduplication

ʔəlčuɬíʔɬəltᵊbəxʷ   It's starting to mist a bit.   LG.

4. ɬəɬk̓ʷúb   red-breasted sapsucker   EK.

ɬə́ɬk̓ʷəb   red-breasted sapsucker   LL., ESi.

298

1.   ɬəp   blink

        ɬə́ptəd Snoh.   eyelash, eyelid

        Cf. ʔəlčupə́ləq̉ᵊb   blinking (flashing on and off)

2.   ɬə́p̉(u)   hang over (as clothes thrown over a line,
                                        a snake looped over a stick)

        See under šəq-t.

        Cf. k̉iɬ, q̉iɬ

        -ut

            ɬp̉úd   hang it up   EK.

        lexical

            ɬp̉ílc   putting the belt on the cultivator   EK.

            ɬə́p̉qs   hung over a point   LL.
                            go over a point   DM.

            sɬə́p̉qs   name for site of the present community
                            of Marysville, Washington

3.   ɬəq̉

        Cf. bá ʔ   wide

            p̉il(i)   flat, wide

        ɬə́q̉t   wide

        lexical

            ɬəq̉ɬəq̉táči ʔ(ac)   young white fir (tree)   MC.

                Cf. t̉úxʷ(əc)

            ɬəq̉táčəd(əc)   white fir (tree)   ESi.

            ɬəq̉tádi ʔ   the width of something   LG.

            ɬəq̉láx̌əd   upper arm   LG.

                Cf. s.ʔílax̌əd

    łə́q̓ulágʷəp   hip, buttocks   LG.

       Cf. xʷíʔləlúgʷəp (from xʷ-ʔil-əlúgʷəp)   LL., EK.

       rejected:

         *łə́q̓tgʷił   LG.

1.   ł(ə)qʷ(u)   wet

     root

       ʔəsłə́qʷ čəd   I'm wet.   EK.

       ʔu.qə́lb čədà łə́qʷ   It rained and I got wet.   EK.

     -ut

       łqʷúd   wet it

     lexical

       łqʷácᵊd   wilted   EK.

     reduplication

       łíʔłqʷ   damp

       tux̌ʷ čəd ʔudx̌ʷłíʔłqʷyuq̓ʷᵊb   LL.

       I just have to wet my throat.

2.   łəx̌   spread out; stiff

     Cf. tix̌(i)   spread,   See łx̌ilč.

     root

       ʔəsłə́x̌ dxʷʔal q̓ilbid   ML.

       It is spread out all the way to the canoe.

       gʷəłə́x̌ čəxʷ   LG.

       You might catch a disease/ become contaminated.

       Cf. čiq̓ʷilcut (under čiq̓ʷ-il-t)

-t

x̌ʷuluɬ q̓ʷasduliča? ti?iɬ ?uɬəx̌t̓əb dxʷ.t̓aq̓t dxʷ?al

tudi? ?al?al   ML.

Nothing but (this special kind of) blanket was
spread out up from shore (clear) to the house.

-a-b

?əsɬx̌ab   stiff

(LG. used this word to describe how people
get when they encounter a power. They often
fall down becoming just stiff and remain that
way until someone finds them and doctors
(baɬad) them.)

ɬx̌abšəd   stiff leg   DM.

1.   ɬəx̌ub   Snoh., SPS   go hunting in the forest (as opposed to along
                                                    the water)

See xʷi?xʷi? (under xʷi?).

Cf. šáyil   Skagit

2.   ɬi   you (pl.)

Cf. gʷəlápu

tix̌ix̌dubut ɬi   Take care of yourselves.   EK.

xʷí?tubš ɬi lə.bà?kʷɬ   LL.
Don't you folks let me get hurt.

húy ɬi   good-bye

?u· ɬì s?i?i?áb   respectful form of address to a group

→
4.   ɬič̓(i)   cut

Compare and contrast the following:

ƛ̓k̓ʷ(u)   chop

x̌iƛ(i)   chop down a tree (Compare jaq̓(a).)

p̓áyəq	hew, make a canoe
ƛ̓al(a)	slice, split open
k̓ʷič(i)/q̓ʷəx̌ʷ	cut into, butcher/clean, operate on
čəɬqíws	cut all up
dxʷ.k̓ič(i)	eviscerate
sik̓ʷ	rip apart
čəɬ	rip a gash (in flesh usually)
pqʷ(u)	cut or break a piece off leaving a larger portion, amputate. (See also under x̌ʷəƛ̓.)
dxʷ.čk̓ápsəb(ᵊd)	decapitate (someone) (Cf. -pqʷúsᵊd.)
čuqʷ(u)	whittle
Cf. also č(ə)x̌, ƛ̓iq̓ʷ(i)	

root

ʔuɬíč čəd	I got cut.	LL.

-it

ʔuɬíčid čəd tə s.qʷíqʷali		EK.
I started to cut hay.		
ʔuɬíčitᵊb čəxʷ ʔu ʔə tə qələb čàčaš		JC.
Did the nasty boy cut you?		

-dxʷ

ɬíčdubut	accidentally cut self

-i-b

ɬíčib	cut cattails for mat making, cut grass for making something	EK.

lexical

ʔuɬíčači(ʔ)b	He cut his finger.	EK.

ʔuƛ́íc̓us čəd	I cut my face.	EK.
ʔuƛ́íc̓usˀb čəd	I got a haircut, I cut my hair.	EK.
ƛ́íc̓yuq̓ʷ	cutting on the throat to remove tonsils	EK.
səxʷƛ́íc̓akʷčup	wood saw	EK.
ƛ́íc̓tadəd	scar	EK.

1. ƛid(i) tie

Compare: xʷə́lkʷ wrap up; intoxicated

  x̌əq wrap around

  gəlk̓ wind around something, entangle

  ƛ̓ač̓ cinch

  x̌ʷaqʷ bind

  ƛ̓iƛ̓p̓abacˀb (See under ƛ̓íp̓(i).)

  x̌ʷúq̓ʷədisˀb (See under x̌ʷúq̓ʷədis.)

  ƛ̓uc(u) tie, knot, wrap up package

Compare also qiq̓(i) 'incarcerate'.

Contrast gəx̌/gʷəx̌ 'get loose, untie'.

root

ʔəsƛid tə təbíƛəd ʔal tə ƛəlày̓? LG.
The rope is tied to the shovel-nose canoe.

təbíƛəd tə ʔəsƛid ʔal tə ƛəlày̓? LG.
The rope is tied to the shovel-nose canoe.

ƛəláy̓ tiʔiƛ ʔəsƛid ʔə tə təbíƛəd LG.
It's a shovel-nose canoe that's tied with a rope.
(As when you see something way out in the water
 and ask what it is.)

təbíƛəd ti dəxʷəsƛids ti ƛəlày̓? LG.
The shovel-nose canoe is tied with a rope.

-t

ʔuƛ́idid   tied it

ƛ́idid   Tie them together.   LL.

ʔuƛ́idid tə x̌əlày? (ʔə tə t́əbíƛəd)   LG.
He tied the shovel-nose canoe (with a rope).

ʔuƛ́idit^əb (ʔə tə s.tùbš) tə x̌əlày? (ʔə tə t́əbíƛəd)   LG.
The shovel-nose canoe was tied (with a rope) (by the man).

t́əbíƛəd ti dəx̌ʷƛ́idids ti x̌əlày?   LG.
He tied the shovel-nose canoe with a rope.

ƛ́idid ʔə kʷi haʔƛ ƛu.xʷiʔəs bələ.pax̌ʷ   JC.
Tie it well so it won't spread apart again.

lexical

ƛidús^əd   Tie the horse.   LG.

sƛídalšəd   pack strap, tumpline   EK.

   Cf. (s)t́k̓ʷálšəd, čəbáʔtəd   tumpline

dəx̌ʷəsƛíd^əgʷiƛ   for tying a boat, a painter   LL.

ƛíd^əgʷiƛ   tie up canoe   LL.

ƛídgʷəs^əd gʷəl gʷə.hàjil   LL.
Tie them together and make them longer.

ʔuƛ́idap   trawling   LL.

ʔuƛ́iʔƛdah^əb   same gloss: trawling   LL., ES.

rejected:

*x̌əláy? ʔə tə x̌ʷìləb (tiʔiƛ) ʔəsƛìd   LG.

1.   ƛik̓ʷ(i)   hook

root

ʔuƛíƛk̓ʷ čəd   I go to fish.   EK.

-it

ɫík\"id — hook it, snag it, catch it — EK.

ʔah ʔəs.qilqiɫiləx\" tiʔəʔ ʔiišəds g\"əɫík\"itʔbəs,
g\"ə.q̓ilitʔbəx\" ʔə tiʔəʔ ship

There were his people despairing [for fear that] he
had been hooked [i.e., kidnapped, cf. sax\"əb-t-b]
[and] carried off on the ship. — VH.
(from old tape of RS.)

lexical

ɫíɫk\"ačiʔ — revolver — EK.

See under x\"últəbàlc.

ɫík\"q(s)šəd — trip — LL.

ɫík\"alik\" — a hook; hook on to something — EK.

-təd

ɫíɫk\"təd — a hook

1. **ɫil** — give food or drink

Cf. ʔab-yi-, ʔəɫ-d

-t

ʔuɫíltʔb ciʔiɫ ʔə tə biàc — LG.
He gave her some meat.

ʔuɫíltʔb čəd — He gave me food. — LG.

x\"íʔ six\" g\"əsɫiltʔbs — ML.
Still he was not given food.

ɫíld (h)əlg\"əʔ — Give them some food. — LG.

ʔuɫíld čəd — I gave him food. — LG.

ləɫílcid čəd — I'm bringing you some food. — LG.

ləɫíɫcid čəd ʔə tə s.ʔə̀ɫˀd   JC.
I'm bringing/giving you food.

ɫuɫíɫtubuɫəd čəd
I'll give you folks some food.

ʔuɫíld čəd ʔə tə biàc   I gave him meat.   LG.

ʔuɫild ciʔiɫ ʔə tə biàc   He gave her some meat.   LG.

biác ti dsɫìld   I gave him meat.   LG.

ɫìxʷ kʷi ɫudsɫílcid   LG.
I'll give you three (things to eat).

ɫìxʷ kʷi ɫudsɫíltubuɫəd   LG.
I'll give you folks three (things to eat).

ɫìxʷ s.ʔuládxʷ ti tudsɫìld (h)əlgʷə?   LG.
I gave them three fish some time ago.

   lexical

   xʷi? gʷat ʔuɫíligʷəd   ML.
   No one gave him food.

1. ɫixʷ   three   (See under dəč̌u?.)

    sɫíxʷəɫdàtil   the third day, Wednesday

    sɫìxʷəɫdát   Wednesday

    lexical

    (s)ɫíxʷači?   thirty, thirty dollars

       rejected: *ɫixʷači?ilc

    ɫixʷágʷəp   3 things to plant, hill up   LG.

    ɫixʷálgʷiɫ   3 canoes   IM.

    ɫíxʷali   3 growing plants

    ɫìxʷálps   3 horses (animals)   LG.

ɫixʷalʔádiʔ	3 sounds; heard it three times
ɫixʷálčup	3 fires
ɫixʷálʔtxʷ	3 houses
ɫixʷáɫič	3 bundles
ɫíxʷəlus	3 squares in making a net, stitches in knitting
ɫíxʷqs	3 points
ʔəsɫixʷúlč ti ds.ʔax̌ʷuʔ	I have 3 baskets (full) of clams. DM.
dxʷsɫíxʷus	3 rows or layers

reduplication

ɫíxʷixʷ	3 people	LL.
ɫíʔɫxʷixʷ	3 children	LL.
ɫəɫíʔxʷixʷ	3 children	LG.

1. ɫí(ʔ)ɫtiàč   fish with line and pole   BT., JC.

   See xʷiʔxʷiʔ (under xʷiʔ.)

   ɫíɫtiàč ʔə kʷə s.x̌ʷədìʔ   JC.
   fish for bullhead with line and pole

2. ɫká̓ʔi   unidentified swamp grass with a flat blade that cuts   LL.

3. ɫqáw̓ʔ   lick, lap   LL.

   Cf. čib(i)   lick, dip

   ʔuɫqáw̓ʔd   [The dog] lapped it up.

4. ɫtqʷ

   gʷəɫtqʷ̓ad   A flock all takes to the air at one time. (Seems to imply a lot of noise too.)   ES.

   Cf. sásaq̓ʷ   (under saq̓ʷ)

1. ɫu- auxiliary prefix 'expected'

    See under gʷə-.

2. s.ɫuáy? inner bark next to sap which is used a lot in basket making, especially the ləqʷá.

    Cf. s.lágʷac SPS

3. (s)ɫub NPS soup EK., LG.

    See under ?əɫ-. Cf. bít? SPS soup

    -txʷ

        ɫúbtxʷ Feed him. (A very emphatic expression.) LL.
                    Feed him soup. LL.

    reduplication

        ɫúbɫub spoon feed a baby LL.

        sɫú?ɫəb a little soup LL.

4. ɫúkʷəɫ sun LL., LG.

    ɫukʷáɫ sun LL.

      Cf. s.x̌ədx̌ídəq̇ Snoq. sun LL.

        sɫukʷálb moon/month LL.

          hìkʷ sɫukʷálb full moon DM.

→

6. ɫúp morning, early

    See under ləx̌.

      ɫu?ɫp a little early

7. ɫúq̇ʷ(u) peel

    lexical

      ɫúq̇ʷəč bald head (lit. 'peeled head')

pútəxʷ ʔəsɬùq̓ʷəč ti ̓ʔiɬ bì.bščəb   ES.
Little Mink was just plain bald-headed.

1. ɬux̌ʷ   bare   JC.

   lexical

→

    ʔəsɬúx̌ʷači ̓ʔ   bare hands   JC.

    ɬúx̌ʷšəd   bare feet   JC.

2. s.ɬú ̓ʔᵊb   dog/chum salmon   LG.
            dried dog salmon   ML., LL.

   See under šab.

   Cf. ƛ̓xʷə́y ̓ʔ   dog/chum salmon   LL., ESi.

    ʔəxʷs.ləkʷ̓dxʷyitᵊ ̓bᵊb jəɬ cə x̌ənimuli ̓ča ̓ʔ ʔə tə
    sɬu ̓ʔᵊms, təlú ̓ʔᵊms   ML.
    It must be that the people want to eat Crow's
    dried dog salmon and dried king salmon.
    (What Raven sang to Crow.)

3. ɬx̌áb   See under ɬəx̌.

4. -ɬx̌á ̓ʔ   lexical suffix 'thigh'

   ʔəs.q̓əč̓q̓əčɬx̌á ̓ʔ crooked thighs

  See under -šad.

5. ɬx̌íl ̓č SPS   stand

   Cf. kiis NPS stand, See under ɬəx̌.

   ʔəs(ɬ)x̌íl ̓č čəd ʔə tə s.tə́k̓ʷəb   JC.
   I'm standing on the log.

6. ɬyá ̓ʔ   shoot a bone into someone out of malice.
          It is done by a shaman.   ES., EK.

  See under x̌əɬ.

λ̓

The sound of this letter is made by pronouncing *t* and *l* simulta-
neously accompanied by an abrupt closure of the vocal cords. [voiceless,
glottalized, lateral alveolar affricate]

1.　λ̓a　　　　　　　　go to some place

> Synonymous with the phrase ʔux̌ʷ dxʷʔal 'go to(ward)'. Note
> that the destination is not marked with a determiner (in
> contrast to constructions with ʔux̌ʷ dxʷʔal: λ̓a x̌ʷuyubalʔtxʷ
> 'to the store' versus ʔux̌ʷ dxʷʔal ti x̌ʷuyubalʔtxʷ 'to the
> store'.) However, the name of the object gone after does
> require a determiner. See remarks under čəɫ 94.1.

　root

ləλ̓á čəd tàwd	I'm on my way to town.	LG.
	I'm going shopping.	LG.
ʔuλ̓á čəd tàwd	I went to town. I'm going to town.	LG.
ləλ̓á čəd ʔàlʔal	I'm going home.	LG.
ləλ̓á ʔàlʔal tiʔiɫ	He is going home.	LG.

　　rejected:

*ləλ̓á čəd dᵊ.ʔàlʔal	LG.
*ləλ̓á ʔàlʔals	LG.

ɫuλ̓à čəd ʔəɫᵊdálʔtxʷ ɫu.tágʷəxʷəd

I'll go to a restaurant when I get hungry.　　　　LG.

> Cf. ɫu.ʔúx̌ʷ čəd dxʷʔal tə ʔəɫᵊdàlʔtxʷ ɫu.tágʷəxʷəd　　LG.
>> Same gloss: I'll go to a restaurant when I
>> get hungry.

ɫuλ̓à čəd x̌ʷuyubálʔtxʷ ɫu.bək̓ʷíləs tə səplə̀l

I'll go to the store when the bread runs out.

λ̓úb čəɫ ʔuλ̓a x̌ʷuyubàlʔtxʷ čəɫa ɫu.tágʷəɫ pù̓ʔtəd　　DM.

Let's go to the store and buy a shirt.

ʔəs.qʷíbəxʷ čəd dxʷʔal kʷi dsƛ̲a tàwd
I'm ready to go to town.

pə(d).táb kʷi ƚ(u)adsƛ̲a xʷuyubàlʔtxʷ   LG.
When are you going to the store?

   Cf. pə(d).táb kʷi ƚ(u)ads.ʔùx̌ʷ dxʷʔal tə xʷuyubàlʔtxʷ LG.
    Same gloss: When are you going to the store?

liludáb tiʔiƚ tə sƛ̲as wàšətəb
He went to Washington, D.C. by train.

-c

ləƛ̲ác čəd tiʔəʔ diʔəʔ   LG.
I'm coming after this.

ləƛ̲ác čəd tiʔəʔ x̌ʷùbt   LG.
I'm getting this paddle.

-txʷ

ləƛ̲átxʷ čəd x̌àčuʔ, ƚu.tít̕əb   LG.
I'm taking her to the lake for a swim.

lexical

  ƛ̲áčup   fetch wood   DM.

  ƚuƛ̲áčup   fetch wood   LG.

reduplication

  ƛáƛčup   fetch wood   ML., DM.

rejected:

  *(ƚu)ƛacut   LG.

1. ƛábuƚ   a mat made from split cedar and placed on
               the bottom of a canoe.   DM., EK.

Some say ƛúbuƚ. See under ƛakʷ(a).

1. ƛ́áč̓   cinch

    See under ƚid(i) 'tie'.

    Cf. ƛ́ip̓(i)   encircle in one's grasp

      p̓ič̓(i)   squeeze

    -b

      pútəxʷ ƛubəƛ̀àč̓ᵊb ci?iƚ ƛaƛačəpəd   ES.
      Ant would just cinch up some more.

    lexical

      ƛ́ač̓əpəd   belt   ES.

        Cf. x̌ʷáqʷabac belt   LG.

      ƛ́aƛačəpəd   ant (small) (lit. 'little cinched up one')
                                         ES.

    reduplication

      ƛ́aƛač̓ᵊb   cinch up   ES.

2. ƛ́áč   abdomen

    Compare: k̓ʷásəd 'stomach, tripe', k̓tú? 'belly, 'bay window'',
      q̓əjáx̌ 'intestines', -dəč lexical for ƛ́ač

3. ƛ́ágʷič   the act of using a ƛəgʷí?čad (which is called
                     č̓əsáy? by some)

    See under cáq̓(a).

    Cf. təpíl

4. ƛ́akʷ/gʷ(a)   stitch; mat make

    types of mats:

      s.ƚágʷid   k̓ʷátaq   ƛúbuƚ/ƛábuƚ

      kʷú?t/q̓ʷú?t   súlič   s.qəq̓ʷús

-at

ƛ́ag^wəd	Stitch it.
ƛ́ag^wət^əb	(The mat) was made.
tuƛ́ag^wat^əb jəɫ	Someone must have stuck the needle.

-š

ƛ́ag^wš ʔal tiʔiɫ	Hook (your needle) in there.	LG.
ƛ́ag^wš (dx^w)ʔal tàdiʔ	Same gloss: Hook (your needle) in there.	LG.

-yi-

ƛag^wyid	Stitch it for him.

-b

ƛ́ag^{wə}b	make mats

-b-yi-

ƛ́ag^{wə}byid	make mats for her

-təd

ƛ́ak^wtəd	cattail needle. They are about four feet long and usually made of iron wood. They are used in making cattail mats.

səx^w-

səx^wƛ́ák^w	a mat making thing	LG.
səx^wƛ́ák^wtəd	a mat making needle	LG.
səx^wuƛ́ák^wtəd	a mat making device	LG.

1. ƛ́áld   See under ƛəl.

2. ƛal   put clothing on; encase; be stranded

-š

ʔuƛálš čəd	I put it on.	LL.

ʔuƛ̓ális čəd tiʔiɬ kəkpù   LL.

I put on my favorite coat.

ʔuƛ̓ális čəd tə d.lupàčiʔ   EK.

I put my gloves on.

ʔuƛ̓ális čəd ti pùʔtəd   LG.

I put my shirt on.

    Cf. ʔu.púʔtədᵊb čəd Same gloss: I put my shirt on.   LG.

      ʔuƛ̓alaɬ čəd puʔtəd   Same gloss: I put my shirt on. LG.

    rejected:

      *ʔuƛ̓ális tiʔiɬ s.tubš   LL.

      *ʔuƛ̓ális ʔə tiʔiɬ s.tubš   LL.

-aɬ

   ʔuƛ̓alaɬ čəd pùʔtəd   I put my shirt on.   LG.

    Cf. ʔuƛ̓ális čəd ti pùʔtəd   Same gloss: I put my shirt on. LG.

-i-b

   ʔuƛ̓álib ʔə tiʔiɬ s.tùbš tiʔiɬ kəpù   LL.

That man put on the coat.

   ʔuƛ̓álib ʔə tiʔiɬ   He put it on.   LL.

   x̌ʷuɬ tuƛ̓álib ti s.ƛaləbac ...   EK.

When he put the garment on ...   EC.

   (ʔuƛ̓álib čəd I was put on (as though I were a coat.)
          I.e., it doesn't make sense.   LL.)

-yi-t-

   ʔuƛ̓áliitᵊb čəd ʔə ciʔiɬ   LL.

She put it on me.

-dxʷ

   ʔuƛ̓áldxʷ čəd   I struggled until I finally got it on,
          e.g., a tight boot.   LL.

ʔu.tálx̌ čəd ʔux̌aldx^w   LG.

I finally succeeded in getting it on.

-tx^w

ʔəsx̌áltx^w ti s.x̀aləbəc   EC.

He had the garment on.

ʔəsx̌áltub til̃ tiʔił   ML.

She lent (the coat) to him.

ʔəsx̌áltub ʔə tə hədli tə d.kəkpu   LG.

Henry is wearing my coat.

    rejected: *ʔux̌áltx^w

lexical

x̌álàbəc^əb   Put your clothes on.   EK.

    Cf. łág^wičaʔb, x^wə́c^əd   take clothing off

sx̌áləbəc   garment

ʔəsx̌əláličaʔ   clothes   LG.

x̌əláličaʔ(ʔ)b   put your clothes on   LG.

x̌álšəd^əb   put your shoes on   EK., LG.

sx̌álšəd   skis, snowshoes   LL.; ML.

ʔux̌álšədid čəd   I put his shoes on him.   LG.

ʔux̌álšədicid čəd   I put shoes on you.   EK.

ʔux̌álšədyid čəd   I put shoes on him for
    (his mother who was too busy
    with the other children.)   LG.

x^wx̌áləp   pot   EK.

-a-b

ʔux̌aláb čəd   I'm stranded.   EK.

-a-b-i-d

ʔəsx̌alx̌alábid čəd   I'm stuck on a problem.   LG.

reduplication

?əsƛ̓aⁱƛ̓aⁱáb čəd   I'm stranded.   LG.

  ?u.ɫə́gʷəɫ čəd šqìqad gʷəl ?əsƛ̓àⁱƛ̓əlalàbəxʷ   LG.
  I left him up hill and now he's stranded.

  ?u.ɫə́gʷəɫ čəd di?ucid gʷəl ?əsƛ̓àⁱƛ̓əlalàbəxʷ   LG.
  I left him across the river and now he's stranded.

1.   ƛ̓al*

root

  ƛ̓áⁱ čəd   me too   LG.

-yi-

  gʷəl ƛ̓uƛ̓áⁱyibəxʷ ti?ə? s.x̌əy̓ùss
  Then they would add its head (i.e., the prow of a ?ə?utx̌s).

-b

  ?əsƛ̓áⁱ⁹b čəd
  I have a habit; I'm used to doing it.

-b-i-t

  ?əsƛ̓áⁱbid čəd   LG.
  I'm used to doing/saying that.

adverb

  ƛ̓áⁱ čəd bə.?áb s.yiq̓us   I have a basket too.   LG.

  ƛ̓áⁱ bəds.gʷà?   That's mine too.   LG.

  ƛ̓áⁱ bə.gʷə̀ɫ ti?iɫ   That's his too.   LG.

  ƛ̓àⁱ čəɫ gʷəbə.gʷí(h)id ti?iɫ ƛ̓ə.ƛ̓iq̓šəd   ML.
  We could also invite Sapsucker.

  ƛ̓áⁱ b(ə)as.?ìstə   They are both the same.   LL.

  ƛ̓àⁱ b(ə)as.?ístə dxʷ?al dəgʷì   The same to you.   LG.

---

* Should be ƛ̓aⁱ in all examples preceding, including and following
  this entry.

λàl b(ə)as.ʔísta tiʔəʔ ʔilaq   MS.
The stern is the same (shape).

gʷə.kʷáxʷac čəxʷ ʔu dxʷʔal kʷi gʷədsλál b(ə)u.hùyud
kʷi s.ʔìsta   JC.
Would you help me to (where) I can also make (one)
like it?

λal čəxʷ b(ə)as.tíx̌ix̌dubut   LG.
You take care of yourself too.

λal bəlču.cùtcut   LG.
He said the same thing.

λál bə.hìkʷ tiʔił ads.dùukʷ   LG.
Your knife there is big too.

λál bə.hìkʷ tə s.dùukʷ ʔə hədli   LG.
Henry has a big knife too.

λàl bə.kiyáʔəxʷ ciʔîł   LG.
She's a grandmother too.

λál čəd bə.ʔàł x̌ʷulàb ʔə dəgʷî   LG.
I'm just as fast as you.

reduplication

λálal uʔxʷ gʷəl lə.bəsàd   LL.
"Early yet, but it's getting dark."

λálal čəd   I'm early.   EK.

λálal tə dsu.təjìl   I go to bed early.   LG.

xʷiʔ kʷ(i) ads.ʔəx̌ kʷi λálal   EK.
Don't come too early!

1.   λal-   sound

      Cf. čux̌(u) 'sharp rattling sound'

          λalx̌   pop, crack   LG.

-t

    ƛə̀lx̌cút   crackling noise   MC.

-b

    x̌ʷúƚ ʔəlčuƛàlˀx̌ˀb t(ə) ad.hùd   LG.
    Your fire is just crackling.

lexical

    ƛə̀lx̌úlč   cranberry ("They are called this because they pop."
                                                          EC.)

    ƛə̀lx̌ə́lc   cranberry   ESi.

lexical

    ƛəládiʔ   noise   EK.

    stáb kʷi ʔuƛəlàdiʔ   What's the sound?

    x̌ʷíʔ gʷədsuƛəlàdiʔ   I didn't make the noise.

    ʔəcá ti ʔuƛəlàdiʔ   I'm the one who's making the noise.

reduplication

    ƛəƛəládiʔ   little noise   EK.

→

2. dxʷs.ƛálb   Clallam

3. ƛáləqəp   See under ʔəƛ.

4. s.ƛálqəb NPS   monster; anything you are afraid of

    Cf. jə́gʷə SPS monster   ESi.

        ʔáx̌ʷədus   Skagit   Basket Ogress

        s.xʷəyúq̓ʷ   Snoh.   Basket Ogress

        ƚx̌ʷúbx̌   Basket Ogress's younger sister   ML., LL.

        qíʔqəƚàdiʔ   daughter of Basket Ogress (lit. 'Little
                                     Uprooted Tree' because her hair, always
                                     messed up, looked like the tangled roots
                                     of an uprooted tree.)

318

See also under čyátkʷu(ʔ).

  sx̌alqəb čəd   I have/am fierce power.   LG.

     rejected:

       *ʔux̌alqəb čəd   LG.

1. ƛ̕áɬᵊb   salt, salty

    -t

      ƛ̕áɬᵊbᵊd   Salt it.

    lexical

      ƛ̕áɬᵊbalikʷ   Same gloss: Salt it.

2. s.ƛ̕áƛ̕akʷ   saw-whet owl   LG., LL.

    Also called x̌ʷúpšəd.

3. ƛ̕áq̓ad   ambushed, surprised

4. ƛ̕áq̓ʷ Snoh.   watertight, solid, strong

    ƛ̕əq̓ʷ Skagit   watertight, solid, strong

      ʔəs.húytxʷ ƛ̕ə̀q̓ʷ   He made it solid.

    Cf. x̌ᵊtádis   hard, solid (like a board)

         qʷíq̓ʷ NPS   strong body, husky

         tíb   able/try to do hard work, expend much
                         physical effort

         wəléx̌ʷ SPS   strong body, husky

5. ƛ̕átəd   a seine, a salmon webbing trap

    See ƛ̕á(ʔ)təd.

6. ƛ̕ax̌   feel cold

Cf. ƛ̓ux̌ʷ   a thing is cold

   t̓əs   weather is cold

    tuq̓ʷub   cold (disease), a cough

ʔəsƛ̓áx̌ čəd yəx̌i ʔalču.šəx̌ʷəb   LG.
I'm cold because the wind is blowing.

ʔəsƛ̓áx̌ čəd gʷə ti ʔu.ɬáč tə hùd   JC.
I'm cold because the fire went out.

t(u)asƛ̓áx̌ čəd gʷəl ʔu.húdičupyic tə d.bàd   LG.
I was cold so my father made a fire for me.

1.   ƛ̓ax̌ʷ   grow, growth (a plant, animal, or people)

ti ʔə ʔ sqʷí ʔ.qʷali ʔ ƛ̓uƛ̓áx̌ʷ   MS.
Grass grows (there).

x̌ʷùləx̌ʷ jəɬ ʔaɬ kʷi gʷədsƛ̓àx̌ʷ   LG.
I wish I'd grow fast.

ləƛ̓áx̌ʷ ɬukʷàɬ   sun rising   EK.

ʔuƛ̓áx̌ʷ tə s.hədəb   spring ('warmth grows')   EK.

ʔuƛ̓áx̌ʷ tə s.t̓əsəb   autumn ('coldness grows')   EK.

həlí ʔ ləƛ̓áx̌ʷ s.t̓ə́k̓ʷəb
a living tree (lit. 'stick/log')   JC.

lexical

sƛ̓áx̌ʷabac   hair (as on a dog)   LG.

   Cf. čá ʔad   dog hair

ƛ̓áx̌ʷayqs   beard (Cf. qʷíd̓əqs)   LL.

sƛ̓áx̌ʷdup   brush, undergrowth, weeds; growing things   LG.

ʔəsƛ̓áx̌ʷədup   too brushy to walk through   LL.

s.tábac ti ʔiɬ sƛ̓àx̌ʷdup   What kind of a tree is that?

   Cf. s.watíx̌ʷtəd

pút čəxʷ ʔəxʷλ̓áx̌ʷus   EK.

Indeed, you have hair all over your face.

1.   λ̓á(ʔ)təd   seine   LL., MS.
                           a salmon webbing trap   LL.

                           (LL. comments that some use this word to
                           mean trap in general, but in his opinion
                           that is bad usage.

                           Compare s.λ̓əlájad (under λ̓əl), təqáp̓ᵊd.

      other nets:

         húyəq   gill net
         ǰiq̓alájəd   set a net
         lúk̓ʷ, q̌ʷúləč   dip net
         λ̓úcič   net webbing
         p̓í.p̓q̓ʷàlikʷ   drifting net
         qʷáqʷɫ, xʷ.šəbtád   bag net
         tiyúʔsəd   hand smelt trap for streams
         ʔəxʷájad   drag net

3.   λ̓ə́bəlus   smooth, even

4.   λ̓ə́bλ̓əbqʷ   salmon eggs that are not dry. They are taken
                           just when fish are ready to spawn.

      See under q̓ə́lx̌.

6.   s.λ̓əgʷádiʔ   earring

7.   s.λ̓əgʷíʔčad   spear used for bottom fish such as flounders,
                           bullheads, etc., including crabs   LL.

      λ̓ágʷič   the act of using a λ̓əgʷíʔčad   LL., ESi.

         Cf. čəsáyʔ   straight spear for bottom fish   EK.

            cacq̓   spear big game on the salt water (under caq̓(a))

            təpíl   spear salmon in a river

1.　　λə́l

    root

        ʔəsλə́l   silent, especially the stillness of the
                         deep forest   VH.

    -t

        λə́ld   Don't touch it. Leave it alone. Forget it. ES.
                    Pay no attention to it. Never mind it.   LG.

        (JC. gives λald 'Pay no attention to it. Never mind it.')

          Compare:

               kʷá?   Leave it alone.

               ʔəxʷ.líligʷədbid   Pay no attention to it.

               x̌ʷá?x̌ʷq̓ʷəd   Distract/disturb something.

               balac-   disturb/distract

               p̓áλaldxʷ   Disregard something.

    -a-but

        λəlábut   Snoh., SPS   understand, listen

          Cf. ləqálbut Skagit   understand

              luh/ləq   hear

              t(ə)kʷádi?   deaf

              pít̓əb   notice, pay attention, understand

              yíč̓əb   notice, see, figure out

    ʔəsλəlábut čəxʷ ?u   Do you understand?   LL., EK.

    xʷi? gʷədsəsλəlábut ?ə kʷi dxʷ.l(ə)šúcid   LL.
    I don't understand Puget Salish.

    xʷí? gʷədsəsλəlàbut   EK.
    I didn't hear (even though I tried to).

-a-but-bi-t

x^wi? g^wəds.tíb ?əsƛəlábut^əbid ti?ił dx^w.l(ə)šùcid   LL.

I don't really understand Puget Salish.

?əsƛəlbutbic čəx^w   You listen to me.   EK.

-ad

túx̌^w čəx^w s.tàlx̌ ti?ił ƛəlàdəx^w ?ə hùydx^w   LL.

You are unusual in that you are able to get the work put together.

g^wə-...-ad

g^wəƛəlád   Stop! Behave, keep still!   EK.

g^wəƛəládəx^w   Stop now!   LL.

x̌^wùɬ ?əsg^wəƛəlád   Stand still!   EK.

?əsg^wəƛəlád tə s.q^wù?q^wa?   Stop drinking.   EK.

dəčáx^w ?əs.k^wədà? g^wəl ?əsg^wəƛəlàd   EK.

(If only) for once he would be still.

g^wəƛəládəx^w čəx^w ?u   Are you stopping now?   LG.

→   other derivation

sƛəlájad   trap   LL.

See under ƛá(?)təd.   See təqáp^əd.

?uƛəlájad čəd dx^w?al ti?ił s.čətx^wəd.
cíck^wəx^w ?u.jùq̓^wud ti?ił ?a?pəlsəc   LL.

I set a trap for that bear.
He's been ruining my little apple trees.

1.   ƛəládi?   See under ƛal-.

2.   ƛəláy?   shovel-nose canoe

See under q̓ilbid.

The ƛəláyʔ was usually poled with a čq̓ap.

ʔəs.ʔəx̌íd kʷi s.ləlíʔ ʔə tiʔəʔ s.dəxʷíɬ dxʷʔal ƛ(ə)lày̓ʔ

What is the difference between a duck-hunting canoe
and a shovel-nose canoe?

x̌ʷəčx̌ʷəjyálus tiʔəʔ s.dəxʷíɬ gʷəl ʔəs.p̓ilp̓ilyálus tiʔəʔ
ƛəlày̓ʔ gʷəl x̌ʷúl gʷəɬ dxʷʔal s.tuləkʷ. s.dəxʷíɬ gʷəɬ
dxʷʔal x̌ʷəlč, dxʷʔal x̌ačuʔ   DM.

A duck-hunting canoe has sharp (i.e., pointed) ends, but
the shovel-nose canoe has flat ends and it belongs just
on the river(s). The duck-hunting canoe belongs to the
saltwater (and) to the lake(s).

ʔabsƛ(ə)láy̓ʔ čəxʷ ʔu   Do you have a shovel-nose canoe? LG.

reduplication

ƛíƛlày̓ʔ   model of a shovel-nose canoe   HD.

compound

sƛəláyʔɬkʷuʔt   sail   LL.

    (kʷuʔt is a kind of mat.)

1. ƛəllá̓ʔ ~ ƛálal   later on (can be on a different day)
                          wait

    Cf. tíɬx̌i   after a while (must be on the same day)

      ʔáciɬ ƛəllà̓ʔ   Wait awhile.

      ƛəllá̓ʔ huʔxʷ   Wait!

      ƛəllà̓ʔ ʔáʔsᵊbš   Wait for me.

      ƛəllà̓ʔ ʔáʔsᵊbuɬ   Wait for us.

      ƛəllá̓ʔ čədà ɬu.qʷíbid   I'll fix it after a while.

      ƛəllá̓ʔ čədà ɬu.gʷáagʷətubicid

      I'll tell you (the story) after a while.

ɬu.gʷáagʷətubicid čəd ƛ̓əlláʔ

Same gloss: I'll tell you the story after a while.

ƛ̓əlláʔ čələpa ɬu.luhəlàdiʔ

You folks will hear it after a while.

1. ƛ̓əlx̌   See under ƛ̓alx̌.

2. ƛ̓əp   deep , beneath (surface)

    Compare šikʷ, gʷəd.

    root

      sƛ̓əp   deep water

        híkʷ sƛ̓əp   It's deep.   DM.

        xʷíʔ lə.tíb sƛ̓əp   It's not too deep.   DM.

    lexical

      ƛ̓iƛ̓pəq   underpants   HD., LL.

      ƛ̓iƛ̓pikʷ   undershirt   HD., LL.

3. ƛ̓ik̓(i) Skagit   adhere

    (This form is recorded as ƛ̓iq̓(i) from the Snohomish consultants.
    It was elicited at an early period in my field work and may be
    an error. Because the Snohomish consultants are now deceased,
    rechecking is precluded. However, a few forms do definitely
    differ between velar and uvular articulation in accord with
    the Skagit versus Snohomish speech areas, e.g., the word for
    sweep, and this may be another case. TH.)

    Compare t̓əq.

    -it

      ƛ̓ik̓id   Stick it on.   LG.

    lexical

      ɬuƛ̓ík̓ƛ̓ik̓aluscid   She will stick your eyes (shut with
                                                    pitch).   LG.

1. λ̓ip̓(i) encircle in one's grasp

Cf. p̓ič(i) 'squeeze', λ̓ač̓ 'cinch'

-it

λ̓uλ̓íp̓id squeezed it LL.

lexical

λ̓íp̓àlbixʷ hold the teat LL.

Cf. p̓íč̓albixʷ milk (a cow) LL.

ʔəsλ̓íλ̓p̓àbəcᵊb hold blanket around self with hand (it's not fastened) LL.

See under x̌ʷuq̓ʷ and ɬid(i).

ʔuλ̓ip̓úsəbᵊd čəd I squeezed his neck. LG.

ʔuλ̓íp̓əpsəbᵊd čəd I choked him. LG.

ʔuλ̓íp̓usc Someone choked me. LG.

2. λ̓íq(i) ~ λ̓q-´ emerge (in general)

Cf. šikʷ, p̓usᵊb, šil

root

ʔuλ̓iq čəd I came out (of a hiding spot). LL.
I came out (of the water). LL.

-it

λ̓íqid tiʔəʔ t̓àltəd Take the "slicing" knife (out of the box). LG.

ʔuλ̓íqitᵊb They let him out. EK.

-dxʷ

xʷíʔ gʷ(ə)adsλ̓íqdubš You can't take me out. ES.

ʔuλ̓íqᵊdxʷ čəd tə d.čàləs I got my hand out. EK.

Cf. ʔuλ̓íqači(ʔ)b čəd
Same gloss: I got my hand out. EK.

ʔuƛ̓íqdubut   (An animal) got out (of its cage).   EK.

xʷíʔ gʷətudsƛ̓íqdubut   EK.
I wouldn't have been able to get out.

-agʷ-il

ʔuƛ̓íqagʷil tiʔił s.čə̀txʷəd tul̓ʔal tiʔił ʔàl̓ʔals   ES.
Bear came out from his house.

-agʷ-i(l)-s

ʔuƛ̓íqagʷis čəd   LL.

I came out of the brush where I had been hiding
(so my friend could see me).

zero grade of root -il

ʔuƛ̓qíl tiʔił s.čə̀txʷəd   LL.

The bear came out of hibernation.

lexical

sƛ̓íqabac   smallpox   EK.

ʔuƛ̓íqači(ʔ)b čəd   I got my hand out.   EK.

ƛ̓íqalihəxʷ tə *beans*   EK.
The beans are sprouting.

ƛ̓íƛ̓iqus   pimples

ƛ̓íqusʔb   stick your face out (the window)   LG.

*dxʷƛ̓íqusʔb   rejected   LG.

dxʷsƛ̓íqusʔb   someone who is always sticking   LG.
his face out

pədƛ̓qúlil   spring of the year   LL.

reduplication

bəƛ̓íqiqəxʷ   It emerged now and again.   ML.

ƛ̓íƛ̓iqus   pimples   EK.

1. λ̓iq̓(i)   Snoh.   adhere

This form is given as λ̓ik̓(i) by LG. who also gives a synonym, t̓əq.

root

?əsλ̓íq̓   It's sticky.   EK.

lexical

?uλ̓íq̓ači(?)b   He signed with his fingerprint.   LL.

?uλ̓íq̓ači(?)c   He stuck it on my hand.   LL.

?əsλ̓íq̓gʷəs   stuck together   LL.

λ̓əλ̓íq̓šᵊd   sapsucker (lit. 'little sticky foot'),
                 a bird of the small animal class,
                 titčulbixʷ   ML.

λ̓íq̓əlčəb   bee's wax   EK.

2. λ̓íw?   escape, get away   ES., LG.

See under təláwil.

lexical

λ̓íw?əp   "a slang word for someone who can't control
                 his rectum"   LL.

3. s.λ̓i?ál?qəb SPS   birds   ESi.
              (Probably more specifically "tree birds"
              as opposed to waterfowl s.q̓ʷáləš, bú?qʷ.
              See Gibbs, p. 312.)

4. λ̓k̓ʷáx̌ad   goose (of unidentified species)

5. λ̓k̓ʷ(ú)   See under łič̓(i).   Cf. č̓iq̓ʷ(i)

-ut

λ̓k̓ʷúd   chop it

λ̓k̓ʷútəgʷəl   chop up one another

1. λláyʔ   See λəláyʔ.

2. λq-   See under λiq.

3. λu-   See under bəs.

ʔəsλúil   thin person   EK.

həláʔbəxʷ čəxʷ x̌əł ti ləλùil   LL.
It looks as if you are getting thinner.

dáyʔ tiʔił cíckʷ sixʷ ləλúil   LL.
He's really getting quite thin.

dáyʔ tiʔił səλúilsəxʷ   LL.
He is getting emaciated.

4. λu-   auxiliary prefix   'habitual'

See under gʷə-.

5. λúb   OK   EK.

root

λúb ʔu   Is that all right?   ES.

λúb ʔu kʷi gʷəds.x̌ʷiłalikʷ   DM.
May I charge it?

xʷiʔ ləλúb ta   That's not all right.   LL.

gʷəλúb ʔu kʷi gʷəds.λalš   DM.
Would it be all right for me to try it on?

-txʷ

(ʔu)λúbtxʷ   That's fine the way it is.   LG.

That's OK (in answer to the question,
'How is it now?' after fixing something). LG.

-il

ɬ(u)asƛúbil čəxʷ ʔə kʷi ɬubəd(s).šùdubicid   ES.
You will be better when I see you again.

-i(1)-s

ʔəsƛúbis tiʔiɬ x̌ə̀čs   He thinks it's all right.   LL.

-il-dxʷ

ƛubildxʷ   agree with him

   ʔuƛubildub ʔə tiʔiɬ dᵊs.càpaʔ ʔi ciʔiɬ dᵊ.kiyàʔ   ES.
   My grandfather and my grandmother agreed to it.

reduplication with [-iɬ] stems

ʔəsƛúƛubiləxʷ čəd   I'm a little better.   LL.

ləƛúƛubil čəd   I'm getting better.   LG.

-a-d

ƛúbad tiʔəʔ yəlyəlàb   The parents agreed.   LG.

ʔuƛúbəd tiʔiɬ dᵊs.càpaʔ ʔi ciʔiɬ dᵊ.kiyàʔ   ES.
My grandfather and my grandmother agreed to it.

adverb

ƛúbəxʷ čəɬ ɬu.ʔə̀ɬᵊd   Let's eat.   DM.

ƛúbəxʷ čəɬ ʔu.gʷàx̌ʷ   We had better go for a walk.   LG.

ƛúb čəɬ ƛa xʷuyubàlʔtxʷ   DM.
Shall we go to the store?

ƛùb čəxʷ ɬu.kʷədád ciʔiɬ dᵊ.bədàʔ   EK.
It is OK for you to take my daughter.

ƛúb ʔəs.ʔìstə   Amen, That's all right.   EK.

ʔəxʷ.cútəb čəd ƛùb xʷíʔ kʷi gʷ(ə)ads.ʔə̀ƛ   HD.
I think it would be better for you not to come.

λ̓ub haac ti?iƚ ƛiyù?səd   A long smelt trap is best.   JC.

other

   ?íƛub   enough   EK.

      xʷí? ləhiƛub kʷ(i) ads.x̌ə̀ƚ   EK.
      You aren't sick enough.

      sí?ƛub dxʷ?al dəgʷí   DM.
      It's just right on you.

   rejected:

      *?iƚƛubil čəd   LG.

1.   λ̓úbuƚ   mat put full length in bottom of a canoe   LL.
     Some say ƛábuƚ. See under ƛakʷ.

2.   λ̓uc(u)   tie, knot, wrap up package
     See under ƚid(i).

     -ut

        λ̓úcud   tie it (knot for a net)   LL., EK.
                        wrap up a package   LL.

     lexical

        λ̓úcᵊgʷasᵊd ƛ̓àʔəbiƚəd   EK.
        Tie the ropes together!

           (LL. uses ƚídgʷəsəd for this!)

        λ̓úcič   net webbing   LL.

           See under ƛá(?)təd.

3.   λ̓úiqs   box, chest   LG., DM., VH.
        Cf. wə́q̓əb   box, chest   EC. and all Snoh. consultants
            wəq̓ə́b   box, chest   JC.

1. λuq̓ʷ(u)   stuff into, plug in

   Synonyms   Antonyms

   čik̓ʷ(i)   swallow, stuff into   ʔəč̓   pull out

                                         x̌əc   pull out, extract

   ʔaq̓-   choke on something   ʔuq̓ʷ(u)/ʔəq̓ʷ(a)   unplug

   čx̌í-   jammed, crowded, stuffed

   t̓(ə)q̓   patch

   λiq̓(i)/λik̓(i)   adhere

   t̓əq   adhere

   -ut

      λúq̓ʷud   Plug it in.   LL.
                     stuff into; hide in a hole   MS.
                     the opposite of ʔəč̓əd   MS.

   lexical

      λuq̓ʷalátxʷ   plug up holes in a building with moss   LG.

      sλúq̓ʷalatxʷ   what is stuffed into a wall   MS.

2. λuxʷ   a thing is cold

   Cf. t̓əs   cold weather

       λax̌   person feels cold

       tuq̓ʷub   cold, cough (disease)

   -il

   ʔəsλúxʷiləxʷ   (The food) is cold now.

                       euphemism for 'someone has died/is dead' LL.

   ʔəsλúxʷil tiʔił kùpi   The coffee is cold.

-il-t

    λ́ux̌ʷild   cool it off   LG.

1.   λ́ux̌ʷλux̌ʷ   oyster (generic)

    ʔəs.ʔəx̌íd kʷi sə(xʷ).xʷíʔs lə.x̌ʷuɫab ʔə tə s.ʔàx̌ʷuʔ
    tiʔiɫ λùx̌ʷλux̌ʷ   JC.
    Why isn't an oyster like a clam?

    gʷəɫ x̌ʷə́lč s.wàtixʷtəd tiʔiɫ λùx̌ʷλux̌ʷ yəxʷ tə s.ʔàx̌ʷuʔ.
    šəqábac ʔə tə s.watixʷtəd tiʔiɫ λux̌ʷλux̌ʷ gʷəl ʔəs.pəd
    tə s.ʔàx̌ʷuʔ. díɫ səs.hùys (h)əlgʷəʔ   JC.
    The oyster and the clam belong to the realm of the sea.
    [But] the oyster is on top of the ground and the clam
    is buried. That is the way they are.

2.   λuy   bump into   DM.

    See under k̓aw-.

    xʷiʔ kʷ(i) adsλúyabəc   Don't run into anything!

    ʔuλúyabəc čəd dxʷʔal tiʔiɫ haʔhaʔɫ ʔaciɫtalbixʷ   EK.
    I ran into (came upon) (some) good people.

3.   λx̌ʷáyʔ Snoh., SPS   dog/chum salmon   LL., ESi.

    pədλx̌ʷáyʔ   dog salmon time   November
                                            autumn

    Cf. s.ɫúʔəb Skagit   dog/chum salmon   LG.

    ML. uses s.ɫúʔəb to mean dried dog salmon

p

This letter stands for a sound very much like that of the English *p*. [voiceless bilabial stop]

→

2. pač(a)   set out (esp. as a gift)   DM.

    See under qʷát.

    -at

        páčad ti?iⱡ s.tabigʷs s.?abyids
        He set out the possessions he was giving.   ES.

3. pádac   SPS   ten

    Cf. ?úlub   NPS   tcn

        pádəc yəxʷ tə dəču?   eleven   ESi., JC.

    lexical

        pàdəcílc   ten dollars   JC.

4. páhᵊb   hazy; windows "steamed" over   LL.

    See under q̓áƛᵊb.

5. pák̓(a)   scatter, distribute

    Cf. xʷəb, ?ix̌ʷ(i)

    -at

        pák̓ad   scatter it /distribute it   LL.

        pák̓atᵊbəxʷ ?ə ti?ə? diⱡdiⱡ kaw̓qs   ML.
        It was distributed by this same Raven.

    -yi-

        x̌ʷuləxʷ čəd ⱡupák̓yid tə ?aciⱡtalbixʷ   ML.
        I'll just distribute (the food) to the people.

1. -pak^w-   lie with hind end up

    ʔudx^wp̓ák^wah^əbitubuł   LL.
    He turned his rear up toward us.

    x̌u.ʔúx̌^wəx^w g^wəl x̌udx^wp̓ák^wah(ə)bəx^w   ES.
    He would go and lie with his rear end up.

    ʔá tiʔəʔ s.čə̀tx^wəd: x̌^wuł ʔəx^wp̓ák^wah^əb   ES.
    There was Bear. He just lay with his rear up.

2. s.pálbəd   calf of leg

    Cf. ǰə́səd; -šad, -ilč, -łx̌aʔ

3. p̓áł   flee, run away out of fright   LL., LG.
                       make self scarce because you are told to   LL.

    See under təláwil.

4. s.pálx̌ad   tide flats   DM.

    Cf. šux̌, s.x^wádəč

5. p(a)q̓^w   smoke of a fire

    See under q^wəš-.

    -b

      pə́q̓^{wə}b   smoke of a fire   ESi.

    g^wə...ad

      x̌^wuł x̌u.bádəš g^wəl x̌u.ʔəx̌ tiʔəʔ sg^wəpq̓^wád ʔə
      tiʔəʔ s.wàtix^wtəd   EC.
      He just would smoke (his pipe) and smoke would
      come over the world.

    lexical

      ʔəx^wp̓áq̓^wus   face blackened by smoke   LL., EK.

        Cf. ʔudx^w.t̓íq̓^wilus čəd   LL.
        The smoke is in my face.

ʔupápq̓ʷàlikʷ   smoked just a few fish   LL.

  Cf. ʔu.tᶖtq̓àlikʷ   Same gloss: smoked just a few fish LL.

1.   pástəd   Caucasian (from English *Boston*)

    Cf. xʷə́ltəb   Caucasian

       páspastəd   many white folks

       pápstəd   white child, endearing way of referring to
                         a white friend

       pápastəd   insulting way of referring to a white man

       pápapstəd   many white children

2.   páx̌   spread

    Cf. ləx̌, tix̌(i)

       ƛ̓ídid ʔə kʷi hà̓ʔɫ ɫu.xʷíʔəs bələpàx̌   JC.
       Tie it well so it won't spread apart again.

→
→
5. s.pá̓ʔc Skagit   bear

       s.čə́txʷəd Snoh.; SPS   bear

6. s.pəču̓ʔ Snoh.   watertight basket made of cedar roots

       yíq̓us Skagit,   s.yált SPS

       reduplication

       spípču̓ʔ   little cedar-root basket

7. dxʷ.pədá̓ʔ   milt

       -a-b

          pədáb   fertilize fish eggs

8.   pəd   dirt, dust, soil, earth; bury

    root

          ʔəspə́d   covered with dirt, dusty, buried

gʷəl ʔəspə́d tə s.ʔáx̌ʷuʔ   But the clam is buried.   JC.

spə́d   dust   EK.

-b

ʔəspə́dᵊb   baked by burying in hot sand or ashes   LG.
            (This form is equivalent to Snoh. ʔəs.pədádub.)

ʔəxʷpə́dᵊb   dust on the surface of the water;
            a pan wanted to put water in is found
            to be dusty   LG.

ʔudxʷpədᵊb It's got dirt/dust in it.   LG.

-agʷ-il

λ̓(u)aspədágʷil ciʔił p̓uày? ʔal pə(d).t̀əs   DM.
A flounder buries itself in winter.

-adub

ʔəspədádub baked by burying in hot sand or ashes   LL.
            (Equivalent to Skagit ʔəs.pə́dᵊb.)

    ʔəspədádub s.pqʷùc   baked potato

    ʔəspədádub səplə̀l   baked bread   LL.

dxʷs₁-

dxʷspədálikʷ one who plants, farmer   LG.

lexical

ʔupədáč̓q̓ʷ   They buried him.   EK.

pədálikʷ   plant

pədálikʷəc   a seed

ʔupədíč   get covered with dirt/dust   EK.

pədíč̣ᵊd   bury it   EK.

    Contrast č̌aʔ(a)

pədíx̌ʷ   soil (not recognized by LL.)   LG.

1. pəd   time of

    See under <u>tab</u>.   Cf. (ʔaləxʷ) k̓ʷid

      tupə́d jəł čà?ᵊb   It must have been time to dig.

      pə(d)táb kʷi łud(s).šudubicid   ES.
      When will I see you?

      pə(d)tábəxʷ kʷi há?ł s.ləx̌il kʷi gʷədəxʷ.bədč̓ᵊbčəł   ES.
      When would be a good day for us to peddle the bull?

      pə(d)táb kʷi gʷ(ə)ads.x̌aƛtxʷ kʷi gʷəds.dəčagʷtxʷbicid   LG.
      When do you want me to visit you?

      pə(d)táb haw̓ə kʷi gʷ(ə)ads.čəwà?til ?ə kʷi
      gʷ(ə)ads.p̓ayəq ?ə kʷi ha?ł s.dəxʷi̓ł   LG.
      When will you ever learn to make a good
      duck-hunting canoe!?

      dił pə(d)táb   any time   ES.

      xʷi? gʷədsəs.(h)áydxʷ pə(d)tàb kʷi łus.?ux̌ʷčəł   LG.
      I don't know when we will go.

      ?əs.(h)áydxʷ čələp ?u pə(d)tàb kʷi s.?ux̌ʷs   LG.
      Do you folks know when he went?

      ?əxʷ.cútᵊb čəxʷ ?u gʷəpə(d)tábəs kʷi gʷə.łči̓ls   LG.
      Do you think he will get here sometime?

      pə(d)tə́s(ᵊb)   winter

      pədhə́dᵊb   summer

      pədƛ̓qúlil   spring (LL.) (LG. gives jəpi̓l)

      pədƛ̓xʷáy?   autumn, November (time of dog salmon)

      pədx̌ʷiwáac   time of (robin) whistling (used for April)

      pədčá?ᵊb   time of digging (camas bulbs) (app. May)

      pədstəgʷád   time of salmonberries (used for June)

pədgʷədbíxʷ   time of blackberries   (used for July)

pə(d)t̓áqa   time of salalberries   (used for August)

pədkʷxʷíc   time of silver salmon   (used for September)

pədxʷíčib   time of elk/deer mating cry   (used for October)

1.   pəjátuɬ   duck hunting; hunting along shore

     See under xʷiʔxʷiʔ.

     ʔəbiləxʷ díɬ kʷši d.ʔálalš kʷi ʔupəjátuɬ ...   ML.

     If it would be my brothers who are duck hunting ...

     ƛupəjátuɬ (h)əlgʷəʔ čaʔkʷ, tiʔiɬ ʔàlalšs   ML.

     They would be duck hunting out from shore, her brothers.

2.   pəɬt   thick (dimension)

     Cf. t̓əq   thick (like dough pressed together)

       ɬəqt   wide

   -il

     pəɬtíl   It got thick.   LG.

3. s.pə́qʷ   boil (disease)

     (Also recorded s.p̓ə̂kʷ.)

     See under x̌əɬ.

4.   pəqʷ(u)   break a piece off (leaving a larger portion)

     See under xʷəƛ, ɬič̓(i).

   -ut

     pqʷud   break it off   LL., LG.

     pqʷútəb   cut off   LG.

-yi-

    pəqʷyíd   Break off a piece so he can have some.   LG.

lexical

    ʔupəqʷšádit°b   amputate a leg, cut leg off   LL.

    ʔupqʷúsᵊd   decapitated him   LL.

      Cf. ʔu.xʷƛápsəbᵊd   broke his neck   LL.

      Cf. (d)xʷ.čƛápsəbᵊd   decapitate him   LL.

rejected:

    *ʔudxʷpqʷúsᵊd   LL.

1. s.pə̀təbqíd   man's name, maternal grandfather of DM.

→

3. pəx̌áy(ʔ)ac   log, dead tree   JC.

4. pəx̌cút   spouting of a whale

5. s.pícx̌ʷ   the myth name of s.x̌ʷəx̌ʷíʔ   LL., ESi.

                        See Ballard, p. 49.

6. pígʷəd   power song and/or power dance of any type LG.

    Cf. s.tílib, sə́x̌ᵊb

      ʔəlčupígʷəd   He's singing a power song.   LG.

    reduplication

      pígʷpigʷəd   powwow   EK.

7. piit   bed (western style)   (from English *bed*
                                             by way of Chinook Jargon)

    Cf. ləlwáʔs

      ƛáɋagʷil dxʷʔal tə piit   Lie down on the bed.

1. s.piláykʷ   fresh-water bullhead   CB.

     s.təbáykʷ   fresh-water bullhead   DM.

2. xʷ.pípt   SPS   shirt   ESi.

     Cf. púʔtəd   NPS   shirt

3. s.pipídəq   jealous   LG.

4. s.píqʷuc, s.páyqʷuc   potato; arrowhead plant, wapato

       s.píʔqʷuc   EK.

       s.pqʷúc   LL.

       s.píqʷulc   VH.

       s.pìqʷúc   ESi.

       See Elmendorf, p. 127.

5. s.píš   fish scales   LG., LL.

6.   píšpiš   cat

      pípšpiš   kitten

      píšpišpiš   cats

      pípipšpiš   kittens

7.   pítᵊb   notice; pay attention to; understand

     Cf. yíčᵊb, ƛəlábut, ləqálbut

     -b

       <u>pít</u>ᵊb   notice

       ʔəs<u>pít</u>ᵊb čəd   I understand.

-i-t

xʷi? gʷədsəspíteᵊbid   I didn't pay attention to it.

1.   pixʷ(i)   shake down

See under xʷis(i), xʷít(il), pus(u).

root

píxʷ čəd   "This means something but I don't know   LG.
                how you'd say it in English."

-it

?upíxʷid   knock it off, shake it off   LL.

píxʷid tə ?apəls   Shake the apples down.   LG.

-yi-

píxʷyic ?ə tə ?apəls   Shake the apples down for me.   LG.

lexical

(dxʷ)pixʷá(hᵊ)b   Brush your bottom off. (Said to
                  someone who has been sitting in
                  the dust.)   LG.

čḱusəd tə cəxʷupìxʷalikʷ   LG.
I felled (the cones by hitting the tree) with a cane.

rejected:

*píxʷicut, *píxʷᵊb, *píxʷib, *píxʷdubut   LG.

I suggested ?upíxʷᵊdxʷ čəxʷ and LG. accepted it, but
seemed to prefer ?upíxʷildxʷ čəxʷ. The gloss for both
was the same, viz., 'You dropped it.'

-il

?upíxʷil   (A pine cone/ a leaf) fell.   LG.

?upíxʷil čəd   I fell (from a tree).   LG.

cày ʔəspíxʷil tə d.x̌ə̀č   JC.

I'm completely disorganized. "This is a slang use of
píxʷil."

píxʷil   fall apart   "This meaning is also a slang use."   JC.

-il-t

píxʷild

Drop it (down to me because I can't reach it).   LG.
This is equivalent to x̌ʷit̓ild.   LG.

ʔupíxʷilt^əb ʔə ti s.tubš tə x̌ʷìləb   LG.
The man dropped the rope.

-il-dxʷ

ʔupíxʷildxʷ čəd   I dropped it.   LG.

lexical

ʔupíxʷilalc čəxʷ ʔə t(ə) ad.pàʔkʷ   LG.
You dropped your pipe.

rejected:

*pixʷagʷil   "That would mean x̌ʷtágʷil. Some other group
              might say pixʷagʷil. I would understand it;
              but we don't [use it]. I've never heard it."   LG.

*ʔupíxʷil čəd ʔə tə s.p̓íp̓əlkʷ   LG.

*ʔupíxʷil čəd ʔə tə ckùsəd   LG.

*s.p̓íp̓əlkʷ tə cəxʷpìxʷil   LG.

*ʔupíxʷiltxʷ čəd tə s.p̓íp̓əlkʷ   LG.
"That would mean 'I throw the cone' but it's not right."   LG.

1.   plála?   See plíla?(ac).

2.   pli   Spirit, Holy Ghost   (from French *esprit*?)

1.　plîlaʔ(ac)　　　wild cherry (tree)

　　Cf. plálaʔ　　　　LL.

　　　k̓ʷəlwástəd ʔə tə plìləʔac　　　　　　　　MC., LG.
　　　birch tree (lit. 'in-laws of the wild cherry tree')

2.　plúlʔk̓ʷəd　　　"fungus on a tree"　　　　　　　　　　AS.

3.　pᵊ́łə́x̌　　　what is put on a person's possessions (esp.
　　　　　　　　clothing) in order to gain power over him　VH.

　　Cf. x̌əč̓adad, s.qəlálitut

　　See Elmendorf, p. 527

4.　pq̓-

　　　pq̓áləqəp　　flat, tasteless

　　See under -qəp.

5.　pt-

　　Cf. dx̌ʷ.cút̓ᵊb, t̓úk̓ʷ/gʷ(u)

　　　ptídəgʷəsᵊb

　　　　ʔuptídəgʷəsᵊb čəd　　　I'm thinking.　　　EK.

　　　　tux̌ʷ čəd ʔuptídəgʷəsᵊb　I'm just thinking.　EK.

　　　　sptídəgʷasᵊb　　　　memory, mind, character　EK.

　　　　hàʔł sptídəgʷəsᵊb　　　good memory, mind, character　EK.

　　　　gʷəl čəd ʔəs.t(ə)łíldxʷ tułʔal bək̓ʷ dᵊsptìdgʷəsᵊb　EC.
　　　　And I believe with all my thoughts.

　　　　yəx̌i čəxʷ huy ləs.k̓ʷax̌ʷac liłʔal tiʔił haʔł ʔads.gʷaʔ
　　　　ʔadsptídəgʷəsᵊb　　　　　　　　　　　　　EC.
　　　　Because you are helping me through Thine own good
　　　　thoughts.

-i-d

Ɂəlčuptídgʷəsᵊbid   LG.

I'm thinking about someone.

reduplication

Ɂəlčupətptídgʷəsᵊb čəd   I'm thinking.   LG.

1.   púbᵊb   drag anchor, resist being towed through
                             the water

2.   púkʷᵊb

      -b

        púkʷᵊb   pile

          hiɁiɁəbəxʷ Ɂəspúkʷᵊb   too much pile now   LG.

        spúkʷᵊb   hill

          Cf. s.bádil   mountain

      -b-t

        púkʷᵊbᵊd   pile it up   LG.

      -yi-

        púkʷᵊbyid   pile it for someone   LG.

      reduplication

        spúkʷpukʷᵊb   hilly

      rejected:

        *púkʷᵊbid, *púkʷud

3.   pús   SPS   aunt
      Ɂəpús NPS   aunt
      See under s.qa.

1.   pus(u)   project through the air, throw

    See xʷis(i) 'brush off', ƛ̓uč̓(u) 'shoot'.

    Cf. xʷəb   throw, discard; throw someone down

       pak̓(a)   scatter, distribute

       píxʷ(i)   shake down

       ʔix̌ʷ(i)   throw out; sweep

  root

    ʔupús čəd   I got hit. E.g., an apple fell on me;
                 in baseball I got hit with/by a wild pitch.   LL.

    ʔupús čəd ʔə tiʔiɬ s.tubš   LL.
    I got hit by that man('s body) flying through the air
    at me.

       Rejected: *ʔupús tiʔiɬ s.tùbš   LL.

    xʷîʔtubš ɬi ləpús   LL.
    Don't you folks let me get hit.

  -ut

    ʔupúsud čəd   I threw it.   LL.

       ʔupúsud čəd tə ds.yayaʔ ʔə t(ə ʔ)əs.bulux̌ʷîlc
       I threw the ball at my friend.

  -dxʷ

    ʔupúsdubš čəxʷ   You happened to hit me.   ES.

    ʔəs.x̌ác čəd gʷəpùsᵊdxʷəd   LL.
    I'm afraid that I might hit him.

    ʔəs.x̌ác čəd gʷəpùsdubicidəd   LL.
    I'm afraid that I might hit you.

  -txʷ

    ʔupústub čəd   LG.
    Someone picked me up and threw me.

-il

ʔupúsil čəd	I threw.	LL., LG.

ʔupúsil čəd ʔə tə (ʔəs).bulux̌ʷílc   LG.
I threw the ball.

s.p̓íp̓əlkʷ tə cəx̌ʷpùsil   LG.
I threw with a pinecone.

ʔəs.bulux̌ʷílc tə cəx̌ʷpúsil   LG.
I threw the ball.

dx̌ʷspúsil   a (baseball) pitcher   LL.

-il-dx̌ʷ

ʔupúsildx̌ʷ čəd t(ə ʔ)əs.bulux̌ʷílc   LG.
I threw the ball.

-il-yi-

łupúsilyicid čəd   I'll throw for you.   LG.

-il-tx̌ʷ

ʔupúsiltub čəd   LL.
I got thrown (as in wrestling).

ʔupúsiltub   It was thrown away.   LL.

ʔupúsiltx̌ʷ čəd   I threw it.   LL.

          I threw it (esp. a living
                    being).   LG.

lexical

ʔudx̌ʷpúsaptʔb čəd   LL.
They threw it at my hind end.

púsqid ʔə ti č̓x̌a?   EK.
He got hit on the head with a rock.

ʔu.x̌ʷítilič čəd čədà pùsqidəx̌ʷ ʔə tiʔił ʔàpəls   LL.
Apples fell on me and hit me on the head.

reduplication

púps	tossing pebbles	LL.
púpsil	throwing it up and down and playing with it	LL.

1. pús^əg^was   the same, even   LG.

x̣ʷúⁱ čəⁱ pús^əg^wəs tə s.(h)àj^əbčəⁱ
We're exactly the same height.

ʔupús^əg^wəs tiʔiⁱ   They are the same size.

2. put   adverb of emphasis

Cf. tib

hay (g^w)əl, pútəx^w ƛ(u)as.bəⁱ tiʔiⁱ s.čətx^wəd   ES.
And then, Bear would get just plumb full.

huy, pútəx^w ƛubə.ƛač^əb ciʔiⁱ ƛaƛačəpəd   ES.
Then, Ant would just cinch up her belt some more.

pútəx^w ʔəs.ⁱúk^wəč tiʔiⁱ bi.bščəb   ES.
Little Mink was completely bald.

(huy, ƛubə.tácəx^w ciʔiⁱ ƛaƛačəpəd) pútəx^w ƛəbə.tílib
And Ant would dance some more and she would really sing some more.

pút čəx^w   You are. (Gloss not clear but EK. was most satisfied with the Snoh.)

pút čəd diʔaʔ   I'm all here.   EK.

3. pux^w(u)   add to, increase the amount of

-ut

púx^wud   add more to it

ʔupúx^wud čəd ʔə k^wi ⁱìx^w bit
I add thirty cents.

lexical

púxʷalikʷ   add in, increase the amount of   EK.

1. púỷ   curve, bend

   Cf. q̓əč   crooked

    x̌ʷuɫáb ʔəspùỷ. díɫ səs.dáʔatᵊbs ʔə tiʔəʔ spuỷáləpəbš.
    yəx̌ì tiʔəʔ s.túləkʷ ʔə tiʔəʔ spuỷàləpəbš gʷəs ʔəspúỷpuỷ MS.
    Just like a curve. They are called the people of the
    bend [i.e., Puyallup] because their river is full of
    bends.
    See Smith, p.9.

2. puʔ(u)   blow; wind

   See under šəxʷᵊb.

  -ut

    púʔud tə l(ə)x̌šàd   Blow out the lamp.   LG.

  lexical

    ʔəlčupúʔalikʷ   It's blowing outside.   LG.

    tíb spùʔalikʷ   It's a really hard wind.   LG.

    púʔtəd NPS   shirt   EK.

     Cf. xʷ.pípt SPS   shirt

     ɫu.təx̌ʷ čəd pùʔtəd   LG.
     I will (go to town to) buy a shirt.

     ɫu.tágʷš čəd ti puʔtəd   LG.
     I will buy the shirt (I've seen before).

     ʔá ʔu kʷi xʷíʔ lə.q̓ič puʔtəd   LG.
     Is there any shirt that is not expensive?

     ʔá ʔu kʷi xʷìʔ lə.q̓ìč ʔə tə pùʔtəd   LG.
     Is there any out of these shirts that is not
     expensive?

-b

ʔupúʔtədᵊb čəd   I put the shirt on.   LG.

Compare:

ʔu.ƛ́álaɬ čəd pùʔtəd

Same gloss: I put the shirt on.

ʔu.ƛ́álš čəd ti pùʔtəd

Same gloss: I put the shirt on.

Contrast:

ʔu.xʷə́cᵊd čəd tə pùʔtəd

I took the shirt off.

reduplication

pípuʔtəd   thin shirt

púʔpuʔtəd   shirts

p̓

The sound represented by this letter is similar to that of p
except for the added simultaneous abrupt closure of the vocal cords,
a sort of catch in the throat. [glottalized bilabial stop]

1.   p̓aa-   See under p̓a?-.

2.   p̓ac̓(a)   sew

        root

?əlc̓up̓ac̓ čəd	I'm sewing.	LG.
səxʷp̓ac̓	sewing machine	EK.
səxʷup̓ac̓	what is used to sew with	LG.
səxʷp̓ác̓təd	a sewing machine	LG.
p̓ác̓təd	a sewing needle	EK., LG.

        -at

p̓ác̓ad	sew it	LL.

        lexical

           p̓ác̓aɫəd (perhaps a misrecording for p̓ác̓aɫx̌əd)

               'strong wind blowing up hard driven spray
                from surface of sea (no big waves)'   LL.

               See under šə́xʷəb.

        rejected:

           *p̓ac̓əb, *səxʷup̓ác̓təd   VH.; LG.

3.   p̓ác̓aɫəd   strong wind blowing up the surface water;
                     hard driven spray

        See under p̓ac̓(a).

4.   p̓ák̓ʷ(a)   See under hud(u).

        -at

           p̓ák̓ʷad   warm it

           p̓ák̓ʷacut warm yourself

351

1. p̓al

    p̓álič   go over a point   DM.

    See under jal.

2. p̓álil   regain consciousness   LG.
                  revive   HD.

    Cf. gʷə.t̓q̓ʷád   faint, pass out

    -t

        p̓álilcut   Come to your senses!, Act your age!
                   (I.e., Behave yourself.)   LG.

3. p̓alq̓   turn(ed) out of shape, bent out of line,
                 shape, position

    See under q̓əč.

    root

        ʔup̓álq̓   It got bent over (from the way it
                         should be).   LG.

    -t

        p̓álq̓əd   Turn it down. Bend it out of shape. LG.

    -i(1)s

        pəlq̓ís   A way of guessing in the bone game, sləhál.
                (It seems to involve guessing two at once
                (hence turned).)

    lexical

        pəlq̓áči?   mole   AS., LG.

         ʔəsp̓əlq̓áči? His hand is turned over as is
                   a cripple's.   LG.

        ʔəsp̓əlp̓əlqšəd   one whose feet are widely turned out AS.

        p̓álq̓usəd   Bend his face back! (shouted in
                 wrestling)   LG.

ʔəxʷp̓álq̓aʔɫdəɫ   Someone who has the lower lip curved
down -- deformed in that way.   LG.

rejected: *p̓álq̓əb   LG.

1.   p̓áƛ-   of no importance

   p̓áƛaƛ   junk, worthless stuff   ES.
   unworthy, nothing of value   EK.

[Note that p̓áƛaƛ, xʷiʔ, x̌aƛ, and x̌ʷuɫ can function as independent and complete predications. However, each is
modified by subordinate predications in a different way.]

as independent predication

   p̓áƛaƛ dxʷʔal ʔəcà gʷ(ə)as.ƛáx̌əs   LG.
   I don't care if she does get cold.

   p̓áƛaƛ gʷə.ʔáhas kʷi səs.čáls gʷəɫu.hùyəs   LG.
   It makes no difference what happens.

   p̓áƛaƛ dxʷʔal ʔəcà gʷ(ə)alču.ʔəx̌íx̌ədəxʷ   LG.
   It doesn't matter to me what you do.

   p̓áƛaƛ dxʷʔal ʔəcà gʷ(ə)alču.ʔəx̌íx̌ədələp   LG.
   I don't care what you folks do.

   tuləs.híwis čəd kʷi bək̓ʷ ʔal ti s.wátixʷtəd p̓àƛaƛ   EC.
   I was into everything of this world that was unworthy.

as head of predication

   tux̌ʷ čəɫ p̓áƛaƛ tu.kʷədálikʷ tuĺʔá   ML.
   We just helped ourselves to worthless stuff from
   there.

   x̌ʷuɫ p̓áƛaƛ tiʔəʔ ds.ʔàbyid   ES.
   I'll just give him junk.

   x̌ʷùɫ p̓áƛaƛ tiʔiɫ s.ʔábyids tiʔiɫ čƛà?   ES.
   He gave only worthless stuff to that rock.

353

huy, ʔábyidəxʷ ʔə tiʔił x̌ʷuĺ p̓aƛaƛ stab   ES.
And then he gave him only worthless stuff.

ʔił-...-il

   ʔiłp̓aƛaƛil   He is getting worse.

-al-dxʷ

   p̓aƛaldxʷ   pay no heed

     Cf. ƛal-d

ʔəbił čəxʷ ʔəsp̓aƛaldxʷ gʷəl tił gʷə.x̌ə́ł kʷ(i) ad.wiw̓su,
gʷə.bakʷł   JC.

If you pay no heed to them, your children might get
sick, might get hurt.

lexical

   p̓áƛucid   worthless talk   DM.

reduplication

   p̓ap̓ap̓ƛaƛ   no-counts, riffraff   ML.

    Equivalent to sdúʔdukʷ. (See under dukʷ(u).)   ML.

1. p̓áyəq   hew out, carve out, make a canoe

   See under łič(i).

   root

     ʔup̓áyəq   hew out, carve out

     dáʔxʷ tup̓áyəq tə d.bàd   My father just made a canoe.

     ləcup̓áyəq   making a canoe

     p̓áyəqəd   adze for making a canoe   Cf. həláytəd

     dxʷsp̓áyəq   canoe maker

2. p̓áʔkʷ   pipe

1. p̓aʔ-   taste it; try to do something

    See under -qəp.

    Compare:

        tíbicut   try hard to do something requiring muscle power

        háy(ʔ)ad   try to learn (from hay 'know'?)

        káwɫᵊb   try, improvise

    -t

        p̓áʔəd   tasted it   LG.

        p̓áʔtəd   (unglossed)   LG.

        tup̓áʔcut čəd dxʷʔal gʷəds.ʔə̀λ   EK.
        I tried to come.

        tup̓áacut čəd dxʷʔal gʷəds.ṭičib
        I tried to swim.

        tup̓áacut čəd dxʷʔal gʷəds.gʷàdədgʷəd
        I tried to talk.

        tup̓áacut čəd dxʷʔal gʷədsəs.làx̌dxʷ   EK.
        I'm trying to think of it.

        ləcup̓áacut čəd čəda ləcu.húd(i)čup   DM.
        I was trying to make a fire.

2. s.p̓ə́č   feces

    See under xʷásil 'wet one's clothes'.

    Cf. sʔəx̌ʷáʔ   urinate (male)

        tiwáʔ   urinate (female)

        čic̓q̓ʷəp   (baby) with feces on buttocks (Cf. čiq̓ʷ)

1.　p̓čəb　　　　　　　　See p̓ə́čəb.

2. (s)p̓ə́čəb　NPS　　　bobcat (lynx)　　　　　　　　　EK., MC.

　　　p̓čə́b　SPS　　　bobcat (lynx)　　　　　　　　　ESi.

3.　p̓ədíl　　　　　　drift up and lodge on shore　　EK., LL.

　　　Cf. ɬálil　　　go ashore, dock

　　　　　p̓əq̓ʷ(ú)　　drift

　　　　　p̓ús°b　　　float

　　　-txʷ

　　　　　ʔəsp̓ədíltub　　It was caused to drift ashore.　ML.

4.　s.p̓ə́kʷ　　　　　(infectious) boil

　　　Also recorded as s.p̓ə́qʷ. See under x̌əɬ.

5.　p̓ələq̓　　　　　　flash, blinking light

　　　See under ləx̌.

　　　-t

　　　　　p̓ələq̓°d　　flash the light on someone/something

　　　-b

　　　　　ʔalč̓up̓ələq̓°b　　　　blinking

　　　reduplication

　　　　　ʔalč̓up̓ə́lp̓ələq̓　　(a traffic light) flashing on and off

→

7.　p̓ə́lxʷəb　Skagit　lungs　　　　　　　　　　　　LG.

　　　Cf. s.cəɬdálbali　Snoh.　　　　　　　　　　　LL.

8.　p̓əɬq̓ʷ　　　　　sprain, get out of joint

　　　See under q̓əč.

pə́ƛ̣q̓ʷáči?   sprain wrist

pə́ƛ̣q̓ʷšád   sprain ankle

pə́ƛ̣q̓ʷùlágʷəp   hip out of joint

1. pə́ƛ̣q̓ʷ Snoh., SPS after

    Cf. bə́lx̌ʷ Skagit   after

    pə́ƛ̣q̓ʷ ?ə tə taɬəgʷət   12:00 o'clock

    čəx̌gʷás ?ə tə spə́ƛ̣q̓ʷ ?ə tə sàli?   2:30 o'clock

    čəx̌gʷásəxʷ ?ə tə spə́ƛ̣q̓ʷ ?ə tə buus   4:30

    ?upə́ƛ̣q̓ʷəxʷ   The sun is going down.

   lexical

    pə́ƛ̣q̓ʷábac   Monday

      Cf. bə́lᵊx̌ʷəɬdàt Skagit   Monday

2. s.pə́ƛ̣q̓ʷ   sucker (freshwater fish)   AS.

   tu?áckʷ   Skagit   LG.

   s.q(ʷ)úb? Snoh.   LL.

   q̓úxʷəd   Nooksack   LG.

3. pə́ƛ̓   Cf. k̓aw-

   -t

   pə́ƛ̓ᵊd   feel it

   pə́ƛ̓tᵊb   be felt

4. pəpáyəqəd(ac) Snoh. rainflower berry (bush)
                     ("If you mess with it, it rains.") LL.

   Cf. hahəláy?təd Skagit   rainflower berry   MC.

1. p̓ə́q̓ac   SPS   rotten wood   ESi.

    p̓q̓ác   NPS   rotten wood

2. p̓əqʷ

    Cf. qʷəqʷ

        ʔup̓ə́qʷəd   popped it   JC.

3. p̓əq̓ʷ(u)   drift, throw into the water

    Cf. p̓ədíl, p̓úsəb

    root

        ʔup̓ə́q̓ʷ   drifted

        p̓q̓ʷáxʷ   drifting now

        ləp̓ə́q̓ʷ tə qʷɬay?   The log is drifting.   LG.

    dxʷ-

        ƛudxʷp̓ə́q̓ʷ tiʔəʔ s.tùləkʷ   LG., EC.
        (Ice) would float in the river.

    -ut

        p̓q̓ʷúd   threw it into the water   LG.

        sp̓ə́q̓ʷucut   What s.ʔuládxʷ are called after spawning,
                       especially the steelhead because they do
                       not die and they eventually revive upon
                       reaching salt water again.   DM.

    lexical

        p̓ip̓q̓ʷálikʷ   drifting net

            See under ƛáʔtəd.

        ləp̓q̓ʷálikʷ   shakes floating down the river   LG.

        ʔəčup̓q̓ʷálikʷ   (The men) are drifting (shakes) down
                       the river.   LG.

358

reduplication

pípəq̓ʷ   drift up and down river estuary
              with the tide   LL.

pə́q̓ʷəq̓ʷ   drift about more or less in one place
              stationary   LL.

rejected: *ʔəlc̓upə́q̓ʷ (čəd)   LG.

1.   p̓əs

     pəsq̓ʷəg̓ʷás   joint   EK.

     pəsq̓ʷəg̓ʷásači?   wrist   EK.

     pəsq̓ʷəg̓ʷá(s)šəd   ankle   EK.

     (EK. also gives q̓ʷəpx̌ʷ(šəd) 'ankle'.)

     spəsq̓ʷšád   ankle   LG.

2.   p̓ič(i)   wring it out

     Cf. ƛ̓ip(i), ƛ̓ač(a)

     -it

     p̓ičid   wring it out   LG.

     lexical

     p̓ič̓albixʷ ci?ə? q̓ʷist   milk the cow   LL.

       Cf. ƛ̓ip̓albixʷ   squeeze/hold the teat   LL.

3.   p̓íč̓t   coals, embers

     Cf. xʷ.(h)údad   ashes

4.   s.p̓ík̓   (pine) marten

5.   p̓íl(i)   flat, broad

     See under šuƛ̓.

Cf. łə́q̓t, ǰač̓

root

ʔəsp̓íl	it's flat	LG.
ʔəsp̓íl	wide, flat (synonym for łə́q̓t)	LL.
ʔəsp̓íl tiʔəʔ s.č̓úp̓č̓ ʔə tiʔəʔ diʔəʔ s.t̓əqxʷ		DM.
The tail of the beaver is flat.		

-it

| p̓ílid | flatten it | |

-b

p̓ílᵊbəxʷ	it flooded	LG.
ʔup̓ílᵊb	high tide	LG.
sp̓ílᵊb	high tide	ESi., EK.
ləp̓ílᵊbəxʷ	The tide is coming in.	LG.
(ʔə)ƛ̓áxʷ tə sp̓ìlᵊb	Same gloss: The tide is coming in.	EK.
ʔup̓ílᵊbəxʷ	The tide came in.	LG.

lexical

ʔəsp̓ilp̓ilálubid	broad shoulders	LL.
p̓ílilc	flat forehead	LG.
ʔəsp̓ilp̓ilyálus tiʔəʔ ƛ̓(ə)lày̓		DM.
The shovel-nose canoe has flattened ends.		

1. s.p̓íp̓əlkʷ   fir cone

2. p̓íq̓ʷ   flatus

reduplication

   p̓íq̓ʷp̓íq̓ʷ   break wind repeatedly

1.   p̓q̓ác   NPS   rotten wood

     Cf. p̓ə́q̓ac   SPS   rotten wood

2.   p̓sác̓   Dolly Varden trout   LL.

     p̓šác̓   Dolly Varden trout   EK.

3.   p̓t̓(a)   put away, tidy up; preserve, save

     Cf. q̓it-   store food

     -t/ -š

        ʔup̓t̓áš čəd   I put it away.   LG.

        p̓t̓áš   preserving (meat)   LG.

        p̓t̓ád t(ə) ad.ʔàlʔal   Tidy up your house.   EK.

     lexical

        p̓t̓ús^əb — rendered below

        p̓t̓úsᵊb   push hair out of face   EK.

        ʔu.q̓ádadid čəd ti dsəsp̓t̓àlikʷ   LG.
        I stole it from my savings.

        tudsəsp̓t̓íg̓ʷsᵊb   LG.
        I had my things stored away, put away neatly.

        t(u)asp̓t̓íg̓ʷsᵊb čəd   LG.
        Same gloss: I had my things stored away, put away
                    neatly.

     rejected: *p̓t̓áb

        Also EK. does not accept p̓t̓áš.

4.   p̓úp̓lab   yeast bread

5.   p̓uq   wild currant   JC.

1. s.p̓ús   kidney   ML.

     Cf. s.čədčəd   kidney   EK.

        č̓ƛ̓alúb   kidney   LG.

2. p̓us^əb   float

     Cf. p̓əq̓ʷ, p̓ədíl

       ʔəsp̓ús^əb   float   HD.

       ʔup̓ús^əbəxʷ   It's floating now, e.g., a log has surfaced.   HD.

       ʔəsp̓ús^əbəxʷ   It floats now (after having been put back in the water this spring.)   LL.

     -dxʷ

       ʔup̓ús^əbdxʷ   Someone got it floating.   HD.

     -agʷ-il

       ʔup̓ús^əbàgʷil tiʔił čxʷ(ə)lùʔ   LL.
     The whale surfaced and floated.

       ʔup̓ús^əbàgʷil čəd   LL.
     I came to the surface. (This can be said only by skin divers and people who are in the water habitually and for long periods of time.)

     lexical

       p̓úp̓s^əbaX̌əd   wooden float for a gill net   LL.

     rejected:

       *p̓ús-ud   HD.

       *p̓ús^əbàgʷis   "Sounds OK but doesn't make sense."   LL.

3. p̓úwəyʔ SPS   flounder

    p̓uáyʔ   NPS   flounder

362

λ(u)as.pədág^wil ciʔił p̓uày̓ʔ ʔal pə(d).t̓əs.

ʔəs.q̓(ə)čáʔłdəł ciʔił p̓uày̓ʔ.

ʔəs.q̓əčq̓(ə)čálus.

A flounder buries itself in the winter.
A flounder has a crooked mouth.
Its face is crooked.   DM.

q

This letter stands for a sound similar to that of k except that the q-sound is made further back in the mouth. [voiceless uvular stop]

1. qa(h)   many, much, a lot

    verb

    -il

        ləqáil ti?ił s.x̌ʷəs   Lots of fat comes.   ES.

        ?uqá(y)il tə sc̉i.c̉qay̓səb   Many more flowers are in bloom. JC.

    head of predication

        qá ti?ə? qyùuqs stə.tùdəqs   ML.
        There were a lot of seagull slaves.

        qá ti?ił ?ìišəds (h)əlgʷə?   ML.
        There were a lot of their friends/relatives.

        qá ti d.tàlə   I have a lot of money.   DM.

        qa qyuuqs   There were a lot of seagulls.   ML.

        qá ?u kʷ(i) ads.yə̀cᵊb   Do you have much news?   ES.

        qá s.či̓q̉ʷil   There was a lot of dirt.

        qáhəxʷ ?acił̉talbixʷ ?əs.q̉ʷu?
        There were a lot of people assembled.

    comparative

        qá tə d.yì̓qus x̌ʷuĺ̉ab ?ə t(ə) ads.gʷà?   LG.
        I have as many baskets as you have.

        ƛal ?u bəqà tə d.yì̓qus x̌ʷuĺ̉ab ?ə t(ə) ads.gʷa?   LG.
        Do I have as many baskets as you have?

        dì̓ł ?ił̉qá tə d.yì̓qus dxʷ?al dəgʷì̓   LG.
        I have more baskets than you.

        In some types of comparative statements lil is used
        instead of qa:

        líl čəd ?ił.lùƛ dxʷ?al dəgʷì̓   I'm a lot older than you.

Both of the following are ungrammatical:

*qa čəd ʔił.luλ̓ dxʷʔal dəgʷi̓

*qa ʔił.luλ̓ čəd dxʷʔal dəgʷi̓

head of subordinate predication

> tələbx̌ q̓i̓l ciʔəʔ ka̓ʔkaʔ tiʔəʔ qa tiʔəʔ šijus,
> kʷi bək̓ʷ s.tab, s.tu̓ʔᵊl, kʷi bək̓ʷ s.tab   ML.
>
> Crow had a canoe full of lots of smelt and
> everything, and herring and everything.

> ʔəy̓dxʷəxʷ qa tiʔəʔ s.ʔulàdxʷ ʔal tiʔił dəču̓ʔ s.tùləkʷ   ML.
>
> He found a lot of fish in one stream.

modifier

> łu.diʔáhəxʷ kʷi qa ʔacił talbixʷ
> There will be a lot of people here.

> təłáxʷ tiʔił qa ʔacił talbixʷ ʔu.q̓ʷuʔᵊd
> Truly, they gathered a lot of people.

head of complement

> hi̓kʷ ʔəs.łáłlil qa ʔal tiʔacəc s.watixʷtəd ʔə
> tiʔił gʷəł dibəł ʔal kʷədi̓ʔ tu.hàkʷ   ML.
>
> Many dwelt in this place that belonged to
> us long ago.

> ʔəs.ʔəx̌i̓d kʷi sqàs kʷi ʔacił talbixʷ ʔal dxʷliləp   EK.
> How many Indians are at Tulalip?

lexical

> siʔáb qahálgʷič̓   a wealthy man   DM.

> dxʷ(s)qáhigʷəd   clever, cunning, crafty   LG.

> λ̓al čəd bəqahigʷəd x̌ʷulab ʔə dəgʷi̓   LG.
> I'm as clever as you.

other derivation

q̲ahəɫ talə čəd	I have a lot of money.	DM.

reduplication

dxʷ(s)qəqáx̌a?	stingy	VH.

    Cf. dxʷ.číx̌

dxʷsqəqáx̌a? čəxʷ	You are stingy.	LG.

rejected:

*qa ?əbstalə čəd		DM.

1.   s.qá   older sibling, child of parent's older sibling

Compare:

by age:	súq̓ʷa?
cross-sex:	?álš
strong blood and emotional tie:	təlíxʷ
sisters married to same man:	?əš̌álgʷəs

366

Chart 1

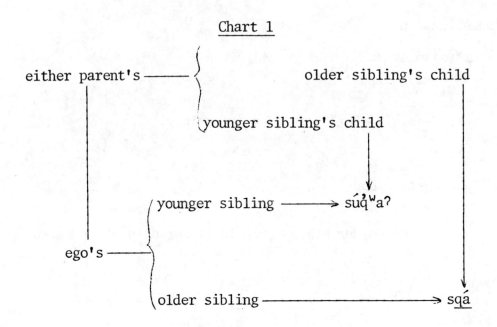

Chart 2

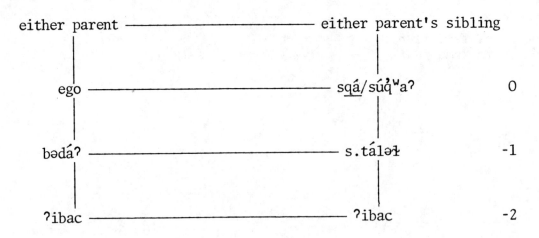

sqíʔqa	little older sibling	LL.
dəxʷsqátəd	older siblings	
sqəqá	older sibling (said humbly)	LG.
sqə́q(ə) Snoqu.	older sibling	LL.
šə́qə́q	older sibling as articulated in a song	ML.
čít sqà	older sibling next to ego	
ʔabsqá čəd	I have an older sibling	LG.
dᵊsqá čəxʷ	You are my older sibling.	LG.

1. qábqəb　　　　　guessing; substitute

2. qac(a)　　　　　lighten, let up

　Cf. x̌əb　　　　(real) heavy

　　xʷəʔáʔxʷəʔ　light weight

　-at

　　qácad　　　　lighten the (canoe) load

　-il

　　ʔuqáciləxʷ ti qə̀lb

　The rain has let up. (It's still raining but not as hard.)

　　See under qəlᵊb.　　Cf. xʷač̓

1.   qácacut   sparking, lightning

     See under ləx̌ 'light'.

2.   qad(a)   back up

     See under jix^w.

     Cf. laq

     -at

qádacut	back up	EK.
ʔəsqádacut	keep back	EK.
qádad	back it up	LG.

     -bi-t

adqádbid	He is behind you.	LG.

       Cf. ad.ləqbíd (from laq)   He is behind you.   LL.

lə.ʔíbəš čəx^w ʔal tiʔəʔ dqədbíd   DM.
You're walking behind me.

ʔəs.g^wədíl ʔal tiʔił adqádbid   LG.
He is sitting behind you.

       Cf. ʔəs.g^wədíl ʔal tiʔił ad.ʔálq̓^wbid   LG.
         Same gloss: He is sitting behind you.

         Cf. *ʔəs.g^wədíl ʔal tiʔił ad.ləqbíd   rejected. LG.

sáx^{wə}b tə čačas d^əqàdbid   LG.
The boy behind me jumped.

ləcu.kʷátač čəd ʔal ti s.bàdil ʔal ti q̀adbid ʔə

ti ʔalʔal čəda ʔu.téčtəč   DM.

I was climbing the mountain behind the house and
I tumbled down.

lexical

qádadiʔ   behind the house   EK.

  Cf. t̓əq̓tálatxʷ   behind the house   DM.
                   (lit.'mountain side of house')

1.   qada   steal

  root

    qáda čəxʷ ʔu ʔə tə s.dùukʷ   LG.
    Did you steal the knife?

    bəqáda tiʔəʔ bəščəb   Mink stole again.   LG.

    ʔuqáda tiʔəʔ luƛ ʔə tə s.ʔuladxʷ   LG.
    The old man stole the salmon.

  dxʷs-

    dxʷsqáda   thief   HD.

  -di-t   (from *-ni-t)

    ʔuqádadid čəd ʔə ti dsəs.p̓tàlikʷ   LG.
    I stole it from my savings.

    ʔuqádaditᵊb čəd jəɫ ʔə tiʔiɫ   LG.
    He must have stolen it from me.

    ʔuqádaditᵊb čəd ʔə ti ds.dúukʷ   EK.
    They stole my knife.

    qádadicut   steal from himself   EK.

    bəqádadidəxʷ tiʔəʔ bəščəb   LG.
    Someone again stole from Mink.

ʔuqádadidəxʷ tiʔəʔ luƛ ʔə tə s.ʔuladxʷ   LG.

Someone stole the salmon from the old man.

tə bə́ščəb ʔuqàdadidəxʷ tə luƛ   LG.

Mink stole from the old man.

bəqádadidəxʷ tiʔəʔ ʔəs.q̓ʷəlb luƛ ʔə tiʔəʔ

s.ʔuladxʷ, tiʔił bəščəb   ML.

He repeated his way by stealing the salmon
the old man had cooked, Mink did.

ʔəxʷsqádadicᵊb   He wants to steal it from me.   LL.

ʔuqádadicid čəd   I stole it from you.   LG.

-d-yi-t

ʔuqádadyid   He stole it for him.   LG.

-d-yi-t-b

ʔuqádadyitᵊb tə luƛ   (preferred)   LG.

Someone stole from the old man.

rejected:

*ʔuqádadidəxʷ tiʔəʔ luƛ tiʔəʔ bəščəb   LG.

1.   qágʷ(a)   scold

      See under cut.

      -at

        ʔuqágʷac čəxʷ   You scolded me.   EK.; LG.

2.   qágʷəlᵊb   continue blowing

      See under šə́xʷᵊb.

3.   qáǰət   hide

      Cf. čaj

1. s.qáǰət   Skagit

    tiʔəʔ sqáǰət gʷəl tu.ʔáləxʷ tiʔəʔ ƛ̓u.cutᵊb *Whidbey Island*
    miʔmaň tiʔəʔ s.watixʷtəd ʔə tiʔəʔ sqaǰət. tulʔal tiʔəʔ
    tu.cutᵊbəxʷ ʔə *Crescent Harbor* gʷəl tiʔəʔ s.niƛ̓ᵊm *Point*.
    gʷəl díɫ tiʔəʔ sqàǰət tulʔal ʔá tiʔəʔ sqàǰət

    The Skagit used to be on this place called Whidbey Island.
    This little land of the Skagit was from what is called
    Crescent Harbor to Snitlem Point. And this is Skagit, where
    the Skagit originated.   MS.

        See Haeberlin and Gunther, p. 9.

    qqáǰətᵊb čəd   I speak Skagit.

    ʔəs.čál kʷ1 gʷəds.dàʔad ʔal ti qqaǰətᵊb
    What do I call it in Skagit.

        rejected:

        *sqaǰətəɫ čəd   LG.

2. qáǰuʔx̌ʷ   raft

3. qakʷ   wrist

        See under p̓əs.

4. ʔəs.qáləkʷ   circle

        Cf. qit(i)

→
6. s.qáləx̌·   digging stick for clams   LL.
                             clam gun, clam fork   LG.

        See under č̓aʔ, s.ʔáx̌ʷuʔ.

7. qáɫqaləx̌ič   killer whale (blackfish)   LG., LL., EK.

8. s.qáwc   potato

        See under s.piqʷuc 'potato'.

1. s.qáyᵊp   See under s.qíp.

2. qayúqʷatx̌   a group in Canada

3. qá?alus   tears

    (Mistake for *qʷá?alus? or directly connected to the Halkomelem?)
    See under qʷu?.

4. qá?kʷ   rest

    ?əcíɫ čəd ɫuqà?kʷ   I'll rest.

    qágʷəxʷ   Rest now.

5. s.qa?qa?gʷəɫ   a respected term for addressing youngsters
                        (The child means a lot to you.)   LG.

        See under hu-.

6. qá?t(a)   See under hud(u).

    root

        ləqá?təxʷ   (His body) is getting warm now (that you've
                       given him blankets). (Said as you touch him.) LG.

    -at

        qá?təd   warm it (as something on a stove -- not an
                       open fire)

7. qá?xʷ(ac)   crab apple (tree)   MC., LG., LL., EK.

8. qcágʷac   ironwood (ocean spray, spirea)

9. qəbəlíd   roll it up   See 373.1.

        Cf. təč 'roll, roll off'

        qəbəlíd t(ə) ads.ɫàgʷid   Roll up your mat.   LG.

→

1. qəbqəbáyus   bat (mammal)   See 372.9.

2. s.qəbqəb̓   edible cartilage in front part of fish nose
                              ("A real treat!")   LL., DM.

    Cf. x̌əp̓ə̓k̓ʷ(əs)

3. qəbúɫ   a large canoe similar to the ʔəʔútx̌s but has a
                       different prow   LL.
                       a canoe similar to the ʔəʔútx̌s only smaller   JC.

    See under q̓il(bid).

4. s.qəbúʔ   breast, milk

→

6. qəd   fornicate

    dxʷ-...-íd

        diɫ (h)aẃəʔ hígʷəxʷ ʔudxʷqədíd tiʔəʔ s.ʔušəbàbdxʷ
        s.bəq̓ʷaʔ ʔə ciʔəʔ čəgʷàss, x̌ʷuʔx̌ʷəyʔ   ML.

        Indeed, he (Kingfisher) really made a cuckold (?)
        of poor Heron by his (Heron's) wife, Diver.

    -b

        ʔuqə́dəb haẃəʔ ʔə tiʔəʔ cədiɫ čə̀tx̌
        She committed adultery with Kingfisher.

    -b-txʷ

        qə́dəbtxʷəxʷ ciʔəʔ čəgʷàs ʔə tiʔəʔ s.bəq̓ʷaʔ, ciʔəʔ x̌ʷuʔx̌ʷəyʔ
        He fornicated with the wife of Heron, this Diver.   ML.

        qə́dəbtúbəxʷ ʔə tiʔəʔ xʷiʔ-lə.haʔɫ čə̀tx̌ ʔal tə s.xʷíʔ
        ʔə tiʔiɫ cədiɫ   ML.
        No-good Kingfisher fornicated (with her) while he
        (Heron) was gone.

→

7. s.qədíx̌   muskrat   ML.

    Cf. s.q̓ə́ɫq̓əɫ   muskrat

1.   qə́dxʷ   mouth

     Cf. -ucid, -aʔɫdəɫ, kaad

2. s.qəjúʔ NPS   squirrel   LL.

   s.qə́juʔ SPS   squirrel   ESi.

3.   qəl-   left (direction, location, position)

     Contrast jəh- 'right'.

         qəlа́čiʔ   left hand

         qəlа́ligʷəd   left side

         adqəlа́ligʷədbid čəd   I'm at your left.

         ʔəs.gʷədíl čəd ʔal t(i) adqəlа̀ligʷədbid
         I'm sitting on your left.

         qəlа́ligʷəds   his left

4. s.qəlа́litut   supernatural power, spirit power

     See Haeberlin and Gunther pp. 69-75, 79-80; and Smith (1940)
     pp. 56 ff.

     Cf. dxʷ.dа́ʔᵊb

     Some types of s.qəlа́litut are the following:

čáyᵊq	s.ƛа́ƛil	tə́stəd
də.dúkʷᵊb	dxʷ.qəlígʷəd	tiyúɫᵊbа́x̌(ad)
s.gʷədílič	s.qíp (s.qа́yᵊp)	túbšadad
dxʷ.híidəʔ	q̓ʷúx̌ʷqəd	s.yúd (s.yə́wᵊd)
jа́ʔabixʷ		ʔəyа́hus

sqəlálitut   spirit power

?átəbəd. ?u.?átəbəd. huy ?u.?átəbəd. sqəlálitut.

hìkʷ (?)əsqəlálitut. tux̌ʷ b(ə)u.?átəbəd   LG.

He died, he died. Yet he died. (He had) power.
(He had) great power and yet he died.

dx̌ʷqəlíg̈ʷəd   a fearless and fierce power that makes
          you very mean   LL.

reduplication

 qəlqəlálitut dream   EK.

  ?uqəlqəlálitutᵊbicid čəd   I dreamt about you. EK.

 qəqəlał̇idəgʷəs coward (not brave enough to go anywhere) EK.

1. qəládi?   up-rooted tree, up-rooted stump LG., ESi., ML.

 qí?qəl̇àdi?   What someone is called if his/her hair is
          all messed up like the roots of an up-rooted
          tree.
          The name of the daughter of Basket Ogress
           See under s.λ̇álqᵊb.

 qəl̇qəládi?   augmentative

  ?áhəxʷ ?al ti?ił ča?kʷ qəl̇qəl̇àdi? kʷi ł(u)adsu.wəlᵊlí?il ML.
  There on the shore in the snags you will be seen once in
  a great while.

2. s.qəlá(y)ǰut   nephew/niece when sibling link is deceased,
         reciprocal of yəláb

 See under qəsí?, s.qá.

3. qə́lb/qə́lᵊb   rain

 Compare:

  ł̇əcᵊb NPS (heavy) mist

  čəbə́š SPS mist

ƛ̓əbx̌ʷíla?	hail
báq̓ʷu?	snow
ƛ̓əlt̓ᵊb	start raining
xʷác̓	stop raining
qácil	rain lets up a bit (though continues)
gə́q̓il	weather clears up
q̓áƛ̓ᵊb	cloud (See also entries listed there.)
qʷubáčəd	rainbow
s.t̓xʷšád	rainbow (LG.)
x̌ʷíqʷədi?	thunder

qəlᵊbáxʷ	It's starting to rain.	LG.

?abiƛ̓əxʷ čəd gʷə.?íbəš, ƛ(u)alc̓uqəlᵊbás čəda gʷə.ƛax̌   LG.
If I walk when it's raining, I get cold.

?əs.qpàli ci dᵊs.qá, ck̓ʷaqid s.x̌aƛs kʷi gʷəsu.?ibəšs
ƛu?uqəlᵊbás   LG.
My older sister is crazy. She likes to walk when it's
raining.

t(u)as.x̌əc čəd gʷə.?əƛəd yəx̌ì? ?uqəlb   EK.
I was afraid to come because it rained.

lexical

?uqəlbíč čəd	I got caught in the rain.	EK.

dxʷ-...-b-il

?əxʷqəlᵊbíl	(The river) is turbid.	LG.
dxʷqə́lb	Baker River	

other

qəlbálqʷu?	rain water	LG.

rejected: *qəl^əbil   LG.

1.   qəlbút   even though

         qəlbút ti?ił s.?ušəbàbdx^w tux̌^w čəx^w ?əs.hig^{wə}d   ES.
         Even though poor you (should) uphold them.

2.   qələb   bad   JC.

      Cf. sa?   NPS   bad

         dił qələb ti?ił ads.hùyud t(i) ad.x̌əč   JC.
         That was bad your making up your mind (that way).

         dиłəx^w qələb ti?ił səs.huys ƛəsə.łəg^{wə}lálιk^ws
         ?ə tə qələb
         It is bad the way it is habitually leaving bad (i.e.,
         droppings).

      -il

         qələbil čələp dx^w?al kàyə?   JC.
         You folks are getting in trouble with grandmother.

      lexical

         qələbig^wəd   body waste   JC.

         qələbus   bad face, ugly   JC.

→

3.   s.qələč   octopus   JC.

      Cf. s.qíbƙ^w

4.   s.qəlíbut(əx^w)   old and infirm

      See under luƛ.

5.   qəl(ə)l-

      Contrast ƙ^wi?át.

-b

ʔəxʷ.qə́ləlᵊb   An insult equivalent to saying "You dirty thing!"
"This is not Skagit. I'm not sure which group
used it. It does not refer to dirt."   LG.

lexical

qəllálus   Someone who has not gone on a power quest, never
followed the training, stayed home and slept.   IM.

One who doesn't learn anything, a good-for-
nothing, impure (like an old wino).   IM.

1. s.qəlíkʷ   Skagit   blanket

Cf. s.ʔíčəb, -iča?

See also:

ǰəsgʷíča? / q̓ʷasdúliča? / q̓ʷastədúliča?   The "old" blanket made
of dog or mountain goat
hair.

təqʷxʷálc

x̌əčiǰálucid (under x̌ač)

2. qəlíl   receive (?)   [Perhaps derived from qa.]

tuqəl̓qəlíləxʷ (h)əlgʷə? tus.tab   EC.
They received many things.

tuqəl̓qəlíləxʷ s.ʔíčəb ciʔił s.k̓ʷuys   EC.
His mother received many blankets.

3. qəlúb   eye

qəl̓qəlúb   eyes

Cf. -alus   lexical suffix 'eye(s)'

čáqalus   eye matter

s.tá?tx̌ʷ   sty (of eye)

1. qə́lʔx̌   dried salmon eggs   MC., LL., ESi.

    Cf. čə́bs, dəwʔáyus (duʔáyus), ƛ̓əbƛ̓əbqʷ

2. qəɫ   wake up

    Cf. ʔitut   sleep

    root

        ʔuqə́ɫ čəd   I woke up.   LL.

        qə́ɫəxʷ SPS   wake up

        qɫáxʷ   NPS   wake up, revive, come to   ES.

        qɫáxʷ tiʔəʔ bəščəb   Mink woke up.   LL.

    -t

        qə́ɫʔd   Wake him up.   LG.

        ʔuqə́ɫc   He woke me up (as was his intention, e.g., he shook my shoulder).   LL.

        qə́ɫcid SPS   woke you

        qəɫcíd NPS   woke you

        ʔuqə́ɫcid čəd ʔu   Did I wake you up?   JC.

        ɫuqə́ɫc čəxʷ ʔal kʷi ɫùʔɫp ʔal təqači?   LL.
    Wake me up tomorrow morning at eight.

        ʔuqə́ɫcáxʷ   He just woke me up.   LL.

        qəɫʔdáxʷ   Wake them up now!   LL.

        ʔuqə́ɫtʔb čəd   He deliberately woke me up!   LL.

        qə́ɫcut SPS   wake (self)

        qəɫcút NPS   wake (self)

        qəɫcútəxʷ ɫi   You all wake up now!   LL.

qə́ɬcutəxʷ, qə́ɬcutəxʷ

gʷə́dil, gʷə́dil

háɡʷəxʷ tu.jàx̌ tə s.wàtixʷtəd

Wake up! Wake up!
Get up! Get up!
For a long time this world has been moving.   JC.

qə́ɬcut, qə́ɬcut!

tílᵊb čəxʷ ʔu.gʷə́dil

ɬu.xʷíʔəxʷ bələ.ʔìtut

Wake up, wake up!
Get up immediately.
(So) you will not fall back to sleep.   JC.

-dxʷ

ʔuqəɬdúbš tə x̌ʷàlituts   His snoring woke me up.

ʔuqəɬdúbutəxʷ   He finally woke himself up. LL.

ʔuqəɬdúbut čəd   I woke up (without an alarm
                                         going off).

1.   qəp   foolish, strange acting

      root

          sqəp   foolish   LL.

          ʔəsqə́p   senile   LL.

          ləqə́p   getting senile   LL.

          qpáli   crazy   LG.

              Cf. kəlísi   crazy

          ʔəsqə́p čəxʷ   You are crazy.   LG.

      gʷə-...-ad

          ʔugʷəqpád   cast a spell on someone, mesmerize
                                         someone   LL.

ʔugʷəqpád čəd   Someone cast a spell on me; I'm
                       anesthetized; I'm not all here.   LL.

gʷəqpát^əb čəd   He anesthetized me.

reduplication

qə́pqəp   kind of foolish

rejected: *qə́p^əd

1.   -qəp   lexical suffix   'smell'

   -àləqəp

      há^ʔɬaləqəp   taste/smell good   EK., LL.

      sá^ʔaləqəp   smell bad (not used with taste)   LL.

      ʔəƛáləqəp   smell

      pq̓áləqəp   flat, tasteless   LG.

   Compare:

      číx̌^əb   rancid   LG.
                       kind of spoiled   VH.
                       a bit too strong to eat   VH.

      c̓áp^əb   sour   EK.
                       sour (as an apple)   LG.

      t̓ác̓^əb   sour (as milk)   LG.
                       bitter   EK.

      sáx̌^əb   bitter   LG.
                       [sax̌]   scrape

      x̌ʷə́c(^əb)   tart   EK.
                       strong (coffee)   LG.
                       [x̌ʷəc]   sharp (knife)

      ƛ̓áɬ^əb   salt

      c̓ás^əb   good taste   LG.
                       delicious   EK.

         s.qəb(i)yá^ʔaləqəp x̌ʷu^{ʔə}lə?   It smells like a skunk.

            Cf. pác̓^əb

1.   qə́p̓   land, alight; cover

     Cf. ƛ̓álil

     root

          ləqə́p̓ dxʷʔal tùdidiʔi   LL.
          (The bird) landed over there.

          ʔuqə́p̓ tə bùʔqʷ ʔal tə qʷùʔ   HD.
          The duck landed on the water.

       -t

          ʔuqə́p̓əd čəd tiʔəʔ hùd   HD.
          I smothered the fire.

       -txʷ

          ʔuqə́p̓txʷ čəd tiʔəʔ ƛulə.sàq̓ʷ   HD.
          I landed the airplane.

     lexical

          qp̓úcid   cover something like a pot or basket   LL.

          x̌qp̓úcid   knee (-cap?)   EK., LL.

2.   qəqíl   See under qəyíqəl̓.

3.   s.qəq̓ʷús   a small mat used to kneel on/in a canoe and
                        sometimes as a covering for lap and knees while
                        a fish is hauled into the canoe

                        (The ƛúbuɫ was put full length in the bottom of
                        the canoe. Then the sqəq̓ʷús was put down.)

     See under ƛakʷ.

4.   qəsíʔ   uncle, male sibling of either parent while that
                        parent is living

          Cf. ʔəpús   aunt

             yəláb   either parent's sibling of either sex when parent
                         is deceased

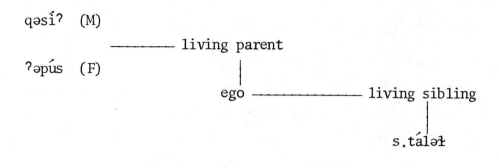

qəsí? (M)

────── living parent

?əpús (F)

ego ────────── living sibling

s.tálət

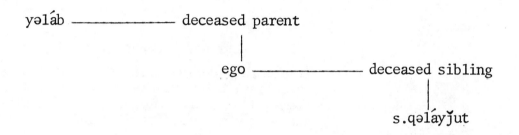

yəláb ─────────── deceased parent

ego ──────────── deceased sibling

s.qəláyǰut

Ego has no special term separating older from younger sibling of parent. However, the distinction is maintained because ego refers to his cousin from an uncle or aunt senior to his own parent as sqa whether or not the cousin is older or younger than himself. Similarly, if the cousin is the child of an uncle or aunt junior to his parent, he calls the cousin suq̓ʷa? even if the cousin is older than he. (See under s.qa.)

The terms yəláb and sqəláyǰut remain in effect while the uncle or aunt and the nephew or niece still live. When they die, they are again called qəsí?, ?əpús, or stálət.

reduplication

qəqsí?   favorite uncle

→

2.   qətqáx̌əd   axilla   LL.

      Cf. gədgáx̌əd   axilla

3. (s)qəyíqəl̓/qə?íqəl̓   not know how to (a loan word from Halkomelem?) LG.

      See under hay 'know'.

Contrast (s)čəwáʔt 'know how to, be good at'.

sqəyíqəl̓ čəd ʔə kʷi ds.x̌àlalikʷ

I don't know how to write.

sqəyíqəl̓ čəd ʔə kʷi gʷəd(s).sàq̓ʷ

I don't know how to fly.

Cf. ʔəsjáƛ̓əb čəd ʔə kʷi gʷəd(s).sàq̓ʷ

Same gloss: I don't know how to fly.

qəqíl   low class

This term is not recognized by LG.

It probably derives from the same source as qəyíqəl̓ and implies incompetence and/or from qəll̓álus and implies lack of ambition and spirit powers. Contrast siʔáb.

1. s.qíbk̓ʷ   octopus (and) squid   LL., ESi.

   Cf. s.qéləč

2. -qid   lexical suffix 'head, top; voice'

   Cf. x̌əy̓ús 'head', -us 'upper part', -ač 'head'

   stress on root/stem

    šáw̓qid   skull   EK., LG.

    qʷúʔqid   crown of head,   EK.
           soft part of baby's head LG.

    (xʷ)čúƛ̓qid whistling swan (lit. 'rattle head') EK., LL.

    k̓áwqid   bump head   EK.

    ʔəs.tíqilqid bushy head   LG.

    ʔəs.qʷəlúbqidəxʷ He's gray now.   LG.

   stress on suffix

    s.čəbqíd   brain   EK., LG.

    ʔu.čəx̌qíd   broken skull   EK.

ʔəs.x̌əɬqíd čəd	I have a headache.	LG.
x̌i.čcqíd	red head	LL.

stress on suffix <u>but root vowel is strong</u>

x̌àc̓qídᵊb	put it over your head	LG.
	cover your head	LG.

stress on suffix <u>but root has strong vowel allomorphs</u>

čə?kʷqídᵊb	wash head	LG.
k̓ʷəlúqid	scalp	EK.

connective element -<u>iya</u>-

šəqiyáqid	tree top	EK., LL., LG.
	mountain top	LL.
	house top	LG.

šəqiyáqid ?ə tə səxʷ.?ígʷəɬ	top of a ladder	LG.
?u.tùgʷiyáqidəxʷ čəd	The water went over my head.	LG., LL.

connective element -<u>əl</u>- with stress on root vowel

qáhəlqìd	lots of hair	HD.
x̌ʷíƛ̓əy(?)əlqid	wool of mountain goat	EK.

connective element -<u>á</u>-

lə.gʷədáqid tə s.ɬàq̓s	He fell on his head.	LG.

dxʷ-...-qid

dxʷ(h)á?ɬqid ?al s.t̓ílib   EK.
He has a good voice for singing.

dxʷ(h)íkʷqid kʷ(i) adsu.gʷàdgʷəd   LL.
Speak in a loud voice!

dxʷ.yəqqídᵊb	Speak up!	LG.
dxʷ.yəqqíd kʷ(i) ads.t̓ílib	Sing loudly!	LG.

1. s.qíg^wəc   deer

     Cf. s.jábtač 'doe', s.x̌^wəláqəd 'buck', yəẃyəɫdáʔ 'fawn',

         húpt 'deer' (LG. only)

     lexical

         sqig^wəcàɫčiʔ   venison   DM., LL., EK.

2. qíɫil   lose one's child through death   EK., LL.

     See under ʔatəb-.

     Contrast particularly with q̓^wíčil.

3. s.qíp   a hunting power (for both sexes)   VH., MC.

     (LG. gives s.qáy^əp)

     See under s.qəlálitut.

4. qíq^əg^wiɫ   a new canoe of any type

     See under q̓ílbid.

5. qiq̓(i)   incarcerate

     See under ɫid(i) 'tie'.

     root

         ʔəsqíq̓ čəd   I'm kept (here).   LL.

     -it

         qíq̓id   hold him against his will but not by tying
                      him or laying hands on him; incarcerate him
                                          HD., EK.

         ʔuqíq̓it^əb čəd   I was arrested.   LL.

     lexical

         qíq̓alik^walʔtx^w   jail, prison   DM.

1. qít(i)   See under jal-.

    See also qáləkʷ 'circle'.

    -it

        qítid   circle around something   ML.

    lexical

        qitálgʷic   circle around me   LG.

        qitúlč   go around the table (An expression used
                        by Shakers for part of their ritual.)   LG.

    reduplication

        qítqitid   many circle around something   ML.

2. qíwx̌   steelhead (rainbow) trout   LL.

    Cf. s.kʷáwəl   steelhead (rainbow) trout

        diɫ ʔu bəs.ʔuládxʷ tiʔiɫ qíwx̌. ʔí. s.ʔuládxʷ
        tiʔəʔ qìwx̌.
        Is a steelhead (also) a salmon? Yes. A steelhead
        is a salmon.

        ʔəs.ʔəxíd kʷi s.ləliʔ ʔə tə qíwx̌ dxʷʔal yubəč.
        tiʔəʔ qíwx̌ gʷəl bíʔbad s.ʔuládxʷ tiʔttiš;
        gʷəl tiʔəʔ yúbəč gʷəl x̌ʷuɫ ʔal jíxʷ s.jəlč
        ƛu.ʔəƛ tiʔəʔ yùbəč. gʷəl tiʔəʔ qíwx̌ gʷəl
        qíləxʷ x̌əƛgʷàsuladxʷ
        How does a steelhead differ from a king salmon?
        The steelhead is a small, narrow salmon. As
        for the king salmon, in the first part of the
        year the king salmon comes; but the steelhead,
        it comes upstream when the year comes together
        (i.e., when winter and spring meet).   MS.

3. s.qíx̌a   (long haired) dog (that was sheared)   EK.

    Cf. s.qʷəbáyʔ 'dog', s.x̌ʷíƛəyʔ 'mountain goat'

1. qíyə?   easy

    qíyə?čəd dxʷ?al s.x̌ʷíƚ   I get lost easily.   LG.

   reduplication

    qi?qiyə́?   JC.

      ƚu.xʷí?əs lə.xʷə̀λ ?ə kʷi qi?qiyə́?   JC.
      So it will not break easily.

2. qí?qəƚàdi?   name of the daughter of Basket Ogress

   See qəládi? 'up-rooted tree or up-rooted stump'

   See under s.λ́álqəb.

3. x̌.qp̓úcid   knee   EK., LL., LG.

4. -qs   lexical suffix   'nose, point'

   Cf. čə̌t- 112.3, tč-

    dí?ƚ kʷi gʷ(ə)adsƚəb.ƚəbč̌qs   LL.
    Your nose might run.

    ?u.šác̓qsəxʷ   He breathed his last.   LL.
             His breath is gone.   LG.

    cƚilqs   nosebleed   LL.

    q̓ítqsə d   hang it from a peg, nail,
             corner of a door, etc.   LL.

      Cf. qítid   Same gloss: hang it from a peg   LL.

    didəč̌á?qs   single barrel rifle   LL.

    sáli?qs   double barrel gun   LL.

    bəq̓ʷáqs   bayonet

     (from s.bəq̓ʷá? 'heron')

    sč̌ə́tqs   point (all kinds)   LL.

ʔílqs   pencil point   LL.

x̌ʷə́cqs   sharp point   EK.

s.jíxʷqs   leader   EK.

ʔəs.q̓ʷu(ʔ)qs   joining of two points   EK.

dxʷ-

gʷədxʷ.tə̀sqscí(d) čəd   LL.
I'll punch you in the nose.

ʔudxʷ.təsqsdúbuɫ   LL.
He punched us in the nose.

ʔudxʷ.ɫíč̓qsə̓d   Someone cut his nose.   LG.

ʔudxʷ.šuk̓ʷilqsə̓dəxʷ ʔə tiʔiɫ ƛuxʷ.(h)ùdad ...   ML., LG.
She grayed their noses with ashes.

     Cf. šúšk̓ʷildəxʷ ʔə tiʔiɫ ƛuxʷ.(h)údad ʔəl kʷi hud   ML.
         She grayed the little ones with ashes from the fire.

ʔəxʷ.šúk̓ʷilqsəxʷ   LG.
Their noses are now grayed.

-ay-qs

qʷəlubáyqs   gray beard, gray whiskers   LL.

s(ə)x̌áyqsə̓b   shave (chin)

qʷidáyqs   beard

     Cf. qʷidáyucid 'beard'

ʔu.tx̌ʷáyqsə̓d čəd   I pulled his beard.   EK.

-qs-ači̓

šišč̓qsàči̓   ring for finger   EK.

q̓ʷx̌qsáči̓   fingernail

yáʔylupqsači̓   ring for finger

č̓ə̓tqsáči̓   finger tips

-q(s)-šad

    q̓ʷx̌q(s)šád   toenail

    ʔuʔí.ʔihəlq(s)šəd čəxʷ   Your toes stink.   LL.

    ɫík̓ʷq(s)šəd   trip (i.e., hook toe)   LL.

lexeme where -qs is a historical component

    káw̓qs   raven

    súp̓qs   hair seal (harbor seal)

    ƛ̓úiqs   box

    bə́qsəd   nose

1.   qtqáč   woodpecker   EK.

     Cf. təqt(ə)qáč   LL.

2.   qx̌íl   open eyes

     qx̌ís   open eyes for special reason

     See under gʷəq̓.

     Cf. číp̓lil 'close eyes', kaad 'open mouth'

3.   qyuuqs   seagull (generic)

     Cf. q̓(ə)čáx̌əd, híkʷ-əs.q̓əyùq̓ʷ

       ʔiqyuuqs   seagulls

     díɫ ʔu bə.bùʔqʷ tiʔəʔ qyùuqs. x̌ʷúl̓əb ʔə tə bùʔqʷ
     tiʔiɫ qyuuqs. ləlíʔak̓ʷbixʷ. xʷíʔ lə.(hə)láʔb
     s.ʔə̀ɫ°d. yáw̓ (hə)láʔb ʔəs.tàg̓ʷəxʷ g̓ʷəl g̓ʷə.huydub
     tiʔiɫ qyuuqs

     Is a seagull a kind of waterfowl? A seagull is like
     a waterfowl, (but) it is a different (sub)class. It
     is not really edible. (You would have to) be really
     hungry before (you) would eat a seagull.   DM.

q̓

The sound represented by this letter is similar to q̠ (discussed on page 363) except for the addition of a simultaneous abrupt closure of the vocal cords. [glottalized, voiceless velar stop]

1. s.q̓áƛ̓   land otter

2. q̓ábəy?   maiden

3. q̓ál   perch (fish)   ESi.

   sə́pkʷ   perch (fish)   LL.

4. q̓al

        xʷi? gʷədsəsq̓álbid   I don't believe it.   LG.

   Compare:

        xʷi? gʷədsəstˀə́ƛ̓ildxʷ   Same gloss: I don't believe it.   LG.

        ?əsqʷácdxʷ čəd   I doubt it.   LG.

        ?əxʷcútˀəb čəd xʷí?   I doubt it.   LL.

5. s.q̓áƛ̓ˀəb NPS   cloud

   See also under q̓ə́lˀəb 'rain'.

   Cf. qʷəšáb 'fog', pə́hˀəb 'haze'

6. q̓ápux̌ʷ   hazelnut; nut in general   LL.

   q̓p̓úx̌ʷ(əc)   hazelnut (tree)   MC., EK.

7. q̓axʷ   freeze

   root

        ?uq̓axʷ   It froze.

        ?əsq̓áxʷ   It's frozen.

        sq̓áxʷ   ice

lexical

q̇áxʷalʔtxʷ   frozen food locker plant

reduplication

q̇áxʷq̇axʷ   freezing (on the level)

1.   q̇ax̌(a)   uncover, bring to light

Cf. q̇ís 'uncover', q̇íkʷ/gʷ 'come partly into view'

Contrast x̌áč̣ 'cover'.

-at

q̇áx̌ad   uncover it,   HD., LL.
                              bring it to light   HD.

łuq̇áx̌əd čəd ti ʔəʔùtx̌əs   HD.
I'm going to uncover the canoe.

q̇áx̌ad   Uncover it, e.g., throw covers off it.   DM.

-dxʷ

ʔəsq̇áx̌ədxʷəxʷ čəd   EK.
It's clearly visible to me now; I see it.

ʔuq̇áx̌ədxʷ čəd ti lə.ʔìbəš   DM.
I got a glimpse of him walking (by).

lexical

ʔuq̇áx̌ičtᵊb   He was uncovered.   LL.

ʔuq̇áx̌ičc   Someone uncovered me.   LL.

ʔuq̇áx̌usc   Someone uncovered my face.   LL.

2.   q̇ax̌ʷ-   See under q̇əx̌ʷ-.

3.   q̇áyx̌əc   Skagit   cascara   MC.

      Cf. ƛ̓ládəc   cascara   ES., ESi.

393

1. s.q̓áʔšəd   NPS   moccasin

    Cf. yáɫšəd/yə́ɫšəd   SPS   moccasin

2. q̓c-

        ʔuq̓cáč   struck back of head against (something)

    Cf. k̓aw- 'touch, bump'

3. q̓cáb   lack, fail to obtain

    Cf. x̌ʷaɫ

        ʔəsq̓cáb čəd   I can't reach (my goal).   JC.

    -il

        ʔəsq̓cábil tə ds.ʔə̀ɬˀd   I'm lacking food.   JC.

4. s.q̓əbyáʔ   Skagit   skunk   LG.

        s.q̓əbyáʔ   Snoh.   skunk   EK.

        s.q̓əbyúʔ   Suqu.   skunk   ESi.

        s.q̓əbiyúʔ Squaxin   skunk   JC.

        s.q̓əbíyəʔ Snoh.   skunk   LL.

5. q̓(ə)č   bent, crooked

    Antonyms are k̓ʷap, cək̓ʷ.

    See also under jal, sídq̓, ɬəlcút.

    Compare:

    p̓álq̓   bend out of line, shape, position

    č̓ə́lp   twist

    čúč̓gʷas   twist in the process of blanket weaving

    puy̓   bend

pə́ƛq̓ʷ   sprain, get out of joint

k̓ʷálč   wrench/twist back

túji1   bend forward, look down

t̓álx̌   bend backwards, lose balance backwards

k̓ʷə́q   fall/lie on the back, lose balance backwards

root

q̓əč   bent, crooked   LL.

-t

ʔuq̓ə́čˀd   I bent it.   ESi.

q̓ə́čtˀb   got bent   LL.

q̓əčq̓čatˀb   made it all crooked   LL.

lexical

ʔəsq̓əčq̓(ə)čáči?   crooked arms   LL.

ʔəsq̓əčq̓(ə)čálus   crooked eyes   DM.

q̓čáx̌ad   SPS   seagull

    Cf. qyúuqs

    x̌ʷi.qʷíq̓ʷ tiʔiɬ q̓(ə)čáx̌ad. tux̌ʷ diɬəxʷ qələ́b tiʔiɬ
    səs.huys ƛ̓əsə.ɬəg̓ʷəlálikʷs ʔə tə qələ́b. ʔəs.bəč
    ʔal ti. ʔəs.bəč ʔal taʔá. x̌ʷi̓ʔəxʷ kʷ əs.háʔɬs

    A seagull is white but it is bad the way it is
    habitually leaving bad (i.e., droppings). A splat
    here. A splat there. It is not good.   JC.

ʔəsq̓(ə)čáʔɬdəɬ ciʔiɬ p̓uày?   DM.
A flounder has a crooked mouth.

ʔəsq̓əčq̓əčšad   crooked legs (from groin to toes)   LL.

ʔəsq̓əčq̓əčɬx̌a?   crooked thighs   LL.

sq̓ə́čqs   Skagit   silver salmon, coho (lit. 'crooked nose')
                                                    VH., LG.

   Cf. s.kʷxʷíc, s.kʷə́xʷic

q̓číc   (by dissimilation from -ič?) bow (archery)

   Cf. čá?suč

?əs.púy̓ ti?ə? q̓ə́číc   The bow is curved.   MS.

1.   q̓əd   slow

   Cf. t̓ababac

   root

      ləq̓əd čəd   I'm going slowly.
      x̌ʷul̓áb čəd q̓ə̀d   I'm real slow.

      -t

      q̓ədcút   Slow down!

2.   q̓əjáx̌   intestines

   See under ƛ̓ač.

3. s.q̓əjú?   (human) hair

      gʷ(ə)asq̓əjú?əs   if it be (considered) his hair

4.   q̓əl

      ?əsq̓əlšád   cramp in the foot

         Cf. q̓əp, q̓up, q̓əyu?us

5.   q̓əl

      q̓ə́ltəd   clout, diaper, sanitary napkin   LG., VH.

         Cf. šádač̓ 'cedar bark clout'

      xʷq̓ə́ltəd ?ə wəl̀is   lichen (lit. 'diaper of frog')   MC.

q̓əláx̌əd   fence

1.   q̓əlᵊb   camp, stay overnight

      łuq̓əlb čəd   I'm going to stay overnight.

      táq̓t ti?ił bəsəsq̓əlbs ?al ti swat.watíx̌ʷtəd   IM.
      It spends the night in trees up on shore.

    -iluł

      q̓əlbíluł   stay overnight

      ləq̓əlbíluł čəd   I'm coming to camp overnight.

2.   q̓əls

      ?əsq̓əls   steam cook

3.   q̓əlx̌   very surprised, dumbfounded

4. (s)q̓əłq̓əł   muskrat   EK., MC., LG.

    Cf. s.qədíx̌   muskrat

5.   q̓əp   gather   See 407.1.   Synonym: q̓ʷu?
    Cf. q̓up, q̓əl, q̓əyú?us

      ?uq̓əp   It formed a lump, (muscle) cramp.   EK.

    lexical

      q̓əpšád   cramp on the leg   EK.

      q̓əpq̓əpəláx̌əd   muscles of the arms   ES.

      q̓əpq̓əpálubid   shoulder muscles   ES.

6.   q̓ə́səd   partition in a longhouse   LG.

7.   q̓ətíl   impatient
    Also recorded k̓tíl by LG.

ʔuq̓ətís^əbš čəx^w ʔu   Did you get tired of waiting for me?   VH.

ʔuq̓ətís^əbuɫəd čəd   I got tired waiting for you folks.

1.   q̓əx̌bíd   hog fennel   MC.

    "It is used like Vicks vapor for treating the common cold."   MC.

2.   q̓əx̌^w-   Also recorded q̓^wəx̌^w- *q.v.*

    q̓əx̌^wqsáči?   fingernail

    q̓əx̌^wq(s)šád   toenail

    Cf. dəx̌-

3.   q̓əyáɫəd   slug, snail   LG., LL., ESi.

4.   q̓əyíl   Skagit   lazy

    Cf. q^wič̓, s.č̓ílč̓il, qəlálus

    ʔuq̓əyíl   He became lazy.

    ʔəsq̓əyíl   He is lazy.

5.   q̓əyúq̓^w   throat   LL., LG.

    Cf. -yuq̓^w, -yus

    hík^w-əsq̓əyùq̓^w   seagull (lit. 'big-throat')   LG., ES.

       Cf. qyúuqs, q̓(ə)č̓áx̌əd

6. s.q̓əywád   unidentified berry. Grows on a low bush with long leaves in the mountains. It looks a little like cranberries. Not particularly good to eat.

7.   q̓əyú?us   scrofula   VH.

    Cf. q̓əl, q̓əp/q̓up

ʔáhəxʷ tiʔəʔ diʔəʔ čačas s.tubš, ʔəsq̓əyq̓əyúʔus   EC.

There is this boy who is crippled.

1.   q̓ibq̓ib   wrinkled

2.   q̓íč   expensive

(hə)laʔb q̓íč ti qʷɬìʔšəd   LG.

The shoes are too expensive.

hiʔáb q̓ìč tiʔiɬ pùʔtəd   DM.

The shirt is too expensive.

→   ʔá ʔu kʷi xʷì? ləq̓íč puʔtəd   LG., DM.

Is there any shirt that is not expensive?

ʔá ʔu kʷi xʷì? ləq̓ìč ʔə tə pùʔtəd   DM., LG.

Is there any out of these shirts that is not expensive?

        rejected:

            * ʔá ʔu kʷi xʷì? ləq̓ìč tə puʔtəd   LG.

    -t

    q̓íččut   keep something to yourself, be unwilling
                      to share information

3.   q̓íkʷ/gʷ-   come partly into view, appear

    Cf. q̓ax̌ 'uncover, bring to light', q̓is 'uncover'

    root

        ʔəsq̓ikʷ   appear, be in view   DM.

        ʔəsq̓íkʷ tiʔiɬ s.qìgʷəc   The deer appeared.   EK.

        ʔəsq̓ígʷəxʷ   It's just visible now.   EK.

        ʔəsq̓ígʷəxʷ gʷəl tux̌ʷ xʷi? gʷəds.kʷəd(d)xʷ   EK.

        It's in sight, but I can't get it (an animal
        being hunted).

lexical

daʔxʷ ʔuq̓íg̣ʷəx̌əd   The edge is showing.   LL.
(e.g., the moon is just
peeking over the hill)

q̓íg̣ʷusᵊb   sticking head out of door or window
to see what's happening   EK.

rejected: *q̓íg̣ʷid

1.   q̓il(i)   get in/on any sort of conveyance -- either
to travel oneself (get on board, mount, ride)
or to load a vehicle (especially a canoe)

                        travel

Cf. ʔux̌ʷ, ʔibəš, ʔuluɬ

root

tuləsq̓íl čəd   I was riding on it.   LL.

ləsq̓íl čəd liɬʔal ti lìlud   I came on the train.   LG.

ləsq̓íl čəd ʔal ti lìlud   I'm riding on the train.   EK.

tələbx̌ q̓il   canoe full   ML.

ʔuq̓íləxʷ ti s.ʔuládxʷ   The salmon are here.   DM.

tiʔəʔ q̓iw̌x̌ gʷəl q̓iləxʷ x̌ə˕gʷasuladxʷ   MS.

As for the steelhead, it travels (upstream) when
the spring and winter come together.

-it

q̓ilid tə s.ʔəɬᵊd čəxʷa ʔux̌ʷtxʷ dxʷʔal dᵊ.q̓ilbid   EK.
Load the food (into the cart) and take it to my car.

xʷiʔ ʔu gʷ(ə)ads.kʷáxʷac, gʷ(ə)ads.q̓íᶅic   LL.
Wouldn't you help me, (and) put me on (the wagon)?

q̓íᶅitᵊbəxʷ dxʷʔal tiʔəʔ q̓ilbid   EK.
It's been put into the canoe.

tux̌ʷ čəd tuq̓ilitᵊb   But I was forced to get on.   LL.

400

-il

q̓íĺil   be on board, mounted

t(u)asq̓iĺil gʷəl tubə.q̓ʷíbəxʷ   EK.
He's been in (the car) and gotten out again.

t(u)asq̓íĺil čəd   LL.
I went along (more just to keep him company).

-agʷ-il

q̓íĺagʷil ʔal tə s.tiqìw   mounted the horse   EK.

q̓íĺagʷil   get in (car, canoe)   EK.

dəxʷq̓íĺagʷil ...   in order to get in (a canoe)   ML.

ʔuq̓íĺagʷil čəd   LL.
I went (and had a definite purpose in going).

-agʷ-il-s

q̓iĺagʷis   (He saw a car going his way so)
                   he caught a ride.   LG.

ʔuq̓iĺagʷis čəxʷ yəx̌i diɬ dəxʷəs.huys tiʔiɬ s.tiqìw   DM.
You ride it because that is what a horse is for.

-agʷ-il-s-b

ʔuq̓íĺagʷisᵊb čəd   Someone got in with me/on me.   LL.

q̓íĺagʷisᵊb tiʔiɬ s.tiqìw   A horse is ridden.   DM.

-bi-t

q̓íĺbid*   canoe (of any class), vehicle of
                 any kind including wagons and automobiles

             See -gʷiɬ.

q̓íʔq̓əlbid   small canoe   LL.

s.tábaɬ q̓ìĺbid   What kind of canoe is that?

---

*Older speakers say q̓íĺbid.

ʔəbsq̓íl̓bid həlgʷəʔ. dày̓ʔəxʷ (h)áʔɬ q̓íl̓bids həlgʷəʔ.   ML.

They have a canoe. Their canoe is very good.

díɬ ʔu bəq̓il̓bid tiʔəʔ s.tiqȋw. xʷiʔ ləq̓íl̓bid gʷəl
q̓ílagʷisᵊb tiʔiɬ s.tiqȋw   ɒM.

Is a horse a vehicle? It is not a vehicle even though
a horse is ridden.

There are six types of canoe distinguished by shape,
function or origin. These are ʔəʔútx̌s, s.dəxʷíɬ, ƛəláy̓?,
s.tiwátɬ, qəbúɬ and s.tᵊk̓íwiɬ. In addition the people
speak of q̓íqᵊgʷiɬ 'a new canoe of any type' and x̌íx̌q̓ᵊwȋɬ
'a racing canoe' (cf. x̌íx̌qalgʷiɬ 'canoe race'). These
last two do not belong to the same classificatory scheme
as the previous six and the vocabulary reflects the difference. The two terms of the second group are formed by
the lexical suffix -gʷiɬ/-wiɬ 'canoe'. The terms in the
first set are not analyzable. (See Elmendorf pp. 170 -
192.)

(1) ʔəs.ʔəx̌ìd kʷi gʷ(ə)adəxʷ.súxʷtəš tiʔiɬ ʔəʔùtx̌s.
(2) tiʔəʔ ʔəʔútx̌s gʷəl híkʷ q̓ìl̓bid. (3) híkʷbid ʔə
tiʔəʔ s.dəxʷȋɬ. (4) gʷəl tiʔəʔ šə́jts gʷəl ʔá tiʔəʔ
s.x̌əy̓ùs. (5) ƛu.húyalcbid tiʔəʔ q̓ìl̓bid gʷəl ƛu.ƛályibəxʷ
tiʔəʔ s.x̌əy̓ùss x̌əɬ ti ʔəs.k̓íis, x̌əɬ ti ʔə(s).šúɬ.
(6) ƛál bəs.ʔìstə tiʔəʔ ʔìl̓aq ʔə tiʔəʔ ʔəs.ʔistə ʔəʔùtx̌s.
(7) gʷəl tiʔəʔ kʷa s.dəxʷȋɬ gʷəl x̌əɬ ti ʔəs.tùjil.
(8) bìʔbad tiʔiɬ sə(s).š(ə)q̓íl ʔə tiʔiɬ šə̀jts. (9) ƛál
bəs.ʔìstə tiʔiɬ ʔìl̓aqs. (10) bìʔbad q̓íl̓bid tiʔiɬ
s.dəxʷiɬ

(1) How would you recognize a Nootka type canoe?
(2) The Nootka type canoe is a big canoe. (3) It is
bigger than the hunting canoe. (4) Its bow has a head.
(5) The canoe would be made and (then) its head would
be added as if it [the head] were standing, as if it
were looking. (6) The stern of this same Nootka type

canoe is the same way. (7) As for the hunting canoe,
it seems to be bent over. (8) The bow is raised a
little. (9) Its stern is the same. (10) The hunting
canoe is a small canoe.   MS.

(1) ʔəs.ʔəx̌íd kʷi gʷəcəxʷ.súxʷtəš tiʔəʔ s.tiwàtɬ.

(2) ʔiɬ.híkʷ səxʷ.ʔùluɬ dxʷʔal tiʔəʔ s.dəxʷîɬ.

(3) híkʷbid ʔə s.dəxʷîɬ yəx̌i dəxʷuʔul.ʔuluɬ ʔə tiʔəʔ
diʔəʔ ʔaciɬtalbixʷ tiʔiɬ s.tiwàtɬ. (4) xʷiʔ ləʔəʔùtx̌s

(5) x̌əɬ ti x̌ʷúləb ʔə tiʔiɬ s.dəxʷîɬ tiʔiɬ səs.huys.

(6) gʷəɬ x̌ʷəlč dəxʷ.ʔuluɬ tiʔiɬ s.tiwàtɬ

(1) How would I recognize a s.tiwatɬ? (2) It is a larger water-going craft than a hunting canoe. (3) It is
bigger than a hunting canoe because people use it for
traveling [not hunting]. (4) It is not a Nootka type.
(5) It seems to be made like the hunting canoe. (6) The
s.tiwatɬ is used on the salt water [not rivers].   IM.

(1) ʔəs.ʔəx̌íd kʷi s.ləlíʔ ʔə tiʔəʔ s.dəxʷîɬ dxʷʔal
ƛəlayʔ. (2) x̌ʷəjx̌ʷəjyálus tiʔəʔ s.dəxʷîɬ. (3) gʷəl
ʔəs.p̓ilp̓ilyálus tiʔəʔ ƛəlàyʔ gʷəl x̌ʷuĺ gʷəɬ dxʷʔal
s.tuləkʷ. (4) s.dəxʷîɬ gʷəɬ dxʷʔal x̌ʷəlč, dxʷʔal
x̌ačuʔ

(1) What is the difference between a hunting canoe
and a shovel-nose canoe? (2) The hunting canoe has
sharp ends. (3) But the shovel-nose canoe has flat
ends and belongs just on river(s). (4) The hunting
canoe belongs on the salt water [and] on lake(s).   IM.

The qəbúɬ is similar to the ʔəʔútx̌s but has a different prow. The s.tiwàtɬ is proportionately wider
than the others. The s.təkíwiɬ is a double-ended
canoe from the s.təkí way to the north.   LL.

parts of a canoe and accessories

š̌ə́jt   bow   ʔílaq   stern (cf. laq 'behind, late')

ʔúdəgʷiɬ	middle of a canoe
x̌əɬəlwíld	thwart
ʔúluɬ	travel over water
ʔišɬ	to paddle (Cf. ʔišil 'fish swims')
x̌ʷúbt	a paddle
k̓ʷádgʷild	a bailer
čq̓áhᵊb	to pole a canoe
čq̓áp	pole for poling a canoe
x̌əƛ́álap	steer a canoe by holding a paddle over the stern
jəlálgʷiɬ	command given paddlers to change sides
xʷácad	carry a canoe (especially a s.dəxʷiɬ) take things off to lighten the load
qʷácad	Same gloss: take things off to lighten the load

-a-b

ʔuq̓ílab čəd ʔə tiʔəʔ s.tàb   LL.
I'm putting my things in.

lexical

ʔá tiʔəʔ dq̓ílaličtubicid
There for you is a load of gifts I (bring).

q̓ílus čəd   getting up the hill   EK.

ləq̓ílilus čəd
I'm now getting up to the top (of the hill).   EK.

1.   q̓íƛt   skunk cabbage, name of Port Gamble Bay   ESi.

   Cf. čú̓ʔk̓ʷ(ali) skunk cabbage   EK., LG., MC.

1. q̓íƛ   wound

   Cf. báʔkʷɫ 'get hurt', ʔíla 'get hurt'

   ʔuq̓íƛʔdxʷ čəd   I wounded him.

   ʔuq̓íƛdub čəd   I got wounded.

   lexical

   ʔəs.čál tiʔiɫ adəxʷq̓íƛqid
   How did you wound your head?

   ʔəs.čál kʷ(i) adəxʷq̓íƛšəd   DM.
   How did you wound your foot?

   rejected: *q̓íƛid

2. q̓íq̓iyagʷəs   limber joint, loose joint

3. q̓íq̓x̌ʷuʔ   short person

   comparison

   ʔiɫq̓íq̓x̌ʷuʔ   shorter   LG.

       This is the opposite of both ʔiɫs.(h)ájəp 'taller
       person' and ʔiɫ.(h)aac 'longer, taller thing'.   LG.

   lexical

   q̓iq̓əx̌ʷuʔáp   short bottomed person   LG.

   sq̓iq̓x̌ʷúʔap   short person, short of stature   LL.

       (These are jocular ways of saying someone is short.)

   rejected: *ʔəsq̓íq̓x̌ʷuʔ   LG.

4. q̓is(i)   peek at something by moving a curtain aside
                           or lifting up something to look under at object

   See under šuɫ.

   Cf. k̓ʷil(i), q̓ax̌(a)

-it

    q̉ísid   Peek at it (by moving a curtain aside or
                             lifting up a cloth and looking under it).   DM.

lexical

    q̉ìsəláx̌əd   arm exposed, rolled up sleeve   DM.

    q̉ìsáq   leg exposed, rolled up pantleg   DM.

    ʔəsq̉ísq̉isàči?   sleeves rolled up   LL.

reduplication

    q̉íq̉sq̉i(s)šəd   legs partly uncovered (e.g., trousers
                             partly rolled up)   LL.

1.   q̉it-   store food

    Cf. p̉t̉-

    tudsəsq̉ít^əbid g^wəl (tə) huy x^wì?əx^w   LL.
    I was keeping it (for later) but it's gone now.

    tudsəsq̉ít^əbid g^wəl huy x^wí?əx^w   LG.
    I had it put away (for lunch) but now it's gone.

    rejected: *ʔəsq̉it, *ʔəsq̉it^əb   LG.

2.   q̉it̉(i)   hang

    See under šəq.

    Cf. k̉iɬ, ɬəp̉

    -it

    q̉ít̉id   Hang it, have something up high,   LL.
                        Put it up!   LG.

    -tx^w

    ʔəsq̉ít̉tx^w čəd   I have it put up. I have it
                           put away.   LG.

lexical

q̓íƛqsᵊd   hang it from a peg, nail, corner of
a door, etc.
have something up high   LL.

1.   q̓ixʷ ~ q̓xʷ- ~ q̓ayxʷ-   upstream

	upstream		downstream
position relative to speaker	q̓íxʷ		ʔáɬx̌ad
direction to current flow	təyíl		qʷíc

q̓íxʷ   (located) upstream   LG.

lədxʷq̓íxʷ čəd   I'm going upstream.   LG.

lədxʷq̓íxʷ   going upriver   LG.

s.tulq̓ixʷ   east (lit.'from upriver')   ES.

lexical

q̓xʷábəc   up above, upper side   EK.

q̓xʷúlgʷədxʷ   eastward   LG., EK.

    Cf. s.tulq̓ixʷ   east   ES.

sq̓íxʷəbš   the Skykomish, the site of
Sultan, Washington   LL., LG.

q̓xʷáx̌ad   upper side (reference to
a spot along the river)   LG.

q̓áxʷqs   upper side of a point   LG.

reduplication

bəsq̓ixʷixʷ   name of a Skagit River extended village (See Sampson,   DM.
p. 22 ff.) Also given as
bəsq̓ayxʷayxʷ.   DM.

1. q̓púd   Gather it.   LG.

2. q̓p̓(u)   pay

    Compare:

        t̓ás(a)   pay for an article

        jəɬálikʷ   marriage payment

        gʷíʔalikʷ   payment of wealth

    -ut

        <u>q̓p̓úd</u>   pay for service   LL.

        <u>q̓p̓úcid</u>   pay you   ES., DM.

    lexical

        <u>q̓p̓álikʷtub</u>   pay for sin, crime, etc.   LL.

3. q̓p̓úx̌ʷ   See under <u>q̓áp̓ux̌ʷ</u>.

4. q̓sáb   not enough

    Contrast <u>ʔíƛub</u> 'enough, sufficient'.

5. q̓úpšəd   leg cramp   LG.

    Cf. q̓əp-, q̓əl, q̓əyúʔus

6. q̓x̌(a)   insult someone, call him names

    -at

    ʔuq̓x̌ad   called him names   VH., LL.

    lexical

    ʔuq̓x̌ábactᵊb   really be given a dressing down
                 for several minutes   LL.

    hayʔ, <u>q̓x̌ábactᵊbəxʷ</u> tiɬ tiʔəʔ kàwqs   ML.
    Then, they called Raven names (behind his back.)

1. q̓(i)yáw? beach worm (used as bait) ESi.

   Cf. s.ʔúləč̓; bálhali?

2. q̓(i)yúq̓ʷ big appetite
   Sort of an insulting term. It would apply
   to kaẃqs. VH.

   See under tagʷəxʷ.

   Cf. k̓yúcʔb

   hikʷ čəd ʔəsq̓(i)yúq̓ʷ VH.
   I have a (very) big appetite.

q^w

The sound for this letter is similar to the *qu* in the English word *queen* except that it is made further back in the mouth. [labialized, voiceless velar stop]

1. qʷác

ʔəsqʷácdxʷ	doubt something	EK.
ʔəsqʷácdxʷ čəd	I doubt it.	LG.

    Compare:

xʷiʔ gʷədsəs.tɬíldxʷ	I don't believe it.	
xʷiʔ gʷədsəs.q̓álbid	Same gloss: I don't believe it.	
ʔəxʷ.cútᵊb čəd xʷìʔ	I doubt it.	LL.

2. x̌ʷi.qʷác   yellow, light green, pale   LL., LG., ESi.

   ʔəsqʷájil   yellowish   LG., ESi.

3. s.qʷágʷapəč   nape, lower part of the back of the head

   Cf. s.qʷəwíč   upper part of back

4. qʷágʷᵊb   sweet   EK.

   qʷágʷᵊb gʷəɬ tə xʷ.sə̀bəd   honey ('sweetness of the bee')   EK.

   -il

   səxʷqʷágʷᵊbᵊbìl   a sweetening thing   JC.

   lexical

   səxʷqʷágʷᵊbàlikʷ   Same gloss: a sweetening thing   JC.

   qʷagʷᵊbàlqʷuʔ   soda pop   VH.

5. qʷálc   boiling

   ʔuqʷálcalikʷ čəd   I'm canning.   EK.

1. qʷáliɬ   pitch (from wood)   MC., ESi., VH., EK.
                      chewing gum   VH.

2. s.qʷáliʔ

    sqʷalíʔabš   Nisqually people

      ... gʷəl tiʔəʔ sqʷíʔqʷaliʔ ƛu.ƛàx̌ʷ dəxʷəs.dáʔətˀbs
      tiʔəʔ diʔəʔ sqʷalíʔəbš dxʷʔal tiʔəʔ sqʷîʔqʷəliʔ
      s.watixʷtəd

      ... and grass (or hay) grows (there) so they named
      the Nisqually for the grassy land.   MS.

    lexical

      sqʷiʔqʷaliʔali   hayfield   LL.

    reduplication

      sqʷíʔqʷaliʔ   hay, grass   MS., LL., EK.

        Cf. sáx̌ʷil

      sqʷíqʷqʷaliʔ   grass (of lawn)   EK.

3. qʷ(a)ɬ(a)   drive, herd; expel, drive off

    -at

      qʷáɬəd   drive it   LL.

        qa qʷíst tiʔiɬ ləqʷàɬəd   LL.
        He was driving a lot of cattle.

      ʔuqʷáɬətˀb čəd   I got kicked out.   ES.

    lexical

      háʔɬ kʷi ƛ(u)adsə(s).šuucbicut ʔal kʷi ƛ(u)adsəqʷɬálps   LL.
      Watch out well for yourself while you drive.

      dxʷsqʷɬálps čəd   I'm a shepherd.   LG.

      ʔəlčuqʷàɬálps čəd   LG.
      I'm driving/herding the animals.
      (Very slow and careful articulation.)

reduplication

    x̌ʷul̕ čəd ʔu.qʷál̕qʷəł   ESi.

    I was simply driven away.

    x̌ʷul̕ čəd ʔu.qʷàl̕əl̕qʷəł   ES.

    (Wherever I went,) I got kicked out.

1.   qʷaqʷ-

        dayʔəxʷ t(u)asqʷaqʷtxʷ tiʔił tu.ʔácəc   ML.

        That was all that was left right there on that spot.

2.   qʷáqʷł   bag net

        See under λ̕áʔtəd.

3.   qʷáq̕ʷ   SPS   raven

        Cf. káw̕qs   NPS   raven

4.   qʷat(a)

        root

            ʔuqʷát   snows   EK., LL.

               Cf. báqʷuʔəb 'snows', təqʷúbəʔ 'any permanently snow
                                         capped peak'

        -at/-aš

           qʷátad   lay it down   EK.

              Cf. bəč(á), ł̕aq̕(á), páč(a)

              ʔuqʷátəd ʔal tiʔił čəgʷálatxʷ   LG.

              laid it down outside

           qʷátaš   lay it down

-agʷ-il

    ʔuqʷátagʷiləxʷ čəɬ   We went to bed.   LL.

       Cf. təjíl, bəčágʷil (under bəč(a))

lexical

    ʔuqʷátič čəd   snowing on me   LL.

       Cf. ʔu.báqʷu(ʔ)bidəxʷ čəɬ   snowing on us   LL.

    qʷatqs   A kind of buʔqʷ. See under báčus.

    qʷatúlč   set the table   LG.

1.   qʷátqs   See under báčus.

This name probably derives from the bird's diving ability.

2.   qʷáwɬᵊb   illustrate

    See under šuɬ.

3. s.qʷáx̌səd   Squaxin

    sqʷáx̌sədəbš   people of Squaxin Island

4.   qʷcá-   See qʷəc.

5. s.qʷəbáyʔ   dog

    sqʷəbqʷəbáyʔ   dogs

    sqʷíʔ(ʔ)qʷəbəyʔ puppy

      sqʷíʔ(ʔ)qʷiqʷəbəyʔ   puppies

→

7.   qʷəbqʷəbč   Oregon grape

8.   qʷəbxʷláx̌əd   elbow   LL.

    qʷəxʷəláx̌əd   elbow   EK.

1. qʷ(ə)c   slide, slip

    -t

      q̲ʷə́cᵊd   slide something   EK., LL.

      q̲ʷə́ctᵊb   got slid   EK., LL.

    -a-b

      q̲ʷcáb   NPS   slip   EK., LL.

       q̲ʷə́cəb   SPS   slip

      ʔuq̲ʷcáb čəd   I slipped.   LL.

        ləcu.čúqʷud čəd tiʔəʔ qʷíꞏ.qʷɫayʔ gʷəl q̲ʷcáb

        tiʔiɫ s.dùukʷ   DM.

        I was whittling a stick and the knife slipped.

    lexical

      ʔuq̲ʷcábšəd čəd   My foot slipped.   LL.

        ʔáɫ ti dsu.təláwil ʔal ti s.q̓àxʷ čəda ʔuq̲ʷcábšəd

        čəda ʔu.bə́č   DM.

        I was running fast on the ice and I slipped
        and fell.

    -agʷ-il

      ʔuq̲ʷcágʷil čəd   I slid down.   EK., LL.

      ʔuq̲ʷíq̲ʷcàwil čəd   I went sledding/skating.   EK., LL.

    -agʷ-i(1)-s

      ʔuq̲ʷcágʷis   I slid down (the bank) after it.   LL.

2. s.qʷədábš   The people of the north fork of the Skagit river.
        See Sampson, p. 27.

3. qʷədís   NPS   whale   LL.

    qʷə́dis   SPS   whale   ESi.

    čxʷ(ə)lúʔ   whale   ES., LL.

1. s.qʷəhálič   a former village on the Nooksack river where there was a log jam that necessitated portaging   LG.

2. qʷəjáb   moss

3. qʷəláʔus(ᵊb)   a blind for duck hunting   ES., LL.

   qʷiqʷəláʔusᵊb   Same gloss: a blind for duck hunting   HD.

   See under xʷi(ʔ)xʷiʔ.

4. qʷəlúb-   gray hair   LL., LG.

   qʷúlub   gray hair   DM.

   Cf. s.q̓əjúʔ   hair

   -us

     qʷúlubus   gray hair   DM.

     ʔuqʷúlubusəxʷ   You're getting gray now.   DM.

     ʔəsqʷəlúbusəxʷ ciʔił   She's getting gray now.   LG.

     qʷúqʷulubusəxʷ čəxʷ   You're getting a bit gray.   DM.

   -adiʔ

     qʷul̓qʷulubádiʔ   gray sideburns   DM.

   -ay-qs

     ʔəsqʷəlubáyqs   gray beard, gray whiskers   LL.

     ʔəsqʷəlubáyqsəxʷ   His beard is gray now.   LG.

   -qid

     ʔəsqʷəlúbqidəxʷ ciʔił   She's gray now.   LG.

5. qʷəlúlt   marsh (along the sound)   LL.

   qʷəlút   marshes that form parallel and near to the sound   FSi., EK.

qʷə́qʷəlùt   lake   ESi.
                   pond   ESi.

Derived from the root *qʷul (non-sea) water?

See under qʷuʔ and note Squamish cognate qʷul 'water'.

Cf. x̌áčuʔ   NPS   lake

Cf. báqʷəb 'cranberry marsh', čə́pdúp 'cattail marsh'   LG.

1.   qʷəlút   marsh tea   LG. MC.

    Cf. qʷəlút   marsh   FSi.

       qʷəlúlt   marsh   LL.

2.   qʷə́łtəd   medium sized sawbill, a buʔqʷ
                  Another name for it is s.xʷíhič.

3.   qʷəlsídəʔ   Quilceeda Creek, Tulalip Reservation ES., JC.
                  (It is the first one encountered going west from Marysville.)   ES.

    qʷəlsídàʔəbš   a person from the vicinity of Quilceeda   ES.

4.   qʷ(ə)qʷ(ə)stáybixʷ   forest dwarf; Eskimo

    See under čyátkʷu(ʔ).

5. s.qʷəqʷíč   a buʔqʷ locally known as war boat, a kind of diver

             LL. says that it is a very small diver of a different class (from other divers).

             In the ancient stories s.qʷəqʷíč gives lots of potlatches because this buʔqʷ is believed to drive the fish toward the shore.

6.   qʷəqʷqʷíʔs   thin, slender

    See under bəs.

-il

q^{w}əq^{w}q^{w}í?sil   getting slimmer

1.   q^w(ə)q^w(ú)   Cf. λ̓əlx̌   pop

    root

      ?uq^{w}ə́q^w It burst.   LL., AS.

    -ut

      ?uq^{w}q^{w}úd čəd   I burst it.   LL.

    -dx^w

      ?uq^{w}ə́q^{w}dx^w čəd   I burst it accidentally.   LL.

    rejected: *q^{w}əq^{w}tx^w LL.

2. x̌^{w}i.q^{w}ə́q̓^{w} white

    lexical

      q^{w}əq̓^{w}ə́x̌əd   black duck (lit. 'white wing')   EK., ESi.

      dx^{w}q^{w}ə́q̓^{w}us   has a white face   EK.

      (x^w)q^{w}ə́q̓^{w}us   bluff of clay or sand (not rock)   LL., EK.

3.   q^{w}əstányə   a woman's name, (one of VH.'s names)
→

5.   q^w(ə)š-

    sq^{w}ə́šəb   smoke   LG.

      Cf. s.tíq̓il   smoke   LL.

      pə́q̓^{w}əb   smoke   ESi.

        sg^{w}ə.pq̓^{w}ád   smoke, fog, clouds   EC.

   ?əsq^{w}ə́šəb   cloudy   JC.

    -a-b

      sq^{w}šáb   fog   HD.

ťəq sqʷšáb	thick fog	LL.
ʔuqʷšáb	fog came in	LL.
ləqʷšáb	fog is coming in	LL.
ʔəsqʷšáb	it's foggy	

1. qʷšəd

   cíckʷəxʷ čəxʷ qʷšəd ʔəxʷs.ťùkʷəb

   It seems as though you want to go home badly.

   didiʔɬ uʔxʷ qʷšəd ʔəxʷs.qəlbáb

   It looks as though it still wants to rain.

2. s.qʷəwíč   upper part of back

   Cf. s.qʷágʷapəč   nape, lower part of the back of the head

3. qʷəʔqʷábac   young fir tree

4. qʷib(i)   fix, prepare, make

   Cf. čəɬ/šəɬ, huy(u)

   root

   ʔəsqʷíbəxʷ čəd dxʷʔal kʷi ds.ƛa tàwd   LG.

   I'm getting ready to go to town.

   -it

   ƛəlláʔ čəd ɬuqʷíbid   LG.

   After a while I'll fix it.

   ʔuqʷíbid čəd x̌ʷùbt tuiʔal tə luƛ s.x̌əlàʔs   LG.

   I made it a paddle out of an old board.

   xʷìʔ kʷ dsqʷíbid tə d.ʔàlʔal   JC.

   I didn't fix my house.

ʔal kʷədiʔ tusqʷibitᵊbsəxʷ tiʔəʔ s.watixʷtəd   ML.
when the world was fixed over.

qʷíbicut   prepare yourself   ES.

qʷibicut čəd dxʷʔal tawd   EK.
I'm getting ready for town.

-yi-

    qʷíbyid   Fix it for him.   ES.

    qʷíbyic ʔə kʷi yiɗus   She made a basket for me.   LG.

-ał

    ʔuqʷíbəł čəd yiɗus   I made a basket.   LG.

    ʔuqʷíbəł čəd x̌ʷubt   I'm making a paddle.   LG.

lexical

    qʷibáyʔstaq   fix the fire   LL.

    qʷíbičup   fix the fire   LL.

    tiʔił dxʷsqʷibdísalikʷ   dentist   LL.

1.   qʷíbikʷs   rock cod of unidentified species
(Sounds like 'fix his face'. LL.)

    Cf. ƛ́ałigʷs(əd)

2.   qʷíc   (travel) with current, downstream
See chart under ɗixʷ.

    ləqʷíc čəd   I'm going downstream   LL., LG.
lexical

    sqʷícqs   point of land   LL.

3.   qʷíc   one who cheats

1. qʷíč   indifferent, unwilling, lazy

    Cf. q̓əyíl   lazy

       ʔəs.lí(h)ililtxʷ čəd   I don't care about it.

       qəllálus   someone who has not gone on a power quest

       s.čílčil   lazy

       ʔəsqʷíč čəd   I'm indifferent to it.   LL.

       ʔəsqʷíč tiʔił   He is unwilling to do something because it is too difficult. LG.

    -bi-t

       ʔəsqʷíčbid čəd   I don't think I am able to do it. LG.

       ʔəsqʷíčbid čəd kʷi gʷəds.dàʔad   LG.
       I don't know what to call it.

2. qʷíd

       qʷídəqs   beard, moustache   LG.

       qʷidáyqs   beard, moustache   LL., EK.

       qʷidáyucid   beard, moustache   LL.

3. qʷíqʷsp   sand fly, gnat   LL., LG.

4. qʷíq̓ʷ NPS   strong in body, husky; solid (object) EK.

    See under ƛaq̓ʷ. Cf. dídti

    Cf. tib(i), wəláx̌ʷ (SPS) Contrast čud 'weak'.

    root

       qʷíq̓ʷ čəd   I'm strong.   LG.

       ... ƛal čəd bəqʷíq̓ʷ   and yet I'm strong. LG.

qʷíq̓ʷcut   brace yourself up   ES.
                           make yourself strong   LG.

?al ti?ił ł(u)adsu.lúⱭil, xʷi? kʷ(i) adsuqʷíq̓ʷcut   ES.
As you are growing up, don't show off your strength.

-il

qʷíq̓ʷil   become strong   IM.

comparison

qʷíq̓ʷ čəd x̌ʷulàb ?ə dəgʷì   I'm as strong as you.   LG.

?iłqʷíq̓ʷ   stronger   LG.

lexical

qʷíq̓ʷqʷiq̓ʷlàx̌əd čəxʷ   You have strong arms.

qʷíq̓ʷqʷiq̓ʷšəd čəxʷ   You have strong legs.

rejected:

*?əsqʷíq̓ʷ čəd, *?əsqʷíq̓ʷəb čəd, *qʷiq̓ʷild, *qʷiq̓ʷis   LG.

1.   qʷíst   Snoh., SPS   bovine

    qʷíqʷst   calf   LL.

    Cf. búsbus   Skagit   bovine

2.   qʷí?ad   Snoh.   yell, call out loudly, telephone

    See under cut.

    Cf. wí?ad   (Skagit)

      ləqʷí?ad ti?ił stùbš   That man is hollering.   LL.

    -txʷ

      ?uqʷí?adtub kʷi ds.dà   HD.
      They called out my name in a loud voice (for all to hear).

    -c

      qʷí?aac   Call him.   LL.

ʔuqʷíʔaac čəd tiʔiʔił   LL.

I attracted their attention by yelling.

-c-b

    qʷíʔaacᵊbš čəxʷ ʔal ču(ʔ)kʷs   LL.

    You telephone me at seven.

reduplication

    ʔuqʷíʔqʷiʔad tiʔiʔił   LL.

    They hollered.

rejected:

    *qʷíʔtəb, *qʷíʔatəb

1.   qʷləstyuʔ   Columbia River smelt

2.   qʷłáyʔ NPS   log, stick

    Cf. s.tə́kʷəb SPS 'log, stick', pəx̌áyʔac 'log'

    lexical

       qʷłíʔšəd Skagit   shoe

         Cf. t̓kʷábšəd Snoh., SPS   shoe

       ʔuqʷłíʔšədᵊb čəd   I put my shoes on.   LG.

         Cf. ʔu.xʷəcšáadᵊb čəd   I took my shoes off.   LG.

       qʷłəy(ʔ)úlč   wooden platter (another name for łaʔx̌) LG.

         Cf. čáwəyʔ(ulč)   modern, store-bought dish

    reduplication

       qʷí(ʔ)qʷłəyʔ   stick, little stick   HD., LL.

       qʷłqʷłáyʔ   logs, sticks

1. s.qʷtáycəd   sturgeon

2. s.qʷúbʔ   sucker (a freshwater fish with white meat and lots of bones)   LL.

     Cf. tuʔáckʷ   sucker

3. qʷulíčut   broth   LG.

4. qʷul(u)   encircle

     Cf. qit(i)

     -ut

         qʷúlud   hug someone   EK.

         qʷulʔqʷulcut   sit with arms crossed and do nothing (lit. 'hug self')

     lexical

         ʔuqʷulusc čəxʷ   You hugged me about the neck.   LG.

5. qʷúləč   dip net   LG.

     See under ƛáʔtəd.

6. qʷúlub-   See under qʷəlúb-.

7. s.qʷútab   disease, sickness   LL., EK.

     See under x̌əɬ.   Cf. túqʷub

         ʔuqʷútab čəd   I caught a cold.   LG.

         ʔəsqʷútab čəd   I have a cold.   LG.

8. qʷuwádbəč   an owl of unidentified species, apparently "what the Snohomish call təkʷtəkʷəlús."   DM.

9. qʷuxʷ (?)   cartilage, gristle

1. qʷúxʷadəb   unripe, opposite of q̓ʷəl.

    Cf. x̌ič   raw (meat)

2. cis.qʷúxʷaɬ   a woman's name; VH.'s mother's name.

                    She was named after her maternal grandfather's grandfather's power which refers to an agate. It means 'bright, can see'.

3. qʷuʔ   (non-sea) water

qʷúbit	(mouth) waters for something	ES.
qʷí(w)ʔqʷuʔ	little water (i.e., a cute way of referrring to the neighborhood creek)	ML.
xʷqʷúʔəd	pail	EK.
ʔəs.táqʷuʔ čəd	I'm thirsty.	EK.

   qʷúʔqʷaʔ

sqʷúʔqʷaʔ	(any kind of a) drink	
ʔuqʷúʔqʷaʔ čəd	I had a drink.	LG.
ʔuqʷúʔqʷadid čəd	I drank it.	LG.

dáʔxʷ čəxʷ b(ə)uqʷùʔqʷadid tə qà qʷùʔ   JC.
You just drank a lot of water.

ʔuqʷúʔqʷadyic	He drank my drink.	LG.

    Cf. tágʷusᵊb   drink by putting face in water, not using a cup (human agent only)
                                       LL., MS.

sqʷúsahᵊb	foam	EK., MS.
qʷubáč(š)əd	rainbow	LL., ESi.
ʔəsqʷubáč(š)ədᵊb	"It's showing out its bright colors."	ESi.

       Cf. s.təx̌ʷšáad   rainbow   LG.

qʷulíčut	broth	LG.

424

qʷúləč	dip net	LG.
qʷùʔlubáʔ	saliva	LG.
ʔuqʷəʔɬubaʔ čəd	I'm salivating.	EK.

lexical

qʷúʔqid	crown of head	EK.
qʷúʔqʷuʔbalus	eyes watering	LL.
Cf. qʷátqʷatəlus	tearful eyes	ES.

-álqʷuʔ

qʷuʔálqʷuʔ	juice	LG.
	a drink that has something in it	JC.
qəlbálqʷuʔ	rain water (LG.'s name for Baker River)	
dxʷs.(h)ədálqʷuʔ	coffee/tea	LG.

Cf. kúpi 'coffee', qʷəlút 'marsh tea'

čəlqʷubəʔ	blackcaps
təqʷubəʔ	any snow-capped mountain

1. s.qʷxʷbíxʷ (ʔ)   hemlock (ʔ)

q̓ʷ

This letter stands for a sound somewhat like *qu* in the English word *queen* but it is pronounced further back in the mouth and the vocal cords are closed abruptly at the same time thus creating a hollow popping sound. [voiceless, glottalized, labialized uvular stop]

1. q̓ʷáač   belch

2. q̓ʷal(a)   tame   MS., VH.

    Cf. k̓ʷəč   wild

    root

       ʔəsq̓ʷál   It is tame.

       ləq̓ʷaləxʷ   It is getting tame.

    -at

       ʔuq̓ʷálad čəd tiʔəʔ x̌àʔx̌əlus   I tamed this raccoon.   VH.

    reduplication

       cisq̓ʷálalq̓ʷal   a woman's name, one of VH.'s names

3. q̓ʷálš/s.q̓ʷálaš SPS   waterfowl

    Cf. búʔqʷ NPS   waterfowl

4. q̓ʷálxʷ   a buʔqʷ with purple feet

                    It is related to qʷəq̓ʷáx̌əd 'black duck'. It is
                    called the treaty duck. ESi. calls it skunk
                    head coot.   ESi., LL.

    (Recorded once as k̓ʷálxʷ.)

5. q̓ʷáq̓ʷəjil   profanity

6. q̓ʷás Cf. k̓ʷás   fish thoroughly dried by smoking   ESi.

    Cf. x̌áx̌yəƛ̓   LG.

       k̓áyayəʔ or k̓ayáyəʔ   "It's smoked with alder."   LL.

426

1. q̓ʷásdùliča?   blanket made of dog and goat hair   LL., ML.

   q̓ʷástədùličə?   garment for doing power dances. It
                        represents the particular power.   LG.

2. q̓ʷáx̌ʷəb   strong and unpleasant odor

   See under sub(u).

3. q̓ʷáʔəb   kelp   EK., LL., ESi.

4. q̓ʷáʔq̓ʷab   seal bark

   Cf. gʷúhəb   dog bark

5. q̓ʷbə́txʷ   water lily   LG., MC.

6. q̓ʷəbxʷáči?   knuckle (?)

7. s.q̓ʷə́cɫ   chipmunk   LL., ESi.

   s.q̓ʷə́c̓ɫ   chipmunk   EK.

   Cf. x̌íx̌iṗič   chipmunk   LG., MC.

8. q̓ʷədíʔq̓ʷ(ac)   cottonwood (tree)   LG., EK.

9. q̓ʷəl   ripe; warm, burn; bake, cook

   See under hud(u).

   Opposite of x̌ič 'raw meat', qʷúx̌adəb 'unripe'.

   root

      q̓ʷəl   ripe, done cooking   LG.

      q̓ʷəláxʷ   It's ripe now.   LG.

      ʔuq̓ʷəláxʷ dəɫ tiʔə? sq̓ʷəláɫəd   EK.
      This berry (must be) ripe now.

dxʷs₂- root

lá?b d(ə)xʷsq̓ʷə́l	It's quite warm.	LG.
Cf. là?b d(ə)xʷs.(h)ə́d	Same gloss: It's quite warm.	LG.

-t

q̓ʷə́ld	cook it	EK.
q̓ʷə́ləd	bake it	LG.

-b

q̓ʷə́lb	cook	LL.
q̓ʷə́lb	cooking it	EK.
q̓ʷə́lb	bake in oven or on outside of fire	LG.

?əs.(?ə)x̌íd kʷi ɬ(u)adsu.hùyud kʷ səplə̀l
ɬ(u)adsq̓ʷə́lᵊb ?al kʷi gʷistə̀lᵊb   JC.
How would you prepare bread to be baked
in the sand?

bə.qádadidəxʷ ti?ə? luƛ ?ə ti?ə? səsq̓ʷə́lbs
s.?uladxʷ ti?ə? bəščəb   LL.
Mink repeats his way by stealing the old
fellow's cooked fish.

bə.qádadidəxʷ ti?ə? ?əsq̓ʷə́lb luƛ ?ə ti?ə?
s.?ulàdxʷ ti?ə? bəščəb
Mink repeats his way by stealing the fish the
old fellow cooked.

sq̓ʷə́lᵊb	barbecued salmon	LG.

-il

?əsq̓ʷəlíl čəd	I'm hot.	EK.

dxʷs₂- root -il

?udxʷsq̓ʷəlíl	Something is hot.	LL.

dáyʔəxʷ sixʷ ʔudxʷsq̓ʷəli̓l ʔal tiʔəʔ s.ləx̣i̓l   LL.

It's a real hot day.

ʔudxʷsq̓ʷəli̓l   weather is warm; water is heated   LG.

ci̓ckʷ (d)əxʷsq̓ʷəli̓l s.ləx̌i̓l   very hot day   EK.

là̓ʔb ʔudxʷsq̓ʷəli̓l   It's gotten really warm.   LG.

-adub

ʔəsq̓ʷəládubəxʷ čəd   My dinner is ready. ("This means
                                      that what I have cooked is ready
                                      for you; so you come to the table.") LL.

čəláłəxʷ čəd gʷəsq̓ʷəlàdubəd   LL.

My dinner is almost ready.

ʔəsq̓ʷəládub s.ʔulàdxʷ   baked salmon   EK.

lexical

q̓ʷəlqi̓d   cooked fish heads (they are cooked
                          and smoke-dried)   LG.

     See under t̓álus.

ʔəs.čal kʷ(i) adəxʷq̓ʷəlus   DM.

How did you burn your face?

     Cf. k̓ʷas

     rejected: *ʔəs.čal kʷ(i) adəxʷdxʷq̓ʷəlus

ʔəxʷq̓ʷəlx̣qs   burned nose (insulting appellation
                             given to Raven. Note that his beak
                             seems cracked.)   LL.

q̓ʷəlx̌šád   burned feet (insulting appellation
                          given to Raven.)   LL.

     The /x̌/ may be from special bird style of talking
     (or being talked about).

reduplication

q̓ʷəq̓ʷəl̓   shot berries   LG., MC.
                          (lit. 'recooked')   LG.

q̌ʷq̌ʷəl̓   huckleberry   ESi.

q̌ʷə́lq̌ʷəl   sweat(ing)   EK., HD., LL.

other derivation

sq̌ʷəlál̓ᵊd berry (in general)   ES., EK.

q̌ʷələstᵊb It was cooked.   ML.

sq̌ʷəldálił̓ᵊd prepared food   LG.

ʔu.x̌ʷəsíld čəd tə s.c̓ìstxʷ ʔə tə hàʔł dᵊsq̌ʷəldálił̓ᵊd

I fattened up my husband with my good cooking.

1. q̌ʷəládiʔ   ear   EK., ESi.

2. q̌ʷələstáb(ac) raspberry   LG.

  Cf. ƛ̓álə   raspberry   EK.

3. q̌ʷə́lq   See under ƛ̓əládiʔ.

  q̌ʷə́lqəd   He's making noise.

  q̌ʷə́lqcút   making noise of itself

4. q̌ʷə́ł̓b   tired   LG., VH. (rejected by DM.)

  See under wáwłqayuʔ.

5. q̌ʷə́łtəbəy̓ unidentified animal

6. q̌ʷəpx̌ʷ(šád) ankle

  (Also recorded p̓əsq̌ʷəgʷásšəd.)

7. q̌ʷəwá(h)ᵊb howl   VH.

8. q̌ʷəx̌ʷ Skagit butcher

  Equivalent to Snohomish k̓ʷič̌(i). See under ł̓ič̌(i).

q̌ʷə́x̌ʷəd tə s.ʔulàdxʷ   Clean the fish.   LG., VH.

łuq̌ʷə́x̌ʷtəb k̓ʷəł

He's going to be operated on, they say.

1. x̌ʷə.q̌ʷəx̌ʷílc   burned forehead, lit. 'blue forehead'

    See under hud(u), q̌ʷix̌ʷ.

2.   q̌ʷəx̌ʷqsáči?   fingernail   LL., EK.

     q̌ʷx̌ʷáči?   fingernail   ESi.

   q̌ʷəx̌ʷqšád   toenail   LL., EK.

    q̌ʷáx̌ʷšəd   toenail   ESi.

3.   q̌ʷəx̌ʷqəd   the force that makes the təstəd go   DM.

    See under s.qəlálitut.

4.   q̌ʷib(i)   disembark

    root

      ʔuq̌ʷib čəd   I go out.   LL.

    -it

      q̌ʷíbid   unload it   LL., EK.

      ʔuq̌ʷíbic   They took me out (because I was injured).   LL.

      ʔuq̌ʷíbitəb čəd   I was forced out.   LL.

    -agʷil

      q̌ʷíbagʷil   get out (of a canoe, car)   EK.

    -agʷ-i(1)-s

      q̌ʷíbagʷis   get off (the bus because one happens to see
                    a friend on the street)   LL.

              get out of (his car because of his insults)

1. q̇ʷíč   See under ʔatəbəd.   Cf. qíḷil

       sq̇ʷíč   widow, widower   EK.

       ʔuq̇ʷíčil   just lost a spouse   EK., LL.

2. q̇ʷiwác   sea moss   LL.

3. q̇ʷíx̌ʷ

       x̌ʷiq̇ʷíx̌ʷ   blue, dark green   LG., LL., ES.

       x̌ʷəq̇ʷíx̌ʷ   blue, dark green   FSi.

       sq̇ʷíx̌ʷ   Negro   EK., ESi.

4. q̇ʷiʔq̇ʷiʔsálbix̌ʷ   short, very strong people with exceptional
                           supernatural power

     See under čyátkʷu(ʔ).

5. s.q̇ʷuháp   stump still rooted   LL., EK.

       s.ʔəlágʷəp   stump   MC.

       Cf. qəládiʔ   up-rooted stump/root
                       end of up-rooted tree

         s.təbágʷapšəd   heel

         s.ʔəlágʷapšəd   heel

6. q̇ʷúlalatxʷ   copper?

7. q̇ʷuɬ(u)

       ʔəsq̇ʷúɬucut   Look out!

         Cf. ʔə(s).šúucbicut

       q̇ʷúɬucut   Excuse me.

1. q̇ʷup̓   shrink, shrivel

    Cf. q̇əyús

    root

        q̇ʷup̓   shrink, shrivel   DM.

    lexical

        ləq̇ʷup̓q̇ʷup̓áči? ʔə tiʔəʔ s.čətxʷəd   ES.
        Bear's hands shrivelled up.

        q̇ʷúp̓q̇ʷup̓əči(ʔ)b   sleeves rolled up   LL.

        q̇ʷúp̓q̇ʷup̓šədˀb   roll up pantlegs   LL.

    reduplication

        ʔəsq̇ʷup̓q̇ʷup̓   He was a cripple.

2. q̇ʷuʔ   gather, collect

    root

        x̌áƛtxʷ čəd kʷi gʷəds.ʔə́ɫˀd ʔəsq̇ʷúʔ ʔə dəgʷi   LG.
        I want to eat with you.

        ʔəs.gʷədíl čəd ʔəsq̇ʷúʔ ʔə màli   LG.
        I sit with Mary.

        ƛlə.ʔibəš ləsq̇ʷúʔ ʔə ʔəcà   (Reverse order preferred.)   LG.
        She walks with me.

        ƛləsq̇ʷúʔ ʔə ʔəca lə.ʔibəšs   (Preferred order.)   LG.
        She walks with me.

        ʔəsq̇ʷúʔ ʔə dibəɫ tə səs.gʷədils (h)əlgʷəʔ   LG.
        They sit with us.

        ci dsq̇ʷúʔ   my girlfriend, wife, mate   EK.

        ti dsəsq̇ʷúʔ   I was with him.   EK.

-t

q̓ʷúʔᵊd	gather it

q̓ʷúʔtᵊb	get gathered	LL.

q̓ʷúʔcut ɫi!	Get together, you all!

-b-i-

ʔəsq̓ʷúʔbid čəd ti d.ʔíišəd	HD.

I am with my people.

ƛ(u)asq̓ʷú(h)uʔbid čəd	I run around with him.	LL.

ɫ(u)asq̓ʷú(h)uʔbicid čəd	LL.

I'll be with you regardless of what may happen.

-ad-b-i-

ʔəsq̓ʷq̓ʷúʔadbid čəd	I room with him.	LL.

lexical

ʔuq̓ʷúʔq̓ʷuʔalikʷ	gathered from all over for a specific purpose	
q̓ʷúʔax̌əd	neighbor	LL., HD.
q̓ʷúʔgʷəsᵊd	put it together	LG., LL.
ʔəsq̓ʷúʔqs	joining of two points	EK.
q̓ʷúʔšəd	close relatives (lit. 'feet together')	LL.
q̓ʷuʔúdaq	close friend (not relative)	EK.
q̓ʷúʔalqʷùʔ	confluence	EK.

reduplication

ʔəsq̓ʷú(h)uʔ čəd	I associate with him. I run around with them.	EK.
ƛ(u)asq̓ʷú(h)uʔbid čəd	I run around with him.	LL.
ɫ(u)asq̓ʷú(h)uʔbicid čəd		LL.

I'll be with you (regardless of what happens).

ti ƛ(u)adsəsq̓ʷúhuʔ   The one you go around with.   EK.

ʔəsq̓ʷ꜀q̓ʷúʔᵊd   I live (in the same house)
                                      with him/them.   ML., EK.

q̓ʷ꜀q̓ʷúʔadčəɬ   our roommate   EK.

ʔəsq̓ʷ꜀q̓ʷúʔadbid čəd   I room with him.   LL.

q̓ʷúq̓ʷúʔalikʷ   gather many from all over
                                      for a specific purpose   LL.

híkʷ čəd ʔuq̓ʷúʔq̓ʷúʔalikʷ   LL.
I gathered them from all over (for the prayer meeting).

　　rejected: *q̓ʷuʔtub

1.   q̓ʷúʔap   a very black bu?q̲ʷ that dives

2.   q̓ʷúʔt   variant form of kʷuʔt q.v.   JC.

　　See under ƛakʷ/gʷ(a).

                      "These mats were sometimes used to eat off." JC.

s

The sound of this letter is similar to the English *s*. [voiceless alveolar fricative]

1.   s-   derivational prefix and syntactic particle
                       expressing absolute modality

2.   -s   a transitive suffix occurring only after -il

3.   -s   his, her, its, their

    See under d- 'my'.

4.   -s   pronominal object suffix 'me'

    See under -bš.

5. dxʷ.sácᵊb   fast flowing water
→
7.   sájᵊb, sájəp   See under haac.

8.   sáli?   two

    Cf. cəb   second, two

        sáli? ti d.pù?təd   I have two shirts.   DM.

    lexical

        sali?ágʷəp   two plants, two things to plant or hill up LG.

        sáli(?)ači? ti?ił ?i kʷi d(ə)ču?   He is twenty-one.   LG.

        sáli(?)ači? ti?ił s.?ulàdxʷ ?i kʷi cəlàc
        There are twenty-five salmon.

        sáli?àli   two plants (growing)   LG.

        səli?álps   two animals

        sali?áɬčup   two fires

        sali?áɬič   two bundles   LG.

sáli?əlus	two squares of a net, two stitches (knitting)	
		LG.
səli?îlc	two dollars	
sáli?qs	double barrel gun	LL.
	two points	LG.
sali?úlč	two baskets, two containers	DM.
dxʷsáli?us	two rows/layers	LG.

reduplication

səsá?li?	two human beings	LL., LG.
sí?ssà?li?	two children	LL.
sá?səli?	two small items	LL.
sáĺsali	two by two	LL.

rejected:

    *díɫ sàli(?)ači? ti?iɫ ?i kʷi d(ə)čủ?

1.   sáq   go in along the surface (as opposed to šič(i))

    root

?usáq	went in along surface	EK.

    lexical

sáqači?	sliver in hand	EK.

2.   saq̇ʷ   fly

    Cf. gʷəɫtqʷád, qəṗ

    root

      ?usáq̇ʷ   It flew.

      ƛusaq̇ʷ (?al ti) liɫ.šə̀q   It flies high.

      ləsáq̇ʷ ci?ə? kà?ka? liɫdᵊ.šəqbìd   LG.
      The crow flew over me.

437

liɬ.šəqbíd ʔə tə d.ʔàlʔal tə səsaq̉ʷ ʔə ciʔəʔ k̉àʔk̉aʔ   LG.
The crow flew over my house.

-txʷ

g̉ʷəsaq̉ʷtubicid   It might fly off with you.

reduplication

saq̉ʷsaq̉ʷ   (many) fly here and there

sáʔsq̉ʷ   fly just a bit

saq̉ʷaq̉ʷ   wheeling in the sky

saq̉ʷaq̉ʷsaq̉ʷ   several flocks wheeling in the sky

sásaq̉ʷ   flock fly away abruptly (as when
                    frightened)

   Cf. sə́səq̉ʷ   quail

1. sáxʷəb   jump or run (fast)

   Cf. təláwil, pə́ɬ, ƛiwʔ

   root

      sáxʷəb dxʷg̉ʷə̀d   They jumped down.

   -i-t

      ʔusáxʷəbid čəd   I jumped (ran) after it.   LL.

   -txʷ

      ʔusáxʷəbtub k̉ʷəɬ ti hədli   LG.
      They say Henry was kidnapped.

   -a-augment

      səʔsxʷáb   a broad jump consisting of two
                        successive leaps, Indian broad jump LL.

      ʔusəʔsxʷáb čəɬ   We broad jumped.   LL.

         Cf. ʔúkʷukʷ

lexical

sàx^wəb?álpsəx^w	They are off! (horses at a race)	LG.
	Start your horse now.	LG.
sá?sx^wəbik^w	jumper (the short jacket cowboys wear), a loan translation from English	ES.

reduplication

sáx^wsax^wəb	many run/jump, someone does a lot of running/jumping	
(lə)sá?sx^wsax^wəb	hopping	LG.
sáx^wax^wəb	scurrying about (more or less in-effectually trying to get things done)	LL.
sá?sx^wəb	run a few short quick steps	LL.
sə?sx^wáb	Indian broad jump	
sáx^wax^wsax^wəb	many run about getting nowhere	

rejected:

*?usáx^wəbis	"What you're trying to say is sáx^wəbid." LL.

1. s(á)x̌(a)   scrape

See under šic(i).

sáxəd	scrape it	EK., LG.

-b

sáx̌^əb	bitter (Skagit only)	LG.
Cf. t̓áč̓^əb bitter		

-b-il

dx^wsáx̌^əbìləx^w	It's beginning to get bitter.	LG.
?u(dx^w)sáx̌^əbil	It got bitter/spoiled, e.g., a pan full of berries.	

lexical

dxʷsx̌áyqsalikʷ	a barber, one who shaves	LG.
səxʷsx̌áyqsᵊb	(electric) razor	LG.
dəxʷsx̌áyqsᵊb	one who shaves	LG.
sx̌áyqsᵊb	shave (scrape chin)	LG., LL.
səx̌sx̌áyqsᵊb	razor	LL.
ʔəxʷsx̌áyqsᵊbᵊbəxʷ	He wants to shave.	LG.
dxʷsáx̌usᵊb	shave (scrape face)	LL.
sx̌úsᵊbəd	straight-edge razor	LL.

rejected:

*ʔəxʷsx̌áyqsəbəxʷ	(when trying to elicit, 'He is clean shaven'.)	LG.
*dəxʷsx̌áyqsᵊd		

1. sáx̌ʷil   grass, hay   LG., ML., LL.

   Cf. s.qʷíqʷaliʔ   grass, hay (under qʷaliʔ)

sáʔsx̌ʷil	(short) grass, lawn	LG.
sáx̌ʷəlàli	hayfield (equivalent to s.qʷiqʷaliʔali)	LL.
sáx̌ʷilàlʔtxʷ	stable, barn	LG.

→

3. saʔ NPS   bad, evil

   Cf. qələb   bad

modifier

   tiʔił tuds.qʷiqʷqʷaliʔ gʷəl ʔu.lək̉ʷtᵊb ʔə ciʔił
   saʔ ad.qʷist   LL.
   My grass was eaten by your bad cow.

-txʷ

   sáʔtubš čəxʷ   You hate me.   EK.

-il

    sá̲ʔil   get in trouble

    huy čəɫ sá̲ʔiləxʷ, *Jimmy*.   We got in bad, Jimmy.   LL.

-bi-t

    xʷsá̲ʔbid   empty (bottle)   LL.

lexical

    sá̲ʔàləqəp   smell bad   (NOT taste bad)   LL.

reduplication

    səʔsəʔá̲ʔqəb   bad words, bad talking   LL.

1.   sá̲ʔkʷəbìxʷ   name of the people along the Sauk and Suiattle
                      rivers.   VH.
                      See Sampson, p. 22ff.

2. dəxʷ.sá̲ʔq   Nooksack   LG.

    bəšxʷsá̲ʔq   Nooksack   VH.

3.   sə̂b

    gʷəsəbâd   be quiet, shut up

  See x̌ʷúbil.

4. -səb   lexical

    -ap.səb

    xʷ(ə)ƛ̕ápsəbəd   Break his neck!   LL.

    xʷ.čk̓ʷápsəbəd   Decapitate him!   LL.

    ʔu.ƛ̕ípəpsəbəd čəd   I choked him.   LG.

    ʔu.čík̓ʷapsəb k̓ʷəɫ They say he gagged/choked. LG.

    čəlíǰəpsəb   upper end of spine, nape   LL., EK.

-ay.səb

  s.čq̉áysəb   flower   EK., LL.

1. xʷ.sə́bəd   bee   LL., EK.

2. dxʷ.sə́d   warm, hot   See həd.

           This form is probably derived from dxʷs.(h)ə́d
           'warm, hot'. However, the s, in some cases at
           least, has lost its status as a prefix and
           come to be treated as the initial consonant
           in the stem.

           This treatment is seen in dxʷsí?səd 'a little
           bit hot', where the s is clearly part of the
           reduplication; and in Puget Salish no prefix
           ever occurs as part of a reduplication.

→

4.   sə́kʷəbác   alder   EK., LL., LG., MC.

   Cf. yəsáwi   alder   ESi.

5.   sə́lp   spin, twist

    See under jal-.

     -t

      sə̀lpcút   spin self

      sə́lsəlpcùt   spin (a top)

    lexical

      sə́lsəlpáligʷəd   whirl around   LG.

6.   səlúsqid   cooked fish heads. They are dried with their
           jaws open. They are used in soups.   ESi.

           LL. gives t̉álus as the equivalent commenting
           that they are cooked and hung to dry.

           LG. gives q̉ʷəlqíd as the equivalent commenting
           that they are cooked and smoke-dried.

7.   sə́pil   pliable, soft   JC.

ɫu.xʷíʔəs həlàʔb ʔə(s)s̲ə̲p̲il tiʔiɫ t̓iyùʔsəd   JC.

A hand smelt trap must not be real soft.

1.   səpl̓ə̀l, səpl̓íl   flour, bread   (from French *farine*?)

(1) ʔəs.(ʔə)x̌íd kʷi ɫ(u)adsu.hùyud kʷ s̲ə̲p̲ə̲l̲ə̲̀l̲
ɫ(u)ads.q̓ʷə̀l̓ᵊb ʔal kʷi gʷístəl̓ᵊb.

(2) ʔəs.láb̓ᵊd c(ə) ad.kàyəʔ.   (3) gʷəl ɫu.húyud
tiʔiɫ gʷìstəl̓ᵊb səpl̓ə̀l ʔə kʷ háʔɫ.

(4) húdčup ʔə kʷi háʔɫ gʷístəl̓ᵊb.   (5) q̓ʷə̀l̓ᵊbəg̓ʷələxʷ
tiʔiɫ gʷístəl̓ᵊb čəxʷə ɫu.líldəxʷ tiʔiɫ hùd.
(6) ʔəs.húydxʷəxʷ čəxʷ tiʔiɫ adsəpl̓ə̀l. (7) čáʔᵊd
tiʔiɫ ʔəxʷs.q̓ʷə̀l̓ᵊb ʔəs.(ʔə)x̌íd kʷi s.ƛ̓əps.
(8) ʔáh̓ᵊdəxʷ tiʔiɫ s̲ə̲p̲l̲̓ə̲̀l̲ čəxʷ(ə) pə́d̓ᵊd ʔə tiʔiɫ
gʷístəl̓ᵊb.   (9) ʔá(h̓ᵊ)dəxʷ čəxʷ tiʔiɫ bələ.hùd.
(10) xʷíʔ lə.qà kʷi hùd gʷə ti gʷə.hùd tiʔiɫ
adsu.q̓ʷəlalikʷ.

(11) ɫ(u)as.(h)áydxʷ čəxʷ ʔəs.(ʔə)x̌íd kʷi ɫusə.q̓ʷə̀l
ʔə tiʔiɫ adsəpl̓ə̀l.   (12) ʔəs.láb̓ᵊd čəxʷ ɫu.šə̀qil ʔə
tiʔiɫ gʷìstəl̓ᵊb.   (13) kʷə́dədəxʷ čəxʷ tiʔiɫ s̲ə̲p̲l̲̓ə̲̀l̲
tul̓ʔal tiʔiɫ tusəs.pə̀ds, čəxʷə jax̌ad.   (14) xʷíʔiləxʷ
tiʔiɫ bəkʷ gʷístəl̓ᵊb, s.číq̓ʷil.   (15) húyəxʷ tiʔiɫ
ads̲ə̲p̲l̲̓ə̲̀l̲.

(1) How would you make bread that is baked in the sand?

(2) Observe your grandmother. (3) She will make sand bread well.

(4) Make a fire on a nice (expanse of) sand. (5) The sand is now heated and you will remove the fire.
(6) You have prepared the dough. (7) Dig (a hole) in the hot (sand) about this deep. [JC. indicated just a bit over two inches.] (8) Now place the bread (in the hole) and bury it in the sand. (9) You replace the burning (wood). (10) The fire should not be much because it might burn your baking (bread).

443

(11) You will know how your bread is baking. (12) You observe the rising of the sand. (13) Now you take the bread from where it was buried, and you shake it. (14) (So) there is no sand, no grime. (15) Now your bread is done.   JC.

"The place where bread was baked was a no-no for us kids. It was marked off with cedar rails, a kind of fence."   JC.

1. sə́pkʷ   perch (fish)   LL.

    Cf. q̓ál

2. xʷ.sáq̓ʷəh   Suquamish as pronounced by ESi. (who is Suquamish).
                          NPS speakers say suq̓ʷábš. See ʔítakʷəbixʷ.

→

4. sə́səq̓ʷ   quail. The term is probably derived from saq̓ʷ 'fly'.   EC.

5. sət̓   Cf. šəq

    sə́t̓əd   lift it

6. səxʷ   grease, fat   JC.

    s.x̌ʷə́s   grease, animal fat   LG.

    səxʷúb   butter clam   EK., LL.

        See under s.ʔáx̌ʷuʔ. Cf. čq̓ʷət̓ 'butter clam'   ESi.

7. səxʷ-   derivational prefix
                          An agent or functioning device that habitually performs an act associated with the stem. Cf. -təd, dəxʷ-
                          See Hoard/Hess, p. 45ff.

    səxʷgʷədíl   chair   LL.

    səxʷx̌ál   pencil, pen   LG.

səxʷʔáx̌ʷuʔᵊb   clam gun   JC.

    Cf. s.qáləx̌

səxʷʔúluɬ   device, means for water travel, q̓ilbid   DM.

səxʷ-as-

səxʷəsq̓ʷúʔil   device for keeping gathered what has been collected, e.g., a book binder   JC.

səxʷ-u-

səxʷuyáyus   tool, what you work with   JC.

1.   səxʷík̓   an unidentified bird which belongs to the class titčulbixʷ   ES., LL.

2.   séx̌   steep

3.   séx̌ᵊb   dance   JC.

    Cf. pigʷəd, júbalikʷ (under jub(u)),tac; čix̌(i), č̓áxʷadiʔ, gʷədáčiʔ; t̓ílib

síʔsx̌ᵊb   "When an adult quietly sings a song and beats a drum, a small child might get up and sort of dance.

    That's síʔsx̌ᵊb. When a child manifests this kind of interest, the adult considers him ready for beginning to instruct."   JC.

4.   -sid   object suffix 'thee'

    See under -bš.

5.   sidq̓   swing aside, turn something, e.g., a handle

    root

     ʔusídq̓   It swung over.

445

-t

   sídq̓ᵊd   Turn it. Turn (a handle).

   sídq̓cut   Move out of the way, move over.

     See under jəx̌, especially under the lexical suffix.

     Cf. dədí?i? (under di?)

reduplication

   sídsidq̓ᵊcut   spin self around

   sísədq̓ᵊd   Turn it just a bit. Swing it just a bit.

    ?í, gʷəbə.?úx̌ʷtxʷ čəxʷ ti?it (?)a; tùx̌ʷ čəxʷ gʷəl ləsísədq̓ᵊd ti?ə? s.gʷədgʷàtəd

    Yes, you could make it go that way; but you are turning (i.e., twisting) the language a bit. MS. [A gentle way of telling the researcher his use of the language was broken.]

1.   sikʷ(i)   tear, take apart, rip apart
                 "This is a forceful word."   LL.

   See under tič(i).

   Cf. x̌ʷət 'tear' (Nisqually), čət 'rip a gash'

   root

    ?ə(s)síkʷ   It's torn.   HD.

   -it

    síkʷid   tear it, take apart, take down; rip apart LL.

    síkʷitᵊb   ripped apart, taken apart LL.

   lexical

    ?usíkʷáliča? čəd   I ripped my clothing. LG.

    ?usíkʷsikʷáliča(?)b ti?it   LG.

    He deliberately ripped up his clothing. (The -b makes it intentional.)

reduplication

     sísik̓ʷid   tear to pieces   LL.

1.   sìk̓ʷwáyuʔ   pronged stick   LL., LG.

    (perhaps sìk̓ʷáyuʔ)

2.   sílalʔtxʷ   tent (lit.'cloth house' from the English *silk*)

3.   sísəd   blow nose   LG.

    See under bə́qsəd (in addendum).

    Cf. púʔu

4.   sítqsᵊb   sniff   LG.

    See under bə́qsəd (in addendum).

    Cf. súpqs, 450.2

5.   sixʷ   intensifying particle

    after predicate head

        b(ə)as.x̌ə́ɬ čəxʷ ʔu sixʷ   Are you sick still again? LG.

        ʔəs.x̌íčil jəɬ sixʷ   He must be cranky.   LG.

        gʷəl ʔá tiʔə káw̓qs sixʷ čà(ʔ)kʷ   ML.
        And there Raven was (of course) down at the shore.

        ʔu.balíic čəd sixʷ ʔə ti d.šiqʷ   HD.
        I forgot my hat again.

        kʷədáxʷ čəxʷ sixʷ   HD.
        You are getting that way again.

    before predicate head

        (hə)láʔb čəxʷ ʔu sixʷ ʔəs.x̌ə́ɬ   LG.
        Are you still very sick?

(hə)láʔb k̉ʷəɬ haw̓əʔ jəɬ <u>six̌ʷ</u> ʔəs.x̌ə́ɬ   LG.

Oh, it is said he still must be real sick.

1.   six̌ʷ-   derivational prefix

                     person serving in the capacity of <u>X</u> for someone else
                     See Hoard/Hess, p. 48ff.

2.   síx̌ʷ(i)   make noise by putting water in motion   LL.

    -it

      ʔudx̌ʷ.bálihigʷəd čəd čəda <u>síx̌ʷicut</u>   LL.

      I forgot myself and made noise with the water.

      <u>síx̌ʷid</u>   make a noise with the water

                 "That would seldom be said because it would mean to do it deliberately, but you wouldn't want to do that. It would frighten the fish and ducks away."   LL.

    reduplication

      ləsíʔsx̌ʷicut tiʔiɬ ǰəsəds   ML.

      His legs are making a little noise (as he (Heron) wades in the shallow water).

3.   siʔáb   See under <u>ʔiʔáb</u>.

4.   stab   See under <u>tab</u>.

5.-ay̓.staq   lexical   'flame'

    Cf. -čup, hud

6.   su   derivational element   'young'

    <u>súq̉ʷaʔ</u>   younger sibling, children of parents' younger siblings

    See entry under <u>súq̉ʷaʔ</u>.

wíw̓su　　　　children

　　Cf. s.táwig^wəɫ, s.táwix^wə?ɫ

?iɫ.t̓ísu　　　　younger

　　diɫ ?iɫt̓í.t̓isu　　　the youngest

1.　　sub(u)　　　　smell

　　Compare: -(alə)qəp

　　　　q̓^wáx̌^wəb　　　strong, unpleasant odor

　　　　x^wák̓^wəb　　　smell of something burning
　　　　　　　　　　　(usually feathers)

　　　　páx̌^əb　　　smell of burning

　　　　?íh^əl　　　stink

　　　　haq^wa-　　　smell it

　　　　c̓áq^əb　　　a strong and unpleasant odor

　　　　x^wás(^əb)　　　the smell of urine

　-ut

　　híwil č(ə)x^wə súbud　　Go and sniff it! Smell it!

　-dx^w

　　x^wi? ?u k^w(i) adsə(s)súb^ədx^w ?əs.q^wàlc čəd ?ə
　　ti?iɫ s.g^wəlùb
　　Don't you smell the chicken I'm cooking?

　-b-dx^w

　　?ə(s)súb^əbdx^w čəd　　I can smell it.

　　?ə(s)súb^əbdx^w čəd ti?iɫ ?u(?ə).ƛ̓àləqəp
　　Same gloss: I can smell it.

2.　　súk̓^wəb　　　　cedar bark still on tree　　　LG., EK., LL.

　　　　　　　　　　act of removing inner (yellowish) cedar
　　　　　　　　　　bark -- NOT the bark itself　　　　ESi.

1. súla   center, opposite of ʔalq̓ʷ.

    súla   (It is lying) in the middle.   LG.

    -t

        súlad   place it in the center   LG.

        súlac   Move me (nearer) to the center.   LG.

        súlàcut   come up in front   DM.

    bi-t

        adsúləbìd   toward the center from you   LG.

            ʔàl tiʔił adsúləbìd   LG.
            It is right there in front of you.

        sùləbíd ʔə tiʔił   toward the center from him   LG.

        dᵊsúlabid   He is toward the center from me.   LG.

        ʔəs.kiis čəxʷ ʔal tiʔəʔ dsuləbíd   DM.
        You are standing in front of me.

    -txʷ

        súlatxʷ   bring it out from the wall   LG.

    -yi-

        tusulayitᵊbəxʷ   Placed them directly in front
                               of him.   ES.

            Cf. qʷátad (under qʷat)

2. súləč̓   See súlič.

3. súlič   mat for making walls

    Also recorded as súləč̓ 'a mat of cedar bark or cattail upon
                           which the bowls of food were set for
                           eating'   LG.

    See under s.łágʷid.

1. súp̓qs   hair seal, harbor seal   LL., ML.

     sú?səp̓qs   hair seal pup

     Cf. ?ášxʷ   hair seal   LG.

       ?ásxʷ   hair seal   ESi. (and in most cognate languages north of Puget Salish)

     Cf. čáyə 'fur seal', ?əšás 'sea lion'

2. súp̓qs   sniff   JC.

     Cf. sítqsᵊb

3. súq̓ʷa?   younger sibling, children of parents' younger siblings. In referring to siblings without regard to seniority, suq̓ʷa? is used, not s.qa.

     See under s.qá.

       ?əbsúq̓ʷə?əxʷ   He already has a younger sibling.   LG.

       adsúq̓ʷa? čəd   I'm your younger brother.   LG.

       čit sùq̓ʷa?   younger sibling next to ego

       súsuq̓ʷə?bitəgʷəl ti?ə? cədił dxʷs.xʷixʷixʷi?   ML.
       (These) younger brothers to each other were hunters.

       ?ə(s)súq̓ʷa? haẃə? ti?a?   VH.
       This (little shaver) is already going to have a little sibling.

4. suq̓ʷábš   Suquamish   LL., MS.

     This name is rendered as xʷ.sə́q̓ʷəb by ESi. See ?ítagʷᵊbixʷ.
     See also Elmendorf, p. 31.

5. -sut   reflexive   See under -bš.

451

1.   suťʔ(u)   draw in

     -ut

          sútutᵊb čəd   I was drawn in.   LG.

     reduplication

          sùsutiʔəʔ   name of site where the town of Mount Vernon,
                         Washington now stands. (The name derives from
                         the fact that there were several establishments
                         here to which many people always felt drawn.)

          ʔəs.łáłlil čəd ʔal ti sùsutiʔəʔ
          I live in Mt. Vernon.

2.   súxʷil   strong cold wind, blustery, stormy

     See under šə́xʷᵊb.

3.   suxʷt-   recognize

     Contrast čáłaʔ 'fail to recognize'.

     See under hay- 'know'.

     -š

          ʔusúxʷtᵊš čəd tə s.tùbš   I recognized the man.   LG.

          ʔusúxʷtᵊš čəd   EK.
          I recognize it (e.g., a sweater I made long ago).

          ʔusúxʷtᵊš čəd tiʔił hədli.   I recognized Henry.   EK.

     pronominal suffixes
     (See remarks under cut-b, p. 58.)

          ʔusúxʷtᵊbš čəxʷ ʔu   Did you recognize me?   EK.

          ʔusúxʷtᵊbicid čəd   I recognized you.   EK.

          x̌əł ti čəd ʔə(s)súxʷtᵊbicid   LG.
          I sort of recognize you.

(1) tuɫčád, tuɫčád tə ʔaciɫtalbixʷ

(2) gʷát čəxʷ. gʷat čəxʷ

(3) xʷíʔ kʷ dsə(s)súxʷtᵊbicid

(4) ʔusúxʷtᵊbš čəxʷ ʔu

(1) From where, from where is this Indian?
(2) Who are you? Who are you?
(3) I don't recognize you.
(4) Do you recognize me?   JC.

-il

cíckʷ čəd ʔusùxʷtil   Indeed I recognize you.   LG.

ʔi. ʔə(s)súxʷtil čəd   LG.

You (it, him etc.) I recognize.

1.   súyqid   man's name. The name of LG.'s son, Fred.

2.   swələq̓   Frog talk. Specifically what Frog would
                           sing to her baby to try to get him to
                           stop crying.   ML.

3.   sʔəx̌ʷáʔ ~ sx̌ʷáʔ   urinate (male)   LL., ML.

     See under xʷás 'wet one's clothes', p̓əč̓ 'defecate'

     Cf. tiwáʔ   urinate (female)

         ʔusʔəx̌ʷáʔ tiʔiɫ   He urinated.   LG.

         ʔu.qʷúqʷadid kʷi sʔəx̌ʷáʔ ʔə kʷi sʔiɫ.ləgʷəbs   ML.
         He drank the urine of another youth.

         ʔəxʷsx̌ʷáʔᵊb čəd   I want to take a leak.   ES.

         ʔudxʷsx̌ʷáʔiluɫᵊb čəd   I need to go urinate.   LL.

             Cf. sgʷi.gʷədilálʔtxʷ   outhouse

         xʷsx̌ʷáʔad   bladder (lit. 'where the urine stays') LL.

š

This letter represents a sound similar to that of the English letters *sh* as in *she* and *shoe*. [voiceless alveolar fricative]

1. -š   a transitive suffix

2. šab(a)   dry

   Cf. ták^{w}il   gone dry   Contrast ł(ə)q^w(ú) 'wet'.

   root

     ʔə(s)šáb   It's dry (anything).   LG.

   dx^w-

     dx^{w}šáb   (A creek, pan of water) is drying up. LG.

     ʔudx^{w}šáb ti ds.q^{w}àlc   What I'm boiling is going dry. LL.

   -at

     šábad   dry it   LG.

   -b

     ʔu.bə́čəd čəx^w, ʔə(s)šáb^{ə}b   JC.
     You lay it down [and] it dries.

   lexical

     šábapsəb   dry throat   DM.

     šábig^{w}əd   (Your) whole insides are dry.   DM.

     ʔəx^{w}šábus   dry face   LG.

     ʔəx^{w}šábus^{ə}b want to have a dry face   LG.

     dx^{w}šábus^{ə}b Dry your face.   LG.

     (hə)lá ʔb čəx^w ʔəx^{w}šábus   LG.
     You (seem) really worried, i.e., dry faced.

     x^{w}šəbús NPS   partly dried fish

       x^{w}šábus SPS   partly dried fish

Cf. k̓áyayə?/x̌ax̌yəƛ 'dried salmon', s.t̓əlú?b 'dried
king salmon, s.ƛú?ᵊb '(dried) dog salmon'

adsxʷšəbús ti?iɬ   That's your partly dried fish.   LG.

adəxʷušəbúsəlikʷ ti?iɬ   That's your fish drying place.   LG.

(This form is preferred to adəxʷušəbús ti?iɬ
which would mean the same thing.)

šabyúq̓ʷ   dry throat   DM.

šabyús   dry throat   DM.

1.   šač̓   ending

See under huy(u).

root

šáč̓əxʷ   That's the ending.   EK.

díɬ šàč̓s   That's the end (of an old story).   EK.

díɬəxʷ hùys, diɬəxʷ šáč̓s   EC.
That's all. That's finished. (EC. concluded one
of her old stories with this.)

?ušáč̓ ti?ə? dsu.yàyus   LG.
I finished what I was working on.

hùy díɬ xʷu?ᵊlə? gʷəsšàč̓əxʷ ?ə ti?iɬ   ML.
That's the end of it, (a very long monologue).

... ɬušáč̓ ?ə ti?ə? s.?íč̓əbs   MC.
... (until he reached) the end of his blanket.

lexical

?ušáč̓qsəxʷ   He has breathed his last.   LL.

šáč̓qs   death; his breath is gone.   LG.

See under ?átəbəd.

1. -ša(a)d ~ -šəd ~ -səd   lexical   'foot, entire leg and foot'

        Cf. -ílč 'leg from knee down'; -ɫх̌áʔ 'thigh'; ǰəsəd 'foot, leg'

        Requires thematic suffix -i- before -t.

            húyutᵊbəxʷ tiʔəʔ dəxʷcícəɫšaadᵊbəxʷ ʔə ciʔəʔ k̓àʔkaʔ
        They made a carpet for Crow's feet.

s.tə̓x̌ʷšáad	rainbow	LG.
s.tə̓x̌ʷšád	cedar root	LG.
ləx̌šád	lamp	LG.

       ʔu.xʷ(ə)ƛ̓šád čəd   I broke my leg.

       ʔəs.čál kʷ(i) adəxʷu.xʷ(ə)ƛ̓šad
       How did you break your leg?

       ʔu.sáxʷəb čəd čəda ʔu.lík̓ʷšəd ʔə tə s.tə̓x̌ʷšəd čəda ʔu.bə́č.
       diɫ cəxʷu.xʷ(ə)ƛ̓šád.
       I was running and I tripped on a root and fell.
       That is how I broke my leg.

         ǰə́səd   foot, leg

       ʔu.x̌əɫšád čəd   I hurt my foot.

       ʔəs.x̌əɫšád čəd   I have a sore foot.

       ʔu.ɫíčšədit̓ᵊb   His leg got cut.

     -qs-šad

čə̓tqᵊ(s)šád	big toe	DM.
s.dəx̌q(s)šád	toe	LG.
kʷədᵊq(s)šádᵊb	Touch your toes!	LG.

2.   šágʷəq   SPS   carrot

      šəgʷáq   NPS   carrot

1.   šal-

   ʔə(s)šálgʷəs   hooked together

2.   šálbixʷ SPS   outside but near house

   Cf. čəgʷálətxʷ NPS   outside, šəjál   go outside

   bə.ʔíbəš dxʷʔal šàlbixʷ   JC.
   He went outside again.

3.   šáqʷil Skagit   cross a river/lake (bodies of water only) DM.

   Cf. túlil   Snoh., diʔúcid (under diʔ), jəlúcid (under jal)

      ʔušáqʷil čəd   I crossed it.   LG.

      šáqʷil čəd dxʷ.diʔùcid   LG.
      I'm going to cross the river to the other side.

   -txʷ

      ʔił.čád ƛəlay? kʷi tušáqʷiltxʷ čəxʷ   LG.
      Which canoe did you take across the river?

4.   šáẃ   bone

   Cf. x̌.dədáẃšəd marrow

   root

      ƛàl bə.káẃkaẃad ti šáẃ   They also chew on bone(s).   LG.

   lexical

      šáẃayucid   jaw

      šáẃ(y)idəgʷəs   collarbone

      šáẃšəd   foot bone

5.   šáẃkʷɫ   mountain beaver (aplodontia)

1. šáyil   Skagit   hunt   DM., LG., MS.

    See under x^wi(ʔ)x^wiʔ.

      dx^wšáyil   hunter

      łušáyil čəd ʔə k^wi s.x̌^wiƛ̓əyʔ   MS.
      I'm going to hunt mountain goat.

2. šəb-   See ƛaʔtəd.

    šə́bəd   A fishing net like a basket with a wide opening but narrows to a point so the fish cannot turn around. It is used in creeks. (LG.) A bag net. s.tídg^wəd tə dəx^wu.čə́ł šəbəd. Cedar boughs are used to make a fish trap [of this type]. LG.

    x^wšəbtád   netting for a ƛaʔtəd   MS.

3. šəbád   enemy

    təlíx^w šəbàd   They are enemies.

    tu.ʔúlułàac̓b čəd ʔə tə dšəbàd   LG.
    My enemy pursued me by canoe.

4. šəg^wáq NPS   carrot   LG., EK., ML.
    šág^wəq SPS   carrot   ESi., (LL.)

5. šəg^wáʔəc   salmonberry sprouts

6. šə́g^wł   road, door, way

    Cf. -ay.ucid

7. šəjál NPS   Go outside!   LL.
    šə́jal SPS   Go outside!

458

Cf. čəgʷálətxʷ (under čaʔkʷ), šalbixʷ

    híwiləxʷ šəjàl   Go on outside!   LL.

    šáajal   many go out   LG.

1.   šəjt   bow, front

See ʔudəgʷ-.   Contrast ʔilaq 'stern'.

    liɬšəjt adsəs.gʷədìl   LG.
    You are sitting in the bow of the canoe.

    ɬušəjt   He was going to get in the bow.   LA.

    šəjt   bow, prow, front seat of an automobile   LL., LG., EK.

2.   šəláʔ   penis

3.   šəɬ Snoh.   make

The Skagit equivalent is čəɬ, q.v.

root

    ƛu.láƙʷtⁱb ƙʷəɬ ʔə tiʔiɬ čàydi tiʔiɬ ƙadəyuʔ
    ƛ̉ususšəɬs (h)əlgʷəʔ s.ɬùb   LL.
    It's said that the Chinese eat rats. They
    make soup of them.

compound

    šəɬbádⁱb   step-father

    šəɬtádⁱb   step-mother

4.   šəƛ   scorch

See under hud(u).

    šəƛšəƛšɬ   a place name of unremembered location
                    meaning 'scorched leaves'   HD.

459

1.   š(ə)p-

    <u>šp</u>ác   comb

  -t

    ʔu<u>šə</u>páj^əd čəd   I combed her hair.

  -b

    <u>šp</u>áj^əb čəd   I combed my hair.

2.   š(ə)q   high, up

  root

    ʔu·, tùdiʔ <u>šə́q</u> haw̓əʔ tə s.ʔa·s   ML..
    There indeed she is up high.

    <u>šə́q</u> ciʔił ʔəs.caq̓ábactubs   ML.
    Up high she is impaled.

  with locative prefixes

    ck̓ʷáqid čəd ɬəliɬ<u>šə̀q</u>   I'll always be on top.   LA.

    ʔu.tə́čt^əb tuɬ<u>šə̀q</u> ʔə tiʔił s.bàdil   EK.
    They rolled it from the top of the mountain.

    ʔu.čúbə čəd dxʷ<u>šqùs</u>   I'm going up hill.   EK.

  -t

    <u>šə́q</u>^əd   Lift it up!   DM.

    ʔu<u>šə́q</u>^əd čəd   LL.
    I picked it up and set it (on the table).

    Compare:

    t̓ágʷt^əd/t̓ágʷt^əš   place on something high, e.g.,
                      a table, high rock

    q̓íɬid   hang it up

    k̓iɬid   hang it on a peg, nail, etc.

    sə́t̓^əd   lift it

ɫpúd   hang over a line, a stick, etc.

bəšəqcútəxʷ sixʷ   She raises herself up again.   LA.

ƛ̓àl sixʷ bušq̓ácut tiʔəʔ kìkəwič   LA.
Little Hunchback raised himself still again.

lexical

-abac

šəq̓ábac   on top of something, e.g., a table   DM.

šəq̓ábac ʔə tə s.wàtixʷtəd tiʔiɫ ƛ̓ùx̌ʷƛ̓ux̌ʷ   JC.
The oyster (lives) on top of the ground.

ʔəs.bə́č (ʔal tiʔiɫ) šəq̓àbac ʔə tə cildàliɫ³d   LG.
It's lying on the table.

gʷəl ʔəs.p̓íl tiʔiɫ šqàbəc ʔə tiʔiɫ č̓ƛ̓aʔ   ES.
And it was flat on top of that boulder.

-ači?

šəq̓áči(ʔ)b   raise your hand   EK.

šišq̓áči(ʔ)d   'Indian' hammer   EK.

-adi?

šəq̓ádi?   on a ledge, on a shelf; hammer, small axe DM.

ʔal ti šq̓ádi?   It is (stored) up above.   LG.

šq̓ádi(ʔ)bid   on top of something   LG.

-alatxʷ

šəq̓álatxʷ   roof   EK.

                upstairs, ceiling, roof;
                above the whole house   LG.

ʔu.húd šəq̓àlatxʷ ʔə tə ʔalʔal   EK.
The roof of the house burned.

-al-ič

šqáličᵂ	high on top (of a mountain)	ES.
	the very top, high on top	EK.

šəqəlíč tiʔił səs.p̀usᵊbs   DM.
It's floating on top of the water.

-ap

dxᵂšqápᵂ	It is high off the ground (talking	
	about a house set on blocks).	EK.

-iqad

tùl̓šq̓íqad tə sə.sàxᵂəbs   LG.
He's running from up the hill.

sáxᵂəb tul̓šq̓ìqad   LG.
Same gloss: He's running from up the hill.

ʔu.ƚəgᵂᵊƚ čəd šəq̓ìqad   LG.
I left them up hill.

-ulgᵂədxᵂ

šq̓úlgᵂədxᵂ	sky, upper-land	EK.

ʔəs.káykəyᵊb ʔu tə šq̓ùlgᵂədxᵂ   LG.
Is the sky blue?

-us

ʔu.čúbə čəd dxᵂšq̓ùs	I'm going up hill.	EK.
x̌ᵂul̓ ʔubəšq̓úsᵊb	He'd just lift up his head.	ES.

-y-alus

šəq(i)yálus ʔə tə *page*	at the top of the page	DM.

-yaqid

šəq(i)yáqid	tree top	EK., DM.

1. šəxʷ

    root

ʔušə̱xʷ	swelled	LL.
ləšə̱xʷ	It's swelling.	LL.

    -b

šə́xʷəb	wind	EK., LL., LG.

    ʔəs.ƛ̕ax̌ čəd yəx̌i ləcušə̱xʷəb
    I'm cold because the wind is blowing.

ší ʔšxʷəb	breeze	LL.

    Compare:

puʔ	blow; wind	
súxʷil	strong wind	
q̓ágʷəlʔb	blowing continuously	
ʔu.č̓ícəxʷ	blowing hard and getting bad at sea	
p̓áč̓aɬəd	strong wind blowing up hard driven spray from surface of sea (no big waves)	
s.túbələ	northwest wind	LL.
stùl.ʔáɬx̌əd	Same gloss: northwest wind	LL.
təgʷáaq̓ʷ	south wind	LL.
stùl.č̓ákʷ	a southerly wind that is dangerous when strong	LL.

2. šic(i)   rub, file

    See under: xʷis(i), t̓ixʷ(i), (pixʷ(i))
        and: ʔik̓ʷ(i) / ʔaq̓ʷ(a) / ʔiq̓ʷ(i), xʷaq̓ʷ

    Compare:

xʷikʷ(i)	čəjq̓ʷəd
sax̌(a)	taš(a)
x̌iq̓(i)	jə̓q̓

root

    ləcušic dxʷʔal tiʔəʔ ʔìlgʷił ʔə tə s.tùləkʷ   MS.
    It rubs against the river bank.

-it

    šícid   Rub it.   LL.

-təd

    šíctəd   a file   EK.

lexical

    ·šíjus   rub on the cutting edge (face)
                     in order to sharpen a knife   LL.

    šíjus   NPS   smelt   LL.
                     (So named because they rub their
                      faces against the river bank to
                      make holes in order to lay eggs.)

        Cf. čaw̓   SPS   smelt

        (1) díł ʔu bəs.ʔulàdxʷ tiʔił šíjus.

        (2) dəčá(ʔ)kʷbixʷ dxʷʔal tiʔəʔ (hə)laʔb s.ʔulàdxʷ
        tiʔəʔ šíjus ləcušíc dxʷʔal tiʔəʔ ʔìlgʷił ʔə tə
        x̌ʷəlč.   (3) gʷəl s.ʔə́ł°d tiʔəʔ šíjus.

        (1) Is a smelt also a (member of the class) 'salmon'?

        (2) The smelt, which rubs its face against the shore
        of the sea, is a different class from the real 'salmon'.
        (3) But the smelt is food.   MS.

1.   š(i)č(i)   stick into, stick through, sheathe, insert

   Contrast with caq̓(a).

    -it

        šíčid   stick it into   LL.

        šíčit°b   stuck into him   EK.

464

ʔu.čúqʷud čəd tiʔəʔ ɫud(s).šíčšičid kʷi dùkʷibəɫ   EK.
I'm whittling these to insert into Transformer.

... gʷəl šičšičitᵊb dxʷʔal cədiɫ   EK.
... and inserted them into him.

lexical

→

šíčidgʷəsᵊb   put a broach on the bosom   LL.

šíčidgʷəstᵊb čəd tiʔiɫ   LL.
He pinned (the badge) on me.

šíščqsàciʔ   ring for finger   EK.

   Cf. s.yaýlúpqsaciʔ

səxʷšíčəlwàʔs   (time to) sheathe the paddles   ML., LL.

reduplication

tiʔiɫ dəxʷ.ʔás tiʔiɫ ʔə(s)šíčšičšàẃ ʔal tiʔiɫ
ǰəsǰəsəd ʔal tə s.qìqʷəc   EK.
That's why there are those extra inserted bones
on the legs of the deer.

1.   šíjtᵊb   surprise attack   LL.

      šíjtᵊb čəɫ   LL.
      We were caught in a surprise attack.
      Fig.: A lot of friends suddenly descended upon us.   LL.

      rejected: *šijid, *šijᵊd   LL.

2.   šijus   See under šic(i).

3.   šikʷ(i)   emerge from water
      See under ƛ(i)q 'emerge', púsᵊb 'float, surface', šíl(i)
                'emerge from beneath'; and šuƛ 'tide goes out,
                river goes down'.

Contrast:

šikʷ	shallow	s.ƛ̓əp	deep
šikʷ(i)	emerge from water	ǰiq̓(i)	immerse, soak

root

ʔušikʷ čəd	I (hit a sandbar while paddling and) was hung up high and dry.	LL.
	I came out of the water.	LL.
ʔušíkʷšikʷ čəd	I ran aground.	LG.
šikʷ	low tide	LG.
ʔə(s)šígʷəxʷ	The tide's gone out.	LG.
ʔə(s)šíkʷ	shallow	LG.
šíkʷ	shallow, water is going down	LG.

Cf. šuƛ NPS 'low tide', s.xʷádəc SPS 'low tide'

-it

šígʷid	Pull it out of the water.	LG.

-agʷ-il

šigʷágʷil	Come out of the water.	ES.
	Get out of the water.	LG.

lexical

ʔušíkʷšədᵊb čəd	take foot out of water	LL.

1. šil(i) come out from under, emerge; dig around to uncover something

Cf. ƛ̓(i)q 'emerge (in general)', šikʷ(i) 'emerge from water'

-it

    ʔušílid čəɬ   We dug around to find [uncover] it
                               (what we had lost).   LL.

-agʷ-il

    šílagʷil   come out of ground   LL.
                            come out from under blankets   LL.

        ʔu.gʷədíl čəd, čədà šìlagʷil   LL.

        I got up and out from under (the blankets).

        ʔušililagʷiləxʷ čəɬ   LL.

        We homebodies finally came out (and went to town).

lexical

    šíldup   digging around looking for something LL.

reduplication

    šíšilus   Said to (or about) a child who does
                             not behave, does not pay attention
                             but does what he wants regardless.   LG.

    šilil-   See under -agʷ-il above.

rejected:

    *šilil (where /-il/ represents the suffix -il and not
         a reduplication of the root)   LL.

→

2.   šíqʷ   NPS   hat   LL.

      šəšíqʷ   hat   LG.

      Cf. s.xʷáyʔs   SPS   hat

         -áliqʷ   lexical suffix   'hat'   LL.

     -b

         ʔušəšíqʷəb čəd   I put my hat on.   LG.

            Cf. ʔu.xʷəcáliqʷəb čəd   I took my hat off.   LG.

lexical

šíqʷac   unidentified plant (lit. 'hat plant'). It
has big leaves. It is good for treating a cold. MC.

1.   šíšəlč   a type of horsetail   LG.

2.   šíšəlč(ac)   yarrow (plant)

3.   šub   disappear

     root

        ʔušub   disappear. He's disappeared.   LG.

        ʔušúbəxʷ   He hasn't come back.   LG.

        ʔušubəxʷ tiʔił s.tubš   LG.
        That man is late, overdue, missing.

     -t

        ʔušúbᵊdəxʷ   You make it disappear.   AS.

     -a-d

        gʷəšəbád   Go away! Disappear!   VH.

          Cf. lilcut

     lexical

        šúbali   death of more than one   LL.

          See under ʔátəbəd.

     reduplication

        šəbšú·b   (She) disappeared (in the dirt).   EK.

4.   šújəʔ   maggot

5.   šúkʷə   sugar (from English (via Chinook Jargon?))

1. šukʷ   powder   VH.

    x̌i.šúkʷ   gray

    -il

        ʔə(s)šúkʷil become gray, light gray

        tu(s)šúkʷil tə šqùlgʷədxʷ   The sky was gray.   LG.

        ʔušúkʷil tə qəlùbs   cataract (of eye)   EK.

    lexical

        dxʷšúkʷilqsidəxʷ ʔə tiʔił xʷ.(h)udad   ML.
        She grayed their noses with ashes.

    reduplication

        šúškʷildəxʷ ʔə tiʔił ƛuxʷ.(h)údad ʔal kʷi ƛu.hùd   ML.
        She grayed (the children) with ashes from the fire.

        šúʔšukʷ Snoh.   an unidentified blue berry

2. šul(u)   pass beneath

    Cf. jəlábac   climb over   dəkʷ/gʷ-   get inside
                                                (bag, cave)

        jəlúlč   go around
        qit(i)   go around

    root

        ʔušúl čəd   LL.
        I was accidentally knocked in the brush.

    -ut

        šúlud   Put it beneath (something).   LL.

    -agʷil

        šúlagʷil   crawl beneath (e.g., a fence)   EK.

    -agʷ-i(1)-s

        ʔušúlagʷis čəd tiʔił s.bəkʷ   LL.
        I crawled under (it) after the ball.

lexical

šúləlwàʔs	Put your paddle in the canoe.	ES.
ʔušulalikʷ	I put something in the oven.	LL.

1.   šuɬ   NPS   see, look

     Cf. lab   SPS

     Compare: k̓ʷal(a)   scrutinize, examine

                gʷəč̓   see, look for

                k̓ʷil(i)   look at from behind something, look at over shoulder

                                    look in on briefly

                q̓is(i)   uncover in order to look at it uncovered, cf. q̓ax̌(a)

                q̓ikʷ   appear, be in view

                wəlíʔ   be visible

    root

ʔušúɬ čəd	I look around.	LL.
t(u)a(s)šúɬ čəd	I was looking on (when something happened).	EK.
x̌ʷùɬəxʷ ʔə(s)šúɬ tiʔəʔ ʔiišəds		ML.
Her friends saw her off.		
t(u)as.x̌əc čəd gʷəšùɬəd	I was afraid to look.	EK.
x̌aƛtxʷ čəd gʷəd(s)šùɬ	I want to see.	EK.
háʔɬ čəxʷ šuɬ	You are good looking.	LL.
cíckʷ čəxʷ haʔɬ šùɬ	You are very good looking.	LL.

       (The Skagit equivalent is: cíck̓ʷəxʷ čəxʷ háʔɬubš
      You are very good looking.   LG.)

dáyʔəxʷ haʔɬ šuɬ ciʔiɬ	She's good looking.	LL.

(ʔəxʷ.cútᵊb čəd) cíckʷ čəd haʔɫ šuɫ   LL.
(I think) I am very good looking.

root (reduced)

ʔudxʷšə́ɫᵊb   look at something through water   LL.

šɫáhadᵊb   watchman, scout   LL.

dxʷšíʔsɫᵊb   window, mirror   ES.

   dxʷšíʔšɫᵊbəd   window, mirror   LG.

   xʷšíʔšɫᵊb   window, mirror   LL.

-c

šúuc   Look at it.   HD.

ʔə(s)šúuc čəd tə háʔɫ s.tùbš   LG.
I'm looking at the good man.

-c-b

ʔušúucᵊb čəd   Someone (came) to see me.   LL.

t(u)a(s)šúucᵊbs čəxʷ ʔal tuds.mìʔman   EK.
You looked after me when I was small.

šúucbicut ʔə kʷi haʔɫ   EK.
Take good care of yourself.

   Cf. tix̌ix̌dubut

ʔə(s)šúucbicut
Look out! (This is equivalent to ʔəs.q̓ʷúɫucut.)

-dxʷ

ʔə(s)šúdxʷ čəd tə háʔɫ s.tùbš   I see the good man.   LG.

dáyʔ čəd ɫušùdubicid   I'll see you later.   EK.

ʔə(s)šudubš čəxʷ   You saw me.   EK.

díʔɫ kʷi gʷə(s)šùdub čəɫ   They might see us.   HD.

gʷəšúdxʷəd čədà gʷə.yə̀cᵊbtxʷ   EK.
If I see him, I'll tell him.

ʔə(s)šúdxʷ čəxʷ ʔu   HD.
Can you see? (I.e., nothing is blocking your view?)

ʔušúdxʷ čəxʷ ʔu ti d.bədà?   HD.
Did you see my son?

-bi-t-

ɫ(u)a(s)šúɫbicid čəd   I'll be looking for you.   EK.

ʔə(s)šúšɫbitᵊb čəd   They are expecting me.   LL.

ʔə(s)šúšɫᵊbid čəɫ tiʔiɫ taʔtami, gʷəl xʷi·ʔ gʷ(ə)as.ɫčils   LL.
We were looking for Thom (to come), but he didn't arrive.

-al-but

ʔə(s)šúɫalbut čəxʷ ʔu   Can you see (not blind)?   HD.

dídiʔɫ (h)uʔxʷ ʔu čəxʷ ʔə(s)šùɫalbut   HD.
Can you still see? (You aren't blind yet?)

xʷíʔəxʷ kʷi ɫub(ə)a(s)šùɫalbuts   ES., HD.
She will not be able to see again.

reduplication

ʔə(s)šúšɫbitᵊb čəd   They are expecting me.   LL.

dxʷšiʔšɫᵊbad/šišəɫᵊbad   window, mirror   ES., LG.

rejected:

*ʔušuucbitᵊb čəd   LL.

1. šuƛ   tide goes out / river goes down

    Cf. šikʷ(i)

    Contrast: šuƛ   river goes down   ǰač   river rises,
                                               river floods

                šuƛ   tide goes out   p̓ilᵊb high tide, flood

šúƛ low tide, tide goes out

ʔušúƛ The tide is going out. LL.

čágʷəxʷ ti šùƛ The tide is out.

ʔə(s)šúƛəxʷ The tide is out. LL.

šúƛ river goes down, tide goes out DM.

Cf. šikʷ ebb tide LG.

s.xʷádəc SPS ebb tide

t

This letter represents a sound very similar to the *t* of the English word *tack*. [voiceless alveolar stop]

1. -t   a transitive suffix

                         /-d/ when final and before certain secondary derivative suffixes

                         /-t-/ elsewhere

2. ta   emphatic particle

kʷà(d)dxʷ čəxʷ tá!	You got it (figured out)!	LL.
ʔəs.λúbiləxʷ čəxʷ ta!		ML.
Indeed you are correct now; all right now!		
λúb tá!	That's all right!	LL.
xʷiʔ lə.λúb ta	Not right.	LL.
díɬ ta!	That's the one!	EK.
díɬ (ta)		
The same! (In answer to the question: Is this yours?)		HD.
... ʔu ta	... isn't it?	LL.

3. ta-

táqʷuʔ	thirst	Cf. qʷúʔ
tágʷəxʷ	hunger	
ʔəstáqʷuʔ čəd	I'm thirsty.	EK.
ʔəstágʷəxʷ čəd	I'm hungry.	EK.
dídiʔɬ čəd ʔəstàgʷəxʷ	I'm still hungry.	EK.
ʔəstágʷəxʷəxʷ čəd	I'm hungry now.	
ɬu.q̓ʷəɬ°b čəd λɬəstàgʷəxʷəd		LG.
I get tired when I'm hungry.		

reduplication

ʔuyə.yú(ʔ)ˋbiləxʷ čəɬ, ʔutətágʷəxʷəxʷ   ML.

We were almost dead, (we) were hungry. (Wolves talking.)

1. tab(a)   thing, what, what?

Cf. čad, čal, gʷat, k̓ʷid, ʔəx̌íd

-at   perform act already mentioned

huy, ʔúx̌ʷəxʷ gʷəl <u>táb</u>ədəxʷ ...   ML.

Then she went, and she went ...

ʔáhəxʷ təjísəxʷ ciʔəʔ x̌ʷùʔx̌ʷəy. ʔáhəxʷ ʔəs<u>táb</u>əd   ML.

Then he lay with Diver. Then he did that (i.e., lay
with her).

reduplication

tábtab sʔu.ʔəɬᵊd	What's he eating?	EK.
státabəb	gossiping	EK.
táʔtabə	serious talk	LL.
tábtabəb	speak a language	LL.

See under <u>cut</u>.

<u>stab</u>   what?, whatever

<u>stab</u> tiʔiɬ	What's that?
<u>stáb</u> əw̓ə ti s.dàʔs	What's it called? LG.
<u>stáb</u> əw̓ə tiʔiɬ tìtčulbixʷ	What is that animal? LL.
<u>stáb</u> tiʔiɬ s.ulàdxʷ	What (kind of) salmon is that? LG.

Cf. <u>stabəɬ</u>

<u>stáb</u> kʷ(i) adəxʷu.j̓ɑ̀ctxʷ tə t(ə)sùlč   LG.

What do you use a drum for?

stáb t(i) adsu.gʷàdədgʷəd   EK.
What are you talking about?

stáb kʷi gʷəds.kʷàxʷacid   EK.
What can I do to help you?

stáb kʷi gʷ(ə)ads.x̌áλtxʷ kʷi gʷ(ə)ads.ʔábyid
c(i) ads.k̓ʷùy   LG.
What do you want to give your mother?

stábəxʷ kʷi ɬuds.x̌áčič   EK.
What am I going to use for cover?

stab kʷi t(u)adsu.huy   What did you do?

stab kʷi səs.huys   What is he like?

stábəxʷ kʷi λ(u)adsu.hùy What have you been doing? LL.

    Cf. ʔəs.ʔəx̌íd kʷ(i) ads.hùy   How did you make out?

stab kʷi λsu.huy ʔə ti ʔə ʔ yubəč
What does a king salmon do?

stab kʷi su.huy(y)itᵊb ʔə t(i) ad.bad tiʔiɬ čačas
What is your father making for that boy?

t̓ábad gʷəstàbəs tiʔiɬ   Guess what that is.   LG.

xʷî ʔ gʷədsəs.(h)áydxʷ gʷəstàbəs kʷi dəx̣ʷ.(ʔ)à ʔs   LG.
I don't know what he is there for.

xʷî ʔ gʷədsəs.(h)áydxʷ gʷəstàbəs kʷi lə.gʷàč̓ᵊd   LG.
I don't know what he's looking for.

xʷí ʔ kʷi stàb dsəs.bap   EK.
I have nothing to do. / I'm not busy.

pə(d)-   when?, where, whenever

  pə(d)táb   when

  pə(d)táb kʷi ɬud(s).šudubicid   ES.
When will I see you again?

pə(d)táb kʷ(i) adəxʷəxʷ.cútᵊb gʷəs.ɫcìls   LG.
When do you think he will arrive?

xʷi? gʷədsəs.(h)aydxʷ pə(d)tàb kʷi ɫus.?úx̌ʷčəɫ   LG.
I don't know when we will go.

?əs.(h)áydxʷ čələp ?u pə(d)tàb kʷi s.?ux̌ʷs   LG.
Do you folks know when he went?

?əxʷ.cútᵊb čəxʷ ?u gʷəpə(d)tábəs kʷi gʷəs.ɫčìls LG.
Do you think he will get here sometime?

-aɫ

  stábaɫ tìtčulbixʷ   What kind of little animal is that? LG.

  stábəɫ əẃə qʷɫày? ti?iɫ ?es.ƛ́ax̌ʷ ?al ti?iɫ   LL.
What kind of wood is that growing over there?

lexical

  stábac   What kind of tree/bush is it?

  stábac ti?iɫ s.ƛax̌ʷdup What kind of tree is that?   LG.

  stəbágʷapšəd   heel   LG.

  stəbálubid Skagit   shoulder   LG., DM.

    Cf. s.?íl?alubid SPS, Snoh. shoulder

  stába(?)kʷᵊbixʷ čəxʷ   LL.
What sort of person are you? (A rather rude way
of asking what group or tribe one belongs to.)

  stábigʷs   belongings, treasure EK.
               possessions   LL.

    (This -igʷs might be from -ikʷs.)

    Cf. s.?úləx̌, s.gʷədígʷs

  stəbəláx̌əd   elbow   LG.

  xʷtábəp   rump, bottom (of anything) EK., LG.

    Cf. x̌ʷáhᵊb   rump   LL.

    s̲t̲ábqs   end   LG.

    xʷt̲ə̲b̲úsači?   palm of hand   LG.

       Cf. xʷ.əcúsàci? (under ?ácus) palm of hand   EK.

    xʷt̲ə̲b̲ú(s)šəd   sole of foot   LG.

1.   tábabac   go slower, take it easy   DM.

      Cf. t̓a(h)á?s, t̓ábabac

2.   tac   dance (from English *dance*)

     Cf. jubalikʷ (under jub(u)), səx̌ᵊb

       huy t̲ácəxʷ ci?ił ƛaƛačəpəd   Then Ant danced.   ES.

       ?ut̲ác   danced   EK.

3. šəł.tádᵊb Snoh.   step-mother, uncle's wife (lit.'make a wife')

      čəł.tádᵊb Skagit   step-mother, uncle's wife

4.   tádi?   a rarely occurring form apparently com-
                          pletely equivalent to t̲údi?, *q.v.*

   See under d̲i̲?.

     tad̲í̲di?i   right there

     t̲ádi? ?àciłtalbixʷ   the people right over there

   -bi-t

     ?u.xʷíʔtil t̲abìd   It fell over there.

      Cf. ?u.xʷíʔtil t̲a ?a It fell there.

5.   tágʷəxʷ   See under t̲a̲-.

6.   tágʷusᵊb   put face in water to drink   LL.

                    drink water without a cup   MS.
                    (used mostly just for humans)

Cf. qʷúʔqʷaʔ 'drink', ǰiq̓(i) 'immerse', túgʷusᵊb (under tukʷ)

1. takʷ-   buy

Compare təxʷ 'buy' and xʷuyub 'sell'.

root

   ʔəstákʷ(əxʷ)   It's bought.   LL.

-š ~ -i-

   tágʷš   Buy it!

   łutágʷš čəd ti pùʔtəd

I'm going to buy the shirt (I saw earlier -- a specific
one I have in mind).

    Contrast łu.téxʷ čəd pùʔtəd

      I'm going to buy a shirt. (I have no
      particular one in mind.)

   łìxʷ stiq.tiqíw tutàgʷš čəd   LG.
I bought three horses.

   tuł.čád kʷ(i) adstàgʷš tə hàʔł púʔtəd   LG.
Where did you buy the nice shirt?

   díł ʔił.čád ʔálʔal kʷi ʔəxʷstàgʷšᵊb čəxʷ   LG.
Which house do you want to buy?

   tu.cùuc tiʔəʔ łutágʷšəd tiʔəʔ s.wàtixʷtəd   MS.
He said I should like to buy this land.

   ʔutágʷib   It's bought.

   ʔəstágʷibəxʷ   It's already been bought (by someone
                who was here before you came back to
                buy it).   LL.

   ʔutágʷibš tiʔił s.tubš   That man bought me.   LG.

-yi-

   ʔutágʷyic ʔə tə s.gəlk̓àlikʷ   LG.
He bought knitting from me.

ʔutáɡʷyic | He bought it for me. | LL.

cədíɬtxʷ kʷi ʔutaɡʷyicid | Let him buy it for you.

rejected: *ʔutáɡʷšyic

-txʷ

ʔəstáɡʷtxʷ | He has it already bought. | LL.

ʔəstákʷtubəxʷ tiʔiɬ | It's been bought. | LL.

lexical

táɡʷalikʷ | going to buy | EK.

ʔutáɡʷəlikʷ | I bought these things. | LG.

-aɬ

Cf. təxʷ (Note that táɡʷaɬ and təxʷ don't allow a determiner to occur with the -ism 'bought'.)

ƛ̓úb čəɬ ʔu ƛ̓a xʷùyubálʔtxʷ čəɬa ɬutáɡʷəɬ púʔtəd | DM.

Shall we go to the store to buy (ourselves some) shirt(s)?

ʔutáɡʷəɬ čəd pùʔtəd | I bought (myself) a shirt. | LG.

rejected:

*ʔutáɡʷtxʷ, *ʔutáɡʷšbid, *ʔutáɡʷdxʷ, *ʔutáɡʷid (In asking for the suffix [-t], LL. supplied the -i- vowel before rejecting this form. I had asked for *táɡʷəd.)
*táɡʷad EK.

1. tálə | money (from English *dollar* by way of Chinook Jargon)

ʔá ʔu kʷ(i) adtàlə | Do you have any money? | DM.

ʔəbstálə čəxʷ ʔu | Same gloss: Do you have any money? | DM.

ʔi. qá ti dtàlə | Yes, I have a lot of money. | DM.

qáhəɬ tàlə čəd | I have a lot of money. | DM.

rejected: *qá ʔəbstàlə čəd | DM.

təqačiʔílc ʔi tiʔił ʔił.čə́x̌ ti dtalə   DM.

I have eight dollars and fifty cents.

lexical

    x̌ʷtáləhàli   purse   ML.

    stáləhali   purse   LG.

    dx̌ʷtálʔtalalus   eye glasses (lit. 'money eyes')   LL.

reduplication

    ʔáʔ ti dtàʔtələʔ   I have a little money.   DM.

1. s.tálət   nephew, niece

    stətálət   young nephew or young niece

    See under qəsíʔ.

2. x.teləx̌ə́čtel   a man's name, LG.'s mother's father (a Chilli-wack name); also the name of LG.'s youngest brother, Willie

3.   talx̌

    ʔutálx̌ čəd ʔu.ƛaldx̌ʷ   I finally succeeded in putting it on.

    làʔbəx̌ stálx̌ ciʔił lə.ʔìbəš   LG.

    She who is walking there (e.g., an old lady) is spry, able, capable.

    tux̌ʷ čəx̌ʷ stalx̌ tiʔił ƛəladəx̌ʷ ʔə huydx̌ʷ

    You are rather unusual in that you are able to get the work put together.

    x̌ʷùl čəx̌ʷ ʔəstálx̌   Keep your spirits up!   LG.

    ʔəstálx̌ (h)uʔx̌ʷ tiʔił   He is still capable.   LG.

   -t

    tálx̌cut   do well   LL.
                    make yourself able, try   LG.

    See under p̓aʔ.

481

x̌ʷúⱡ čəxʷ ʔəstàlx̌cut kʷ(i) ad.x̌ə̀č   LG.

Keep your mind strong!

→

1.   táⱡ(a)   stretch; a unit of measure equal to distance
                                 from finger tip to finger tip with arms ex-
                                 tended sideways, about six feet.

     Contrast x̌ʷiƛ.

     yəlà?c táⱡ ti?iⱡ háac ?ə ti?iⱡ qʷⱡày?   DM.
     That log is 36 feet long.

     ⱡíxʷ tà̀ⱡ kʷ(i) ads.t̓ùgʷyid t(i) ad.?à?yəd   DM.
     Measure off 18 feet for your partner.

     -aⱡ

     The difference between saying ⱡìxʷəⱡtáⱡ and ⱡìxʷ táⱡ
     is that the former is a known measure while the latter
     construction would be used to indicate how much is to
     be marked/measured. DM. The latter construction has a
     wider range of occurrence.

     cəbtáⱡ   12 feet

     ⱡìxʷəⱡtáⱡ   18 feet

       ⱡìxʷəⱡtáⱡ ti?iⱡ hàac ?ə ti?iⱡ də.q̓ìlbid   DM.
       My canoe is 18 feet long.

     bùusəⱡtáⱡ   24 feet

     yəlà?cəⱡtáⱡ   36 feet

     -at

       táⱡad   Measure it!   DM.

         Cf. t̓ukʷ(u)

     lexical

       táⱡtaⱡalači(?)b   extend/stretch arms (or hands)

       táⱡtaⱡlax̌əd   extend/stretch arms (sideways).

1. táqʷšəblù   a woman's name, one of VH.'s names

2. táqʷuʔ   See under ta-.

3. cə.tásiyə   a woman's name, LG.'s mother's father's
                     sibling's daughter
                     also LG.'s oldest daughter (Helen)
                     (a Chilliwack name)

4. táš (tə́š)   on account of, because of, due to

   pútəxʷ łu.čə́dᵊb ʔal tiʔił s.łcìls tiʔił ʔib.ʔibac
   taš s.tə̓ss   EK.
   When the grandchildren arrive, they will really
   shiver from the cold.

   x̌i.čə́c tə̀š tiʔił tus.cáq̓atᵊbs   ML., LL.
   (He is) red on account of his having been speared.

5. taš(a)   stroke lightly; use leg spindle

   See under šic(i).   Cf. łaq

   root

   táš   spin   EK.
                    specifically, use the leg spindle LG.

                    (łaq is used to mean on modern equipment,
                    but many use taš for all spinning.) LG.

   ʔutáš čəd   I spun / I'm spinning.   EK.

   dəxʷutášəd   (modern) spinning wheel   MC.

      Cf. júlaq̓   old fashioned hand kind of spinning wheel
                    (This final consonant might be k̓.)   MC.

   -at

   tášad   massage it   LG.

   tášad   pet it, stroke it lightly,
                    touch it lightly   MS.

                    rub on leg -- a way of spinning
                    by using the leg spindle   LG.

lexical

| ʔutašwíĵᵊd | massaged his back | LG. |
| tašwíčc | Massage my back! | LG. |

reduplication

| tátšad | pet/touch very gently | MS. |

1. tátačulbixʷ · large animal, especially mammals that were
hunted. Contrast títčulbixʷ, a small animal;
a catch-all category for land animals and
small birds that do not belong to any other
class; and ʔacíɫta(1)bixʷ 'human being,
Indian'.

(1) díɫ ʔu bətàtačulbixʷ tiʔiɫ s.tiqàyuʔ.

(2) xʷiʔ lətatačulbixʷ. (3) títčulbixʷ tiʔiɫ s.tiqàyuʔ.
(4) tátačulbixʷ tiʔiɫ s.čòtxʷəd ʔi s.qigʷəc. (5) x̌ʷúləb
ʔə s.qʷəbàyʔ tiʔiɫ s.tiqàyuʔ.

(1) Is a wolf a (member of the class) 'large animal'?

(2) It is not a 'large animal'. (3) A wolf is a 'small
animal'. (4) Bear and deer are 'large animals'. (5) A
wolf is similar to a dog.   IM.

(1) ʔəs.ʔəx̌íd kʷi də(xʷ).xʷìʔs lətàtačulbixʷ tiʔiɫ
s.qʷəbàyʔ.

(2) ləlíʔa(ʔ)kʷbixʷ. (3) títčulbixʷ. (4) xʷiʔ gʷəs.ʔə́ɫᵊds.
(5) tátačulbixʷ gʷəl s.ʔə́ɫᵊd. (6) s.čòtxʷəd, s.qigʷəc,
kʷágʷičəd, s.x̌ʷíƛəyʔ gʷəl s.ʔə́ɫᵊd ʔə kʷi ʔacíɫtalbixʷ.

(1) Why isn't a dog a (member of the class) 'large animal'?

(2) It belongs to a different class. (3) It is a 'small
animal'. (4) It is not eaten. (5) A 'large animal' is food.
(6) Bear, deer, elk, and mountain goat are food for people.
                                                 IM.

1. s.táwixʷə?ł   Skagit   children, plural of čačas

    Cf. s.táwigʷəł   Skagit   children

       wíẃsu   Snoh.   children

    Contrast <u>bədá?</u> 'one's own child(ren)'.

2. táx̌   fall forward (on to face)

    Cf. dxʷ.bílcəp   fall on rump

       ḱʷəq   fall on back

3. táy

    root

      lə<u>táy</u>   coming to raid

    -c

      ?u<u>táy</u>cᵊb   They went after them (on a raid).

    Cf. tígʷil   hide self and family from enemy raiding party

4. s.tá?ł   two pronged salmon harpoon   EK., LG., ESi.

    See under <u>čəsáy?</u> and <u>təpíl</u>.

    reduplication

      stí?ta?ł   small spear   ESi.

5. tč̓-

    Cf. č̓ət- 112.3, -qs-

    lexical

    -adi?

      ?u<u>tč̓adi?</u>   point with finger   LL.

      ?u<u>tč̓adi?</u>əxʷ ti?ə? čačas   The boy is pointing.

-us

ʔutč̓ə́usəd   point it out   LL., LG.

ʔutč̓ə́uscidəxʷ čəd   I point it out to you.

1.   tə   article   'known to addressee'

     See under ti.

2.   təb-   See under tab.

3.   təbáš   crave

     Cf. x̌aƛ   want, like

       ʔəstəbáš čəd kʷi s.bàdəš

       I'm craving a cigarette.

4.   s.təbáykʷ   fresh-water bullhead   DM.

     Cf. s.piláyk̓ʷ   fresh-water bullhead   CB.

5.   s.tə́bcə?   a kind of horse clam   FSi.

     s.tə́bjə?   ESi.

     Cf. há?əc   horse clam, black nose clam

6.   tə́bəd   knot of a tree

7.   təbəwí?   finally

8.   tə́bɫ   ochre

     təblík̓ʷ   apply ochre

9.   s.təbtábəɫ   grizzly bear   LL., AS., LG.

     Cf. s.čátqɫəb   Skyk.   grizzly bear   LL.

1.　　təč　　　　　　　　roll; roll off, fall off

　　　Cf. qəbəlíd　　　roll it up

　　　root

　　　　ʔutə́č čəxʷ　　　You are falling off.　　　　　　　EK.

　　　　ʔutə́č　　　　　　It rolled.　　　　　　　　　　　　EK.

　　　-t

　　　　ʔutə́ǰəd　　　　　He rolled it.

　　　lexical

　　　　təǰábac　　　　　sea cucumber. (It looks like a cucumber,
　　　　　　　　　　　　　grows to about 5 inches, swims in loops
　　　　　　　　　　　　　or corkscrew motions.)
　　　　　　　　　　　　　　　　　　　　　　　　　LL., EK., JC.

　　　reduplication

　　　　titǰálikʷ　　　　a game of rolling stones to see who can
　　　　　　　　　　　　　roll them farthest.　　　　　　　JC.

　　　　See under ʔukʷʔukʷ.

　　　ʔutə́čtəč čəxʷ　　　You fell off.　　　　　　　　　　EK.

　　　tuləcu.kʷátač čəd ʔal ti s.badil čəda ʔutə́čtəč　　DM.
　　　I was climbing the mountain and I fell.

2.　s.tə́čəb　　　　　　chub, small fish

3.　təč̓-　　　　　　　See under tč̓-.

4.　-(t)əd　　　　　　suffix indicating utensil

　　　Cf. səxʷ-　　　　See also Hoard/Hess, p. 46ff.

5.　tədə́qsəd　　　　　an unidentified waterfowl, a kind of buʔqʷ

6.　təgʷáaq̓ʷ　　　　　south wind

　　　See under šə́xʷəb.

1. s.təgʷád   salmonberry   EK.

   s.tə́gʷəd   salmonberry   ESi.

   Cf. jətgʷád   Skagit   salmonberry   LG., MC.

   A member of the class s.q̓ʷəlátᵊd.

2.   təjíl   go to bed

   Cf. qʷátagʷil   go to bed

     híwil təjìl   Go to bed.   EK.

     ƛ́alal tə dsutəjìl   I go to bed early (a general act).   LG.

     ƛ́alal tə dstəjìl   I'm going to bed early (on this
                                                   occasion).   LG.

     ʔəxʷs.ʔítutᵊb, gʷəl xʷiʔ gʷəstəjìls   LG.
     He's sleepy, but he won't go to bed.

     ləlwáʔsəd tə cəxʷutəjìl   LG.
     A 'longhouse shelf/bed' is what I want to go to bed on.

   -i(1)-s-b

     ʔəstəjísᵊb ciʔə?   One in bed with her.   ES.

     ʔutəjísᵊb (h)əlgʷə?   They went to bed with them.   LL.

   -i(1)-s-bi-t-b

     gʷəl ləstəjísbitᵊbəxʷ (h)əlgʷə?   ES.
     And (these men) were in bed with them.

     ʔutəjísbitᵊb (h)əlgʷə?   LL.
     They went to bed with them for sex.

   reduplication

     títəjìl   lie down for a little while   EK.

       Cf. bəčágʷil   lie down

         ɬáq̓agʷil   lie down

1. təjúcid   answer

     See under <u>cut</u>.

        hay, <u>təjúci</u>(d)cid čəd   Now I answer you.

        <u>təjúci</u>(d)c   Answer me!

        <u>təjúci</u>(d)d   Answer him!

2. təǰ-   See under <u>təč</u>.

3. tək^w [Probably error for <u>təq^w</u> meaning difficult to break, tough to snap in two.]
    Cf. x̌aƛ̓

4. s.tək^{w}áb   waterfall   DM.

5. tək^{w}tək^{w}əlús   great horned owl   LG., LL., ESi., MS., DM.

    Cf. číit(ə)bix^w, q^{w}uwábdəč   other names for same bird   LG., DM.

      ƛ̓al bə.x̌íbx̌ib ti?iɬ tək^{w}tək^{w}əlùs   DM.
      The great horned owl is also a bird of prey.

6. təláwil   run

    Cf. sáx^{w}əb, páɬ, ƛ̓iw?

    -tx^w

      <u>təláwil</u>tx^w operate a machine; exercise (a horse)

    Note: The attenuative of təláwil, títəlàwil, means to run less fast but does not <u>restrict or shorten</u> the distance covered, while the attenuative of sáx^{w}əb, sá?sx^{w}əb, limits the distance but not the <u>speed</u>.

      ?u<u>təláwil</u> čəd   I run.   EK.

      dídi?ɬ čəd lə<u>təlàwil</u>   I'm still running.   EK.

      <u>təláwil</u>əx^w q̓iyàƛəd, <u>təláwil</u>əx^w EK.
      Run slug, run! (A gambling song.)

t(u)as.x̌ə́c čəd gʷətəlàwiləd   I was afraid to run.   EK.

x̌aƛ(txʷ) čəd gʷədstəlàwil   I want to run.   EK.

ʔəs.xʷák̓ʷil čəd ʔə ti dstəlàwil   EK.
I'm tired of running.

ʔáɬ ti dsutəlàwil čəda ʔu.ɬík̓ʷšəd ʔə ti s.tə̀x̌ʷšəd   DM.
I was running fast and I tripped on a root.

-i(1)-s

    təláwis   Run after it!   LG.

    lətəláwis tə spàʔc   He's running after the bear.

-i1-txʷ

    təláwiltxʷ tiʔiɬ   Run (operate) that!   ES.

    ɬutítəlàwiltxʷ tiʔiɬ dˀs.tiqìw   ES.
    Run my horse about a bit.

      Cf. sáxʷəbtxʷ   kidnap someone

reduplication

    títəlàwil   jog   EK.

1.   təlíxʷ   full-blood siblings who are emotionally "close"

    See under s.qá.

2.   təls

    lətə́lsšəd   a kind of dance wherein the feet are moved
                    only inches but very, very fast. Sort of
                    "drumming" the feet.

      Cf. júbalikʷ (under jub(u)), səx̌ˀb, tac

    tə̀lsáči?   beat with the hands very, very rapidly

      Cf. cix̌(i) and ƛ̓itəd

1.   təɬ   true

     See cə̓kʷ 'straight', ləq̓áɬil 'correct', q̓al 'believe'.

     Contrast kʷacdxʷ 'doubt'.

     root

          təɬ   true   EK.

          gʷəl gʷətɬáxʷ ʔu   Can it be true?   HD.
                              Is it the truth?   HD.

          tə́ɬ ʔù   Is that so/true?

     adverb

          tə́ɬ čəxʷ ʔu ʔu.šùdxʷ kʷi bùus s.pàʔc   LG.
          Did you really see four bears?

          tə̀ɬ ʔu dəgʷí   Is that really you?   LL.

          ʔu.tᶿúc̓utᶿb čəd, čədà tᶦùc̓ᵊdub təɬ   LL.
          They shot at me and they sure hit me.

     -il-dxʷ

          ʔəstɬíldubicid čəd   I believe you.   EK.

          xʷiʔ gʷədsəstɬíldxʷ I don't believe it.   EK., LL., LG.

          gʷəl čəd ʔəstɬíldxʷ tuĺʔal bək̓ʷ dᶿs.pətìdgʷəsᵊb   EC.
          And I believe with all my thoughts.

     -txʷ

          tə́ɬtxʷ   Let it be true!   LG.

          tə́ɬtxʷ t(i) adsu.gʷàagʷəd   Tell the truth!   LG.

2.   tə́ɬəɬ   arrive safely

          ... čələpa ɬutə́ɬəɬ ʔə kʷi hàʔɬ   ML.
          ... and you folks will arrive safely in a good way.

| ɬutə́ɬəɬ čəd | I will arrive safely. | LG. |
| tutə̀ɬəɬdúbutəxʷ čəxʷ | You arrived safely. | LG. |

1.   təp(á)   stab (using knives or short handled cutting implements)

     Cf. caq̓ 'jab, poke', čəsáy?

     root

| tə́p čəd | I got stabbed. |

     -at

ʔutpád čəd	I stabbed him.
ʔutəptpátubuɬ	He stabbed us.
tpátᵊb	get stabbed
tpád	have knife in hand ready to use on someone LL.

     -il

| ʔutpíl   Snoqu. | speared (fish)
spear salmon in a river
use a čəsáy?   DM. |

       Cf. cácq̓   spear big game on the salt water

         ƛ̓ágʷič   spear crabs, and bottom fish

     reduplication

| ʔutəptpátubuɬ | He stabbed us. |

2.   təpíkʷsəd   name for Oyster Bay at southern end of Puget Sound

→

4.   təq(a)   close, block

     -at

| dxʷtqád tə š̓ə̀gʷɫ | Shut the door. | LG. |

dxʷtq̓ácut   Shut the door.   LG.

-dxʷ

təqdúbəxʷ ʔə tiʔəʔ cədiɬ dukʷibəɬ   ML.
Transformer blocked her route.

lexical

tq̓áči?   eight (lit.'closed hand(s)')

tq̓áči?ači? ?i kʷi tq̓àči?   eighty-eight

?úlub ?i kʷi t(ə)qàči? s.bəkʷàči? s.jə̀lč̓ ?i
kʷi cəlacàči? ?i kʷi cəlàc   year 1855 MS.

t(ə)qači?ílc ?i tiʔiɬ ?iɬ.čə̀x̌ ti d.tàlə DM.
I have eight dollars and a half.

stq̓álikʷ   a fish weir (i.e., it is blocked) LL.

t(ə)q̓ápᵊd   dam, trap, head something off DM.

 See s.ƛ̓əlajəd (under ƛ̓əl).

t(ə)q̓úcid   Shut the door.   EK.

 (rejected by LG.)

t(ə)q̓úsᵊd

t(ə)q̓úsᵊd tiʔiɬ s.tuʔtələkʷ   LG.
They (beavers) block the stream.

reduplication

təqq̓áči?   eight people

títq̓àd   close but not tightly, close for a moment

1. təqtq̓áč   woodpecker (generic?)   LL.

 Cf. qtq̓áč woodpecker   EK.

2. təq̓   slap LG. gives ɬaq̓ʷ.

 See under k̓aw.

-t

    táq̓ᵊd   slap him

    ʔutə́q̓c ʔal ti qə̀dxʷ   He slapped me on the mouth.

    ʔutə́q̓c čəxʷ   You slapped me.

lexical

    tq̓áči?c   slapped my hand

     ʔutq̓áči(ʔə)d čəd ługʷə.x̌əlàdəxʷəs
     I slapped his hand so that he would stop.

    tq̓úsc   slapped me in the face

    tq̓ùstᵊb   slapped in the face

    tq̓áʔłdəlitᵊb   slap on the mouth

reduplication

    títk̓ᵊd   pat it

1.   t(ə)qʷ-adiʔ*   deaf

    Cf. luh, ləq 'hear', x̌əlábut 'understand'

    ʔəstqʷádiʔ   deaf, not understand   LL.

     ʔəstqʷádiʔ čəd ʔə tiʔił ʔàcixtalbixʷúcid
     I'm deaf to the Indian language.

      Cf. xʷiʔ gʷədsəs.x̌əlábut ʔə kʷi dxʷ.l(ə)šùcid   LL.
       I don't understand Puget Salish.

      xʷiʔ gʷədsəs.ləqálbutbid tə ʔàcixtalbixʷúcid LG.
       I don't understand the Indian language.

    reduplication

    ʔutìtqʷádiʔcut   LL.
    He's making believe he can't hear/understand.

---
* V.H. points out this form should be t(ə)kʷ-adiʔ.

1. təqʷxʷálc   blanket -- white with a black stripe on each end. "They were very expensive and highly, very highly, thought of."   LL.

     See under s.qəlíkʷ, -iča?.

2. təs   hit with fist

     See under k̓aw-.

     -t

        ?utə́sᵊd   Someone hit him with fist.

        ?utə́sᵊc   Someone hit me with fist.

        ?utəsᵊcíd   Someone hit you with fist.

        ?utə́stᵊb

        təstágʷəl   boxing (lit.'hit each other')   EK.

     lexical

        ?utsáči(?)b čəd   I pounded my hand.   EK.

        ?udxʷtsáladi?dᵊb čəd   LL.
        I wanted to sock him in the temple.

        t(ə)sádi?   hit (ceiling) with boards; drum   MS.

        tsálikʷ   pound (as hammer and nail)   EK.

        tsúlč   a drum   EK.

           cəxʷut(ə)sálikʷ ti t(ə)sùlč   LG.
           I use a drum to pound on.

        títsyàx̌əd   knock on the door   EK., ML.

        títsucid   knock on the door   LL.

     reduplication

        títsᵊd   tap it with fist

        títstàgʷəl   boxing, sparring   EK.

        dxʷstítstagʷəl   boxer

1. tə́stəd   a power similar to s.gʷədílič but it always remains inside the building. It is used to purify the hall before and after a ceremony.

                 It is a pair of long poles painted with tə́bł (ochre). Cedar bark and deer hooves are tied to the top of it.   LG., EK.

                 It is a single pole.   DM., MS.

                 It is caused to run by q̇ʷúx̣ʷqəd and only one man hangs on to it.   DM.

     -uł

        təstəduł   comes from təstəd (i.e., one's ancestors had this power.)   MC.

    See under s.qəlálitut.

2. təš   kill, beat up

    See under gʷəlál-.

    root

        ʔutə́š k̓ʷł ti qəsiʔs   His uncle beat him up.   LG.

        dəxʷtəšs ʔaʔ   That one caused the trouble.   LG.

           (that one is ʔa.)

        dił dsəxʷtəš ʔáʔ (tiʔił)   LG.
        That's the one who beat me up.

    -txʷ

        dəxʷtə́štxʷs ʔáʔ   LL.
        That is what he used to kill him.

        sáliʔqs tiʔił dəxʷtəštùbs ʔáʔ   LL.
        They killed him with a double-barrel rifle.

        1. təš č̓ʎ́áʔ tiʔił s.pusutᵊbs ʔə tiʔił wiw̓su   LL.

        2. ʔu.púsutᵊb ʔə tiʔił wiw̓su təš č̓ʎ́àʔ   LL.

        3. ʔu.púsutᵊb ʔə tiʔił wiw̓su ʔə tiʔił č̓ʎ́àʔ   LL.

        1, 2 and 3 mean: The children threw rocks at it.

rejected:

*téšəd, *téšc, *téštxʷ, *təšíl, *təš čəd, *təšəb

1.   tətíʔc   vein

2.   tətíʔəd   humming bird   EK., LL.

3.   tətlálkʷɫ   a single-shot gun

      See under xʷúltəbàlc.

4. s.tətúpəɫ   spider

5.   tətyíqa   younger brother of Mink

6.   təxʷ   buy

Compare takʷ 'buy' and xʷuyub 'sell'. təxʷ differs from takʷ in that the latter is used when the buyer has a specific item in mind. Compare ɫutéxʷ čəd púʔtəd 'I'm going to buy a shirt (but have no particular one in mind).' with ɫu.tágʷš čəd ti púʔtəd 'I'm going to buy the shirt (I saw earlier).' See comments under čəɫ, 94.1.

root

    ɫutéxʷ čəd səplàl   I'm going to buy some bread.

    ɫutéxʷ púʔtəd tiʔiɫ   He will buy a shirt.   LG.

    ds.x̌áƛ kʷi dstə̀xʷ t(ə)sulč.   I want to buy a drum.   LG.

    ds.x̌áƛ kʷi stə̀xʷs t(ə)sùlč   I want him to buy a drum.

    ʔutə̀xʷ čəd s.tiqìw   I bought a horse.   LG.

-txʷ

    lətéxʷtxʷ čəd š.šìqʷ cə d.ʔàlš   LG.
    I've come to buy a hat for my sister.

    lətə̀xʷtxʷyíd čəd š.šìqʷ cə d.ʔàlš   LG.
    Same gloss: I've come to buy a hat for my sister.

rejected:

   *táxʷəb, *táxʷəd, *təxʷád, *təxʷíl, *táxʷc, *təxʷyíd

1.   təx̌   chapped (?)

   ʔəstəx̌t(ə)x̌ábšəd   chapped feet   DM.

   ʔəstəx̌t(ə)x̌ábači(ʔ)b čəd   I have chapped hands.   DM.

      Cf. t̓əsʔbáʔɬdəɬ   chapped lips   LL.

   stətxəbšád   toes spread out (?)   LG.

2. s.táxʷəb   ring-necked pheasant   EC., LG.

   Cf. s.gʷəlúb   ring-necked pheasant   LL., ESi., MS.

3.   t(ə)x̌ʷ(u)   pull, drag

   See under x̌əc.   Opposite of x̌əd.

   -ut

      tx̌ʷúd   Pull it!   EK.

      t(u)as.x̌əc čəd gʷətx̌ʷúdəd   I was afraid to pull it. EK.

   -t-agʷəl

      titx̌ʷútəgʷəl   tug-of-war (lit.'pull one another')

         See under ʔúkʷukʷ 'play'.

   lexical

      tx̌ʷúsʔd   Drag it!   LG.

      x̌kʷúsʔd č(ə)xʷa tx̌ʷùsʔd   Turn it over and drag it. LG.

      ʔutx̌ʷáyqsʔd čəd   I pulled his beard.   EK.

      lətəx̌ʷgʷíɬ (h)əlgʷə?   LG.
      They're dragging the canoe (over a portage).

dxʷtəx̌ʷtx̌ʷálačədᵊb   LL.

A man who drags his testicles on the ground.

ʔudxʷtəx̌ʷtx̌ʷáhᵊb   LL.

He's dragging his hindend around.

1.   təyíl   proceed upstream (for analysis see under q̓ix̌ʷ.)

      ʔutəyíləxʷ tə s.ʔulàdxʷ   EK.
      The salmon are going upriver.

2.   ti   article
                                     1. new information
                                     2. emphasis

                          Determiner System

→

basic   secondary

                  known to addressee

tə   cə (from tsə)

                  new information, emphasis

ti   ci (from tsi)

                  hypothetical, vague, remote

kʷi   kʷsi

                  modifiers, pronouns

this   tiʔəʔ   ciʔəʔ (from tsiʔəʔ)

these   tiʔiʔəʔ (distributive of tiʔəʔ)   no distributive

this   tiʔacəc

that   tiʔił   ciʔił (from tsiʔił)

those   tiʔiʔił (distributive of tiʔił)   no distributive

1. tib(i)   do something requiring much physical effort,
                               be strong

    See under ƛ̓aq̓ʷ 'watertight'.

    root

        tíb   strong   LG.

        tíb tə dsu.yàyus   I work hard.   LG.

    -it

        <u>tibicut</u>   try hard (to do something physical)
                     Try your best! (What is said to one who
                     is trying to lift something very heavy.) LG.

        ʔutíbɪcut ʔu.təlàwɪɫ tə hùpt   LG.
        The deer tried its best to run.

        xʷiʔ gʷəds.həlàʔb ʔutìbɪcut   LL.
        I didn't really try very hard (to do something physical).

        With <u>tíbicut</u> compare:

            p̓áacut   try

            háy̓ad   try to learn (from <u>hay</u> 'know')

            k̓áwɫ°b   try, improvise

    modifier

        <u>tíb</u> s.pù?alikʷ   It's a real hard wind.   LG.

        xʷiʔ čəd lətìb háʔɫ   I'm not so well.   LL.

        xʷîʔ lə<u>tib</u> líl   He hadn't gone very far.   ML.

        xʷîʔ lə<u>tib</u> s.ƛ̓ə̓p   It's not too deep.   IM.

        xʷîʔ gʷəds<u>tíb</u> ʔəs.ƛ̓əlábut°bid tiʔiɫ dxʷ.1(ə)šùcid   LL.
        I don't really understand Puget Salish.

    reduplication

        stíbtib   strong person   LG.

            Cf. qʷíq̓ʷq̓ʷiq̓ʷlàx̌əd čəxʷ   You have strong arms.

stíbtib čəd x̌ʷulàb ʔə dəgʷí   I'm as strong as you.   LG.

Cf. qʷíq̓ʷ čəd x̌ʷulàb ʔə dəgʷí

Same gloss: I'm as strong as you.

1.   tídtid   radio, phonograph

ʔu.tílibtxʷ čəd tiʔił tídtid

I played the radio/phonograph.

2.   s.tíd^əgʷəd   cedar branches (especially when they are put to
                       some use). Often they are used for tying things.

See under təbíłəd.

stídgʷəd tə dəxʷu.čəł šə̀bəd

Cedar boughs are used to make a fish trap.

łu.ʔúləx̌ čəł ʔə kʷi hãac stíd^əgʷəd   JC.

We will collect long cedar boughs (to use in making a
smelt trap).

čə́x̌^ədə̀xʷ čəxʷ tiʔił adstíd^əgʷəd   JC.

Split your cedar branches.

3.   tígʷil   hide self and family from enemy raiding party

Cf. čaj, c̓alcut (under c̓al), qajə̀t

4.   tíǰ   muscle, sinew

5.   tiləb   adverb   'right away, suddenly, unexpectedly'

tìləb čəd łu.ʔúx̌ʷ   I'm going right now.   ES.

tíləb čəxʷ ʔu.gʷədìl łu.xʷíʔəxʷ bələ.ʔìtut   JC.
Get up right now so you won't (go back to) sleep.

tíləbəxʷ tàq̓təxʷ tiʔił s.łalíl ʔə tiʔił čxʷəlù?   ES.
The whale landed way up on shore.

gʷəl tíləbəxʷ tu.cuuc tiʔə? diʔə? s.tùbš   EC.
And then he said to this (here) man

tíləbəxʷ tiʔił s.xʷi? ʔə tiʔə? čiyúuqʷ   EK.
All at once the wart was gone.

łu.xʷíʔəs tiləb lə.jiǰ   JC.
So it does not break right away.

tiləb ʔu kʷi s.łixʷəłdàt kʷi łub(ə)ads.łčil ʔal kʷi d(ə)ču? EK.
Will you come again Wednesday next week?

tiləb ʔu kʷi s.cəbdàt kʷi łub(ə)ads.łčil   EK.
You won't come again until Tuesday?

1.   tilil

      x̌ʷuì čəxʷ cixʷtílilᵊb   Behave yourself.

         Cf. ƛ̓əlábut   Listen!

2.   tiì   'not present'   particle of the noun phrase --
                                         it precedes the determiner if
                                         a determiner occurs.

      ʔu.x̌ʷíì tiì tiʔił ƛucəxʷu.x̌àl   LL.
      It's lost that which I use to write with.

      ʔu.x̌ʷíìdxʷ čəd tiì tiʔił ƛucəxʷu.x̌àl   LL.
      I lost that which I use to write with.

      xʷuʔᵊlə? čəd ʔu.ʔíx̌ʷᵊdxʷ tiì tiʔił   LL.
      I must have thrown it out.

      hay, k̓x̌ábactᵊbəxʷ tiì tiʔə? kàw̓qs   ML.
      Then they called Raven names (behind his back).

ʔu.ʔəx̌íd hawə̀ʔ <u>tiⱡ</u> ti bads   LG.

What happened to his father?

ʔu.ʔəx̌íd əwə̀ <u>tiⱡ</u> dəxʷu.x̌a(h)ᵊbs   LL.

What's causing him to cry?

ʔu.x̌áhᵊbid hawə̀ʔ <u>tiⱡ</u> tiʔə̀ʔ bads   LL.

He's crying because his father is out of sight.

1.   tíⱡx̌i   after a while (later on during the <u>same</u> <u>day</u> only)

      Cf. ƛ̓əllàʔ (ƛ̓álal)   later on (can be on a different day); wait

2. s.tiqáyuʔ   wolf

      (often pronounced s.təqáyuʔ)

      See s.wáxʷiʔⱡ 'litter of whelps'.

        stiqtiqáyuʔ   wolves

        ʔistiqáyuʔ   wolves

      (1) díⱡ ʔu bə.tàtačulbixʷ tiʔiⱡ <u>stiqàyuʔ</u>. (2) xʷiʔ
lə.tátačulbixʷ. (3) títčulbixʷ tiʔiⱡ <u>stiqàyuʔ</u>. (4) xʷúⱡəb
ʔə s.qʷəbày̓ʔ tiʔiⱡ <u>stiqàyuʔ</u>.

      (1) Is a wolf (classed as) a 'large animal'? (2) It is not
(classed as) a 'large animal'. (3) A wolf is a 'small animal'.
(4) A wolf is like a dog.   DM.

3.   tíqil

      ʔəs<u>tí</u>qil   bushy   LG.

    lexical

      ʔəs<u>tí</u>qilqid   bushy head

        Cf. qíʔqəⱡàdiʔ (under qəládiʔ)

1. s.tiqíw   horse

      (often pronounced s.təqíw)

         stítqiw   pony, foal

         stiqtiqíw   horses

    (1) díɫ ʔu bə.q̓ìlbid tiʔəʔ stiqìw.

    (2) xʷiʔ lə.q̓ìlbid gʷəl q̓ílagʷisᵊb tiʔiɫ stiqìw.

    (3) ʔəs.ʔəx̌íd kʷi də(xʷ).xʷìʔs lə.q̓ìlbid tiʔəʔ

    stiqìw.   (4) xʷiʔ lə.q̓ìlbid yəx̌i tàtačulbixʷ.

    (5) həlí tiʔiɫ stiqìw, xʷiʔ lə.q̓ìlbid.

    (6) ʔu.q̓ílagʷis čəxʷ yəx̌i díɫ dəxʷəs.huys tiʔiɫ

    stiqìw.   (7) gʷəl xʷíʔ gʷəsu.cùtcuts gʷə.q̓ìlbidəs.

    (1) Is a horse a [kind of] q̓ilbid?

    (2) It is not a q̓ilbid even though a horse is
ridden. (3) Why isn't a horse a q̓ilbid? (4) It
is not a q̓ilbid because it is an animal. (5) A
horse is alive, [but] a q̓ilbid is not. (6) You
ride it because that is what a horse is for.
(7) But it wouldn't be said to be a q̓ilbid.   DM.

2. s.títaɫ   a very small kind of owl   DM.

3. s.títaʔɫ   wild people

    See under čyátkʷu(ʔ).

4. títčulbixʷ   small animal

    See under tatačulbixʷ.

5. s.tiwátɫ   a type of canoe

    See under q̓ilbid.

1. tiwá?   urinate (female)

    See under x^{w}ásil and contrast s.?əx̌^{w}á?.

      ?utiwá? ci?ił   She urinated.

2. tix^w(i)   bail out a boat

    Cf. k̓^{w}ad(a) 'dip it out', yaλ̓(a) 'dip it out; gore; fetch water

    -it

      tíx^{w}id   bail out a boat   LL.

      ?utíx^{w}icut   bail out (?)   LL.

      dəx^{w}utíx^{w}icut   That's what we use to bail it out.   LL.

        Cf. dəx^w?uyáλ̓^{ə}b   thing to dip water with   LG.

          k̓^{w}ádg^{w}ild   bailer (made of cedar bark)   EK.

3. t(i)x̌(i)   spread

    Cf. łəx̌, pax̌

    root

      ?əstíx̌   It's spread.   LG.

    -it

      tíx̌id   spread it out   LG.

    -dx^w

      ?utíx̌dx^w čəd   I took care of it.   LG.

      ?əstíx̌dx^w čəd   I'm taking care of him.   LG.

      ?əstíx̌dubš   Someone is taking care of me.   LG.

      łu.hà?ł k^{w}i ł(u)adsəstíx̌^{ə}dx^w Take good care of it.   HD.

      ?əstíx̌dx^w one who protects a new dancer   DM.

lexical

ʔəstíx̌ədiʔ	salmon cooked all in one piece -- opened out and backbone removed	HD.
tíx̌alc	spread out one's arms quickly to protect oneself or to keep canoe from hitting shore	HD.
ʔəstíx̌qid	spread head (i.e., long hair every which way)	LG.

Cf. qəládiʔ

reduplication

tíx̌ix̌dubut. ɫi	Take care of yourselves.	LG.
tíx̌ix̌dubut čələp	Same gloss: Take care of yourselves.	LG.
x̌ál čəx̌ʷ b(ə)astìx̌ix̌dubut		LG.
You take care of yourself too.		
ʔəstíx̌ix̌dubut	Take care of yourself.	ES.

1. tiyùɫʔbáx̌(əd) — a power which provides great abundance. See under s.qəlálitut. For people living near the sound, it is encountered at a great depth in the sound, while those living up river find it on mountains.

2. tiʔəʔ — demonstrative 'this'

 tiʔiʔəʔ — these

 See under ti.

3. tiʔiɫ — demonstrative 'that'

 tiʔiʔiɫ — those

 See under ti.

4. tíʔttiš — narrow

 Compare: bəs, x̌ú-, qʷəqʷqʷíʔs; k̓ilc

Contrast: baʔ, ɫəq̓t, p̓íl(i)

1. təqʷúbəʔ   any permanently snow-capped peak

      See q̓ʷát(a).   Cf. báqʷuʔ(b) 'snow(ing)'

2. tə̓ʷáč   golden-eye, a buʔqʷ

3. tu-   auxiliary prefix   'remote in time or space'

      See under gʷə-.

4. -tu-   variant of -txʷ 'causative'

5. s.túbələ   northwest wind   LL., ES.

      See under šə́xʷəb.

6. s.túbš   man

     stúbubš   men

     stútubš   boy

     stúutubš   boys

     stúʔtəbš   a single man (among many women)

     -adad

       tubšadad   "a mean spirit, thunder and wind usually follow this dance"   LL.

                equivalent to the Skagit's q̓ʷə́x̌ʷqəd   LG.

                warrior's song/dance   HD.

              See under s.qəlálitut.

8. x̌i.túč   SPS   black

     Cf. x̌i.bə́č   NPS   black

1. s.túdəq   slave

    stútədəq   child of slave

    stətúdəq   distributive, i.e., 'slaves all about'

    -il

        tu.xʷúyubtub čəd čəda tùdəqíləxʷ
        I was sold and then I became a slave.

2. túdi?   over there (equivalent to tadi?)

    Perhaps from tu di?.   See under di? 'side'.

      ?əs.ɫaɫlil ?al tudi? q̓ìxʷ   He lives way upstream.

      ?al tùdi? líl   far away

      gʷát kʷ(i) (?)al tudi?   Who is over there?   JC.

      túdi?di?i tə ds.x̌àƛ   I want that one over there.

3. tújil   bend forward; look down

    synonym: jəqíl crawl
                 have head down

    opposite: t̓álx̌(cut)   bend backwards

       (k̓ʷálč(cut))   bend back too far

    opposite: x̌əpúsəb   lift head up, straighten up

       (cək̓ʷcút)   straighten posture

    See under q̓(ə)č 'bend'.

     tújil   bend over (forward), look down   LG., EK.

       xʷi?əxʷ gʷədsutújil   I can't bend over.   LG.

        Cf. xʷi?əxʷ gʷədsutújildubut
         Same gloss: I can't bend over.

-i(1)-s

tú jis   bend over in order to pick something up

-il-dxʷ-

xʷí? gʷədstújildubut   EK.
I can't bend over any more.

xʷi?əxʷ gʷədsutújildubut   I can't bend over.   LG.

1.   tukʷ   immerse, soak more thoroughly than jiq̓(i)

See under jiq̓(i).

root

?utúkʷ čəd   (Because it was late, I was careless about
                selecting a camp site, and the) tide came
                over me (while I slept).

lexical

?utúgʷusᵊb   dunked face in water

    Cf. tágʷusᵊb

?utugʷiyáqid   The water went over (my) head.

?əstugʷiyaqid   The water is over (my) head.

2.   tuk̓ʷ(u)   dead sound, pounding sound

See under k̓aw-.   Cf. kʷixʷi-, čuƛ̓u-

-ut

túk̓ʷud   make pounding sound

lexical

-ap

túk̓ʷəp   clapping or slapping sound at rear; outboard
                motor

-us

túk̓ʷus   clapping or slapping sound in front; automobile

1. s.túləkʷ   river

  stúɫtuləkʷ   rivers   LG.

  stúʔtələkʷ   creek   JC.

   Cf. jəɫíxʷ creek

   stuləgʷábš   Stillaguamish   EK., ESi., LG.

   ƛ̉áʔtəd ʔə tiʔəʔ bəstúləkʷ

   the seine (used) by those (people who) have a river

2. s.túligʷəd   blood

   Cf. cɫíl

3. tulil Snoh., SPS cross a river (or any body of water)

   Cf. šáqʷil Skagit; diʔúcid (under diʔ), jəlúcid (under jal)

   ʔutúlil čəd I crossed the water.   EK.

   čədíbac stùlil a fir log for crossing a stream EK.

4. túlq   name of the site of Carnation, Washington

5. tul(u)   interpret

  -ut

   túlud   Translate it.   HD.

   ʔalčutulud čəd tə s.x̌àl I'm reading the letter. LG.

   x̌ʷùɫ čəd ʔutúlud tə s.tìlib I just read the song. LG.

   túlud . follow one's own blaze   EK.

  lexical

   túlalikʷ interpret   LL., EK.

   dxʷstúlalikʷ   interpreter   LL.

    Cf. ʔílalikʷ interpret   LG.

1. tuɬ   from

Cf. dxʷ- 'toward', liɬ- 'by what route, by what means,
located where'

tuɬ-čad

    tuɬčád čəxʷ   Where are you from?   LL.

    tuɬčádəxʷ čəxʷ   Where are you coming from?   LG.

    tuɬčád kʷ(i) ads.tàgʷš tə haʔɬ puʔtəd   LG.
    Where did you buy the nice shirt?

tuɬ-čaʔkʷ

    tuɬčáʔkʷ   south wind (lit.'from the sea')   LG.

tuɬ-haʔkʷ

    adəxʷu.xʷíʔxʷiʔ tuɬhàʔkʷ
    tuɬháʔkʷ adəxʷu.xʷìʔxʷiʔ
    ck̓ʷáqid ɬ(u)ads.gʷàʔ
    ɬ(u)ads.gʷáʔ ck̓ʷàqid

    Where you hunted and fished from long ago
    From long ago where you hunted and fished
    Always that will be yours
    That will be yours always.   MS.

tuɬ-šəq

    ʔu.téčtᵊb tuɬšə̀q ʔə tiʔiɬ s.bàdil   EK.
    They rolled it from the top of the mountain.

    sáxʷəb tuɬšqìqad   Run from up the hill.   LG.

    tùɬšqíqad tə sə.sàxʷəb   LG.
    He's running from up the hill.

tuɬ-ɬaq̓t

    tuɬɬáq̓t tiʔəʔ su.ʔə̀ƛ̓ ʔə tiʔəʔ qʷ̀ùʔ   ML.
    From on up above this water came.

511

tuɫ-ʔal   tuɫʔal is usually pronounced /tuʔləl/.

tùɫʔal čəd jìjəlálič   I'm from Seattle.   LL.

tuɫʔál čəd s.qàǰət   I'm from Skagit.   LG.

tu.líɫc tuɫʔal kʷi bək̓ʷ tucəxʷəs.hìwil   EC.
He took me away from all I used to get into.

ʔu.bápədəxʷ čəd tuɫʔal ti s.yayus   EK.
I bothered him from his work.

tuɫʔál kʷi t(u)ads.líɫc tuɫʔal kʷi bək̓ʷ tucəxʷəs.hìwil   EC.
You took me away from all I used to get into.

ʔiɫ.(h)á²ɫ tuɫʔal kʷi xʷî²   EK.
It's better than nothing.

gʷəl čəd ʔəs.tɫíldxʷ tuɫʔal bək̓ʷ dəs.ptìdgʷəsᵊb
And I believe it with all my thoughts.

búusəɫdat tuɫʔal ti tuds.ʔə̀ɫᵊd   DM.
I haven't eaten for four days.

→ comparison

ʔiɫ.lúƛ čəxʷ tuɫʔal ʔəcà   You are older than I.   LG.

     Cf. ʔiɫ.lúƛ čəd dxʷʔal dəgʷî   I am older than you.

ʔiɫ.čáčas čəxʷ tuɫʔal ʔəcà   You are younger than I.   LG.

ʔiɫ.qá t(ə) ad.yìqus tuɫ²al tə ds.gʷà² dᵊ.yiqus
You have more cedar-root baskets than I have.

ʔiɫ.háac ti²iɫ ad.q̓ìlbid tuɫ²al ti²ə² d.q̓ìlbid   LG.
Your canoe is longer than mine.

ʔiɫ.x̌áb ti²iɫ wə̀q̓əb ²al tùdi² tuɫ²al ti²ə² wə̀q̓əb ²al ti²ə²
That chest over there is heavier than this chest right here.

-iɫ

tuɫiɫ   foreigner   EK.

tuɫiɫ s.bək̓ʷá²k̓ʷbixʷ   foreigners   LL.

1.   túq̓ʷub   a cough   LG., EK.

     See under x̌əɬ 'sick, hurt'.

        ʔəstúq̓ʷub čəd   I have a cough.   LG.

        túq̓ʷubali   coughing kind of TB   LG.

          ʔəstúq̓ʷubali čəd   I have the coughing kind of TB.   LG.

2.   tux̌ʷ   adverb   'and yet; merely, just, nearly'

     VH. glosses tux̌ʷ as 'and yet, on the other hand'; but in
many sentences the glosses are 'just, merely, simply', i.e.,
apparently synonymous with x̌ʷul. It is also glossed as 'and
then'. Its significance seems to be to contrast clauses (the
first of which may only be known from context).

        tux̌ʷ čəd ʔudxʷɬi.ʔɫqʷ yùq̓ʷəb   LL.
        I just have to wet my throat.

        túx̌ʷ čəd ʔu.ʔíbibəš   I'm just going for a walk.   LG.

        túx̌ʷ čəd ʔu.ptídəgʷəsˀb   I'm just thinking.   EK.

        tùx̌ʷ čəd ʔəs.béčtxʷ   I've just got it lying there.   ES.

        tùx̌ʷ čəɬ p̓áʎaʎ tu.kʷədálikʷ tuɫʔáʔ   ML.
        We only took (helped ourselves to) the worthless
        stuff from there.

        túx̌ʷ ʔu.ɫíčdubš   He just cut me.   LG.

        tùx̌ʷ (h)əlgʷəʔ x̌əɬ ti ʔu.šəɬ qʷíqʷəʎqʷəʎ   LL.
        They were just picking on one another.

        tux̌ʷ ʔu.ʔúx̌ʷ   He went anyway.   LG.

        tux̌ʷ čəxʷ s.talx̌ tiʔiɬ ʎəládəxʷ ʔə huydxʷ   LL.
        You are rather unusual in that you are able to get
        the work put together.

... hìkʷ ʔəs.qəlálitut, **tux̌ʷ** b(ə)u.ʔátəbəd   LG.

He had great power and yet he died.

gʷə.yáyus čəd, gʷəl **túx̌ʷ** čəd ʔəs.q̓ʷə̀ɫ ᵊb   LG.

I ought to work but I'm too tired.

(hə)là ʔb s.(h)àjəp, čəda **túx̌ʷ** bəs.(h)àjəp

dxʷʔal cədiɫ

I'm just as tall as he is.

həlaʔb **tux̌ʷ** ʔu.ɫíčic   LL.

He really meant to cut me.

həlaʔb **tux̌ʷ** ʔəxʷs.ɫičtubuɫ ᵊb   LL.

He really wants to cut us.

ʔu.púsiltubš čəxʷ gʷəl **túx̌ʷ** day? čəxʷ ɫu.x̌ə̀ɫə̀ɫx̌əč   HD.

You have thrown me (in wrestling), but you are only
to be sorry. (I.e., You're really going to catch it.)

ʔu.jùbdubut čəd **túx̌ʷ** = **túx̌ʷ** čəd ʔu.jùbdubut   LL.

I accidentally kicked myself.

ʔu· **tùx̌ʷ** siʔáb. ʔu.bəčálq čəɫ ʔə tiʔə?

ʔu· siʔáb. **tux̌ʷ** čəɫ ʔu.bəčálq ʔə tiʔə?   ML.

Oh, Sir! We only killed this (game).

ʔu.ɫík̓ʷšə(d)dub čəd **tux̌ʷ**   LL.

Just hooked my foot by accident.

-haxʷ   **tux̌ʷhaxʷ** is usually pronounced /tx̌ʷə́xʷ/.   LG.

tux̌ʷəxʷ čəɫ ʔudxʷ.huyigʷᵊdid tam   LL.

We will simply satisfy Thom now.

λ̓əll ʔá huʔxʷ **tùx̌ʷəxʷ** ɫu.ɫčìl (h)əlgʷə?   LG.

Wait until they get here.

tux̌ʷəxʷ ɫu.ɫčìl (h)əlgʷə? čəxʷa ɫu.huydáliɫ ᵊd   LG.

Wait for them to get here and then prepare the food.

túx̌ʷəxʷ čəd ɫu.ʔùx̌ʷ   I'll go after awhile.   LG.

gʷə.hawə? <u>tux̌ʷəxʷ</u> x̌bə.lìlil   ML.

Just as soon as he would go away...

reduplication

túx̌ʷux̌ʷ ?u.tàb   It wasn't much of an event.   ML.

túx̌ʷux̌ʷ ?u.tab ?ə kʷi s.čəbíd   ML.

It wasn't much of a thing with the bark.

→

2.   tu?(u)   spit

   -ut

      ?utú?ud čəd   I spit on it.

      ?utú?utᵊb ti?ił s.tùbš   That man got spit on.

   -ad

      stú?ad   spit, saliva

      ?utú?ad čəd   I spit (not aiming at anything).

   lexical

      ?udxʷ<u>tu?ustubuł</u> ?ə ti?ił ?əs.cùt ?ə ti!

      They spit in our faces with what they said just so!

   rejected:

      *?utú?atᵊb ti?ił s.tùbš

      *?utú?ad čəd ti?ił s.tùbš

3.   tu?ackʷ   sucker (a freshwater fish with white meat
                              and lots of bones)

   Recorded tuwáctxʷ from IM.

4.   tu?áłəd   king salmon (?)   ESi.

   Cf. yúbəč NPS   king salmon

      sáčəb SPS   king salmon   [addendum]

1. -tx^w   lexical suffix   'building'

   ʔəs.čúl̓tx^w   a rented house

   -al̓ʔtx^w   a building

   -alatx^w   building in a larger conceptual frame,
                        e.g., reference to a house in directions;
                        some act being performed on a house

2. -tx^w   'causative'

   Pronounced /-tu-/ before -b, /-tx^w/ elsewhere.

3. tx^wəl   See dx^wʔal.

t̓

The sound of this letter is similar to that of t except for the
addition of a simultaneous abrupt closure of the vocal cords; a sort
of 'exploded' t. [glottalized, voiceless alveolar stop]

1. t̓ábabac   slow down

    Cf. q̓əd 'slow' Cf. tábabac

        t̓ábabac t(i) adsu.gʷəgʷàdgʷəd   Talk slowly.

        t̓ábabac ɬu.bàkʷɬ čəxʷ   Slow down or you'll get hurt.

        x̌ʷultxʷ t̓ábabəc   Go slowly.   EK.

        x̌əɬ tì t̓ábabəctxʷ   A little bit slower (please).   ES.

2. t̓ábad   guess

        t̓ábad gʷəs.tàbəs ti?iɬ   Guess what that is.   LG.

        t̓ábad ɬu.?əx̌ìdəd   Guess what I'm going to do.   LG.

        t̓ábad gʷədxʷ.čàdəd   Guess where I'm going to go. LG.

        t̓ábad gʷə.čàdəs kʷi ɬuds.t̓àɬlil   LG., DM.
        Guess where I'm going to live.

            rejected:

                *t̓abad gʷə.čadəs gʷə.ɬaɬliləd

        x̌ʷ u l̓ čəd ɬut̓ábəd   Let me guess.

3. t̓ábid   fur, animal hair

        ?əst̓ábidabac   human body hair

4. t̓áčad   shape it

5. t̓áč̓əb   bitter (taste)   EK.
                       sour (as sour milk); spoil   LG.

        See under -qəp.

-a-b

    ʔutáčab   bile   LL.

lexical

    táčᵊbàlikʷ   Make it sour.   LG.

1.   tád-

    stádač   log jam   DM.

    stádaq   caught in the branch of a tree

      táʔtədàq   a game: Shoot a blunted arrow up into a cottonwood tree until it gets caught. Then shoot other arrows at the first one trying to get it down again. (See ʔúkʷukʷ.)

    tədús   sit together

      Cf. gʷədíl

2.   tagʷt   placed on top of something high

    See under šə́q-t.

root

    tágʷt(əxʷ)   noon   LG., LL., EK.

      Cf. cqʷúɫ   post, day

    ʔəstágʷt ti ƛuiqs ʔal ti cildàliɫᵊd
    The box is on the table.

    ʔəstágʷt tiʔiɫ s.xʷîʔxʷiʔləp   ML.
    Your (pl.) game (that you are hunting) is up on it (the rock).

    ləstágʷt čəd liɫʔal tə s.tiqìw   LG.
    I'm riding on the horse.

  -t or -š

    ʔutágʷtᵊd   laid it on top   EK.

ƛ́agʷtˀəd   Place it on top of something high.   LL.

ƛ́agʷtˀəš   Put it up!   LG.

-agʷ-il

    ʔəsƛ́agʷtagʷil ʔal tiʔił č̓ʎ̀aʔ   ML.

    (The seal) placed himself high up on that rock.

lexical

    xʷƛ́agʷtəp Skagit   chair   LG.

    dxʷƛ́əgʷtá(hˀ)b   sit on a chair   LG.

        Cf. səxʷ.gʷədíl Snoh.   chair

reduplication

    ƛ́áƛgʷˀt(əxʷ)   noon time   LG.

1.   ƛ̓ahá̓ʔs   slow down   DM.

    Cf. tábabac; laq(il)

    ƛ̓ahá̓ʔs gʷ(ə)adsgʷə.gʷàdad   talk slowly, talk softly DM.

2.   ƛ̓ákʷil   gone dry

    See under šab(a) 'dry'.

3.   ƛ̓al(a)   slice, split open

    See under łič̓(i).

    root

        sƛ̓ál   sliced (fish)   LG.

    -at

        ƛ̓álad   slice it   LG.

    -təd

        ƛ̓áltəd   a knife used specifically for slicing
                       "The blade is set in a cedar stick."

lexical

> t̓álus   cooked fish heads -- "They are cooked and hung up to dry."   LL.
>
> LG. gives q̓ʷəlqíd commenting that they are cooked and smoke-dried.
>
> ESi. gives səlúsqid commenting that they are dried with jaws open. They are used in soups.

other derivation

> stəlú?b   fish split open and dried by sun and wind
>   LG., LL., ESi.
> (This was usually a king salmon (i.e., yúbəč).)

See also under šab(a).

> Cf. s.łú?ᵊb   dried dog salmon   LL.
>
> xʷ.šəbús   fish that's smoked only a few days
>
> k̓ayáyə?, x̌áx̌yəƛ, q̓ʷás   fish thoroughly dried by smoking

1.   t̓álx̌   lose balance backwards

See under q̓(ə)č.

> Cf. k̓ʷalč̓   bend backwards
>
> xʷíč̓ič̓ab   balance, teeter, stagger
>
> łík̓ʷšəd   stumble

root

> xʷi?txʷ lət̓álx̌   Don't let him fall over backward. (Said to someone holding a baby.)

-t

> t̓álx̌ᵊd   Bend him backwards! (Shouted to someone who is wrestling.)
>
> Cf. k̓ʷálč̓ᵊd   bend him over backwards

520

ʔalčutálx̌cut   bending self backward

táłx̌cut means the opposite of tujil.

lexical

ʔəstálx̌qs   pug nose

1.   táɬ(a)   crossways

-at

táɬəd   Put it crossways.

táɬətᵊb   It was put crossways.

-tx̌ʷ

ləstáɬtx̌ʷ   Carry it crossways (because you won't be
                     able to manage it any other way).

-ab

ʔəx̌ʷtáɬab   It is across the trail.

-il

ʔutáɬil   It has fallen across (my road, door, etc.)

-ag̈ʷ-il

táɬag̈ʷil   Lie crosswise!

táɬag̈ʷis   lie crosswise for some reason

-il-dx̌ʷ

ʔutáɬildx̌ʷ   It has accidentally fallen across (my road,
                     door, etc.).

-il-tx̌ʷ

ʔəstáɬiltx̌ʷ   He has it crossways (as in criticizing someone's
                     work).

lexical

táɬusəd   beam (in building)

Cf. səx̌ʷ.táx̌ʷəlik̈ʷ

ʔəstáɬtaɬšəd He is cross-footed. (an insult)

1. táɬigʷs(əd) rock cod LL., ESi.

Cf. qʷíbikʷs

2. táqa salalberry LG., MC., EK., ESi.

→

3. táq̓t landward, opposite of čaʔkʷ

See under čaʔkʷ.

Cf. čubə 'up from water's edge'

root

táq̓t tiʔiɬ bəsəs.q̓əlbs ʔal ti swat.watixʷtəd DM.
Up on shore it spends the night in trees.

sáxʷəb tiʔəʔ bə̀sčəb liɬtáq̓t ML.
Mink ran along the top (of the bluff).

ʔá kʷi ƛb(ə)asʔiɬtàq̓ts ML.
He would be there again up from shore.

tíləb dxʷtáq̓təxʷ tiʔiɬ s.ɬalil ʔə tiʔiɬ čxʷ(ə)lùʔ ES.
All at once the whale landed way up on shore.

tiʔiɬ s.k̓ʷil ʔə tiʔiɬ bibščəb dxʷtáq̓t ES.
Little Mink looked up landward.

-bi-t

díɬ ʔu ads.gʷàʔ ad.táʔɬ ti ʔəs.ɬáq̓ (ʔal tiʔiɬ) tàq̓tbid
ʔə ti ʔàlʔal LG.
Is that your salmon spear lying behind the house?

lexical

təq̓tálatxʷ 1. up in the woods behind a house LL.
2. landward side of the house (outside of it on the land side) LG.

ƛ́əq̓tádiʔ   landward side of a house (inside)   LG.

ƛ́əq̓táladiʔ (ʔə ti ʔalʔal)   landward side of the house   LG.

ƛ́əq̓táyucid   upper side of the road   LG.

ti ʔalʔal ƛ́əq̓táyucid ʔə tə šəg̓ʷɬ   LG.
The house on the upper side of the road.

1. s.ƛ́áqʷu   liver   LL., LG.

     Cf. s.č̓álub

2.   t̓as(a)   pay

     See under q̓p̓(u).

     -at

          ʔut̓ásədəxʷ čəd   I paid for it.   LG.

          t̓ásətᵊb   It's paid for.   LG.

     -yi-

          ʔut̓ásyid čəd   I paid him.   LL.

          t̓ásyitᵊb   pay someone for a particular
                              article he bought for you   LL.

     -b-il

          ʔut̓ásᵊbiləxʷ čəd   I paid for it.   LL.

          ɬut̓ásᵊbil čəd ʔə tə dsəs.x̌ʷíƛ̓alikʷ   LG.
          I will pay for what I owe.

          díɬəxʷ dəxʷut̓àsbilčəɬ   ES.
          That's why we are paying him.

     -b-il-du-but

          ʔut̓ásᵊbildubut čəd   I paid (my bill).   LL.

3.   t̓áxʷ(a)

     -at

          t̓áxʷad   lay boards on a beam   AS.

523

lexical

 səxʷƛ̓áxʷalikʷ   beam (architecture)   AS.

  Cf. ƛ̓áɬusəd   beam in building

1. ƛ̓áyəd

  ləƛ̓áyəd   claiming (?)   EK.

2. s.tá?txʷ   sty (of eyelid)

  See x̌əɬ 'sick', qəlúb 'eye'.

3. ƛ̓čsúšəd (?)   (logger's) cork shoe   ES.

  Probably ƛ̓čú(s)šəd from tuč(u).

  See under ƛ̓k̓ʷábšəd 'shoe'.

4. ƛ̓əbádi?   'cheeks' of a fish   LL.

  ƛ̓əbá?adi?   cheeks of a fish   LG.

   táltalədi?   (lit. 'money on side')   ESi.

5. ƛ̓əbá?   fall into water; drown   EK.

  Compare ǰiq̓(i); gʷal, x̌ƛ̓ab; dxʷ.bəč̓əb

   tu.cùuc čəd gʷə.xʷí?əs gʷəsu.k̓ʷíts dxʷ?al tə s.tùləkʷ,
   gʷəl kʷi ƛ̓əbƛ̓əbá?   LG.
   I told him not to go down to the river, he might
   fall in.

6. ƛ̓əb

  ƛ̓əbš   braid

 -t

  ƛ̓əbšᵊd   Braid it.

lexical

t̓əbšáydid	Braid her hair.	LG.
ʔəst̓əbt̓əbšáydiʔ	braided hair	LG.
ʔəst̓əbt̓əbšáydi(ʔ)d	braided hair	LG.

reduplication

t̓át̓əbìɬəd	ropes

other derivation

t̓əbíɬəd   Snoh.   rope

    Cf. x̌ʷíləb

s.t̓ətəgʷúlač̓	fishing twine
dəxʷəs.ɬíd̓gʷiɬ	for tying a boat
plilá ʔ	wild cherry bark (often used as rope)
s.tíd̓gʷəd	cedar branches when they are put to some use, generally used for tying things

1.   t̓ə́bt̓əb   winter wren (?)   LG., LL.

2.   t̓əbxʷ   Skagit   gooseberry   MC.

      č̓q̓áb   Snoh.   gooseberry   LL.

      č̓áq̓ab   Suqu.   gooseberry   ESi.

3.   t̓əbxʷíl   buzzing and biting of a fly

4.   t̓ə́č̓   gall

5. s.t̓əč̓ás   name for Budd Inlet; name now applied to Olympia, Washington

    st̓əč̓ásəbš   people who live by Budd Inlet

1. t̓əd   in a row, lined up

    root

       ʔəst̓ə́d   It (e.g., cord wood) is stacked in a row.

    -t

       t̓ə́dəd   put them in a row

    lexical equivalent, -us:

       dxʷ.d(ə)č̓ág̓ʷus   one row/layer

       dxʷ.sáliʔus   two rows/layers

       dxʷs.ɬíxʷus   three rows/layers

       dxʷs.búusus   four rows/layers

       dxʷs.cəlácsus   five rows/layers

       dxʷs.yəlʔacus   six rows/layers

       dxʷ.č̓úʔkʷsus   seven rows/layers

       dxʷ.k̓ʷídusəxʷ   How many layers?

       dxʷ.qáhusəxʷ   many layers

    reduplication

       t̓ədt̓ədád   put them in rows

2. t̓ədús   See under t̓ad-.

3. t̓(ə)k̓*   patch

    Cf. ƛ̓iq̓(i) 'adhere', t̓əq 'adhere'; ƛuk̓ʷ(u) 'plug in, caulk',

       čik̓ʷ(i) 'stuff into, caulk'

    root

       ʔəst̓ə́k̓   patched

    -t

       t̓ə́k̓əd   patch it

*t̓(ə)k̓ should read t̓(ə)q̓ in all examples preceding, including and following this entry.

lexical

ʔutk̓álgʷiɫ   patch canoe on side or gunnel

ʔəstk̓álgʷiɫ   patched canoe side or gunnel

reduplication

t̓əktk̓ád tiʔiɫ ad.q̓ilbid Patch up your canoe.

1. s.t̓(ə)k̓ʷəb

 t̓ək̓ʷ-

  st̓ə́k̓ʷəb SPS   log, stick; wood(s)

   Cf. qʷɫáyʔ NPS log, stick; pəx̌áyʔac log, dead tree

   ʔust̓ə́k̓ʷəb s.yàyus He's working in the woods. JC.

 lexical

  st̓k̓ʷábac   wood parts, wood pieces JC.

  st̓k̓ʷálšəd   tumpline   LL., LG.

   Cf. s.ɫidálšəd, čəbá(ʔ)təd

  t̓k̓ʷábšəd Snoh. SPS shoe

   Cf. qʷɫíʔšəd (under qʷɫáyʔ), t̓čsúšəd (logger's) cork shoe

 reduplication

  st̓ít̓k̓ʷəb   stick   ESi.

2. s.t̓əljíxʷ   medicine   EK., JC.

3. t̓əlk̓ʷ   uvula

4. t̓əlqáy   soak

 See ǰiq̓(i).

t̓əlqáyᵊd   soak something in water

ʔux̌ʷ čəd ɫut̓əlqáy   I'm going to soak (the dried fish).

1.   s.t̓əlúʔb   See under t̓al(a).

2.   t̓əĺqáyd   side (?)

3.   t̓əɫ-

     t̓əɫqídᵊb   see into the future, foretell future (?)   AS.

     t̓ɫáyačib   Same glosses: see into the future, foretell future

4.   t̓ə̀nsəwíc   Chinese slippers "Brown shell lying on its back, collected at low tide; look like snails."
                                          LG.

   See ʔáx̌ʷuʔ.

5.   t̓əq   1. thick (like dough pressed together)
                   2. adhere   LG.

   Cf. pə́ɫt 'thick' (dimension); ƛ̓iq̓(i) 'adhere'

   root

     t̓ə̀q s.qʷšáb   thick fog   LL.

     ʔəst̓ə̀q   It's stuck to something.   DM., LG.

   lexical

     t̓qálikʷ   1. make bread   LG., LL. (See under q̓ʷəl.)
                2. plaster   DM.

       ƛ̓u.ʔá(ʔ)dəxʷ ʔal tiʔəʔ diʔəʔ st̓qàlikʷs   DM.
       (The beaver) puts it where he plasters.

       ʔəst̓qálicaʔ čəxʷ   There is something stuck on your clothing.   LG.

       t̓qíǰᵊd tiʔəʔ diʔəʔ təqápᵊds   DM.
       (The beaver) plasters its dam.

ʔəstáqšád čəxʷ   There is something stuck to your
shoe, leg, foot.   LG.

other derivation

stáqxʷ NPS   beaver
stqáxʷ SPS   beaver   BMc.

(1) ʔəs.ṗíl tiʔəʔ s.čuṗč ʔə tiʔəʔ diʔəʔ stáqxʷ.
(2) xʷíʔ lə.tíb híkʷ tiʔəʔ stáqxʷ.   (3) ƛu.xíƛəp.
(4) díɬ tiʔəʔ dəxʷ.(h)ac(h)əc ʔə tiʔəʔ jədis.
(5) ƛu.xíƛid tiʔəʔ diʔəʔ s.watíxʷtəd.   (6) ƛu.jéctxʷ
dxʷʔal tiʔəʔ su.húyuds tiʔəʔ təqápᵊds.   (7) díɬ
səs.húy ʔə tiʔəʔ stáqxʷ.

(1) A beaver has a wide tail. (2) A beaver is not
very big. (3) It fells (trees). (4) That is why (its)
teeth are long. (5) It fells trees. (6) It uses them
to make its dam. (7) This is what a beaver is like.

(1) díɬ dəxʷəs.dàʔatᵊbs ʔə tiʔəʔ stáqxʷ dxʷʔal tiʔəʔ
bəsu.húyuds tiʔəʔ ʔalʔals, ƛsutqíjᵊds tiʔəʔ diʔəʔ
təqápᵊds.   (2) gʷəl ƛu.čáxʷad tiʔəʔ diʔəʔ pədíxʷ.
(3) ƛu.ʔá(ʔ)d tiʔəʔ diʔəʔ stqàlikʷs.   (4) díɬ tiʔəʔ
diʔəʔ ƛu.čəxʷá(hᵊ)b tiʔəʔ dəxʷəs.ʔəƛ ʔə tiʔəʔ s.daʔs,
dxʷʔal tiʔiɬ ƛus.dáʔatᵊbsəxʷ ʔal kʷi stáqxʷ.

(1) He is called "sticker/plasterer" (i.e., beaver)
because of the way he makes his house, [how] he plasters his dam. (2) He hits the mud. (3) He puts it
where he plasters. (4) He hits with his tail [and]
this is where his name comes from, why he is called
the "sticker/plasterer".

→

2. s.táqí*   a people from far to the north   ML.

lexical

stáqíwiɬ   a double-ended canoe

See under qilbid, p. 400, 402 and under -gʷiɬ, p. 174.

_____

* Should be s.təkí in all examples preceding, including and following
this entry.

1. ṭəqṭqác   vine maple   MC., LG., DM.

      Cf. kyú?kiwəc   vine maple   EK.

           s.čuču?łəc   vine maple   ESi.

→

3. ṭəq̓ʷ(u)   snap (in two) a flexible object

      See under x̌ʷəƛ̓.

      root

          x̌ʷùl ?iłṭəq̓ʷ ?ə ti?ə? x̌ə̀pàyəc
          just short of (the top of) the cedar tree

      -ut

          ṭə́q̓ʷud   break it (a string/rope); stop a song

      -txʷ

          ?utə́q̓ʷtxʷ   He stopped the song.
                            (This is done by making an abrupt spreading motion
                            with the arms, palms down as a signal for the drum-
                            mers to stop (as when they are not getting the
                            rhythm right).)

      -ad

          (?u)gʷətq̓ʷád   faint, pass out   EK., LG., ES.

            Cf. p̓álil   regain consciousness

      lexical

          ṭəq̓ʷgʷás   come apart

4. ṭə́s   cold weather

      See under hud(u).

      Cf. ƛ̓áx̌   person feels cold (sensation)

           ƛ̓úx̌ʷ   a thing, e.g., food, is cold

           túq̓ʷub   cold, cough (disease)

-t

čə́sˀᵊd   decold it   LG.
                       bake it   LL.
                       warm it (put it close to an open fire)   LG.

čəscút dxʷʔal tə hud   Warm yourself by the fire.

čəscút ʔə tə hud   Same gloss: Warm yourself by the fire.

Contrast čə́sˀᵊd with qaʔt(a).

-b

čə́s(ˀᵊb)   cold weather

ʔəsčəsˀᵊb čəd ʔal tiʔəʔ *Hawaii*.   I'm wintering in Hawaii.

čəsˀᵊbáxʷ   It's cold now.   LL.

pə(d)čə́s(ˀᵊb)   winter   EK.

ʔu.ƛ́axʷ tə sčə̀sˀᵊb   autumn (i.e., growing of winter)   EK.

-b-lexical

čəsˀᵊbáʔɬdəɬ   chapped lips   LL.

-il

ʔáliləxʷ kʷi sə.čitils kʷi səčsils   EC.
Now it's getting close to cold weather.

-adub

ʔəsč(ə)sádub   bake on an open fire with embers and ashes
                       and gravel piled around but not over it.
                       You use some sort of pan.   LL.

1.   s.čə̀təgʷúlačˀ   fishing twine

    See under čəbíɬəd.

2.   čə́ttqʷiʔ   See títtqʷiʔ.

531

1. t̓əx̌   Cf. ləč̓, šəq

    t̓x̌ábid   Step over it.

2. s.t̓əx̌ʷšáad   rainbow   LG.

    Cf. qʷubáč̓(š)əd   (under qʷuʔ)

3. s.t̓əx̌ʷšəd   root (esp. cedar root)   EK., MC.
                      ancestors (fig.)   EK.

    s.t̓əx̌ʷšád   root   DM., LG.

    Cf. qəládiʔ   up-rooted; qʷəbəláx̌ʷ   root of any kind

4. t̓ičib   wade out, swim

    Cf. gʷəcíl   wade/stand in shallow water

        t̓ít̓əb   bathe

         t̓it̓it̓əb   swimming

        ʔíšil   (a fish) swims, swim within water

    root

        ʔut̓íčib   wade, swim   EK.

          ʔut̓íčib dxʷ.diʔucid ʔə tə s.tùləkʷ   EK.
          He waded/swam across the river.

        tut̓íčib čəd   I swam/waded out.   LG.

        t(u)as.x̌ác čəd gʷət̓íčibəd   I was afraid to swim.   EK.

        dxʷst̓íčib   swimmer   LG.

          tudxʷst̓íčib čəd   I used to be a swimmer.   LG.

    -i-t

        ʔut̓íčibid   He swam/waded out after it.   LL.

    rejected: *t̓íčibis

1. t̕igʷ(i) ~ t̕iwił   thank, pray

     -it

         ʔut̕ígʷid čəd   Thank you.   EK.

             Cf. dáhədubš, həlíi(ʔ)dubš čəxʷ, ck̕ʷálìdxʷ

         t̕íwił čəd   I pray.   EK.

         st̕íwił   religion   EK.

     - iluł

         ʔut̕íwiłiluł   go to church   EK.

     lexical

         t̕iwiłál̕ʔtxʷ   church   EK., LG.

→
3. t̕íləqʷ SPS   wild strawberry   ESi.

     Cf. s.číʔyu NPS   wild strawberry

4. t̕ílib   sing

     See under cut.   Cf. yáwdᵊb

         huy, t̕ílibəxʷ tiʔił bìbščəb   Then Little Mink sang.   ES.

         lət̕ílib ʔal tiʔił ʔílgʷił ʔal tiʔəʔ s.wàtixʷtəds (h)əlgʷəʔ ML.
         She was going along singing by the shore of their world.

         ƛ̕əlcut̕ílib čəd łu.yàyusəd   I sing when I work.   LG.

         dxʷ.(h)áʔɬqid čəxʷ ʔal t(i) adst̕ilib   EK.
         You have a good voice when you sing.

         gʷəl tiʔə́ʔəxʷ tiʔił tust̕ilibs   ES.
         And this is what she sang.

         dxʷ.(h)áʔɬqid čəxʷ ʔal təst̕ilib   EK.
         You have a good voice while singing.

-tx^w

ʔutílibtx^w čəd   I sang it to him.   LG.

ʔutílibtɬ^w čəd tiʔiɬ tìdtid   LL.
I played the radio/phonograph.

t(u)əlčutílibtubš   He was singing to me.   LG.

-yi-

ʔutílibyid čəd   I sang for him.   LL.

lexical

stílibəx̌əd   an unidentified type of song   LG.

rejected: *tilibid

1.   tíq̓^w   smoke, murk

See under q^w(ə)š.

-il

stíq̓^wil   smoke   LL.

   Cf. páq̓^{wə}b, q^wəšəb

ʔudx^wtíq̓^wilus čəd   The smoke is in my face.   LL.

   Cf. ʔəx^w.páq̓^wus   face blackened by smoke   LL.

ʔəx^wtíq̓^wil   river is murky   LG.

   Cf. ʔəx^w.qələbíl   Same gloss: river is murky
                         (lit. 'rain water')

-b

dx^wtíq̓^{wə}b ti s.tùlak^w   The river is murky.   LL., LG.

ʔəx^wtíq̓^{wə}b   murky water   LG.

ʔudx^wtíq̓^{wə}bdx^w   render turbid   LG.

lexical

tíq̓^walik^w   smoke meat   LL.

?utíⁱtq̓ʷàlikʷ   smoke just a few fish   LL.

?upá.pq̓ʷàlikʷ   Same gloss: smoke just a few fish   LL.

1.   t̓ísəd   arrow, bullet

     t̓ít̓səd   small projectile

2.   t̓ísu   Cf. luλ 'old'

     ?iɬt̓ísu   younger

     ?iɬt̓ísu čəxʷ tuʎ?al ?əcà   LG.

     You are younger than I (speaking to a sibling or other relative).

       (?iɬ.čácas replaces ?iɬt̓ísu when speaking to a non-relative.)

     lexical

     t̓isux̌álqsaci?   little finger

     reduplication

     díɬ ?iɬt̓ít̓isu   the youngest one

3.   t̓it̓ᵊb   bathe   EK.
                           bathe for spiritual cleansing   LG.

     Cf. ča?kʷ, t̓ič̓ᵊb

     root

     ?əxʷst̓it̓ᵊbᵊb   He wants to bathe.   LG.

     -txʷ

     ?alčut̓it̓ᵊbtxʷ tə bədà?s   She's bathing her baby.   LG.

     ?əxʷst̓it̓ᵊbtxʷᵊb tə bədà?s   She wants to bathe her baby.   LG.

     reduplication

     ?ut̓ít̓it̓ᵊb   swam   EK.

     ?əs.xʷák̓ʷil čəd ?ə ti dst̓it̓it̓ᵊb   EK.

     I'm tired of swimming.

ʔu.ʔúx̌ʷ dxʷ.diʔi ʔut́i̓tit̓ᵊbiluɫ   LL.

He went over there to go swimming.

(ɫu)ʔúx̌ʷ čəɫ ɫutítit̓ᵊb ʔal kʷi tìⅼ̓x̌i?   LG.

We will go bathing after a while.

1.   títədàči(ʔ)b   loping (of a horse)

      Cf. lə.cíx̌ači(ʔ)b   trotting   (under cíx̌(i))

2.   s.títələ?   young animal such as fawn, calf, colt

      Cf. tátačulbixʷ   large animal

          títčulbixʷ   small animal

          s.wáxʷiʔɫ   litter of whelp wolves (still with mother)

          yəw̓yəɫdá?   fawn (one year old)

3.   títtqʷi?   NPS   butterball/bufflehead, a bu?qʷ   LL.

      Cf. tə́tt̓ᵊqʷi?   SPS   ESi., LL.

4.   títx̌əlá?   grasshopper   ML.

5.   tixʷ(i)   brush off, shake off

      Cf. pixʷ(i), xʷis(i)

      -it

          ʔutíxʷid čəd ti?iɫ   I brushed (something) off it.   LL.

          xʷuⅼ čəd ɫutíxʷid tə d.kəkpù   LG.

          I'll just shake (the dust) off my little coat.

          ʔutíxʷicut tə s.qʷəbay?   The dog shook himself off.   LG.

      -il-dxʷ

          ʔutíxʷildxʷ čəxʷ   You got it brushed off.   LG.

lexical

ƛ̓ix̌ʷáličaʔc   brush my clothes off while wearing them   LG.

reduplication

st̓í̓tix̌ʷ   red huckleberry   MC., EC.

st̓ə̓tíx̌ʷ   red huckleberry   LG.

other derivation

st̓íx̌ʷib   red huckleberry. "They are gathered by
             shaking or brushing against the bush."   LL.

st̓x̌ʷíb   red huckleberry   ESi.

rejected:

*ʔəst̓ix̌ʷ, *ʔut̓ix̌ʷ, *t̓ix̌ʷil   LG.

1.   t̓íx̌təd   a man's name. "He was a great warrior."   ES.

2.   ƛ̓iyúʔsəd   hand smelt trap for streams   JC.

See under ƛ̌a(ʔ)təd.

(1) húyudəxʷ čəɬ kʷi ƛ̓iyùʔsəd.

(2) ɬu.ʔúləx̌ə d čəɬ kʷi hàac s.tìdə gʷəd. (3) ƛ̌úb hàac
ti ʔiɬ ƛ̓iyùʔsəd. (4) čə́x̌ə dxʷ čəxʷ ti ʔiɬ s.tìdə gʷəd.
(5) ɬu.xʷí̓əs həlàʔb ʔə(s).sə́pil ti ʔiɬ ƛ̓iyùʔsəd. (6) k̓ʷid.
(7) ʔəbíl̓ t(ə)qàči ʔ, x̌ʷə̀l, pàdac kʷi gʷəs.tidə gʷəd.
(8) gə́lk̓ə dxʷ; ƛ̓íxʷ búus rows kʷi gʷ(ə)ads.gə̀lk̓ə d. (9)
q̓ʷú̓ʔə dəxʷ ʔal ti ɬ(u)adsəxʷu.kʷə̀dəd čəxʷə ɬidid. (10)
ʔu.bə́čəd čəxʷ ʔal ti c̓albid. (11) ʔə(s).šábə b. (12)
ʔəbíləxʷ čəxʷ ʔu.xʷi̓(ʔ)xʷi ʔ čəxʷə ʔu.ĵíq̓id ɬu.xʷí̓əs lə.xʷə̀ƛ̌
ʔə kʷi qi ʔ.qiyə́ ʔ.

(1) We are now going to make a smelt trap.
(2) We will collect long cedar branches. (3) A long smelt
trap is best. (4) You split the cedar branches. (5) [But]

the smelt trap must not be real pliable. (6) How many?
(7) Perhaps eight, nine, [or] ten [split] cedar branches.
(8) Now wind/knit them together; three [or] four rows of
braiding you do. (9) Gather it where you will hold it
[i.e., the ends] and tie it. (10) Lay it in the shade.
(11) It dries. (12) When you go fishing, soak it so it
will not break easily.   JC.

1.   ƛ̕iʔ(i)   ring (a bell)

      Cf. ƛ̕ilib 'sing', ƛ̕idtid 'radio, phonograph'

      -it

          ƛ̕iʔid   ring it

          ƛ̕iʔyid   ring the bell for him

          ƛ̕iʔyidəxʷ gʷəl gʷə.ʔə́ƛ̕   Ring it for him to come.

      lexical

          dəgʷítxʷ kʷi ʔuƛ̕iʔalikʷ   You ring the bell.

          ƛ̕iʔalikʷyicid   Let him ring it for you.

          dəgʷítxʷ kʷi ʔuƛ̕iʔalikʷyid   You ring the bell for him.

2.   ƛ̕kʷ-   See under ƛ̕əkʷ-.

3.   ƛ̕qədiʔac   hemlock   LL., MC.

          ƛ̕íƛ̕qədiʔac   young hemlock   MC.

4.   ƛ̕uč(u)   shoot

      root

          ʔuƛ̕úč čəd   I got shot.   EK., LL.

538

-ut

    t̓úc̓ud   shot it   EK.

    q̓(ə)č̓ícab tə st̓ùc̓uds tə s.q̓ìgʷəc   LG.
    He shot the deer with a bow.

    ʔut̓úc̓utᵊb čəd   They shot at me. They shot me.

    q̓(ə)č̓ícab tə st̓uc̓utᵊbs ʔə tə s.tùbš tə s.q̓ìgʷəc   LG.
    The man shot the deer with a bow.

    ʔut̓úc̓utəgʷəl   shot one another on purpose   LL.

-dxʷ

    ʔut̓úc̓utᵊb čəd, čədà t̓ùc̓ᵊdub təɬ   LL.
    They shot at me and they surely hit me.

    ʔu.k̓ʷəƛc čəd, čədà t̓ùc̓ᵊdxʷ tiʔiɬ dᵊq̓ì.q̓ilbid   ES.
    I missed and hit my little canoe.

    ʔut̓úc̓ᵊdxʷ čəd gʷəl tux̌ʷ čəd ʔu.k̓ʷəƛc   EK.
    I shot at it but I missed.

    ʔut̓úc̓ᵊdub čəd   LL.
    I got shot (but they weren't necessarily trying
             to hit me).

    ʔut̓úc̓dəgʷəl   shot one another accidentally   LL.

-il

    t̓úc̓il   shoot   EK., LL.

    t̓úc̓iləxʷ   He has shot now.   EK.

    t̓ísəd tə cəxʷt̓úc̓il   I shot the arrow.   LG.

    ʔut̓úc̓il čəd tə q̓(ə)č̓ic   I shot the bow.   LG.

         rejected: *ʔut̓úc̓il čəd ʔə tə t̓ísəd

-il-txʷ

    ʔut̓úc̓iltxʷ čəd tə t̓ìsəd   I shot the arrow.   LG.

rejected:

*ʔutúčiltxʷ čəd tə q̓(ə)čìc   LG.

*ʔutúčildxʷ

lexical

ʔutúčadiʔ čəd cut ɬ(u)as.x̌əcàs   LL.
I shot at random just to scare him.

túčalikʷ   go shooting   JC.

reduplication

tútutč   bee sting   EK.

tútčil   shoot more than once   LL.

1.   túkʷ(u)   measure, figure out

Cf. taɬ(a); dxʷ.cutᵊb, ptídəgʷəsəb

-ut

túgʷud   measure it; figure it

túgʷud tiʔiɬ qʷɬáyʔ   Measure that log.   DM.

túgʷud ʔəs.ʔəx̌id kʷi s.ba(ʔ)wiɬ ʔə t(i) ad.q̓ílbid   DM.
Measure how wide your canoe is.

túgʷucut   think over

lexical

túkʷtəd   tape measure, ruler

reduplication

ʔalčutútugʷucut čəd   I'm thinking it over a lot.

2.   túkʷ   go home

ʔáliləxʷ kʷi (gʷə)cəxʷt̓úk̓ʷ   It's time for me to go home.

-txʷ

lət̓úk̓ʷtub ʔə ti d.bàd tə s.qìgʷəcałči? ləs.čəbád   DM.
My father took the venison home back packing it.

1. t̓úxʷ(əc)   white fir (tree)   MC.

    Cf. łəq̓łəq̓táči?(ac)   young white fir (tree)
                          nickname for the tree, i.e. 'wide hands'
                                                       MC.

    Cf. łəq̓táčəd(əc)   white fir   ESi.

        qʷə?qʷábac   young fir tree   MC.

2. s.t̓x̌ʷ   See under s.təx̌ʷšáad

3. t̓u?   hole through something

    Cf. lu?   hole in the ground, a hole in something,
                          but not through it;

        k̓ʷúlu?   hollow

        ?əst̓ú?   (The cloth) has a hole in it.

4. s.t̓ú?ə1   herring   LL., ESi.

5. s.t̓ú?q̓ʷ   small feathers (as would be used in pillows)
                                                       EK., LL.

    Cf. číčal   long feathers with thick 'stems';

        s.k̓ʷík̓ʷəlč   eiderdown

6. t̓ú?xʷəc   hemlock

    Cf. t̓q̓ədí?ac 'hemlock', s.k̓ʷúpəc 'hemlock'

u

This letter stands for a sound which English speakers tend to hear as being sometimes similar to that of *oo* in *boot* and sometimes *oa* in *boat*.

1. -u-   lexical connective   See 8.2.
2. -u-   aspectual prefix 'completive'
3. -ubuɬ   object suffix   'us'

   See under -bš.

4. -ubuɬəd   object suffix   'you (pl.)'

   See under -bš.

5. -ucid   lexical suffix   'gap, opening'

   The various English glosses for -ucid are not as abstract as the real significance of the suffix. The meaning of -ucid is clearer when it is contrasted with other lexical suffixes which have the same glosses:

mouth	-ucid	opening or hole in the face
mouth	-aʔɬdəɬ	the parts of the mouth, e.g., lips
river	-ucid	the opening in the ground, what needs to be crossed
river	-gʷiɬ	the means of travel
door	-ucid	the opening to pass through
door	-y-ax̌ad	the hinged object attached to one side

   This suffix sometimes requires the thematic suffix -i- before -t, but speakers vary greatly in their use of it.

-ucid   'mouth, language; door, lid; river

bəqʷúcid	Skagit	kiss	LG.
ləkʷúcid	Snoh.	kiss	EK.

ləlíʔucid	foreign language	
dəxʷəs.cútucid ʔə tiʔəʔ qyuuqs	language the seagulls use	ML.
t(ə)qúcid	Shut the door.	EK.
ʔuq̓ʷúcidᵊb	Open the door.	LL.
diʔúcid	other side of the river	
s.čəgʷúcid (s-čaʔkʷ-ucid)	island	EK., LG.
x̌k̓ʷúcid	cover, top, lid	
q(ə)p̓úcid	cover a pot or basket	LL.
x̌.q(ə)p̓úcid	knee (-cap?)	EK., LL.

-ay-ucid 'road; chin, jaw'

diʔáyucid	other side of the road	
čəgʷáyucid (čaʔkʷ-ay-ucid)	lower side of the road	
jəháyucid	right side of the road	
šaẁáyucid	jaw	
s.gʷədáyucid	chin	
qʷídáyucid	beard, moustache	

    Cf. qʷidáyqs

c̓ú(h)àyucid	weak chin	ES.

    See under c̓ud.

x̌i̓c̓iláyucid	shame in the mouth	ES.
liláyucid	stubborn, mean	EK.

-ucd- 'lunch, dinner' Cf. s.ʔə́ɫᵊd, -aɫc̓iʔ

ʔábucdid	I take him his lunch/dinner.	LG.

1. -údaq   lexical suffix   'friend'

     q̓ʷuʔúdaq   close friend (not a relative)   LG.

2. -udəq   lexical suffix   'conference, parley, agenda'

    See under cut.

     s.tàb kʷ(i) ads.jìxʷúdəq   What is first on your agenda?   LL.

3. -ul-   lexical connective   See 8.2.

4. -ulč   lexical suffix   'container'

     s.kʷədúlč   container   LG.

     k̓ʷidúlč   How many containers?   LG.

     łìxʷúlč   three containers   LG.

     háʔłùlč   nice basket   LL.

     t(ə)súlč   drum   EK.

     č̓(a)xʷúlč   clubbed in abdomen   LL.

     čàwəyʔúlc   store-bought dish   LG.

     qʷłəy(ʔ)úlč   wooden platter   LG.

     č̓əgʷúlč   wash dishes

     s.ʔìlúlč   side of a box, cup, etc.   LG.

5. -ulgʷədxʷ   lexical suffix   'land'

     š(ə)qúlgʷədxʷ   the land above, sky   EK.

     gʷədúlgʷədxʷ   the land below   EK.

6. -uł   a suffix meaning to proceed to some place in order to perform the action of the underlying stem. It occurs only with -il stems.

júbalikʷiluɫ	go to (a) dance: júbalikʷ dance
q̓əlbíluɫ	go camping: q̓ə́l^əb camp, stay over night
c̓əbəbíluɫ	go berry picking: c̓ə́bəb pick berries
t̓íwiɫiluɫ	go to church: t̓íwiɫ pray
gʷədíluɫ	go (there) to sit down: gʷədíl sit

1.   -uɫ   This suffix designates family origin.

    Cf. -aɫ

s.duhúbšuɫ čəd	I am from/of the Snohomish.	LL., MC.
tə̀stədúɫ	(have) tə̀stəd power from one's ancestors	MC.
s.gʷədíličùɫ	(have) s.gʷədílič power from one's ancestors	MC.

2.   -us   lexical suffix   'upper part, head, face, hair'

    Cf. -qid, -alus, -əlus

c̓əlpús^əd	turn head (of a horse while riding)	
ɫidús^əd	tie (a horse) with the reins	LG.
š(ə)qús	up hill Cf. -iqad	
š(ə)qús^əb	lift head	ES.
x̌(ə)pús^əb	straighten posture	EK.
xʷəbəbús^əb	turn head (face away and deliberately not listen)	LL.
s.ʔácus	face	
s.x̌əy(ʔ)ús	head	
x̌áʔ.x̌əlus	raccoon (lit. 'little marked face')	
qəlúbus	gray hair	
t(ə)x̌ʷús^əd	drag it	LG.

545

x̌(ə)k̓ʷúsᵊd	cover it	EK.
ʔudxʷ.c̓ágʷusᵊb	He washed his (own) face.	LG.
dxʷ.(h)áʔɬus	white face	EK.
dxʷ.ɬíc̓usᵊb	cut hair	LG.
ʔəxʷ.páq̓ʷus	face blackened by smoke	LL., EK.
dxʷ.qʷq̓ʷús	white face	
xʷ.qʷq̓ʷús	bluff of clay or sand (not rock)	LL., EK.
dxʷ.sáx̌usᵊb	shave (lit. 'scrape face')	
ʔudxʷ.túʔustubuɬ	(They) spit in our faces.	LL.

-us-ači?

xʷ.tabúsači?	Skagit	palm of hand
xʷ.ʔəcúsači?	Snoh.	palm of hand

-us-alikʷ

kʷədúsàlikʷ	drive team, buggy, car	LG.

Cf. qʷ(a)ɬ(a)

dxʷ.x̌ác̓usalikʷ	pull the blinds/shades	LG.

-us-alps

kʷədùsálps	lead an animal	LG.

Cf. qʷ(a)ɬ(a)

-u(s)-šəd

xʷ.tabú(s)šəd	Skagit	sole of foot
xʷ.ʔəcú(s)šəd	Snoh.	sole of foot

w

The sound represented by this letter is very similar to that of *w* in English spelling. [voiced glide to higher back position]

1. s.wádəbš   the people east of the mountains; Warm Springs Reservation

2. wa(h)i

       ʔuwáhi čəd   I couldn't help it.   LL.
                                I feel bad about it.   LL.

       ƛuwáhi tə s.čáčasčəɫ ƛu.jàƛˀb   LL.
       Our child made a mistake unintentionally.

3. ʔu.wáq̓ʷsˀb   lightning   ESi.

     Cf. qácacut 'sparking' (There is no word for lightning as such.)   LL.

       ʔalčulí.ləx̌ tə x̌ʷíqʷədiʔ   lightning   LG.

4. wáq̓waq̓   an unidentified kind of small frog   ML.

       wáw̓q̓waq̓   baby frog of this kind   ML.

     Cf. s.wəq̓íq̓, wəlís

5. wášətəb   Washington

6. s.wátix̌ʷtəd   land, world, place

     Cf. s.watíx̌ʷtəd

       ləlíʔ swàtix̌ʷtəd   strange land

       ʔílax̌əd ʔə tiʔəʔ swàtix̌ʷtəd   MS.
       the ends of the earth

       qə́ɫcutəxʷ, qə́ɫcutəxʷ   Wake up! Wake up!
       gʷə́dil, gʷə́dil   Get up! Get up!
       hágʷəxʷ tu.jàx̌ tə swátix̌ʷtəd   For a long time this world is moving (i.e., people have been up and about for a long time). JC.

s.tə́čas s.dà? ?ə ti?ə? swàtixʷtəd   MS.
Stə́čas is the name of the place.

   reduplication

   swáẃtixʷtəd   little land   LL.

   swáẃwaẃtixʷtəd   lots, plots   LL., LG.

   swátwatixʷtəd   nations   LG.

s.watíxʷtəd   all manner of plants, the entire plant kingdom   LG.

   Cf. s.wátixʷtəd

   ?u.?ígʷəł čəd ?al ti?ə? swatìxʷtəd   DM.
   I was climbing a tree.

      Cf. cqʷuł

   s.tábał swatìxʷtəd   What kind of growing thing/tree is that? DM.

      Cf. s.tábac

   reduplication

   swatwatíxʷtəd   trees   DM.

   swáẃtixʷtəd   small shrubs   LG.

   swàẃwaẃtíxʷtəd   middle sized growth   LG.

      Cf. s.λ́áx̌ʷdup

(1) ?əbíl xʷi? kʷi ł(u)səs.túkʷləp til čələp gʷə.?ə́ydúp
?ə kʷi swàẃtixʷtəd. (2) s.táb ti?ił swàẃtixʷtəd. (3)
s.táb kʷi gʷəds.dà?əd. (4) xʷí? kʷi gʷədsəs.(h)áydxʷ
s.tàb ti?ił swàẃtixʷtəd ?al ti s.ləx̌íl. (5) gʷəl
b(ə)as.cútᵊb čəł ?ə ti?ił lùλluλ. (6) swáẃtixʷtəd gʷəl
?á ?al ti s.wàtixʷtəd. (7) s.táb kʷi λəsu.huys (h)əlgʷə?.
(8) λələłə́čiləxʷ ti s. łàx̌il gʷəl łu?íb.?ibəšəxʷ (h)əlgʷə?.
(9) λu.?íbəš ?u; ?u.saq̓ʷ ?u. (10) xʷí? kʷi gʷàt

ʔəs.(h)àydxʷ. (11) ʔu.(ʔə)x̌íx̌əd (h)əlgʷəʔ. (12)
ʔəs.láb^ədxʷ ti bə́kʷ s.tàb, kʷi łəsəs.yàyus ʔə tiʔił
t̓àqaʔəc, gʷə́dbixʷəc, bə̀kʷ s.tab. (13) ʔu.lábab^əd
(h)əlgʷəʔ. (14) tùx̌ʷ łəsəxʷəs.(h)áydxʷs (h)əlgʷəʔ,
"ʔí; háʔł kʷi səs.yàyus ʔə kʷi t̓àqaʔəc tiʔił. (15)
łu.x̌áx̌ʷ^ədxʷ kʷi haʔł s.ʔə̀ł^əd."

(16) ʔəbíl̓ čəxʷ c̓ac̓as čəxʷə xʷíʔ lə.tùkʷ ʔal kʷi
səs.łáx̌ils gʷə.sáxʷ^əbtub čəxʷ. (17) s.tə́kʷəb. (18)
ʔəbíl̓ čəxʷ ʔu.kʷàtač ʔal kʷi s.tə́kʷəb, ʔəbíl̓ ʔəs.ʔátəbəd,
ʔəs.bə́č tiʔił s.tə́kʷəb gʷəl gʷə.sáq̓ʷtubicid.

(1) If you (folks) are not at home, you be found [and
taken] by the swaw̓tixʷtəd. (2) What are the swaw̓tixʷtəd.
(3) What can I call them? (4) To this day I don't know
what the swaw̓tixʷtəd are. (5) But the elders told us
(6) [that] the swaw̓tixʷtəd are on this earth. (7) What
deeds do they perform? (8) When night comes, they travel all over. (9) Do they walk or do they fly? (10) No
one knows. (11) What do they do [and how]? (12) They
see to everything, the salalberry bush, the blackberry
vines, everything. (13) They look them over (14) so
they may know, "Yes, that salalberry bush is working
well. (15) It will grow good food."

(16) If you are a child, and you are not home at
night, you might be kidnapped. (17) A log. (18) Perhaps
you climb on a log, even a dead log lying [on the ground],
it might fly off with you.

1.	s.wátu	woman's name, MS.'s mother's mother
2.	wáwəxʷ	join in eating. The food is set on the table and people pick out what they want as breaking off pieces of meat or taking handfuls of pop-corn, etc.

See under ʔəł-.

→		
3.	wáwłqayuʔ	very tired (This is a 'big' word.) LL.

549

Cf. xʷákʷil, q̓ʷə́ɫˀb   tired

yúbubil   (body) is tired out, doesn't feel well LG.

k̓t̓íl   grow tired, become impatient

1. s.wáxʷəbš   marmot/woodchuck/groundhog   LG., LL.

2. s.wáxʷiʔɫ   litter of whelp wolves (still with mother)

    Cf. -iʔɫ, s.tiqáyuʔ

3. way   adverb 'finally'

    ƛu.gʷádil gʷəl bə.ʔíšil dxʷ.q̓íxʷ. wàyəxʷ gʷəl
    lúʔucut   LG.

    They leap (out of the water) and swim upstream and
    finally they spawn.

4. -waʔs   lexical suffix

    ʔay̓wáʔs   change

    ʔay̓wáʔsaličaʔ(ʔ)b   change clothes   LG.

    ʔay̓wáʔsuličaʔ(ʔ)b   change clothes   DM.

    (See also -alwáʔs.)

5. s.wədáʔx̌   mountain blueberry   MC., EK., ESi.

6. s.wədəbš   Swinomish

    ʔə(s)swə́dəbš tiʔiɫ dˀs.ɫáɫlil   DM.
    I live in Swinomish.

7. s.wəlád   promise

tu.hùyut^əb ʔə tiʔəʔ <u>swəlád</u> tiʔəʔ ʔaciɫtalbix^w   MS.

A promise was made to the people.

1.   wələ́x̌^w   SPS   strong   JC.

   Cf. q^wiq̓^w   NPS   strong

   -il

       <u>wələ́x̌^wil</u>   become strong   DM.

2.   wəlís   unidentified kind of small frog   LG.

   Cf. wáq̓waq̓   frog   ML.

       s.wəq̓íq̓   frog   ESi.

       x^w.q̓əltəd ʔə <u>wəlìs</u>   lichen ('diaper of frog')   MC.

3.   s.wəlítùb   a man's name, DM.'s father-in-law

4.   wəlíʔ   appear, be visible

   See under <u>šuɫ</u>.   Contrast <u>čal</u>- 'obstruct the view'.

   root

       ləwəlíʔəx^w tə ɫùk^wəɫ   The sun appeared.   LG.

       ləwəliʔəx^w tə s.ɫuk^wàlb   The moon appeared.   LG.

       x^wiʔəx^w g^w(ə)adsəswəlíʔ g^wə.ƛalš tə s.ƛalabəc   EC.
       You cannot see (him) when the garment is put on.

   -il-s

       x^wiʔəx^w g^wəsəs<u>wəlí(ʔ)</u>is   He was not visible.   EC.

   -yi-

       <u>wəlíʔyid</u>   Show it to him.   LG.

reduplication

    wə́ləlíʔil   appear from time to time   ML.

    ʔáhəxʷ ʔal tiʔił čaʔkʷ, qə́l.qəladiʔ kʷi ł(u)adsuwə́ləliʔil MC.

    There down on the snags (and driftwood) you [Mink] will appear now and then.

1. s.wəlús   young man of noble parentage   EC., LG.

    (Apparently this word does not occur in Snohomish.)

2.   wə́q̓əb Snoh.   box, chest

      Cf. wəq̓əb SPS, ƛúiqs Skagit

        wíwq̓əb   little box   LL.

        wíwiwq̓əb   little boxes   LL.

3. dxʷ.wə́qʷłali   knife sheath

4. wəq̓ʷús   an unidentified 'diver', a <u>buʔqʷ</u>   MS.

5. s.wəwáʔ   cougar   EK., LL., ESi.

      s.wə́wəʔ   cougar   JC.

      swəw̓wáʔ   little cougar   EK.

6. -wič   lexical suffix   'back (of body)'

    Cf. -ič

      ʔudxʷ.ləxʷ<u>wíč</u>c   He stabbed me in the back.   LG.

      s.kəw<u>íč</u> NPS   humpback

      x̌álw<u>ič</u> s.q̓əbyàʔ   striped skunk   EK.

1. s.wíhič   another name for q^wə́ɫtəd, a medium sized sawbill, a buʔq^w   LL.

2. wíəx̌^w   SPS   lost   JC.

   Cf. x̌^wiɫ   NPS   lost

   -bi-t

      wíəx^wbidəx^w čəd tiʔiɫ tə dsu.ʔá   JC.
      I lost it [where] my place is.

3. wíliq̓^w(i)   ask a question

   root

      x^wiʔ k^w(i) adswíliq̓^w   Don't ask!   JC.

   -it

      ʔuwíliq̓^wid čəd   I asked him.   LG.

      wíliq̓^wid həlg^wəʔ ciʔəʔ ʔalš   They asked (their) sister.

      wíliq̓^wit^əbəx^w   He was asked.   EK.

   -tx^w

      wíliq̓^wtx^wəx^w (h)əlg^wəʔ   EK.
      They asked (for her to be their son's bride).

4. -wiɫ ~ -wil-   variant of -g^wiɫ, *q.v.*

5. səs.wíx̌ab   Mrs. Lamont's Indian name. This was presented to her in the proper, formal Indian way. It was given to her by an uncle who got it from the tiyúɫbax̌ power that inhabits the bottom of the Sound.

6. wíwsu   children   EK., LG.

   (-su 'young')

   Cf. čáčas   child

Cf. s.táwix^wə?ɬ   children   EC.

    s.táwig^wəɬ   children   LG.

1.   wiyáx̌(ə)čtəd   man's name, LG.'s mother's mother's sister's younger son

2.   wí?-   Skagit   announce in a loud voice

     Cf. q^wí?ad   Snoh.   announce in a loud voice

     See under cut.

       wí?əd   holler

          x^wi? g^w(ə)adswí?əd   Don't holler!

      wí?aac   hello

          x^wí? k^w(i) adswí?aac^əbš   Don't telephone me.

          ?uwí?aacəx^w ti?ə? bàds ?i cə s.k̓^wùys
          He called his father and his mother.

          ?áh ?u k^wi ?uwí?aac čəx^w ?əs.ləqálbut
          Is there someone you call who would understand?

3.   s.wúq^wad   loon, a bu?q^w   LL., ESi., LG.

     s.wúq^wa   loon   DM., MS.

     (1) ?əs.?əx̌íd k^wi s.ləli? ?ə tə x̌^wətís dx^w?al swùq^wa.

     (2) bì?bad ti?ə? x̌^wətís. (3) g^wəl ti?ə? swúq^wa g^wəl diɬ hík^wbid dx^w?al ti?ə? x̌^wətís. (4) ?iɬ.hík^w. (5) g^wəl ti?ə? x̌^wù?x̌^way? g^wəl (hə)la?b bì?bad. (6) x̌əɬ ti di.d(ə)čák^{wə}bix^w ti?i?ə? di?ə?.

     (1) What is the difference between a silver diver and a loon?

     (2) A silver diver is small. (3) A loon is bigger

554

than a silver diver. (4) It is bigger. (5) And the little diver is really small. (6) It is as though they were of a different class.

In the old stories Loon and x̌əsáwq̓ are brothers and their sister is Little Diver.

1. wúx̌təd   sweat house

x̌ʷ

The sound of this letter is similar to that of the English combination *wh* as in *which* or *when*. The English sound, however, is a bit softer (and harder to hear) because the mouth is open a little wider for it than for x̌ʷ. [voiceless, labialized velar fricative]

1. x̌ʷ-   derivational prefix
                                 See Hoard/Hess, pp. 53ff.

x̌ʷbá(ʔ)wiɬ   width of a canoe   x̌ʷ(h)údad   ashes

x̌ʷcqʷúɬ   day   LG.   x̌ʷlábali   bottle

x̌ʷčiɬqs   an unidentified kind   x̌ʷɬídič   bow string   MS.
             of a very large oyster
                              ML.   x̌ʷláɫbuɫəd ŠƮ̓Š window   JC.

x̌ʷčupč   tail   LG.   x̌ʷšəbtád   netting   MS.

2. x̌ʷa

ʔəsx̌ʷáacəb čəd   They want my company.

3. x̌ʷac(a)

    -at

x̌ʷácad   take something off it to lighten it   LG.

x̌ʷácatəb   carry (rather than drag) a canoe   LL.

   x̌ʷácatəbəx̌ʷ tiʔəʔ s.dəx̌ʷiɬ   ML.
   They carried the hunting canoe.

4. x̌ʷač   stop raining   (VH. gives x̌ʷač.)

    See under qə́lʔb.   Contrast ɬə́ltʔb.

    ʔux̌ʷáč(əx̌ʷ)   It stopped raining.

5. x̌ʷah   forbid

    Compare x̌aʔx̌aʔ, x̌ʷiʔ.   Contrast x̌aƛ 'want'.

556

-c

tuxʷáac čəd — I didn't permit him to. — LG.

ʔəsxʷáac cə čəgʷàs gʷə.ʔùx̌ʷəs dxʷ.čád — LG.
He doesn't want (his) wife to go anywhere.

ʔəsxʷáac tə s.gʷədgʷatədčəɬ — LG.
She's stingy with our language.

ʔəsxʷáacᵊbš tə ds.čistxʷ — LG.
My husband doesn't want me to do things.

ʔuxʷáacbicid čəd — I don't want you to. — EK.

tuxʷáac čəd ʔə kʷi gʷəs.ʔùx̌ʷs — LG.
I didn't permit him to go.

tuxʷáac čəd gʷəl x̌ʷuɬ ʔiɬ.ʔùx̌ʷ — EK.
I told him not to go but still he went.

-i(1)-s

xʷáhis — deny/deprive of something — LL.

-yi-

ʔəsxʷáyid čəd — I don't want him to take it. — LG.
I didn't give it (to someone). — EK.

ʔəsxʷáyic ti ʔiɬ — He doesn't want me to take it. — LG.
He doesn't want me to have it. — EK.

ʔəsxʷáyic ʔə kʷi gʷədsčulalc ʔə kʷi xʷəltəbàlc — LG.
He doesn't want me to lend the rifle.

ʔuxʷáyitubuɬəxʷ — He doesn't want us to take it. — LG.
He won't let us have it. — LL.

xʷíʔ. tuxʷáyid čəd — LG.
No. I didn't want him to take it.

1. xʷáj(a) *

See under gʷəlald.

---

* Should be x̌ʷáj(a) in all examples preceding, including and following this entry.

ʔux̌ʷájatᵊb   Several families were slaughtered.   LL.

x̌ʷájad   wipe out a village, annihilate the
                    whole populace   MS.

1.   x̌ʷák̓ʷᵊb   smell of something burning (usually feathers)

     See under sub(u).

2.   x̌ʷak̓ʷil   tired

     See under wáwɫqayuʔ.

        ʔəsx̌ʷák̓ʷil   He is tired.

        ʔəsx̌ʷák̓ʷiləxʷ čəd   I'm tired.

        dáyʔəxʷ čəd ʔəsx̌ʷàk̓ʷil   I'm very tired.

        pùtəxʷ čəd ʔəsx̌ʷák̓ʷil   Same gloss: I'm very tired.

        ʔəsx̌ʷák̓ʷil čəd   LG.
        I'm a little tired / I'm not quite myself.

        ʔəsx̌ʷák̓ʷil čəd ʔə ti ds.ʔîbəš   EK.
        I'm tired of walking.

     -il-bi-t-

        ʔəsx̌ʷák̓ʷilbidəxʷ čəd   LL.
        I'm tired of it (from my own lack of energy, enthusiasm, etc.)

     -i(1)-s

        ʔəsx̌ʷák̓ʷisəxʷ čəd   LL.
        I'm tired of it (because it is dull or fatiguing).

     -i(1)-s-b

        x̌ʷák̓ʷisᵊbəxʷ čəd ʔə tiʔiɫ siʔàb   ES.
        That gentleman is tired of me.

-i(1)-s-bi-t-

ʔəsx̌ʷák̓ʷisbitubuɫəd čəd   I'm tired of you folks.   LL.

-i(1)-s-bi-t-b

ʔəsx̌ʷák̓ʷisbitᵊbəxʷ čəd ʔə tiʔəʔ ɫədsu.jəlàx̌ad   LL.
They are tired of me, my visits.

rejected: *x̌ʷák̓ʷild

1.   x̌ʷáq̓ʷ   Mount Rainier (lit. '(sky) wiper')

See under x̌ʷís(i), t̓íx̌ʷ(i).

2.   x̌ʷas-   See under sub(u).

Cf. sʔəx̌ʷáʔ   urinate (male)

tiwáʔ   urinate (female)

p̓ə́c̓   defecate

-il

ʔux̌ʷásil   wet one's clothes   LL.

-b

x̌ʷásᵊb   the smell of urine   LG.

rejected: *d(x̌ʷ)x̌ʷásᵊb

lexical

d(x̌ʷ)x̌ʷásᵊbap   (Your) bottom smells.

3. s.x̌ʷáyʔs SPS   hat

Cf. šiqʷ NPS   hat, -aliqʷ

reduplication

sx̌ʷáʔx̌ʷiʔs   little hat   ESi.

1. x^wcáb   empty

    See under x^wəc.

2. x^wəb   throw, discard; throw someone down

    See under pus(u).   Cf. paḱ(a), ʔix̌^w(i)

    -t

        x^wə́b^əd   throw it (away)   LL., DM.
                        throw him down (must be a person
                                  as in wrestling)   LG.

        x^wəbt^əbáx^w got thrown now   LL.

        x^wə́bt^əb   He got thrown down.   LG.

    -dx^w

        ʔux^wə́b^ədx^w He threw it without intending to. LL.

    reduplication

        x^wəbəbús^əb   LG.

        He turned his face around and didn't listen.
        That is "sort of like jálalqùs^əb".   LG.

    rejected: *ʔəsx^wə́b čəd   LG.

3. x^wəc   take (clothing) off

    Cf. łag^wiča(ʔ)b   take clothing off
    (LL. says that some would use x^wəc to mean unplug something
    (i.e. ʔúq̓^w(u)) but such usage he considers to be careless
    or sloppy.)

    -t

        x^wə́c^əd   take (clothing) off   LL., LG.

    -ab

        x^wcáb   empty

560

lexical

ʔəsx̣ʷcáliqʷ	have hat off	LL.
x̣ʷəcdáliɫᵊd	fast (lit. 'take off eating')	LG.

Cf. ƛ̓əlá?ɫdəlb 'stop eating', x̣ʷi?əɫdálb 'dieting, fasting'

1. x̣ʷəlk̓ʷ wrap around; intoxicated

See under ɫid(i).

root

sx̣ʷə́lk̓ʷ	drunk	LG.
ʔəsx̣ʷə́lk̓ʷ	is drunk	LG.
ləx̣ʷə́lk̓ʷ	is getting drunk	LG.
ləsx̣ʷə́lk̓ʷ	is going along drunk	LG.

-t

ʔux̣ʷə́lk̓ʷᵊd čəd ʔə s.qəlìkʷ cə d.bədà?		LG.

I wrapped my daughter in a blanket.

x̣ʷə́lᵊk̓ʷᵊd	wrap it up	LG.

-tx̣ʷ

ʔəsx̣ʷə́lk̓ʷtx̣ʷ	wrapped around with a blanket	LL.

Cf. x̌ʷúq̓ʷᵊdisᵊb, ƛ̓i.ƛ̓pabacᵊb

lexical

sx̣ʷə̀lk̓ʷqíd	kerchief	EK.
ʔəsx̣ʷə̀lk̓ʷqíd	crazy in the head	EK.

reduplication

ʔux̣ʷíx̣ʷəl̓k̓ʷawis čəd		LL.

I was playing goofy to sort of entertain.

1. xʷə́ltəb   Caucasian

    Cf. pástəd

      x̲ʷə̀ltəbálc   gun

        Cf. ƛ́iƛk̉ʷači?   revolver

           tətlákʷɫ   a single shot gun

           didč̉á?qs   single barrel gun

           sáli?qs   double barrel gun

2. xʷəɫ   See under xʷi?-əɫ.

3. xʷəƛ̉   break rigid object in two

    See under ƛič̉(i).

    Cf. t̉əq̉ʷ(u)   snap flexible object (e.g., break string/rope)

      čəx̌   crack, split (e.g., break a plate); half

      jix̌(i)   collapse, break off and fall; motor break down, be out of order

      pəqʷ(u)   break or cut a piece off (leaving a larger portion)

    root

      ?ux̲ʷə́ƛ̉ tə d.jədìs   I broke my tooth.   EK.

      ?u.ǰíq̉id ɫu.xʷí?əs lə̲x̲ʷə̀ƛ̉ ?ə kʷi qi?.qiyə̀?

      Soak it so it will not break easily.

    lexical

      x̲ʷƛ̉úlgʷiɫ   broken rib   EK., LL.

      dxʷx̲ʷə̉ƛgʷás   half (a sack)   EK.

      ?ux̲ʷƛ̉ápsəbᵊd   broke his neck   LL.

        Cf. ?u.pqʷúsᵊd   decapitated him   LL.

     rejected: *ud(xʷ)xʷƛ̉ápsəbᵊd   LL.

562

1. xʷəš   throw, broadcast, distribute goods

    See under pus(u).

    -t

      xʷə́šʷᵊd   throw it, broadcast it, give it away

    lexical

      xʷšálikʷ   seeding by hand; potlatching

        Contrast pəd.

2. s.xʷə́t   thrush, salmonberry bird

3. s.xʷə́t̓   See under xʷít̓- ~ xʷt̓-.

4. s.xʷəyúq̓ʷ Snoh.   Basket Ogress   ML.

    Cf. ʔáx̌ʷədus 'Basket Ogress', ɬx̌ʷúbx̌ 'younger sister of Basket Ogress'

5. xʷəʔáʔxʷəʔ   light weight; opposite of x̌əb.

      ʔiɬxʷəʔáʔxʷəʔ   lighter

        ʔiɬxʷəʔáʔxʷəʔ tiʔəʔ q̓ilbid dxʷʔal tiʔiɬ q̓ilbid   LG.
        This canoe is lighter than that canoe.

6. xʷíč̓ič̓ab   balance, teeter, stagger

      Cf. t̓álx̌   lose balance backwards but not quite fall

        ɬík̓ʷšəd   stumble

        ləxʷíč̓ič̓ab ti lə.ʔùx̌ʷ   He is staggering as he goes along.

7. xʷíč̓ib   mating cry of deer and elk

      pədxʷíč̓ib   time of elk mating cry, twelfth moon from the
                          one in December

1. xʷíduɬ   melancholy

     Cf. xəɬx̌əč

         dáyʔəxʷ čəd ʔəsx̲ʷíduɬ   I feel very melancholy.   EK.

2. s.xʷíhič   a medium sized sawbill, a buʔqʷ. It is also
                     designated as qʷə́ɬtəd.   DM.

3. xʷikʷ(i)   scrape, rub hard

     See under šic(i).

       -it

           x̲ʷíkʷid   Scrape it. Rub it. Rub it hard.   LL.

           ʔux̲ʷíkʷitubuɬ   He rubbed us (down).   LL.

           ʔux̲ʷíkʷicut tiʔiɬ s.qʷəbàyʔ ʔal tiʔiɬ šəgʷɬ   LL.
           The dog is rubbing himself against the door.

           x̲ʷíkʷicut   rub self to toughen body   LG.

       lexical

           ʔux̲ʷíkʷəgʷəs   two things (e.g., canoes) happen to
                       rub together   LL.

4. xʷis(i)   brush off (e.g., rug, tablecloth)

     Cf. t̓ixʷ(i), pixʷ(i), xʷaq̓ʷ, ʔix̌ʷ(icut), ʔiq̓ʷ(i) ~ ʔik̓ʷ(i), pak̓(a)

       -it

           x̲ʷísid   brush it off (e.g., rug, tablecloth). (Not to
                     be used for brushing off clothes that you have
                     on. Rather use t̓ixʷ(i).)

           ʔux̲ʷísicut tə s.qʷəbàyʔ   The dog shook himself off.   LG.

       cisx̲ʷísaɬ   the name of LG.'s mother's mother. It derives
                   from the way she danced, sort of making motions
                   as if brushing off her lap as she danced. (Her
                   other name was cis.yúyud.) LG. was named
                   cisx̲ʷísaɬ after her.

1. xʷít- ~ xʷt́-   fall/drop from a height

 Compare:

 1. píxʷil   2. bə́č/łáq̓(a)   3. dxʷ.bílcəp

         q̓ʷát(a)   k̓ʷəq

 4. č̓əxʷtᵊdábut   5. t̓əbáʔ   6. jáq̓(a)

          gʷál   x̌íʌəpəd

          x̌t̓áb

 7. xʷíc̓ic̓ab   8. təč

   t̓álx̌

   łík̓ʷšəd

root (weak grade)

  <u>sxʷət̓</u>   waterfall   LL.

   Cf. s.təkʷáb   waterfall

    q̓xʷáʔłdəł   above a waterfall

    gʷədáʔłdəł   below a waterfall

-il

  ʔuxʷít̓il tə biác dxʷʔal tə hùd   The meat fell into the fire.   LG.

  dxʷʔal tə húd tə <u>sxʷít̓il</u> ʔə tə biàc   LG.
  Into the fire fell the meat.

  <u>xʷít̓ilə</u>xʷ tə łùkʷəł   sun setting   EK.

  ʔəs.x̌ə́c čəd gʷəx<u>ʷít̓il</u>əd   I'm afraid I'll fall.   EK.

  ʔux<u>ʷít̓il</u> čəd   I fell (from a high place).   EK.

  ʔəs.x̌ə́c čəd gʷəx<u>ʷít̓il</u>əxʷ čəxʷà gʷə.ləčdùbš   LL.
  I'm afraid you'll fall and crush me.

-il-t

  <u>xʷít̓il</u>d   Drop it! Knock it down!   LL.

x^wíti̧ld (Equivalent to píx^wild.)   LG.
Drop it (down to me because I can't reach it).

ʔux^wíti̧ld čəd   I knocked it down (to the ground).   LL.

ʔux^wíti̧lt^əb čəd   They lowered me.   LL.

-il-dx^w

ʔux^wíti̧ldx^w čəd   I happened to drop it.   LL.

ʔux^wíti̧ldub (ʔə ti̧ʔiɫ) tə biàc dx^wʔal tə hùd   LG.
He accidentally dropped the meat into the fire.

ʔəs.x̌ə́c čəd g^wəx^wíti̧ldubšəx^w   LL.
I'm afraid you'll cause me to fall (if you don't
stop shaking the limb.)

ʔəs.x̌ə́c čəd g^wəx^wíti̧ldubicidəd   LG.
I'm afraid I'll cause you to fall.

lexical

ʔux^wíti̧lič čəd ʔə tə yi̧q̓us   The cedar-root basket fell on me. LG.

ʔux^wíti̧lič čəd ʔə tə x^w.làbəli   The bottle fell on me.   LG.

reduplication

x^wíx^witi̧l   small item(s) fall(s)   LL.

x^wítx^witi̧l   large items fall   LL.

rejected:

*ʔux^wít̓ čəd, *ʔud(x^w)x^wít̓^əb, *x^wíti(l)s

-ag^w-il

cút^əbəx^w čəd g^wəx^wt̓ag^wiləd   ML.
I was told to come down (at once)!

-ag^w-i(l)s

ʔux^wt̓ág^wis   He climbed down after it.   LG.

-agʷ-il-txʷ

  xʷʔtágʷiltub   Bring him down.

-ad

  ʔuxʷʔtád čəd   I took it down (from under the roof).   LL.

1.   xʷíʔ   no, not

  Compare x̌áʔx̌aʔ, xʷah.   Contrast ʔi 'yes'.

  root

    ʔəxʷ.cútəb čəd xʷíʔ   I think not.   LL.

      Cf. ʔəs.qʷácdxʷ čəd 'I doubt it.'

    ʔəxʷ.cútəb čəd ƛub xʷíʔ kʷi gʷ(ə)ads.ʔə́ƛ̓   HD.
    I think it would be better for you not to come.

    ʔiɬ.(h)áʔɬ dxʷʔal kʷi gʷəsxʷíʔs   LG.
    It is better than nothing.

    ʔiɬ.(h)áʔɬ tulʔal kʷi xʷiʔ   Same gloss: It is better than nothing. EK.

    xʷíʔ gʷə(l) ləxʷíʔ   LG.
    None and still none. (This was said while unsuccessfully digging for clams.)

    xʷíʔ kʷi gʷát   No one.   EC., JC.

     xʷíʔ gʷə.gʷát   Same gloss: No one. LG.

     xʷíʔ kʷi gʷát gʷ(ə)u.kʷə́d(d)xʷ tiʔəʔ cədiɬ EC.
     No one got this.

    xʷíʔ kʷ(i) ads.wíliq̓ʷ Don't ask. JC.

    xʷíʔ kʷ(i) ads.ʔə́ƛ̓ Don't come. EK.

    xʷíʔ kʷ(i) ads.láqil Don't be late. EK.

    xʷíʔ kʷ(i) ads.hùydxʷ tiʔíɬ Skagit Don't eat that! LG.

xʷíʔ kʷ(i) ads.húydubš   Skagit   Don't eat me!   LG.

xʷíʔ kʷi sgʷə.jákʷədləp   Don't you folks move.   LL.

xʷíʔ kʷi gʷ(ə)ads.ʔùx̌ʷ   Don't go.   LG.

xʷíʔ kʷi gʷ(ə)ads.x̌ə́ɬ   You will not get sick.   LG.

xʷiʔ gʷədsəs.(h)áydxʷ   I don't know.

　xʷíʔ gʷədsəs.(h)áydxʷ gʷəs.tàbəs kʷi dəxʷ.(ʔ)às   LG.
　I don't know what he is there for.

　xʷíʔ gʷədsəs.(h)áydxʷ pə(d).tàb kʷi gʷ(ə)ads.ʔùx̌ʷ   LG.
　I don't know when you will go.

xʷíʔ gʷəd.yíq̓us   I don't have a basket.   LG.

xʷíʔ gʷəd.tálə   I don't have (any) money.   DM.

xʷíʔ gʷəds.qʷəbàyʔ   I don't have a dog.   LG.

xʷíʔəxʷ gʷ(ə)as.dékʷ   Nothing is inside now.   LG.

xʷíʔ gʷəsu.léqs   He doesn't hear.   LG.

xʷíʔ gʷəds.bə́ɬ   I didn't get full.   LG.

xʷíʔ gʷəƛ̓su.ʔúsils   It doesn't dive.   DM.

xʷíʔ gʷəƛ̓su.ƛ̓íčibs   It does not swim.   DM.

xʷíʔ gʷətus.ʔábyitᵊbs ʔə tiʔəʔ ʔaciɬtalbixʷ tiʔəʔ
Governor Stevens   MS.
The Indians did not give it to Governor Stevens.

gʷəl xʷíʔəxʷ tiʔiɬ s.ƛ̓àlabəc   EC.
But there was no garment.

xʷíʔəxʷ tiʔəʔ diʔəʔ s.tùbš   There was no man.   EC.

bə.sáx̌əd tiʔəʔ j̓əsəds dxʷʔal kʷi gʷəsxʷíʔs kʷi
gʷəsəsìʔ.sx̌ʷicuts ʔal ti sə.gʷəčiss tiʔiɬ s.x̌ʷədìʔ
ʔi tiʔiɬ p̓í.p̓uayʔ liɬ.ʔílgʷiɬ
He scraped his legs so that he wouldn't make even a little
noise as he waded in the shallows after bullhead and little
flounder along the shore.   ML.

Same construction with modal particles

xʷíʔ kʷədáʔ kʷi gʷəs.qə̀lᵊbs   Maybe it won't rain.   LG.

xʷíʔ kʷədáʔ gʷ(ə)ads.ʔə̀ƛ   Maybe you will not come.   LG.

xʷíʔ hàwəʔ gʷ(ə)ads.ʔùx̌ʷ   Oh! You didn't go!   LG.

xʷíʔ xʷuʔᵊləʔ gʷəds.ʔùx̌ʷdubut   It is doubtful that I can go. LL.

Same construction with adverbs

xʷíʔ kʷ(i) ads.x̌ʷùləx̌ʷ lìlusbic   LL.
Don't just turn (remove) your face away from me.

xʷíʔ ʔu kʷi ƛ(u)ads.həláʔb ʔu.x̌ə̀łqìd   LL.
You don't get much of a headache, do you?

xʷiʔ lə-   'exclude; be not a member of; exclude from participation
        in a particular act or state'

xʷíʔ lə.dìł   He is not the one.   ML.

xʷíʔ lə.q̓ílbid   It is not a canoe.   DM.

xʷíʔ lə.ʔəʔútx̌s   It is not a Nootka type canoe.   DM.

łúp. xʷíʔ lə.łúb   (I said) morning; not soup.   LL.

xʷíʔ ləs.tíləqəb, čtílqʷəb   MS.
It is not (pronounced) stiləqəb (but rather) čtílqʷəb.

xʷíʔ lə.qá   It is not much.   LG.

xʷíʔəxʷ lə.qá ti d.tàlə   I don't have much money.   DM.

xʷíʔ lə.lìl   almost (lit. 'not far')

    xʷíʔ lə.lìl gʷə.díłgʷasəs   They are almost alike.   EK.

    xʷíʔ lə.lìl čəda báliic ʔə gʷəds.ʔàbyicid ʔə kʷi tàlə   EK.
    I almost forgot to give you the money.

xʷíʔ-lə.háʔł   (You) no-goodnik!   ML.

xʷíʔ ləbə.lúƛ   They too are not very old.   ML.

xʷíʔ ləd.bád tiʔiɬ   He is not my father.   LG.

xʷíʔ ləds.gʷá?   It is not mine.   LG.

xʷíʔ čəxʷ ləds.yàya?   You are no friend of mine.   LG.

xʷíʔ čəd lə.ʔáciɬtalbixʷ   I'm not Indian.   LG.

xʷíʔ čəd lə.ʔə̀ɬᵊdíluɬ   I didn't come to eat.   LG.

xʷíʔ čəxʷ lə.lùƛ x̌ʷuƚáb ʔə ʔəcà.   LG.
You are not as old as I am.

xʷíʔ čəd lə.lùƛ x̌ʷuƚáb ʔə dəgʷì   LG.
I am not as old as you.

xʷíʔ čəd lə.x̌ʷuƚàb ʔə dəgʷì kʷi gʷəds.lùƛ   LG.
Same gloss: I am not as old as you. (lit. 'I am not like
         you, my age.')

xʷíʔ lə.dxʷʔal tiʔìɬ   Not that way! (direction)   LG.

   Cf. dxʷʔal tiʔə́?   This way!   LG.

xʷíʔ lə.dxʷʔal tə s.tùləkʷ kʷ(i) ads.təlàwil   LG.
Not toward the river may you run!

xʷíʔ čəd lə.tùƚdiʔə̀?   I'm not from here.   LG.

Same construction with modal particle

xʷíʔ čəxʷ sixʷ lə.bàkʷɬ   Don't get hurt still again!!   LG.

Same construction with modifiers

xʷíʔ lə.tíb s.ƛ̕əp   It is not too deep.   DM.

xʷíʔ lə.dídti dxʷ.dà?ᵊb   He is a shaman not to be taken lightly.
                                                LG.
xʷíʔ lə.(hə)láʔb s.ʔə̀ɬᵊd   It is not really food.   DM.

xʷíʔ lə.tíb híkʷ tiʔə? s.tə̀qxʷ   A beaver is not very big.   DM.

xʷíʔ lə.(hə)láʔb qà ti ds.ʔə̀ɬᵊd   LG.
I didn't really eat very much.

Same construction as a part of larger constructions

díɫ də(xʷ)xʷíʔs lə.búʔqʷ tiʔiɫ   DM.
That is why it is not a waterfowl.

ʔəs.čál tiʔiɫ də(xʷ)xʷíʔs lə.buʔqʷ tiʔiɫ s.bəq̓ʷá?   DM.
Why isn't a heron a [member of the class] waterfowl?

ʔəs.(ʔə)x̌íd kʷi sə(xʷ)xʷíʔs lə.x̌ʷuɫab ʔə tə s.ʔáx̌ʷuʔ
tiʔiɫ ƛ̓úx̌ʷƛ̓ux̌ʷ   JC.
Why isn't an oyster like a clam?

ʔəs.ʔəx̌íd kʷi də(xʷ)xʷíʔs ləs.ʔuládxʷ ciʔiɫ p̓uáy?
Why isn't a flounder a [member of the class] salmon?

ʔá ʔu kʷi xʷíʔ lə.q̓íč pùʔtəd   DM.
Is there any shirt that is not expensive?

ʔá ʔu kʷi xʷíʔ lə.q̓ìč ʔə tə puʔtəd   DM.
Is there any out of these shirts that is not expensive?

gʷə.kʷáxʷatubuɫəd čəd cut ləxʷíʔələp lə.bákʷɫ   LL.
I should help you folks so you will not get hurt.

    rejected:

    *xʷiʔ čəd lə.ʔùx̌ʷ   "It doubts itself as you say it." LL.

xʷiʔ-as

ɫuxʷíʔəs həlaʔb ʔə(s).sə́pil tiʔiɫ ṫiyùʔsəd   JC.
A smelt trap must not be real pliable.

ɫídid ʔə kʷi hà?ɫ ɫuxʷíʔəs bələ.pàx̌ʷ   JC.
Tie it so it will not spread apart again.

ʔu.ĵíq̓id ɫux̌ʷíʔəs lə.xʷə̀ƛ̓ ʔə kʷi qiʔ.qiyə́ʔ   JC.
Soak it so it will not break easily.

-t 'refuse'

t(u)asxʷíʔ²d c(i) ad.ʔíbac   ES.
Your grandniece refused him.

díɫəxʷ tudəxʷ.ɫyá?t°bs ?ə ti?ə? dxʷ.dà??b ?al ti?iɫ
tusx̱ʷì?°ds   ES.

That shaman shot a bone into her because she had refused him.

-txʷ   '(do) not cause'

x̱ʷí?txʷ lə.bàkʷɫ   Don't let him get hurt!   EK.

x̱ʷí?tubš ɫi lə.xʷìtil   Don't you folks cause me to fall! LL.

x̱ʷí?txʷ ɫi lə.sàxʷəbtub   LL.

Don't you folks let anyone kidnap him!

-il   'become non-existent'

x̱ʷí?il   gone, used up   EK.
                    euphemism for die   LL.

   Cf. bəkʷíl, ?átəbəd

bə̂kʷ ?ux̱ʷí?il   It's all gone.   JC.

x̱ʷí?iləxʷ ti?iɫ bə̂kʷ gʷìstal°b   JC.

There is no sand at all.

tùx̌ʷəxʷ k̓ʷidəládxʷəxʷ gʷəl ɫux̱ʷí?il   ES.

In just a few years, it (her eye) will be gone.

gə́lk̓°d ti?iɫ ?iɫ.šə̀q dxʷ?al dəxʷəsx̱ʷí?ils dxʷ?al ti?iɫ s.λ̓əps JC.

Entwine the top so that it disappears into the bottom.

-əɫ

?əsx̱ʷ(i?)ə́ɫ tàlə čəɫ   We are out of money.   VH.

?əsx̱ʷ(i?)ə́ɫ čəɫ tàlə   Same gloss: We are out of money. VH.

-əɫ-il

?ux̱ʷ(i?)əɫíl tàləčəɫ   Our money is gone.   VH.

lexical

x̱ʷì?əɫdálb čəd   I am dieting, fasting.   LG.

   Cf. xʷəcdáliɫ°d 'fast', λ̓əlá?ɫd°lb 'stop eating'

other derivation

    xʷíʔxʷiʔ   hunt, forage, gather food

      See under bək̓ʷ(u).

      Cf. pəjátuɬ   duck hunt, hunt along the shore

        qʷəláʔusᵊb   duck hunt (by using a blind)

        šáyil/ɬəx̌úb hunt in the forest

adəxʷuxʷíʔxʷiʔ tuɬ̓.hàkʷ   MS.
Where you hunted and fished from long ago.

ʔəbíɬ̓ čəxʷ ʔuxʷíʔxʷiʔ   When you go fishing.   JC.

dᵊs.x̌áƛ kʷi gʷədsxʷíʔxʷiʔ ʔə kʷi bù̓ʔqʷ   DM.
I want to hunt waterfowl.

ʔu.k̓ʷəɬdúb ʔə cə sù̓q̓ʷaʔ tə sxʷíʔxʷiʔs   LG.
(My) younger sister spilled (what she had) gathered,
i.e., berries or clams, etc.

  -bi-t

    ləxʷíʔxʷiʔbid čəd tə s.q̓ʷàlš   JC.
    I want to hunt waterfowl.

    ƛəcəxʷuxʷíʔxʷiʔbid kʷi ča̓ʔuʔ   JC.
    I use it to catch smelt.

  dxʷsxʷíʔxʷiʔ   a hunter, a food gatherer

    Cf. dxʷs.ɬəx̌úb/dxʷ(s).šáyil, dxʷs.ʔúbədì̓ʔ

1.   xʷíxʷəlàčəl   man's name, LG.'s husband's father (George).
                  The name is Chilliwack.

2.   xʷúpšəd   saw-whet owl   LL., DM., MS.

    Also called s.ƛ̓áƛak̓ʷ.

3.   xʷuxʷúbid   larynx

1. xʷuyub   sell

    Cf. tágʷ(š) 'buy', təxʷ 'buy'

    -i-t

        ʔuxʷúyubid čəd   I sold it to him.   LG.

        ʔəsxʷúyubic čəxʷ   You sold it to me.   EK.

        xʷúyubic ʔə kʷi cəlàc s.ʔáx̌ʷuʔ   Sell me five clams.   DM.

    -i-t-b

        xʷúyubitᵊb čəd   He sold it to me.   LG.

    -txʷ

        xʷúyubtxʷ   Sell it!   HD.

        ʔuxʷúyubtubš čəxʷ   You sold me.   EK.

    -txʷ-b

        tuxʷúyubtubəxʷ tiʔił ʔàlʔal   LG.
        That house is sold.

        ʔəxʷsxʷúyubtubᵊb   They want to sell it.   ES.

    -txʷ-yi-

        ʔuxʷúyubtxʷyid čəd ci d.ʔìbac   LG.
        I sold it for my granddaughter.

           Cf. ʔu.tágʷyic ʔə tə s.gəlgàlikʷ   LG.
              He bought knitting from me.

    lexical

        xʷùyubálʔtxʷ   store   LG.

        ƛúb čəł ʔu ƛa xʷuyubàlʔtxʷ   Shall we go to the store?   DM.

2. xʷuʔᵊləʔ   a model particle 'maybe, I guess so'

    See under jəł.   Cf. kʷədáʔ

after predicate head

ʔí. ʔá huʔxʷ xʷuʔəˀləʔ kʷi dtaʔ.təla, ʔəs.dəkʷ   ML.
Yes, there still, (I) guess, is my little bit
of money in it.

ʔu.gʷəlált̓əbəxʷ xʷuʔəˀləʔ ʔə tiʔəʔ s.bəq̓ʷaʔ   ML.
Maybe Heron beat her up.

tu.bát̓ət̓əbəxʷ xʷuʔəˀləʔ ʔə tiʔəʔ ʔacit̓talbixʷ   ML.
Perhaps the people treated her (shamanistically).

t̓u.qəlˀb xʷùʔəˀləʔ   Maybe it will rain.   LG.
                            I think it's going to rain.

lə.ʔíbəš ʔal ʔítut xʷuʔəˀləʔ   LG.
He's walking in a daydream so it would seem.

after first adverb

ƛúb čət xʷùʔəˀləʔ ʔu.q̓ʷúʔəˀd kʷi bəkʷ tìtčulbixʷ   ML.
Maybe we had better gather all the little animals.

cíck̓ʷ xʷuʔəˀləʔ (hə)láʔb ʔəs.x̌ə̀t tiʔit   LG.
He must be very sick.

initially

xʷuʔəˀləʔ čət gʷəs.šúbalihəxʷ   LL.
Maybe we'll be dead.

xʷuʔəˀləʔ čəd ʔu.ʔíx̌ʷədxʷ tit̓ tiʔit   LL.
I must have thrown it out.

xʷúʔəˀləʔ tuləcu.hùdud tiʔit q̓ʷt̓ayʔ   LG.
They must have burned the logs.

xʷúʔəˀləʔ haʔt gʷə.ʔəƛáhəxʷ   LG.
Maybe you should come.

xʷúʔəˀlə(ʔha)xʷ jət ʔu.t̓čil   I hope he comes.   LG.

     rejected: *xʷuʔəˀləxʷ čəd jət ʔu.t̓čil   LG.

xʷúʔᵊləʔ tus.xʷíʔ ʔə ciʔił tukiyàʔčəł   EK.

Suppose our grandmother weren't even around.

    Cf. tus.xʷíʔ ʔə ciʔił kiyàʔčəł xʷùʔᵊləʔ   EK.

       Same gloss: Suppose our grandmother weren't
            even around.

xʷuʔᵊləʔ sə.ʔibəš ʔal tiʔəʔ ʔil.gʷił ʔə tə x̌ʷəlč   ML.

He was probably walking along the beach of the Sound.

xʷúʔᵊləʔ ʔə kʷi (s).ʔàlalustubs   ML.

Maẏbe someone has done something to her.

xʷuʔᵊləʔ ʔal kʷi jixʷ tiʔił p̓ap̓ap̓ƛaƛ, ʔal jixʷ
tiʔəʔ x̌aʔx̌əlus   ML.

I guess first [came] the riffraff, first [came]
Raccoon.

x̌

The sound of this letter is a little like the sound made when gargling, it resembles the "French *r* ". [voiceless, uvular fricative]

1. s.x̌ác

    1. prick, stick

        Cf. cáq̓(a)

    2. inner fibers of dried fir bark (very fine and tiny, present only when dried out)

    Compare s.čəbíd.   Contrast s.ƚuáy?, s.lagʷac.

    lexical

    sx̌áx̌ajᵊdis   name of a creek in the Skagit valley. The name derives from the prickly growth along its banks. CB.

2. x̌ac

    ?u.x̌acx̌acᵊb   quarreling

    Cf. x̌aƛil

3. x̌ácbid   lunch (carried with one)   EK., JC.

4. x̌ac̓-   cover

    Cf. ləx̌ʷ-, pəd, x̌k̓ʷúcid (under x̌ək̓ʷ(u))

    Contrast q̓áx̌(a).

    lexical

    sx̌ác̓ič   covering   EK.

    ?əsx̌ác̓ič   cover, lid   EK.

    s.tábəxʷ kʷi ƚudsx̌ác̓ič   EK.
    What are you going to use for cover?

    x̌əc̓iȷ́álucid   a blanket for covering knees and legs while riding in a wagon or canoe   LL.
    See under s.qəlikʷ.

    x̌ác̓iȷᵊd tə tibu   Cover the table.   EK.

577

x̌áčičtᵊb	He got covered.	LG.
x̌áčijᵊb ʔə tə s.qʷəlìkʷ		LG.
Cover yourself with the blanket.		
x̌àčqídᵊb	Put it over your head.	LG.
x̌áčucid	any kind of covering	LG.
ʔəsx̌áčusᵊb	have face covered	LG.
(dxʷ)x̌áčùsᵊb	Cover your face.	LG.
rejected: *x̌áčad		LG.

1. x̌áču?   NPS   lake

Cf. cáləł, qʷəlúlt

   ʔəs.ʔəx̌íd kʷi s.λ̀əp ʔə ti?ił x̌áču? ʔal ti?à? DM.
   How deep is the lake here?

2. x̌áhᵊb   cry

Synonymous with ʔíub.   See under cut.

Cf. číqicut 'scream, loud crying', jáq- 'mourn'

root

ʔəsx̌áab	I'm full of cry.	VH.
ʔalčux̌áab čəd	I'm crying.	LG.
x̌ʷì? kʷ(i) adsx̌áab	Don't cry.	LG.
ʔəxʷx̌áabᵊb čəd	I feel like crying.	LG.

-i-t

  ʔux̌áhᵊbid haẁə? tiì ti?ə? bàds LL.
  He's crying because his father is out of sight.

ʔux̌áabicutəxʷ čəd	I'm crying.	VH.
ləcux̌áabicutəxʷ čəd	Same gloss: I'm crying.	VH.

reduplication

x̌áx̌ahᵊb an infant crying LL.

1. s.x̌áhus big river sawbill, a bu?qʷ; the wife
of Coyote LL., MS.

2. x̌ájaƛad pry it up, pry it open

See under x̌əc.

?ux̌ájaƛatᵊb It was pried open.

3. x̌al(a) mark, write, decorate

See under x̌iq̓(i). Cf. x̌əjk

root

?əsx̌ál tə ds.dà? My name is written. LG.

?u.kʷəd(d)xʷ ti sx̌al He received a letter. HD.

?alču.túlud čəd tə sx̌àl I'm reading the letter. LG.

səxʷx̌ál thing for writing, pen, pencil, etc. LG.

dəxʷux̌ál ?ə kʷi sgʷə.gʷàdad LG.

tape recorder (lit. 'what is used to mark the words')

-at or -š

x̌álad čəxʷ t(ə) ads.dà? Write your name. ES.

x̌álad kʷ(i) ads.dà? Write your name. HD.

-š

x̌álš t(ə) ads.dà? Write it, your name. ES.

ƚux̌álš čəd kʷi ds.dà? I'll write my name. EK.

?ux̌álš čəd I wrote it down. LL.

-at-sut

   x̌alacut   having a picture taken   EK.

     ʔux̌alacut čəd   I'm having my picture taken.   EK.

     łu.ʔúx̌ʷ čəł dxʷʔal ti čằʔahalʔtxʷ čəła łu.lábᵊd
     kʷi sx̌àlacut ʔu.čằʔa   JC.
     We will go to the playhouse and we will see what
     picture is playing.

-at-sut-txʷ

     ʔux̌alacut(t)ub čəł   We had our picture taken.   HD.

     ʔux̌alacut(t)ubicid čəd   I took your picture.   EK.

-yi-   NPS

     ʔux̌ályic ʔə tə sx̌àl yəx̌i čəd ʔu.k̓ʷásači?   LG.
     Write the letter for me because I burned my hand.

     łux̌ályicid čəd   I'll drop you a line.   EK.

-ši-   SPS

     ʔux̌álšic tə d.bàd ʔə tə sx̌àl   JC.
     My father wrote me a letter.

-dxʷ

     háy x̌álᵊdxʷ kʷ(i) ads.dà?   Write your name.   LL.

     ʔux̌áldubš   LL.
     They have my name (and they are using it against me).

-txʷ

     ʔux̌áltub ʔə tiʔił sx̌àl   LL.
     He was asked to write the letter for someone.

-təd

     x̌áltəd   writing utensil, pencil, pen

580

lexical

-ali

  x̌álali   post office, postman   LL.

-alikʷ

  ʔux̌álalikʷ čəd dxʷʔal hədli   I wrote to Henry.   EK.

  ʔalc̓ux̌álalikʷ   He's writing a letter.   LG.

  tu.k̓ʷásači̓ čəd gʷəl ʔux̌álalikʷyic ci ds.k̓ʷúy
  dxʷʔal d.qəsì   LG.
  I burned my hand so my mother wrote to my uncle for me.

-alʔtxʷ

  x̌álalʔtxʷ   school   LL.

-qsači̓

  t̓isux̌álqsači̓   little (i.e., 'young') finger   EK.

     See under dəx̌-.

-us

  dxʷx̌álusᵊbəxʷ tiʔił x̌àʔx̌əlus   ML.
  Raccoon marked his face.

  dxʷx̌álusᵊbəxʷ ʔə tiʔił x̌ʷi.qʷə́q̓ʷ ʔi tiʔił x̌i.bə̀č
  ʔal tiʔił s.ʔàcus   ML.
  He painted his face white and black (on the face).

-wič

  ʔux̌álwičt̓ᵊb čəd   They wrote on my back.   LL.

reduplication

  x̌áʔx̌əlus   NPS   raccoon

     Cf. bəlúps   SPS   raccoon

  ʔəsx̌ál̓x̌əl   speckled   EK.
                         striped   EK.

rejected:

    *x̌ált^əb, *x̌álbit^əb

1.   x̌álšəd   bridge

2.   x̌aƛ̓   want, like

    Compare <u>təbáš</u> 'crave'.   Contrast <u>jilid</u> 'dislike someone'.

    possessive affixes

(hə)la?b čəxʷ d^əs<u>x̌aƛ̓</u>	I really want you.	LG.
s<u>x̌áƛ̓</u>čəł kʷi (gʷə)su.ƚilihčəł	We like to sing.	LG.
s<u>x̌áƛ̓</u>s kʷi su.?ə́ƚ^əds (h)əlgʷə?	They like to eat.	LG.
d^əs<u>x̌áƛ̓</u> kʷi ds.?ə́ƚ^əd	I want to eat.	LG.
ƛ̓uds<u>x̌áƛ̓</u> ti?iƚ kùpi	I like coffee.	LL.
d^əs<u>x̌áƛ̓</u> tə biàc	I like meat.	LG.
d^əs<u>x̌áƛ̓</u> kʷi špàc	I want a comb.	LG.
d^əs<u>x̌áƛ̓</u> kʷi gʷ(ə)as.tágʷš kʷi bə.dəčù? u?xʷ pù?təd		LG.
I need to buy one more shirt.		
d^əs<u>x̌áƛ̓</u> kʷi d.šudubicid	I want to see you.	LG.
d^əs<u>x̌áƛ̓</u> kʷi gʷəds.?ìtut	I want to sleep.	LG.
d^əs<u>x̌áƛ̓</u> kʷi dsu.təlàwil	I like to run.	LG.
čád kʷi gʷ(ə)ads<u>x̌àƛ̓</u>txʷ kʷi gʷ(ə)ads.gʷədìl		DM.
Where do you want to sit?		

    -txʷ

?ux̌áƛ̓txʷ čəd	I want it.	LL.

      Cf. hâ?ƚtxʷ 'like it, enjoy it'

Cf. ?ux̌áƛ̓ildxʷ čəd	I got to liking him.	LL.
	I sure like him.	LL.

ʔəsx̌áƛtxʷ čəxʷ ʔu kʷi kupi   EK.
Do you want some coffee?

x̌áƛtxʷ čəd kʷi ds.qʷùʔqʷaʔ ʔə kʷi làb
I want a drink of whisky.

x̌áƛtxʷ čəd kʷi gʷəds.təlàwil   I want to run.   LG., EK.

x̌áƛtxʷ čəd kʷi gʷ(ə)ads.təlàwil   LG.
I want you to run.

x̌áƛtxʷ čəd gʷəd(s).sàxʷəb   I want to run/jump.   EK.

x̌áƛtxʷ čəd gʷəd(s).šùɬ   I want to see.   EK.

x̌áƛtxʷ čəd gʷəds.ʔəɬˀd   I want to eat.   EK.

x̌áƛtxʷ čəd gʷəds.ʔùx̌ʷ   I want to go.   EK.

ʔiɬ.čádgʷəs ʔə ti təstəd kʷi gʷ(ə)adsx̌àƛ
Which drum would you like?

-il-dxʷ

ʔux̌áƛildxʷ   I got to like him.   LL.
                        I sure like him.   LL.

  Cf. ʔux̌àƛtxʷ čəd   I want it.   LL.

x̌áƛildxʷ tiʔiɬ ləliʔ sɬə.ɬàdəy   EK.
He wants different women.

tux̌àƛildub ʔə tiʔiɬ dxʷ.dáʔˀb s.tubš ʔal tudiʔ lil   ES., HD.
A shaman from far away wanted her.

-il-d-ˀgʷəl

ʔácəc tiʔiɬ tux̌àƛildəgʷəl   ES.
There was a couple who fell in love.

gʷəl tiʔəʔ s.ɬádəy ʔi tiʔiɬ s.túbš
gʷəl cíckʷ t(u)asx̌àƛildəgʷəl   ES.
And this woman and that man. They really were in love.

1.   x̌áƛaləp   See under x̌əƛáləp.

2.   x̌aƛ   difficult

    Cf. təkʷ

        x̌áƛ s.yàyus   hard work   EK.

        x̌áƛdup   impassable brushy place   LG.

    -il

        x̌áƛil   begin to get difficult

3.   x̌áƛil   argue

    See under cut.   Cf. x̌ac 576.2

    Contrast x̌ix̌q̓cut (under x̌íx̌q̓).

    -il

        x̌áƛil   argument that ends in a fight   LL.

        ʔux̌áƛil   argue, talk rough, fight verbally   LL.

        ʔu.ʔúx̌ʷtubəxʷ kʷəɬ dxʷʔal kʷədi(ʔ) ʔux̌áƛil   LL.
        It's said he's been sent to the war (WW1).

        hay gʷəl x̌áƛiləxʷ tiʔiɬ ƛàƛačəpəd ʔi tiʔiɬ s.čətxʷəd   ES.
        Then Ant and Bear argued.

    -il-s

        ʔux̌áƛx̌aƛis   stick up for him, defend him   LL.

    reduplication

        x̌áƛx̌aƛil   quarrel   LL.

        x̌áƛx̌aƛis   stick up for him, defend him   LL.

        ʔux̌áx̌aƛil   squabble (as did Crow's seagull slaves)

    rejected: *x̌áƛis   LL.

1. ʔəs.x̌ápdup   scab   EK.

2. x̌áq̓əwʔ   dried backbone removed from a fish   LG., ESi.

    Cf. s.x̌əx̌(ə)č   backbone of a fish

      c̓uʔbid   fish bone

3. x̌átx̌at   mallard, a <u>buʔq^w</u>   LL., MS.

4. x̌áw̓s   Skagit   new, fresh

    Cf. łáw̓t   Snoh.   new

    lexical

      <u>x̌áw̓sulq^wł</u>   a new dancer

5. x̌áx̌aʔ   forbid

    Cf. x^wiʔ

      x̌ax̌ax̌á·d   forbid a child to do something

6. s.x̌ax̌aʔ   See under <u>x̌áʔx̌aʔ</u>.

7. s.x̌áx̌əlč   sword fern   LG., MC.

    s.x̌əx̌əlč   sword fern   LL.

8. x̌áx̌əƛusəc   thistle (perhaps burdock)   MC., EK.

9. x̌áx̌atib   See under <u>x̌aʔx̌aʔtib</u>.

10. x̌áx̌yəƛ   fish thoroughly dried by smoking   LG.

    See <u>x^w.šəbús</u>, <u>s.t̓əlúʔb</u>, and <u>s.łúʔᵊb</u>.

    Cf. k̓áyayəʔ ~ k̓ayáyəʔ   Same gloss.   LL., LG.

      k̓^wás   Same gloss.   ESi., JC.

1. x̌ayᵊb   laugh

    root

         ʔux̌áyᵊb   laughed   EK.

         ʔalčux̌áyᵊb čəd   I'm laughing.   LG.

         ləx̌áyᵊb čəd   I'm laughing as I come along.   LG.

         ʔəsx̌áyᵊb   laughing

         ʔəxʷ(s)x̌áyᵊbᵊb čəd   I feel like laughing.   LG.

    -dxʷ

         ʔux̌áyᵊbdubš   He made me laugh.   LG.

    -txʷ

         x̌áyᵊbtubš   smiled at me   LG.

         x̌áyᵊbtub   smiles at him   LL.

            ʔəxʷx̌áyᵊbus tiʔəʔ ʔəsx̌áyᵊbtub   LG.
            Smile as if I were smiling. (What the lúƛluƛ used
            to say when someone whom they didn't know smiled
            at them.)

    -i-t-

         x̌áyᵊbic   laughed at me (mocking)   LG.

         ʔux̌áyᵊbic   laughed at me   LG.

         ʔudxʷx̌áyᵊbusbic ciʔiɬ   She smiled at me.   LG.

         ʔudxʷx̌áyᵊbusbid čəd   I smiled at her.   LG.

         dxʷx̌áyᵊbusbid   smiles at him   LL.

    lexical

         ʔəxʷx̌áyᵊbus čəd   I'm smiling.   LG.

    reduplication

         x̌áʔx̌ayᵊb   giggle   JC.

    rejected: *ʔudxʷx̌áyᵊbusbš   LG.

→

1. s.x̌áy̓us   See under s.x̌əy̓ús.

2. s.x̌áy̓ay̓   (fish) gills   LG.

        s.x̌əyáy̓   gills   EK., LL.

        Cf. s.čay(ʔ)t SPS   gills   LL.

3. s.x̌áʔaʔ NPS   littleneck/steamer clam   EK.
        See under s.ʔáx̌ʷuʔ.   Cf. k̓ʷúx̌ʷdiʔ SPS

4. s.x̌áʔədxʷ   toad   LG., LL.

        s.x̌aʔádxʷ   toad   MC.

5. x̌áʔx̌aʔ   great, sacred
        Cf. k̓ʷiʔát

        x̌áʔx̌aʔ dxʷdàʔᵊb   a great shaman   DM.

        x̌áʔx̌aʔ s.qəlálitut   great power   DM.

        lexical

        x̌áx̌aʔəɬdàt   Sunday, i.e., great day   EK.

        other derivation

        sx̌áx̌aʔ   in-law

            sx̌ax̌ax̌aʔ   in-laws

            See under s.k̓ʷəlwás.

6. x̌áʔx̌aʔtib   be in a hurry
        See under ʔáɬ 'fast'.

            ʔəsx̌áʔx̌aʔtib čəd   I'm in a hurry.   LG.

            s.tábəxʷ k̓ʷi ƛ(u)adəxʷəsx̌àʔx̌aʔtib   LL.
            What are you in a hurry about?

ʔəsx̌áʔx̌aʔtib dxʷʔal kʷi gʷəds.hùyalc ʔə ti d.ʔàlʔal   LG.

(I'm) in a hurry to finish my house.

ʔəsx̌áʔx̌aʔtib dxʷʔal kʷi gʷəs.łàʔs   LG.

He is in a hurry to get there.

ʔəsx̌áʔx̌aʔtib čəd dxʷʔal kʷi gʷəds.hùyalc ʔə ti dsu.yàyus.

I'm in a hurry to finish my work.

ʔəsx̌áʔx̌aʔtib čəd dxʷʔal kʷi gʷəds.hùyalc ʔə ti dsu.p̓àyəq

ʔə ti ƛ(ə)làyʔ

I'm in a hurry to finish making the shovel-nose canoe.

1.   x̌əb   (very) heavy   LL., DM., LG.

   Opposite of xʷəʔáʔxʷəʔ 'light weight'.

      x̌əb ʔu tiʔił wəq̓əb   Is the box heavy?   DM.

      x̌əb tiʔił wəq̓əb   That box is heavy.   LG.

      ʔiłx̌əb tiʔił wəq̓əb ʔal tùdiʔ tulʔal tiʔəʔ wəq̓əb ʔal tiʔáʔ   LG.

      That box over there is heavier than this box right here.

2.   x̌əc   fear

      root

         híkʷ čəł ʔux̌əc   We were greatly frightened.   HD.

         ʔəsx̌əc čəd   I'm afraid.   EK.

         ʔəsx̌əc čəd gʷə.ʔùx̌ʷəd   I'm afraid to go.   EK.

         t(u)asx̌əc čəd gʷə.šùłəd   I was afraid to look.   EK.

         t(u)asx̌əc čəd gʷə.tìčibəd   I was afraid to swim.   EK.

         t(u)asx̌əc čəd gʷə.ʔəλ̓əd yəx̌ì ʔu.qəlˀb   EK.

         I was afraid to come because it rained.

         ʔəsx̌əc čəd gʷə.c̓əlpšədəd gʷə.təlàwiləd ʔə kʷi ʔàł   ML.

         I'm afraid that I might turn my ankle if I run fast.

588

?əsx̌ə́c čəd gʷə.làx̌ᵊbicəs   LL.

I'm afraid he might remember (the argument) he had with me.

?əsx̌ə́c čəd gʷə.làx̌dubšəs   LL.

I'm afraid he might remember me.

?əsx̌əc čəd ?ə ti?it s.qʷəbày?   LG.

I'm afraid of that dog.

?əsx̌ə́c čəd ?ə kʷi (gʷə)ds.təlàwil   LG.

I'm afraid to run.

-dxʷ

?ux̌ə́cᵊdxʷ čəd ti?it s.tùbš   I scared that man.   LL.

-bi-t

?əsx̌əcbícid čəd   I'm afraid of you.   EK.

?əsx̌əcbíc čəxʷ   You're afraid of me.   EK.

?əsx̌əcbíd čəd tə s.qʷəbày?   I'm afraid of the dog.   LG.

?əsx̌əcbíd ti?it s.qʷəbày?   Someone is afraid of that dog.   LG.

?əsx̌əcbítᵊb ?ə ti?it s.tubš   That man is afraid of it.   LG.

?əsx̌əcbítᵊb ?ə ti?it s.tùbš tə s.qʷəbày?   LG.

The man is afraid of the dog.

reduplication

?əsx̌í(?)x̌əcᵊbid čəd   I'm a little afraid of it.   LL.

     (The /?/ seems to be optional.)

1.   x̌əc   pull out, extract

Synonyms

     xʷəc   take off   ?əč̓   pull out
     x̌ajaƛ(a)   pry open/up   ?əq̓ʷ(a)   unplug

                ?uq̓ʷ(u)   unplug

Antonyms (See under ƛuq̓ʷ(u).)

589

-t

?ux̌ə́cˀd   pull it out

x̌ə́cˀd tə s.ťuˀqʷ   plucking feathers

?əsx̌ə́c čəd gʷəx̌ə́cˀdəd   I'm afraid to pull it out.

lexical

?ux̌cíč   weed (a garden), pull up from ground

1.   x̌ə́č   counters used in bone game

2.   x̌(ə)čádiˀ   corner

   See s.x̌əx̌(ə)č̌   backbone of a fish

   ?əs.cqʷúɫ x̌əčadiˀ ?ə ti ?alˀal
   It's up on end in the corner of the house.

3.   x̌əč   mind, inner thoughts, sense, understanding; count

   Cf. ptídəgʷəsˀb

   root

      x̌əč   mind, inner thoughts   LL.
                  mind, understanding   MS.

      ?əbsx̌ə́č   He's sensible.   LG.

      ?u.hígʷiləxʷ tiˀiɫ x̌ə̀čs   He's got his courage now.   LL.

      ?əs.ƛ̓úbis tiˀiɫ x̌ə̀čs   He thinks he's all right.

      xʷìˀ lə.x̌ʷúl diɫ kʷs(i) ads.ɫàdəyˀ kʷ(i) adsx̌ə̀č   LL.
      Don't think only about your woman.

      ?əs.ˀídigʷat kʷ(i) adsx̌əč   What do you think of it?   JC.

   -t

      ?ux̌ə́čˀd čəd   I'm counting.   EK.

      ?alčux̌ə́čˀd tə s.paˀpaˀc He's counting the bears.   LG.

x̌ə́č̣ᵊd k̓ʷídid kʷi diʔà?   Count how many people are here.   DM.

-ab

x̌č̌áb   more thoughtful   EK.

-ádad   cast a spell

x̌ᵊč̌ádadid   put a spell on someone   VH.

   Cf. x̌ícis (under x̌icil), pᵊɫə́x̌

lexical

ʔəs.ʔəx̌íd kʷi (səs)x̌č̌àlc ʔə tiʔə? pù?təd   DM.
What is the price of this shirt?

   Note: ...*sx̌č̌àlc... is not grammatical.

x̌ʷəlilc ʔi kʷi x̌ʷəlbít ʔi kʷi ʔiɫ.čəx̌bít tiʔiɫ x̌əč̌àlc
ʔə tiʔiɫ pú?təd   DM.
That shirt is 9.95 dollars.

ʔalc̓ux̌č̌álikʷ   He's counting.   LG.

s.tábəxʷ kʷi səs.hùys ʔal tiʔə? s.ɫukʷàlb ʔal kʷi
səsx̌əč̌əɫdàts   LL.
What is the date?

other derivation

šəɫx̌ə́č̣ᵊb   what one has made up his mind to do,
                   law, order, edict, proclamation   HD.
                   (Equivalent to Skagit čəɫx̌ə́č̣ᵊb.)

   haʔɫ kʷi gʷəs.čálatᵊbs t(i) ads.gʷa? adsšəɫx̌ə́č̣ᵊb
   ʔal ti s.watixʷtəd
   It be good that thy own will be followed on earth.
   (From a translation of the Pater Noster.)

   x̌ə́ɫəɫx̌əč̌   sorry, sad, broken-hearted

1.   x̌əd   push

   Cf. hiq(i) 'push, shove'   Opposite of təx̌ʷ(u) 'pull, drag'

-t

ʔux̌ədcíd čəd	I pushed you.	LG.
ʔux̌ə́dᵊd	Push it.	EK.

lexical

x̌ədálusəd	mat creaser	VH.
x̌ədústəd	mat creaser	LG.

reduplication

x̌ədx̌ədáči(ʔ)b	pushing hands away	LG.
x̌ədx̌ədyálc	pushing with the hands	LG.

→

2. x̌ədi-   save

-t

x̌ədíhᵊd	preparing it
ʔəsx̌ədíhᵊd čəd ʔə tiʔił s.čiʔyu	I saved the strawberries.
ʔəsx̌ədí(i)c	Save me some.

rejected: *x̌ədíyic

3. x̌ənimúliča?   myth name of káʔka? 'Crow' who is the sister of
                       káẉqs 'Raven'

4. s.x̌ədíʔac   devil's club   MC., EK., ESi.

5. x̌ə́kʷəd   salmon sticks, sticks for 'baking' salmon

    Cf. k̉i?

6. x̌ə́kʷ(u)   turn it over face down

    Cf. jal-   turn to reverse side

592

root

ʔux̌ə́k̓ʷ čəd	(The canoe) turned over with me in it.	
	("This expression is not much used. Rather we would say, 'ʔux̌k̓ʷíč čəd'.")	LL.
ʔux̌ə́k̓ʷ čəd	I turned over.	LG.

-ut

ʔux̌k̓ʷúd	He turned it over.	HD., LL.
	He turned it down.	EK.
x̌k̓ʷúd	Turn it over.	LG.
ʔəsx̌k̓ʷúcut čəd	I was crouched low.	EK., ES.

Cf. x̌itáhᵊb 'squat'

-agʷil

| x̌əx̌k̓ʷágʷil | turn over | LL. |

xʷíʔ kʷi dxʷ.čád ƛusu.ʔùx̌ʷčəɬ. dàyayʔ ʔal tiʔə?
dəxʷəsx̌k̓ʷágʷilčəɬ   LL.

We never go anywhere. We're just here where we stay crouched (low).

lexical

| x̌k̓ʷáp | the back part of a chicken that is eaten | LL. |
| ʔux̌k̓ʷíč čəd | (The canoe) turned over with me in it. | LL. |

Cf. gʷal 'capsize'

x̌ək̓ʷgʷíɬ	Turn the canoe over.	LG.
x̌k̓ʷúcid	cover, lid	LG.
ʔəsx̌k̓ʷús tiʔiɬ	He has his head down.	LG.

Cf. jəq̓íl   crawl, have head down

ʔəsx̌k̓ʷús k̓ʷəɬ ʔə ti sə.p̓ə̀q̓ʷs   LG.

(The drowned person) was drifting face down, they say.

x̌k̓ʷúsᵊd	turn it over	LG.
x̌k̓ʷúsᵊd ləx̌šàd	cover the lamp	EK.
x̌k̓ʷúsᵊb ʔə tə s.ʔìčəb	cover head with blanket	EK.

reduplication

x̌əx̌k̓ʷág̓ʷil	turn over	LL.

1.   x̌ə́jk   write fast, scribble, shorthand   LL.

    Cf. x̌al(a)

ɫux̌ə́jkᵊd čəd	I'll scribble it down.	ES.

2.   x̌əlábac   1. hollow cedar tree
                          2. name for Illabot Creek, a tributary of the
                                       Skagit River

3.   s.x̌əlá́ʔs   board (wood)

4.   x̌əlídup   floor

    Cf. -ali

5.   x̌ə́ɫ   sick

    Cf. bakʷɫ 'get hurt', q̓iƛ(dxʷ) 'wound', čud 'weak (muscles), sickly'

       dukʷahᵊb 'not quite well'

    root

ʔəsx̌ə́ɫ čəd	I'm sick.	LG.
ʔəsx̌ə̀ɫ tə d.qə̀dxʷ	My mouth hurts.	EK.
xʷiʔ kʷi səsx̌ə́ɫs	He is not sick.	EK.
xʷiʔ kʷi sx̌ə́ɫs	He didn't get hurt.	EK.
xʷiʔ kʷ(i) adsx̌ə́ɫ	Don't get sick.	EK.
ck̓ʷáqid čəxʷ ɫ(u)asx̌ə̀ɫ	You will always be sick.	EK.

b(ə)asx̌ƚáxʷ čəxʷ ʔu   Are you sick again?   EK.

dídiʔƚ čəd ʔəsx̌ə̀ƚ   I'm still sick.   EK.

dídiʔƚ ʔəsx̌ə̀ƚ ʔə tiʔiƚ   He is still sick.   EK.

xʷíʔ kʷi dsəs.(h)àydxʷ kʷi səsx̌ə̀ƚ ʔə hədli   EK.
I didn't know Henry was sick.

xʷíʔ lə.ʔiƛub kʷ(i) adsx̌ə̀ƚ   EK.
You aren't sick enough (to warrant going to the hospital).

ʔəbiləxʷ čəd həláʔb gʷət(u)asx̌ə̀ƚ gʷəl xʷiʔ gʷəds.ƚčíl.   LL.
x̌ʷuƚ čəd gʷətuʔál ʔàlʔal
If I had been real sick, I would not have come.
I would have been home.

ʔi·. gʷətu.ʔúx̌ʷ čəƚ gʷə.xʷíʔəs ti ʔəs.həláʔb čəƚ
x̌ə̀ƚx̌əƚ čəƚà (ʔə)s.čúd
Yes. We would have gone, but we are much too sick,
too much under the weather (lit.'(too) weak').

-il

ʔəsx̌əƚx̌ƚíl (h)əlgʷəʔ   They are sick.   LL.

ʔəsx̌əƚx̌ƚíl čəƚ   We are sick.   LL.

cíckʷ k̓ʷəƚ (h)əlgʷəʔ ʔəsx̌əƚx̌əƚíl   LG.
It is said they are very sick.

lexical

ʔux̌əƚdís   I have a toothache.   EK.

x̌əƚyúq̓ʷ   sore throat   EK.

    x̌əƚyúq̓ʷ čələp   You folks have sore throats.   EK.

ʔəsx̌ƚádis   He is sickly.   LL.

in compound

ʔəsx̌ə̀ƚəƚx̌ə̀č   feel bad (mentally)
                   feelings hurt, sad   ML.

Cf. xʷíduƚ 'melancholy', xʷíʔalusbid 'miss (not having
                                        someone around)'

reduplication

> ʔəs.dúkʷab čəd.   ʔu.wəlíʔil sixʷ ti dsx̌ìʔx̌ɬ   LL.
> I'm not so well. My little sickness has (re)appeared.

> ʔəsx̌ə́ɬx̌əɬ čəɬ   We are sick.   LL.

> ʔəsx̌əɬx̌ɬíl čəɬ   We are sick.   LL.

> ʔəsx̌əɬx̌ɬíl (h)əlgʷəʔ   They are sick.   LL.

rejected:

> *ʔəsx̌(ə)ɬíl čəd   LL.

> *ʔəsx̌əɬx̌əɬ čəɬ   LG.

1.   x̌əɬ   as if, like, seem

Cf. x̌ʷuɬ-ab

root

> x̌əɬ čəd ti s.paʔc   I feel like a bear.   LG.

> bə.x̌ʷiʔ čəɬ lə.hix̌ʌub gʷə.húyucutəxʷ x̌əɬ (ɬi) ʔə
> kʷi ʔəs.ʔìstəʔ   LL.
> We are not enough to do anything in this either.

> x̌əɬ čəd ʔə(s).súxʷtᵊbicid   I sort of recognize you. LG.

x̌əɬ in construction with ti clauses

> həlá ʔbəxʷ čəxʷ x̌əɬ ti lə.x̌ùiɬ   LL.
> It looks as if you are getting thinner.

> x̌əɬ ti x̌ʷiʔ gʷəs.k̓ʷə̀ɬᵊds   LG.
> I don't think he spilled it.

> x̌ʷiʔ x̌əɬ ti   No, I guess. (Equivalent to x̌ʷuʔᵊləʔ.)

> x̌ə̀ɬ ti ʔəs.cùt   It's something like that.   LL.

> x̌ə̀ɬ ti ʔa kʷi səs.húy ʔə tiʔəʔ c̓ə̀tx̌   ML.
> It seems as if (something) is wrong with Kingfisher.

gʷəl x̌ə̵ɫ ti díɫ c(i) ad.ʔàlš ti ʔiɫ ʔu.cùtcut   ML.

It seems like it's your sister who's talking.

díɫəxʷ dəxʷəs.čcíls.   x̌ə̵ɫ ti λ(u)as.cɫíl ti ʔə? ʔal ti   ML.

That's why its red. Just as though it were bleeding
right there.

ʔəs.(h)áydub ʔə ti ʔiɫ cədiɫ bəščəb. huy x̌ə̵ɫ ti

bədxʷ.qahigʷəd ti ʔiɫ bəščəb. gʷəl x̌ə̵ɫ ti b(ə)as.dúkʷil

Mink knew what was up as if Mink were clever and as
though he were preternatural.

gʷəl x̌ə̵ɫ ti s.táb kʷi gʷəs.dàʔatəbs   ML., LL.

It's hard to say just what it could be called.

x̌ə̵ɫ ti x̌ʷi.qʷác   It's almost greenish-yellow.   ML., LL.

mí ʔmad gʷəs.ʔíšɫs (h)əlgʷəʔ x̌ə̵ɫ ti λə.ʔəx̌íd lə.ʔùx̌ʷəs   ML., LG.

They only had to paddle a little, and it would really go.
(It would go without much effort.)

x̌ə̵ɫ ti x̌íyəx̌i   kind of bashful   LG.

x̌ə̵ɫ čəd ti t(u)as.x̌íyəx̌i   I was kind of bashful (then).   LG.

ʔə(s).šúɫ x̌ə̵ɫ ti bəqsəd   It looks like a nose.   MS.

x̌ə̵ɫ ti x̌ʷúləb ʔə ti ʔiɫ s.dəxʷiɫ ti ʔiɫ səs.huys   DM.

It seems to be made like the hunting canoe.

1.   x̌ə̵ɫalwíld   thwart   LL.

2.   x̌ə̵ɫtəd   a man's wife's brother and male cousins, a man's
                    sister's husband and male cousins

    See under s.kʷəlwás.   Contrast čəbás.

    reduplication

       x̌ə̵ɫx̌ə̵ɫtəd   wife's brothers, sister's husbands

1. x̌əƛ   bite

     -t

        x̌ə́ƛˀəd   bite it   EK.

        ʔux̌ə́ƛtˀəb čəd ʔə tə tìtčulbix̌ʷ   The insect bit me.   EK.

     lexical

        dx̌ʷx̌ə́ƛahˀəb   'chewing on your rear'   LL.

        ləsx̌ˀəƛálc ʔal tə s.čupč̓ ʔə ti k̓ʷatad   EK.
        (While travelling along) the mice were biting
          the tails of the ones(ahead in order to hang on).

        x̌ƛálikʷ   bite (into something to eat)   EK.

           ʔux̌ƛálikʷ čəd ʔə tə *apple*   EK.
        I took a bite of the apple.

        x̌íx̌ƛˀədup   snack, lunch   EK.

        x̌ˀəƛgʷás   come together   VH.

           x̌ˀəƛgʷásuladx̌ʷ   spring (lit. 'where/when the ends of)
                                             the year come together') MS.

        x̌íx̌ƛùstəgʷəl   converse (lit.'bite each others'
                                             faces a little')   LL.

     other derivation

        x̌əƛyáčəd   a type of spear so named because
                                       it looks as though it bites. It was
                                       used to hit behind the salmon's head. VH.
                                       See under čəsáyʔ.

2. x̌əƛáləp   steering by using a paddle   LG., ML.

     x̌áƛaləp   Same gloss: steering by using a paddle ESi.

3. x̌ˀəpúsˀəb   lift head up, straighten up

     Synonym: cək̓ʷcút   Opposite: tújil   look down, bend forward

                                    jəqíl   crawl, have head down

1. (s)x̌əṗáb   cockles. One of the class of s.ʔáx̌ʷuʔ.   LG., LL.

    s.x̌ə́pəb   cockles   ESi.

    See under s.ʔáx̌ʷuʔ.

2.   x̌əṗk̓ʷ   See under k̓aw(a).

    dày?əxʷ ?ux̌ə́ṗk̓ʷəd ti šàw̓   ESi.
    (A dog) sure was chewing up the bone and doing it noisily.

    x̌ə́ṗək̓ʷəd   chew something hard that makes noise   LG.

    lexical

     sx̌ə́ṗ(ə)k̓ʷ   edible cartilage in front part of fish nose
               ("A real treat!")   LG.

       x̌ə́ṗk̓ʷəs   Same gloss.   ESi.

         Cf. s.qə́bqəb̓   Same gloss.   LL.

3.   x̌əq   wrap around

    See under łid(i).

    -t

     x̌ə́qəd   Wrap string/cloth around it.   LL.
                Tie it.   LL.
                Wind it around.   EK.

    lexical

     x̌qábacəd   Wind it around some bundle.   EK.

     x̌qáhustəb   tie (rag) over eyes   EK.

     səsx̌qí?łs ?əs.kəkì?txʷ   ML.
     She has the baby tied in a cradle board.

4.   x̌əṡtád   nit

5.   x̌ətádis   hard, solid (like a board)   EK.
                 very hard wood   LL.

    See under ƛ̓aq̓ʷ.

1. x̌ʔt̓áb   fall out of a canoe into the water, fall overboard
                                                                         LG.

      x̌ə́t̓əb   fall into water   ESi.

      See under x̌ʷiti̓l, ǰíq̓(i).   Cf. t̓əbá?, gʷál

      Contrast təč̓.

           ?ux̌t̓áb čəd tul̓?al tə d.ƛ(ə)lày?   LG.
           I fell out of the shovel-nose canoe.

2. x̌ʔt̓íč   name of a slough near Lyman, Washington   CB.

3. x̌əwáwq̓   unidentified kind of big diver, a bu?qʷ. In
                          mythology, this character has a brother,
                          swúqʷad 'Loon', and a sister x̌ʷú?x̌ʷəy? 'Little
                          Diver'.   LL.

4. s.x̌ə́x̌(ə)č̓   backbone of a fish   EK., LG.

      See under x̌(ə)č̓ádi?.

      Cf. x̌áq̓əw?   dried backbone removed from a fish

           č̓ú?bid   fish bone

5. s.x̌ə́x̌əlč   See under s.x̌áx̌əlč.

6. s.x̌əyáy̓   See under s.x̌áy̓ay̓.

7. s.x̌əy̓ús   head

      Cf. -qid, -us

           ?u.qə́p̓ cə bibu?qʷ ?al tə dsx̌əy̓ús   LG.
           The little bird landed on my head.

           (1) ti?ə? ?ə?útx̌s gʷəl híkʷ q̓ìlbid. (2) gʷəl ti?ə?
           šə́jts gʷəl ?á ti?ə? sx̌əy̓ùs. (3) ƛu.húyalcbid ti?ə?
           q̓ìlbid gʷəl ƛu.ƛályibəxʷ ti?ə? sx̌əy̓ùss.

(1) The Nootka type canoe is a big canoe. (2) Its
bow has a head. (3) The canoe would be made and (then)
its head would be added. MS.

derivation

sx̌áy̓us   1. boiled salmon heads   LL.
                                 2. head   ESi.

sx̌x̌áy̓us   heads   LL.

1.   x̌i-   prefix with certain color terms

     Cf. x̌ʷi-

        x̌ibə́c̓   black

        x̌ičəc   red

        x̌išúk̓ʷ   gray

2.   x̌ib(i)   grab with pressure (as a hawk would do), claw

     See under x̌iq̓(i) and kʷəd(a).

     -it

        ʔux̌íbid   He grabbed/clawed it.   LG.

        ʔux̌íbic ti pìšpiš   LG.
        The cat clawed (grabbed, scratched) me.

        ʔux̌íbic čəxʷ   You grabbed me.   LG.

        ʔux̌íbitubuɫəd čəɫ   We grabbed you folks.   LG.

        ʔux̌íbitəb čəd ʔə tə pìšpiš   The cat clawed me.   EK.

     lexical

        ʔəsx̌ibabac   It is hanging on with its claws.   EK.

        x̌ʷuɫ čəd ʔux̌íbigʷsəb   LG.
        I just grabbed my things (not having time to pack
                           carefully).

ʔux̌íbustəgʷələxʷ   scratch each other up (as in fighting)   LL.

ʔux̌ìbᵊwíčdubš čəxʷ   You clawed my back.   LG.

reduplication

     ʔux̌íbx̌ibic   It clawed me all up.   LG.

     ʔux̌íbx̌ibid   Gathered it up.   LG.

     x̌íbx̌ib   chicken hawk; general term for bird of prey

(1) díɬ ʔu bəx̌ibx̌ib tiʔiɬ čìxʷčixʷ

(2) ʔí; x̌íbx̌ib tiʔəʔ čìxʷčixʷ

(1) Is a fish hawk a bird of prey?
(2) Yes; a fish hawk is a bird of prey.

(3) díɬ ʔu bəx̌ìbx̌ib tiʔiɬ yəx̌ʷəlàʔ

(4) ʔi; ƛál bəx̌ìbx̌ib tiʔiɬ yəx̌ʷəlàʔ

(3) Is an eagle a bird of prey?
(4) Yes; an eagle is also a bird of prey.

(1) díɬ ʔu bəx̌ìbx̌ib ciʔiɬ s.ƛaƛakʷ

(2) ʔí; ƛál bəx̌ìbx̌ib ciʔiɬ s.ƛaƛakʷ

(3) gʷəl ƛál bəx̌ìbx̌ib tiʔiɬ təkʷtəkʷəlùs

(1) Is a screech owl a bird of prey?
(2) Yes; a screech owl is also a bird of prey
(3) and a "large-eyed" owl is a bird of prey, too.

1.   x̌icil   angry

     Cf. dúkʷtxʷ 'angry', čígʷil 'irritated, disgusted, impatient';

       x̌ac-, x̌áƛil

     -s

     x̌ícis   hex someone because of anger

       Cf. x̌ᵊčádadid 'put a spell on someone'

-b

x̌ícilᵊb   grumpy, kind of angry   LG.

-bi-t

x̌ícilbid   angry with him

1.   x̌íc̓   raw (meat)

    Compare qʷúx̌ʷadᵊb 'unripe' and c̓ikʷ.

2.   x̌íc̓il   shame, guilt   EK.

    Cf. x̌ídub, x̌íx̌i

    ʔəsx̌íc̓il čəd dxʷʔal ti dsu.bədč̓ᵊbid tiʔił   LG.
    I'm guilty of having told him a lie.

    lexical

    x̌íc̓ilàyucid   shame in the mouth   ES.
    (When the lips quiver, one will soon be embarrassed.)

    ʔəsx̌íc̓ilus   contorted, distorted face from
                       bad feelings   LG.

3.   x̌id   See under ʔəx̌íd.

4.   x̌ídib   growl

5.   x̌ídub   catch someone doing something wrong

    híkʷ čəd ʔu.hùytub ʔal tiʔił dᵊsx̌ídub   LL.
    They really gave it to me when they caught me at it.

    ʔux̌ídub čəd ʔə ciʔił dᵊs.łàdəyʔ   LL.
    My woman caught me at it.

6.   x̌ík̓ʷ   ugly, mean, rough; strange appearance

                  "A person can be called this if he is ugly
                  even though his personality is good."   LL.

harsh talker, rude; ugly in appearance   LG.

root

    putəxᵂ čəxᵂ ƛux̌ík̓ᵂ   You're getting real ugly.   LL.

-il

    ʔəsx̌ík̓ᵂil čəd   I'm mean.   AS.

-b

    x̌ík̓ᵂəb   lonesome; be quiet, be still

      See under x̌ᵂubil.

    ʔux̌ík̓ᵂəb ʔal ti s.ləx̌il   (We) got lonesome today.   EK.

    x̌əɬ ti ʔəsx̌ík̓ᵂəb ti s.wàtixᵂtəd   LG.
    Soft, strange stillness in the land as though the
    world were lonesome.

    ʔəsx̌ík̓ᵂəb tə *Thom*   Thom is lonesome.   LG.

1.   x̌ílix̌   war, battle, fight

    Cf. yábuk̓ᵂ   fight;

      x̌ác(x̌acəb)   quarrelling

      x̌áƛil   argue

2.   x̌iƛ(i)   fell (a tree)

    See under ɬič̓(i).   Cf. jáq̓(a)

    -it

      ʔux̌íƛid   He cut it down.   EK.

      ƛux̌íƛid tiʔəʔ diʔəʔ s.wətíxᵂtəd   DM.
      [A beaver] fells the tree(s).

lexical

ʔux̌íƛap	chop a tree down	LL., EK.
	fell a tree, undercut a tree	DM.
ƛux̌íƛəp ʔə tiʔəʔ s.wətìxʷtəd		DM.
[A beaver] fells trees.		
x̌íƛəpəd	fell a tree by burning	LG.
dxʷsx̌íƛap	tree-feller, lumberjack	LL.

1.   x̌íp̓(i)   scratch (and leave a mark)

       See under x̌íq̓(i).

      -it

          x̌íp̓id   scratch it and leave a mark

             (This might be a misrecording for x̌ib(i).)

2.   x̌íx̌ip̓íč   Skagit   chipmunk   LG., MC.

       Cf. s.q̓ʷə́cɫ   Snoh., SPS   chipmunk   LL., ESi.

3.   x̌íq̓(i)   scratch, esp. to relieve an itch, čə́lpəb

       See under šic(i).

       Synonyms: x̌ʷíč̓(i), x̌ib(i), ʔix̌(i), x̌al(a), x̌əjk, x̌íp̓(i)

      -it

          x̌íq̓id   scratch it to relieve an itch   LG., HD., LL.

          ʔux̌íq̓ic tə pìšpiš   The cat scratched me.   LG.

          ʔalc̓ux̌íq̓icut tiʔəʔ s.pàʔpaʔc   LG.

         The bears are scratching themselves.

          ʔux̌íx̌iq̓icut   (a dog) scratching itself   LL.

      -dxʷ

          x̌íq̓dxʷ   scratch   LL.

lexical

ʔalcux̌íq̓əbàcᵊb	He's scratching his body.	LG.
x̌íq̓qídic	Scratch my head.	LG.
ʔalcux̌ìq̓qídᵊb	He's scratching his head.	LG.
x̌ìq̓ᵊwíčc	Scratch my back.	LG.
ʔux̌ìq̓ᵊwíčc ciʔił	She scratched my back.	LG.

reduplication

ʔalcux̌íq̓x̌iq̓itᵊb ʔə cə pìšpiš tə xʷ.tág̓ʷtap	LG.
The cat is scratching the chair.	
x̌íx̌iq̓icut	(a dog) scratching itself	LL.
	(This form would not much be used for people.)	

rejected:

*ʔəsx̌íq̓ tə ƛ̓ələ̀y?	LG.

1. x̌iṭahᵊb   squat

Cf. x̌k̓ʷucut (under x̌ək̓ʷ(u))

root

    ʔəsx̌iṭá(h)b čəd   I'm squatting.

-txʷ

    x̌iṭá(h)btxʷ   make him squat

-bi-t

    x̌iṭá(hᵊ)bid   Squat next to him.

rejected:

    *x̌iṭid, *x̌iṭad, *x̌iṭapᵊb, *x̌iṭábalps, *x̌iṭabəp, *x̌iṭabahəb

2. x̌íx̌i   shame

Cf. x̌ičil

x̌í·x̌i·   For a shame!

ʔəsx̌íx̌i čəd dxʷʔal ti dsu.bədč̌ə̌bid tiʔił
I'm ashamed that I lied to him.

reduplication

x̌íyə̌x̌iʔ   bashful   LG.

   x̌ə̌ł čəd t(u)asx̌íyə̌x̌iʔ   I was kind of bashful then.   LG.

ʔəs.č̌ál kʷ(i) adəxʷəsx̌íyə̌x̌íʔ kʷi gʷ(ə)ads.ʔùx̌ʷ
Why are you reluctant to go?

1.   x̌ix̌q̓   get the best of someone, compete; refuse   LG.

   root

      ʔux̌íx̌q̓ čəd   I won't (do something).   EK.

      tux̌íx̌q̓ tə diʔəʔ s.tùbš dxʷʔal ha(ʔ)kʷ   EK.
      This man refused for a long time.

         Cf. xʷiʔə̌d

      dxʷsx̌íx̌q̓   a racer, debater   LG.

   -t

      xʷiʔ kʷ(i) adsux̌íx̌q̓cut   Don't argue/answer back.   LG.

   lexical

      x̌ix̌q̓ə̌wíł   racing canoe   LL., DM.

      x̌íx̌q̓algʷíł   canoe race   LG.

      x̌ix̌q̓álps ((h)əlgʷəʔ)   horse race   LL.

      səxʷx̌íx̌q̓ s.tiqìw   race horse   LL.

      səxʷx̌ìx̌q̓álps   race horse   LG.

2.   x̌páyʔəc   cedar tree   HD., ESi.

      x̌ix̌páyʔəc   small cedar tree   LL.

1.   x̌tádis   See under <u>x̌ᵊtâdis</u>.

x̌ʷ

The sound of this letter resembles the noise made when gargling with the lips rounded as if pronouncing the English letters *oo* at the same time. [voiceless, labialized, uvular fricative]

1.   x̌ʷáhᵊb   rump   LL.

        Cf. xʷ.tábap   rump

2.   x̌ʷálitut   snore

        Cf. under ʔítut.

3.   s.x̌ʷáluʔ(əc)   willow (tree)   MC.

          x̌ʷəx̌ʷáluʔ(ac)   willow (tree)   LG.

          cəx̌ʷáluʔ   willow   ML.

          s.čáp(ac)   willow (tree)   ESi.

4.   x̌ʷaƚ   lack control

     root

          ʔəsx̲̌ʷáƚ   what someone can't comprehend, can't master   LL.

              Cf. q̓cáb

          ʔəsx̲̌ʷáƚ čəd   I'm too weak to carry it; it's too

                                    heavy for me.   LL.

          ʔux̲̌ʷáƚ čəd   I was defeated; I lost a game;

                                    I couldn't catch any fish.   LL.

             Contrast čəl-.

     -dxʷ

        lə(ʔə)xʷsx̲̌ʷáƚdxʷᵊb   He wants to get the best of him.   LL., ML.

     -bi-t

        ʔəsx̲̌ʷáƚbicut čəd   I give up (because my body is fatigued). LL.

            Contrast dxʷ.x̌ʷaƚigʷəd.

ʔəsx̌ʷálbid čəd   I can't control it.   EK.
                           I can't handle it.   ES.

                           I can't quite use it (due to my lack of ability, knowledge, etc.)   LL.

ʔux̌ʷálbid čəd   I lost it; it's too heavy for me to lift. LL.

(Equivalent to ʔux̌ʷal čəd 'Lost it.', meaning game/fish got away.)

ʔəsx̌ʷálbid čəɫ ʔə tə s.ʔùx̌ʷ dx̌ʷʔal tə s.q̓àx̌ʷ
We can't control it when it goes on the ice.

x̌ʷálig̓ʷədbid čəd ʔə tiʔiɫ su.cùtcuts (h)əlg̓ʷə?   EK.
I gave up on what their plans were.

ʔux̌ʷálbid tiʔiɫ dx̌ʷs.qada   LL.
They didn't catch the thief.

ʔux̌ʷálbitᵊb tiʔiɫ dx̌ʷs.qada   LL.
They didn't catch the thief.

ʔux̌ʷálbitᵊb ʔə tiʔiɫ s.čʼətx̌ʷəd tiʔiɫ s.tùbš   LL.
The bear didn't get the man.

ʔux̌ʷálbitᵊb ʔə tiʔiɫ s.tùbš tiʔiɫ s.q̓ìg̓ʷəc   LL.
The man lost the deer.

ʔux̌ʷálbitᵊb ʔə tiʔiɫ s.tubš   LL.
The man lost it.

x̌ʷálbitᵊb ti s.čʼətx̌   ML.
They didn't catch the Kingfisher.

lexical

ʔudx̌ʷx̌ʷálig̓ʷəd čəd

I give up (because it is too much for me to figure out or my patience has given out).

Contrast ʔəsx̌ʷálbicut.

dx̌ʷx̌ʷálig̓ʷəd   He gave up.   EK.

ʔudx̌ʷx̌ʷálig̓ʷədbidəx̌ʷ čəd   I give up; I have to give up. LL.

reduplication

ʔəsx̌ʷàɬx̌ʷalí1c čəd

I can't manage my legs (from knees down).
(An expression meaning that one is very tired from walking.)

1. x̌ʷaqʷ-   bind

See under ɬid(i) 'tie'.   Cf. xʷə́1ə́kʷ 'wrap up, drunk'

lexical

    x̌ʷáqʷabac   belt   LG.

       Cf. ƛ̓áčəpəd

    x̌ʷáqʷabàcəb   bind yourself with a belt; something
                you tie around your waistline   LG.

    ʔəsx̌ʷáqʷqid   He's got a band around his head.   LG.

    ɬux̌ʷàqʷqídəb čəd   I'm going to put a band around my head.   LG.

    x̌ʷəx̌ʷqʷáləqid   headband   EK.

reduplication

    x̌ʷəx̌ʷqʷáləqid   headband   EK.

rejected: *x̌ʷáqʷad, *x̌ʷáqʷəb   LG.

2. x̌ʷaq̓ʷ(a)   worry, bother

Cf. bap(a), bəɬbíd (under bəɬ), (ʔ)idaw1-, dukʷucut

root

    x̌ʷáq̓ʷ   worry   LL.

    ʔəsx̌ʷáq̓ʷ čəd   I'm busy.   LG.

    x̌ʷùɬ sixʷ cədíɬ kʷi səsx̌ʷáq̓ʷ   He will just be a bother.   EC.

-at

    ʔalčux̌ʷáx̌ʷq̓ʷad ti?iɬ s.tubš   LG.
    Something is bothering that man.

... kʷ(i) adsux̌ʷáʔx̌ʷq̓əd tiʔił s.čətxʷəd   JC.

Don't pay any attention to that bear.

dxʷx̌ʷáx̌ʷaq̓ʷacut   She worked herself up.   LL.

-bi-t

ʔəsx̌ʷáq̓ʷbid čəd   I'm too busy, I'm troubled.   LG.

ʔəsx̌ʷáq̓ʷbid čəd ʔə tə d.bədà?   LG.

I'm bothered by my son.

x̌ʷáx̌ʷəq̓ʷbidəxʷ ciʔə? ʔàlš dxʷʔal kʷi gʷədəxʷ.(h)əlíʔis   ML.

He worried about how to make his sister well.

-bi-t-b

ʔəsx̌ʷáq̓ʷbitᵊb čəd ʔə ci ds.k̓ʷùy   LG.

I'm a bother to my mother.

ʔux̌ʷáx̌ʷq̓ʷbitᵊb ʔə tiʔə? ʔàlš, kaẃqs   ML.

Her brother, Raven, worried about her.

lexical

ʔux̌ʷáq̓ʷigʷəd čəd dxʷʔal ti spa.pstədčəł   ML.

I'm worried about our young white boy.

dxʷx̌ʷáq̓ʷigʷəd čəd   I'm worried.   LL.

reduplication

x̌ʷáx̌ʷaq̓ʷəxʷ tiʔə? kàẃqs   Raven is worrying now.   LL.

dxʷx̌ʷáx̌ʷaq̓ʷacut   She worked herself up.   LL.

ʔalću̓x̌ʷáx̌ʷq̓ʷad tiʔił s.tubš   LG.

Something is bothering that man.

... kʷ(i) adsux̌ʷáʔx̌ʷq̓əd tiʔił s.čətxʷəd   JC.

Don't pay any attention to that bear.

1. s.x̌ʷásəb   soapberry, Indian ice cream   LL., Esi.

612

Cf. s.x̌ʷúsəb   soapberry, Indian ice cream

    s.x̌ʷúʔsəb   soapberry, Indian ice cream

1.   x̌ʷəc   sharp (knife), tart (taste)

See under -qəp.

Cf. jəq̓ 'grind', jəq̓ús 'sharpen'

root

    x̌ʷə́c   sharp (knife, axe); tart

       xʷíʔ lə.laʔb x̌ʷə́c ti kupis   LG.
       His coffee isn't very strong.

   -b

    dxʷx̌ʷə́jᵊb   strong/tart tasting   EK., LG.

      láʔb dxʷx̌ʷə̀jᵊb tiʔił kupis   LG.
      His coffee is real strong.

      xʷíʔ lə.laʔb dxʷx̌ʷə́jᵊb ti kupis   LG.
      His coffee isn't very strong.

   lexical

    x̌ʷə́cqs   sharp point   EK., LG.

    x̌ʷəcx̌ʷəjyálus tiʔəʔ s.dəxʷíł   DM.
    The hunting canoe has sharp ends.

2. s.x̌ʷədíʔ NPS   bullhead (fish)

    s.x̌ʷə́diʔ   SPS

    sx̌ʷíʔx̌ʷədìʔ or sx̌ʷíx̌ʷədìʔ   small bullhead

    Cf. s.č̓ábək̓ʷ

3.   x̌ʷəj-   See under x̌ʷəc.

1. x̌ʷə́l   nine

    x̌ʷə́ləl   nine people

        x̌ʷəlálc̓up   nine fires   LG.

        x̌ʷəlálič̓   nine bundles   LG.

        x̌ʷəlálus   nine squares in net making or nine
                      stitches in knitting   LG.

        x̌ʷəlílc   nine dollars   DM.

            x̌ʷəlílc ʔi kʷi x̌ʷəlbít ʔi kʷi ʔił.čəx̌bít
            tiʔił x̌əčàlc ʔə tiʔił pú̓ʔtəd   DM.
            The shirt is 9.95 dollars.

        x̌ʷə́lqs   nine points   LG.

2. s.x̌ʷəláqəd   buck (deer)   See s.qíg̓ʷəc.   VH.

3. x̌ʷə́lč   sea, ocean, sound, salt water

    Contrast qʷuʔ 'freshwater'.

4. x̌ʷə́ƛ̓t   pillow

5. s.x̌ʷə́qʷəb   thunderbird   MS.

    Cf. x̌ʷíqʷədiʔ 'thunder'

6. x̌ʷəs   fat   LG., JC.

    Cf. bəqʷ, s.x̌ʷújəʔ, səxʷúb

    root
        sx̌ʷə́s   grease   LG.

    -il
        ʔux̌ʷ(ə)síləxʷ tə s.qʷəbày?   The dog is getting fat.   LG.

-il-t

ʔuẋʷ(ə)síld čəd tə bùsbus   I fattened up the bull.

ʔuẋʷ(ə)síld čəd tə s.čistxʷ ʔə tə haʔɬ dᵊs.q̓ʷəldáliɬᵊd   LG.
I fattened up (my) husband with my good cooking.

rejected: *ẋʷ(ə)sí(l)s   LG.

1.   ẋʷəš   scatter

      Cf. xʷis(i)

      root

          ʔəsẋʷə́š   It is scattered.   VH.

      -t

          ẋʷəš̀ᵊd   Scatter it!   VH.

      lexical

          sẋʷəšqíd   scatter brained (a loan translation from
                            English)   VH.

2.   ẋʷə́t   SPS

      Cf. sik̓ʷ(i) NPS

          ʔəsẋʷə́t   It's torn.   HD.

→
3.   ẋʷətís   silver diver (or 'regular' diver), a buʔqʷ

      (1) ʔəs.ʔəẋíd kʷi s.ləliʔ ʔə tə ẋʷətís dxʷʔal s.wúqʷa.

      (2) tiʔəʔ s.wúqʷa gʷəl diɬ hík̓ʷbid dxʷʔal tiʔəʔ ẋʷətís.

      (3) ʔiɬ.hík̓ʷ.   (4) gʷəl ẋʷù̓ʔẋʷəyʔ gʷəl (hə)laʔb bì̓ʔbad.

      (5) tiʔəʔ ẋʷətís gʷəl hík̓ʷbid dxʷʔal ciʔəʔ ẋʷù̓ʔẋʷəyʔ?

      (1) What is the difference between a regular (or silver)
      diver and a loon?

      (2) A loon is bigger than a regular diver. (3) It is
      bigger. (4) But the little diver is real small. (5) The
      regular diver is bigger than the little diver.   MS.

615

1. x̌ʷəx̌ʷáyu fly (insect) LG., EK.
   Cf. x̌áyux̌ʷaʔ

2. s.x̌ʷə́x̌ʷc̓q̓ʷ river snipe LL., MS.

   A small, blackish diver and good swimmer.
   It eats trout eggs. It's mostly in creeks
   and rivers. LL.

   In mythology he is a tricky sort of guy.
   He makes up lies to scare people. He is
   tásyəwaʔq (but not so much as Coyote). LL.

3. x̌ʷəyʔcíd whitefish

4. s.x̌ʷəx̌ʷíʔ See s.x̌ʷíʔ.

5. x̌ʷəʔx̌ʷíƛ̓alikʷ See under x̌ʷíƛ̓.

6. x̌ʷi- prefix with certain color terms

   Cf. x̌i-

       x̌ʷiqʷác light green, yellow

       x̌ʷiqʷə́q̓ʷ white

       x̌ʷiq̓ʷix̌ʷ dark blue, dark green

7. x̌ʷic̓(i) plow land (EK. and HD. also use this word to mean
   mark up, scratch. LL. and LG. do not.)

   See under x̌iq̓(i).

   -it

       x̌ʷíc̓id Mark it. Plow land. HD.

   lexical

       ʔudxʷx̌ʷíc̓us čəd I scratched my face. EK.

       x̌ʷíc̓ədup plow LG.

       ʔalc̓ux̌ʷíc̓dupəxʷ čəd I'm plowing now. LG.

reduplication

    pùtəxʷ x̌ʷíčx̌ʷič   All scratched up.   HD.

1.   x̌ʷíkʷ(i)

    ʔux̌ʷíkʷicut   (The fire) blazed up.   EK.

    See under hud(u).

2.   x̌ʷíləb   Skagit   thread   LG.

    See under təbíɫəd.

3.   x̌ʷil-

    ʔəsx̌ʷílič   kneel

        Cf. x̌qpúcid 'knee' (under qəp̓)

4.   x̌ʷiɫ   NPS   lost, turned around

    Cf. wíəx̌ʷ   SPS   lost

    root

    ʔəsx̌ʷiɫ čəd   I'm lost.   EK.

    ʔux̌ʷíɫ čəd diʔiʔaʔ   I got lost right here.   EK.

    ʔux̌ʷíɫ čəd ʔal tiʔəʔ tàwd   I'm lost in this town.   LL.

    ʔux̌ʷíɫ čəd ʔal tudiʔ tàq̓t   I got lost way up mountainward. LL.

    ʔux̌ʷíɫ tiɫ tiʔiɫ ƛ̓ucəxʷu.x̌al   LL.
    It's lost that which I use to write with.

    ʔux̌ʷíɫ ti d.tàlə   lost my money   EK.

    qíyə čəd dxʷʔal sx̌ʷiɫ   EK.
    I got lost/turned around easily.

    xʷiʔ ʔu kʷ(i) adsəsx̌ʷiɫ   Are you lost?   EK.

-t

    ʔəs.ʔəx̌íd kʷi dsəsx̌ʷìłcid   How much do I owe you?   DM.

    łu.tásad čəd tiʔił dsəsx̌ʷìłcid   DM.
    I'll pay you what I owe you.

-dxʷ

    ʔux̌ʷíłdxʷ čəd tił tiʔił λ̓ucəx̌ʷu.x̌al   LL.
    I lost that which I use to write with.

    hi siʔáb, x̌ʷiʔ ləx̌ʷíłdxʷ t(i) ad.tàlə   LL.
    Hey buddy, don't lose your money!

-bi-t

    x̌ʷíłbid   the person whose wife, fiancee etc. was
                    stolen away.   LG.

-alc

    ʔux̌ʷíłalc čəd   I lost it.   EK.

    ʔux̌ʷíłalcbid čəd   I lost it.   LL.

    ʔux̌ʷíłalc čəd ʔə ti ds.k̓ʷ(ə)qʷə̀b   I lost my axe.   EK.

    ʔəsx̌ʷíłálc čəd ʔə ti čáagʷəs   I lost (my) wives.   EK.

    ʔux̌ʷíłálc čəd ʔə ci mali   Mary and I broke up.   EK.

-alikʷ

    λ̓ùb ʔu kʷi gʷədsx̌ʷíłalikʷ   May I charge it?   DM.

reduplication

    ʔəsx̌ʷílił   She is lost.

    (DM. said this after a woman had come to the door to
    ask directions.)

1.   x̌ʷíλ̓   unit of measure from thumb tip to tip of middle
                            finger while fingers are spread. This word is
                            not used in measuring fish. Fish are either hikʷ
                            or miʔman.   DM.

Compare ta̱ɫ(a) and t́ukʷ(u).

cə́b x̌ʷìƛ	two "spans"	DM., LG.
ɫíxʷ x̌ʷìƛ	three "spans"	DM.

lexical

   x̌ʷəʔx̌ʷíƛʌlikʷ   inch worm

      See s.čə́kʷ, s.ʔúləč̓.

rejected: *ɫíxʷəɫ x̌ʷiƛ   DM.

1.   s.x̌ʷíƛəyʔ   mountain goat, a tátačulbixʷ

sx̌ʷíx̌ʷƛəyʔ	kid	
x̌ʷíƛəyʔáɫčiʔ	mountain goat meat	DM.
x̌ʷíƛəyʔəlqìd	wool	LG.

2.   x̌ʷíqʷədiʔ   thunder

    Cf. s.x̌ʷə́qʷəb

x̌ʷíqʷadi(ʔ)b	It's thundering.	EK.
ʔalčuli.ləx̌ tə x̌ʷìqʷədiʔ	lightning	LG.

3.   x̌ʷítx̌ʷit   "summer" seagull (present around Tulalip in August)   LL.

4.   x̌ʷiw-   whistle

    See under cut.

   -t

     x̌ʷíwəd   whistle   LG.

   -c

     x̌ʷìwáac   Whistle at him.   LG.

     pədx̌ʷiwáac   time of whistling (robins), the fifth moon from the December one   HD.

reduplication

ʔalčux̌ʷíʔx̌ʷəw̓əd ti ʔił   He is whistling a tune.   LG.

1. s.x̌ʷí   Oregon grape   JC.

2. s.x̌ʷíʔ or s.x̌ʷəx̌ʷíʔ unidentified kind of small bird. It's myth
                             name is s.pícx̌ʷ, *q.v.*

3. s.x̌ʷiʔáb SPS   traditional story, myth   ESi., JC.

    See under cut.

    Cf. s.yəhúb NPS   traditional story, myth

        sx̌ʷiʔx̌ʷiʔábigʷəd   an improvised, non-traditional, story
                             told to children specifically for their
                             instruction in proper behavior   JC.

4. x̌ʷúbil   Be quiet! Shut up!   EK., LG.

    Cf. gʷə.səbád, gʷə.ƛ̓əlád, x̌ik̓ʷəb

    Contrast dx̌ʷ.yəqqíd̓əb 'Speak up!'

5. x̌ʷúbt   canoe paddle

    Cf. lexical suffix -alwaʔs; ləláb 'oar', ʔišł 'paddle' (verb)

        č̓uʔƛac tə dəx̌ʷu.čəł x̌ʷùbt
        Maple wood is what paddle(s) are made out of.

→
7. s.x̌ʷújəʔ   fat from fish when it is attracting flies and
                           maggots   JC.

    Cf. x̌ʷəs

        sx̌ʷújədàlił̓d   fat of a fish; a fat fish   JC.

8. x̌ʷúk̓ʷədis   buttoned, hooked, fastened   VH.

    (This word is recorded as x̌ʷúq̓ʷədis from LL.)

    See under łid(i) 'tie'.

620

1. x̌ʷul(u)

    Cf. čit

    -ut

        x̌ʷúlud dxʷʔal tiʔił   Put it near that.

        ləx̌ʷúlucut čəd
        I'm moving myself next to someone (to talk to him).

2. x̌ʷul   adverb   'merely, just that and nothing else'

        x̌ʷul čəł yələlʔàc   There are only 6 of us.   LG.

        x̌ʷul čələp ʔu ču(ʔ)kʷs   Are there only 7 of you?   LG.

        x̌ʷul čəxʷ ʔu.gʷuhub   You'll just bark.   ES.

        x̌ʷul čəd ʔu.x̌íbigʷsᵊb   LG.
        I just grabbed my things (because there was no time to pack).

        łu.ʔá· čəxʷ x̌ʷul ł(u)ads.yúbil   ES.
        You'll be there until you die.

        x̌ʷul čəd łu.táb^ᵊb   Let me guess.   EK.

        x̌ʷul ləbíʔ.bəlx̌ʷəd   He passed him by just a bit.   ML.

        gʷəl x̌ʷúl ʔił.təx̌əgʷàs kʷi s.ʔux̌ʷs   ML.
        And (got) just halfway.

        x̌ʷul páƛaƛ tiʔəʔ łuds.ʔàbyid   ES.
        I'll just give him junk.

        x̌ʷùl ʔəlču.ƛáləx̌ᵊb t(ə) ad.hud   LG.
        Your fire is just a crackling.

        x̌ʷùl čəxʷ ʔəxʷ.líligʷədbid   LG.
        Don't pay any attention to it.

        x̌ʷùl čəxʷ ƛ(u)as.qʷíq̓ʷcut   LG.
        Just build yourself up now (encouraging a sick person).

        x̌ʷúl čəxʷ ʔu.kʷàd   Just let it go (like that).   VH.

x̌ʷúl̓ gʷəɬ dxʷʔal s.tùləkʷ   It belongs just on river(s).   DM.

gʷə.háw̓ə? x̌ʷul̓ ʔu.ɬəgʷəldxʷ ciʔə? čəgʷàs   ML.
He found out what had transpired at home when he left
(his) wife.

x̌ʷul̓əxʷ ləs.cɬíl ti ʔəxʷ.gədgyax̌əds   ML.
He was just bleeding under the arms.

təláwil gʷəl x̌ʷul̓əxʷ ʔu.bə̀č   He ran until he fell.   ES.

x̌ʷul̓əxʷ ʔu.lə̀k̓ʷəd čáləsab   EK.
They ate by hand (because they had neither fork nor knife).

x̌ʷul̓əxʷ jəɬ xʷiʔ gʷədsəxʷs.ʔìtutᵊb   LG.
I just wish I weren't so sleepy.

x̌ʷúl̓əxʷ čəxʷ jəɬ gʷə.ʔə̀ƛ̓   I hope you will come.   LG.

xʷiʔ ləx̌ʷul̓ diɬ kʷs(i) ads.ɬadəyʔ kʷ(i) ads.x̌əč   LL.
Don't think only about your woman.

ləx̌ʷúl̓əxʷ ʔə kʷi tà.ɬəgʷət   It will soon be noon.   LG.

xʷiʔ kʷ(i) adsx̌ʷul̓əxʷ lílusbic!   LL.
Don't just remove your face from me.

diɬəxʷ tudəxʷx̌ʷúl̓səxʷ   That was that.   ML.

x̌ʷulul̓ bəčác tiʔə? diʔə? *basket* ʔəs.hùytub ʔə ciʔə?
diʔə? s̓.ƛ̓àlqəb   LG.
Basket Woman had made the basket all out of snakes.

-ab   similar to, like, as

  Cf. x̌əɬ, 596.1

x̌ʷúl̓əb ʔə ʔəcà   He's just like me.   EK.

xʷìʔ ləx̌ʷúl̓əb ʔə dəgʷì   He is not like you.   EK.

x̌ʷúl̓əb ʔə tə bù?qʷ tiʔiɬ qyuuqs   DM.
A seagull is like a waterfowl.

x̌ʷúl̓əb ʔə s.qʷəbàyʔ tiʔił s.tiqàyuʔ   DM.
A wolf is like a dog.

gʷəl bə.q̓ʷaq̓ʷab x̌ʷul̓áb ʔə tiʔił ƛu.cutcut ʔə tiʔił
sup̓qs ʔəl ʔəł əs.t̓agʷtəs   ML.
And he barked again just the way a hair seal sounds
when it is put up on it.

ʔu.q̓ʷàq̓ʷab čəxʷ x̌ʷúl̓əb ʔə tiʔił ƛəsəs.hùy ʔə tiʔił sùp̓qs   ML.
Bark just the way a hair seal does.

ʔəbíiləxʷ gʷ(ə)usà.saq̓ʷ gʷəl gʷ(ə)ucútcut x̌ʷúl̓əb ʔə tiʔił
Whenever they would fly, they would talk like that.

haʔł kʷi gʷəs.čalatᵊbs t(i) ads.gʷaʔ ad(d)šəł.x̌əčᵊb ʔal
ti s.watixʷtəd x̌ʷul̓ab ʔə təs(u).čalad t(i) ads.gʷaʔ
ad(s)šəł.x̌əčᵊb ʔal di šəq
Fiat voluntas tua, sicut in celo, et in terra.

ƛub čəxʷ ʔu.baliicyitubuł ʔə tə jək̓ʷadədčəł x̌ʷul̓ab ʔə
təs(u).baliicyid čəł tə ləliʔ ʔacił̓talbixʷ ʔə tə
jək̓ʷadəds dxʷʔal dibəł
Et dimitte nobis debita nostra, sicut et nos dimittimus
debitoribus nostris.

x̌ʷul̓áb ʔə ti bàds ti s(h)ájᵊbs tiʔił ləgʷəb   LG.
That youth is as tall as his father.

x̌ʷul̓áb ʔu ʔə ti bàds kʷi s(h)ájᵊbs ʔə tiʔił ləgʷəb   LG.
Is that youth as tall as his father?

s(h)ájᵊb tiʔił ləgʷəb x̌ʷul̓àb ʔə ti bàds   LG.
That youth is as tall as his father.

s(h)ájᵊb čəd x̌ʷul̓ab ʔə dəgʷi   LG.
I'm as tall as you are.

ƛal ʔu bə.qà tə d.yìq̓us x̌ʷul̓áb ʔə t(ə) ads.gʷaʔ   LG.
Do I have as many cedar-root baskets as you have?

λál čəd bə.ʔàɬ x̌ʷułàb ʔə dəgʷì   LG.

I'm just as fast as you.

lúʎ čəxʷ ʔu x̌ʷułàb ʔə tiʔiɬ s.tùbš   LG.

Are you as old as that man?

xʷíʔ čəd ləx̌ʷułàb ʔə dəgʷì kʷi gʷəds.lùʎ   LG.

I'm not as old as you are.

xʷíʔ čəd lə.lùʎ x̌ʷułàb ʔə dəgʷì   LG.

I'm not as old as you are.

1. x̌ʷúʎ(u)   chew up

    See under k̓aw(a).

        x̌ʷúʎud   chew it

                         "A rougher word than k̓aw(a). It's less elegant.
                         Or it can refer to what some animal did, i.e.,
                         chewed up my sheep."   LL.

2. x̌ʷuq̓ʷədis   pin with a straight pin   LL.

    (This word is recorded as x̌ʷúkʷədis from VH.)

    See under ɬid(i) 'tie'.

    Cf. ʔəsʎi.ʎpabacəb   hold blanket around self with hand.
                              (It's not fastened.)

    Cf. ʔəs.xʷə́lkʷtxʷ   wrapped around with a blanket

        x̌ʷúq̓ʷədisəd   pin with a straight pin in order
                              to put a wrap on someone   LL.

        ʔux̌ʷúq̓ʷədisəb čəd   I pin a wrap about myself with
                              a straight pin.   LL.

3. s.x̌ʷúsəb   See s.x̌ʷásəb.

4. x̌ʷúx̌ʷəyʔ   hell diver, a buʔqʷ

    x̌ʷúʔx̌ʷəyʔ   little hell diver. In the old stories she is
                         the sister of s.wúqʷad and x̌əwáwq̓, and wife of s.bəq̓ʷáʔ.

(1) gʷəl tiʔəʔ s.wúqʷa[d] gʷəl diɬ hikʷbid dxʷʔal tiʔəʔ x̌ʷətís. (2) gʷəl tiʔəʔ x̌ʷúʔx̌ʷəyʔ gʷəl (hə)láʔb bìʔbad. (3) x̌əɬ ti di.d(ə)č̓akʷbixʷ tiʔiʔəʔ diʔəʔ. (4) tux̌ʷ ləcu.ʔúsil. (5) tiʔəʔ x̌ʷətís gʷəl hík̓ʷbid dxʷʔal ciʔəʔ x̌ʷùʔx̌ʷəyʔ. (6) x̌ʷúʔx̌ʷəyʔ gʷəl x̌ʷuɬab ʔə gʷəds.cut bìʔbad

(1) The loon is bigger than the regular (or silver) diver. (2) And little hell diver is real small. (3) (It is) as though they belong to a different class (of waterfowl). (4) But it does dive. (5) The regular diver is bigger than the little hell diver. (6) Of the little hell diver I would just say it is small.   MS.

1.   x̌ʷúyšəd   name for Camano Head, the southern tip of
                          Camano Island.   EK.

y

The sound represented by this letter is very similar to that of *y* in English spelling. [voiced glide to higher front position]

1. -y-   lexical connective

    See under -al-.

2. yábuk̓ʷ   fight

    Cf. x̌ílix̌ 'battle, fight, war'

3. s.yált   SPS   watertight cedar-root basket

    Cf. s.pəču̓?   Snoh.

        yíq̓us   Skagit

4. -yalus   lexical suffix   'end, edge'

    Cf. -ax̌ad

      ?ilyálus   end (of a table)

      di?yálus   on the end, the other end

      ɬəq̓yálus   edge (of a table)

      gʷədyálus   lower end (of a sheet of paper)

        x̌álad t(i) ads.dá? ?al ti s.gʷədyálus   JC.
        Write your name on the bottom edge.

      šəqyálus ?ə tə *page*   top of the page

      čət̓ʷyálus   end (of something)

      x̌ʷəjx̌ʷəjyálus ti?ə? s.dəxʷíɬ gʷəl ?əs.p̓ìlp̓ilyálus
      ti?ə? ƛ̓əlay?   DM.
      A hunting canoe has sharp (pointed) ends, but a
      shovel-nose canoe has flat ends.

5. yál?šəd   See under yəl.

1. yáƛ(a)   fetch water; gore; partitive of water

    Cf. k̓ʷad(a) 'dip out water', tixʷ(i) 'bail out a boat'

    -at

        yáƛəd   dip it out   LG., EK., LL.

        ʔuyáƛətᵊb ʔə ciʔiɫ qʷist   HD., EK., LL.
        He was gored by a cow.

        ʔəxʷyáƛatᵊbᵊb čəd ʔə ciʔiɫ qʷist   LL.
        The cow wants to hook me.

    -yi-

        yáƛyic   Get me some water.   EK.

        tuyáƛyid čəd   I got her some water.   EK.

        hi̓wil, yáƛyic ʔə kʷi qʷù?   Go, get me some water.   LG.

    -b

        yáƛᵊb   carry water   HD., LG.
                                     get water, dip out   LL.

        t(u)asyáƛᵊb čəd   I was carrying water.   EK.

    lexical

        yáƛalikʷ   getting water   LL.

        ʔəxʷyáƛ   puddle   LG.

        suyáƛ   name of village near Darrington,
                                     Washington   LG.

    rejected: *yáƛil

2. yápəntukʷ   woman's name, VH.'s daughter, Lois; named
                             by VH.'s father

3. xʷ.yátacut   man's name, LG.'s husband, Richard

1. -yaqid   lexical suffix   'the very top'

    Cf. -qid

       šəqyáqid   tree top, roof

2. yáwdᵊb   spirit power song   LG.

    Cf. ƛilib, s.qəlálitut

       ƚuyáwdᵊb čəd   I'll sing my power.   LG.

3. yaw̓   See under yəhaw̓.

4. s.yáya?   (perhaps s.ya?ya?)   relative, friend

    syə̀yá?ya?   relatives, friends

    Cf. ?íišəd, ?á?yəd, q̓ʷú?udaq

5. yáyus   work

    root

       ?uyáyus čəd ?al di?àbac ?ə ti?iƚ s.c̓ə̀tqs   DM.
       I'm working on the other side of the point.

       gʷəyáyus čəd   I can work.   LG.

       ƚuyáyus čəd   I will work.   EK.

       ləcuyáyus, ləcuyáyus, ləcuyáyus, ck̓ʷáqid ləcuyàyus   ES.
       (Ant) is working, working, working, always working.

       xʷi? gʷədsyàyus   I will not work.   EK.

       ?əxʷyáyusᵊb čəd   I need to work. I want to work. LG.

       čád kʷ(i) adsuyáyus   Where do you work?   DM.

       čád kʷ(i) adsəsyáyus Same gloss: 'Where do you work?',
                              but the preceding example is preferred. DM.

-bid

    ýáyusbid   work at it   LL.

rejected:

    *čad kʷ(i) adsƛ̉uyayus

1.   s.yaẏlúpqsači?   ring for finger

       Cf. šiščqsači? (under šič̉)

2.   yá?ɬ   adverb   'unrealized wish, be unable'

       yà?ɬ čəd ?əxʷs.?íbəš̉əb   I want to walk but can't.   LG.

       yà?ɬ ?əxʷ.x̌áyəbusəb   LG.
       He is trying to smile but can't.

3.   yəbál?txʷ   head office, Indian agency

       (Perhaps derived from ?i?ab-?al?txʷ.)

4.   yəc-   tell, report, inform; news

      See under cut.

      -t

        ?uyə̀cc čəxʷ   You told me.   LL., LG.

          xʷi? kʷ(i) adsyə̀cc   Don't tell on me.   HD.

        ?uyə́ctubuɬ čəxʷ   You told on us.   LL.

        ?uyə́cəd čəd   I told it (in response to question,
                             "Did you tell it?")   LL.

        yə́ccut   tell all about own hunting trip,
                        latest adventure, etc.   LG.

      -yi-

        yəcyíd   report for him   LG.

-b

ʔuyə́cᵊb čəd	I told it.	LL.
xʷiʔ gʷədsuyə̀cᵊb	I never tell.	HD.
syə́cᵊb	news	
qá ʔu kʷ(i) adsyə̀cᵊb		ES.

Do you have lots of news? (A common greeting.)

xʷiʔ gʷədsyə́cᵊb

I haven't any news. (The typical answer to the preceding question.)

-bi-t

yəcᵊbíc	He told on me (and really made a good story of it).	LG.

-b-yi-

yəcᵊbyíd	inform someone for him	LG.

-b-txʷ

ʔuyə́cᵊbtxʷ (h)əlgʷəʔ	They told him.	EK.
ʔuyəcᵊbtúb čəd	He told me.	ES.
ʔuyəcᵊbtúbš	Tell me.	VH.

yəcᵊbtúbš ʔəs.x̌ìd kʷ(i) ɫ(u)adsu.hùyud kʷə səpləl   JC.

Tell me how you would make bread.

ʔuyəcᵊbtúbicid čəd	I told you.	EK.
xʷìʔ kʷ(i) adsyəcᵊbtúbš	Don't tell me.	EK.
xʷìʔ kʷ(i) adsyə́cᵊbtxʷ kʷi gʷàt	Don't tell anyone.	HD.

ʔəx̌íd əẁə gʷəyəcᵊbtùbšəxʷ ʔəs.gʷə́q̓ tiʔiɫ dxʷši?.šɫᵊb   ES.

Why didn't you tell me the window was open?

reduplication

ʔuyəcyəcác čəxʷ	You have been babbling around about me.	LL.

rejected:

    *yəc^əbt^əb, *yəcib   LL.

1.   yəháw̓   proceed

     Also pronounced simply yáw? and occasionally haw?.

     as head of a predicate

         bəyəháw̓tx^w (čəx^w)   Again go ahead.   ES.

         yəháw̓tx^w   Go ahead.   EK.

         x^wí? g^wədsyáw̓ ?u.q̓p̓ùd   I don't have to pay him!   ES.

     as adverb

         yəhàw̓ bə.?ílid   Please repeat that.   ES.

         hàw̓ wíliq̓^w   Go ahead, ask!   ES.

         yəháw̓ s.qaǰət^əb   Say it in Skagit!   VH.

         yáw̓əx^w čəx^w ɫu.q^wí?ac^əbš   HD.
         I'll wait for you to phone me.

         ?əs.dúk^w tə d.?àl?al. yáw̓əx^w čəd ɫu.q^wìbid   JC.
         My house needs repairing. Now I'll have to fix it.

         yáw̓ (hə)lá?b ?əs.tàg^wəx^w g^wəl g^wə.huydub ti?iɫ qyuuqs   DM.
         (You would have to) be really hungry before (you) would
         eat a seagull.

2.   yədwás   Skagit   heart

     Cf. s.čáli?, -idg^was

3.   s.yəyəhúb   NPS   traditional old story

     also just s.yəhúb

     Cf. s.x̌^wi?áb   SPS   traditional old story

     -tx^w

       yəyəhúbtx^w   recite a myth   ML.

1. yəl-   both, pair

         yəlgʷásbid   Put it on both sides.   LG.

         yəlábcəd   trousers   ESi., LL.

           yəyəĺábcəd   panties   LL.

           Cf. cqíws   Skagit   trousers

         yəláči?   both hands

           Cf. jəláči?   SPS   six

         yəla?c   NPS   six

         ɬíxʷači?əxʷ čəd ?i kʷi yəla?c   I'm 36 now.   LG.

         gʷíhači? čəd ?ə kʷi yəla?cìlc ?i kʷi ?iɬ.čəx̌   DM.
         Lend me six dollars and fifty cents.

           yəlà?cəɬtáɬ   six taɬ, about 36 feet   DM.

           yəlà?c táɬ   Same gloss: six taɬ, about 36 feet DM.

           yəlˀə́lá?c   six people   LL.

           yəla?cálič   six bundles   LG.

           yəla?cálčup   six fires   LG.

2. yəláb   either parent's sibling of either sex when
                     parent is deceased

    See under qəsí?.

      Cf. s.qəláyǰut   the reciprocal of yəláb

         s.bálucid   in-law when link is dead

3. yəlyəláb   ancestors

    See under bədá?.

1. yəpyáptəd   a man's name, LG.'s husband's brother, John

2. yəq-

      dxʷyəqqídᵊb   Speak up!   LG.

      dxʷyəqqíd kʷ(i) ads.t̓ílib   Sing loudly.

      dxʷyəqqíd ɫu.gʷáagʷədəs   She talks loud when she talks.

3. yəsáwi   alder   ESi.

    Cf. s(ə)k̓ʷəbác   alder   LG., MC.

        sək̓ʷəbác   alder   EK., LL.

4. yəwáɫ   particle, an intensifier

    diɫəxʷ yəwáɫ liɫ.laq   She was the very last.

5. yəẃyəɫdáʔ   fawn, one year old deer   VH.

    See under s.qígʷəc 'deer'.

6. yəxʷ   SPS   a particle providing for the addition of
                     items (or people) to the predicate complement

    See under ʔi (the NPS equivalent).

7. yəx̌í   adverb   'because, for what reason'

    ʔəs.ƛ̓áx̌ čəd yəx̌i ʔəl̓cu.šə́xʷᵊb   LG.
    I'm cold because the wind is blowing.

    x̌ályic ʔə tə s.x̌àl yəx̌i čəd ʔu.k̓ʷásači?
    Write the letter for me because I burned my hand.

    híkʷbid ʔə s.dəxʷi̓ɫ yəx̌i dəxʷuʔul.ʔuluɫ ʔə tiʔəʔ
    diʔəʔ ʔaciɫtalbixʷ   DM.
    It is bigger than a hunting canoe because people
    use it for travelling.

xʷi? lə.q̓ílbid yəx̌i tàtačulbixʷ   DM.

It is not a vehicle because it is an animal.

1. yə́x̌ʷəd   flint, arrowhead

2. yəx̌ʷ(ə)lá?   eagle

   díɬ ?u bə.x̌ìbx̌ib ti?iɬ yəx̌ʷəlá?. ?i. ƛ̓ál bə.x̌ìbx̌ib
   ti?iɬ yəx̌ʷəlá?
   Is an eagle also a bird of prey? Yes. An eagle is
   also a bird of prey.   DM.

3. yəydú?   swing   EK.

   ?alčuyəy̓dú?   swinging (in a swing)   LG.

     yəydú?ac   honeysuckle   EK.

     yaydú?ac   honeysuckle   MC.

4. s.yəylúpqsàči?   ring (for finger)

   (Also recorded as s.yay̓lúpqsači?, *q.v.*)

5. -yi- NPS   secondary suffix marking transferred agent

   -ši- SPS

   (Suffixes having two forms, one occurring finally and the other
    not, have the "final" one before -yi-.)

       ?ábyid   give it to him   ?ab   have; reach, extend

       ?íšɬyid   paddle in his   ?íšɬ   paddle
                    place

       ?úx̌ʷyid   fetch it for him; ?úx̌ʷ   go
                    go in his place

       ?úx̌ʷtxʷyid   take it for him   ?úx̌ʷtxʷ   take it

634

1. yíčᵊb   notice, observe, see; figure out

    Cf. pítᵊb

    -bid

        ʔuyíčᵊbid čəd tiʔił   I noticed that.
                                    I happened to understand.

        ʔuyíčᵊbitᵊb čəd
        They caught on to me (the shenanigans I was up to).

            (This is equivalent to ʔugʷə.háytub čəd.)

2. yíq̓(i)   work something into a tight place, "worrying" it
                             into place; make/ weave cedar-root baskets

    Cf. ʔəqʷál   weave a blanket

        ƛ́agʷ(a)   stitch, make mats

        t̓əbš   braid

        gəlk̓   entwine; make a clam basket

    -it

        yíq̓id   weave it   HD.

        yíq̓idəxʷ   weave it now   HD.

    -b

        syíq̓ib   basket (in general)   LL.

        yíq̓ibəxʷ čəxʷ   Weave a basket!   HD.

        ʔuyíq̓ib ciʔił s.łàdəyʔ ʔə tə s.p(ə)čùʔ   LL.
        That woman made a basket.

    lexical

        yíq̓us   watertight basket made of cedar roots   LG.

            Cf. s.pəčúʔ Snoh., s.yált SPS

Cf. s.gʷəlúlč   loosely woven basket

    xʷ.ʔáx̌ʷaʔəd   clam basket

    ləqʷá   a soft, pliable basket made of s.łuáyʔ

    -ulč   container

other derivation

    yíq̓ibad   awl for weaving

1.   yíyəq̓ʷ   pocket knife

   Cf. s.dúukʷ, t̓áltəd

2.   yúbəč NPS   king salmon

   x̌ʷuł ʔal jíxʷ s.jə̀lč̓ x̌u.ʔə́x̌ tiʔəʔ yùbəč   MS.
   In the first part of the year the king salmon comes.

   yúʔibəč   blackmouth   LL.

   Cf. tuʔáłəd king salmon   ESi.
     sač̓əb Muck. king salmon

3.   yúbil   starve; (animals) die

   See under ʔatəbəd '(humans) die'; and compare tágʷəxʷ 'hunger'.

   lexical

    yúbiligʷəd miscarriage (lit. 'dead inside')   LL.

   reduplication

    yúyəbil   (a chick, puppy) dies   LG.

    yəyúbil   They are starving.   LG.

    yúbyubil   They (distributive) are starving.   LG.

    yúyuyəbil children are starving   LG.

    yúbubil   (The body) is tired out/ doesn't feel well. LG.

    See x̌əł, 593.5; dukʷab.
    yúʔybilàwil someone plays dead   LL.

1. yuhú?ud   interjective particle   'You see?, See there!,
                                                   I told you so!'

2. yúla?   wild celery

3. -yuq̓ʷ   Snoh.   lexical suffix   'throat'

    Cf. -apsəb 'neck'

    ?əxʷ.x̌əɬyúq̓ʷ čəxʷ ?u   Do you have a sore throat?   LL.

    tux̌ʷ čəd ?udxʷɬí?.ɬqʷyuq̓ʷəb   LL.
    I just have to wet my throat.

    q̓əyúq̓ʷ   throat

4. -yus   Skagit   lexical suffix   'throat'

    Cf. -apsəb 'neck'

    ?u.ɬíč̓yusəb   He cut his own throat.   LG.

    ɬídyusəd   Tie it about the neck.   LG.

    λ̓ip̓yusəd   Choke him.   LG.

    Cf. λ̓ip̓əpsəb

5. cis.yúyud   woman's name, LG.'s mother

6. yú(?)   slang for ha?ɬ   EK.

    pút yu su.ləllícut ?ə ti?ə? šíqʷs   ML.
    His hat was changing (colors) very prettily.

7. yú?qʷ   an old salmon that has already spawned
                                 and is about to die

8. yú?yu?bəč   butterfly

ʔ

The sound represented by this letter is made by closing the vocal cords abruptly, a kind of catch in the throat, as in the English negative word *uh-uh*. [glottal stop]

1.   ʔa   be located

    Cf. ʔal, ɫaʔ

    (Does not occur with the aspectual prefixes u-, as-, lə-.)

    root

        ʔá ti sup̓qs ʔal tə ʔá   ML.
        There is Hair Seal right there!

        ʔá ɫiʔiɫ s.čə́ɬxʷəd ʔal kʷədiʔ dəxʷəs.ɫáɫlils   ES.
        There was Bear where he lived.

        ʔáhəxʷ tiʔəʔ diʔəʔ čačas ʔal tiʔəʔ sx̌a.x̌ax̌aʔs
        This young man stayed with his in-laws.

        ʔá tiʔəʔ syə.yəhùb dxʷʔal ʔàdad tiʔiɫ s.čə́ɬxʷəd ʔi
        ciʔiɫ ƛàƛačəpəd   ES.
        There is an old story pertaining to Bear and Ant.

        bəʔá tiʔiɫ ʔukʷàl.k̓ʷalčcut   ML.
        He (Hair Seal) is still there bending himself backwards.

        ƛàl bəʔá ʔal kʷídiɫ   VH.
        It was there too at Quinault.

        dídiʔɫ uʔxʷ ʔu ʔà   Is it still there?   LL.

        xʷiʔəxʷ tiʔəʔ diʔəʔ s.tubš dxʷʔal kʷi gʷəsʔás   EK.
        No man was there.

        xʷíʔ kʷi dsəs.(h)áydxʷ kʷi sʔàs kʷi ʔəs.x̌ə̀ɫ   EK.
        I didn't know anyone was sick.

        ʔəs.ɫáɫlil tiʔiɫ s.čə́ɬxʷəd ʔal kʷədiʔ dəxʷʔàs   LG. from ES.
        Bear lives there where he is.

        diɫ tudəxʷʔá kʷi tuds.capaʔ ʔi kʷi tuds.čabiqʷ   VH.
        That is the place where my grandfather and great
        grandfather (were from).

ɫčíltubəxʷ dxʷʔà   He was brought to there.   VH.

yəx̌i tu.ɫálil kʷi *ship* dxʷʔa   VH.
Because the ship docked there.

tuʔʔáhəxʷ gʷəl tu.háydubəxʷ ʔə kʷi dxʷs.λ̀alb kʷi
gʷəsu.lə̀k̓ʷəds (h)əlgʷəʔ tiʔəʔ gʷəɫ pàstəd s.ʔə̀ɫəd   VH.
From there (it was that) the Clallam learned to
eat of the Whiteman's food.

ʔá ʔu kʷ(i) ads.ʔáx̌ʷuʔ   Do you have any clams?   DM.

ʔí. ʔá ti ds.ʔáx̌ʷuʔ   Yes. I have some clams.

  Cf. ʔəbsʔáx̌ʷuʔ čəxʷ ʔu (under ʔabs-)

      ʔəbsʔáx̌ʷuʔ čəd   (under ʔabs-)

lílil čəxʷ tuʔʔal tiʔiɫ (ʔ)a   Get away from that.   LG.

díɫtxʷ tiʔiɫ ʔa   He's the one.   LG.

-t

ɫuʔácid čəd   I will put you there.   ML.

ʔáhədəxʷ   put it there   LG., EK.

ʔátəbəxʷ tiʔəʔ q̓ìlbid   The canoe was put out.

gʷəl ʔuʔátəb tiʔəʔ x̌əɫ ti s.gʷistalb   VH.
And (something) like sand was put there.

-bi-t

x̌ʷùbálijəbidəxʷ ʔal tiʔiɫ ʔəbíds ʔə ti   ML.
She threw it on her back having it right there.
(As she said this, ML. reached behind and touched
 her back between the shoulder blades.)

in derivation

ʔəλá   come here

ʔədá   come near/here   LG.

ʔácəc   be located right there
                                   It is there. ("If someone is looking for
                                   something, I say, ʔácəc.")   LG.

ʔácəc uʔxʷ ʔu   Is it still there?   LL.

ʔácəc tiʔił bəščəb   Mink was there.   ML.

ʔácəc tiʔił tu.x̌ax̌ildəgʷəl tuíʔal tiʔił tus.wiw̓sus (h)əlgʷəʔ ES.
There was a couple who loved each other from childhood.

dày̓ʔəxʷ t(u)as.qʷàqʷtxʷ tiʔił tuʔácəc   ML.
That was all that was left right there on that spot.

ʔácəc xʷuʔᵊlə ʔal kʷədiʔ dəxʷ.ʔàs ʔə tiʔił d.bədbədáʔs
(This long phrase is what was given for the English
 concept *family*.)

xʷí·ʔəxʷ gʷəs.x̌ʷú·bil ʔə ciʔəcəc wàq̓waq̓ ʔu.cutcut   ML.
This Frog does not quit talking.

ƛubəxʷ čəd x̌ʷuləxʷ łu.ʔíx̌ʷid ciʔəcəc waq̓waq̓ dxʷʔal
tiʔəʔ ʔəs.c̓əp̓àlič   ML.
I had better just throw this Frog into the swamp.

tubə.dáʔᵊbəxʷ (h)əlgʷəʔ ʔi tiʔəcəc təkʷtəkʷəlùs   ML.
They had a child, (Frog) and this Owl.

xʷíʔəxʷ gʷəs.x̌ʷúbil ʔə tiʔəcəc bìʔ.bədaʔs   ML.
This little child doesn't shut up.

kʷədátᵊbəxʷ ʔə ciʔəʔ waq̓waq̓ tiʔəcəc bìʔ.bədaʔs   ML.
Frog took this little child.

łu.ʔàl čəxʷ c̓əp̓álič kʷi ł(u)adəxʷ.ʔá x̌ʷəbtᵊbáxʷ ʔəs.q̓ʷuʔ
ʔə tiʔəcəc biʔ.bədáʔᵊbs mìʔman̓ səs.bədáʔᵊbs ciʔəʔ cədił
waq̓waq̓   ML.
In the swamp is where you will be, thrown down together
with this little child, the small one Frog bore.

lə.ʔíbəšəxʷ ʔal tiʔacəc lił.ʔilgʷił   ML.
He was walking right here at the very water's edge
of the beach.

1.   ʔab   reach, extend

　　-t

　　　ʔábcutəxʷ dxʷʔal kʷi gʷəs.cáq̓at^əbs   ML.
　　　It (Seal) extended itself so that they could spear it.

　　-yi- (-ši-)

　　　ʔábyid   Give it to him.   LG., HD., LL.

　　　ʔuʔábyicid čəd ʔə tə tàlə   I gave you the money.   EK.

　　　ʔə(s).šúdxʷ čəd ti x̌uiqs ʔə tiʔə(ʔ) ads.ʔábyid ti s.tùdəq   LG
　　　I see the box you gave the slave.

　　　dəc̓uʔ s.tab gʷəl xʷíʔ gʷətusʔàbyit^əbs ʔə tiʔəʔ ʔàcił̓talbixʷ
　　　tiʔəʔ *Governor Stevens.*
　　　One thing the Indians did not give to Governor Stevens.

　　　ʔábšic   SPS   Give it to me.   ESi.

　　　ʔábšid   SPS   Give it to him.   HD.

　　lexical

　　　ʔábači(ʔ)b   reach with hand   LG.

　　　ʔábalikʷ   give away   VH.

　　　ʔábaq^əd   return something (borrowed)   HD., EK., LG.
　　　　　　　　　give a lift   LL.

　　　ʔábgʷəs   delivering (moving, carrying) belongings   LG.

　　　　ʔəx̣txʷáxʷ (h)əlgʷəʔ tiʔəʔ s.tàbs ʔal tiʔəʔ dádatu
　　　　ʔuʔàbgʷəsəxʷ (h)əlgʷəʔ   LG.
　　　　They bring their things with them in the morning
　　　　piece by piece.

　　　　ʔuʔábgʷəs (h)əlgʷəʔ ʔal tiʔəʔ q̓xʷàbac ʔal tiʔəʔ st^əkʷàb   EC.
　　　　They brought them piece by piece to the upriver side
　　　　of the bend, to st^əkʷàb.

| ʔábšədᵊb | take a step | LG. |

| ʔabʔabšadᵊb | sticking out one foot after the other as does a heron while stalking fish | ML. |

| ʔábucdid čəd | I take him his lunch, dinner. | LG. |

ʔabs-   prefix denoting possession

Compare constructions with ʔabs- to those involving ʔa and possessive affixes.

| ʔabsʔáx̌ʷuʔ čəxʷ ʔu | Do you have any clams? | DM. |

| ʔabsʔáx̌ʷuʔ čəd | I have some clams. | DM. |

| ʔəbsx̌əč | He is sensible. | LG. |

| ʔábsʔə̀ɬᵊd čəd | I have some food. | LG. |

| ʔəbsbədbədáʔiləxʷ (h)əlgʷəʔ | They had children. | LG. |

| ʔábstàlə čəd | I have money. | LG. |

ʔábstà ʔtəla čəxʷ ʔu
Do you have a little money?   LG.

xʷúʔᵊlə ʔabstàlə   He might have money.   LG.

x̌ʷúləxʷ jəɬ gʷ(əʔ)abstàlə ti d.suq̓ʷaʔ   LG.
I hope my younger brother has money.

bək̓ʷ s.táb ʔəsʔəbstàlətxʷ (h)əlgʷəʔ   EK.
They had to have money for everything.

tuʔəbsqəlík̓ʷ čəd ʔə ti x̌ʷi.qʷə̀q̓ʷ   LG.
I had a white blanket.

| ʔəbsyíq̓us čəd | I have a basket. | LG. |

λál čəd b(əʔ)àbsyíq̓us   I have a basket too.

ɬuʔəbsyíq̓us čəd ʔal kʷi dùkʷəɬdat   LG.
I'll have a basket tomorrow.

rejected:

*ʔabstəqáči ʔilc čəd

1. ?ac-   center (of something round or enveloping?)
                                 Always bound to a lexical.

Compare especially ?udəgʷ-. See also ?acəc under ?a.

Other bound locative roots are c̆ət-, jəh-, qəl-, and ?udəgʷ-.

Similar locative roots that are often but not always bound
are di? and ?il.

?ácap	in the center of the bottom	LL.
s?ácgʷəs	middle of the body, waistline	EK.
	small of the back	LL.
?ácgʷił	middle of lake/river	
?ácigʷəd	inside	

    tu?ácigʷədil c̆əd   I was inside (the whale).

    łixʷdát ti?ił ?àcigʷəds (h)əlgʷə? ?ə ti?ił c̆əxʷ⁼lù?
    Three days they were inside the whale.   ES.

s?ácus	face
xʷ?əcúsac̆i?	palm of hand
xʷ?əcú(s)šəd	sole of foot

    rejected: *?acabac   DM.

2. ?acíł   wait

    Cf. ?á?s

?acíł c̆əd łu.qà?qʷ	I'll rest.
?acíł c̆əd ?u.c̆əgʷùlc̆	I'll wash the dishes first (before I leave).

?acíł ?ugʷə.ƛəlàd tə s.pà?c gʷəl ?u.qʷu?qʷa?   LG.
The bear stopped for a drink.

bəkʷ lə.təláwil tə s.pa?c ?i tə hupt gʷəl ?acíł ?ugʷə.ƛəlad
tə s.pa?c gʷəl ?u.qʷu?qʷa? gʷəl bə.təlawiləxʷ
The bear and deer were running and the bear stopped for a
drink and then ran again.

ʔacíł xʷiʔgʷ(ə) ads.ʔùx̌ʷ	Don't go yet awhile.
ʔacíł ʔaʔs (h)əlgʷəʔ	Just wait for them.
ʔacíł ƛəlláʔ	Wait awhile.
ʔacíł ʔíʔixʷəd	I'm humbling myself.

1. ʔáciłtalbixʷ, ʔáciłtəbixʷ   1. people as opposed to all other animals, plants and other dwellers on this earth

2. Indian as opposed to all other races. Contrast pástəd, x̌ʷəltəb; s.q̓ʷix̌ʷ, čáydi.

2. ʔáčədà·   an exclamation of mild surprise, often (but not always) about something that is unfortunate

3. ʔádad   pertain to, be characteristic of

ʔá tiʔəʔ s.yəyəhùb dxʷʔal ʔadad tiʔíł s.čətxʷəd ʔi
ciʔíł ƛàƛačəpəd   ES.
There is an old story pertaining to Bear and Ant.

díł tu.šáč tiʔíł dxʷʔal ʔàdad k̓aʔkaʔ   ML.
That's the end of that (story) pertaining to Crow.

túx̌ʷ ds(y)àdad   It's just my way.   LL.

4. ʔádəkʷ   each and everyone of you

   Cf. bək̓ʷ 'all'

5. ʔádʔad   magpie

6. ʔágʷalᵊb   yawn

   ʔágʷəlᵊb   EK.

   ʔáʔəgʷàlᵊb   LG.

7. ʔágʷaq   groan

→

1. ʔájəlus   bright (color)

    <u>ʔájəlus</u> x̌i.čə̀c   bright red

2. ʔájq-   meet

   -dxʷ

     ʔuʔájqᵊdxʷ čəd ti *John*   I met John.   EK.

     dày ̓ čəd łuʔájqᵊdubicid   I'll meet you later.   LL.

   reduplication

     ʔəxʷsʔáʔəjəqbidᵊb čəd ci s.k̓ʷuy ʔal s.təqači ̓   LG.
     I have to meet my mother at eight.

     dày ̓ čəł łuʔáʔjᵊqᵊdubut   We will meet later.   HD.

3. ʔal   be located at or by some specific point in time
          or space, location with reference to something named

    Cf. ʔa   be located, be there in time or space

     q̓ixʷ   and words of that class

     čit   and words of that class

     <u>ʔàl</u> ʔálʔal ʔu kʷ(i) ads.čistxʷ   ES.
     Is your husband home?

       Cf. diʔə ̓ ʔu kʷ(i) ads.čistxʷ   ES.
         Is your husband here?

     ʔáhəxʷ tiʔə ̓ diʔə ̓ čačas <u>ʔal</u> tiʔə ̓ sx̌a.x̌ax̌aʔs
     This boy stayed with his in-laws.

     ʔá tiʔił s.čətxʷəd <u>ʔal</u> kʷədiʔ dəxʷəs.łałlils   ES.
     There was Bear where he lived.

     <u>ʔàl</u> tiʔił ł(u)adsu.lúƛil, xʷíʔ kʷ(i) adsu.qʷíq̓ʷcut   ES.
     As you are growing up, don't show off your strength.

ɫu.qə́ɫc čəxʷ ʔal kʷi ɫùʔ.ɫp ʔal təqàči?   LL.
Wake me up tomorrow at eight.

ʔàl s.búus   4 o'clock   LG.

ləs.cíl tiʔiɫ ǰəsəds ʔal tiʔiɫ sə.ʔibəšs
Her feet (go along) protected when she walks.

huy, siʔáb, cíckʷ siʔab, ciʔə? kàʔkaʔ ʔàləxʷ kʷi
tusəs.hùys ʔàciɫtalbixʷ   ML.
This Crow was high class, very high class, when she
was made as a human.

See also under dxʷʔal, liɫʔal, and tuɫʔal.

-il

    ləʔálíləxʷ čəd tə ʔùdəgʷič   I'm getting to the center.   EK.

    ʔálíləxʷ kʷi gʷəcəxʷ.tùkʷ   It's time I should go home. EK.

    ʔálil kʷədìʔ tudəxʷ.ɫàlils   ML.
    Until she came to the place where she went ashore.

2. ʔálalus

    díɫ ʔálalus tiʔiɫ   That is what happened.   LG.

    díɫ ɫ(u)adʔàlalus   That is what is going to happen to you. LG.

3. ʔalču-   See ləcu-.

4. s.ʔáləp   thigh, hind leg   EK., LL.

    -ɫx̌aʔ   thigh

5. ʔáləšək   turtle   EK.

6. ʔálətàɫ   a man's name; one of Martin Sampson's names

1. ʔalq̓ʷ   away from center, away from fire

      Opposite of <u>sula</u>.   Cf. ɬal(a); qad(a)

         ʔálᵊq̓ʷ   away from center   LG.

         <u>ʔalq̓ʷ</u> tiʔəʔ adsəs.gʷədil   DM.
         You are sitting in the back.

      -t

         ʔálᵊq̓ʷᵊd   Take it away from the fire.   LG.

         <u>ʔalq̓ʷ</u>cut   move away from, get back from   EK.
                        Go to the back (and sit down).   DM.

      -bi-t

         ʔàlq̓ʷbíd   behind something (inside a building)   DM.

         (ti) d<u>ʔalᵊq̓ʷbí</u>d   behind me (away from the fire/
                         center of the house)   LG.

         ɬu.kʷədácid čəd ʔal ti d<u>ʔalᵊq̓ʷbí</u>d   LG.
         I'll take you from behind me.

         ɬu.kʷədácid čəd čədà ɬu.ʔál ti d<u>ʔalq̓ʷbí</u>d   EC.
         I'll take you and put (you) behind me.

         dᵊʔal<u>q̓ʷbí</u>d tiʔəʔ adsəs.gʷədil   DM.
         You are sitting behind me.

         ʔəs.gʷədíl ʔal tiʔiɬ ad<u>ʔalq̓ʷbí</u>d   DM.
         He is sitting behind you.

2. ʔálš   sibling cross-sex

    ʔálalš   siblings cross-sex

    See under <u>s.qa</u>.

         ləlí ʔu c(i) ad<u>ʔàlš</u> ci ʔu.cutcut   ML.
         Isn't that your sister who is speaking?

ʔəbiɫəxʷ díɫ kʷši dʔálalš kʷi ʔu.pəjátuɫ   ML.

Perhaps it is my brothers who are duck hunting.

jəgʷáʔ dxʷsxʷixʷi.xʷiʔ tiʔiɫ x̌əɫx̌əɫtəds, ʔálalš

ʔə ciʔəʔ čəgʷàss   ML.

His brothers-in-law were expert hunters, the brothers
of his wife.

čádəxʷ t(i) adʔàlš   Where is your brother?   EK.
                            (Asked of a woman.)

s.qá dᵊʔàlš   EK.

my older sister, my female cousin of my parent's
older sibling

1.   ʔálʔal   house

     Cf. -alʔtxʷ

     ʔáʔalʔal   hut

       ʔəsʔálʔəlᵊb   He's making a home.

2.   ʔaɫ   fast

     Cf. x̌ax̌atib 'hurry'

Note the similarity between ʔaɫ and x̌aƛ̓ in their occurrence
with possessive affixes.

     root

       ʔáɫ tə dsə.təlàwil   I'm running fast.   EK., LG.

       ʔáɫ ti sə.təlàwils   He can run fast.   LG.

       ʔáɫ ti dsu.təlàwil čəda ʔu.ɫáq̓   DM.

     I was running fast and I fell.

       ʔáɫ ti dsu.təlàwil ʔal ti s.q̓àxʷ čəda ʔu.qʷcábšəd

     čəda ʔu.ɫáq̓

     I was running fast on the ice and I slipped and I fell.

ʔáɬ kʷ(i) ads.hùyud   Do it fast!   JC.

ck̓ʷáqid <u>ʔáɬ</u> kʷi ƛu.pàɬs   ML.
He always gets away quickly.

x̌ʷuiləxʷ jəɬ <u>ʔáɬ</u> kʷi gʷəds.ƛàx̌ʷ   LG.
I wish I'd grow fast.

ʔəbìiləxʷ <u>ʔáɬ</u> kʷi gʷədsə.ʔibəš čəda gʷə.ɬáʔ ʔal
kʷi dùkʷəɬdat   LG.
If I walk fast, I'll get there tomorrow.

lə.təláwil čəd ʔə tə <u>ʔàɬ</u>   I'm running fast.   EK.

ƛàl čəd bəʔáɬ x̌ʷuiab ʔə dəgʷi   LG.
I'm just as fast as you.

-t

ƛ(u)adəxʷəsʔáɬcut   What are you in a hurry about? LL.

xʷiʔ gʷədsəsʔáɬcut   I'm not in a hurry.   LL.

ʔáɬcut! ʔáɬcut!
ʔəs.ʔáʔs t(i) ads.càpaʔ   JC.
Hurry! Hurry!
Your grandfather is waiting.

xʷiʔ bələʔáɬšubicid   Don't speed!   JC.

1.   ʔáɬx̌ad   (located) downstream: opposite of q̓ixʷ.

See under q̓ixʷ.   Compare qʷic.

 lədxʷʔáɬx̌ad čəd   I'm going downstream.   LG.

dxʷʔáɬx̌ad   go downstream   EK.

    lədxʷ.ʔáɬx̌ad is synonymous with lə.qʷíc.

lexical

    ʔàɬx̌ədábac   downstream side   EK.

    ʔəɬx̌ádqs   the lower side of a point   EK.

1. ʔaq̓

       ʔuʔáq̓g^wił   He choked (by getting something caught in
                          his throat).
                     catch in the throat

   See under čik̓^w(i), ƛuq̓^w(u).

2. ʔásx^w   hair seal (harbor seal)   ESi.

   See under súp̓qs, 450.1.

3. ʔášx^w   hair seal (harbor seal)   LG.

   See under súp̓qs, 450.1.

4. ʔátəbəd   die

   Cf. yúbil, šubali, qíⱡil, q̓^wíčil

      ʔuʔátəbəd   He died.   EK.

      ʔátəbəd; ʔuʔátəbəd. s.qəlálitut; hík^w s.qəlàlitut.
      túx̌^w b(ə)uʔàtəbəd   LG.

      He died; he died. He had power, great power;
      and yet he also died.

   Euphemisms for ʔatəbəd:

      s.káyuiləx^w   become a ghost   LL.

      ʔəs.ƛúx^wiləx^w   become cold   LL.

      ʔu.šác̓qsəx^w   breathed his last   LL., LG.

      x^wiʔil   become nothing, be used up,
                         be gone

5. ʔáx̌^wuʔ   clamming

      łuʔáx̌^wuʔ čəd   I will go clamming.   EK.

-b

łuʔáx̌ʷuʔᵊb   I will go clamming.   DM.

-iluł

łuʔáx̌ʷuʔiluł čəd   I should go clamming.   DM.

səx̌ʷʔáx̌ʷuʔᵊb   clam gun   JC.

  Cf. s.qáləx̌

x̌ʷʔáx̌ʷaʔəd   clam basket; the large one left on
                                   the beach into which everyone empties
                                   her x̌ʷʔíʔx̌ʷaʔəd.

  Cf. s.ʔáx̌ʷuʔalc

x̌ʷʔíʔx̌ʷaʔəd   the small clam basket each person has
                                   with her as she digs. Periodically, she
                                   empties this into the x̌ʷʔáx̌ʷaʔəd.

  See under yíqib.

łu.gə́lkʷᵊd čəd kʷi sʔàx̌ʷuʔalc   JC.
I'm going to make a clam basket.

ʔáx̌ʷədus   Basket Ogress   LG.

  Cf. s.x̌ʷəyúq̌ʷ   Basket Ogress   ML.

  See under s.ƛ́álqəb 'monster'.

sʔáx̌ʷuʔ   butter clam; clam used in general

  s.tábał sʔáx̌ʷuʔ   What kind of clam is it?   DM.

Kinds of clams:

  čq̌ʷə́t   butter clam   ESi.

    Cf. səx̌ʷúb, s.ʔáx̌ʷuʔ

  háʔəc   horse clam (black nose clam)   EK., ESi., MS.

  híʔhaʔəc   eastern clam   ESi.

gʷídəq   geoduck   ESi.

k̓ʷúxʷdiʔ   littleneck (steamer)   ESi., JC.

  Cf. s.x̌áʔaʔ

səxʷub   butter clam   EK., LL

  Cf. c̓q̓ʷət̓, s.ʔáx̌ʷuʔ

s.təbcəʔ   horse clam different from the haʔəc.
            It is rounder and does not have the
            corners like the black nose.   ESi.

t̓ənsəwíč   Chinese slippers   LG., MC.

s.x̌áʔaʔ   littleneck (steamer)   EK.

  Cf. k̓ʷúxʷdiʔ

s.x̌əp̓áb NPS cockle   LG., LL.

  s.x̌əp̓əb SPS   ESi.

s.ʔáx̌ʷuʔ   butter clam   MS., VH.

  Cf. səxʷúb, c̓q̓ʷət̓

(1) háʔəc gʷəl láʔb hikʷ s?àx̌ʷuʔ. (2) gʷəl ʔəs.p̓íl
ti?əʔ čáwəyʔs. (3) gʷəl tux̌ʷ (h)uy ʔəs.búlux̌ʷ ti?əʔ
čàwəyʔ ʔə ci?əʔ s.x̌əp̓áb. (4) gʷəl ti?əʔ s?áx̌ʷuʔ gʷəl
ʔùdəgʷabacbid ʔə ti?əʔ saliʔ   MS.

(1) The horse clam is a really big clam. (2) And its
shell is flat. (3) In contrast the shell of the cockle
is round. (4) [In size] the butter clam is between the
[other] two.

(1) ʔəs.ʔəx̌íd kʷi sə(xʷ).xʷì?s lə.x̌ʷuɫab ʔə tə s?àx̌ʷuʔ
ti?iɫ ƛùx̌ʷƛux̌ʷ

(2) gʷəɫ x̌ʷəlč s.wàtixʷtəd ti?iɫ ƛùx̌ʷƛux̌ʷ yəxʷ tə s?àx̌ʷuʔ.
(3) šəqábac ʔə tə s.watixʷtəd ti?iɫ ƛùx̌ʷƛux̌ʷ gʷəl ʔəs.pə́d
tə s?àx̌ʷuʔ. (4) díɫ səs.hùys (h)əlgʷəʔ   JC.

652

(1) Why isn't an oyster like a clam?

(2) The oyster and the clam belong to the realm of the sea. (3) [But] the oyster is on top of the ground and the clam is buried. (4) That is the way they are.

1.   ʔàyəyáš   incompetent, clumsy (Children would taunt someone
                                                          by chanting this.)

     rejected: *ʔəsʔayəyáš

2.   ʔáyil   store something /cache it

       -t

       tu.q̓ʷúʔˀd (h)əlgʷəʔ gʷəl ƛuʔáyild (h)əlgʷəʔ
       They gathered it and cached it.

3.   ʔaỷ   change

       -txʷ

       ʔáỷtxʷ   trade it/ exchange it

     lexical

       ʔáỷgʷas   exchange

         ʔaỷgʷəsálica(ʔ)b   change clothes   LG.

       ʔaỷwáʔs   change

         híwil. ʔaỷwáʔsˀd   Go change it.

         ƛuʔàỷwáʔsalicaʔˀb čəd   I'm going to change my clothes.

4.   ʔáʔəgʷàlˀb   See under ʔágʷalˀb.

5.   ʔaʔs   wait

       Cf. ʔacíɬ

     root

       ʔacíɬ ʔaʔs (h)əlgʷəʔ   Just wait for them.   LG.

?áʔsˀbš   wait for me

?áʔsbuɬ   wait for us

-il

dˀs.x̌áƛ kʷi gʷədsəs?àʔsil dxʷʔal kʷi t̓à.t̓gʷət

I want to wait until noon.

-b

?əs?áʔsˀb čəxʷ ʔə t(i) ads.càpaʔ   JC.

Your grandfather is waiting for you.

-bi-t

?əs?áʔзˀbitˀb čəxʷ ʔə t(i) ads.càpaʔ   JC.

Your grandfather is waiting for you (so you two
can do it).

1.   ?áʔyəd   friend of one's own sex, a pal
                      "no blood connection"   LL.
                      "man only"   EK.

    Cf. q̓ʷúʔudaq   close friend, not a relative   LG.

        q̓ʷəʔúdaq   close friend, not a relative   EK.

    Cf. s.yáyaʔ   relative, friend
                  "touch of family connection" LL.

       ?íišəd   relative, friend
                  "more in the family than s.yayaʔ" LL.

2.   ?ə   particle linking <u>agent</u>, <u>instrument</u>, and <u>manner</u>
                      words and phrases to predication. (Sometimes
                      also <u>time</u> and <u>location</u>, but these are most fre-
                      quently introduced by ?al.)

    agent: ?u.júbutˀb čəd ?ə ti s.tiqìw

              The horse kicked me.

    instr.:   ?u.púsud čəd ?ə tə č̓ƛaʔ

              I hit him with a rock / I threw at him with a rock.

manner: šúucbicut ʔə kʷi hà̀ʔɫ

Look after yourself well.

ʔə also relates possessor to possessed

poss.:   ti s.tiqíw ʔə tiʔiɫ s.tùbš

        horse   that man

That man's horse.

1.   ʔəbíĺ   if, whenever, perhaps, either...or, whether...or

díɫ s.tab ads.ɫilc. ʔəbíĺ qʷuʔ. ʔəbíĺ s.qəbuʔ.   LL.

Give me something to drink. Either water or milk.

díɫ s.tab, ʔəbíĺ biàc, ʔəbíĺ ɫàẃt s.ʔuladxʷ   EK.

Everything [was cooked like that] whether meat or
fresh salmon.

ʔəbíĺəxʷ čəxʷ ɫubə.yàyus ʔə kʷi s.hùyud ʔə tiʔiɫ

tiyù̀ʔsəd. gʷə.kʷáx̌ʷac čəxʷ ʔu dxʷʔal kʷi gʷəds.ƛál

b(ə)u.hùyud kʷi s.ʔìstə

If you are going to continue working at making that
smelt trap, would you help me so I can also make (one)
likewise.

ʔəbíĺəxʷ xʷiʔ kʷi ɫ(u)ads.x̌ʷubil, ƛubəxʷ čəxʷ ʔu.lilcut   LL.

If you won't shut up, you had better go away.

ʔəbíĺəxʷ di·ɫ kʷši d.ʔàlalš kʷ(i) ʔu.pəjátuɫ

Perhaps it would be my brothers who are duck hunting...

                                 (ML. quoting Crow)

ʔəbíĺ čəxʷ bə.ťáq̌t ʔal ti s.watixʷtəd   EC.

Perhaps you will go up again in that place.

ʔəbíĺəxʷ gʷ(ə)usà.saq̌ʷ gʷəl gʷ(ə)ucút.cut x̌ʷuɫəb ʔə tiʔiɫ   ML.

Whenever they would fly, they would talk like that.

ʔəbíĺəxʷ (h)əlgʷəʔ ƛu.ʔəx̌id gʷəl ƛu.ƛəládiʔ (h)əlgʷəʔ?   ML.

Whenever there is anything wrong with them, they make noise.

ʔəbíˑləxʷ čəd həláʔb gʷət(u)as.x̌ə̀ɫ gʷəl xʷíʔ gʷətuds.ɫčil

<u>If</u> I had been real sick, I wouldn't have come.

-as

ɫílc ʔə kʷi qʷuʔ ʔəbíˑləs xʷíʔ kʷi s.qəbùʔ   LL.

Give me some water, <u>if</u> you don't have any milk.

ɫílc ʔə kʷi qʷùʔ, ʔəbíˑləs gʷəl b(ə)as.qəbùʔ   LG.

Give me <u>either</u> water <u>or</u> milk.

ʔəbíˑləs gʷəl diɫ ti s.túbš gʷəl diɫ ʔu ti bədáʔs, tu.ɫčil   LG.

It was <u>either</u> that man <u>or</u> was it his son who came.

ʔəbíˑləs čədà ɫu.šudxʷ   I might see him.   LG.

1. ʔəbs-   See under <u>ʔabs-</u>.

2. ʔəcá   NPS   I/me

ʔə́cə   SPS   I/me

The independent and emphatic counterpart to -<u>ad</u>.
See <u>čədíɫ</u> and <u>díɫ</u>. Belonging to the same class as ʔəcá are
<u>dəgʷi</u> 'you (sg.)', <u>díbəɫ</u> 'we/us', and gʷəlápu 'you (pl.)'

ʔəcá kʷi ɫu.kʷədátəb   I am the one who will be taken.

ʔəcá ti hə̀di   It's me, Henry.

diɫ ʔəcá t(i) as.(h)aydxʷ   I am the one who knows it.

dəb ʔəcá tiʔiɫ λə.x̌ə̀ɫqìd   I'm the one who gets the headache (not you).   LL.

λləs.q̓ʷúʔ ʔə ʔəcà lə.ʔìbəšs   It's with me that she walks.

ʔiɫ.čáčas čəxʷ tuˑlʔal ʔəcà   You are younger than I am.   DM.

3. ʔəcəládiʔ   place name, site of Utsalady on Camano Island   JC.

4. ʔə́čʔəč   stutter, stammer

See under <u>cut</u>.

656

1. ʔəč̓

    ʔə́c̓ʷəd   pull it out   EK.
                    pull it out, opposite of ƛ̓uq̓ʷ(u), q.v. MS.

    See under x̌əc.

2. ʔədá   come here (Probably derived from ʔa-t plus -a.)

    Cf. ʔəƛ̓á   Same gloss: come here

3. -ʔəhad-   talk

    See under cut.

    s.táb t(i) adsudxʷʔəhàdəd   EK., LG.
    What are you really talking about?

    -bi-t

    ck̓ʷáqid ʔalc̓udxʷʔəhàdədbid ʔə tə ʔìišəds   LG.
    She's always talking about her people.

4. ʔəkʷyíqʷ   four generations removed from ego, both ascending
                    and descending, i.e., great, great grandparent
                    and great, great grandchild

    See under bədáʔ.

5. ʔəlc̓u-   See under ləcu-.

6. ʔəlíqs   even

7. s.ʔəlʔəlbíxʷ   unidentified berry, a mountain blueberry that grows
                   on a low bush and is sweet

8. ʔəɬ   food, eat

    The most frequent suffix is -d. It is homonymous
    with [-d ~ -t-] with which it is not to be confused.
    The construction ʔəɬ-d structures like bare roots
    and like roots plus -il and -b.

Compare: húydxʷ, bə́q̓əd, k̓aw-, wáwəxʷ, čətx̌ʷəd, lə́k̓ʷdxʷ,

     čík̓ʷ(i), ƛ̓úbtxʷ.

See also -daliƛ^əd.

<u>ʔə́ƛ^əd</u>   eat

ləs<u>ʔə́ƛ^əd</u> čəd   I've eaten.   EK.

ʔuʔə́ƛ^əd tə bùsbus ʔə tə sàx̌ʷil   LG.
The bovine ate the grass.

    *ʔuʔə́ƛ^əd tə sàx̌ʷil ʔə tə bùsbus   LG.
    *The grass ate the bovine. I.e., nonsense.

sáx̌ʷil tə suʔə́ƛ^əd ʔə tə bùsbus   LG.
The bovine ate the grass.

sáx̌ʷil tə suʔə́ƛ^əds   It ate the grass.   LG.

tábtab suʔə́ƛ^əd   What are (you) eating?   EK.

ƛ̓úbəxʷ čəƛ ƛuʔə́ƛ^əd   Let's eat.   LG.

júʔiləxʷ ʔə tiʔə? ƛusʔə́ƛ^əd ʔə ci s.ƛ̓àlqəb ʔə tiʔə?
qa wìw̓su   LL.
He enjoyed (the thought of) the monster's eating
the many children.

<u>sʔə́ƛ^əd</u>   food

čáydi sʔə́ƛ^əd   Chinese food   LG.

  Cf. čáydidàliƛ^əd   (make a regular diet of)   LG.
                     Chinese food

jixʷáƛ d^ə(s).cìlalikʷ ʔə kʷi cəbáb sʔə́ƛ^əd   LG.
It's the first time I took a second helping.

-txʷ

ʔə́ƛtúb čəd   fed me   LL.

-t-agʷəl

<u>ʔə́ƛtágʷəl</u>   Feed one another.   LL.

658

-d-iluɬ

ʔu.ʔúx̌ʷcˀb ʔə tiʔiɬ s.tùbš ciʔiɬ s.ɬàdəyʔ dxʷʔal
kʷi gʷəsʔəɬdíluɬs (h)əlgʷəʔ   LL.

The man went after the woman to take her to lunch.

-d-iluɬ-bi-t

ck̓ʷàqid ʔuʔəɬdíluɬbitubuɬ   LL.

He always (comes and wants to) eat off us.

-adəp

ʔuʔəɬádap čəd   I gave a feast.   LL.

ʔuʔəɬádapbicid čəd   I gave you a feast.   LL.

ʔuʔəɬádapbitubuɬəd čəd   I gave you all a feast.

ʔuʔəɬádap čəd dxʷʔal dəgʷì   I gave you a feast.

ʔuʔəɬádap čəd dxʷʔal gʷəlàpu   I gave you all a feast.

reduplication

sʔíʔɬˀd   a little food

ʔìʔɬádˀb   eat berries as you pick them   LG.
                                 (Sometimes a synonym for č̓əbəb.)

other derivation

xʷə̀cdalíɬˀd   fast (lit. 'take off eating')   LG.

s.q̓ʷəláɬˀd   berry, fruit (lit. 'ripe food')

ʔəɬádəp   banquet

ʔəɬˀdálʔtxʷ   restaurant

   ʔìʔɬdálʔtxʷ   hamburger stand   LL.

rejected:

*ʔə̀ɬtˀb, *ʔəɬádˀb

1. ʔəɬ   ʔəɬ expresses the attendent circumstances of an act, the purpose for which something is done. It is glossed with various English conjunctions and prepositions, e.g., 'for, of, with, like, when'. Compare -əɬ.

x̌ʷuláb ʔə tiʔiɬ ƛ(u)cut.cut ʔə tiʔiɬ sup̓qs ʔəɬ ʔəs.t̓agʷtəs   ML.

Just what the hair seal would say <u>when</u> he was put up on it (a big rock).

cùkʷ háʔɬ s.pàʔc ʔə̀ɬ ʔəs.ʔátəbədəs   LG.

Only is a bear good <u>when</u> it's dead.

lə.təláwil tə hupt ʔəɬ ti s.pùʔəlikʷ   LG.

The deer <u>runs</u> <u>like</u> the wind.

2. ʔəƛ̓   come toward

Contrast: ʔux̌ʷ   go   synonym: ɬčíl   arrive

               ɬəgʷɬ   leave it   ɬáʔ   arrive there

               ƛ̓a   go   ʔədá   come here

root

ʔə̀ƛ̓ čəxʷ ʔal kʷi dadatu   Come in the morning.   EK.

xʷíʔ kʷ(i) adsʔə̀ƛ̓ ʔal kʷi ɬùʔ.ɬp   EK.

Don't come too early.

ɬáw̓t lə ʔə̀ƛ̓ c̓qàysəb   Flower just coming out.   EK.

t̓íʔyidəxʷ gʷə ʔə̀ƛ̓   Ring it for him to come.   EK.

t(u)as.x̌ə́c čəd gʷə ʔə̀ƛ̓əd yəx̌i ʔu.qə́lb   EK.

I was afraid to come because it rained.

-c

ʔə́ƛ̓c   come after it

-txʷ

ʔə́ƛ̓txʷ tə x̌pày̓   Bring that cedar!   LG.

ʔə́ƛ̓txʷ tə s.dùukʷ   Bring (me) the knife.   LG.

-bi-t

　　ʔəƛbíds　　　　　　on this side　　　　　　　　　LG.

lexical

　　ʔəƛáləqəp　　　　　　smell

　　　s.táb tiʔiɬ ʔuƛàləqəp　　What's that smell?　　EK.

　　ʔəƛáyucid　　　　　this side of the road　　　　EK.

　　ʔíʔƛqs (ʔə tə s.čə́tqs)　a bit on this side of the point　LL.

　　dxʷʔəƛúsʔb　　　　Look this way!　　　　　　　LG.

reduplication

　　ʔíʔƛqs　　　　　　a bit on this side　　　　　　LL.

-a

　　ʔəƛá　　　　　　come here

　　　Cf. ʔədá　　　come here　　　　　　　　LG.

　　ʔəƛá bəlkʷ　　　Come back!　　　　　　　LG.

　　ʔəƛá s.kʷukʷi (or) s.kʷúkʷi ʔəƛà　　　　　　EK.
Come here, nice little girl!

　　ʔəƛáhəxʷ　　　　Come on!　　　　　　　EK.

　　　ƛáhəxʷ čəxʷ ʔíʔɬʔd　Come on! Eat a little!　LL.

　　　háʔɬ gʷəʔəƛáhəxʷ　(You) should come.　　LG.

　　ʔəƛáxʷ ɬu.ʔúx̌ʷ čəɬ dxʷʔal tàwd　　　　LG.
Come on! Let's go to town.

　　ʔəƛáxʷ ɬu.qʷuʔqʷaʔ čəɬ ʔə kʷi ku.kpi　　LG.
Let's have some coffee.

1.　ʔəpús　NPS　　aunt, female sibling of either parent
　　　　　　　　when that parent is living

　　pus　SPS

　　See under qəsíʔ 'uncle'

Cf. yəláb   either parent's sibling of either sex when parent is deceased.

Ego has no special term separating older from younger sibling of parent. However, the distinction is maintained because ego refers to his cousin from an uncle or aunt senior to his own parent as s.qa whether or not the cousin is older or younger than himself. Similarly, if the cousin is the child of an uncle or aunt junior to his parent, he calls the cousin suq̓ʷəʔ even if the cousin is older than he.

reduplication

ʔəpʔəpús	aunts	
ʔíʔpùs	aunty	EK.
ʔíʔəpus	aunty	LG.

1. ʔəqʷál   weave a blanket

Cf. čúčgʷas   twisting in the process of weaving blankets

ʔəšálgʷəs   interwoven; two sisters married to the same man

Cf. yíq̓(i)   weave/make a blanket

ƛ́ágʷ(a)   stitch/make a mat

2. s.ʔəqʷəlíč   back (of body)   LG., EK., LL.

Cf. s.ʔíličəd   Same gloss: back (of body)   LL.

3. ʔəq̓ʷ   equivalent to ʔuq̓ʷ(u), *q.v.*

See under x̌əc.

root

... jixʷbídəxʷ ʔə tiʔəʔ diʔəʔ łusʔəq̓ʷ ʔə tiʔəʔ diʔəʔ su.pìgʷədčəł   EC.

... before our pigʷəd will be opened, i.e. begun.

lexical

-y-ax̌əd

    dxʷʔəq̓ʷyáx̌ədalikʷ   open the door

    dxʷʔəq̓ʷyáx̌ədid   open the door

    ʔəxʷʔəq̓ʷyáx̌əd   The door is open.

    dxʷʔəq̓ʷyáx̌ədyic   Open the door for me.

-ucid

    ʔəq̓ʷúciid   open it

1.   ʔəs-   See under as-.

2.   ʔəšálgʷəs   two sisters married to the same man
                           ("It means 'interwoven'." LL.)

                           (Probably composed of [ʔəs-šal-gʷas].)

    See under s.qá, ʔəqʷál.

3.   ʔəšás   sea lion

    See under súp̓qs.

4. dxʷ.ʔə́t̓əb   clear

    dxʷ.ʔə́t̓əb c̓ƛ̓àʔ   agate

5.   ʔəx̌áʔ   snowgoose

    Cf. ƛ̓k̓ʷáx̌ad   unidentified goose

6.   ʔəx̌íd   NPS   what act/state, why not (do something)

    x̌íd   SPS

    Compare: čal, k̓ʷid, tab, čad, čayɫ, gʷat, gət, ʔidigʷət

ʔuʔəx̌íd   What happened?   EK.

ʔuʔəx̌íd čəxʷ   What did you do to yourself
                                  (that you have your arm in a cast)?

   Cf. x̌ʷúl čəxʷ ʔu ƛ(u)as.ƛúbil
    Have you been getting along OK?

ʔuʔəx̌ídəxʷ čəxʷ   What did you (just now) do to yourself?

ʔəsʔəx̌íd   How is it?   LG.

  gʷəl ʔəsʔəx̌íd tiʔił s.čətxʷəd   ES.
  And what's with Bear?

ʔəsʔəx̌ídəxʷ čəxʷ   How are you? (Less polite than čal
                                  among the Skagit.)

ƛ(u)asʔəx̌ídəxʷ čəxʷ   How have you been getting along?   LL.

ʔəx̌íd əwə gʷə.yəcᵊbtùbšəxʷ ʔəs.gʷəq̓ tiʔił dxʷši̓ʔ.šłᵊb   ES.
Why didn't you tell me the window was open?

ʔəx̌íd haẁəʔ gʷə.təlàwiləxʷ   EK.
Why don't you run?

ʔəx̌íd kʷa   NPS   perhaps   Cf. x̌ʷú̓ʔᵊləʔ?   EK.

ʔəx̌íd la   SPS   perhaps   HD.

yəx̌í ʔuʔəx̌íd   why?   EK.

ʔəsʔəx̌íd kʷ(i) ads.lùƛ   How old are you?   EK.

ʔəsʔəx̌íd kʷi s.qas kʷi ʔaciłtalbixʷ ʔal dxʷ.liləp   EK.
How many Indians live at Tulalip?

ʔəsʔəx̌íd s.ǰəlč kʷi gʷəsu.yayusbidčəł   LL.
How many years would we have to work at it?

ʔəsʔəx̌íd kʷi s.háac ʔə tiʔił ad.q̓ílbid   DM.
How long is your canoe?

ʔəsʔəx̌íd kʷi s.(h)ájəp ʔə t(i) ad.bad   DM.
How tall is your father?

ʔəsʔəx̌íd kʷi gʷ(ə)adsu.ǰə̀ctxʷ tiʔəʔ q̓ìlbid   DM.

What do you use a canoe for?

ʔəsʔəx̌íd kʷi s.ləlì̓ʔ ʔə x̌ʷətìs dxʷʔal s.wùqʷad

How does a silver diver differ from a loon?

ʔəsʔəx̌ídəxʷ kʷ(i) adəxʷəs.tàgʷəxʷ   LG.

Why are you hungry?

ʔəsʔəx̌íd kʷi gʷ(ə)adəxʷ.súxʷtəš tiʔił ʔəʔùtx̌s

How would you recognize a Nootka type canoe?

ʔəsʔəx̌íd kʷi də(xʷ).xʷì̓ʔs lə.q̓ìlbid tiʔəʔ s.tiqìw

Why isn't a horse a *q̓ilbid* ?

ʔəsʔəx̌íd kʷi də(xʷ).xʷì̓ʔs ləs.ʔulàdxʷ ciʔił p̓uày?

Why isn't a flounder a salmon?

with adverb

  bək̓ʷ (ʔ)əsʔəx̌íd   all kinds (of color)   ML.

  bək̓ʷ ʔəsʔəx̌íd səs.huys   LL.

  Someone who is not consistent. A guy who always has
  something wrong with him.

  pút ləʔəx̌ìd lə.ʔùx̌ʷəs   ML.

  How wonderfully it [the canoe] would go!

  x̌əł ti λ̓ələ(ʔə)x̌íd lə.ʔùx̌ʷəs   ML.

  Without much effort it would go.

  t̓ábad łuʔəx̌ìdəd   Guess what I'm going to do?   LG.

-txʷ

  λ̓(u)adsəxʷu[ʔə]x̌ix̌ə̓txʷ tiʔił   JC.

  What do you do with that?

  ʔəlc̓uʔəx̌íx̌tub ʔə t(i) ad.bad tə čáčas   LG.

  What is your father doing to the boy?

-b-il

    [ʔə]x̌íd^əbil   incident   JC.

lexical

    ʔəsʔəx̌ídəlus   What color is it?   LG.

    ʔəsʔəx̌ídəlus tiʔił   What color is that?   LG.

reduplication

    ʔuʔəx̌íx̌^əd čəxʷ   What are you doing?   EK.

    ʔuʔəx̌íx̌^əd   What's being done?   HD.

    ʔalču ʔəx̌íx̌^əd əw̓ə čəxʷ! ʔu.púsdubšəxʷ čəxʷ   LG.
    What are you doing?! You've hit me now!

1.   ʔəxʷájad   drag net

    See under x̌á(ʔ)təd.

    lexical

    dxʷsʔəxʷəjádəb   a fisherman who uses a drag net

2.   ʔəyáhus   a power which would shoot someone with little
                       worms that would eat him. This is the only
                       power that no human could ever obtain. (See
                       s.qəlálitut.)   AS.

3. dxʷ.ʔə́yəb   clear water; name of a village on the South
                       Fork of the Nooksack River. It was famous as
                       a place for spear fishing because it was so
                       easy to see the fish there.   LG.
                       (Also recorded as dxʷʔíʔəb.)

4.   ʔə́y̓dxʷ   find it

    ʔuʔə́y̓dxʷ čəd   I found something.   LG.

    ʔuʔə̀y̓dxʷ úʔxʷ čəxʷ ʔu kʷi ʔàlʔal   LG.
    Have you found a house yet?

bəʔəy̓dxʷ tiʔəʔ cədiɬ k̓aʔk̓aʔ   ML.
Again he found Crow.

tuʔəy̓dúbš čəxʷ   You found me.   LG.

tuʔəy̓dúbicid čəd ʔal t(i) adsəs.x̌ʷiɬ   LG.
I found you when you were lost.

1.   ʔəʔútx̌s   Nootka type canoe (also called Chinook and family canoe)

See under q̓ilbid.

2.   ʔi   yes

3.   ʔi   NPS   additive particle   'and'

Cf. yəxʷ   SPS; ʔi- 'collective'

tu.ɬčís̓b čəɬ ʔə tiʔəʔ s.tubš ʔi ciʔiɬ čəgʷàs ʔi tiʔiɬ bədbədaʔs
A man and (his) wife and their children came to us.

tu.šúdxʷ čəɬ ʔi mali
We saw it and Mary (i.e., Mary and I saw it).

ʔúlub ʔi kʷi ɬixʷ   ten and three, i.e., thirteen

4.   ʔi-   derivational prefix   'collective'

ʔisčə́txʷəd   bears

ʔiqyúuqs   group of seagulls

ʔiƛ̓úb   enough

sʔiƛ̓úbəxʷ tə s.hìkʷs   That's big enough.

Contrast: ʔəs.ƛ̓úbil   It's (big) enough.   LG.

5.   ʔi-

ʔílaq   stern, back seat of a car   EK.

ʔíʔˀlaq(b)   the second singer, the one who answers
                    another's song

1.   ʔíbac   grandchild

     See under bədaʔ.

     ʔíbibac   small/dear grandchild

     cixʷʔíbac   grandchild's spouse (See under s.kʷəlwás.)

2.   ʔíbəš   travel on land, walk

     Contrast with ʔúluɫ 'travel by water'.

     Compare gʷaX̌ʷ and see under ʔuX̌ʷ.

     root

         ləʔíbəš čəd   I'm walking (right now).   LG.

         ʔalču̓ʔíbəš čəd   I have to walk all the time.   LG.

         dídiʔɫ čəd ləʔìbəš   I'm still walking.   LG.

         ʔəxʷsʔíbəš̌ˀb čəd   I want to walk.   EK.

         dˀs.X̌áƛ kʷi sʔíbəšəxʷčəɫ   I want us to go now.   LG.

         ƛ̓ləs.q̓ʷú̓ʔ ʔə ʔəcà ləʔìbəšs   She walks with me.   LG.

     -txʷ

         ʔuʔíbəštxʷ   He dated her (lit. 'caused her to
                                               land travel')

     lexical

         ɫuʔíbəš(š)əd čəɫ   We are going on foot.   LG.

     reduplication

         ʔíbibəš   pace back and forth

             tú̓X̌ʷ čəd ʔuʔìbibəš   I'm just going for a walk.   LG.

         ʔíbʔibəš   walk all about

1. s.ʔíč̓əb   blanket   LL., EK.

       See under s.qəlík̓ʷ.

           s.ʔíč̓ʔič̓əb   blankets   EK.

2. dxʷ.(ʔ)idáwligʷəd   worry

       Cf. dxʷ.x̌ʷaq̓ʷigʷəd

3.   ʔidigʷat   What say?

       See under cut. (Some people say ʔidgʷat.)

           ʔuʔídigʷət čəxʷ   What did you say?   LL., EK., JC., LG.

           ʔalču̓ʔídigʷət ciʔəʔ s.buluх̌ʷìlc   LG.
           What are you talking about? You round (fore)head!

           ʔəsʔídigʷat kʷ(i) ads.x̌əč̓   JC.
           What do you think of it (e.g., a plan to do something)?

4.   ʔíhəl   smell bad, stink   LL., LG.

       See under sub(u).

           ʔuʔíʔihəlq(s)šəd čəxʷ   Your toes stink.   LL.

5.   ʔígʷəɬ   climb a tree, ladder, stairway (Skagit only)
                         (as opposed to climbing a hill or mountain)

       Cf. kʷatač

       -txʷ

         ʔígʷəɬtxʷ   take something up stairs
                      make someone climb a tree

       -c-b

         ʔìgʷəɬáacᵊb   climbed after them

       other derivation

         səxʷʔígʷəɬ   ladder

ti lə.jə́k̓ʷ səxʷʔíg̓ʷəɬ   escalator

    Cf. səxʷ.k̓ʷátač   Snoh.   ladder

rejected: *ʔíg̓ʷəɬtəd

1. (s)ʔíišəd   relative, friend
                 "More in the family than s.yayaʔ."   LL.
                 "s.yayaʔ is more a relation while ʔíišəd
                 is more a friend."   DM.
                 "It can mean the people of one's own "tribe"
                 as well as relative."   JC.

    See under ʔáʔyəd.

2.   ʔik̓ʷ(i)   Snoh. equivalent to ʔiq̓ʷ(i), *q.v.*

3.   ʔil   begin

    Compare with the suffix -il, 208.3.

      ʔíləxʷ tə s.ʔə́ɬᵊd   They began to eat.   EK.

      ʔíləxʷ tə s.təlàwil   They began to run.   EK.

4.   ʔíla   hurt

    Cf. baʔk̓ʷɬ, q̓iƛ̓(dxʷ), x̌əɬ

    ʔəs.čál tiʔiɬ adəxʷʔìla   How did you get hurt?   DM.

   rejected:

    *ʔəs.čál tiʔiɬ adəxʷʔilaqid

5.   ʔil(i)   lean against, prop up; side; edge

    Compare dəš, diʔ.

    root

      ʔəsʔíl   leaning on something   EK.

-it

ʔílid	prop it up; put a brace under it	EK.
ʔəsʔílicut	leaning against something	EK.

lexical

sʔíladiʔ	side of house	EK.
ʔilálap	side of a tree	EK.
ʔiláx̌əd ʔə tiʔəʔ s.wàtix̌ʷtəd	the ends of the earth	MS.
ʔílqs	point of a pencil	LL.
	end of rope, tape	LL.
ʔilǰiqad	bank/slope down to a river or lake	LL.
sʔílgʷił ʔə tiʔəʔ x̌ʷəlč	shoreline	LL.
sʔilálgʷił	side of a canoe	EK.
sʔiláligʷəd	whole side	EK.
	side, one side as opposed to the other	LG.
sʔilúlč	side of a box, cup, bucket	EK.
dx̌ʷʔílalədiʔ	cheek	
sʔílʔalubid	shoulder	LL.

      Cf. s.təbálubid (under tab) 'shoulder'   LG.

sʔílax̌əd	arm, hired hand	EK., LL.
x̌ʷiʔləlúgʷəb	buttocks, hip	EK., LL.

    Cf. x̌ʷ.tábəp   rump

sʔílidəgʷəs	chest of body	
sʔílilc	forehead	
sʔíličəd	back	LL.

    (Rejected by EK. who gives s.ʔəqʷəlíč. This is also accepted by LL. and LG.)

ʔilyálus	end (of a table)

1. ?il(i)   sing, repeat, interpret

    See under cut and t̓ílib.

    Perhaps etymologically related to hil(i).

    root

    　　?íləxʷ čəxʷ   You sing!

    　　dəgʷítxʷ kʷi ?u?il̓   You sing!

    -it

    　　bə?ílid   Repeat it. Say it again.   LG.

    　　　　("The more polite way of saying this is ?əs.čál əwə ?əs.čàl." LL.)

    lexical

    　　lə?ilálikʷ   He's interpreting.   LG.

    　　　　Cf. tulalikʷ 'interpret'

2. ?ił-   partitive. Denotes a part of some larger unit.

    　　?iłčad   which one?, either one

    　　　　Cf. díł čad 'either one'

    　　?iłčə́x̌   half   LL.

    　　xʷə́cᵊd ti?ił ?iłgʷəd   Take that from the bottom.   LG.

    　　bə.kʷədátᵊbəxʷ ?ə ci?ə? s.ƛ̓àlqəb bə.díiču? gʷəl bə?iłgʷə́d   ML.
    　　Again this ogress took another one from the bottom.

    　　dił ?iłs(h)ájəp ti?ił ?iłdi?i?
    　　That person on the other side is taller.

    　　?ił(h)á?ł tul̓?al kʷi xʷi?   (It is) better than nothing.   EK.

    　　?iłjixʷ   better

    　　　　?iłjìxʷ čəxʷ ?əs.láx̌ᵊdxʷ   You remember better (than I)   EK.

    　　?iłt̓ísu   younger   LG.

ʔiɫkʷə́lq   others, more, some   LL.

  tiʔiɫ x̌átx̌atəxʷ kʷi ʔiɫkʷə́lq   ML.
  Some of them were mallards.

  ciʔiɫ bəʔiɫkʷəlq ʔaciɫtalbixʷ   LG.
  ... these other people.

ʔiɫláq ʔàciɫtalbixʷ   the latter people   ML.

ʔiɫjíxʷ   first

  tí·ləb kì.kəwič tiʔiɫ ʔiɫjìxʷ   ML.
  Right away Little Hunchback was first.

  kʷədátˀbəxʷ kì.kəwič tiʔiɫ ʔiɫjixʷ   ML.
  Little Hunchback was taken first.

ʔiɫlúƛ   older   EK.
                            He's the oldest.   LG.

  tə ʔiɫlúƛ dˀ.bəda?   my older son   HD.

diɫ ʔiɫqá tə d.yəq̓us dxʷʔal dəgʷi   LG.
I have more baskets than you.

xʷə́cˀd tiʔiɫ ʔiɫšə̀q   Take that off the top.   LG.

  (Cf. xʷə́cˀd tiʔiɫ šə̀q   Take the top one off. LG.)

ʔiɫx̌ə́b tiʔiɫ wə̀q̓əb ʔal tùdi? tuĺʔal tiʔə? wə̀q̓əb ʔal tiʔá? LG.
That box over there is heavier than this box right here.

ʔiɫčíčətq   a small pinch of it

ʔu.qʷú(?)qʷadid kʷi s(ʔə)x̌ʷà? ʔə kʷi s(ʔ)iɫlə̀gʷəbs   ML.
He drank the urine of another youth.

xʷuʔˀlə? sə.ʔíbəš ʔal tiʔə? ʔilgʷiɫ ʔə tə x̌ʷəlč ʔá kʷi
ƛəbəsʔiɫtáq̓ts gʷəl ʔá kʷi sʔiɫčà(?)kʷs   ML.
He was probably walking along the beach of the sound
up the bank and down by the water.

  (The ʔiɫ- here perhaps refers to relatively further up
   the bank and then closer to the water.)

x̌ʷul̓ ʔil̓wíʔad   He just kept hollering.   LG.

tu.x̌ʷác čəd gʷəl x̌ʷul̓ ʔil̓ʔùx̌ʷ   EK.
I told him not to but he still went.

x̌ʷùl̓ ʔil̓sáx̌ʷəb tiʔił s.čə̀txʷəd   EK.
The bear just ran.

gʷat kʷi łusʔił̓húygʷəss   ML.
Whom will she be able to get together with?

1.   ʔiq̓ʷ(i)   wipe, mop

See under x̌ʷis(i).   Note ʔik̓ʷ(i).

-it

ʔíq̓ʷid   wipe it   LG.

  Cf. ʔík̓ʷid wipe it   EK.

lexical

ʔíq̓ʷidup   mop the floor   LG.

  Cf. ʔík̓ʷidup   EK.

ʔíq̓ʷšad   rug   LG.

ʔík̓ʷusəd   towel   HD.

2.   ʔístə   thus, in such manner

Perhaps reduced from *ʔístaʔ.

ʔal tudiʔ ʔístə   way over on the side   LG.

ʔəsʔístə tiʔił   It's like that.   LG.

ʔú ʔəsʔístə haw̓əʔ   Oh, is it like that?   LG.

ʔí ʔəsʔístə   Yes, it is.   LG.

ƛ̓ál b(ə)asʔìstə   So be it; Amen.

ƛ̓al b(ə)as?istə ?al ti?ə?   EK.

It was like this (in the old days).

ƛ̓àl čəxʷ b(ə)u.húyud ?əs?ístə bə.ti dsu.húyud ti ds.gʷà?   JC.

You can also make one just as I have made mine.

hík̓ʷ(h)ikʷ. ?á ti?iɬ ?əs?ístə ?ə ti?ə?   EK.

They (the roasted salmon) were big. They were about
like this. (She spread her hands to indicate size.)

s.táb kʷi ɬ(u)as?ístə čəɬ   JC.

How are we going to go about this?

?u?ístə ti?iɬ čačas   1. That is what happened to the child. JC.
                      2. The child is doing that.   JC.

?əs?ístətxʷ ?ə ti?iɬ   Leave it like that.   LG.

?əs?ístətxʷ   Leave it that way.   LG.

kʷá?ᵊd x̌ʷuɬtxʷ ?əs?ístə   Let it be that way.   LG.

-b

?əs?í?istəb čəlàp   This is where you folks stay.   LL.

gʷə́diləxʷ čəxʷ ?al ti čəxʷa ?í?istəb   FSi.

You sit down there and you stay there.
(As in talking to a child.)

?əs.?í?istəb ti?iɬ s.bəq̓ʷà? ?i ci?iɬ x̌ʷù?x̌ʷəy?   ML.

Heron and Little Diver were staying there.

-bi-t

?ístəbid ?al ti ?àl?al   On this side of the house.   LG.

t(ə) ad?ístəbid   Right beside you.   LG.

?ístəbids   beside it, on the side of it   LG.

reduplication

?əs?í?istəb ti?iɬ s.bəq̓ʷà? ?i ci?iɬ x̌ʷù?x̌ʷəy?   ML.

Heron and Little Diver were staying there.

(According to LG. ?i?istəb implies humble status.)

1. ʔiš

    -il

        <u>ʔíšil</u>   fish swims

           See under <u>tíčib</u>.

        ʔuʔíšil ti s.ʔulàdxʷ ʔal tiʔəʔ gʷədálgʷiɫ   DM.

        The salmon swam under the canoe.

        ƛu.gʷádil gʷəl bəʔíšil dxʷ.q̓ixʷ

        They jump amd they swim upstream.

    -ɫ

        <u>ʔíšɫ</u>   (to) paddle

          Cf. x̌ʷúbt   a paddle

             -alwaʔs   lexical suffix 'paddle'

             ləláb   oar

        ʔuʔíšɫ čəd ʔə tə q̓ilbid   I paddle the canoe.   EK.

        míʔmad kʷi sʔíšɫs (h)əlgʷəʔ   They barely paddled.   MC.

    -ɫ-š

        <u>ʔuʔíšɫš</u> čəd   I paddled it.   LL.

        ʔu.hílitᵊb čəd ɫəʔíšɫšəd   LL.

        I was told to paddle it (so they could see how good I was).

    -txʷ

        <u>ʔuʔíšɫtub</u>   try out a new canoe   LL.

        <u>ʔuʔíšɫtub</u> tə q̓ilbid   EK.

        They paddled the (racing) canoe.

    -yi-

        <u>ʔíšɫyic</u>   Paddle for me.   LG.

rejected:

    *ʔišłib ʔə tiʔił s.tubš   *ʔišłib ʔə tiʔił ƛ̓ələ̀yʔ   LL.

1. ʔítakʷᵊbixʷ   Suquamish   LL., VH.

    Cf. suq̓ʷábš   Suquamish   LL., MS.

      xʷ.sə́q̓ʷᵊb   Suquamish   ESi.

2. ʔítut   sleep

(Etymologically ʔit plus reflexive component -ut.)

Contrast qəł 'wake up'.

root

    ʔítutəxʷ   Go to sleep.   LG.

    ʔəsʔítut   He's asleep.   LG.

    ʔəxʷʔítutᵊb čəd   I'm sleepy.   LG.

    x̌ʷuləxʷ jəł x̌ʷiʔ gʷədsəxʷsʔítutᵊb   LG.
    I wish I weren't so sleepy.

    jəgʷá dxʷsʔìtut   a great one for sleeping   LL.

-dxʷ

    ʔítutdubut   oversleep   LL.

compound

    s.qəlálitut   power (supernatural)

    x̌ʷálitut   snore

    (Also: səsaʔalítut 'bad dream'.)

      hìkʷ čəd ʔusə.saʔalítut tu.łax̌   LG.
      I had a real bad dream last night.

      ʔuqəl.qəlálitut čəd   I had a dream.   LG.

1. ʔíub   cry

     See under cut.

     (Same meaning as x̌áhᵊb.)

     Cf. číq̇icut   scream, loud crying

     root

        ʔuʔíub čəd   I cried.   EK.

        ʔuʔíubəxʷ   She cried.   EK.

        ʔuʔíub čəɬ bək̓ʷ s.ɬax̌il   We cried all night.   EK.
        ("Of course the luƛluƛ cried only in the early morning,
          off by themselves so they would not disturb others." EK.)

     -i-t

        ʔuʔíubid haw̓əʔ tiɬ tiʔəʔ bads   LL.
        He is crying because his father is out of sight.

2. ʔixʷ-   derivational prefix   'spouse'

     See Hoard and Hess, pp. 50ff.

        ʔixʷčačas   young spouse

        ʔixʷsəsáʔliʔ   two spouses

        ʔixʷdxʷspáyəq   spouse is a canoe-maker

        ʔixʷčəgʷás   acting as wife

3. ʔix̌   (something gets) scratched

     See under x̌iq̇(i).

     root

        ʔəsʔíx̌ tə ƛəlàyʔ   The canoe is scratched.   LG.

     -dxʷ

        ʔuʔíx̌ᵊdub jəɬ tə ƛəlàyʔ   LG.
        Somebody must have scratched the canoe.

1.   ʔix̌ʷ(i)   throw away

  See under pus(u) and xʷis(i).

  root

    ʔuʔíx̌ʷ čəd   I was thrown things (gifts) for
                        helping in the power song.   LL.

    ʔuʔíx̌ʷ   throwing blankets or money   LL.

      Cf. pák̓(a), pač̓(a)

  -it

    ʔíx̌ʷid   Throw it.   LL., EK.
                        Throw it away.   EK.
                        Throw it out.   LG.

    ʔíx̌ʷitᵊb   It was thrown.   LL.

    ʔíx̌ʷic ʔə tiʔił tabiłəd   Throw the rope to me.   LL.

    ʔíx̌ʷicut   sweep   LG.

    səxʷʔíx̌ʷicut   broom

  -dxʷ

    ʔuʔíx̌ʷᵊdxʷ čəd tiʔił   I threw it away without thinking. LL.

    xʷuʔᵊləʔ čəd ʔuʔíx̌ʷᵊdxʷ tił̓ tiʔił   LL.
    I must have thrown it out.

  lexical

    ʔíx̌ʷᵊduptᵊb   thrown out (and scattered)   LL.

  reduplication

    adsixʷʔíʔix̌ʷəd   I'm humbling myself.   LG.

2.   ʔiyáł   a woman's name, LG.'s husband's mother. (Per-
                        haps a Nooksack name.)

3.   ʔiʔáb   wealth

    siʔáb   nobleman, wealthy man, sir

sí?i?əb (or maybe sí?iyəb)   sort of high class   ML.

ci si?áb   noblelady, madame, wife of a si?áb

?í?iyəb   young man who is related   LG.

?i?áb   endearing term of address to a little boy   LG.

-il

?iyábil (or perhaps ?i?ábil)   rich   LG.

1. ?i?áab?aɬ   a woman's name, LG.'s mother

    cisi?áabaɬ   a woman's name, LG.'s father's mother's sister.
    This woman's daughter's daughter is Emma Conrad.
    Also the name of LG.'s younger daughter, Isabel.

3. ?u   interrogative particle
    mutually exclusive with čad, čal, k̓ʷid, tab,
    ?əx̌id, ?id(i)gʷat

4. ?u-   See under u-.

5. ?u·   interjection 'oh!'

6. ?údaw?   tallow

7. ?údəgʷ-   middle (This morpheme is always bound to a lexical.)

    See under ?ac-.

    -abac

    ɬu.kí(i)stxʷ čaləp ?al ti?iɬ ?ùdəgʷabac   EC.
    You folks stand him up in the middle.

    ?ùdəgʷábac 1. in the middle of some defined enclosure,
                   e.g., field, room, some unit of measure DM.
                2. in the middle (of a table)   DM., LG.

-ič

   liⱦʔúdəgʷìč   in the middle   EK.

   x̌ʷuⱡəxʷ ʔuʔúdəgʷiȷ̌iləxʷ ʔal tiʔiⱦ ʔalʔal   EK.
   She got only to the middle of the house.

   ʔúdəgʷìč   middle of house, rope, pile of things, road   EK.
                     middle of house, room   DM.

-(gʷ)iⱡ

   ʔal tiʔiⱦ ʔúdəgʷiⱡ kʷ(i) ads.q̓il   LA.
   You ride in the middle (of the canoe).

   liⱦʔúdəgʷiⱡ   LG., DM.
   Someone is in the middle of the canoe.

   liⱦʔúdəgʷiⱡ čəxʷ   LG.
   You sit in the middle of the canoe.

rejected:

   *ʔúdəgʷadiʔ, *ʔúdəgʷap   LG.

1.   ʔúgʷus   teach

root

   ʔúgʷus   give directions, show, demonstrate,   DM.
                 teach   LG.

-t

   ʔúgʷusəd   Teach him.   LG.

   ʔúgʷusc ʔə kʷi q.qàȷ̌ətəb   Teach me Skagit.   LG.

    xʷìʔ kʷi gʷátəxʷ kʷ(i) uʔùgʷusc   LG.
    No one taught me.

   ʔalču̓ʔúgʷustəb tiʔiⱦ   teaching him   LG.

-aɬ

ʔúgʷusaɬ	teach a child	LG.

ʔalčuʔúgʷusaɬ He's teaching his child. LG.

ʔal s.buusəɬdát tə dsuʔugʷùsáɬ ʔə tə q.qàǰətəb LG.
On Thursday I'm teaching Skagit.

dxʷsʔugʷusaɬ teacher LG.

ʔugʷus(aɬ)ál?txʷ school LG.

-aɬ-bi-t

ʔalčuʔúgʷusaɬbitˀb ti?iɬ LG.
teaching it to him

ʔuʔúgʷusaɬbic čəxʷ You taught me. LG.

lexical

-ucid

ʔúgʷucidid teach, put it in the mouth LL.

dxʷsʔúgʷucidid teacher LL.

ti?iɬ ʔuʔúgʷucidid ti?iɬ wiẃsu ʔə ti?iɬ s.x̌al LL.
He who teaches the children to write.

1. ʔúkʷukʷ NPS play

Cf. čáʔa SPS play

Some games: ʔu.čəcxʷíÍč shinny: sdə.dúkʷˀb unidentified and undescribed game; s.ləhál bone game;
səʔ.sxʷáb 'Indian broad jump' consisting of two suc-
cessive leaps; ti.tǰálikʷ a game of rolling stones to
see who can roll them the farthest; ti.tx̌ʷúdəgʷəÍ tug-
of-war; táʔ.tədàq a game wherein a blunted arrow is
shot into a cottonwood tree until it gets caught. Then
other arrows are shot at the first one to see who can
shoot it out of the tree.

See Haeberlin and Gunther, pp. 62-66, Elmendorf, pp. 224-245 and Smith, pp. 206-227.

-bi-t

ʔúkʷukʷbicid	make fun of you	AS.
ʔúkʷukʷbic	make fun of me	AS.
ʔúkʷukʷbitᵊb čəd	make fun of me	AS.

1. s.ʔuládxʷ   NPS   general term for all sea-going fish (salmon and trout) that spawn in fresh water creeks and rivers

    Cf. s.čədádxʷ   SPS   salmon

     s.ʔúʔ(ə)ladxʷ   name of a class of fish

    Cf. s.łúʔᵊb, λxʷáyʔ   dog salmon, chum

     hədú   humpback, pink

     yúbəč, sáčəb   king, spring, chinook, tyee

     s.q̓əčqs, s.kʷxʷíc   silver, coho

     s.číʔł, s.cəq̓í, s.cəwád, xʷ.bádiʔ   sockeye, red, blueback

     qíwx̌, s.kʷáwəl   steelhead, rainbow trout

     yúʔibəč   grilse (blackmouth)

     yúʔqʷ   old salmon that's spawned and ready to die

2.   ʔúlal   cattail   LL.

   ʔúlʔulal   cattails

   ʔúlalali   cattail place   ESi.

3. s.ʔúləč   worm (generic)   EK.
                a fishing worm, large, found in rotten logs   LG.

    Cf. s.čək̓ʷ 'worm, bug', x̌ʷəʔ.x̌ʷiλalikʷ 'inch worm'

1. ʔúləx̌   obtain   LG.

    ləʔúləx̌ čəd ʔə kʷi s.ʔàx̌ʷuʔ   JC.
    I'm on my way to gather clams.

    łuʔúləx̌ čəd ʔə kʷi s.ʔàx̌ʷuʔ   VH.
    I should gather clams.

    x̌ál čəd gʷəbəʔùləx̌yid kʷi s.ʔulàdxʷ ʔə ti čìx̌čix̌   ES.
    For Fish Hawk, I also can get salmon.

    sʔúləx̌   unidentified kind of mussel like "thing
              from which beads and earrings are made"   LL.
              dentalium   LL., JC.
              possessions   LL., LG.
             (In this sense see under s.tábigʷs.)

    səxʷʔúləx̌əgʷəl   property container   JC.

2. ʔúlub NPS   ten

   Cf. pádac SPS   ten

    ʔúlub ʔi kʷi d(ə)c̓uʔ   eleven

    ʔúlubəłiləxʷ   ten times   EK.

   lexical

    ʔùlubac̓čup   ten fires

    ʔulubác̓ʔič   ten bundles

    ʔúlubəlus   ten squares in a net, ten stitches
                    in knitting   LG.

    ʔúlubìlc ʔi kʷi d(ə)c̓uʔ   eleven dollars

    ʔúlubqs   ten points

   reduplication

    ʔululúʔb   ten people

1. ʔúluɫ   travel by water

    Contrast with ʔíbəš 'travel on land'.

    root

        bələʔúluɫ (h)əlgʷəʔ   ML.
        They are travelling some more (by canoe).

        ʔúluɫəxʷ ciʔəʔ k̓aʔk̓aʔ
        (Then) Crow took a canoe trip.

    reduplication

        ʔúʔuluɫ   move residence   EK.

        ʔúluluɫ   boat riding   EK.

2. dxʷ.ʔúlus   a willing worker   ES.

                one who has patience and is interested in
                what he is doing   EK.

3. ʔúp̓(u)   sit on lap

    root

        ʔuʔúp̓ čəd   I sat on his lap (without the intention of
                    either of us).   LG.

    -ut

        ʔuʔúp̓ud tiʔiɫ ʔíbac   LL.
        She put her grandson on her lap.

        ƛáhəxʷ. ʔuʔúp̓ucid čəd   LL.
        Come on! I'll put you on my lap.

        ʔəsʔúp̓ud čəd   LG.
        I'm holding (this child) on my lap.

        ck̓ʷáqidəxʷ x̌àƛtxʷ gʷ(ə)adsəsʔúp̓ud   LL.
        You always want to be on his lap.

ʔuʔúp̓utᵊb ʔə tiʔił s.càpaʔ tiʔił ʔìbac   LL.

ʔuʔúp̓utᵊb tiʔił ʔìbac ʔə tiʔił s.càpaʔ   LL.

Both are glossed: The grandfather put the grandchild
                   on his lap.

ʔəsʔúp̓utəg̓ʷəl hawə́ʔ tiʔiʔə́ʔ

He put her on his lap.

-txʷ

ʔuʔúp̓txʷ čəd   I sat her on his lap.   LG.

ʔuʔúp̓tubš   They brought the baby to me.   LG.
                   He made me hold her on my lap.   LG.

-bi-t

ʔəsʔúp̓bid čəd tiʔił   I'm sitting on his lap.   LG.

híwil. ʔúp̓bid tiʔił   Go sit on his lap.   LG.

rejected: *(ʔu)ʔúp̓ᵊb

1.   ʔuq̓ʷ(u)   pull out, unplug

See under x̌əc.

-ut

ʔúq̓ʷud   Pull it out.   EK.

lexical

ʔuq̓ʷúci(d)cid čəd   I opened the door on you;
                          I opened the door and there you were. LL.

ʔuq̓ʷúci(d)txʷ   Pull it out.   LL.

ʔuʔuq̓ʷúcidᵊb   opened the door (lit. 'un-
                      plugged it')   LL.

reduplication

ʔúʔuq̓ʷud   Pull it part way out.   EK.

1. ʔúsil   dive

    Compare the lexical suffix -us 'head, upper part; face, hair'

    xʷiʔ lə.búʔqʷ tiʔəʔ s.bəq̓ʷáʔ yəx̌i ... xʷiʔ gʷəx̣̌suʔúsils   DM.
    A heron is not (classed as) a buʔqʷ because it does not
    dive.

    -s

    ʔúsis   dive after something

2. ʔúšəb   pity   LG.

    ʔəsʔúšəb   kindness   EK.

    -i-t

    ʔúšəbic   Pity me.   EK.
                   Pity me; help me.   LG.

    ł̓əʔúšəbic čələp   You folks pity me!   LG.

    ʔúšəbid   Pity him.   EK.

    ʔúšəbitubuł   Pity us.   EK.

    ʔúšəbitᵊb   He was pitied.   EK.

    -a-b-dxʷ

    sʔušəbábdxʷ   poor ("sort of a good word; always
                       willing to help")   EK.

    ʔušəbábdxʷ čəd   I'm poor.

    díbəł sʔušəbàbdxʷ ʔal ti s.wàtixʷtəd   EK.
    We poor ones on earth.

        Cf. həwúʔ

    -a-b-dxʷ-il

    ʔuʔùšəbábdxʷil čəd   I'm in trouble/difficulty. ES.

    -t-d-a-but

    ləʔùšəbtədábut čəd dxʷʔal dəgʷiʔ   I'm asking help of you. ES.

1. ʔut̓əb   stretch

    sʔútub   rubber ball

   lexical

     ʔúʔtəbikʷ   a stretch shirt, e.g., a T-shirt, especially a form fitting one   LL.

     ʔəxʷʔútʔutalus   stretched eyes, slant eyes, sleepy eyes (an insult for Bear)   LL.

2. ʔux̌ʷ   go

    Synonyms: ƛá 'go to'; híwil 'go ahead'; ɬə́gʷɬ 'leave someone/something'; ʔə́ƛ 'come'; ʔíbəš 'go by land'; ʔíʔlɪɬ 'go by water'.

   root

     ʔúx̌ʷ čəd ɬu.bəq̓ʷìčaʔ ʔə kʷi hùd   LG.
     I'm going (out) to pack wood on the shoulder.

     ʔəs.x̌əc čəd gʷəʔùx̌ʷəd   I'm afraid to go.   EK.

     pút lə.ʔəx̌id lə ʔùx̌ʷəs   How wonderfully they would go!   MC.

     tuʔəxʷsʔúx̌ʷəb čəd   I wanted to go.   EK.

     x̌aƛtxʷ čəd (kʷi) gʷədsʔùx̌ʷ   I want to go.   EK.

  -c

     tuʔúx̌ʷcəxʷ ciʔiɬ sɬà.ɬdəyʔs   He went to his girl.   ES.

     tuʔúx̌ʷcəxʷ   He went after them.   ES.

     gʷəʔúx̌ʷc čəd gʷədxʷ.təsəxʷ čəlàdi(ʔ)d   ES.
     I'll go over there and hit him in the side of the head.

  -c-yi

     ʔúx̌ʷcyic   Go after it for me.   LG.

  -c-b

     ʔuʔúx̌ʷcᵊb   He went after him.   LL.

ʔuʔúx̌ʷcᵊb ti d.bədàʔ   They went to get my son.   HD.

ʔúx̌ʷcᵊbəx̌ʷ   Go get it!   LL.

-dxʷ

xʷiʔ xʷuʔᵊləʔ gʷədsʔúx̌ʷdubut   LL.
It is doubtful that I can go.

-txʷ

ɬuʔúx̌ʷtxʷəxʷ tiʔəʔ   He is going to take this now.   EK.

-txʷ-yi-

ʔúx̌ʷtxʷyic   Take it for me.   LG.

-txʷ-b

ʔuʔúx̌ʷtub ti d.bədàʔ   They took my son.   HD.

-yi-

ʔúx̌ʷyic   Go for me.   LG.

1.   ʔúʔəd   agree strongly; say 'yes'

     ʔúhuʔəd   agree by lending vocal support
as someone is talking to you

Addendum

3.1

-ač   lexical suffix   'head'

       Cf. -qid

4.1

ad-   thy

       See under d- 'my'.

8.3

-alačəd   lexical suffix   'testicles'

       Cf. bâčəd

     dxʷ.təx̌ʷtx̌ʷálačəd^əb   one who drags his testicles on the ground

8.4

-alatxʷ   lexical suffix   'part of a building'

       Cf. -alʔtxʷ

9.4

-aliqʷ   lexical suffix   'hat'

       Cf. šiqʷ NPS   and   s.xʷáyʔs SPS   'hat'

    ʔu.xʷəcáliqʷ^əb čəd   I took my hat off.   LG.

9.5

-alubid   lexical suffix   'shoulder'

       Cf. s.təbálubid Skagit   'shoulder'

         s.ʔí1ʔalubid   Snoh. SPS   'shoulder'

    ʔəspíƚ.pilálubid   broad shoulders   LL.

9.6

-alus   lexical suffix   'eye, color'

        Cf. -us; qəlúb

    ʔudxʷ.x̌əɫx̌ɫálusəxʷ čəxʷ ʔu   Are your eyes aching?   LL.

    ʔəxʷ.ʔútʔutàlus   sleepy eyed, slant eyed
                              (lit. 'stretched eyes')   ML.

    qʷátqʷatàlus   tears   ES.

    ʔu.gʷəc̓əlúsᵊb čəd   I looked around for it.   LL.

    təkʷtəkʷəlús   great horned owl

    č̓ítəlus   surprised (lit. 'near eyed')   EK.

    ʔájəlus   bright (color)   EK.

    ʔəs.ʔəx̌ídəlus   What color is it?   EK.

    ʔəs.č̓uɫəyʔàlus   leaf color

9.7

-alwaʔs   lexical suffix   'paddle'

        Cf. x̌ʷubt

    qʷiq̓ʷəlwáʔs   strong with a paddle

        ʔu.hílitᵊb čəd ɫu.ʔíšɫšəd gʷəl háydub gʷəl qʷiq̓ʷəlwáʔsəd   LL.
        They told me to paddle so they could find out how strong
        I was with a paddle.

    səxʷ.šíc̓əlwàʔs   (time of year to) sheathe the paddles ML., LL.,
                                                                ES.

    šúləlwàʔs   Put your paddle in the canoe.   ES.

    s.ɫàdəyʔəlwáʔs   a woman's paddle   LL.

9.8

-alʔtxʷ   lexical suffix   'building'

        Cf. -alatxʷ, ʔálʔal

10.1

-ał   derivational suffix that designates class membership

     s.tábał   What kind of ____ is it?

     s.duhubšəł čəd   I am from Snohomish.   LL.

10.2

-ał   a derivational suffix

        With action stems, it indicates that the agent
acts with his own interests paramount. It is mutually exclusive with transitive suffixes and the
(obligatory) patient may never have a determiner.
Stems formed with -ał behave much like the small
class of roots typified by təx^w 'buy' and čəł/šəł
'make'.

     ʔu.húyəł čəd x̌^wùbt   I made myself a paddle.   LG.

     ʔu.q^wíbəł čəd x̌^wùbt   Same gloss: I made myself a paddle. LG.

       Cf. ʔu.čə́ł čəd x̌^wùbt   I made a paddle.   LG.

     ʔu.čáləł čəd pìšpiš   I chased the cat.   LG.

     ʔu.čáləł pìšpiš tə s.q^wəbày?
The dog chased itself a cat.

     káw̓kawəł šàw̓ həlg^wə?   They chew for themselves bones. LG.

     káw̓kawəł (h)əlg^wə? ʔə ti šàw̓   LG.
Same gloss: They chew for themselves bones.

     káwəł čəd šàw̓   I chew a bone for myself.   LG.

     káwəł šàw̓ čəd   Same gloss: I chew a bone for myself.

     ʔu.tág^wəł čəd pù?təd   I bought myself a shirt.   LG.

       Cf. ʔu.tə́x^w čəd pù?təd   I bought a shirt.   LG.

x^wəł   (from x^wi?-əł)

     ʔəs.x^wə́ł ǰəsəd   He was without leg(s).   EC.

ʔəs.xʷə̀ɬ tálə čəɬ   We are out of money.   VH.

ʔəs.xʷə̂ɬ čəɬ tàlə   Same gloss: We are out of money.   VH.

10.3

-aɬˀd 'food'

   derivational element in s.q̓ʷəláɬˀd 'berries, fruit'
                              (lit. 'ripe food')

   Cf. ʔə́ɬˀd, -daliɬˀd

11.2

-aq   lexical suffix 'forked'

   ƛ̓í.ƛ̓pəq   underpants   LL.

      Cf. ƛ̓əp

   q̓isáq   exposed leg   DM., LL.

   tá̓ʔ.tədàq   a game wherein a blunted arrow is shot into
                     a cottonwood tree until it gets caught. The
                     first one to shoot it down wins.   DM.

15.3

báčəd   testicles

      Cf. -alačəd

16.5

xʷ.bádiʔ   sockeye   (Snoqu.)   EW.

      Cf. s.čí̓ʔɬ (Skagit), s.cəqí (Snoh.), c̓əwádxʷ (Muck.)

24.1

bəč̓lúlaʔ   ant   BMc., EJ.

under 30.4

In place of

bəlqʷəyíʔqʷəb   JC. gives

bəlqʷíbigʷəd   'somersault'.

32.2

bə́qsəd   nose

  Cf. -qs and note the following:

ɬə́bc̓qs	mucus	LL.
sísəd	blow the nose	LG.
sítqsᵊb	sniff	LG.
sup̓qs	sniff	JC.

37.1

biq̓(i)   press down on

 -t

  bíq̓id   Press down on it.   LG., VH.

  làʔb ʔəsbíq̓itᵊb tiʔəʔ ƛ̓àʔtəd dxʷ.gʷəd   MS.
  The net is pressed down strongly.

47.1

cə́jx̌əlqid   pull wool apart after washing to make it fluffy.
                      BMc., EJ.

49.5

cə́wəɬ SPS   hungry

  Cf. tág̓ʷəxʷ NPS

694

under 51.3

cìldáliⁱⁱ⁄əd   table   LG.

63.4

čapx̌   SPS   cedar root   BMc.

s.ṭə́x̌ʷšəd NPS   cedar root

      Cf. qʷəbəláx̌ʷ

63.8

c̓awqʷ-   Yakima   Cf. tú̓bšədàd (Addendum)

    -b

      c̓áwqʷᵊb   speak Yakima   DM.

lexical

      c̓áwqʷucid   Yakima language   DM.

66.5

c̓əbíq̓i-t-ᵊb   scratched someone   BMc.

      Cf. x̌iq̓(i), x̌ib(i), x̌ip̓(i), ʔix̌

70.4

c̓əwádxʷ   sockeye   BMc.

s.c̓əwád   sockeye   EW.

      Cf. s.c̓í̓ʔⁱ (Skagit), s.cəqí̓ (Snoh.), xʷ.bádiʔ (Snoqu.)

72.4

čikʷ   raw   LG.

      Cf. x̌ič̓

      tiʔəʔ tátačulbixʷ ʔəsčìkʷ   fresh animal (meat)   EC.

72.8

čiq̓ʷ(i)   split

> See under ɫič(i).   Cf. čəx̌; čuqʷ(u), ƛ̓k̓ʷ(u)

lexical

čiq̓ʷá(ʔ)k̓ʷčup   split wood

> ləcučiq̓ʷák̓ʷčup čəd tiʔiɫ cəxʷ.ƛ̓k̓ʷšád   DM.
> I was splitting wood. That's how I cut my foot.

80.3

čábk̓ʷ   cloud(y)   BMc., EJ.

under 80.4

> diɫ.čàd   either one   LG.

under 80.4

> ʔiɫ-

> ʔiɫčàd   which one; either one   LG.

92.4

s.čədádxʷ   SPS   salmon and sea-going trout, general term

> Cf. s.ʔuládxʷ   NPS

101.6

čubáliali   name for White Horse Mountain

> See s.x̌ədəlwáʔs (Addendum).

under 105.3

> With čáčas compare ɫisu, 534.2, especially when
> occurring with the partitive prefix.

696

under 106.1

      sčáčəjəp   little cedar bark skirt   LL.

108.1

   s.čáyəp   skirt   LG.

     Cf. s.čájəp

112.3

   čəš

     ʔučəšálbixʷ   suckle

under 114.1

     -ut

     čxʷúd   add it to something   LG.

       čxʷúd t(i) ads.čàyəp   Lenghten your skirt.   LG.

114.4

   číčq̓ʷəp   (baby) with feces on buttocks
    See under s.p̓áč.

115.1

   čiɫ(i)   praise   VH.

     Cf. k̓ʷədíid

123.1

   -daliɫᵊd   lexical suffix 'food'
             (especially food viewed from a continuative
             or iterative aspect)

         Cf. ʔəɫᵊd

   cildáliɫᵊd   (dining) table
   čàydidáliɫᵊd   making a regular diet of Chinese food
     Contrast čáydi s.ʔə̀ɫᵊd   Chinese food   LG.

s.(h)uydáliłᵊd	food preparation
xʷəcdáliłᵊd	fast (lit. 'take off eating')
s.x̌ʷújə(ʔ)dàliłᵊd	fat of a fish JC.

124.3

s.dáwdwał   man's name; Jimmy Price's father's name

135.4

didti   powerful

   Cf. qʷiq̓ʷ

   xʷíʔ lədídti dxʷ.dàʔᵊb   He is a shaman not to be taken lightly. LG.

under 155.1

   lexical

   cáy čəł (ʔ)ugə̀q̓ᵊbič   We are really having sunny weather.

155.2

gəq̓ád   open it   BMc.

163.2

s.gʷáʔac   salmonberry sprouts   BMc.

under 173.3

   xʷ.bá(ʔ)wił   width of a canoe

under 196.1

   hudáyʔstaq   open fire pit   DM.

217.2

jáʔabixʷ   a kind of s.qəlálitut

219.2

    jə́lč   See under ǰə́lč.

223.1

    jíjəgʷaʔ   Muck.   bug   EJ.

                            This includes fly, ant, spider, etc.
                            but not snake.

under 228.4

        ʔúlub ʔi kʷi təqàči? s.bəkʷ̓ači? sjə̂lč ʔi tiʔə?
        cəlácači? ʔi tiʔə? cəlàc   MS.
        Ten and eight hundred year(s) and fifty-five, i.e., 1855

under 231.2

        kày?káwič   the SPS name for Little Hunchback   JC.

under 243.2

      -dxʷ

        kʷá?dubut   manage to get away

under 252.2

        k̓ʷás   fish thoroughly dried by smoking

          Cf. q̓ʷás

under 254.4

      -t

        ʔukʷ̓ədícut čəd   I am praying.   BMc.

      lexical

        k̓ʷədícutal?txʷ   church   BMc.
          Cf. t̓igʷ(i) ~ tiwił

265.4

    -lap   your (pl.)

        See under d̲- 'my'.

275.2

    ləq̓ʷay?   plate   EJ.

        Cf. ɬa?x̌

under 278.2

        DM. gives sləhíb.

284.2

    -lula?

      bəčlúla?   ant

      təplúla?   spider

under 293.3

        tux̌ʷ ɬəbčúɬ tə dàbut   LL.
        a little hard earned money (figurative)

300.3

    ɬičá?a SPS   net   EW., BMc., EJ., BT.

under 302.1

      x̌ʷɬídič   bow-string

307.5

    (s)ɬúlac   brant

under 308.1

    ɬúx̌ʷabac   naked   BT.

317.1

    ƛ́álagʷil   spawning   BMc.

under 320.1

    See also qəč̓áp in Addendum.

320.2

    ƛ́əbč-

        ʔəsƛ́ə́bč̓ə̓d čəd tiʔiɬ   I am listening to that.   BMc.

        ʔəsƛ́ə́bč̓cid čəd   I am listening to you.   EJ.

320.5

    ƛ́əbx̌ʷílaʔ   hail   LG., BT.

under 321.1

    lexical

        ƛ́əlá́ʔɬdəlb   stop eating

            Cf. xʷəcdáliɬə̓d 'fast', xʷiʔəɬdálb 'dieting, fasting'

        ƛ́əlúsə̓bəx̀ʷ   Behave yourself.   BMc.

        ƛ́əlax̌ad   fence

333.1

    pác̓ə̓b   odor of skunk   LG.

    Cf. -qəp, 381.1 and sub(u)

335.3

 pax̌ʷəb   smell of burning   LG.

  Cf. -qəp, 381.1 and sub(u)

335.4

 s.páyqʷuc   See under s.píqʷuc.

339.2

 pətq   pierce, go completely through

  Cf. caq̓(a), saq, šič̓(i)

  x̌ʷuləx̌ʷ ƛu.caq̓atᵒb gʷəl pə́tq   He was stabbed and pierced.   ML.

  gʷəl bələpə́tq ti?ił s.caq̓ads   His jab penetrated completely
                 through (Kingfisher).   ML.

355.6

 pə́łəlqid   card wool   BMc., EJ.

371.5

 qaləp

  ?əsqaləp   unmarried person (of either sex)   VH.

372.10

 qəbə́təd   SPS   axe

  Cf. s.k̓ʷ(ə)qʷə́b   NPS   axe

373.5

 qəč̓áp   an unidentified type of salmon trap made
           out of cedar boughs   LG.

  See ƛa?təd.

under 373.6

>   -bi-t

>   >   ʔuqədᵊbíd tiʔəʔ ṡ.čə̀tx̌ tiʔəʔ dəxʷ.gʷəláltᵊbs ʔə tiʔəʔ
>   >   ṡ.čistxʷs s.bəq̣ʷaʔ   ML.
>   >   Kingfisher committed adultery with her, so her husband,
>   >   Heron, beat her.

under 377.2

>   other derivation

>   >   qə́ləleb   bad   LG.

>   >   qəlálšti   have the bad luck to get injured

>   >   >   ʔuqəlálšti čəd   I had bad luck and got hurt.   LG.

383.1

>   qə́sqᵊb   chattering all the time; converse

>   See under cut, kə́skᵊb.

under 398.2

>   ʔá ti ds.yə̀cᵊb cay q̣ič   I have very important business.   BMc.

412.6

>   qʷəbəláxʷ   root(s) of any kind

>   Cf. ṡ.tə́xʷšəd, čapx̌

416.4

>   qʷəsyúʔ   porpoise   DM.

435.6

    saċəb   Muck.   king salmon

        Cf. yubəč   NPS

439.2

    say   nervous, fidgety, at loose ends, excited

       tu₀xʷə́łil s̀ày ci tuds.k̓ʷuy   VH.
       Mother used to get into traumatic states.

441.3

    səhí?wəhš   Sahəhwamish   "The name sort of means the people
                                     at the head of the bay."   JC.

       See Smith (1941), p. 204.

443.3

    sə́səq   thimbleberry   EW.

       Cf. łáqə?

under 463.1

      xʷší̓ċəp   safety pin

       Cf. x̌ʷúq̓ʷadis

466.1

    šiƛ(i)

      -it

       šiƛ(i)cut   brag   DM., VH.

under 469.1

      -txʷ   show, demonstrate

       šúłtxʷəxʷ ?əs.?əx̌íd kʷi gʷəs.pədəds
      Then they showed them how to plant (potatoes).   VH.

under 480.3

    -dxʷ

      stáb əẃə ƛ(u)adstáĺx̌ᵊdxʷ ti syalt   BMc.
      What do you use a cedar-root basket for?

      ƛutáĺx̌ᵊdxʷ čəd ƛu.ʔúluɫ čəd.   BMc.
      I use a canoe to travel by water.

      ƛutáĺx̌ᵊdxʷ čəd ƛu.ʔútud čəd s.x̌ʷiƛalqid   BMc.
      I use it to spin with.

491.3

    təplúlaʔ   spider   Cf. s.tətúpəɫ   EJ.

under 498.2

In SPS the system is somewhat different. In addition to the
forms given here, there is šə and sə used with items known
to exist but whose location is in doubt. The forms tiʔəʔ
and ciʔəʔ do not exist, their place being taken by ti and
ci; and finally there is a distinction between tiʔiɫ and
ti(i)ɫ. The former is used as an independent pronoun and
the latter as a modifier.

506.7

    túbšədàd   Yakima

      Cf. čawqʷ- (Addendum)

under 510.1

    tùĺʔálxəd   northwest wind

514.1

    túx̌ʷ   runner of a vine; what trails along the ground   EW.

      ƛ(u)astúx̌ʷtux̌ʷ ʔal tiiɫ s.watix̌ʷtəd   BMc.
      It sends runners on the ground (a blackberry bush).

-agʷil

    túx̌ʷəgʷi   crawl esp. of a snake or other such thing.

      tux̌ʷəgʷi tiił bəc̓ac   The snake crawls.   BMc.

under 521.2

    reduplication

      t̓át̓qaʔəc   miniature salalberry bush. "This plant is important for medical purposes."   JC.

528.1

    s.t̓əqáx̌ʷ SPS   beaver   BMc.

529.2

    t̓ə́qus SPS   blind

      Cf. bádil

532.2

    (s)t̓ik̓iwił   double-ended canoe that originated among the stikí

      See under q̓ílbid.

under 548.2

    -txʷ

      wáwəxʷtub   He was allowed to join in their eating. VH.

585.2

    x̌áyux̌ʷaʔ SPS   fly (insect)

      Cf. x̌ʷəx̌ʷáyu

706

591.1

s.x̌ədəlwá?s   Upper Skagit name for Mt. Hagen (across the river
                       from White Horse Mt.)

        See čubáliali (Addendum).

                       sx̌ədəlwá?s stole čubáliali (which/who has burned
                       looking sides) and hid her where she now stands
                       and is hard to see (from the Skagit side).

under 614.2

    -t

        ?ux̌ʷə́t^ə d čəd šə sxʷ.pipt   I tore my shirt.   BT.

619.6

x̌ʷudx̌ʷud   converse

        Cf. cut

643.8

dxʷ.?ãha   name of a group of Skagit living along the
                    Samish river and to the north of it.   DM.

                    See Sampson, pp. 2 and 25-27.

645.1

?ãlacut   go on spirit power quest

under 645.2

        díɫ tu?ãlalus ti?iɫ   That is how it happened.   LG.
    -txʷ

        díɫ tu?ãlalustxʷs   That is how he was treated.   LG.

        díɫ tu?ãlalustubš   That is how he treated me.   LG.

679.2

ʔíʔixʷəd

      sixʷ.ʔíʔxʷəd   age mate, peer, one of the same generation   VH.

English Index

approach s.o./s.th. und. 116.2

~ April (time of (robin) whistling)
   und. 337.1/und. 618.4

argue 583.3

arm, hired hand und. 669.5,
   upper arm und. 298.3, lower arm,
   hand lex. suff. 3.2

go around, over some obstruction
   212.2

arrest und. 386.5

arrive 293.5, arrive there 292.1,
   arrive safely 490.2

arrow, bullet 534.1, arrow quiver
   119.3, arrowhead, flint 633.1

arrowhead plant, wapato; potato
   340.4

article 498.2 (cə 45.3, ci 50.2,
   kʷi 248.3, kʷsi 249.2, tə 485.1,
   ti 498.2)

as....as und. 315.1; as, like,
   similar to und. 620.2; as if,
   like, seem 595.1

ashes und. 196.1

go ashore, land a boat/canoe,
   dock/moor a boat 289.1

ask a question 552.3, ask, invite,
   call to 172.2

associate with und. 432.2

surprise attack 464.1

pay attention to, notice, understand 340.7, pay no attention,
   don't touch, leave alone und.
   321.1, don't pay attention und.
   278.5

~ August (time of salalberries) und.
   337.1

aunt 344.3, 660.1

territorial authority of person or
   group (deriv. pref. bəs-) 34.2

automobile und. 508.2

autumn und. 319.1/und. 529.4, und. 332.3/
   und. 337.1

go, get away und. 278.5, away from center,
   away from fire 646.1

after a while und. 323.1, 502.1

awl for weaving und. 634.2

axe 256.4, 372.10

axilla 383.2, axilla, tickle 154.1

baby und. 39.2, unnamed baby 232.2,
 1ex. suff. 209.4

back (of body) 661.2, und. 669.5
 1ex. suff. 551.6, upper part
 of back 417.2, back, cover
 1ex. suff. 204.1, back (of head)
 und. 265.5, backbone of humans,
 mammals 68.1, backbone of a fish
 599.4, dried backbone removed
 from a fish 584.2, backpack,
 carry on back 89.1, back part
 of chicken that is eaten und.
 591.6, back seat of a car 666.5,
 back up 368.2

bad, bad luck 377.2, bad, evil
 439.3, bad, worthless 143.1,
 bad news to come und. 260.4,
 getting worse und. 352.1

bag, pocket und. 132.1

bail out a boat 504.2, bailer
 und. 173.3/250.2

bail out of jail, get loose, untie 156.2

bait for fishing 17.4

bake on open fire und. 529.4, bake
 by burying in hot sand or ashes
 und. 335.8, bake, cook, ripe;
 warm, burn 426.9

balance, teeter, stagger 562.6,
 lose balance backwards 519.1

bald head und. 307.7

ball 26.2, rubber ball und. 687.1

sound of banging, pounding 248.6

bank, hill, incline, slope 1ex. suff.
 209.3, river banks washed away 39.1

barbecue, burn body, roast 252.2,
 barbecued salmon und. 426.9

barber und. 438.1

bare 308.1

bark, esp. fir bark 91.1, cedar bark
 still on tree 448.2, inner bark
 265.3, 307.2, inner fibers of dried
 fir bark 576.1, pry bark off 285.2,
 cedar-bark skirt 106.1

dog bark 175.3, seal bark 426.4

barnacles 76.4

bashful und. 605.2, have head down being
 bashful und. 221.1

basin, pan und. 51.3

basket (in general) und. 634.2, loosely
 woven basket 170.4, soft, pliable
 basket 275.1, water tight cedar-root
 basket 335.6, 625.3, clam basket und.
 649.5, make basket und. 154.5, Basket
 Ogress 562.4, und. 649.5, Basket Ogress's
 daughter's name 388.2

bat (mammal) 373.1

bathe, bathe for spiritual cleansing
 534.3

battle, fight, war 603.1

bayonet und. 33.1/und. 388.4

be thus; make, do, finish 197.2

walk along beach und. 171.1/212.2

beam (in building) und. 520.1

bear 335.5, black bear 97.3, grizzly
 bear 85.4, 485.9

beard und. 319.1, beard, moustache
419.2

beat up, kill 495.2, (cougar) beats
to death (or injures severely) with
tail und. 107.3

beaver und. 527.5, 528.1, mountain
beaver 456.5

because, for what reason 632.7,
because of, due to, on account
of 482.4

become und. 197.2, becoming; begin;
reach or achieve a state or position 208.3

bed (western style) 339.7, go to bed
und. 411.4, 487.2, bedsheet; mat,
mattress 288.1

bee 441.1, bee sting und. 537.4,
bee's wax und. 327.1

before (in time or space), first
223.4

begin 669.3, begin; reach or achieve
a state or position; becoming
208.3, in the beginning und. 223.4

behave self! und. 321.1, und. 351.2,
501.1, unladylike behavior und.
64.3, story to induce proper
behavior und. 619.3

behind, last 265.5, behind s.o./s.th.
und. 368.2, und. 646.1

belch 425.1

believe und. 490.1, don't believe
391.4

belly 263.4, belly (slangy and mildly
insulting) 239.4, bellyful und. 270.1

belonging to 170.5, belongings, possessions, treasure und. 474.1, move
belongings und. 640.1

below, under und. 165.2

belt und. 311.1, und. 610.1, put belt
on cultivator und. 298.2

beneath, under 468.2

bend, curve 348.1, bend forward, look
down 507.3, bent, crooked 393.5,
bent out of line, shape, position;
turned out of shape 351.3

blackberry 169.1, time of blackberries
(~ July) und. 337.1, mountain blueberry 549.5, swamp blueberry 42.1,
cranberry und. 316.1, wild currant
360.5, blue elderberry 72.5, red
elderberry 62.2, gooseberry 63.6,
69.6, 524.2, huckleberry und. 426.9,
blue/black huckleberry 66.4, red
huckleberry und. 535.5, rainflower
berry 178.3, 356.4, raspberry 289.2,
429.2, blackcaps (raspberries, *q.v.*)
93.6, salalberry 521.2, time of salalberries (~ August) und. 337.1,
salmonberry 221.4, 487.1, salmonberry sprouts 457.5, 163.2, time of
salmonberries (~ June) und. 337.1,
soapberry, Indian icecream 611.1,
wild strawberry 101.4, 532.3, thimbleberry 290.1, 443.3, thimbleberry
sprouts 67.1

unidentified berry 397.6, unid.
blueberry und. 468.1, unid.
berry, a mt. blueberry 656./,
dried berry of unid. variety
236.2, unid. berry plant und.
91.2, pick berries 248.4, pick
fruit/berries 66.3

beside und. 671.2

do one's best und. 231.3

bet, wager und. 22.5

better see und. good

big 190.4, big, heavy set, fat
32.4

bile und. 516.5

bind 610.1, binder, device for
keeping gathered und. 443.7

birch tree und. 254.6/und. 334.1

birds 327.3, unid. bird 444.1,
unid. kind of small bird 619.2,
small unid. shore bird 72.2,
bird of prey (general) und. 600.2

bite 597.1, buzzing and biting of a
fly 524.3

bitter und. 438.1, bitter, sour,
spoil 516.5

black 24.4, 506.8, shiny black cloth
124.4, (face) blackened by smoke
und. 334.5

bladder und. 452.3

blanket 378.1, 494.1, 668.1, blanket
for covering knees and legs und.
576.4, dog/goat hair blanket 228.5,
426.1, hold blanket around self w.
hand und. 325.1

(the fire) blazed up 616.1

bleed und. 48.3

blind 16.3, 529.2, blinded by too bright
light 78.3, blind for duck hunting
414.3, pull blinds/shades und. 544.2

blink 298.1, blinking light, flash 355.5

block, close 491.4

blood 509.2, mixed blood und. 99.3/und.
161.1

blow, wind 348.2, und. 462.1, continue
blowing 370.2, blowing hard and getting
bad at sea 100.2

blue, dark green 431.3, sky blue, azure
und. 231.7, getting blue, bruised 111.3

bluff of clay or sand und. 416.2

(think about s.th. and) blurt it out 169.4

board (wood) 593.3, lay boards on a beam
522.3, board which was pounded to keep
time und. 165.2

get on board, mount, ride 399.1

bobcat (lynx) 355.2

body, bulk lex. suff. 2.2, body waste
und. 377.2

boil, fry und. 73.3, boil, cook 409.5
boiling, bubbling, spring of water 30.6,
infectious boil 338.3, 355.4

bone 456.4, backbone (humans and mammals)
68.1, (fish) 599.4, fish bone 78.1,
bone game 270.4

borrow 38.2, borrow, lend items other
than money 102.2

both, pair 631.1

bother, worry 610.2

bottle und. 264.1

bottom lex. suff. 10.6

bovine 420.1

bow (archery) 66.1, und. 393.5

bow, front 458.1

box, chest 330.3, 551.2

boxing und. 494.2

boy und. 506.6, endearing term
of address to a little boy
und. 678.3

bracelet 64.1

brag 466.1

braid 523.6

brain 66.2

branch, limb 106.7

brave und. 190.4

bread, flour 442.1, yeast bread
360.4

break a piece off (leaving larger
portion) 338.4, tough to break
488.3, break rigid object in
two 561.3, break s.o.'s neck
und. 440.4, break (string/
rope); stop a song und. 529.3,
break down, collapse 225.1, break
up (one's engagement) und. 616.4,
broken skull und. 107.3, broken
down, nothing, worthless und.
143.1, broken-hearted und. 589.3

early breakfast und. 275.5

breast, milk 373.4

bridge 581.1

bright (light) 78.3, brightness,
sunshine 155.1, 171.2, bright
(color) 644.1

bring und. 659.2, und. 293.5

broad, flat 358.5

broadcast, throw 562.1

broom und. 678.1

broth 422.3

brother, brother-in-law und. 646.2,
brother-in-law, wife's male cousin
596.2

bruised, dark red 96.4, bruised, getting blue 111.3

brush off 563.4, brush off, shake off
und. 341.1, 535.5

brush, undergrowth, weeds und. 319.1
impassable brushy place und. 583.2

bubbling up, spring of water, boiling 30.6

buck (deer) 613.2

bug, worm (generic) 67.6, bug (incl.
fly, ant, spider) 223.1

build, make 94.1, building lex. suff.
9.8, 515.1, part of a building lex.
suff. 8.4

bullet, arrow 534.1

bullhead 612.2, fresh-water bullhead
340.1, 485.4

bulk, body lex. suff. 2.2

bump into 332.2, bump, touch 237.1

burn, fire, (fire)wood, light (s.th.)
196.1, burn, warm; bake, cook; ripe
426.9, burn body, roast, barbecue
252.2, burned forehead 430.1, fell a
tree by burning und. 603.2

burst 416.1

bury; dust, dirt, soil, earth 335.8,
   bury it! und. 204.1

bushy 502.3

busy 19.3, busy, troubled und. 610.2

but, next, and 169.5

butcher an animal 257.4, 429.8

butterfly 636.8

buttocks, hip und. 298.3, und. 669.5
   buttocks, money, forehead lex. suff.
   208.4

buttoned, hooked, fastened 619.8

buy 496.6, buy (special item in
   mind) 478.1, buy (for a wife)
   220.1

buzzing and biting of a fly 524.3

skunk cabbage 119.6, 403.1

cache, store s.th. 652.2

cackle 263.3

calf of leg 334.2

call, name 126.1, call out loudly,
    yell, telephone 420.2, call to,
    ask, invite 172.2, call names,
    insult 407.6

blue camas, crow potato 62.1

camp, stay over night 396.1

can, metal container 231.5, can-
    ning und. 409.5

candles und. 196.1

cane, walking stick 54.4, 75.2

canoe und. 399.1, canoe, water
    way; curved side; narrow pas-
    sage way lex. suff. 173.3,
    double-ended canoe 528.2, 532.2,
    large canoe 373.3, Nootka type
    canoe 666.1, shovel-nose canoe
    322.2, small, fast canoe 134.3,
    canoe used on salt water 503.5,
    canoe full und. 399.1, make a
    canoe 353.1, try out a new canoe
    und. 675.1, put paddle in canoe
    und. 468.2

can't 628.2, und. 393.3

capable, able, succeed und. 480.3

capsize 160.1

capture und. 244.1

carbuncle boil 90.1

carcass; kill game und. 22.5

card wool 355.6

take care of und. 504.3, take care of,
    look after und. 469.1, don't care
    und. 352.1

carpet und. 51.3

carrot 455.2, 457.4

carry 555.3, und. 244.1, carry on back,
    backpack 89.1, carry on shoulder
    und. 32.4, carry wood up from beach
    und. 101.7

cartilage, gristle 422.9

carve out, hew out, make a canoe 353.1
    carving tool und. 187.2

cascara 392.3

casket und. 232.1

cat 340.6

cataract (of eye) und. 468.1

barely catch s.o. und. 244.1, catch up
    with und. 83.1, catch s.o. doing s.th.
    wrong 602.5, catch a disease 299.2,
    catch a ride und. 399.1, catch it,
    hook it und. 303.1, clothing caught
    in a door und. 238.6, get caught
    (arrow in branches) und. 517.1, get
    caught in rain, darkness und. 204.1

cattail 682.2, cattail needle und. 311.4

Caucasian 335.1, 561.1

caulk; narrow; swallow; stuff into 100.3

causative (-tx^w) 506.4, 515.2

cave und. 285.3

cedar tree 606.2, hollow cedar tree 593.2,
    cedar branches (when put to use) 500.2,
    cedar root 63.4, 531.3

ceiling, roof, upstairs und. 459.2

wild celery 636.2

ten cent 37.3, five, fifty cent
und. 99.3

center 449.1, 642.1

a certain party 156.1

certainly, surely, indeed 247.1

chair und. 165.2/und. 443.7, und.
517.2

change, exchange 652.3, change,
different 271.4, change, transform 142.4, change lex. suff.
549.4, wind changes und. 218.1,
command to change side of canoe
on which one is paddling und.
212.2, 'change affected' suffix
12.3, 153.14, 179.3, 'change in
resolution' suffix 203.1

chapped (?) 497.1, chapped lips
und. 529.4

character, memory, mind 343.5
be characteristic of, pertain
to 643.3

chase, follow 83.1

always chattering und. 64.3, chattering all the time; converse
233.1, 383.1

one who cheats 418.3

cheek und. 669.5, 'cheeks' of a fish
523.4

chest of body und. 669.5

chest, box 551.2

wild cherry (tree) 343.1

chew (food) 236.3, chew up 623.1,
chew (as an insect) 118.1

chew noisily 598.2

chickadee 68.2

one's own child 24.5, any child 105.3,
children 484.1, 552.6, lose one's
child through death 386.2, said to
(or about) child who does not behave
und. 465.1, resp. term for address.
youngsters (child means a lot to you)
372.5

chin und. 165.2, chin, jaw; road lex.
suff. und. 541.5

Chinese 86.1

Chinook jargon 92.5

chipmunk 426.7, 604.2

choke, catch in throat 173.3/649.1,
choke on s.th. und. 100.4, choke
s.o. und. 325.1, 440.4

chop 327.5

church und. 254.4, und. 532.1

cinch 311.1

circle 371.4, circle around 387.1

claiming (?) 523.1

Clallam 317.2

list of clams und. 649.5, black nose
clam 181.1, butter clam 76.2, 443.6,
und. 649.5, Chinese slippers 527.4
cockles 598.1, Eastern clam 195.2,
geoduck 172.1, a kind of horse clam
485.5, horse clam 181.1, littleneck/
steamer clam 263.1, 586.3, clamming
649.5, clam digging stick, clam gun,
clam fork 371.6, clam gun und. 443.7

class membership (deriv. suff.) 10.1,
153.7, low class und. 383.3

718

container und. 244.1, container lex.
suff. 543.4, metal container, can
231.5
become contaminated und. 299.2
'continuitive' (asp. pref.) 269.2,
645.3, 656.5
contorted, distorted face from bad
feelings und. 602.2
lack control 608.4, 'not in full
control' (trans. suff.) 152.2
converse und. 157.2, und. 597.1,
619.6, converse; chattering all
the time 233.1, 383.1
cook und. 209.2, 234.4, cook, bake;
ripe; warm, burn 426.9, overcooked 39.3, overcooked, well-
done 36.3, cooking und. 197.2,
way of cooking with a stick over
fire 239.2
cool it off und. 331.2
copper (?) 431.6
copulating (?) 252.1
corner 589.2
corpse, ghost 232.1
be correct, get s.th. right 274.2
cottonwood (tree) 426.8
cougar 551.5
cough 512.1
count; mind, inner thoughts, sense,
understanding 589.3, counters used
in bone game 589.1, no-counts und.
143.1, und. 352.1
courage und. 190.4/und. 589.3
court a girl und. 18.3

female cousin, older sister und. 646.2,
male cousin, brother-in-law 596.2
cover, lid, top 104.5, und. 591.6, cover,
back lex. suff. 204.1, cover s.o./s.th.
278.1, 576.4, und. 591.6, cover; land,
alight 382.1
coward und. 374.4
coyote 35.6
crab 35.1
crab apple (tree) 372.7
crack, split; half 99.3, cracking und.
239.2, crack, pop und. 316.1
cradle board und. 232.2
crafty, clever, cunning 363.1
cramp, lump 396.5, leg cramp 407.5, cramp
in foot 395.4
sandhill crane, a kind of buʔqʷ 278.2
crave 485.3
crawl (like a snake) und. 514.1, crawl,
have head down 221.1
crazy 232.4, crazy, foolish, senile und.
380.1, crazy, turned head und. 560.1
creative activity lex. suff. 9.3
creek 220.3
creek names und. 264.1, und. 576.1, 593.2
creeper, runner of vine 514.1
bird's crest und. 233.5
cripple und. 432.1, crippled (scrofula)
und. 397.7, hand turned over as is a
cripple's und. 351.3
crooked, bent 393.5
cross body of water und. 138.2, und. 212.2,
456.3, 509.3

cross-footed (insult) und. 520.1,
  crossways 520.1

crouched low und. 591.6

crow 238.1, myth name of crow 591.3

crowded, jammed, stuffed; too tight,
  squeezed into 120.3

crown of head, soft part of baby's
  head und. 384.2/und. 423.3

crush, smash 36.5, crush, come down
  hard on und. 269.3

cry 577.2, 677.1, loud crying, scream-
  ing 115.3, stop s.o. from crying
  182.1

cunning, crafty, clever und. 363.1

cure by a shaman, Indian doctor 19.2

curve, bend 348.1, curved side; narrow passage way; canoe, water way
  lex. suff. 173.3

cut 300.4, cut all up 68.5, cut up,
  stab 275.4, cut down, fell 603.2,
  cut off und. 338.4

(usually cylindrical) object lex. suff.
  8.5

dam, trap und. 491.4

damp, a little wet 20.2, und. 299.1

dance und. 226.1, 444.3, 477.2,
    'drumming' dance 489.2

grow dark 34.3, darkness, night
    291.3

date (of month) und. 589.3

dawn, getting light 241.2, und.
    275.5

day 123.2, und. 54.9, und. 275.5

dead 'on the otherside' und. 138.2,
    'corpse' und. 232.1, 'is cold
    now' und. 331.2, 'breathed his
    last' und. 454.1, 'be used up'
    und. 566.1, play dead und. 635.3,
    hang up the dead und. 239.1

deaf 493.1

debater, racer und. 606.1

decapitate und. 75.1, und. 338.4

decay, rot 115.4

decold it und. 529.4

decorate, mark, write 578.3

deep 324.2

deer 197.1, 386.1

defend und. 583.3

delicious und. 106.6

demonstrate, show und. 469.1,
    demonstrate, teach 680.1

demonstrative 498.2

dentalium und. 683.1

dentist und. 417.4

deny, deprive of s.th. und. 555.5

deprive of s.th., deny und. 555.5

device for (deriv. pref. səxʷ-) 443.7

devil (of Christian concept) 278.3

devil's club 591.4

diaper, clout, sanitary napkin 395.5

die 649.4, 'breathe one's last' und.
    454.1, 'gone, used up' und. 566.1
    (animals) die; starve 635.3, death
    of more than one und. 467.3, lose
    one's child through death 386.2, lose
    spouse through death und. 431.1

different, change 271.4, different from
    und. 129.1

difficult 488.3, 583.2

dig, dig out, loosen ground for planting
    108.2, time of digging (camas bulbs)
    (~ May) und. 337.1, dig up s.th. buried
    173.1, dig around to uncover s.th.; come
    out from under, emerge 465.1

dignity, graciousness 222.1, dignity, high,
    personal respect und. 190.4

dinner, lunch und. 541.5

dip, lick 71.2, dip out 250.2

Big Dipper (constellation), elk 241.3

dirt, muddy und. 36.5, dirt, dust, soil,
    earth; bury 335.8, dirt, filth, infec-
    tion und. 115.4, dirty, soiled 96.5

disappear 467.3

discard, throw; throw s.o. down 559.2

disease, sickness 422.7, catch a disease
    und. 299.2

disembark 430.4

disgusted, irritated, impatient 114.[5]

dish up, upbear, place on/in receptacle
    51.3

dislike 223.3

be completely disorganized (slang) und. 341.1

dissatisfied with und. 143.1

distorted, contorted face (from bad feelings) und. 602.2

distract, disturb 17.2

distribute, scatter 333.5, 'distributive' lex. suff. 145.2, 'group viewed distributively' lex. suff. 13.2

disturb, distract 17.2, disturb (animals), make run about und. 16.7

dive 686.1

divide into two equal parts, halve 48.2

do, finish; be thus; make 197.2, make do, try, improvise; do fumblingly, inadroitly 231.3, well-done, overcooked 36.3

dock/moor a boat 289.1

Indian doctor, shaman 127.1, cure by an Indian doctor 19.2

doe 211.1

dog 412.5, (long haired) dog (that was sheared) 387.3, dog/goat hair blanket 228.5

dolls und. 24.5

dollar und. 208.4

door, way, road 457.6, door, lid lex. suff. und. 541.5

double (barrel gun) und. 435.8

doubt s.th. 409.1, und. 56.4

down 165.2, down, downhill und. 146.3 go down to water's edge 261.2, (located) downstream 648.1, (travel) with current, downstream 418.2, (work) is getting me down und. 22.5

drag, pull 497.3

draw in 451.1

dream und. 374.4, und. 676.2

dress 249.4

drift, throw into water 357.3, drift up and lodge on shore 355.3, -wood und. 218.1

drink und. 423.3, put face in water to drink 477.6

drip 175.1

drive, herd; expel, drive off 410.3, drive team, buggy, car und. 544.2

drop it und. 341.1, droppings und. 377.2

drown und. 22.5, und. 229.2, drown; fall into water 523.5

drum; hit (ceiling) w. boards und. 494.2 sort of 'drumming' the feet 489.2

dry, dry up 453.2, dried herring eggs 110. fish thoroughly dried by smoking 237.2, und. 252.2, 425.6, 584.10

duck see waterfowl, duck sound 45.2

due to, on account of, because of 482.4

dumbfounded, very surprised 396.3

dust, dirt, soil, earth; bury 335.8

Duwamish und. 132.1

forest dwarf, Eskimo 415.4

dwell 289.4

each and everyone 643.4, each other
7.2
eager 67.5
eagle 633.2
ear 429.1, ear, side, sound lex.
suff. 5.3, earring 320.6
early, morning und. 123.2, 307.6,
early und. 315.1
earth, dust, dirt, soil; bury
335.8
east und. 406.1
easy 388.1, take it easy, go slower
477.1
eat, food 656.8, eat, put in mouth
201.2, 271.1, join in eating
548.2
edge, end 625.4, edge, side appendage lex. suff. 12.4, edge; side;
lean against, prop up 669.5, on
the edge (of table) und. 290.2,
edge (of moon) showing und. 398.3
egg see herring, salmon
eiderdown 260.3
eight und. 491.4
either one und. 80.4, either one,
which one? und. 671.2, either...
or 654.1
elbow 412.8, und. 474.1
eleven und. 333.3
elk, Big Dipper 241.3
embers, coals 358.3
emerge 325.2, emerge from water
464.3, emerge, come out from under; dig around to uncover s.th.
465.1

adverb of emphasis 'put' 347.2, emphatic particle 'ciɬ' 52.1, emphatic
particle 'hawə?' 179.2, emphatic particle 'ta' 473.2, contrastive emphatic
'dab' 122.2
empty 559.1, empty (bottle) und. 439.3
encase; be stranded; put clothing on 312.2
encircle, hug 422.4, encircle in one's
grasp, squeeze 325.1
end und. 474.1, end, edge lex. suff.
625.4, end, point und. 112.4, ending
454.1
endearing address 195.4, for a little boy
und. 678.3, for mother, for a little
girl und. 263.2
enemy 457.3
enjoy 230.1
enough und. 328.5/und. 666.4, not enough
407.4, get more than enough und. 31.2,
36.4
entangle, wind around s.th.; entwine 154.5,
entangled, mixed up, messed up 19.1
enter a building 186.2
equipment, gear, tackle 5.1
escape 327.2
escalator und. 668.5
Eskimo, forest dwarf 415.4
even 656.6, even, smooth 320.3, even, the
same 347.1, even more und. 223.4, even
though 377.1
evening und. 291.3
eventually, soon 163.3
ever since und. 280.2

everyone und. 26.3/und. 161.2, und.
38.3, each and everyone of you
643.4

everywhere und. 80.4, und. 146.3

evil, bad 439.3, evil thoughts 15.2

eviscerate 238.5

exaggerate, lie, fib 25.1

examine, scrutinize, look over,
size up 251.2

exchange, trade it und. 652.3

excited, nervous, fidgety, at loose
ends 439.2

exclamation of mild surprise 643.2

excuse me 431.7

exercise a horse; operate a machine
und. 488.6

exhortative 179.1, exhortative to
story teller 178.1

'expected' (aux. pref.) 307.1

expel, drive off; drive, herd 410.3

expensive 398.2

(arm, leg) exposed, rolled up sleeve,
pantleg und. 404.4

extend, reach 640.1

extinguish 287.2

extract, pull out 588.1

eye 378.3, eye, color lex. suff. 9.6,
cataract of eye und. 468.1, close
eyes 72.7, open eyes 390.2, stretch-
ed eyes, slant eyes, sleepy eyes
und. 687.1, eyes, watering und. 423.3,
eyebrow 55.1, eyelash, eyelid und.
298.1, eye matter 63.7, eye glasses
154.4, und. 479.1

figure out, measure 539.1, figure
out; notice, observe, see 634.1

file, rub 462.2

fill/full (container) 270.1

filth; open sore 111.4, filth,
infection, dirt und. 115.4

dorsal fin 262.3, pectoral fin
area 68.3, 72.6

finally 485.7, 549.3

find it 665.4, find out 169.4,
und. 180.2

finger und. 134.4, und. 388.4, und.
3.2, little finger und. 534.2,
und. 578.3, fingernail 397.2,
430.2, und. 388.4, finger tip
und. 388.4, sign with fingerprint und. 327.1

finish, be thus; make, do 197.2

Douglas fir 91.1, white fir 540.1,
und. 298.3, young fir 417.3

fire, (fire)wood, light (s.th.);
burn 196.1, firewood, a laid
fire lex. suff. 103.2, stick
of firewood 112.2, open fire
pit und. 196.1, away from fire
646.1, take off/out of fire
288.3, fire dept. und. 287.2

fire, dismiss s.o. from employment
und. 197.2

first, before (in time and space)
223.4, und. 280.2, und. 671.2

seagoing fish (generic) 682.1,
unid. bottom fish 29.2, 109.5,

dogfish 250.1, skate fish 249.1, 249.5,
big skate fish 253.3, whitefish 615.3,
fish thoroughly dried by smoking 237.2,
und. 252.2, 425.6, 584.10, fish split
open and dried by sun and wind und. 518.3,
(fish) swims 675.1, fish bone 78.1,
fish heads und. 518.3, cooked fish heads
441.6, edible cartilage in front part
of fish nose 373.2, und. 598.2, fish
skin 251.1, fishtail 247.5, fish (hook)
und. 303.1, fish with line and pole
306.1, fish (hunt) und. 566.1, fishing
twine 530.1, fish weir und. 491.4

does not fit und. 143.1

five 48.1

fix, prepare, make 417.4, is not fixed
right und. 143.1

flame lex. suff. 447.5

flash und. 275.5, flash, blinking light
355.5

flat, broad 358.5

flat, tasteless 343.4

flatus 359.2

flea 120.1

flee, run away out of fright; make self
scarce because told to 334.3

flesh, skin of human or salmon 77.2

red-shafted flicker 67.3

flint, arrowhead 633.1

float (verb) 361.2, wooden float 106.3,
wooden float for gillnet und. 361.2,
ice, shakes floating down the river
und. 357.3

flock taking to air at one time
306.4, flocks wheeling in the
sky und. 436.2

it floods, river rises 228.2,
flooded, high tide und. 358.5

floor 593.4, floor, ground lex.
suff. 206.3

flounder 361.3

flour, bread 442.1

flower 75.4, 248.7

fly (insect) 585.2, 615.1, sandfly, gnat 419.4, fly (verb)
436.2

foam und. 423.3

fog, smoke, clouds 416.5

follow, chase 83.1

food, eat 656.8, food lex. suff.
123.1, 209.2 food (deriv. el.)
10.3, give food (?) 288.2,
give food or drink 304.1

foolish, strange acting 380.1

foot, leg 229.1, foot, entire
leg and foot lex. suff. 455.1,
foot race 103.3, foot of a
tree, hill und. 165.2, feet
widely turned out und. 351.3

for 659.1, 'for s.o.' (deriv.
pref. six^w-) 447.1, for, in
s.o.'s place 633.5, for (the
purpose of) und. 146.3

forage, gather food, hunt und.
566.1

forearm, hand 85.1

forbid 555.5, 584.5

forecast the weather 254.2

foreigner und. 38.3/ und. 271.4, und. 26.3/
und. 510.1

forehead, buttocks, money lex. suff. 208.4
burned forehead 430.1, flat forehead
und. 358.5

foretell future und. 222.2, und. 527.3

forget 17.5

fork und. 49.3, forked lex. suff. 11.2

fornicate 373.6

four 42.5

freeze 391.7

fresh, new 291.2, 584.4

Friday und. 48.1

close friend und. 432.2, friend lex. suff.
543.1, friend, relative 627.4, 669.1
friend (of one's own sex), pal 653.1

unid. kind of small frog 546.4, 550.2
frog talk 452.2

from 510.1, from (family origin) 544.1

front, bow 458.1, in front of und. 223.4

pick fruit, berries 66.3

fry 73.3

do fumblingly, inadroitly; try, improvise,
make do 231.3

full (from food or drink) 31.2, fill/
full (container) 270.1

make fun of und. 681.1

fungus on a tree 343.2

fur, animal hair 516.3

foretell future und. 222.2, und. 527.3

gall 524.4

gambling song und. 488.6

list of games und. 681.1, bone
game 270.4, a way of guessing
in the bone game und. 351.3,
game of rolling stones und.
486.1, game of shooting blunted arrows und. 517.1, shinny
92.1, broad jump und. 437.1,
unid. sort of game and power
und. 143.1

gang up on und. 86.4

gap, opening 541.5

garment und. 312.2

gather it 396.5, gather, collect
432.2, gather food, hunt, forage und. 566.1, gather it up
und. 28.1, und. 600.2, device
for keeping gathered und. 443.7

gear, tackle, equipment lex. suff.
5.1

one of same generation, age mate
679.2

get, hold, take 244.1, get item
und. 309.1, get the better of,
win 67.7, get the best of s.o.,
compete; refuse 606.1, get the
best of s.o. und. 608.4, get
in/on any sort of conveyance
399.1, not get along too well
with s.o. und. 278.5, (animal)
gets out (of cage) und. 325.2
get up from prone position, sit

down und. 165.2

ghost, corpse 232.1

giggle und. 585.1

gills 64.5, 586.2

girl, little woman und. 287.4, girl, endearing term und. 263.2, girlfriend,
wife, mate und. 432.2

give und. 640.1, give food (?) 288.2,
give food or drink 304.1, give up und.
608.4

glad, happy 190.3

get glimpse of s.o. und. 16.7, und. 392.1

glitter, sparkle 69.1

gloves 285.1

gluttony und. 270.1

gnat, sand fly 419.3

go 687.2, go for a walk, stroll 162.1,
go ahead, be ahead; go away 194.2,
go around/over some obstruction; reverse the side of, turn over/around
212.2, go for what reason? 86.2, go
home 539.2, go in along surface 436.1,
go over a point 351.1, go to some place
309.1, go to (event mentioned in stem)
543.6, gone, used up, die und. 566.1

mountain goat 618.1, goat/dog hair blanket
228.5

gobble food 98.1

good 182.2, slang for good 636.6, be good
at, know how to 98.2, good-looking
70.5, und. 469.1, good-bye und. 197.2,
und. 300.2, no-good 154.2, good-for-
nothing, impure und. 377.5,

better und. 325.5, und. 671.2,
better than und. 182.2, und.
223.4

goose (of unid. species) 327.4

gore; partitive of water; fetch
water 626.1

gossiping und. 474.1

grab und. 244.1, grab with pressure,
claw 600.2

graciousness, dignity 222.1

grandchild 667.1, grandmother
234.2, grandmother, voc. 231.6,
grandfather 44.7

Oregon grape 412.7, 619.1

grass, hay und. 410.2, 439.1, unid.
swamp grass 306.2, sharp, white
grass used as trim on baskets
und. 112.4

grasshopper 535.4

gray und. 468.1, und. 600.1, gray
hair 414.4

grease, fat 443.6, und. 613.6

great 586.5

great-grandchild, great-grandparent
105.2, gr-gr-grandchild, gr-gr-
grandparent 656.4, gr-gr-gr-grand-
child, gr-gr-gr-grandparent 69.3

greedy (person) 238.3

light green, yellow, pale 409.2, und.
615.6, dark green, dark blue und.
615.6, green, leaf color und. 119.7

grind, sharpen 221.2

gristle, cartilage 422.9

groan 643.7

loosen ground for planting, dig, dig
out 108.2, ground, soil 335.8, ground,
floor lex. suff. 206.3

groundhog/marmot/woodchuck 549.1

'group viewed distributively' lex. suff.
13.2, 'homogeneous group or cluster'
lex. suff. 38.3

blue grouse 29.1

grow, growth (a plant, animal or people)
319.1, growth, shrubs, trees und. 546.6,
grow up (to a purpose) und. 284.3

growl 602.4, growl, complain 20.4

grumpy und. 601.1

guess 516.2, I guess so, maybe 573.2,
guessing; substitute 367.1, a way of
guessing in the bone game und. 351.3

guest, company und. 141.1

guilt, shame 602.2

gully und. 111.1

gums und. 217.4

gun und. 561.1, single-shot gun 496.3,
double barrel gun und. 435.8

have a habit und. 315.1, 'habitual'
(aux. pref.) 328.4

hackles of dog und. 233.5

hail 320.5

human hair 395.3, human body hair
und. 516.3, gray hair 414.4,
long hair every which way und.
504.3, hair, head, face, upper
part lex. suff. 544.2, animal
hair, fur 109.2, 516.3, und.
319.1, have hair done und. 43.1,
hair stand on end und. 233.5,
get haircut und. 300.4, push
hair out of face und. 360.3

half; crack, split 99.3, half
(of quantity) und. 161.1, und.
671.2, half (a sack) und. 561.3
half-sibling 34.2/52.2

halibut 104.3

halve, divide into two equal parts
48.2

hammer, small axe und. 459.2

hand, forearm 85.1, hand, lower
arm lex. suff. 3.2, hand turned over as is a cripple's und.
351.3

can't handle, lose it und. 608.4
handle (on utensil) und. 244.1

hang on with claws und. 600.2, hang
on peg, nail 239.1, hang over
(as clothes thrown over line)
298.2, hang up high 405.2

happen 645.2

happy, glad 190.3, make self happy, have
a good time und. 182.2

hard, solid 598.5, try hard; strong und.
499.1, hard, difficult und. 583.2

hardtack 273.1

two-pronged salmon harpoon 484.4

harsh talker, rude 602.6

hat 466.2, 558.3, hat lex. suff. 9.4

hate und. 439.3

have und. 637.1, und. 640.1, have nothing,
poor 189.2

chicken hawk und. 600.2, fish hawk 73.2,
74.2

hay, grass und. 410.2, 439.1

hazelnut, nut in general 391.6

hazy, windows "steamed" over 333.4

he, him 11.4

head 599.7, head lex. suff. 3.1, head,
top, voice lex. suff. 384.2, head,
face, hair, upper part lex. suff. 544.2,
side of head 63.1, back of head und.
265.5, have head down und. 591.6,
have head down, crawl 221.1, lift head
up, straighten up 597.3, fall on head
und. 165.2, toss head from side to side
und. 211.3, headband und. 610.1, head
off s.th. und. 491.4

heal, recover health und. 189.1

healthful und. 189.1

hear 273.3, 282.4

heart 63.2, 630.2

(very) heavy 587.1, heavy set, fat, big
32.4

pay no heed und. 352.1

heel und. 474.1

hello und. 553.2

help 242.2, help, pity und. 686.2
can't help it, feel bad about
546.2

hemlock 249.3, 537.3, 540.6
hemlock (?) 424.1

her (poss.) 435.3, her, she 11.4

herd, drive; expel, drive off
410.3

here 141.1, come here und. 637.1,
656.2

heron 33.1

herring 540.4, dried herring eggs
110.1

hew out, carve out, make a canoe
353.1

hex s.o. because of anger und. 601.1

hibernate 113.2, come out of hibernation und. 325.2

hiccup 187.1

hide und. 62.4, 81.1, 370.3, hide
self and family from enemy raiding party 500.3, hide in a hole
und. 331.1

high, up 459.2, high, up (free in
air) und. 280.2, sort of high
class und. 678.3

hill 344.2, hill, incline, slope,
bank lex. suff. 209.3, go up
hill und. 101.7/und. 459.2,
getting up the hill und. 399.1

him, he 11.4

hip, buttocks und. 298.3, und. 669.5

his 435.3

hit with fist 494.2, hit, club und. 107.3,
hit (ceiling) with boards; drum und.
494.2, get hit und. 345.1

hoe 273.2

hold, take, get 244.1

hole in ground; hole in s.th. but not through
it 285.3, hole through s.th. 540.3

holler und. 553.2, und. 420.2

hollow 262.4

Holy Ghost, spirit 342.2

home und. 647.1, go home 539.2

honey und. 409.4

honeysuckle 633.3

hook (verb) 303.1, hooked together 456.1,
hooked, fastened, buttoned 619.8

hoop 22.2

hope ('maybe, I guess so') und. 573.2

horn, antler 159.1

horse 503.1

horsetail (scouring rush) 41.4, type of
horsetail 467.1

hot, warm 185.3, hot und. 426.9

house 647.1, house post 133.1

how? 82.2, und. 662.6, how many 257.5,
und. 363.1/und. 662.6

howl 429.7

hug und. 422.2

humbling self und. 642.2, und. 678.1

humming bird 496.2

humpback 231.2, 233.3, exhortative to caution
against becom. humpbacked 178.1

hundred und. 26.3

hunger 473.3, hungry 49.5

hunt 457.1, hunt, forage, gather
   food und. 566.1, go hunting in
   the forest 300.1, duck hunting,
   hunting along shore 338.1

get hurt 21.1, 669.4, hurt, sick
   593.5

be in a hurry 586.6, und. 647.2

husband 116.1

husky, strong in body; solid
   (object) 419.4

hut und. 647.1

'remote, hypothetical' (article)
   248.3, 249.2

I, me 4.2, 92.3, 655.2, (121.1)

ice und. 391.7, ice floating in river und. 357.3

Indian ice cream, soapberry 611.1

as if, like, seem 595.1, if, whenever, perhaps, either...or, whether...or 654.1

illustrate 412.2

imagined, vague 241.1

immerse, soak 229.2, immerse, soak more thoroughly 508.1

impassable brushy place und. 583.2

impatient, disgusted, irritated 114.5, become impatient, grow tired 239.3, 396.7

important, big und. 190.4, important (expensive) und. 398.2, of no importance und. 352.1

improvise, make do, try; do fumblingly, inadroitly 231.3

impure, good-for-nothing und. 377.5

do inadroitly, fumblingly; try, improvise, make do 231.3

incarcerate 386.5

inch worm und. 617.1

incident und. 662.6

incline, slope, bank, hill lex. suff. 209.3

incompetent, clumsy 652.1

increase the amount of, add to 347.3

indeed, surely, certainly 247.1

indifferent, unwilling, lazy 419.1

Indian, people und. 38.3/643.1

infection und. 115.4

old and infirm 377.4

inform, tell, report; news 628.4

inherit 106.2

injure, kill 170.2

in-law und. 586.5, in-law relationship 254.6, brother-in-law, wife's male cousin 596.2, in-law when link is deceased 18.3, siblings-in-law 109.4, -in-law (deriv. pref. cix^w-) 53.2, go to live with in-laws 261.1

insert, sheathe; stick into, stick through 463.1

inside a small, confining place 132.1, inside lex. suff. 207.1, inside (center und. 642.1, inside (a building) und. 186.2

insult s.o., call him names 407.6, insult und. 377.5, und. 63.7, sort of insult 408.2

intensifying particle 446.5, 632.4

interjection 'hey!' 124.1, 'oh!' 679.5

interpret, translate 509.5, interpret, sing, repeat 671.1

interrogative particle 679.3

interwoven, two sisters married to same man 662.2

intestines 395.2

in(to) und. 146.3

introduce self und. 268.1

intoxicated; wrap around 560.1

invite, ask 211.4, invite, call to,
    ask 172.2

iron, knife 145.3

ironwood (ocean spray, spirea)
    372.8

irritated, impatient, disgusted
    114.5

island und. 86.4/und. 541.5

it 11.4, its 435.3

itch 93.5

jab, poke 44.8, 53.1, jab, spear
   49.3

jail und. 386.5

jammed, stuffed, crowded 120.3,
   log jam und. 517.1

jaw und. 456.4, jaw, chin; road
   lex. suff. und. 541.5

Steller's jay, one who talks
   too much 231.7

jealous 340.3

jellyfish 232.3

jerk, tug, move 51.2

join in eating 548.2, joining of
   two points und. 432.2

joint 358.1, get out of joint
   355.8

joke und. 230.1

juice und. 423.3

~ July (time of blackberries)
   und. 337.1

jump, run (fast) 437.1, the jumping of salmon 159.2

~ June (time of salmonberries)
   und. 337.1

junk, worthless stuff 352.1

just, merely 620.2, just, nearly,
   merely; and yet 512.2

lack, fail to obtain 393.3

ladle, spoon 289.5

ladder und. 241.4, und. 668.5

lake, 44.6, 577.1, lake, pond
und. 414.5, middle of lake/
river und. 173.3

lamp und. 275.5

land, world, place 546.6, land
lex. suff. 543.5

land, alight; cover 382.1, land
a boat/canoe 289.1

landward 521.3, go up landward,
proceed away from shore 101.7

language und. 157.2, language,
mouth lex. suff. und. 541.5,
Salish language, what is
understandable 275.3, speak
a language und. 474.1

lap, lick 306.3, lap, marrow,
lick lex. suff. 12.1

larynx 572.3

last, behind 265.5/und. 280.2,
the last (only) 55.3, 125.1

late und. 265.5, later on, wait
323.1

the latter und. 671.2

laugh 585.1

law, order, edict, proclamation
und. 589.3

lay it down und. 411.4

layer/row, lined up 525.1

lazy 101.1, 397.4, lazy, indifferent, unwilling 419.1

leader und. 223.4, leader of a school of
fish 159.2, lead an animal und. 544.2

leaf (in general) 119.7

lean, be on side 133.2, lean against, prop
up; side; edge 669.5

learn und. 98.2, und. 180.2

leave, leave behind 295.2, leave it alone,
let it go 243.2, leave alone, pay no
attention, don't touch und. 321.1, left
(over) 411.1

on a ledge, shelf und. 459.2

left (direction, location, position) 374.3

leg, foot 229.1, entire leg and foot;
foot lex. suff. 455.1, hind leg, thigh
645.4

lend, borrow items other than money 102.2,
lend money und. 172.2, lend clothing
und. 312.2

lengthen, add more 114.1

let it go, leave it alone 243.2, let s.o.
out und. 325.2, let up, lighten 367.2

level und. 47.2

lichen und. 395.5/und. 550.2

lick, dip 71.2, lick, lap 306.3, lick,
lap; marrow lex. suff. 12.1

lid, top, cover 104.5, und. 591.6, lid,
door lex. suff. und. 541.5

lie/fall on back 256.2, lie, set or fall
from stand. position 290.2, lie with
hind end up 334.1, lie down for a little
while und. 487.2

lie, fib, exaggerate 25.1

life und. 189.1

lift it 443.5, und. 459.2, lift, raise (self) up und. 459.2, lift head up, straighten up 597.3

light 275.5, getting light, dawn und. 171.2, 241.2, light s.th. burn, fire, (fire)wood 196.1, bring to light, uncover 392.1

light weight 562.5, lighten weight 555.3, lighten, let up 367.2

lightning 546.3, 618.2, lightning, sparking 368.1

like, want 581.2, like, enjoy und. 182.2

like, as 659.1, like, as, similar to und. 620.2, like, seem, as if 595.1

tiger lily bulb 44.5

limb, branch 106.7

limber joint, loose joint 404.2

lined up, row/layer 525.1

lip curved down, deformed und. 351.3, lips lex. suff. und. 14.1

listen, understand und. 321.1, listen to 320.2, listen, hear! und. 273.3, und. 282.4

little, small 39.2

live, alive 189.1, live, dwell 298.4, living (and growing) und. 319.1

liver 85.2, 522.1

lizard 131.2

load a vehicle (esp. canoe) 399.1

locate, point out 268.1, be located 637.1, 644.3, located where, by what route, by what means 280.2

location names 16.1, 18.2, und. 24.5, 32.1, und. 34.2, und. 69.6, 90.2, 96.3, 99.1, 100.1, 109.3, 110.4, und. 118.5, und. 119.6, 131.4, 137.1, und. 174.1, 190.1, 195.3, und. 212.2, 220.2, und. 232.1, 247.3, und. 262.4, und. 278.5, und. 291.3, und. 298.2, und. 371.1, 403.1, und. 406.1, 414.1, 415.3, und. 451.1, 491.2, 509.4, 524.5, 546.5, 599.2, 624.1, und. 626.1, 655.3, 665.3

lock (w. key) und. 270.5

log, stick 421.2, log, stick; wood(s) 526.1, log, dead tree 339.3

lonesome; be quiet, be still und. 602.6

long, tall 176.1

look, see 469.1, look at, look after und. 264.2, look down; bent forward 507.3, look for, seek, search for 165.1, look over, size up, examine, scrutinize 251.2, look out! 431.7, look from behind (peek) 260.4

get loose, untie, bail out (of jail) 156.2 get loose, let out (of jail) 171.6, at loose ends, excited, nervous, fidgety 439.2, loose joint, limber joint 404.2 loosen ground for planting, dig, dig out 108.2

loping (of a horse) 535.1

lose it, can't handle und. 608.4
   lost, turned around 616.4, lost
   552.2

a lot, many, much 363.1

lots, plots und. 546.6

loud 632.2

louse 41.2

love, want each other und. 581.2
   two lovers walking about und.
   162.1

low class und. 383.3, lower side
   und. 86.4, lower edge/world
   und. 165.2

lucky 260.1, good luck und. 242.2

lullaby 282.3

lumberjack und. 603.2

Lummi (language) 269.1

lump 24.3, lump, cramp 396.5

lunch, dinner und. 541.5, lunch,
   bite und. 597.1, lunch (carried with one) 576.3

lungs 355.7

luster, shine (as fur) 173.2

lynx (bobcat) 355.2

meat 35.5, meat lex. suff. 10.4,
red meat, red cloth und. 5.2,
white meat, white shirt und.
5.2

mechanical device breaks down
225.1

medicine 526.2

meet 644.2

melancholy 563.1

melt, thaw 217.1

memory, mind, character 343.5,
memorize und. 266.1

the event mentioned 135.5

merely, just 620.2, merely, just,
nearly; and yet 512.2

mesmerize s.o., cast a spell on
s.o. und. 380.1

messed up, mixed up, entangled 19.1

middle 679.7, middle, center of
642.1, middle voice -b 15.1

after midnight und. 99.3

might, eventually und. 163.3, modal
particle emphasizing probability,
maybe, might 246.1

milk, breast 373.4, milk the cow
und. 38.3/358.2

milt 335.7

mind, memory, character 343.5, mind,
inner thoughts, sense, understanding; count 589.3

mink 35.2, 66.2, younger brother of
Mink 496.5

mirror, window und. 469.1, mirror-like
water, good weather 278.4

miscarriage und. 635.3

miss (target, person) 256.1

mist 90.3, heavy mist prior to a general
rain 293.4

make mistake unintentionally 546.2, mistaken, confused 17.3

mixed up, messed up, entangled 19.1, mixed
up, confused und. 214.1

moccasin 393.1

molasses 40.1

mole und. 351.3

Monday und. 31.1, und. 356.1

money 479.1, money, forehead, buttocks
lex. suff. 208.4, money, hard earned
(fig.) und. 293.3

a kind of monster und. 79.1, 217.6, monster, anything you are afraid of 317.4

month/moon und. 307.4

moon; full moon und. 307.4

moor, dock a boat 289.1

mop, wipe 669.2, 673.1

get more than plenty, have more than enough
und. 31.2, 36.4, more, some, others und.
671.2, even more und. 223.4

morning, early und. 123.2, 307.6

mosquito 110.3

moss 414.2, sea moss 431.2

mother 175.2, 263.2

outboard motor und. 508.2

mount horse und. 399.1

mountain 16.4

mountain names 30.1, 101.6, und.
 272.2, 558.1, 591.1

mourn 215.1

mouse 253.2

moustache, beard 419.2

mouth 374.1, mouth, language
 lex. suff. und. 541.5, parts
 of the mouth lex. suff. 14.1,
 put in mouth, swallow 32.3,
 put in mouth, eat 201.2, und.
 271.1, open the mouth 231.1

move 222.2, move, jerk, tug 51.2,
 move, shake 216.1, und. 211.3,
 move rapidly 16.7, move rapidly in a small area 26.1, move
 belongings und. 640.1, move
 residence und. 684.1

much, a lot, many 363.1

mucus 293.3

muddy, dirt und. 36.5

mumbling 154.3

murk, smoke 533.1

muscle, sinew 500.4, muscles of
 arms, shoulder und. 396.5

muskrat 373.7, 396.4

unid. kind of mussel und. 683.1

must be (would seem) und. 219.4,
 must be (kʷaʔ 'not absolutely
 certain') 243.1

my (I, me) 121.1

myth, traditional story 619.3,
 myth name of Crow 591.3,
 recite a myth und. 630.3

nail (of finger, toe) 397.2, 430.2

nailing 73.1

naked und. 308.1

names see immediately after creek,
location, man, mountain, rock,
river, woman; name, call 126.1,
unnamed baby 232.2

nape, lower part of the head 409.3

narrow 505.4, narrow; swallow; stuff
into; caulk 100.3, a narrow place
und. 238.6

nations und. 546.6

navel 30.1

near 116.2, come near/here und. 637.1,
put, move near 620.1

nearsighted und. 251.2

nearly, merely, just; and yet 512.2

front part of neck 54.6, neck lex.
suff. 11.1

necklace 228.1

cattail needle und. 311.4

negligent 247.2

Negro und. 431.3

neighbor und. 432.2, next door
neighbor und. 138.2

nephew, niece 480.1, nephew, niece
when sibling link is deseased 375.2

nervous, fidgety, at loose ends,
excited 439.2

net 300.3, bag net 411.2, dip net
284.1, 422.5/und. 423.3, drag
net und. 665.1, drifting net
und. 357.3, gill net 201.3,

basket-like fishing net 457.2, set
a net und. 229.2, net webbing und.
330.2

stinging nettles 67.4

new, fresh 291.2, 584.4

news; tell, report, inform 628.4

next, then 180.1, 201.1, next, but, and
169.5

nickname for unid. duck 45.2

niece, nephew 480.1, niece, nephew when
sibling link is deceased 375.2

night, darkness 291.3, spend night, camp
overnight und. 396.1

nine 613.1

nipping at the heels und. 236.3

Nisqually 410.2

nit 598.4

no, not, nothing 566.1

no-counts, riffraff, rabble und. 143.1

nobleman, noblelady und. 678.3

noise und. 316.1, make noise 429.3,
make noise by putting water in motion
447.2

Nooksack 440.2

noon und. 517.2

northwest wind 506.5, und. 510.1

nose 32.2, nose, point lex. suff. 388.4,
pug nose und. 519.1, blow nose 446.3,
nose run und. 293.3

nothing, not, no 566.1, nothing to do,
not busy und. 474.1

notice; pay attention to; understand 340.?
notice, observe, see; figure out 634.1

~ <u>November</u> (dog salmon time) und.
   337.1/und. 332.3

just <u>now</u> 124.2, 128.1

a <u>number</u> of, how many? 257.5

<u>hazelnut</u>, nut in general 391.6

canoe paddle 619.5, paddle lex.
suff. 9.7, paddle (verb) und.
675.1

pail und. 423.3

paint und. 578.3, paint self red
und. 282.1

pair, both 631.1, pair lex. suff.
161.1

pale, yellow, light green 409.2

palm of hand und. 134.4, und. 474.1/
und. 544.2, und. 642.1

pan, basin und. 51.3

paraphernalia 169.2

child of parent's older sibling
365.1

park (a car) 289.1

parley, agenda, conference lex.
suff. 543.2

particle ʔə 653.2

modal particle 'maybe, might' 246.1,
'quotative' 255.2, 'surely, certainly, indeed' 247.1, 'uncertain'
243.1

the particular one (who), the very
(one) 46.2

partition in a longhouse 396.6

partitive. Denotes part of some
larger unit 671.2

pass, surpass, after in time and
space 31.1

pass out, faint und. 529.3

narrow passage way; canoe, water
way; curved side lex. suff.
173.3

pat it und. 492.2

patch 525.3

one who has patience 684.2

pay 407.2, pay for an article 522.2,
marriage payment 220.1, payment of
wealth in retribution und. 172.2

permanently snow-capped peak 506.1

peck (as a bird) und. 73.1

peek, peer 260.4, peek at s.th. by moving
obstruction aside or up 404.4

peel 307.7

peer, peek 260.4

peer, age mate 679.2

pen, pencil und. 443.7

penis 20.3, 458.2

penny und. 91.2

people, Indian 643.1, people of lex. suff.
41.1

people, groups of Indians - people way
up river 34.2, people along Skagit
River und. 101.7, people who live(d)
at site of Steilacoom, Wash. 119.4,
'people of the big rocks' und. 190.4,
Skagit group who lives along or near
the Nookachamps River 145.1, group of
Skagit living along the south fork of
the Skagit River 234.1, group in Canada
372.2, people of the north fork of the
Skagit River 413.2, short, very strong
people with exceptional supernatural
power 431.4, people along the Sauk and
Suiattle Rivers 440.1, wild people
503.3, stíkí und. 532.2, people who live
by Budd Inlet 524.5, a people from far

to the north 528.2, people east of
the mountains; Warm Springs Reservation 546.1, a group of Skagit
along the Samish River and to the
north of it 643.8, people (in
general) who have a river und.
509.1

perch (fish) 391.3, 443.1

perhaps 654.1, und. 662.6

pertain to, be characteristic of
643.3

pester, annoy und. 19.3

pet it, stroke, touch lightly und.
482.5, pet (loveable stray animal) und. 28.1

ring-necked pheasant 170.3, 497.2

phonograph, radio 500.1

pick berries/fruit 66.3, 248.4, pick
on s.o. und. 86.4, pick s.o./s.th.
up und. 292.1

have picture taken und. 578.3

pierce, go completely through 339.2

pig 233.2

pigeon 185.1

pile 344.2

pillow 613.4

pimples und. 325.2

straight pin, tooth 137.2, pin with
a straight pin 623.2, pin on und.
463.1

pinch 70.3, 238.6

white pine (tree) 63.10, und. 226.1

pipe 353.2

pitch (from wood) 410.1

(baseball) pitcher und. 345.1

pity 686.2

place, land, world 546.6, place where
lex. suff. 9.2, place where (an act
occurs) (deriv. pref. dəxʷ-) 134.2,
in s.o.'s place, for 633.5, place on/
in receptacle; dish up; upbear 51.3

war plane und. 173.3

plant und. 335.8, plant kingdom und. 546.6,
a planter und. 290.2

plaster (as does beaver) und. 527.5

plate 275.2, plate, platter 293.1

wooden platter und. 421.2, platter, plate
293.1

play 109.1, 681.1

plead a cause und. 197.2

pliable, soft 441.7

plots, lots und. 546.6

plow land, mark up, scratch 615.7

pluck feathers und. 588.1

plug in, stuff into 331.1

pocket, bag und. 132.1

point, end, tip 112.4, point, nose lex.
suff.388.4,point of land 268.1, point
out, locate 268.1, point (out) und.
484.5

poke 51.1, poke, jab 44.8, 53.1

pole for poling a canoe 69.5

pond, lake und. 414.5

poor, have nothing 189.2, poor, to be
pitied und. 686.2

pop, crack und. 316.1, popped it
    357.2

porpoise 248.1, 416.4

possessions und. 683.1, possessions,
    belongings, treasure und. 474.1,
    possessions, things lex. suff.
    208.1, indispensable possession
    und. 244.1

reach or achieve a state or position,
    becoming, begin (voice suff. -il)
    208.3

post, sticking up und. 54.9

post office, postman und. 578.3

pot und. 312.2

potato 371.8, potato, arrowhead plant,
    wapato 340.4, crow potato, blue
    camas 62.1

potlatch und. 172.2, und. 562.1

pound (as hammer and nail) und. 494.2,
    sound of pounding, banging 248.6

pour, spill 255.1

powder 468.1

a kind of power 169.3, a kind of
    sqəlálitut 217.2, supernatural
    power, spirit power 374.4, a
    mean spirit und. 506.6, have/be
    fierce power und. 317.4, become
    stiff und. 299.2, spirit (or other
    power) seizing s.o. und. 244.1,
    have power from one's ancestors
    544.1, power inside a building
    495.1, power for procuring food
    64.4, the spirit power that pro-

vides an abundance of fish and game
190.2, a hunting power (for both sexes)
386.3, power which provides great abundance 505.1, force that makes a təstəd
go 430.3, unid. sort of game and power
und. 143.1, a power which would shoot
s.o. with little worms 665.2, shoot bone
into s.o. (shaman) 308.6, what is put on
a person's possessions in order to gain
power over him 343.3, cast a spell on
s.o., mesmerize s.o. und. 380.1, go on
spirit power quest 645.1, someone who
has not gone on a power quest und. 377.5,
short, very strong people with exceptional supernatural power 431.4, spirit
power song 627.2, power song and/or
power dance of any type 339.6, garment
for doing power dances und. 426.1

powerful 135.4

powwow und. 339.6

praise 115.1, praise s.o., thank s.o.
    254.4

pray und. 172.2, und. 254.4, pray, thank
    532.1

independent predication marker č 80.1

aspectual prefix 'completive' 679.4, 541.2,
    'continuitive' 269.2, 645.3, 656.5,
    'progressive' 268.3, 153.1, 'static'
    662.1, 11.3, 153.10

auxiliary prefix 'anew' 22.1, 'expected'
    307.1, 'habitual' 328.4, 'remote in
    time or space' 506.3, 'subjunctive'
    164.1

rabbit und. 253.4

rabble, riffraff, no-counts
und. 143.1, und. 352.1

raccoon 30.7, und. 578.3

foot race 103.3, (canoe, horse)
race und. 606.1

radio, phonograph 500.1

raft 371.2

raid 484.3

rain 375.3, start raining, sprinkle
297.3, stop raining 555.4, rain
has let up und. 367.2, rainbow
und. 423.3, 531.2

raise (self) up, lift und. 459.2

rancid 101.3

move rapidly 16.6, move rapidly
in a small area 26.1

rat 236.1, 238.2

rattle made of deer hoves 262.2,
sharp rattling noise 103.1

raven 231.4, 411.3

raw (meat) 72.4, 602.1

(electric) razor und. 438.1

reach, extend 640.1

almost ready und. 83.1

really, very 187.3, really do s.th.
(intens. part.) 211.2

rear s.o. und. 284.3

'reason for', 'place where' (deriv.
pref. dəx^w-) 134.2, go for what
reason? 86.2

receive (?) 378.2

reciprocal 7.2

recite the history of a people 271.3

recognize 451.3, fail to recognize 85.3

recounting of past und. 266.1

rectum 49.4, slang for can't control
rectum und. 327.2

red 91.2/und. 600.1, 248.5, 282.1, dark
red und. 96.4

edible reed 19.4

reflexive 42.4, 450.5

refuse und. 566.1, refuse; get the best
of s.o./compete 606.1

related 75.7, affinal relationship 254.6,
relative, friend 627.4, 669.1, close
relatives und. 432.2

religion und. 532.1

reluctant und. 605.2

remember 266.1

remind und. 266.1

reminiscing und. 266.1

'remote, hypothetical' (article) 248.3,
249.2, 'remote in time and space' (aux.
pref.) 506.3

remove to a distance, far 278.5

rent, borrow und. 102.2

repeat, interpret, sing 671.1

report, inform, tell; news 628.4

resist being towed through the water, drag
anchor 344.1

respect und. 190.4, respected term for
addressing youngsters 372.5

rest 372.4

restaurant und. 656.8

as a result of und. 146.3

return 30.3, und. 293.5, return
s.th. (borrowed) und. 640.1

reverse the side of, turn over/
around, go around/over some
obstruction 212.2

revive, regain consciousness
351.2, revive, wake up, come
to und. 379.2

revolver und. 303.1

abrupt rhythm und. 53.3

rib 270.3, break ribs und. 173.3

rich und. 678.3

ride on horse und. 517.2, ride
on train und. 399.1

riffraff, rabble, no-counts
und. 143.1, und. 352.1

rifle und. 388.4

right away, suddenly, unexpectedly 500.5

right (direction, location, position) 217.7

get s.th. right, be correct 274.2,
und. 47.2; not right und. 143.1

ring for finger und. 285.1/628.1,
633.4, und. 388.4/und. 463.1

ring (a bell) 537.1

rip apart, tear, take apart 445.1,
ripped through 111.1

ripe; warm, burn; bake, cook 426.9

rival 97.2

river 509.1, river lex. suff. und.
541.5, river rises, it floods
228.2, river goes down, tide

goes out 471.1, river banks are washed
away 39.1, narrow part of a river und.
100.4, middle of river/lake und. 173.3,
going up river und. 406.1

river names und. 91.2, 145.1, und. 375.3

road, door, way 457.6, road; chin, jaw
lex. suff. und. 541.5

roast, barbecue, burn body 252.2

robin 256.3, time of (robin) whistling
(~ April) und. 337.1/und. 618.4

rock 111.2, 118.5

rock name und. 190.4

rock, wag, shake 211.3

roll; roll off, fall off 486.1, roll it
up 372.9, rolled up sleeves, pantleg
und. 404.4, und. 432.1

roof, upstairs, ceiling und. 459.2

room with und. 432.2

roots (of any kind) 412.6, cedar root
63.4, root (esp. cedar), ancestors
(fig.) 531.3

rope, string, thread und. 523.6

rot, decay 115.4, rotten wood 357.1,
360.1

rough, ugly, mean; strange appearance
602.6

round, sphere 41.5

row/layer, lined up 525.1, reach end of a
row in commercial harvesting 289.1

row (a boat) und. 271.2

by what route, by what means, located where
280.2

rub about, rub bark together 93.1
rub, file 462.2, rub hard, scrape
563.3
rude, harsh talker: ugly in appearance
602.6
rug und. 673.1
ruin, smash up, shatter 227.2
rump 608.1, rump, bottom (of anyth.)
und. 474.1, fall on rump 36.2
run 488.6, run(fast), jump 437.1,
more than one (person or animal) runs 215.2, make (animals)
run all about und. 16.7, run into
(come upon) und. 332.2, runner
of vine 514.1

sacrum 101.5

sad, brokenhearted, sorry und. 589.3

Sahəwamish 441.3

sail und. 322.2

Salish language, what is understandable 275.3

saliva und. 423.3, und. 514.2

list of salmon und. 682.1
salmon and seagoing trout, gen. term 92.4, blackmouth und. 635.2, dog (chum) salmon 308.2, 332.3, humpback 186.1, king salmon 435.6, 514.4, 635.2, silver (coho) salmon 249.6, und. 393.5, time of silver salmon (~ Sept.) und. 337.1, sockeye salmon 16.5, 49.1, 70.4, 118.4, an old salmon that has already spawned and is about to die 636.7, salmon opened out und. 504.3, barbecued salmon und. 426.9, boiled salmon heads und. 599.7, salmon eggs, not dry 320.4, dried salmon eggs 379.1, fermented salmon eggs 69.4, 134.1, 146.1, salmon sticks, sticks for baking salmon 591.5, salmon spear und. 597.1, two pronged salmon harpoon 484.4, the jumping of salmon 159.2, what salmon are called after spawning und. 357.3, the salmon travel/are here und. 399.1

salt, salty 318.1

the same, even 347.1, the same, also und. 315.1

sand 174.1, sandfly, gnat 419.3

sanitary napkin, clout, diaper 395.5

red-breasted sapsucker 297.4, sapsucker und. 327.1

Saturday und. 116.2

Sauk und. 38.3

save, prepare 591.2, save, preserve; put away, tidy up 360.3, save (life) und. 189.1

wood saw und. 300.4

say, tell 56.4

scab 584.1

fish scales 340.5

scalp und. 254.5/und. 384.2

scapula 75.5

scar und. 300.4

make self scarce because told to; flee, run away out of fright 334.3

scare s.o. und. 587.2

scatter 614.1, scatter, distribute 333.5

scavenge 35.3

school und. 578.3, und. 680.1

scold (verbally) und. 157.2, 370.1

scorch 458.4

scout, watchman und. 469.1

scrape 438.1, scrape, rub hard 563.3

scratch esp. to relieve itch 604.3, scratch (as a cat) und. 600.2, scratch (and leave a mark) 604.1, scratch, plow land, mark up 615.7, scratched s.o. 66.5, (s.th.) gets scratched 677.3

scream, loud crying 115.3

scribble, shorthand, write fast
593.1

scrofula 397.7

scrutinize, look over, size up,
examine 251.2

scurry about und. 437.1

sea, ocean, sound, salt water
613.3, blowing hard and getting
bad at sea 100.2

sea cucumber und. 486.1

seagull 390.3, und. 393.5, und.
397.5, summer seagull 618.3

fur seal 64.2, hair (harbor) seal
450.1, 649.2, 649.3, seal bark
426.4

sea lion 662.3

seashell (of any type) 107.1

seaward, toward the water 86.4

seaweed 287.1

search for, look for, seek 165.1

second, two 46.1, second singer
und. 666.5

see 264.2, see, look 469.1, see,
notice, observe; figure out
634.1, you see? see there! 636.1
see into the future und. 3.2/und.
527.3, near sighted und. 251.2

seed und. 2.3/und. 335.8, seeding
by hand und. 562.1

seek, search for, look for 165.1

seem, as if, like 595.1, 'so it
would seem' (mod. part.) 219.4

seine, salmon webbing trap 318.5, 320.1

select it (out of many) 37.2

for self (deriv. suff.) 10.2

sell 573.1

send s.o. on errand 97.1, send to do task
und. 190.4

senile und. 380.1

sense, understanding, mind, inner thoughts:
count 589.3, sensible und. 640.1

separated (?) 113.1, be separated (from
rest of group) und. 278.5

~ September (time of silver salmon) und.
337.1

sequence connector 'a' 1.1

set down, fall from standing position 22.5
set, lie, or fall from stand. pos. 290.2
set out (esp. as a gift) 333.2, set the
table und. 411.4, set out for s.o. und.
268.1, sun setting und. 564.1

land settlers, und. 206.3/und. 244.1

seven 78.2

sew 350.2

go to bed for sex und. 487.2, have sex
und. 215.3

shadow und. 62.4

shake, move 216.1, shake, rock, wag 211.3,
the shaking of the Shakers, shiver
(from cold or fear) 110.5, shake down
341.1, shake off, brush off 535.5, shake
self off (animal) und. 563.4

shakes floating down the river und. 357.3

shallow und. 464.3

shaman, Indian doctor 127.1, cure by a
shaman 19.2, bone shot into s.o. by
shaman und. 308.6

shame 605.2, shame, guilt 602.2,
shame in the mouth und. 541.5

shank (of leg) lex. suff. 209.1

shape it 516.4

share equally und. 48.2, be able
to share in receiving (usually
food) 76.1, be unwilling to
share information und. 398.2

shark 250.1

sharp (knife), tart (taste) 612.1,
sharpen, grind 221.2

shatter, ruin, smash up 227.2

shave und. 438.1

she, her 11.4

knife sheath 551.3, sheathe, insert;
stick into, stick through 463.1

sheep 265.1

on a shelf, ledge und. 459.2

shepherd und. 410.3

shine (as fur), luster 173.2,
shine (as sun) und. 171.2

battle ship und. 173.3

shirt 340.2, und. 348.2, shirt lex.
suff. 208.2, white shirt und. 5.2

shiver (from cold or fear), the
shaking of the Shakers 110.5

shock, surprise 93.7

shoe und. 421.2, und. 526.1, (logger's) cork shoe 523.3

shoo! 234.3

shore, edge of water und. 173.3,
shoreline und. 280.2, und. 669.5,
proceed away from shore 101.7,
be down on shore und. 261.2

shoot 537.4, shoot a bone into s.o. out
of malice (Indian doctor) 308.6

short person 404.3, short cut und. 47.2

shorthand, write fast. scribble 593.1

shoulder und. 474.1, und. 669.5, shoulder
lex. suff. 9.5

shove, push; too (excessively) 193.2

show, demonstrate und. 469.1, show, teach
680.1, show, point out und. 268.1

shrink, shrivel 432.1

shrivel, shrink 432.1

shrubs, trees, growth und. 546.6

shut (door) und. 491.4, shut up, be
quiet 171.4/440.3, shut up! be quiet!
619.4

older sibling 365.1, older sibling next
to ego und. 116.2, younger sibling
450.3, younger sibling next to ego
und. 116.2, sibling cross-sex 646.2,
siblings-in-law 109.4, full-blood
siblings emotionally close 489.1,
either parent's sibling of either sex
when parent is deceased 631.2, half-
sibling with mother in common und. 263.2

sick, hurt 593.5, some member of one's
family is sick 287.3, sickness, disease
422.7, unid. sickness 78.4, get sick
and tired 62.3, get sicker, worse und.
143.1, sickly, cloth, meat lex. suff.
und. 5.2, sickly, weak (muscles) 76.5

side; edge; lean against, prop up 669.5
side, sound, ear lex. suff. 5.3, side
appendage, edge lex. suff. 12.4, side
of head 63.1, be on side, lean 133.2

to/at the side of 138.2, this side
und. 659.2, side (?) 527.2, side
ache und. 173.3

sigh, sharp, fairly loud (as old
people do) 48.3

sign with fingerprint und. 327.1

silent, stillness of deep forest
und. 321.1

similar to, like, as und. 620.2

sin und. 218.1

sinew, muscle 500.4

sing 532.4, sing, repeat, interpret
671.1, second singer und. 666.5

single man und. 506.6, single (unmarried) person of either sex
371.5, single barrel gun und.
129.1

sink und. 22.5

sister, female cousin und. 646.2,
sister's husbands, wife's brothers
und. 596.2, two sisters married
to same man, interwoven 662.2

sit down 50.4, sit together und. 517.1,
sit on lap 684.3

six 219.1/und. 631.1

size up, examine, scrutinize, look
over 251.2

sizzle 49.2

Skagit 371.1

skate see under fish

skate, sled und. 413.1

ski, snowshoe und. 312.2

skin of human or salmon; flesh 77.2
fish skin 251.1, skin, hide 254.5

cedar bark skirt 106.1, 108.1, 'modern'
skirt 249.4

skull und. 384.2

skunk 393.4

sky und. 543.5

Skykomish und. 406.1

give slack 36.1

slap 291.1, 492.2

slaughter, annihilate und. 556.1

slave 507.1, catch for a slave und. 244.1

sled, skate und. 413.1

sleep 676.2, sleeping platform 272.2

slender, thin 415.6

slice, split open 518.3

slide, slip 413.1

slip, slide 413.1

sliver und. 436.1

slope, bank, hill, incline lex. suff.
209.3

slow 395.1, slow down 516.1, 518.1, go
slower, take it easy 477.1

slug, snail 397.3

small, little 39.2

smallpox und. 325.2

act smart und. 35.6

smash, crush 36.5, smash up, shatter, ruin
227.2

smell 178.5, 448.1, 317.3, und. 659.2
smell lex. suff. 381.1, smell bad
und. 439.3, smell bad, stink 668.4,
smell of burning 335.3, smell of s.th.
burning (feathers) 557.1, smell of urine
und. 558.2

smelt 107.2, 464.2, Columbia river
smelt 421.1

smile und. 585.1

smoke, fog, clouds 416.5, smoke,
murk 533.1, smoke of fire 334.5,
smoke fish und. 334.5

smooth, even 320.3

smother und. 382.1

snack, lunch und. 597.1

snail, slug 397.3

snake 22.3

snap (in two) 529.3

sneak up on s.o., stalk 110.6

sneeze 178.6

sniff 446.4, 450.2

river snipe 615.2

Snohomish 142.3

Snoqualmie und. 38.3/und. 143.1

snore 608.2/und. 676.2

snotty nose und. 293.3

snow (noun) 20.1, snow (verb)
411.4, permanently snow-capped
peak 506.1

snowgoose 662.5

snowshoe, ski und. 312.2

soak 526.4, soak, immerse 229.2,
soak, immerse more thoroughly
508.1

soda pop und. 409.4

soft, pliable 441.7, soft part of
baby's head und. 384.2

soil, dirt, dust, earth; bury
335.8, soiled, dirty 96.5

sole (fish) 63.9

sole (of foot) und. 474.1, und. 544.2,
und. 642.1

solid, hard 598.5, solid, strong, watertight 318.4, solid (object); strong in
body, husky 419.4

some, more, others und. 671.2

somersault 30.4

gambling song und. 488.6, stop a song;
break (a string/rope) und. 529.3, unid.
type of song und. 532.4

soon, eventually 163.3, as soon as und.
135.5

open sore, filth 111.4, sore throat und.
593.5

sorry, sad, brokenhearted und. 589.3

sound, salt water, sea, ocean 613.3

sound 316.1, sound, ear, side lex. suff.
5.3, dead sound, pounding sound 508.2

soup 38.1, 307.3

sour (like a sour apple) 106.5, (turned)
sour, spoil; bitter (taste) 516.5

south wind 486.6, und. 86.4/und. 510.1

sparking, lightning 368.1

sparkle, glitter 69.1

spawning und. 285.3, 317.1

speak, give speech 157.2

salmon spear und. 597.1, straight spear
for crabs and bottom fish 112.1, spear
used for bottom fish 320.7, spear, jab
44.8, spear big game on the salt water
und. 44.8, spear salmon in a river und.
491.1, act of using spear for bottom
fish 311.3

speckled, striped und. 578.3

cast a spell on s.o., und. 380.1, und. 589.3

sphere, round 41.5

spider 496.4, 284.2/491.3

spill, pour 255.1

spin 289.6, spin, twist (whirl) 441.5, spin; stroke lightly 482.5, spin self around und. 444.5, hand spinning wheel 226.3, (modern) spinning wheel und. 482.5

upper end of spine und. 68.1/440.4

spirit, Holy Ghost 342.2, keep spirits up und. 480.3, get started (under influence of a spirit) und. 293.5; see also under power.

spit 514.2

split 72.8, split, crack; half 99.3, split open, slice 518.3

spoil; sour (as sour milk), bitter (taste) 516.5

spoon, ladle 289.5

spouse (deriv. pref.) 677.2

spouting of whale 339.4

sprain, twist, turn 110.7, sprain, get out of joint 355.8

hard driven spray; strong wind blowing up the surface water 350.2

spread (apart) 335.2, spread (out) 504.3, spread out; stiff 299.2

spring of water 43.2, 43.4, spring of water, bubbling up, boiling 30.6

spring season und. 337.1, und. 325.2, und. 597.1, und. 185.3/und. 319.1

sprinkle, start raining 297.3

sprout (verb) und. 325.2, thimbleberry sprouts 67.1, salmonberry sprouts 163.2

spruce tree 68.4

square in a net und. 129.1

squat 605.1

Squaxin 412.3

squeeze und. 325.1, squeezed into, too tight (clothing) und. 120.3

squid 384.1

squint und. 64.3

squirrel 374.2

stab 491.1, stab, cut up 275.4

stagger, balance , teeter 562.6, stagger, totter und. 215.3

stagnant water, swamp 69.2

stalk prey und. 110.6, stalk, stick out one foot after the other und. 640.1

stammer, stutter 655.4

stand up 233.5, 308.5, stand in shallow water, wade 164.2, stand still! und. 321.1

star 104.2, evening star und. 291.3

starve; (animals) die 635.3, starved 240.1

reach or achieve a state or position; becoming; begin (voice suff. -il) 208.3

'static' (asp. pref.) 11.3

stationary (won't move) 21.3

stay over night, camp 396.1

go steady und. 244.1

steal 369.1

steam cook 396.2, windows "steamed" over, hazy 333.4, steamboat und. 173.3/und. 196.1

steep 444.2

steering by using a paddle 597.2, steer to right or left und. 297.1

step, stalk und. 640.1, step over 531.1, step on und. 269.3

step-relatives und. 94.1, step-mother, uncle's wife 477.3

stern, back end und. 265.5, stern, back seat of a car und. 138.2, 666.5

stick, log; wood(s) 526.1, stick, log 421.2 pronged stick 446.1, walking stick, cane 54.4, 75.2, stick of firewood 112.2, a split stick for roasting und. 239.2, sticks used in the bone game und. 67.7, sticks for keeping time und. 107.3, digging stick for clams 371.6, salmon sticks, sticks for baking salmon 591.5

stick, prick 576.1, stick on, adhere 324.3, 327.1, stick into, stick through; sheathe, insert 463.1, stick (face) out (of window) und. 325.2, stick head out of window und. 398.3

sticky und. 327.1

stiff; spread out 299.2

Stillaguamish und. 509.1

be still, be quiet; lonesome und. 602.6 stillness of deep forest, silent und. 321.1

still 135.2, still, yet 201.4

bee sting und. 537.4

stingy 74.1, und. 363.1

stink, smell bad 668.4

stitch; mat make 311.4, stitch in knitting und. 129.1

stomach, tripe 253.1

stop und. 321.1, stop, wait 642.2, stop, break up song und. 529.3, stop s.o. from crying 182.1

store (noun) und. 573.1

store food 405.1, store, cache s.th. 652.2, store away neatly und. 360.3

trad. story, myth 619.3, 630.3, story und. 157.2

storm see wind

stove und. 196.1

stubborn, mean und. 278.5

be stuck on a problem und. 312.2

up-rooted stump, up-rooted tree 375.1, stump still rooted 431.5

straight 47.2, straighten up, lift head up 597.3

be stranded; put clothing on; encase 312.2

strange acting, foolish 380.1, strange appearance; ugly, mean, rough 602.6

stray animal und. 28.1

upstream 406.1

stretch 687.1, stretch; unit of measure 481.1

strike back of head against 393.2

string, thread, rope und. 523.6

striped, speckled und. 578.3

stroke lightly; spin 482.5

stroll, go for a walk 162.1

strong 550.1, strong in body, husky;
solid (obj.) 419.4, strong; try
hard 499.1, strong, solid, watertight 318.4, strong (taste) und.
612.1

stubborn, mean und. 541.5

get stuck on 194.1

stuff into, plug in 331.1, stuff
into, caulk; narrow; swallow
100.3, stuffed, crowded, jammed und. 120.3

sturgeon 422.1

stutter 257.3, stutter, stammer 655.4

sty (of eyelid) 523.2

'subjunctive' (aux. pref.) 164.1

substitute; guessing 367.1

succeed, able, capable und. 480.3

in such manner, thus 673.2

suck 77.1

sucker (fish) 356.2, 422.2, 514.3

suckle 112.3

suddenly 142.1, suddenly, unexpectedly, right away 500.5

suffix provid. for a change in resol.
(-i-) 203.1, asp. suff. 'change
affected' 12.3, 179.3, deriv. suff.
of unknown signif. (-a$_2$-) 1.3,
deriv. suff. (agent puts himself
into the act) 7.1, class membership 10.1, for self 10.2, obj.
suff. 'me' 40.2, 'thee' 35.7,

444.4, 'us' 42.2, 'you(pl.)' 42.3, sec.
suff. (-bi-) 35.4, (-yi-) 633.5, thematic
suff. (-a$_1$-) 1.2, trans. suff. (not in
full control) 152.2, -c 44.1, -s 435.2,
-š 453.1, -t 473.1, voice suffix 'reach
or achieve a state or position; becoming;
begin' 208.3

sugar 467.5

summer und. 185.3/und. 337.1

sun 307.4, sunset 257.2, sun rising und.
319.1, und. 356.1, sunshine, brightness
155.1

Sunday und. 586.5

support (?) 127.2

suppose, maybe und. 573.2

Suquamish 443.2, 450.4, 676.1

surely, certainly, indeed 247.1

surpass, pass, after in time and space 31.1

surprise, shock 93.7, surprised, 'near
eyed' und. 116.2, very surprised, dumbfounded 396.3, surprised, ambushed 318.3,
exclamation of mild surprise 643.2

suspicious 254.3

swallow, put in mouth 32.3, swallow, stuff
into, caulk; narrow 100.3

swamp, stagnant water 69.2

whistling swan und. 384.2, 'rattle head'
und. 103.1

sweating und. 426.9, sweat house 554.1

sweep und. 678.1

sweet 409.4

swell 462.1

swim und. 534.3, swim, wade out 531.4

swing 633.3, swing aside, turn s.th. 444.5

Swinomish 549.6

table und. 209.2

taboo, cleansed, pure 262.1

tackle, equipment, gear 5.1

tag along und. 30.1

tail, coccyx 119.8, fishtail
und. 113.1

take what one finds 28.1, take und.
687.2, take, get, hold 244.1
take s.o. lunch, dinner und.
640.1, take apart, rip apart
tear 445.1, take (clothing) off
und. 288.1, 559.3, take off/out
of fire 288.3, take parts out
of s.th. 50.5, a flock takes to
the air at one time 306.4, take
daughter away (because husband
treats her badly) und. 278.5,
take out und. 325.2, take s.o.
along und. 309.1

talk 56.4, 226.2, 656.3, serious
talk und. 474.1, one who talks
too much 231.7, talk over
(among themselves) und. 56.4,
und. 157.2, worthless talk
und. 352.1

tall, long 176.1, tall (person)
435.7

tallow 679.6

tame 425.2

tape recorder und. 157.2

tart (taste), sharp (knife) 612.1

it has good taste 106.6, taste/
smell good und. 381.1, tasteless,
flat 343.4, taste it; try to do
s.th. 354.1

taught, tight 54.8

tavern und. 264.1

tea, coffee und. 185.3/und. 423.3,
marsh tea 415.1

teach 680.1

tear, take apart, rip apart 445.1,
torn 614.2

tears 372.3

teeter, balance , stagger 562.6

telephone, yell, call out loudly 420.2,
und. 553.2

tell, say 56.4, tell (to do s.th.) 193.1,
tell, report, inform; news 628.4,
I told you so! 636.1

temper tantrum, fall down flat 114.2

ten 333.3, 683.2, ten cents 37.3

tent 446.2

territorial authority (deriv. pref.) 34.2

testicles 15.3, testicles lex. suff. 8.3

than und. 146.3, und. 278.5, und. 510.1

thank, pray 532.1, thank, praise s.o.
254.4, thank for gift of food /drink
122.3, thank you 54.2, 56.1, und. 189.1

that (dem.) 54.1, 505.3, the thing
that, the one who 135.5, in
order that/to 56.3

thaw, melt 217.1

thee see you (sg.)

their 435.3, their, they, them
188.1

them, they 11.4, them, they, their
188.1

then, next 180.1, 201.1, (well)
then 14.2

there 477.4, 507.2, und. 637.1

they, them 11.4, they, them, their
188.1

thick (dimension) 338.2, thick; adhere 527.5

thief und. 369.1

thigh, hind leg 645.4, thigh lex.
suff. 308.4

thin 34.1, thin (person) 328.3, thin,
slender 415.6

thing, what, what? 474.1, things,
possessions lex. suff. 208.1

think und. 56.4, 343.5, think of,
remember und. 266.1, think over
und. 539.1

thirst 473.3

this (dem.) 53.4, 505.2, this
(there) und. 637.1

thistle 584.8

thou see you (sg.)

even though 377.1

inner thoughts, sense, understanding,
mind; count 589.3, evil thoughts
15.2, thoughtful und. 589.3, go along
(with s.o.) in one's thoughts und. 83.1

thread und. 523.6, 616.2

three 305.1

throat 397.5, throat lex. suff. 636.3,
636.4, catch in throat, choke 649.1,
cut on throat to remove tonsils und.
300.4

throw, broadcast 562.1, throw away 678.1,
throw, discard; throw s.o. down 559.2,
throw, project through air 345.1, throw
into the water, drift 357.3, throw self
down flat, fall down flat all spread out,
fall down hard (temper tantrum) 114.2

through (bleed through the mouth) und.
280.2

thrush, salmonberry bird 562.2

thumb und. 284.3

thunder 618.2, thunderbird 613.5

Thursday und. 42.5

thus, in such manner 673.2

thwart 596.1

thy see your (sg.)

tickle, axilla 154.1

tide goes out/ river goes down 471.1,
ebb tide und. 464.3, tide flats 334.4,
high tide, tide coming in und. 358.5

tidy up, put away; preserve, save 360.3

tie 302.1, tie, knot, wrap up package
330.2, tie, wind around und. 598.3

tight, taught 54.8, too tight, squeezed into (clothing) und. 120.3, struggle into s.th. tight (clothing) und. 312.2

time of, season 337.1, time of camas tubers (~ March) und. 62.1, time of dog salmon (~ Nov., autumn) 332.3, just get there in time und. 293.5

tip of finger und. 112.4

tired 429.4, very tired 548.3, tired, tired of 557.2, grow tired, become impatient 239.3, 396.7, (body) tired out, not feel well und. 635.3, extreme fatigue und. 128.4

in order to/that 56.3, in order to und. 146.3, to, toward und. 146.3

toad 586.4

tobacco 16.2

toe und. 134.4, big toe und. 113.1, toenail und. 388.4, und. 397.2, 430.2

come together und. 161.1/und. 597.1, sit together 517.1

tomorrow und. 123.2

tongue 289.3

too (also) und. 315.1

too (excessively) und. 193.2

tool und. 443.7

tooth 217.4, tooth, straight pin lex. suff. 137.2, toothpick 92.2, teeth mostly extracted und. 111.1

top, cover, lid 104.5, top, head; voice lex. suff. 384.2, the very top lex. suff. 627.1, on top und. 459.2, placed on top of something high 517.2, just short of (the top of) a tree und. 529.3

topple, fall over; fell s.th. 215.3

torso area lex. suff. 206.2

tossing pebbles und. 345.1

touch, bump 237.1, touch it und. 292.1, don't touch, leave alone, pay no attention und. 321.1

toward 146.3, 515.3, toward the water, seaward 86.4

towel und. 673.1

trachea 48.3, 217.3

track (of animal) und. 97.1, track (verb) 254.1

trade, exchange it und. 652.3

train 280.1

trampled und. 269.3

transform, change 142.4, transformer und. 142.4

transitive 473.1

translate, interpret 509.5

trap und. 321.1, trap, dam und. 491.4, salmon webbing trap, seine 318.5, 320.1, hand smelt trap for streams 536.2, unid. salmon trap made of cedar boughs 373.5

travel, wander, be unstable 218.1, travel on land, walk 667.2, travel by water 684.1, (travel) with current, downstream 418.2, travel, get in/on any sort of conveyance 399.1, water travel device und. 443.7

trawling und. 302.1

treasure, belongings, possessions und. 474.1

trees, shrubs, growth und. 319.1, und. 546.6, tree (upright cylindrical object) lex. suff. 2.3, tree, unid. 16.6, dead tree, log 339.3, up-rooted tree, up-rooted stump 375.1, tree knot 485.6

from a different tribe, others und. 38.3

trip (hook toe) und. 303.1, und. 388.4

tripe, stomach 253.1

trotting und. 53.3

get in trouble und. 377.2, und. 439.3, be in trouble/difficulty und. 686.2

trousers 54.7, 631.1

trout (general) 257.1, salmon and seagoing trout, gen. 92.4, chub, a small trout 486.2, Dolly Varden trout 360.2, steelhead (rainbow) trout 242.1, 387.2

true 490.1, tell the truth und. 47.2

try, improvise, make do; do fumblingly, inadroitly 231.3, try to do s.th., taste it 354.1, try to learn s.th. und. 180.2

Tuesday und. 46.1, und. 123.2

tug, move, jerk 51.2, tug-of-war und. 497.3

tule (swamp grass) 260.2

tumpline und. 89.1, und. 302.1, und. 526.1

turbid (river) und. 375.3

turn, sprain, twist 110.7, turn over/around, go around/over some obstruction, reverse the side of 212.2, turn it over face down 591.6, turn (handle), swing aside 444.5, turn off (to the right or left) 297.1, turn(ed) out of shape, bent out of line, shape, position 351.3, turned around, lost 616.4, turning of seasons, year 228.4, turning spring 220.4, turn over on und. 204.1

turtle 645.5

twins 118.2

twist, turn, sprain 110.7, twist, spin 441.5, twist back (of body), wrench 250.3, twisting in the process of weaving blankets 119.5

twitch und. 51.2

two 435.8, two, second 46.1, which (of two) und. 161.1

ugly, bad face und. 377.2, ugly, mean, rough; strange appearance 602.5

umbrella und. 62.4

unable und. 419.1

'uncertain' (modal particle kʷaʔ) 243.1

uncle, male sibling of either parent while that parent is living 382.4, uncle's wife, step-mother 477.3

uncover, bring to light 392.1

under, beneath und. 165.2, 468.2

undergrowth, brush, weeds und. 319.1

underpants und. 324.2

undershirt und. 208.2/und. 324.2

understanding, mind, inner thoughts, sense; count 589.3, understand, have straight und. 47.2, understand, listen und. 321.1, understand, hear und. 273.3, understand; notice; pay attention to 340.7, what is understandable, Salish language 275.3, not understand und. 214.1, not understand, deaf und. 493.1

underwear und. 165.2

unexpectedly, right away, suddenly 500.5

make mistake unintentionally 546.2

unladylike behavior und. 64.3

unload und. 430.4

unmarried person of either sex 371.5

unnamed baby 232.2

unplug, pull out 685.1

unripe 423.1

be unstable, travel, wander 218.1

untie, bail out (of jail), get loose 156.2

until (toward then) und. 146.3

unwilling, lazy, indifferent 419.1

unworthy, nothing of value 352.1

up, high und. 146.3/459.2, up, high (free in air) und. 280.2, up above, upper side und. 406.1, upper part, head, face, hair lex. suff. 544.2

upbear, place on/in receptacle; dish up 51.3

uphold und. 190.4

go upriver und. 146.3/406.1

up-rooted tree, up-rooted stump 375.1

upstairs, ceiling, roof und. 459.2

proceed upstream 498.1

urinate (female) 504.1, urinate (male) 452.3, smell of urine und. 558.2

us, we 10.5, 96.1, 135.1, 42.2 (obj. suff.), 541.3 (obj. suff.)

use s.th. 228.3, und. 480.3, used up, gone, die und. 566.1

be used to und. 315.1

utensil 486.4

uvula 526.3

vague, imagined 241.1

vein 496.1

venison und. 386.1

very 45.1, 50.3, 125.1, 187.3,
the very one 46.2

vibrate, quiver, wriggle 297.2

come partly into view, appear
398.3, obstruct the view
62.4

be visible, appear 550.4, clearly visible und. 392.1

visit und. 129.1, und. 212.2,
und. 222.2, short visit
(peek in on) und. 260.4, be
visited und. 293.5

voice und. 157.2, voice; head, top
lex. suff. 384.2, weak voice
und. 76.5

vomit 227.3

wade out, swim 531.4, wade, stand
in shallow water 164.2

wag, shake, rock 211.3

waist line und. 161.1

wait 652.5, wait, stop 642.2, wait,
later on 323.1

wake up 379.2

walk, travel on land 667.2, walk
along beach und. 171.1/und. 212.2

wander, travel, be unstable 218.1

want, like 581.2, want to 417.1,
want s.o.'s company 555.2

wapato, potato; arrowhead plant
340.4

war, battle, fight 603.1, war cry
118.3

warm, hot 185.3, 441.2, warm, burn;
bake, cook; ripe 426.9, warm self,
s.th. 350.4, und. 529.4, warm it
(on stove), (body) getting warm
372.6

wart 74.3

wash 64.6, river banks washed away
39.1

body waste und. 377.2

watch s.o. und. 264.2, watchman,
scout und. 469.1

(non-sea) water 423.3, salt water,
sea, ocean, sound 613.3, water's
edge und. 280.2, fast flowing
water 435.5, stagnant water, swamp
69.2, mirror-like water (not a

ripple on it), good weather 278.4, go
down to water's edge, to a body of water
261.2, partitive of water; fetch water;
gore 626.1, water went over head und. 384.2

waterfall 488.4, und. 564.1, below, above
a waterfall und. 14.1

waterfowl, generic 43.3, 425.3, waterfowl
unid. 15.4, 24.2, 412.1; 486.5, 551.4, big
diver 599.3, unid. duck 45.2, brant 307.5,
buʔqʷ with purple feet 425.4, a very black
buʔqʷ that dives 434.1, black duck und.
416.2, blue head, blue bill 30.2, butter-
ball/buffle head 535.3, golden eye 506.2,
hell diver 623.4, loon 553.3, mallard
584.3, big river sawbill 578.1, medium
sized sawbill 415.2, 552.1, 563.2, small
sized sawbill 135.3, silver diver 614.3,
war boat 415.5, sandhill crane 278.2

watertight, solid, strong 318.4

waterway, canoe; curved side; narrow passage
way lex. suff. 173.3

wave (of water) 227.1

bee's wax und. 327.1

way, road, door 457.6, way, road lex. suff
und. 541.5, be in s.o.'s way und. 274.2,
put out of way und. 278.5, which way?
und. 280.2

weak (muscles), sickly 76.5, und. 608.4

we, us 10.5, 96.1, 135.1

wealth 678.3, wealthy und. 363.1

wear out 70.6, worn out (and now no good)
und. 143.1

weasel 295.1

bad weather und. 143.1, cold weather
529.4, good weather, calm, no
storm und. 182.2, good weather,
mirror-like water 278.4, weather
cleared up und. 155.1, forecast
the weather 254.2

weave a blanket 661.1, weave/make
cedar-root basket; work s.th.
into a tight place 634.2

Wednesday und. 305.1

weeds, brush, undergrowth und. 319.1

fish weir und. 491.4

(feel) not well und. 143.1

wet 299.1, a little wet, damp 20.2,
wet one's clothes und. 558.2

whale 104.4, 413.3, killer whale
(blackfish) 371.7, inside (a
whale) und. 207.1

what? und. 161.2, 474.1, 662.6
what say? und. 82.2, 668.3
what time? und. 257.5

when 659.1, when? und. 337.1, und.
474.1, whenever 654.1

where? 80.4, und. 146.3, where
from? und. 80.4

whether...or 654.1

which one?, either one und. 80.4/
und. 671.2, which of you (two)
und. 161.2, which way? und.
280.2

after a while und. 323.1, 502.1

whirl around und. 441.5

whisky 264.1

whistle 618.4, time of (robin) whistling
(~ April) und. 337.1

white 416.2/und. 615.6, white face und.
544.2, white man und. 335.1

whittle 104.1

the one who, the thing that 135.5, who?
161.2, whose? und. 161.2/und. 170.5

why, how? 82.2, 662.6

wide 298.3, wide, width measured from
inside 20.6

widow, widower 431.1

wife 92.6, wife, mate, girlfriend und.
432.2, wife's brothers, sister's husbands und. 596.2

wild 253.4, very vicious wild Indians 79.1

willow 50.1, 63.3, 608.3

wilted und. 299.1

win, get the better of 67.7

wind around s.th.; entwine, entangle
154.5, wind around, tie, wrap around
und. 598.3

wind und. 462.1, wind, blow 348.2, strong
wind 451.2, strong wind blowing up the
surface water; hard driven spray und.
350.2, NW-wind 506.5, und. 510.1, S-wind
486.6, und. 510.1, wind changes und.
218.1

window, mirror und. 469.1, window und.
264.2

windpipe , go down wrong pipe 69.5

wing (of bird, airplane) 110.2

winter und. 337.1/ und. 529.4, winter (verb)
und. 529.4

wipe, mop 669.2, 673.1

with 659.1

wolf 502.2, litter of whelp wolves 549.2

woman 287.4

woman's names 41.3, 55.2, 124.6, und. 203.2, 219.3, und. 222.1, und. 263.2, 272.1, 388.2, 416.3, 423.2, und. 425.2, 482.1, 482.3, 548.1, 552.5, und. 563.4, 626.2, 636.5, 678.2, 679.1

wood(s), log, stick 526.1, driftwood und. 218.1, rotten wood 357.1, 360.1

woodchuck/groundhog/marmot 549.1

woodpecker 390.1, 492.1

wool lex. suff. und. 384.2, pull wool apart to make it fluffy 47.1, card wool 355.6

word und. 157.2

work 627.5, a willing worker 684.2, work s.th. into a tight place; make/weave cedar-root baskets 634.2

all worked up und. 610.2

world, land, place 546.6

worm (generic) 682.3, worm, bug (generic) 67.6, beach worm 408.1

worry und. 143.1, 668.2, worry, bother 610.2

worthless, bad 143.1

would be, must be und. 219.4

wound 404.1

wrap around 598.3, wrap up package, tie, knot 330.2, wrap around; intoxicated 560.1

winter wren (?) 524.1

wrench, twist back (of body) 250.3

wriggle, vibrate, quiver 297.2

wring it out 358.2, wring neck und. 110.7

wrinkled 398.1

wrist 358.1, 371.3

write, decorate, mark 578.3, write fast, scribble, shorthand 593.1

be wrong und. 214.1

Bibliography

Ballard, Arthur C. Mythology of Southern Puget Sound. *University of
Washington Publications in Anthropology* 3. 31-150, 1929.

Collins, June McCormick. *Valley of the Spirits*. University of Washington Press, 1974.

Elmendorf, W. W. *The Structure of Twana Culture*. Washington State
University. Pullman, Washington, 1960.

Gibbs, George. *Dictionary of the Niskwalli. Contributions to North
American Ethnology I*. Washington, D. C., 1877.

Gunther, Erna. *Ethnobotany of Western Washington*. University of
Washington Press. Seattle, 1945.

Haeberlin, Hermann and Erna Gunther. *The Indians of Puget Sound*.
University of Washington Press. Seattle, 1952 (reprinted).

Hoard, James E. and Thos. M. Hess. *Studies in Northwest Indian Languages*.
Sacramento Anthropological Society Paper II. Sacramento, California,
April 1971.

Roberts, Natalie. *A History of the Swinomish Tribal Community*.
PH. D. Dissertation, University of Washington, 1975.

Sampson, Martin J. *Indians of Skagit County.* Skagit County Historical
Society. Mount Vernon, Washington, 1972.

Sapir, Edward. *Central and North American Languages*. Encyclopaedia
Britannica, (14th Edition, 1929) 5: 138-141.

Smith, Marian W. The Coast Salish of Puget Sound. *American Anthropologist*
43. 197-211, 1941.

___. *The Puyallup-Nisqually*. Columbia University Press. New York, 1940.

Snyder, Warren A. *Southern Puget Sound Salish Texts, Place Names and
Dictionary*. Sacramento Anthropological Society 9. Sacramento,
California, 1968.

Thompson, Laurence C. The Northwest. *Current Trends in Linguistics*, edited
by T. A. Sebeok, Vol. X, 1973.

Thompson, Laurence C. and M. Terry Thompson. Language Universals, Nasals,
and the Northwest Coast. *Studies in Linguistics in Honor of George L.
Trager*. Mouton, The Hague, 1972 [1973].